United States

HARCOURT BRACE SOCIAL STUDIES

Series Authors

Dr. Richard G. Boehm

Claudia Hoone

Dr. Thomas M. McGowan

Dr. Mabel C. McKinney-Browning

Dr. Ofelia B. Miramontes

Dr. Priscilla H. Porter

Series Consultants

Dr. Alma Flor Ada

Dr. Phillip Bacon

Dr. W. Dorsey Hammond

Dr. Asa Grant Hilliard, III

HARCOURT BRACE & COMPANY

Orlando Atlanta Austin Boston San Francisco Chicago Dallas

New York Toronto London

 Visit The Learning Site at http://www.hbschool.com

Series Authors

Dr. Richard G. Boehm
Professor and Jesse H. Jones
Distinguished Chair in
Geographic Education
Department of Geography and
Planning
Southwest Texas State University
San Marcos, Texas

Claudia Hoone
Teacher
Ralph Waldo Emerson School #58
Indianapolis, Indiana

Dr. Thomas M. McGowan
Associate Professor
Division of Curriculum and
Instruction
Arizona State University
Tempe, Arizona

Dr. Mabel C. McKinney-Browning
Director
Division for Public Education
American Bar Association
Chicago, Illinois

Dr. Ofelia B. Miramontes
Associate Professor of Education
and Associate Vice Chancellor
for Diversity
University of Colorado
Boulder, Colorado

Dr. Priscilla H. Porter
Co-Director
Center for History–Social Science
Education
School of Education
California State University,
Dominguez Hills
Carson, California

Series Consultants

Dr. Alma Flor Ada
Professor
School of Education
University of San Francisco
San Francisco, California

Dr. Phillip Bacon
Professor Emeritus of Geography
and Anthropology
University of Houston
Houston, Texas

Dr. W. Dorsey Hammond
Professor of Education
Oakland University
Rochester, Michigan

Dr. Asa Grant Hilliard, III
Fuller E. Callaway Professor of
Urban Education
Georgia State University
Atlanta, Georgia

Media, Literature, and Language Specialists

Dr. Joseph A. Braun, Jr.
Professor of Elementary Social
Studies
Department of Curriculum and
Instruction
Illinois State University
Normal, Illinois

Meredith McGowan
Youth Services Librarian
Tempe Public Library
Tempe, Arizona

Rebecca Valbuena
Language Development Specialist
Stanton Elementary School
Glendora, California

Grade-Level Consultants and Reviewers

Eunice Anderson
Teacher
Sobey Elementary School
Flint, Michigan

Dr. Ira Berlin
Professor
Department of History
University of Maryland
at College Park
College Park, Maryland

Dr. Eugene H. Berwanger
Professor
Department of History
Colorado State University
Fort Collins, Colorado

Dr. Glen Blankenship
Program Director
Georgia Council on Economic
Education
Atlanta, Georgia

Dr. John Henrik Clarke
Professor Emeritus
Department of Africana &
Puerto Rican Studies
Hunter College
New York, New York

Jewel Farris
Teacher
Northmore Elementary School
West Palm Beach, Florida

Dr. Donald L. Fixico
Professor
Department of History
Western Michigan University
Kalamazoo, Michigan

Kathryn M. Glaser
Staff Development Trainer
Edison Township School District
Edison, New Jersey

Dr. Lois Harrison-Jones
Former Superintendent of Boston,
Massachusetts, Public Schools
and Richmond, Virginia,
Public Schools

Dr. Donald Hata
Professor of History
California State University,
Dominguez Hills
Dominguez Hills, California

Cathy M. Johnson
Supervisor
Office of Social Studies
Detroit Public Schools
Detroit, Michigan

Amy Keller
Resource Teacher
Orange County Public Schools
Orlando, Florida

Patricia A. Kissel
Teacher
Jupiter Farms Elementary School
Jupiter, Florida

Timothy L. Mateer
Principal
East Petersburg Elementary School
East Petersburg, Pennsylvania

Marie A. McDermott
Teacher
Kingsbury School
Waterbury, Connecticut

Adell Miles
Teacher
Escatawpa Elementary School
Moss Point, Mississippi

Keith D. Miller
Teacher
Oak Hill Elementary School
Orlando, Florida

Dr. Howard H. Moon, Jr.
Coordinator of Language Arts/
Social Studies
Kenosha Public Schools
Kenosha, Wisconsin

Richard Nichols
(Santa Clara Pueblo Tewa)
Vice President
ORBIS Associates
Washington, D.C.

Dr. Estelle Owens
Chairman of the Social Studies
Division and Professor of
History
Wayland Baptist University
Plainview, Texas

Debra L. Powell
Teacher
Jacksonville Heights Elementary
School
Jacksonville, Florida

Dr. L. Anita Richardson
American Bar Association
Chicago, Illinois

Dr. Linda Kerrigan Salvucci
Associate Professor
Department of History
Trinity University
San Antonio, Texas

Karen R. Santos
Teacher
George G. White
Middle School
Hillsdale, New Jersey

Dr. Stephen L. Schechter
Director of Council for
Citizenship Education
Russell Sage College
Troy, New York

Carolyn Smith
Teacher
Farragut Intermediate School
Knoxville, Tennessee

Dr. Judith B. Smith
Supervisor of Humanities
Baltimore City Public Schools
Baltimore, Maryland

Marita A. Smith
Teacher
Sunrise Elementary School
Ocala, Florida

Dr. Mary Jane Turner
Senior Education Advisor
Close Up Foundation
Alexandria, Virginia

Printed in the United States of America

ISBN 0-15-320106-1

2 3 4 5 6 7 8 9 10   048   03 02 01

Contents

An Olmec statue

Dora Pino

Amerigo Vespucci

Motecuhzoma

Unit

3

Our Colonial Heritage 166

CHAPTER 5

Junípero Serra

CHAPTER 6

A British colonist

4

John Adams

Mercy Otis Warren

5

Abigail Adams

George Washington

6

Mary Prosser

Juan Seguín

7

Frederick Douglass

Edwin Jennison

x

8

An Asian woman

A cowhand

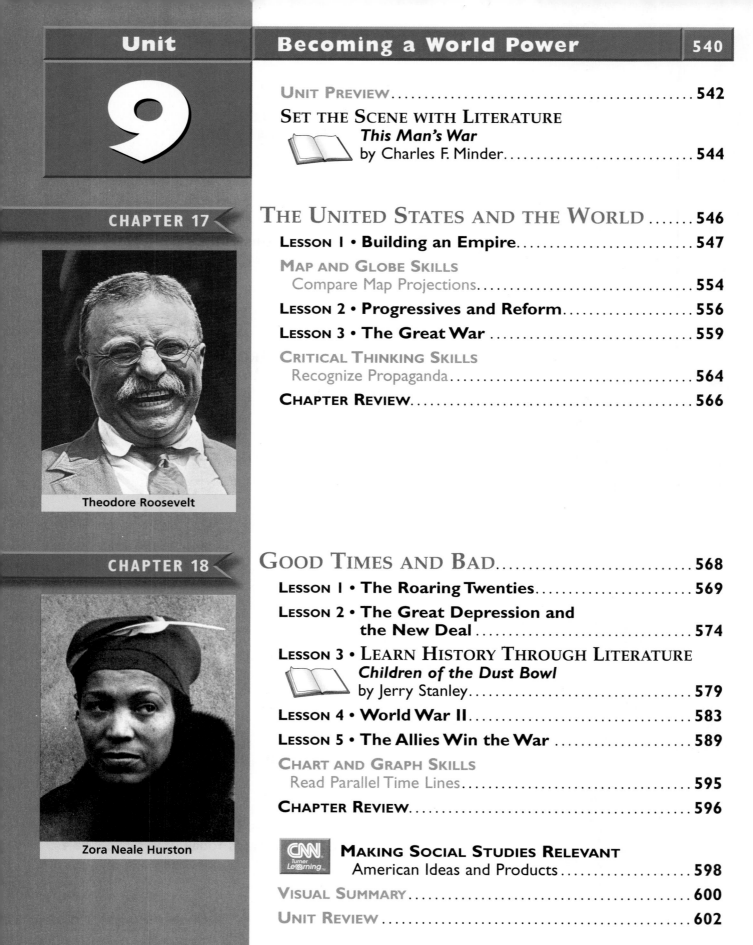

Theodore Roosevelt

Zora Neale Hurston

The Lincoln Memorial, Washington, D.C.

F.Y.I.

F.Y.I.

Features

Maps

Time Lines

F.Y.I.

Charts, Graphs, Diagrams, and Tables

Atlas

Contents

Atlas

The World: Political

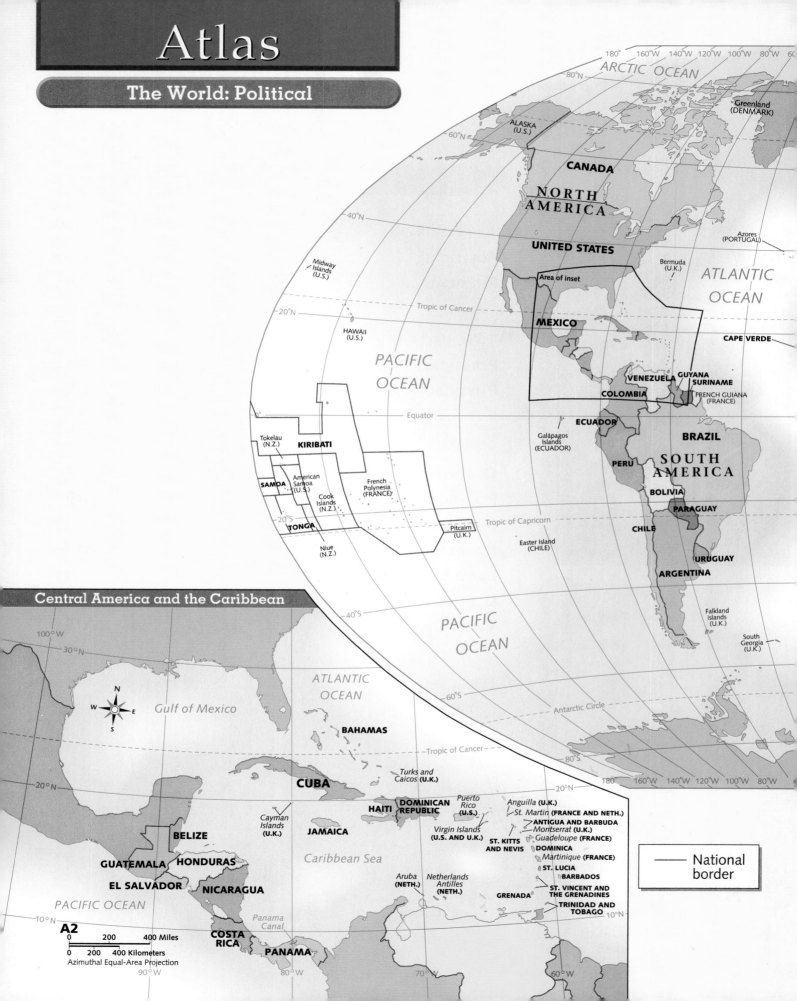

ARCTIC OCEAN

80°N

Greenland (DENMARK)

60°N

ALASKA (U.S.)

CANADA

NORTH AMERICA

40°N

UNITED STATES

Azores (PORTUGAL)

Midway Islands (U.S.)

Area of inset

Bermuda (U.K.)

ATLANTIC OCEAN

20°N

Tropic of Cancer

MEXICO

HAWAII (U.S.)

CAPE VERDE

PACIFIC OCEAN

VENEZUELA   GUYANA   SURINAME

COLOMBIA   FRENCH GUIANA (FRANCE)

Equator

ECUADOR

Galápagos Islands (ECUADOR)

BRAZIL

Tokelau (N.Z.)

KIRIBATI

SOUTH AMERICA

PERU

American Samoa (U.S.)

SAMOA

Cook Islands (N.Z.)

French Polynesia (FRANCE)

BOLIVIA

PARAGUAY

20°S

CHILE

TONGA

Tropic of Capricorn

Pitcairn (U.K.)

Easter Island (CHILE)

URUGUAY

Niue (N.Z.)

ARGENTINA

40°S

PACIFIC OCEAN

Falkland Islands (U.K.)

South Georgia (U.K.)

60°S

Antarctic Circle

80°S

180   160°W   140°W   120°W   100°W   80°W

Central America and the Caribbean

100°W

30°N

N W E S

Gulf of Mexico

ATLANTIC OCEAN

Tropic of Cancer

BAHAMAS

20°N

CUBA

Turks and Caicos (U.K.)

Cayman Islands (U.K.)

HAITI

DOMINICAN REPUBLIC

Puerto Rico (U.S.)

Anguilla (U.K.)

St. Martin (FRANCE AND NETH.)

BELIZE

JAMAICA

Virgin Islands (U.S. AND U.K.)

ANTIGUA AND BARBUDA

Montserrat (U.K.)

Guadeloupe (FRANCE)

GUATEMALA   HONDURAS

Caribbean Sea

ST. KITTS AND NEVIS

DOMINICA

Martinique (FRANCE)

EL SALVADOR

NICARAGUA

Aruba (NETH.)

Netherlands Antilles (NETH.)

ST. LUCIA

BARBADOS

ST. VINCENT AND THE GRENADINES

PACIFIC OCEAN

GRENADA

Panama Canal

TRINIDAD AND TOBAGO

10°N

A2

0   200   400 Miles

0   200   400 Kilometers

Azimuthal Equal-Area Projection

COSTA RICA

PANAMA

90°W   80°W   70°W   60°W

10°N

National border

Atlas

The World: Physical

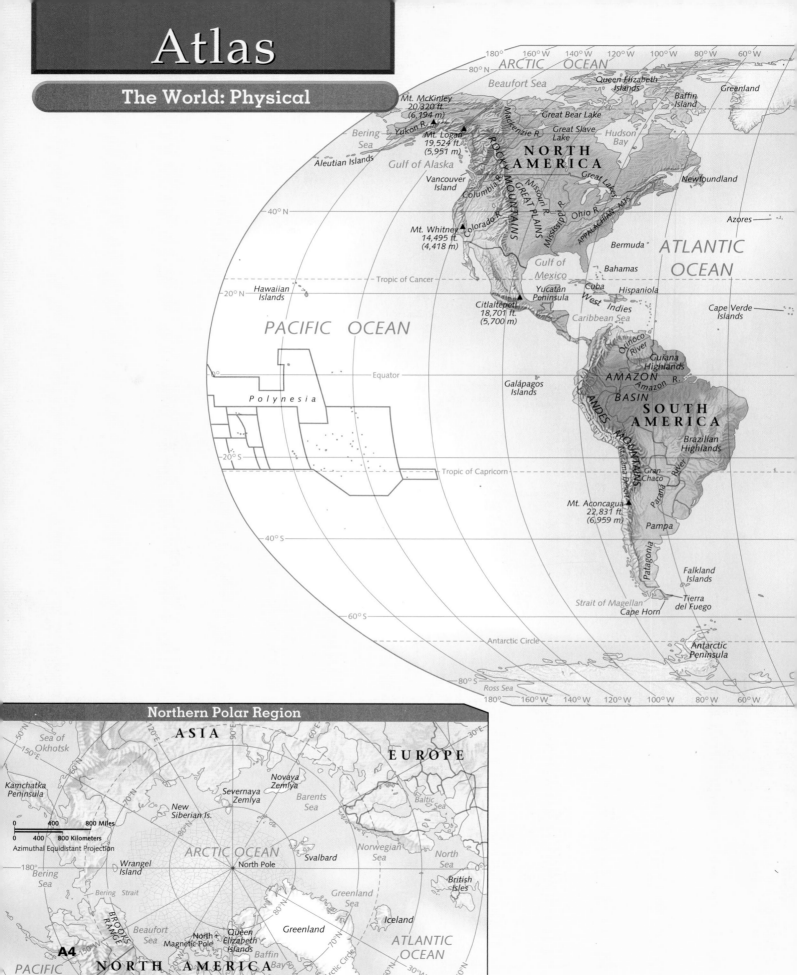

ARCTIC OCEAN

Beaufort Sea

Queen Elizabeth Islands

Baffin Island

Greenland

Mt. McKinley 20,320 ft. (6,194 m)

Yukon R.

Bering Sea

Mt. Logan 19,524 ft. (5,951 m)

Aleutian Islands

Gulf of Alaska

Vancouver Island

Great Bear Lake

Great Slave Lake

Mackenzie R.

Hudson Bay

Newfoundland

NORTH AMERICA

ROCKY MOUNTAINS

GREAT PLAINS

Missouri R.

Ohio R.

Mississippi R.

Great Lakes

APPALACHIAN MTS.

Azores

Columbia R.

Mt. Whitney 14,495 ft. (4,418 m)

Colorado R.

Bermuda

ATLANTIC OCEAN

Tropic of Cancer

Gulf of Mexico

Bahamas

Yucatán Peninsula

Citlaltépetl 18,701 ft. (5,700 m)

Cuba

Hispaniola

West Indies

Caribbean Sea

Cape Verde Islands

PACIFIC OCEAN

Hawaiian Islands

Polynesia

Equator

Galápagos Islands

Orinoco River

Guiana Highlands

AMAZON BASIN

Amazon R.

SOUTH AMERICA

ANDES MOUNTAINS

Brazilian Highlands

Tropic of Capricorn

Gran Chaco

Atacama Desert

Paraná River

Mt. Aconcagua 22,831 ft. (6,959 m)

Pampa

Falkland Islands

Patagonia

Strait of Magellan

Cape Horn

Tierra del Fuego

Antarctic Circle

Antarctic Peninsula

Ross Sea

Northern Polar Region

Sea of Okhotsk

Kamchatka Peninsula

ASIA

Novaya Zemlya

Severnaya Zemlya

Barents Sea

EUROPE

Baltic Sea

New Siberian Is.

0   400   800 Miles

0   400   800 Kilometers

Azimuthal Equidistant Projection

Wrangel Island

ARCTIC OCEAN

North Pole

Svalbard

Norwegian Sea

North Sea

Bering Sea

Bering Strait

Greenland Sea

Iceland

British Isles

A4

BROOKS RANGE

Beaufort Sea

North Magnetic Pole

Queen Elizabeth Islands

Baffin Bay

Greenland

ATLANTIC OCEAN

Arctic Circle

NORTH AMERICA

PACIFIC OCEAN

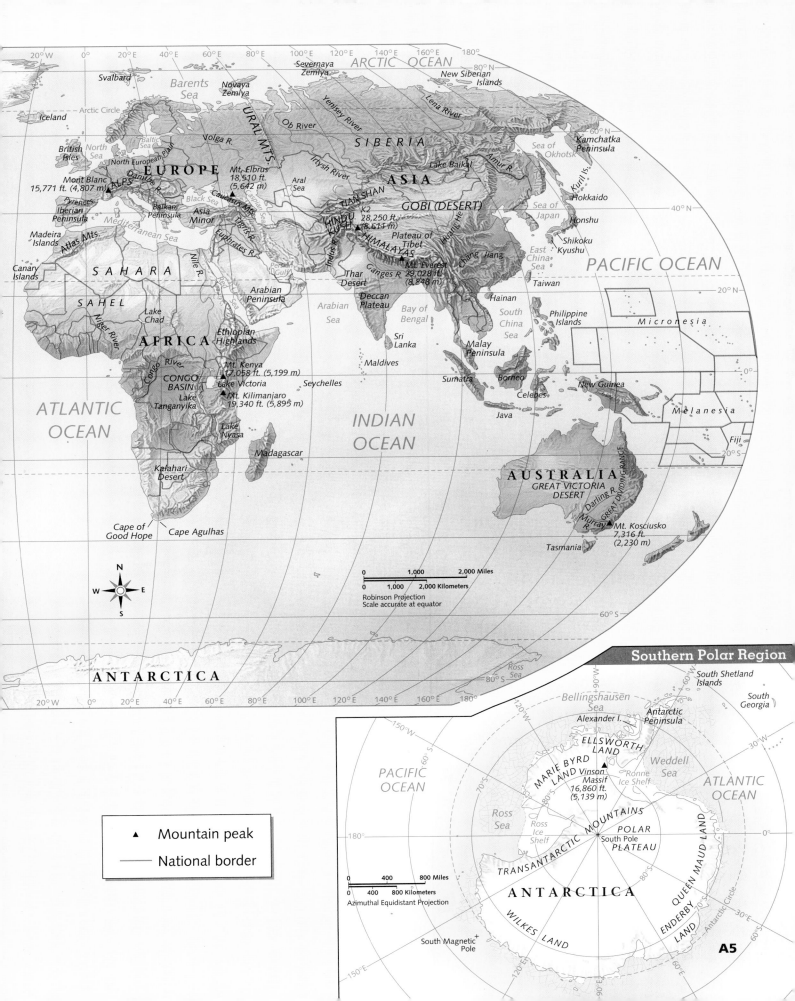

ARCTIC OCEAN

EUROPE

20°W · 0° · 20°E · 40°E · 60°E · 80°E · 100°E · 120°E · 140°E · 160°E · 180°

Svalbard
Iceland
Arctic Circle
Barents Sea
Novaya Zemlya
Severnaya Zemlya
New Siberian Islands
80°N

British Isles
North Sea
Baltic Sea
North European Plain
Volga R.
URAL MTS.
Ob River
Yenisey River
Lena River
SIBERIA
Kamchatka Peninsula
60°N

Mont Blanc 15,771 ft. (4,807 m)
ALPS
Danube R.
Balkan Peninsula
Black Sea
Asia Minor
Caucasus Mts.
Mt. Elbrus 18,510 ft. (5,642 m)
Aral Sea
Caspian Sea
Irtysh River
ASIA
Lake Baikal
Amur R.
Sea of Okhotsk
Kuril Is.
Hokkaido
Sea of Japan
40°N

Pyrenees
Iberian Peninsula
Mediterranean Sea
Tigris R.
Euphrates R.
Persian Gulf
HINDU KUSH
TIAN SHAN
K2 28,250 ft. (8,611 m)
HIMALAYAS
GOBI (DESERT)
Plateau of Tibet
Mt. Everest 29,028 ft. (8,848 m)
Huang He
Chang Jiang
Honshu
Shikoku
Kyushu
East China Sea
PACIFIC OCEAN

Madeira Islands
Atlas Mts.
Canary Islands
SAHARA
Nile R.
Red Sea
Indus R.
Thar Desert
Ganges R.
Deccan Plateau
Bay of Bengal
Taiwan
South China Sea
Hainan
20°N

SAHEL
Lake Chad
Arabian Peninsula
Arabian Sea
Sri Lanka
Philippine Islands
Micronesia

Niger River
AFRICA
Ethiopian Highlands
Mt. Kenya 17,058 ft. (5,199 m)
Maldives
Malay Peninsula
0°

Congo River
CONGO BASIN
Lake Victoria
Mt. Kilimanjaro 19,340 ft. (5,895 m)
Lake Tanganyika
Seychelles
Sumatra
Borneo
Celebes
New Guinea
Java
Melanesia

ATLANTIC OCEAN
Lake Nyasa
INDIAN OCEAN
20°S
Fiji

Kalahari Desert
Madagascar
AUSTRALIA
GREAT VICTORIA DESERT
Darling R.
Murray R.
GREAT DIVIDING RANGE
Mt. Kosciusko 7,316 ft. (2,230 m)

Cape of Good Hope
Cape Agulhas
Tasmania

N
W · E
S

0 · 1,000 · 2,000 Miles
0 · 1,000 · 2,000 Kilometers
Robinson Projection
Scale accurate at equator

Ross Sea
60°S

ANTARCTICA
80°S

20°W · 0° · 20°E · 40°E · 60°E · 80°E · 100°E · 120°E · 140°E · 160°E · 180°

▲ Mountain peak
— National border

Southern Polar Region

South Shetland Islands
South Georgia
Bellingshausen Sea
Alexander I.
Antarctic Peninsula
ELLSWORTH LAND
Weddell Sea
ATLANTIC OCEAN

PACIFIC OCEAN
MARIE BYRD LAND
Vinson Massif 16,860 ft. (5,139 m)
Ronne Ice Shelf
QUEEN MAUD LAND

Ross Sea
Ross Ice Shelf
TRANSANTARCTIC MOUNTAINS
South Pole
POLAR PLATEAU
ENDERBY LAND

ANTARCTICA
WILKES LAND
Antarctic Circle

0 · 400 · 800 Miles
0 · 400 · 800 Kilometers
Azimuthal Equidistant Projection

South Magnetic Pole

A5

Atlas

Western Hemisphere: Political

ARCTIC OCEAN

Beaufort Sea

Viscount Melville Sound

Baffin Bay

Greenland
(DENMARK)

Bering Strait

Great Bear Lake

Foxe Basin

Davis Strait

Arctic Circle

ALASKA
(U.S.)
• Fairbanks

Yukon River

Great Slave Lake
• Yellowknife

Hudson Strait

• Anchorage
• Whitehorse
• Juneau

Mackenzie River

Liard River

CANADA
Lake Athabasca

Hudson Bay

Labrador Sea

60° N

Gulf of Alaska

Peace River

• Edmonton

Athabasca R.

Saskatchewan R.

Lake Winnipeg

James Bay

St. Lawrence River

• St. John's

Bering Sea

• Calgary
• Saskatoon

• Vancouver

Puget Sound

• Seattle
• Regina

• Winnipeg

UNITED STATES
• Thunder Bay

Great Lakes

⊛ Ottawa
• Quebec
⊛ Montreal

Gulf of St. Lawrence

• St. John
• Halifax

Columbia R.

Snake R.

• Portland
• Boise

• Toronto
• Detroit
• Cleveland
⊛ Albany
• Boston

• Chicago

• Salt Lake City

Great Salt Lake

• Indianapolis

• New York City
• Philadelphia
⊛ Washington, D.C.

• Reno

Missouri R.

• Denver

• St. Louis

• Richmond
• Norfolk

• San Francisco

Colorado R.

• Las Vegas

• Memphis

• Raleigh

• Atlanta

ATLANTIC
OCEAN

• Los Angeles
• San Diego

• Phoenix
• Tucson

• El Paso

Rio Grande

• Dallas

• Houston

Mississippi R.

• Charleston
• Savannah

• Hermosillo

• San Antonio

• New Orleans

• Jacksonville
• Tampa

30° N

Tropic of Cancer

• Honolulu

MEXICO

• Chihuahua

• Monterrey

Gulf of Mexico

• Miami

BAHAMAS
• Nassau

HAWAII
(U.S.)

• Durango

• Tampico

• Havana

CUBA

HAITI
• Port-au-Prince

PACIFIC
OCEAN

• León

(star) Mexico City

JAMAICA

• Santo Domingo

PUERTO RICO (U.S.)

• Guadalajara

• Puebla
• Veracruz

BELIZE

• Kingston

DOMINICAN REPUBLIC

• Acapulco

GUATEMALA
⊛ Belmopan

• Guatemala City
• San Salvador
⊛ Tegucigalpa
HONDURAS

Caribbean Sea

EL SALVADOR
⊛ Managua
• San José

NICARAGUA
⊛ Panama City

• Maracaibo

GUYANA

COSTA RICA
PANAMA

• Caracas

VENEZUELA

SURINAME
• Paramaribo

• Medellín

⊛ Georgetown
• Cayenne

FRENCH GUIANA (FRANCE)

• Cali
⊛ Bogotá

COLOMBIA

Rio Negro

Amazon R.

• Belém

• Quito

• Fortaleza

0°

Equator

Galápagos Islands
(ECUADOR)

• Guayaquil

ECUADOR

• Manaus

Tapajós River

Xingu R.

Tocantins R.

• Iquitos

• Recife

São Francisco R.

• Trujillo

PERU

BRAZIL

• Salvador

• Lima

• Cuzco

Lake Titicaca

• La Paz

• Brasília

• Belo Horizonte

FRENCH
POLYNESIA
(FRANCE)

• Arequipa

⊛ **BOLIVIA**

• Goiânia

• Campo Grande

• Rio de Janeiro

• Papeete

• Sucre

• São Paulo

Tropic of Capricorn

• Antofagasta

Paraguay R.

PARAGUAY

• Salta

⊛ Asunción

• Curitiba

• San Miguel de Tucumán

Paraná R.

• Pôrto Alegre

CHILE

• Córdoba

30° S

• Valparaíso
⊛ Santiago

• Rosario

URUGUAY
⊛ Buenos Aires
⊛ Montevideo

0   1,000   2,000 Miles

• Concepción

• La Plata

• Mar del Plata

0   1,000   2,000 Kilometers

• Valdivia

• Bahía Blanca

Miller Cylindrical Projection

ARGENTINA

N
W   E
S

—— National border
⊛ National capital
• City

A6

Falkland Islands
(U.K.)

South Georgia
(U.K.)

• Punta Arenas

150° W   120° W   90° W   60° W   30° W

Atlas

ARCTIC OCEAN

North Magnetic Pole

Ellesmere Island

Queen Elizabeth Islands

Melville Island

Devon Island

Baffin Bay

Greenland

Viscount Melville Sound

Banks Island

Beaufort Sea

Point Barrow

Victoria Island

Baffin Island

Brooks Range

Foxe Basin

Arctic Circle

Davis Strait

Mt. McKinley 20,320 ft. (6,194 m)

Yukon River

Mackenzie Mts

Great Bear Lake

Mackenzie River

Hudson Strait

Cape Farewell

60° N

Alaska Range

Yukon Plateau

Great Slave Lake

Liard River

Labrador Sea

Mt. Logan 19,524 ft. (5,951 m)

Gulf of Alaska

Peace River

Athabasca R.

Lake Athabasca

Hudson Bay

James Bay

Labrador

Alaska Peninsula

Kodiak Island

Coast Mountains

Saskatchewan River

Lake Winnipeg

CANADIAN SHIELD

Aleutian Islands

Queen Charlotte Islands

ROCKY

GREAT

NORTH AMERICA

Newfoundland

Gulf of St. Lawrence

Vancouver Island

Cascade Range

Coast Ranges

Snake R.

MOUNTAINS

PLAINS

Great Lakes

St. Lawrence R.

Nova Scotia

Puget Sound

Black Hills

Missouri R.

Mississippi R.

Bay of Fundy

Cape Cod

Long Island

Sierra Nevada

Great Salt Lake

GREAT BASIN

Platte R.

INTERIOR PLAINS

Ohio R.

APPALACHIAN MTS.

Mt. Whitney 14,495 ft. (4,418 m)

Colorado R.

Arkansas R.

Ozark Plateau

Cape Hatteras

Death Valley (lowest point in N.A.) -282 ft. (-86 m)

Sonoran Desert

Rio Grande

Sierra Madre Occidental

Sierra Madre Oriental

COASTAL PLAIN

ATLANTIC OCEAN

30° N

Baja California

Gulf of California

Gulf of Mexico

Bahamas

Tropic of Cancer

Hawaiian Islands

Yucatán Peninsula

Cuba

Greater Antilles

Hispaniola

Puerto Rico

PACIFIC OCEAN

Citlaltépetl 18,701 ft. (5,700 m)

Lesser Antilles

Lake Nicaragua

Caribbean Sea

Isthmus of Panama

Lake Maracaibo

Llanos

Orinoco R.

Guiana Highlands

Chimborazo 20,561 ft. (6,267 m)

Galápagos Islands

Rio Negro

Amazon R.

Cape São Roque

Equator

Line Islands

AMAZON BASIN

Marquesas Islands

ANDES

Tapajós R.

Xingu River

Tocantins R.

São Francisco River

Brazilian

Cook Islands

Tuamotu Archipelago

Society Islands

Huascarán 22,205 ft. (6,768 m)

Mato Grosso Plateau

Lake Titicaca

Highlands

SOUTH AMERICA

Paraguay R.

Tropic of Capricorn

Altiplano

Atacama Desert

Gran Chaco

Iguazú Falls

Paraná R.

Uruguay R.

30° S

Mt. Aconcagua 22,831 ft. (6,959 m)

Rio de la Plata

MOUNTAINS

Pampa

Valdés Peninsula (lowest point in S.A.) -131 ft. (-40 m)

0   1,000   2,000 Miles

0   1,000   2,000 Kilometers

Miller Cylindrical Projection

Patagonia

▲ Mountain peak

▼ Point below sea level

— National border

≈ Waterfall

N
W   E
S

Falkland Islands

South Georgia

Strait of Magellan

Tierra del Fuego

Cape Horn

A7

150° W   120° W   90° W   60° W   30° W

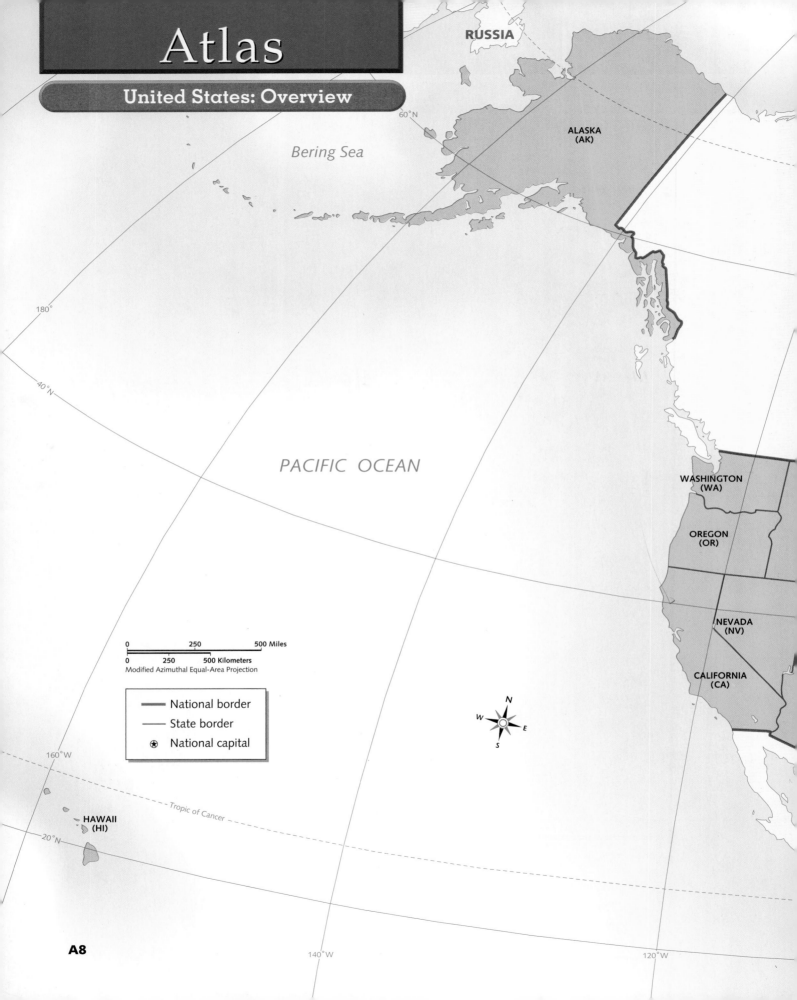

Atlas

United States: Overview

RUSSIA

60°N

Bering Sea

ALASKA
(AK)

180°

40°N

PACIFIC OCEAN

WASHINGTON
(WA)

OREGON
(OR)

NEVADA
(NV)

| 0 | 250 | 500 Miles |
| 0 | 250 | 500 Kilometers |

Modified Azimuthal Equal-Area Projection

CALIFORNIA
(CA)

National border
State border
National capital

N
W   E
S

160°W

Tropic of Cancer

HAWAII
(HI)

20°N

140°W

120°W

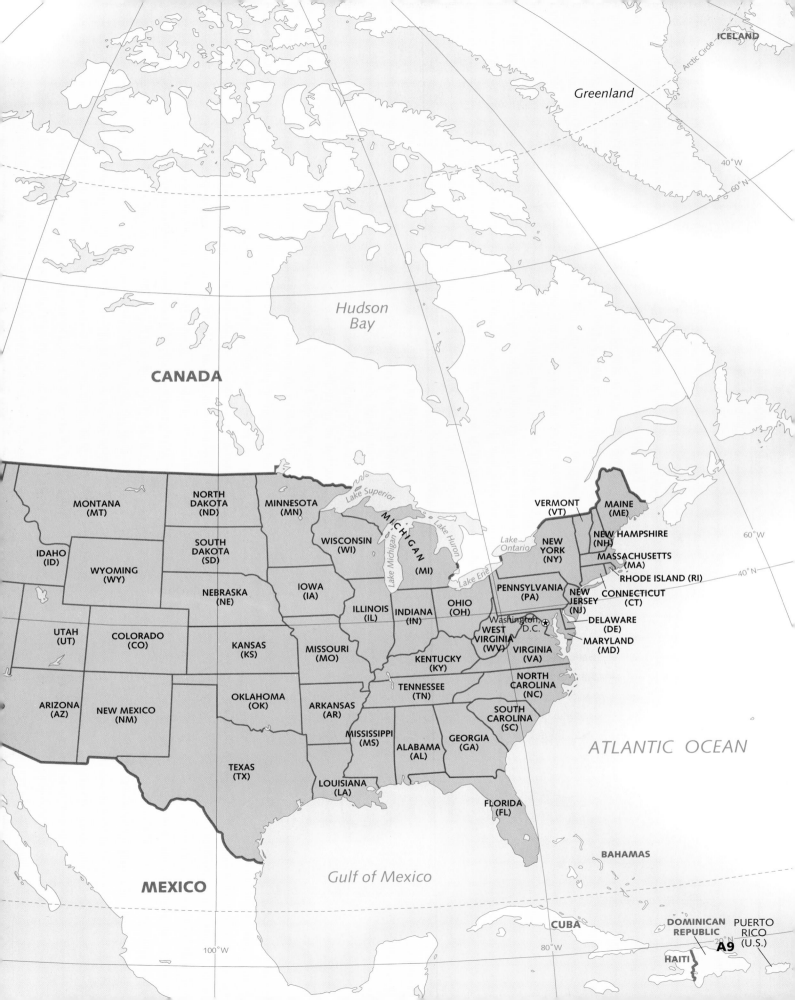

ICELAND

Greenland

CANADA

Hudson
Bay

Lake Superior

MONTANA
(MT)

NORTH
DAKOTA
(ND)

MINNESOTA
(MN)

VERMONT
(VT)

MAINE
(ME)

IDAHO
(ID)

WYOMING
(WY)

SOUTH
DAKOTA
(SD)

WISCONSIN
(WI)

MICHIGAN
(MI)

Lake Huron

Lake
Ontario

NEW
YORK
(NY)

NEW HAMPSHIRE
(NH)

MASSACHUSETTS
(MA)

RHODE ISLAND (RI)

UTAH
(UT)

COLORADO
(CO)

NEBRASKA
(NE)

IOWA
(IA)

Lake Michigan

Lake Erie

PENNSYLVANIA
(PA)

CONNECTICUT
(CT)

ILLINOIS
(IL)

INDIANA
(IN)

OHIO
(OH)

Washington,
D.C.

NEW
JERSEY
(NJ)

DELAWARE
(DE)

KANSAS
(KS)

MISSOURI
(MO)

WEST
VIRGINIA
(WV)

MARYLAND
(MD)

ARIZONA
(AZ)

NEW MEXICO
(NM)

OKLAHOMA
(OK)

ARKANSAS
(AR)

KENTUCKY
(KY)

VIRGINIA
(VA)

TENNESSEE
(TN)

NORTH
CAROLINA
(NC)

SOUTH
CAROLINA
(SC)

TEXAS
(TX)

MISSISSIPPI
(MS)

ALABAMA
(AL)

GEORGIA
(GA)

ATLANTIC OCEAN

LOUISIANA
(LA)

FLORIDA
(FL)

MEXICO

Gulf of Mexico

BAHAMAS

CUBA

DOMINICAN
REPUBLIC

PUERTO
RICO
(U.S.)

HAITI

A9

Arctic Circle

40°W

60°N

60°W

40°N

100°W

80°W

20°N

Atlas

United States: Political

RUSSIA

ARCTIC OCEAN

ALASKA

CANADA

170° E

70° N

120° W

Arctic Circle

Yukon River

60° N

Fairbanks

Yukon River

60° N

Anchorage

Bering Sea

180°

250   500 Miles

250   500 Kilometers

Juneau

PACIFIC OCEAN

50° N

170° W   160° W   150° W   140° W   130° W

CANADA

120° W   110° W

Seattle
Tacoma
Olympia
WASHINGTON
Spokane

Great Falls

Portland
Columbia River
Helena
MONTANA

Salem
OREGON
IDAHO
Billings
Yellowstone R.

Eugene

Boise

Snake River

WYOMING
Pocatello

Casper

40° N

Great Salt Lake
Ogden
Salt Lake City
Cheyenne

Reno
NEVADA
Provo

Sacramento
Carson City
UTAH
Denver

San Francisco   Oakland
San Jose
Colorado River
Colorado Springs

PACIFIC OCEAN

130° W

Fresno
COLORADO
Pueblo

CALIFORNIA
Las Vegas

Bakersfield

Santa Fe

Flagstaff
Albuquerque

30° N

Los Angeles
San Bernardino
ARIZONA
NEW MEXICO

San Diego
Phoenix
Roswell

Tucson

El Paso
Rio Grande

Legend

Northeast	National capital
Southeast	State capital
Middle West	Major city
Southwest	National border
West	State border

MEXICO

N
W   E
S

160° W   PACIFIC OCEAN   155° W

Honolulu
HAWAII

20° N

Hilo

100   200 Miles

100   200 Kilometers

250   500 Miles

250   500 Kilometers

Albers Equal-Area Projection

20° N

120° W   110° W

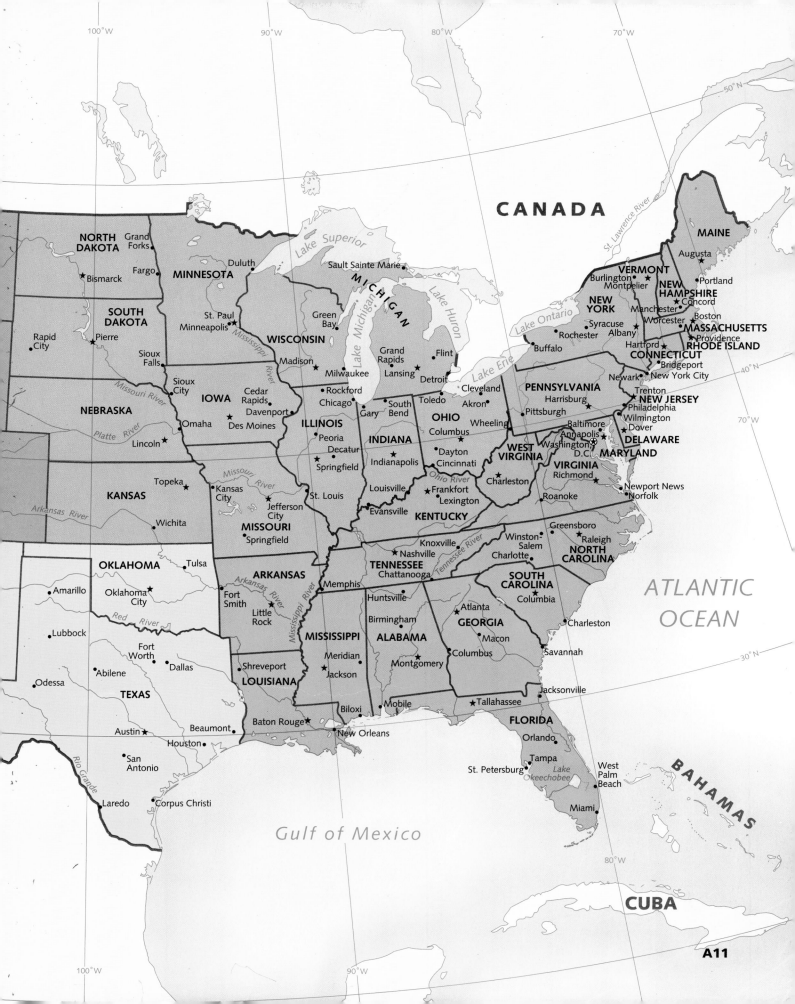

Atlas

United States: Physical

CANADA

RUSSIA

ARCTIC OCEAN

170° E

Brooks Range

70° N

120° W

ALASKA

Seward Peninsula

St. Lawrence Island

Yukon River

60° N

Arctic Circle

CANADA

Mt. McKinley 20,320 ft. (6,194 m) △

Alaska Range

Yukon River

60° N

Bering Strait

Bering Sea

Gulf of Alaska

50° N

Aleutian Islands

Kodiak Island

180°

150° W

140° W

130° W

Legend

- Arid
- Evergreen forest
- Grassland
- Mixed forest
- Mountains
- Tundra
- National border
- State border
- ▲ Mountain peak
- △ Highest point
- ▼ Lowest point

PACIFIC OCEAN

Coast Ranges

Cascade Range

WA

Mt. Rainier 14,410 ft. (4,392 m) ▲

Mt. St. Helens 8,364 ft. (2,549 m) ▲

Columbia River

Mt. Hood 11,235 ft. (3,427 m) ▲

OR

Columbia Plateau

Bitterroot Range

ID

Salmon River Mountains

Snake River

ROCKY

Fort Peck Lake

MT

Yellowstone River

Bighorn Mts.

Teton Range

Wind River Range

WY

Great Divide Basin

Front Range

MOUNTAINS

Cape Mendocino

Sacramento River

Sierra Nevada

Pyramid Lake

Donner Pass

Lake Tahoe

NV

GREAT BASIN

Great Salt Lake

Wasatch Range

Uinta Mts.

Mt. Elbert 14,433 ft. (4,399 m) ▲

San Juan Mts.

Sangre de Cristo Mts.

Coast Ranges

Central Valley

San Joaquin R.

Mt. Whitney 14,495 ft. (4,418 m) ▲

Death Valley -282 ft. (-86 m) ▼

Mojave Desert

Lake Powell

Colorado River

Lake Mead

Grand Canyon

UT

CO

Colorado Plateau

Point Conception

CA

Channel Islands

30° N

Salton Sea

Imperial Valley

Sonoran Desert

AZ

Baldy Peak 11,403 ft. (3,476 m) ▲

NM

Guadalupe Peak 8,749 ft. (2,667 m) ▲

Rio Grande

130° W

MEXICO

HAWAII

160° W

155° W

PACIFIC OCEAN

Kauai

Niihau

Oahu

Molokai

Lanai

Maui

Kahoolawe

20° N

Hawaii

Mauna Kea 13,796 ft. (4,205 m) ▲

0   100   200 Miles

0   100   200 Kilometers

N
W   E
S

0   250   500 Miles

0   250   500 Kilometers

Albers Equal-Area Projection

20° N

120° W

110° W

A12

CANADA

ME
Moosehead Lake
▲ Mt. Katahdin 5,267 ft. (1,605 m)

Lake of the Woods
Upper Red Lake
Lower Red Lake
Mesabi Range
Leech Lake
Mille Lacs Lake

Isle Royale
Lake Superior
Keweenaw Peninsula

Upper Peninsula

Lake Champlain
VT
Green Mts.
▲ Mt. Washington 6,288 ft. (1,917 m)
NH
Cape Ann

Lake Sakakawea

ND

MN

WI
Wisconsin River

Lake Huron

NY
Adirondack Mountains
Connecticut R.
White Mts.
MA
Cape Cod

SD
Lake Oahe

Mississippi River

Lake Michigan
Lower Peninsula

MI
Lake St. Clair

Lake Ontario
Niagara Falls
Finger Lakes
Hudson R.
CT
RI

Black Hills

Lake Winnebago

Lake Erie

PA

Allegheny Mts.
Potomac R.
MD
NJ
Long Island

G
North Platte R.
Sand Hills
NE
Platte River
South Platte R.

IA

IL
Illinois River
Wabash River

IN

OH

WV
VA
James R.
DE
Delaware Bay

R
E
A
T

I N T E R I O R
P L A I N S
Missouri River

Missouri River

MO

CENTRAL PLAINS

Ohio River

KY
Cumberland Gap
Mt. Mitchell 6,684 ft. (2,037 m) ▲
Roanoke R.

APPALACHIAN MOUNTAINS

Cape Charles
Chesapeake Bay
Albemarle Sound

Smoky Hills

Lake of the Ozarks
Harry S. Truman Reservoir

KS

Ozark Plateau

Lake Barkley
Cumberland R.

P
I
E
D
M
O
N
T

NC
Cape Fear River
Cape Hatteras

Red Hills

P
L
A
I
N
S

Arkansas River

Mississippi River

TN

Cape Fear

OK
Canadian River
Ouachita Mountains
Lake Texoma

AR

Stone Mountain ▲
Chattahoochee R.
Clark Hill Lake
Savannah River
Oconee R.
SC

Llano Estacado

Red River

MS

GA

Altamaha R.
Okefenokee Swamp

COASTAL

Sabine River

Tombigbee R.
Alabama R.

Brazos River

Toledo Bend Reservoir
LA

AL

TX

Pecos River

Edwards Plateau
Colorado River

Sam Rayburn Reservoir

P L A I N
Lake Maurepas
Lake Pontchartrain

St. Johns River

Cape Canaveral

FL

ATLANTIC OCEAN

Rio Grande

Galveston Bay

Mobile Bay

Mississippi Delta

Tampa Bay
Lake Okeechobee

BAHAMAS

Cape Sable
Everglades
Florida Keys
Straits of Florida

Gulf of Mexico

CUBA

A13

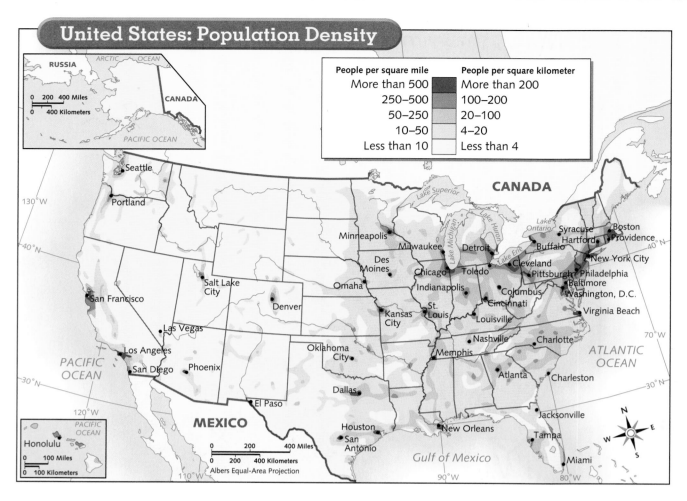

United States: Population Density

People per square mile
- More than 500
- 250–500
- 50–250
- 10–50
- Less than 10

People per square kilometer
- More than 200
- 100–200
- 20–100
- 4–20
- Less than 4

RUSSIA
ARCTIC OCEAN
CANADA
PACIFIC OCEAN
0 200 400 Miles
0 400 Kilometers

Seattle
Portland
San Francisco
Salt Lake City
Las Vegas
Los Angeles
San Diego
Phoenix
Denver
El Paso

130°W
40°N
30°N
120°W
110°W

PACIFIC OCEAN

Honolulu
PACIFIC OCEAN
0 100 Miles
0 100 Kilometers

MEXICO

Minneapolis
Milwaukee
Des Moines
Chicago
Omaha
Indianapolis
Kansas City
St. Louis
Oklahoma City
Dallas
Houston
San Antonio
New Orleans

Detroit
Toledo
Cleveland
Pittsburgh
Columbus
Cincinnati
Louisville
Nashville
Memphis
Atlanta

Buffalo
Syracuse
Hartford
Boston
Providence
New York City
Philadelphia
Baltimore
Washington, D.C.
Virginia Beach
Charlotte
Charleston
Jacksonville
Tampa
Miami

CANADA
Lake Superior
Lake Michigan
Lake Huron
Lake Erie
Lake Ontario

ATLANTIC OCEAN
Gulf of Mexico

90°W
80°W
70°W

0 200 400 Miles
0 200 400 Kilometers
Albers Equal-Area Projection

United States: Land Use and Resources

- Manufacturing
- Farming
- Grazing
- Forest
- Little-used land

- Fishing
- Oil or natural gas
- Coal
- Iron
- Copper

- G Gold
- S Silver
- L Limestone
- U Uranium
- Zn Zinc

RUSSIA
ARCTIC OCEAN
CANADA
Anchorage
PACIFIC OCEAN
0 200 400 Miles
0 400 Kilometers

Seattle
Portland
San Francisco
Los Angeles
San Diego
Denver
El Paso
Fort Worth
Dallas
Houston

Minneapolis
Milwaukee
Des Moines
Chicago
Omaha
Indianapolis
Kansas City
St. Louis
Cincinnati

Detroit
Cleveland
Pittsburgh
Buffalo
Boston
New York City
Philadelphia
Baltimore
Washington, D.C.
Charlotte
Atlanta
Jacksonville
New Orleans

CANADA
Lake Superior
Lake Michigan
Lake Huron
Lake Erie
Lake Ontario

PACIFIC OCEAN
ATLANTIC OCEAN
Gulf of Mexico

MEXICO

130°W
40°N
30°N
120°W
110°W
90°W
80°W
70°W

Honolulu
PACIFIC OCEAN
0 100 Miles
0 100 Kilometers

0 200 400 Miles
0 200 400 Kilometers
Albers Equal-Area Projection

A14

United States: Climate

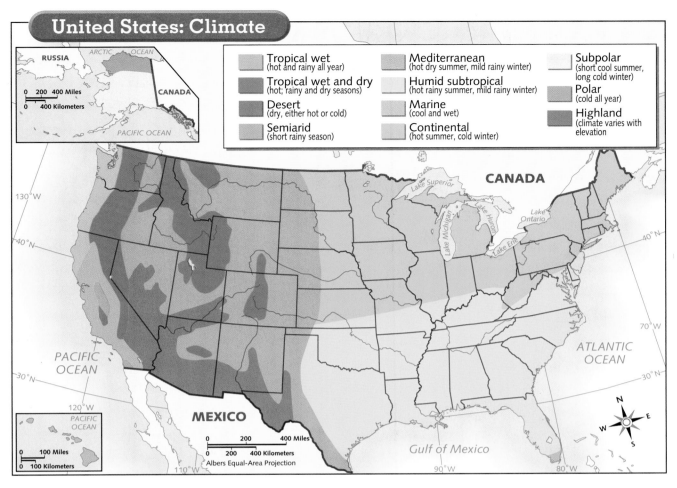

Tropical wet (hot and rainy all year)

Tropical wet and dry (hot; rainy and dry seasons)

Desert (dry, either hot or cold)

Semiarid (short rainy season)

Mediterranean (hot dry summer, mild rainy winter)

Humid subtropical (hot rainy summer, mild rainy winter)

Marine (cool and wet)

Continental (hot summer, cold winter)

Subpolar (short cool summer, long cold winter)

Polar (cold all year)

Highland (climate varies with elevation)

United States: Vegetation

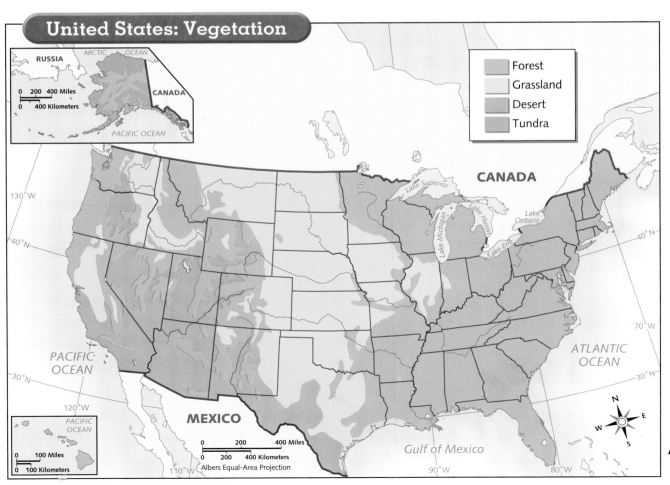

Forest

Grassland

Desert

Tundra

A15

Atlas
Geography Terms

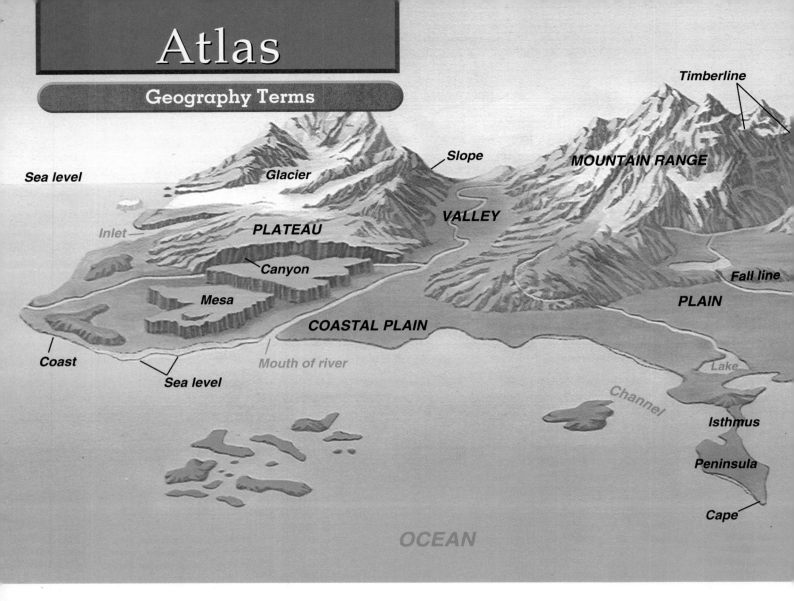

Timberline

Sea level

Slope

Glacier

MOUNTAIN RANGE

VALLEY

Inlet

PLATEAU

Canyon

Mesa

Fall line

PLAIN

COASTAL PLAIN

Coast

Mouth of river

Sea level

Lake

Channel

Isthmus

Peninsula

Cape

OCEAN

basin bowl-shaped area of land surrounded by higher land

bay body of water that is part of a sea or an ocean and is partly enclosed by land

bluff high, steep face of rock or earth

canyon deep, narrow valley with steep sides

cape point of land that extends into water

channel deepest part of a body of water

cliff high, steep face of rock or earth

coast land along a sea or ocean

coastal plain area of flat land along a sea or ocean

delta triangle-shaped area of land at the mouth of a river

desert dry land with few plants

dune hill of sand piled up by the wind

fall line area along which rivers form waterfalls or rapids as the rivers drop to lower land

floodplain flat land that is near the edges of a river and is formed by the silt deposited by floods

foothills hilly area at the base of a mountain

glacier large ice mass that moves slowly down a mountain or across land

gulf body of water that is partly enclosed by land but is larger than a bay

harbor area of water where ships can dock safely near land

hill land that rises above the land around it

inlet a narrow strip of water leading into the land from a larger body of water

island land that has water on all sides

isthmus narrow strip of land connecting two larger areas of land

lake body of water with land on all sides

marsh lowland with moist soil and tall grasses

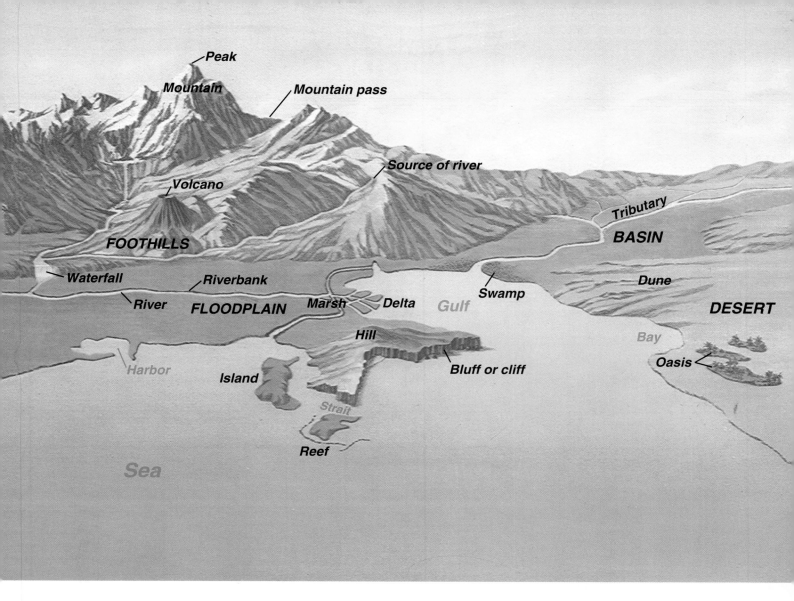

mesa flat-topped mountain with steep sides

mountain highest kind of land

mountain pass gap between mountains

mountain range row of mountains

mouth of river place where a river empties into another body of water

oasis area of water and fertile land in a desert

ocean body of salt water larger than a sea

peak top of a mountain

peninsula land that is almost completely surrounded by water

plain flat land

plateau area of high, flat land with steep sides

reef ridge of sand, rock, or coral that lies at or near the surface of a sea or ocean

river large stream of water that flows across the land

riverbank land along a river

sea body of salt water smaller than an ocean

sea level the level that is even with the surface of an ocean or sea

slope side of a hill or mountain

source of river place where a river begins

strait narrow channel of water connecting two larger bodies of water

swamp area of low, wet land with trees

timberline line on a mountain above which it is too cold for trees to grow

tributary stream or river that empties into a larger river

valley low land between hills or mountains

volcano opening in the Earth, often raised, through which lava, rock, ashes, and gases are forced out

waterfall steep drop from a high place to a lower place in a stream or river

WHY STUDY SOCIAL STUDIES?

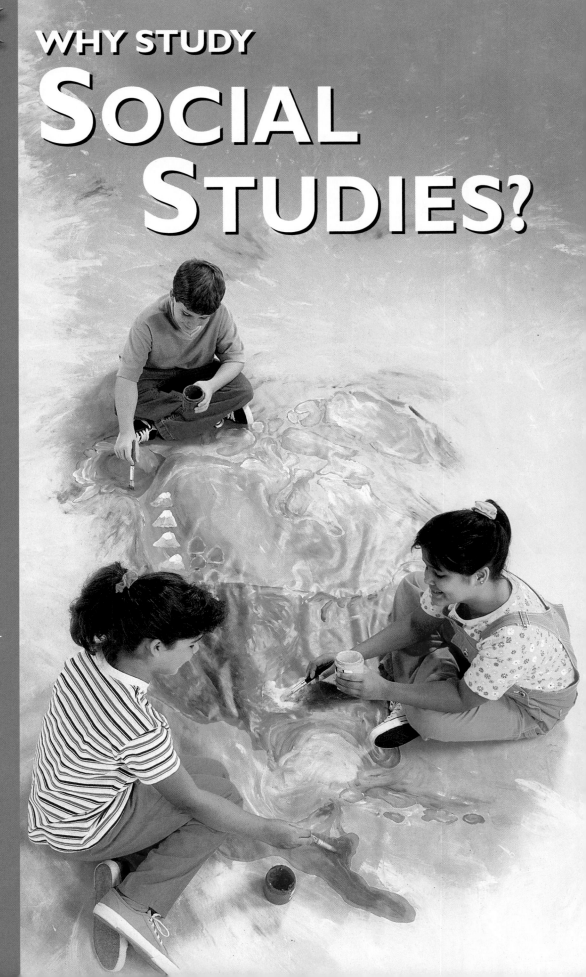

"*Every one of you already holds the important office of citizen. Over time you will become more and more involved in your community. You will need to know more about what being a citizen means. Social studies will help you learn about citizenship. That is why social studies is important in your life.*"

The authors of
Harcourt Brace
Social Studies

The Themes of Social Studies

Think about the many groups of which you are a part. Your family, your class, and your community are different kinds of groups, and you are a member of each one. You are also a member—or **citizen**—of your town or city, your state, and your country. Citizens work to improve the many groups to which they belong and to make their world a better place.

To help you think, feel, and act as a citizen, *Harcourt Brace Social Studies* begins every lesson with a question. That question connects the lesson to one or more of five themes, or key topics, of social studies. Citizens need to understand these themes in order to make decisions. Each question also links you to the lesson's story, helping you see how the story relates to your own life. The lesson helps you learn about being a citizen by letting you see how people from many places and times have thought, felt, and acted. Each lesson will help you organize your thinking around one or more of the following five themes of social studies.

In this painting by Howard Chandler Christy, American leaders are shown in 1787 signing the Constitution, the plan of government for the United States. By taking part in government, these leaders were carrying out the office of citizen.

Commonality and Diversity

In some ways people everywhere are alike. We all have the same basic needs for things such as food, clothing, and shelter. We all laugh, get angry, and have our feelings hurt. These are examples of our commonality (kah•muh•NA•luh•tee), or what we all share. At the same time, we need to understand that each person is different from everyone else. We each have our own ways of thinking, feeling, and acting. That is our diversity (duh•VER•suh•tee). Learning about commonality and diversity can help you see that every person is unique and deserves understanding and respect.

All people are alike in some ways, but each person has different ways of thinking, feeling, and acting.

Conflict and Cooperation

Because people are different from one another, they sometimes have conflicts, or disagreements. People can often settle their conflicts by cooperating, or working together. In social studies you will learn about the disagreements people have had in the past and about many of the ways people have found to settle their disagreements. You will also learn ways to cooperate and to settle conflicts in your own life.

Continuity and Change

While some things change over time, other things stay the same. Many things have stayed the same for years and will probably stay the same in the future. This means that they have continuity (kahn•tuhn•OO•uh•tee). Understanding continuity and change can help you see how things in the world came to be as they are. You will learn how a past event, or something that has happened, may have helped shape your life. You will also learn how present events can help you make better decisions about the future.

Individualism and Interdependence

Citizens can act by themselves to make a difference in the world. Their actions as individuals (in•duh•VIJ•wuhlz) may be helpful or harmful to other citizens. Much of the time, however, people do not act alone. They depend on others for help, and others depend on them. People depend on one another in families, schools, religious groups, government groups, and other groups and organizations. Such interdependence (in•ter•dih•PEN•duhns) connects citizens with one another.

Interaction Within Different Environments

People's actions affect other people. People's actions also affect their environment (in•VY•ruhn•muhnt), or surroundings. This is true of their physical environment, their home environment, their school environment, and any other environments of which they may be a part. Their environments affect them, too. Understanding such interactions is important to understanding why things happened in the past and why things happen today.

Understanding interaction is important for understanding social studies. The subjects that make up social studies are all related. You will learn, for example, that history—the study of the past—is related to geography—the study of the Earth's surface and the way people use it. Civics and government, or the study of how people live together in a community, is related to economics, or the study of how people use resources. And all of these subjects are related to the study of culture. **Culture** is a people's way of life, including their customs, ideas, and practices. These subjects interact with one another to tell a story. Together they tell how people have lived over time and how they have made contributions as citizens. Understanding this story will help you learn how to hold the office of citizen.

REVIEW *What are the five themes of social studies?*

When you take part in student government or other groups, you are also carrying out the office of citizen. Understanding each of the themes of social studies will help you make decisions as a citizen.

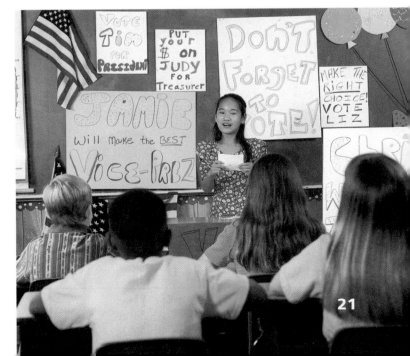

21

Read Social Studies

1. Why Learn This Skill?

Social studies is made up of stories about people, places, and events. Sometimes you read these stories in library books. At other times you read them in textbooks like this one. Knowing how to read social studies can make it easier to study and do your homework. It can help you find important ideas and learn about people, places, and events.

2. Getting Started

Your book is divided into ten units. At the beginning of each unit, you will find several pages that will help you preview the unit and predict what it will be about.

▲

Each unit begins with a short overview of the unit and a list of the social studies themes it teaches. You will also read about a project you can complete as you study the unit.

▲

The Unit Preview has a map that shows where some of the important events you will read about took place. It also has a time line that shows the order in which the events happened. There may be a story line that shows some of the people, places, or events.

▲

Each unit has at least one literature selection that helps you understand the time and place you are studying. The literature selection may be a story, or it may be a poem or a song.

3. The Parts of a Lesson

Each unit has two chapters, and each chapter is divided into lessons. The first page of a chapter and the beginning and end of a lesson are shown below.

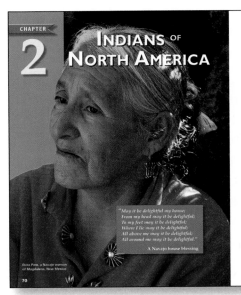

This question helps you see how the lesson relates to life today.

This statement gives you the lesson's main idea. It tells you what to look for as you read the lesson.

These are the new terms you will learn in the lesson.

Each new vocabulary term is highlighted in yellow and defined.

Each lesson, like each chapter and each unit, ends with a review. The review questions and activities help you check your understanding and show what you know.

4. Understand the Process

You can follow these steps to read any lesson in this book.

1 Preview the whole lesson.
- Look at the title and the headings to find out what the lesson is about.
- Look at the pictures, the captions, and the questions to get an idea of what is most important in the lesson.
- Read the Focus question at the beginning of the lesson to see how the lesson relates to life today.
- Read the Main Idea statement to find out the main idea of the lesson.
- Look at the Vocabulary list to see what new terms you will learn.

2 Read the lesson to learn more about the main idea. As you read, you will come to a number of questions with the label **REVIEW**. Be sure to answer these questions before you continue reading the lesson.

3 When you finish reading the lesson, say in your own words what you have learned.

4 Look back over the lesson. Then answer the Lesson Review questions from memory. These questions will help you check your understanding of the lesson. The activity at the end of the review will help you show what you know.

5. Some Other Parts of Your Book

Your textbook has many other features to help you learn. Some of them are shown below.

▲ The skills lessons help you build basic study skills. They also help you build citizenship skills as you work with others.

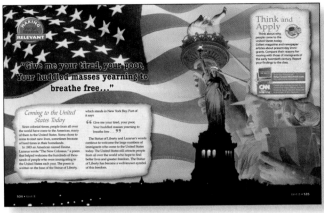

▲ The feature called Making Social Studies Relevant helps you see how social studies is connected to your life and the lives of other people.

▲ The Counterpoints pages help you understand the different points of view people may have about certain issues.

At the back of your book is a section called *For Your Reference*. It includes the following reference tools.

- How to Gather and Report Information
- Almanac
- American Documents
- Biographical Dictionary
- Gazetteer
- Glossary
- Index

6. Think and Apply

Use the four steps in Understand the Process each time you read a lesson in *Harcourt Brace Social Studies*.

History

istory helps you see the links between the past and the present. It also helps you understand how things that happen today can affect the future. History is about what happened last month and last year as well as in the ancient past.

As you read about the people, places, and events of the past, ask yourself the four questions below. They will help you think more like a historian, a person who studies the past.

- What happened?
- Who took part in it?
- How and why did it happen?
- When did it happen?

What Happened?

To find out what really happened in the past, you need proof. You can find proof by studying two kinds of sources—primary sources and secondary sources. Historians use these kinds of sources in writing history.

Primary sources are the records made by people who saw or took part in an event. They may have written down their thoughts in a journal. They may have told their story in a letter or a poem. They may have taken a photograph, made a film, or painted a picture. Each of these records is a primary source, giving the people of today a direct link to a past event.

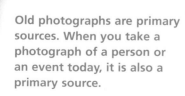

Old photographs are primary sources. When you take a photograph of a person or an event today, it is also a primary source.

A **secondary source** is not a direct link to an event. It is a record of the event written by someone who was not there at the time. A magazine article, newspaper story, or book written at a later time by someone who only heard or read about an event is a secondary source. A newspaper may include both primary sources and secondary sources.

When there are no written records of an event, historians gather proof through oral histories. An **oral history** can be either a primary or a secondary source, depending on the events a person describes. Oral histories tell the experiences of people who did not have a written language or who did not write down what happened. Oral histories can be recorded by writing down an interview with someone. Today they also can be recorded by making an audiotape or a videotape of the interview.

As you read this book, you will read many kinds of primary and secondary sources. The stories told in each lesson contain primary sources—the words and photographs of people in the past—as well as secondary sources written by historians. Maps, graphs, literature, pictures, and diagrams also help tell the stories you will read.

Newspapers help keep citizens aware of the events occurring all over the world. Newspapers and this textbook contain both primary and secondary sources.

You may gather information about the past through interviews.

Who Took Part in It?

To understand the stories of the past, you need to know something about the people who took part in the stories and about the times and places in which people lived. This will help you understand their actions and feelings. This understanding is called **historical empathy**.

By reading the words of people of the past, you can come to understand their **perspective**, or point of view. A person's perspective will depend on whether that person is old or young, man or woman, rich or poor. Perspective is also shaped by a person's culture and race. Your understanding of history will grow as you study the many perspectives of the people who took part in the stories. You will see that all people, even those living in other places and times, are a lot like you.

History lets you come face to face with people from the past.

How and Why Did It Happen?

Many events in history are linked to other events. To find the links between events, you will need to identify causes and effects. A **cause** is any action that makes something happen. What happens because of that action is an **effect**. Historians have found that most events have many causes and many effects.

To understand an event, you need to analyze its causes and effects. When you **analyze** something, you break it into its parts and look closely at how those parts connect with one another. Once you have analyzed an event, you can summarize it or draw a conclusion about how or why it happened.

When Did It Happen?

One way to tell or write a story of the past is to put the events in the order in which they happened. This presents the story's **chronology** (kruh•NAH•luh•gee), or time order. As you read this book, you will notice that it is organized by chronology. The events described at the beginning of the book happened before the events described at the end of the book.

You will see many time lines in this book. They will help you understand each story's chronology. A time line is a diagram that shows the events that took place during a certain period of time in the order in which they happened. Time lines may show a period of a month or a year. Others may show a period of 10 years, 100 years, or 1,000 years. Time lines can help you understand how one event may have led to another.

REVIEW *What questions should you ask yourself when you read about the past?*

Time lines help you understand *when* in the past something happened.

Work Together in Groups

1. Why Learn This Skill?

Many of the projects you do in social studies will be easier if you work with a partner or in a group. Each of you can work on part of the project. For a group project to succeed, each member needs to cooperate with the others. Knowing how to work together is an important skill for students and for all citizens.

2. Understand the Process

Suppose your group were asked to do a project, such as presenting a short play about everyday life long ago. You might find it helpful to follow a set of steps.

1 Organize and plan together.
   - Set your goal as a group.
   - Share your ideas.
   - Cooperate with others to plan your work.
   - Make sure everyone has a job.

2 Act on your plan together.
   - Take responsibility for your work.
   - Help one another.
   - If there are conflicts, talk about them until they are settled.
   - Show your group's finished work to the class.

3 Talk about your work.
   - Discuss what you learned by working together.
   - Discuss what could have been done differently to improve how your group worked together.

3. Think and Apply

Follow the steps above for working together as you take part in the activities in *Harcourt Brace Social Studies.*

These students are preparing for a class play about life in the British colonies in the Americas.

Geography

The stories you will read in this book all have a setting. The setting of a story includes the place where it happens. Knowing about places is an important part of geography. **Geographers**, people whose work is to study geography, think about the following five topics or questions when they study a place.

- **Location**
  Where is it?
- **Place**
  What is it like there?
- **Human-environment interactions**
  How does this place affect the lives of people living there?
  How do people living there affect this place?
- **Movement**
  How and why do people, ideas, and goods move to and from this place?
- **Regions**
  How is this place like other places? How is it different?

Asking yourself these questions will help you understand the setting of a story. These five topics are so important that many people call them the five themes of geography.

Location

Everything on the Earth has its own location. To tell exactly where you live in your town or city, you can use the names and numbers of your home address. To find your **absolute location**, or exact location, on the Earth, you can use the numbers of your "global address." These numbers appear on a pattern of imaginary lines drawn on maps and globes. You will read more about these lines on pages 34–36 when you review how to read a map.

The location of a place can also be described in relation to the location of other places. You describe the **relative location** of a place when you say what it is near. You might say that the bus stop is on the corner by the gas station, or you might also say that the city of New Orleans is southeast of the city of St. Louis.

Place

Every location on the Earth has a place identity made up of unique features that make it different from all other locations. A place can be described by its **physical features**—landforms, bodies of water, climate, soil, plant and animal life, and other natural resources. Many places also have **human features**—buildings, bridges, farms, roads, and the people themselves. People's culture also helps form a place's identity.

The Golden Gate Bridge is a human feature that helps make the San Francisco skyline unique.

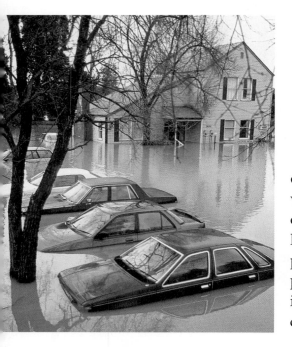

People are affected by the environment when floods cover the ground with muddy water.

Human-Environment Interactions

Humans and the environment interact, or affect each other. People interact with their environment in different ways. Sometimes they change it. They clear land to grow crops. They build cities and towns. Sometimes people pollute the environment. The environment can also cause people to change the way they act. People who live in cold places wear warm clothing. Sometimes things that happen in nature, such as hurricanes, tornadoes, and earthquakes, cause great changes in people's lives.

Movement

Each day, people in different parts of the country and different parts of the world interact with one another. People, products, and ideas move by transportation and communication. Geography helps you understand the causes and effects of this movement. It also helps you understand how people came to live where they do.

An air traffic controller helps track the movement of airplanes.

Regions

Areas on the Earth with features that make them different from other areas are called **regions**. A region can be described by the physical features, such as mountains or a dry climate, that exist there. A region can also be described by its human features, such as the language most of its people speak or the way they are governed. Sometimes a region is described by its political, cultural, or economic features.

Regions are sometimes divided into smaller regions that are easier to compare. Some geographers who study the Earth's surface and its people divide the United States into regions named for their relative locations—Northeast, Southeast, Middle West, Southwest, and West.

The states in each region are alike in many ways. They are all in the same part of the United States. They may have the same kind of landforms, climate, and natural resources. The people who live in those states often earn their living in the same ways. Dividing the 50 states into regions makes the geography of the United States easier to understand.

REVIEW *What are the five themes of geography?*

LEARNING FROM DIAGRAMS The 50 states are often grouped into five regions. The states in each region are all in the same part of the country.

■ *In which region of the United States is your state located?*

Regions of the United States

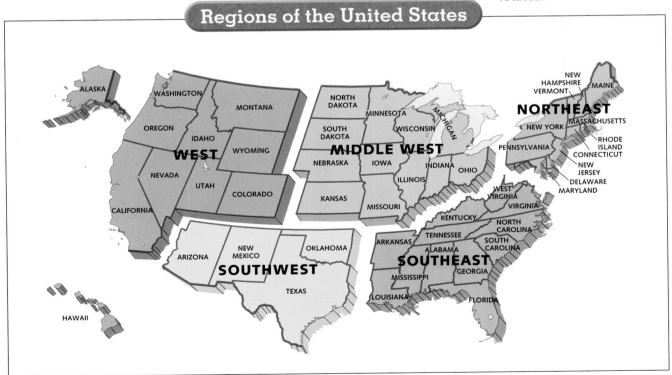

Read a Map

1. Why Learn This Skill?

To answer questions about the world around you, you need information. One way you can get this information is by studying maps. Maps tell you about the world by using one or more of the five themes of geography. Knowing how to read and understand maps is an important skill both for learning social studies and for taking action as a citizen.

2. The Parts of a Map

Maps are drawings that show the Earth or part of the Earth on a flat surface. To help you read maps, mapmakers add certain features to most maps they draw. These are a title, a map key, a compass rose, a locator, a map scale, and an inset map. Mapmakers may also put a grid of numbered lines on maps to help people locate places more easily.

The **map title** tells the subject of the map. What is the title of the map shown on page 34? A map title may also help you understand what kind of map it is. Physical maps show landforms and bodies of water. Sometimes, shading is used to help you see where the hills and mountains are located. Political maps show cities and national boundaries, or borders. Many of the maps in this book are historical maps that show the United States as it was in the past. Historical maps often have dates in their titles. When you look at any map, look for information in the title to find out what the map is about.

⊛ National capital

★ State capital

━━━ National border

── State border

The **map key**, sometimes called a map legend, explains what the symbols on the map stand for. Symbols may be colors, patterns, lines, or other special marks, such as circles, triangles, or squares. According to the map key for the map on page 34, stars are used to show state capitals. What symbol is used to show the national capital?

The **compass rose**, or direction marker, shows the **cardinal directions**, or main directions— north, south, east, and west. A compass rose also helps you find the **intermediate directions**, which are between the cardinal directions. Intermediate directions are northeast, northwest, southeast, and southwest.

The **locator** is a small map or picture of a globe. It shows where the area shown on the main map is located in a state, in a country, on a continent, or in the world. The locator on the map of the United States on page 34 is a globe that shows the continent of North America. The United States is shown in red.

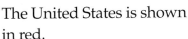

The **map scale** compares a distance on a map to a distance in the real world. A map scale helps you find the real distance between places on a map. Each map in this book has a scale that shows both miles and kilometers.

Map scales are different, depending on the size of the area the map shows. Look at the map of the United States on page 34. On that map are two smaller maps—one of Alaska and one of Hawaii. A small map within a larger map is called an **inset map**. The boxes around Alaska and Hawaii show that they are inset maps. Inset maps have their own scales. Inset maps make it possible to show places in greater detail or to show places that are beyond the area shown on the main map.

The north-south and east-west lines on a map cross each other to form a pattern of squares called a **grid**. The east-west lines are **lines of latitude**. The north-south lines are **lines of longitude**. This grid helps you find the absolute location, or global address, of a place.

3. Understand the Process

Use the map of Illinois on this page to answer the following questions.

1. What is the title of the map?
2. What five states share a border with Illinois?
3. Find the map key. Which symbol is used to show the state capital?
4. Find the compass rose. In which direction would you travel if you went from Peoria to Rockford?
5. Find the locator. How is the location of Illinois shown?
6. Find the map scale. How long is the line that stands for 90 miles?
7. About how many miles is it from Springfield to Decatur?
8. Find the inset map. What area is shown in the inset map?
9. What line of latitude is closest to Elgin?
10. What line of longitude is closest to Naperville?

4. Think and Apply

Look again at the map of Illinois. Find the different parts of the map, and discuss with a partner what information the map gives you about Illinois.

Illinois

State capital / State border

WISCONSIN, IOWA, MISSOURI, INDIANA, KENTUCKY

Chicago Area

Civics and Government

Civics and government is the study of citizenship and the ways in which citizens govern themselves. A government is a system of leaders and laws that helps people live together in their community, state, or country. In the United States, citizens have an important part in making the government work. The laws that guide the actions of people are written and carried out by citizens.

In *United States* you will find out how the United States government works today. You will read about the people and events that shaped the government in the past. You will also learn about citizenship and the rights and responsibilities of citizens.

Economics

An **economy** is the way people in a country use its resources to meet their needs. The study of how people do this is called economics. In this book you will read about how people in the past made, bought, sold, and traded goods to get what they needed or wanted. You will learn how the economy of the United States came to be what it is today—an economy in which businesses are free to offer for sale many kinds of goods and services.

Culture

In this book you will learn about the people of the past who shaped the present. You will learn who these people were, what they looked like, and how they spoke and acted. You will explore their customs and beliefs and their ways of thinking and expressing ideas. You will look at their families and communities. All these things make up their culture. Each human group, or **society**, has a culture. This book will help you discover the many cultures that are part of our country's story, both past and present. You will also learn about our country's **heritage**, or culture that has come from the past and continues today.

REVIEW *What kinds of things do you learn when you study civics and government, economics, and culture?*

THE ANCIENT AMERICAS

The story of how the earliest peoples came to what is known today as the Americas begins many thousands of years ago. Historians do not know exactly where the first peoples of the Americas came from or when they arrived.

One thing, however, is certain. After early peoples arrived, they slowly moved throughout North and South America. Over time they developed many different ways of life. Today we know them by many different names, such as Cree, Zuni, Iroquois, and Aztec. Together they are known as Native Americans or American Indians. They were the first Americans.

◄ This painting by Tom Lovell, titled *Pecos Pueblo,* shows American Indians from the 1500s trading in the Southwest.

UNIT THEMES

- Commonality and Diversity
- Conflict and Cooperation
- Continuity and Change
- Interaction Within Different Environments

Unit Project

Create a Map Complete this project as you study Unit 1. Working with several classmates, draw a large outline map of North America. As you read about an American Indian group, add it to your map. Draw pictures to illustrate examples of the foods the first Americans ate, the clothing they wore, and the shelters they built. Display your map in the classroom.

ARCTIC OCEAN

Beaufort Sea

Ellesmere Island

Brooks Range

Yukon River

Bering Sea

Alaska Range

Aleutian Islands

Gulf of Alaska

Coast Mountains

Victoria Island

Great Bear Lake

Mackenzie River

Great Slave Lake

CANADIAN

ROCKY MOUNTAINS

GREAT PLAINS

Lake Winnipeg

Vancouver Island

Columbia River

Cascade Range

Coast Ranges

Missouri River

Mississippi River

PACIFIC OCEAN

GREAT BASIN

Great Salt Lake

Sierra Nevada

Colorado River

Arkansas River

Coast Ranges

Sonoran Desert

Baja California

Gulf of California

Rio Grande

Sierra Madre Occidental

Sierra Madre Oriental

Rio Balsas

0 500 1,000 Miles
0 500 1,000 Kilometers
Modified Azimuthal Equal-Area Projection

N
W E
S

| 15,000 years ago | 12,500 years ago | 10,000 years ago | 7,500 years ago |

North America

Baffin
Bay

Baffin
Island

Greenland

Labrador
Sea

Hudson
Bay

Labrador

S H I E L D

Newfoundland

Lake
Superior

St. Lawrence River

Lake
Huron

Lake
Ontario

Lake
Michigan

L. Erie

APPALACHIAN MOUNTAINS

Ohio   River

*ATLANTIC
OCEAN*

COASTAL PLAIN

Gulf of
Mexico

B a h a m a s

Cuba

Yucatán
Peninsula

Hispaniola

Puerto
Rico

C a r i b b e a n   S e a

5,000 years ago   **2,500** years ago   **Present**

Northwest Coast
PAGE 71

Southwest
PAGE 76

Great Plains
PAGE 81

Eastern Woodlands
PAGE 85

Middle America
PAGE 90

The People Shall Continue

THE PEOPLE
•Shall Continue•
by Simon Ortiz

American Indians have a very long history in North and South America. Many of their stories tell of the beginnings of the Earth as well as their beginnings as a people. Read now how one writer, an Acoma poet named Simon Ortiz, describes the earliest years of American history, when the first Americans—who called themselves the People—settled throughout the land.

This Acoma pot from a pueblo in New Mexico was used to store food.

MANY, many years ago, all things came to be.
The stars, rocks, plants, rivers, animals.
Mountains, sun, moon, birds, all things.
And the People were born.
Some say, "From the ocean."
Some say, "From a hollow log."
Some say, "From an opening in the ground."
Some say, "From the mountains."
And the People came to live
in the Northern Mountains and on the Plains,
in the Western Hills and on the Seacoasts,
in the Southern Deserts and in the Canyons,
in the Eastern Woodlands and on the
    Piedmonts.
Some People fished, others were hunters.
Some People farmed, others were artisans.
Their leaders were those who served the
    People.
Their healers were those who cared for the
    People.
Their hunters were those who provided for
    the People.
Their warriors were those who protected the
    People.

Artworks such as this Bella Coola
sun mask (left) and the Crow
butterfly (above) help tell the
story of Indian peoples' long
history.

43

The teachers and the elders of the People
all taught this important knowledge:
"The Earth is the source of all life.
She gives birth.
Her children continue the life of the Earth.
The People must be responsible to her.
This is the way that all life continues."
The People of the many Nations visited
each other's lands.
The People from the North brought elk meat.
The People from the West gave them fish.
The People from the South brought corn.
The People from the East gave them hides.
When there were arguments,
their leaders would say,
"Let us respect each other.
We will bring you corn and baskets.
You will bring us meat and flint knives.
That way we will live a peaceful life.
We must respect each other, and
the animals,
the plants, the land, the universe.
We have much to learn from
all the Nations."

Nevertheless, life was always hard.
At times, corn did not grow and
   there was famine.
At times, winters were very cold
   and there was hardship.
At times, the winds blew hot
   and rivers dried.
At times, the People grew uneasy
   among themselves.
The learned men and women talked with
   each other
about what to do for their People,
but it was always hard.
They had to have great patience
and they told their People,
     "We should not ever take anything
      for granted.
     In order for our life to continue,
     we must struggle very hard for it."

When they tell their stories, Indian storytellers open
and close this Kwakiutl (KWAH • kee • oo • tel) mask by
pulling a string. The Eastern Woodlands
serving basket (above) was
made in the 1700s.

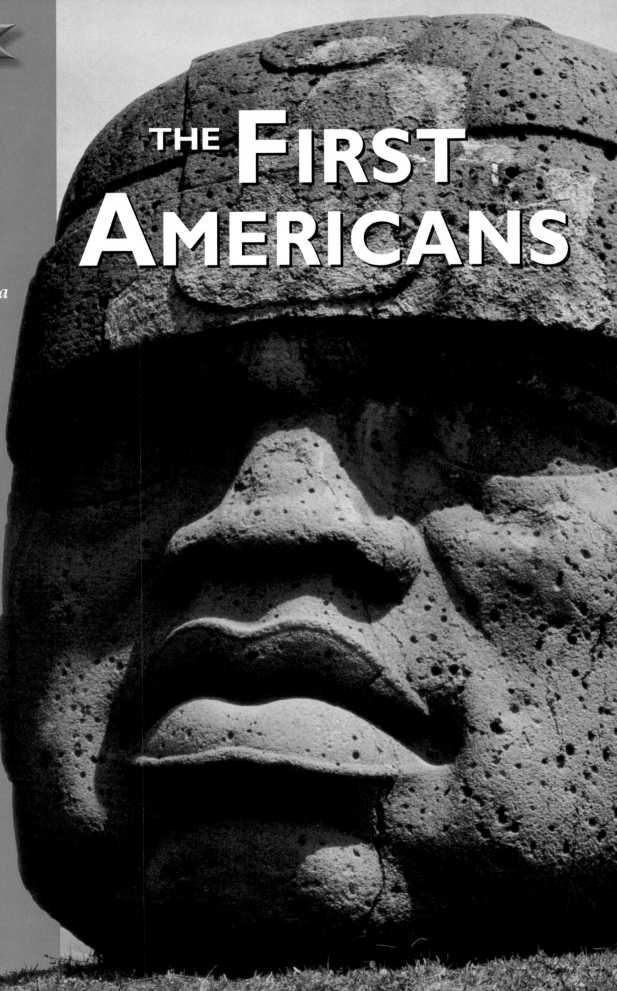

THE FIRST AMERICANS

*"My forebears
have been in
North America
for many
thousands of
years. . . .
[Their]
resources
were few, as
we think of
them from
our vantage
point in the
twentieth
century. . . ."*

N. Scott
Momaday
from *America
in 1492*

An ancient stone
head carved by the
Olmec people

The Search for Early Peoples

LESSON

1

FOCUS
How does the environment affect the ways people today move from place to place?

Main Idea   As you read, think about how the environment affected the ways early peoples moved from place to place.

Vocabulary

migration
glacier
band
nomad
theory
culture
archaeologist
artifact
evidence
origin story

Humans have always been on the move. From the earliest times until today, people have wandered the Earth. Sometimes their journeys are fast-moving, exciting adventures. Other times their movements are so slow that they are hard to notice. It was in just this way—very, very slowly— that early peoples first moved from place to place.

Over the Land Bridge

At a number of times in its history, the Earth has had long periods of freezing cold. During these periods, known as the Ice Ages, people who lived anywhere but near the equator shivered through long, hard winters.

Life could not have been easy in those wintry times. Days, even weeks, were spent inside small shelters made of animal skins. Fires inside helped keep people warm while icy winds blew outside. The weather was not as cold during the short summers, but melting ice turned the frozen ground into fields of mud.

Many groups of people, however, still set out into these cold lands. During hundreds of thousands of years, their ancestors had traveled from Africa into Europe and Asia. Now some groups in this great **migration**, or movement, turned northward to the vast area of Asia known today as Siberia.

These early peoples did not travel alone. They followed huge Ice Age animals that they hunted for food. One such animal was the mammoth—a giant, hairy elephant. The hunters depended on these animals to survive. They ate the meat and used the fur, skins, and bones to make clothing, shelters, and tools.

The last Ice Age started about two million years ago and ended about 10,000 years ago. At times it was so cold that

An Ice Age mammoth

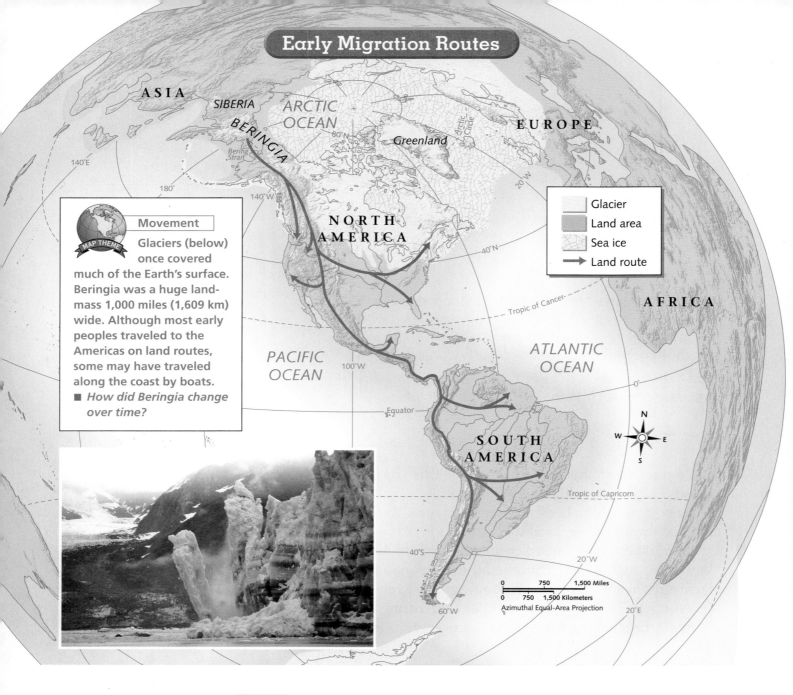

Early Migration Routes

ASIA

SIBERIA

BERINGIA

Bering Strait

ARCTIC OCEAN

80°N

Greenland

Arctic Circle

EUROPE

140°E

180°

140°W

NORTH AMERICA

40°N

20°W

AFRICA

Tropic of Cancer

PACIFIC OCEAN

100°W

ATLANTIC OCEAN

0°

Equator

SOUTH AMERICA

Tropic of Capricorn

20°W

N
W   E
S

40°S

0   750   1,500 Miles
0   750   1,500 Kilometers
Azimuthal Equal-Area Projection

60°W

20°E

Legend:
- Glacier
- Land area
- Sea ice
- Land route

MAP THEME — Movement

Glaciers (below) once covered much of the Earth's surface. Beringia was a huge land-mass 1,000 miles (1,609 km) wide. Although most early peoples traveled to the Americas on land routes, some may have traveled along the coast by boats.

■ *How did Beringia change over time?*

---

huge sheets of ice called **glaciers** formed over much of the land. So much water was locked up in the glaciers that the oceans became shallower.

The Bering Strait, a narrow strip of water that today separates Siberia and Alaska, also became shallower. Over time, hundreds of miles of land that had been under water were uncovered. This strip of land connected Asia and North America. The land bridge joining the two continents is known as Beringia (buh•RIN•gee•uh).

Most scientists believe that the first humans to find Beringia were bands of hunters from Siberia. A **band** is a small group of people who work together to do activities, such as hunting. At that time, bands were probably made up of only one or two families.

Many bands probably crossed into north-western Siberia and Beringia. They probably traveled only a few miles in an entire lifetime. Wanderers like these hunters, who have no settled home, are called **nomads**.

Finally, after thousands of years, the hunters reached what is today Alaska. But there they—and the animals they followed—had to stop. Huge glaciers blocked their path. They could go no farther.

Then, about 12,000 years ago, the climate changed. The Earth began to warm up. Over the years, some of the glaciers started to melt. The oceans began to rise, once again covering Beringia. At the same time, a narrow path opened between two melting glaciers that covered what is now Canada. It was as if one door behind the hunters closed as another door in front of them opened. The animals followed the path between the glaciers. The hunters followed the animals, slowly making their way farther and farther into the Americas. These hunters became the first Americans.

REVIEW *What was Beringia?*

New Discoveries

If this **theory** (THEE•uh•ree), or possible explanation, about the land bridge is correct, the first people arrived in the Americas about 12,000 years ago. But could they have been here earlier? Many scientists today say yes.

Once early peoples moved into the Americas, they settled all over both continents, in time reaching the southern tip of South America. Each native group developed its own **culture**, or way of life. Some groups lived in cities. Others were nomads who roamed the plains. Some made their clothing of furs and skins, while others made theirs of cotton. They lived in large wooden lodges, grass huts, tents made of animal skins, and steep cliff dwellings. They spoke thousands of different languages.

To build and develop such different cultures must have taken a great deal of time. Some scientists now argue that it must have taken much longer than 12,000 years.

But how could people have arrived earlier? It turns out that Beringia was uncovered at another time during the last Ice Age—from 45,000 to 75,000 years ago. Asian hunters could have crossed then into North America on dry land. It is also possible that the first Americans did not cross the land bridge at all. Instead, they could have traveled along the coast of Beringia to the Americas by boat.

Scientists who study the cultures of people long ago are known as **archaeologists** (ar•kee•AH•luh•jists). In recent years archaeologists have made discoveries that seem to prove the "early arrival" theory. One of the most important was at a dig, or an archaeological site, located in southwestern Pennsylvania. There, the archaeologists discovered an Ice Age campsite they called the Meadowcroft Rock Shelter. At the campsite they found a number of **artifacts**, or objects that early peoples had made. These artifacts are 14,000 to 15,000 years old. A few are more than 19,000 years old.

These archaeologists are searching for ancient objects at a dig in southwestern Pennsylvania. White tags identify the different layers of earth they have uncovered.

There are other discoveries that also support the early arrival theory. In Monte Verde (MOHN•tay VAIR•day), Chile, archaeologists have uncovered stone tools and animal bones that are 13,000 years old. And in Brazil they found stone chips that may have been made by early peoples. Some archaeologists believe these artifacts are 30,000 years old.

Although the number of artifacts found is growing, some archaeologists are still not convinced. They believe that there is not enough **evidence**, or proof, that people arrived in the Americas any earlier than 12,000 years ago. Some so-called artifacts, they say, are not artifacts at all. What one person believes is a stone tool shaped by humans could really be a stone shaped by nature—by wind or water.

Archaeologists today continue to search for more evidence from the past. Each new discovery brings new information about the first Americans.

REVIEW *What is the early arrival theory?*

Origin Stories

The Indian peoples themselves have many different stories about the origins of their lands and their beginnings long ago. These stories tell of the peoples' beliefs about the world and their place in it. Such stories are called **origin stories**.

Some origin stories are much like the story of Creation in the Bible that tells how the world was made. The Blackfoot people, for example, tell a story of how Old Man the Creator made the animals and plants and formed the prairies and mountains. He made a woman and her child from clay and brought them to life.

Animals and natural surroundings such as mountains, rivers, rocks, and trees play an important part in many origin stories. The Huron (HYUR•ahn) people tell a story that says in the beginning the Earth was covered with water. Dry land was formed from a bit of soil taken from under the claws of a turtle. The turtle had picked up the soil after diving

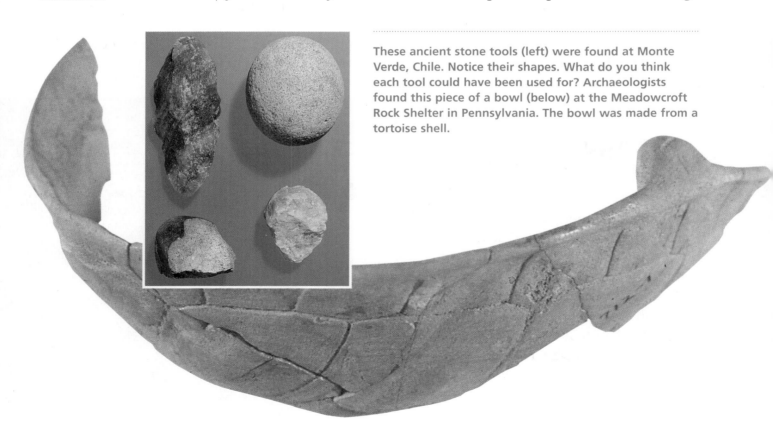

These ancient stone tools (left) were found at Monte Verde, Chile. Notice their shapes. What do you think each tool could have been used for? Archaeologists found this piece of a bowl (below) at the Meadowcroft Rock Shelter in Pennsylvania. The bowl was made from a tortoise shell.

This Pueblo clay figure (above left) shows the importance of storytellers to their listeners. In some origin stories, animals like the elk (above right) are able to talk to humans.

to the bottom of the ocean. Because of this story, some Indian people today still use the name Turtle Island for the Americas.

Even though no one knows exactly when the first people arrived in the Americas, all agree that it was thousands of years ago. It was so long ago that the descendants of the first Americans—the American Indians— have no memories of distant homelands. They do not tell stories of faraway places where their ancestors once lived. They tell stories of the Americas.

REVIEW *Why are origin stories important to Indian peoples?*

LESSON I REVIEW

Check Understanding

1. **Remember the Facts** In what ways did the Ice Ages change the Earth's environment?

2. **Recall the Main Idea** How did the environment affect the ways early peoples moved from place to place?

Think Critically

3. **Think More About It** What skills would have been important to help the early peoples survive during the Ice Ages?

4. **Explore Viewpoints** Why do some people believe that the first Americans arrived about 12,000 years ago? What evidence do others give to support the early arrival theory?

Show What You Know
Diorama Activity Make a diorama of an Ice Age scene that shows bands of people or herds of giant mammoths. Display the diorama in your classroom.

Use a Map to Show Movement

1. Why Learn This Skill?

Some information is easiest to understand when it is shown in a drawing. One way to understand the movement of people over time is to use a map. Look at the map on page 53. It shows the movement of early peoples as they migrated into North America and, over time, settled throughout the continent. Maps like this can help you understand the ways in which geography affects the movement of people. Learning to read this map will help you understand other maps like it as you learn more about the story of the Americas.

2. Directions on a Map

To use a map to describe movement, you first need to understand direction. A direction marker called a compass rose is found on most maps. The compass rose shows the cardinal directions and the intermediate directions.

These two ancient tools were found at Meadowcroft Rock Shelter, an Ice Age campsite.

The compass rose on the map on page 53 is located at the bottom of the map. The compass rose shows the arrow with the *N* for north pointing toward the top of the map. This means that south is toward the bottom of the map, east is toward the right, and west is toward the left.

The north arrow on a compass rose points to what is called true north. True north is in the direction of the North Pole. On some maps the compass rose may be placed so that the north arrow is not pointing straight up toward the top of the map. The north arrow of the compass rose may point toward another part of the map. However, the arrow always points north, toward the North Pole. And south is still opposite north, and east is still opposite west.

Look at the map on the next page. The purple route arrows show the directions in which early peoples traveled. The arrows do not stand for the exact routes taken. They show only the general direction people might have followed. It is important to remember how slowly early peoples moved from place to place. Bands traveled only a few miles in a lifetime, so the migration took many generations.

3. Understand the Process

Now that you know about the use of the compass rose and route arrows in showing movement on a map, you can answer these questions.

1 On the map on page 53, find the archaeological site of Owl Cave. With your finger, trace the route from Owl Cave to Quad. In what direction did you move your finger?

2 Trace the route that goes from Claypool to Meadowcroft. In what direction did people most likely travel to get to Meadowcroft from what is now the middle of the United States?

Climate, landforms, and other physical features affected the movement of early peoples. As they encountered barriers to travel, they often changed the direction of their migration.

3 Why do you think early peoples did not travel farther east into what is now Canada before they moved south?

4 Why do you think one route in what is now the western part of the United States turned northwest?

4. Think and Apply

Use the information on the map and what you already know about the geography of the United States to write a paragraph about the movement of early peoples. Describe one of the routes shown on the map. Explain the directions in which the people moved along the route and the physical features they might have seen along the way. Share your paragraph with a classmate.

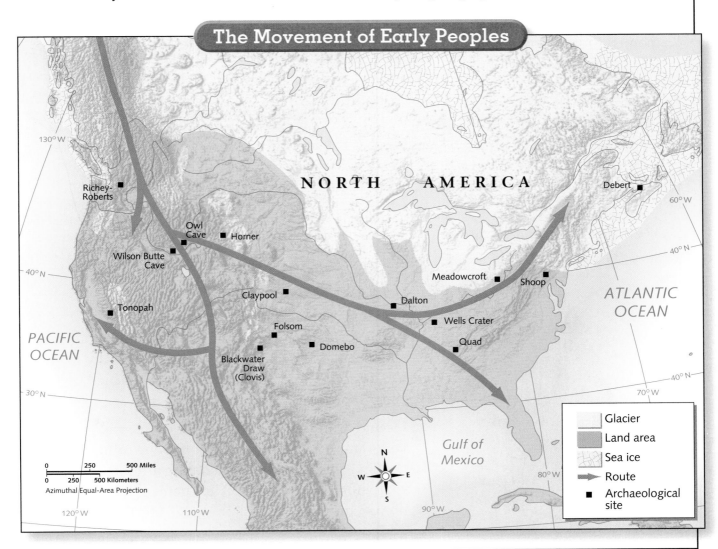

The Movement of Early Peoples

NORTH AMERICA

PACIFIC OCEAN

ATLANTIC OCEAN

Gulf of Mexico

130° W
60° W
40° N
40° N
30° N
40° N
70° W
120° W
110° W
90° W
80° W

Richey-Roberts
Debert
Owl Cave
Horner
Wilson Butte Cave
Meadowcroft
Shoop
Tonopah
Claypool
Dalton
Wells Crater
Folsom
Quad
Domebo
Blackwater Draw (Clovis)

0   250   500 Miles
0   250   500 Kilometers
Azimuthal Equal-Area Projection

N W E S

Glacier
Land area
Sea ice
Route
Archaeological site

How Long Have People

No one really knows how long people have lived in the Americas. For many years archaeologists agreed that the first people in the Americas arrived by crossing Beringia no more than 12,000 years ago. These people, called the Clovis (KLOH•vuhs) people, were named for the place in New Mexico where their stone artifacts were discovered. Many archaeologists now believe that people may have reached the Americas more than 20,000 years ago.

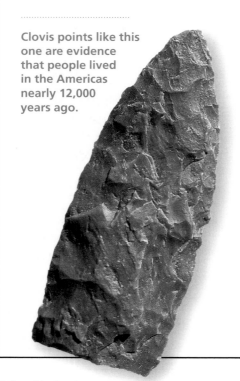

Clovis points like this one are evidence that people lived in the Americas nearly 12,000 years ago.

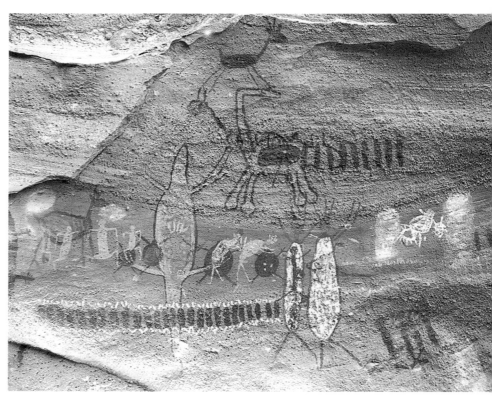

The walls and ceiling of a cave at Pedra Furada, Brazil, are covered with paintings of animals. Archaeologists disagree about how old some of the artifacts found there really are.

Jacques Cinq-Mars

Jacques Cinq-Mars (ZHAHK SANK MAR) of the Archaeological Survey of Canada studied the Bluefish Caves in Canada's Yukon Territory. The caves are in an area that people from Siberia could have reached by crossing Beringia. Cinq-Mars said:

66 I found a bone flake in one of the caves, and two years later I found the mammoth bone from which the flake was chipped, both dating around 24,000 B.P. [before the present]. . . . It's good evidence for human presence . . . certainly at 25,000 B.P. 99

Lived in the Americas?

Vance Haynes

Many archaeologists still think that the Clovis people were the first to migrate to the Americas. Vance Haynes, a professor at the University of Arizona, studied evidence in layers of rock in the ground. The layers on top are the newest. Layers below are older. Haynes said:

> I've spent a good part of a lifetime as a geologist, as well as an archaeologist, and from Clovis up I've seen one layer after another with artifacts, while from Clovis down there's nothing human. . . . Hardly a year goes by that there isn't a new site that's claimed to be old, but they all fall away . . . unless you're a believer.

Glenn Morris

Glenn Morris works for the American Indian Anti-Defamation Council in Colorado. He believes that the Indian peoples did not come to the Americas from Siberia or anywhere else. He believes they have *always* been in the Americas. Morris said:

> The problem with the Bering Strait theory is that it is wrong, not only according to indigenous [native] peoples' creation stories and histories, it is also wrong according to a growing body of Western research. . . . Digs at Lewisville, Texas, San Diego, California, and Pedejo Cave, New Mexico, have revealed [uncovered] human remains at 38,000, 44,000, and 48,000 years old. . . . By contrast, the oldest human remains found in the Siberian region of northern Asia . . . are a mere 20,000 years old! Other scientific evidence . . . indicates that a migration did occur, but the footprints went in the other direction, from the Americas to Asia!

Compare Viewpoints

1. What evidence does Cinq-Mars have for his view? Why does Haynes disagree?

2. What evidence does Morris have for his view? How does his view differ from those of Cinq-Mars and Haynes?

3. A Yakima Indian once said, "I . . . did not come here. I was put here by the Creator." Which of the three views would this person most likely support?

Think and Apply

Historians and scientists often use physical evidence, such as artifacts, to support their views. However, people do not always agree on what the evidence means. Use newspapers or magazines to identify some disagreements today that are based on the meaning of physical evidence.

Main Idea Read to find out what the ancient Indians did when their environment changed.

Vocabulary

technology	religion
extinct	tribe
agriculture	surplus
maize	specialize

Ancient Indians

As early peoples made their way across the Americas, the climate of the Earth continued to change. Over thousands of years, it became drier and warmer. In some places, lakes slowly dried up. In other places, grassy meadows turned to sand. Without water and food, the huge Ice Age animals began to die out. Many of the first Americans had depended on these animals for food, clothing, and shelter. Now they had to find new ways to survive.

Giant-Mammal Hunters

Compared to the mighty mammoth, standing 14 feet (4.3 m) high at the shoulder and weighing about 5 tons, early hunters seemed small and weak. Their spears were little more than sharpened sticks. In time they tied sharpened stones to the ends as spear points. Some hunters carried clubs and axes. Yet they survived mainly by tracking the mammoths and other giant Ice Age mammals and killing them when they could.

The earliest native hunters were nomads who lived in small bands. As they trailed behind the giant animals, they gathered

LEARNING FROM DIAGRAMS Due to the size and strength of the mammoths, ancient Indians often had to work together when hunting the giant animals. Each of the hunters in this diagram is using an atlatl to bring down the mammoth. The atlatl allowed the hunter to throw a spear with deadly force while staying a safe distance away from the target.

■ *Why do you think it was important for hunters to work together?*

1 The hunter rests the spear on the atlatl.

2 The hunter sets the spear in motion.

56

fruits, nuts, and roots for food. They lived in caves or in tents made from animal skins. Their tools and weapons were made mostly from sticks, animal horns, and bones. From time to time, different peoples invented new tools, such as the atlatl (AHT•lah•tuhl), or spear-thrower. They also found new ways of sharpening stones or of leading animals into a trap. But such improvements came slowly.

About 11,600 years ago, something very important happened. Someone found a way to make a spear point by a process called flaking. First, a piece of bone or stone was used to knock off flakes, or thin pieces, from flint or another type of stone. The flakes were knocked off until the stone formed a sharp point. The point was then fluted, or hollowed out, on one or both sides. This made it easier to fasten the point tightly to a spear.

These delicate yet deadly spear points are called Clovis points. They are named after the town of Clovis, New Mexico, where they were first found. Archaeologists call the early Indians who made these spear points the Clovis people. Other artifacts of the Clovis people have been found in places from Alaska to the Andes Mountains.

TECHNOLOGY

The Atlatl

The atlatl, or spear-thrower, was an important weapon used by early hunters. Although archaeologists are not certain when it was invented, they do know that it was used in North America at least 10,000 years ago. Atlatls were spear holders 2 to 3 feet (61 to 91 cm) long and made of wood. The spear rested in a groove against a base at the end of the atlatl. The hunter held on to the atlatl and then snapped it forward with a whiplike motion to send the spear toward its target. The motion of the atlatl made the spear travel with much greater speed and force than it would have had alone.

3 The spear is released from the atlatl.

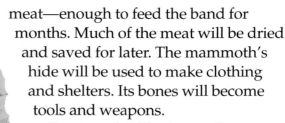

Clovis points were one of the important improvements in technology for early peoples. **Technology** is the use of scientific knowledge or tools to make or do something. You may not think of sharpened stones as technology. But these spear points were just as important to the Clovis people as computers are to many people today. Clovis points were razor-sharp, making them the best weapons early hunters had ever had.

Imagine one band of early peoples moving closely behind a herd of mammoths they have been tracking for weeks. Finally the hunters see what they are looking for! In the shallow water of a small lake is a giant woolly mammoth taking a drink.

Looking over the area, the hunters quickly realize that they are not the only ones interested in the mammoth. A saber-toothed tiger, eager to sink its 8-inch (20.3-cm) teeth into the animal, is also watching, waiting to make its move.

The hunters move in quickly and quietly to get the mammoth before the tiger does. On a signal from their leader, they throw their spears. The Clovis points easily pierce the mammoth's thick skin. After wounding the animal, the hunters close in to finish the job, driving spears into the mammoth's heart and neck.

The band then sets to work. They waste little of the fallen animal. From this one kill, they get about 2 tons of

Clovis points were 1.5 to 5 inches (3.8 to 12.7 cm) long and very sharp. These points were fastened tightly to spears so they could be used again and again.

meat—enough to feed the band for months. Much of the meat will be dried and saved for later. The mammoth's hide will be used to make clothing and shelters. Its bones will become tools and weapons.

Even so, the Clovis people cannot carry everything with them as they move on. Some of the kill must be left behind. This does not seem important to them. After all, there is always another herd of mammoths or other animals just ahead.

Over the next thousand years, however, the giant mammals would become **extinct** (ik•STINGT), or die out. The drier climate was drying up lakes and rivers and killing the tall, lush grasses that the animals ate. By about 10,000 years ago, most of the animals weighing 100 pounds (45.4 kg) or more, such as mammoths, horses, camels, and saber-toothed tigers, were gone from the Americas.

REVIEW *Why were Clovis points so important to early hunters?*

Food Gatherers

As the environment changed and the huge Ice Age animals died out, early peoples had to change their ways of life. Life no longer centered around the hunting of giant mammals. People began to fish and to hunt more of the smaller animals. They also began to gather and store more plants for food. These changes in the way people lived took place from about 9,000 years ago to 3,000 years ago.

Because they did not follow herds of large animals, food gatherers stayed in places a little longer than hunters. In time they learned where certain plants grew best and at what time of year the

American Indians used these decoys about 3,000 years ago to hunt ducks. The decoys are made of reeds—water plants that grow along the shores of lakes and rivers.

plants became ripe. Their bands then traveled to these places each season to gather food.

Picture one band of food gatherers, moving from their winter camp to their summer camp. After days of walking, they finally reach the marshy tidelands near the river where they will spend the summer. The people set up camp in the shelter of a large rock along a hillside. Then both the women and the men begin to prepare the food.

First, the women empty their willow baskets of the seeds and nuts they have gathered along the way. Then, they use flat stones to grind the food into flour. Next, they mix the flour with water and put the dough in a cooking basket. They put the basket on stones that have been heated in the fire and wait for the dough to cook.

While the women make the bread, the men skin the animals they have killed that day. They often hunt raccoons, deer, antelope, and otters, but today's meal will be rabbits. The men then heat up more stones in the fire and place the rabbits on a wooden rack to roast.

After the meal the women check and repair the knives and baskets they will use to gather plants the next day. The men check and repair the spears and nets they will use to

hunt and fish. Finally, they lie down in their shelters to sleep. At dawn they will be up again, ready to begin another day of searching for food.

To this day some native peoples gather foods that grow wild in nature. Some Ojibwas (oh•jib•WAYZ), for example, gather wild rice that grows near the Great Lakes.

REVIEW *What changes did early peoples make when the giant Ice Age animals became extinct?*

Early Farmers

Over time some American Indians changed their way of life as food gatherers. They took the first steps toward a new technology that would change their lives forever. They began to plant seeds and grow some of their own food. This was the beginning of **agriculture**, or farming, in the Americas.

Indian peoples in Central America were among the first to develop agriculture in the Americas. Some of the earliest farmers lived in the Tehuacán (tay•wah•KAHN) Valley in central Mexico. There archaeologists have found evidence of farming that dates from

7,000 years ago to 4,700 years ago. The early farmers of the valley harvested at least 12 kinds of corn, as well as avocados, squash, pumpkins, and beans.

Corn, or **maize** (MAYZ), was the most important food grown in the Americas. Maize gave early peoples more food than any other crop. For this reason, they thought of maize as a gift from their gods. This idea was part of the Native American peoples' **religion**, or beliefs about God or gods. The religion of many early peoples centered around a number of gods that helped to explain the many qualities found in nature. Among these were a sun god and a rain god.

For some Native American groups, growing their own food meant that they no longer had to move from camp to camp. They could settle and stay in one place, build stronger homes,

Ears of corn appear on this carving of a god. The god is believed to bring good harvests. Early corn, or maize, was much smaller than the corn grown today.

and form villages. With more food, people lived longer, and their population grew. In time, bands of people joined together to form tribes. A **tribe** is a group made up of many bands of people with a shared culture and land.

Agriculture also meant that people no longer had to spend all their time searching for food. For once, they had a food **surplus**, or more than was needed. Now people could spend more time doing other things to help their tribe. Soon they began to **specialize**, or work on one job they could do well. Early peoples were no longer only hunters, gatherers, or farmers. Some specialized in making pots, weaving, or trading.

REVIEW *What changes did farming bring about in the lives of some ancient Indians?*

LESSON 2 REVIEW

Check Understanding

1 Remember the Facts Why did the giant Ice Age mammals become extinct?

2 Recall the Main Idea What did the ancient Indians do when their environment changed?

Think Critically

3 Personally Speaking Would you rather have lived as a hunter, a food gatherer, or a farmer? Explain your answer.

4 Past to Present List five changes in technology that are important to our lives today.

5 Cause and Effect What effect did Clovis points have on the lives of early Indians?

Show What You Know

Mural Activity Recall what you read about the ways of life of the hunters, food gatherers, and early farmers. Select one group and make a mural that shows how the group lived in the Americas. Give your mural a title and write a caption that provides additional information. Display completed murals and share them with your classmates.

Identify Patterns on Time Lines

1. Why Learn This Skill?

In history there are a great many events that took place over a long period of time. An easy way to understand events in history is to look at a time line. Knowing how to read a time line can help you understand the order in which events happened in the past and the amount of time that passed between those events.

2. Understand the Process

A **time line** is a diagram that shows the events that took place during a certain period of time. It looks something like a ruler marked in dates instead of inches. Like inches marked on a ruler, the dates on a time line are equally spaced. The earliest date is on the left end of the time line. The most recent date is on the right end. To read the events in the order in which they happened, you read from left to right.

Time lines can show events that took place during any period of time. Some time lines, for example, show events that took place over a **decade**, or a period of 10 years. Others show events that took place over a **century**, or a period of 100 years. Some even show events that took place over a **millennium**, or a period of 1,000 years.

The time line below shows dates from the ancient past to the present. Notice the letters

B.C. and *A.D.* in the middle of the time line. Many people today identify years by whether they took place before or after the birth of Jesus Christ. Years before the birth of Christ are labeled *B.C.* This stands for "before Christ." Years after the birth of Christ are labeled *A.D.* This stands for the Latin words *Anno Domini*, which mean "in the year of the Lord."

An event that happened in 100 *B.C.* took place 100 years before the birth of Christ. An event that happened in *A.D.* 100 took place 100 years after the birth of Christ. What year is it now? What letters would be used with this year? The answer is *A.D.*, but because every year in modern times is *A.D.*, the letters are usually not used.

You may also see the letters *B.C.E.* or *C.E.* with dates. The abbreviation *B.C.E.* stands for "before the Common Era." It is sometimes used instead of *B.C.* The abbreviation *C.E.*, which stands for "Common Era," is sometimes used in place of *A.D.*

3. Think and Apply

Make a time line that shows events in your life. Start with the year you were born. Then add other years in which something important happened. Display your time line in the classroom.

B.C. and A.D. Time Line

2000 B.C.				B.C. A.D.			A.D. 2000
	1500 B.C.	1000 B.C.	500 B.C.		A.D. 500	A.D. 1000	A.D. 1500

FOCUS

How are the ways of life of people today different in different parts of the world?

Main Idea Read to learn about the different ways of life of early peoples living in different parts of the Americas.

Vocabulary

civilization   drought
temple   kiva
pyramid
cultural diffusion
earthwork
pueblo
adobe
mesa

This Olmec mask was found in a temple near what is today Mexico City. It is a little over 4 inches (10.2 cm) high.

Early Civilizations

With farming and settled life, American Indian cultures grew and changed. Over time, people in different cultures came to hold different beliefs, speak different languages, and live in different ways. Three of these early peoples were the Olmecs (AHL•meks), the Mound Builders, and the Anasazi (ah•nuh•SAH•zee).

The Olmecs

For hundreds of years the artifacts of a people called the Olmecs lay hidden beneath thick jungle growth. When the artifacts were found, archaeologists learned that the Olmecs had built one of the earliest civilizations in the Americas. A **civilization** is a culture that has well-developed forms of government, religion, and learning.

The Olmecs lived in the green river valleys along Mexico's east coast as early as 1500 B.C. So many later groups learned so much from the Olmec culture that it has become known as the "mother civilization" of the Americas.

Powerful priests governed the Olmecs, and many activities of daily life centered around religion. The Olmecs believed in many gods. One of the most important was the rain god. The Olmecs believed that the rain god appeared as a jaguar (JA•gwar), a large, spotted cat. To honor the gods, the Olmecs built great stone **temples**, or places of worship. Some of the temples were built on the tops of pyramids. A **pyramid** is a building with three or more sides shaped like triangles. The sides slant upward toward a point at the top. The Olmecs made the tops of their pyramids flat and built temples there.

Near the temples were paved roads that led to other buildings and a marketplace. Government leaders lived in this central area. Most other people lived in nearby villages. Huge stone faces looked out over the villages. Some stone faces weighed as much as 20 tons each. Olmec artists may have carved the faces to look like their rulers' faces.

The Olmecs carved giant stone heads from basalt (buh•SAWLT), a kind of volcanic rock. They moved the statues from miles away by floating them down rivers on rafts.

Religious services held in the temples were important to the people. The priests standing before the crowds wore bright-red robes covered with jaguar skins. On their heads they wore bird feathers and flowers.

The Olmecs developed their own number system, writing system, and calendar. Their writing used pictures to stand for words or ideas. They also traded with people from civilizations that were hundreds of miles away in present-day Mexico and Central America. The Olmecs also traded with people along the coast of the Gulf of Mexico. Trade gave people a chance to meet and exchange ideas. In this way Olmec culture spread to other places. This process is called **cultural diffusion**.

No one knows how the Olmec civilization came to an end. We do know, however, that by A.D. 300 the Olmec civilization had been replaced by other civilizations. Yet Olmec ideas had spread through trade and lived on in other cultures.

REVIEW *Why is the Olmec culture called the "mother civilization" of the Americas?*

The Mound Builders

About the same time that the Olmec people were building a civilization in Mexico, a people called the Adenas (uh•DEE•nuhz) were also building a civilization. The Adena people lived in the Ohio River valley from about 1000 B.C. to A.D. 200.

The Adena people were the first of several ancient civilizations known as Mound Builders. The Mound Builders lived in the eastern half of what is today the United States. The Mound Builders got their name because of the large mounds, or hills of earth, that the people built. These mounds are called **earthworks**.

One of the most famous Adena earthworks, the Serpent Mound, is about 5 feet (1.5 m) high, 20 feet (6.1 m) across, and 1,330 feet (405.4 m) long. The mound does not look like much from the ground, but when you look at it from the air, you can see that it forms the shape of a snake.

Nobody knows why the Adena people built the snake-shaped mound. Perhaps it was built for religious purposes. Archaeologists do know that many smaller mounds were built to bury the dead.

Archaeologists believe that the most important people were given the fanciest mound burials. First, the Adenas covered the body of the person who had died with a kind of paint made of reddish-colored earth. Red was the color of blood and of life. The Adenas believed the red paint would allow the person's spirit to live on after death. Then, they laid the body on a bed of bark strips set in the floor of a small house.

To help the dead enjoy their life after death, the Adena people placed jewelry, clay pipes, beads, and other goods around the body. Then they went outside and set the house on fire. After the house had burned down, they covered the ashes with earth. Over time more people would be buried in the mound, and the mound would rise higher.

About 300 B.C. a second, larger mound-building civilization began to take shape in the middle of what is now the United States. This was the Hopewell civilization. The culture of the Hopewells grew to be the strongest in the region for nearly 500 years.

The Hopewells had great skill in arts and crafts. They made ceramic pots, woven mats, and figures carved from bone, wood, and metal. They made spear points and knives from obsidian (uhb•SIH•dee•uhn), a hard, shiny, black stone. They wore clothing made of animal skins and jewelry made from copper and shells.

Like Olmec goods and ideas, Hopewell goods and ideas spread far and wide through trade. This trade reached from the Atlantic Ocean to the Great Plains and from Lake Superior to the Gulf of Mexico. Hopewell traders were often away from home for weeks at a time, visiting trading centers hundreds of miles away.

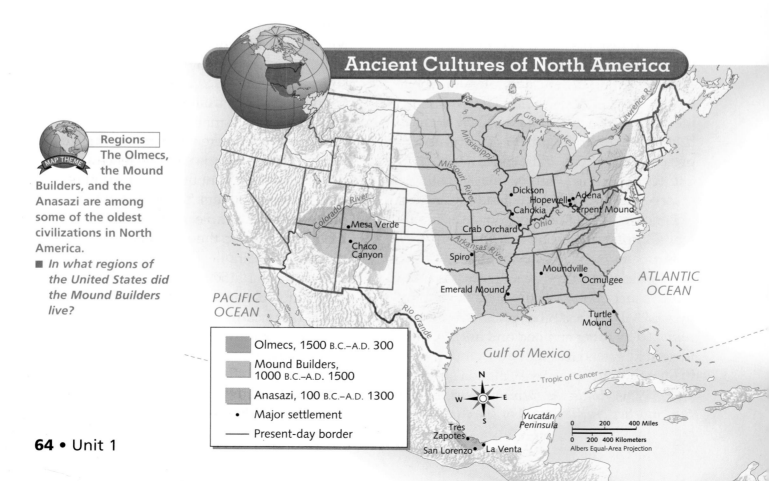

Regions The Olmecs, the Mound Builders, and the Anasazi are among some of the oldest civilizations in North America.

■ *In what regions of the United States did the Mound Builders live?*

Ancient Cultures of North America

Olmecs, 1500 B.C.–A.D. 300
Mound Builders, 1000 B.C.–A.D. 1500
Anasazi, 100 B.C.–A.D. 1300
• Major settlement
— Present-day border

The Serpent Mound (above) is in southern Ohio. Other Adena mounds are shaped like birds, tortoises, and people. A Hopewell artist made this eagle in flight (left) out of copper.

The greatest mound-building civilization was that of the Mississippians. It developed in the Mississippi River valley about A.D. 800. The Mississippians lived in hundreds of towns and several large cities. They built huge mounds, some nearly as big as a football field. Some of these high, box-shaped mounds had large temples built on top.

The largest Mississippian city was near where East St. Louis, Illinois, stands today. By A.D. 1200 as many as 40,000 people lived in this city, called Cahokia (kuh•HOH•kee•uh).

Picture the large city of Cahokia, dotted with 85 different mounds, as it looked one autumn morning. The powerful chief, who is both priest and ruler, has just come out of his house on the flat top of the huge main temple mound. He and the other priests are getting ready to greet the sun god and ask his blessing on the corn harvest.

Monk's Mound, where Cahokia's chief is standing, is 110 feet (33.5 m) high and covers 16 acres. It took the people more than 300 years to build. They had to carry soil to the mound one basketful at a time.

Below Monk's Mound is the large town square. It is already filling up with thousands of people gathering for worship. Later, the square will be used as a marketplace.

Looking over his lands, the chief looks past the square to the smaller mounds that have houses on top, where other important people live. Outside the large wooden fence around the city, he sees the houses of the farmers, hunters, and workers. The people are hurrying toward the temple, and the chief's thoughts return to the religious service that is about to begin.

By about A.D. 1500 the Mississippian civilization began to break down. War, hunger, or sickness may have played a part. Slowly, the Mississippian culture, the last of the great mound-building civilizations, ended.

REVIEW *Why did the Mound Builders construct earthworks?*

The Anasazi

From about 100 B.C. to A.D. 1300, another early civilization grew up in the dry lands of what is today the southwestern United States. This was the civilization of the Anasazi, or "Ancient People."

The Anasazi lived in groups of houses that Spanish people later described as **pueblos** (PWEH•blohs). *Pueblo* is the Spanish word for "town" or "village." Pueblos were multi-storied and made of adobe (ah•DOH•bay) bricks or stone bricks.

Adobe is a mixture of sandy clay and straw that is dried into bricks. The Anasazi had to carry wood for roof beams from miles away, but adobe and stone were near at hand.

Most pueblos were built on top of **mesas** (MAY•sahz), or high, flat-topped hills. The buildings had few windows or doors on the lower levels. People moved from one level to another by using ladders.

One great Anasazi settlement was Pueblo Bonito, or "beautiful town." Pueblo Bonito was built beneath the towering rock walls of Chaco (CHAH•koh) Canyon, in what is today New Mexico. It was made up of 800 rooms and housed more than 1,200 people. Nearly 5,000 people lived in smaller villages nearby. The villages were connected by paved roads, which also served as trade routes.

The Anasazi built some pueblos into the sides of high cliffs, far out of the reach of enemies. One, the pueblo at Mesa Verde (MAY•sah VAIR•day), in present-day Colorado, is known as the Cliff Palace. Rising three stories high, the pueblo has 200 rooms. As many as 1,000 people may have lived there.

Even though their land was very dry, the Anasazi grew fields of corn, squash, and

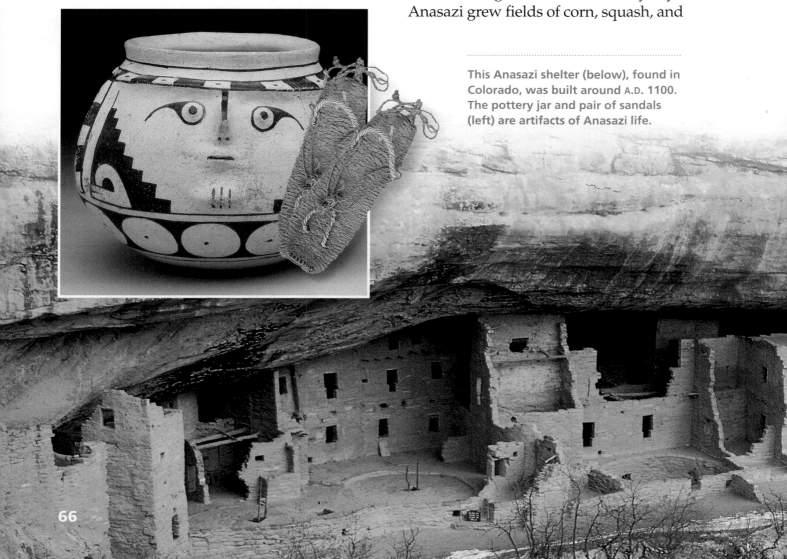

This Anasazi shelter (below), found in Colorado, was built around A.D. 1100. The pottery jar and pair of sandals (left) are artifacts of Anasazi life.

beans. They planted their seeds deep in the ground to get the most water out of the soil. They also dug holes and ditches to store water for use in drier times. In case a long dry spell, or **drought**, should come, they saved enough dried corn in clay jars to feed the people for up to two years.

Religion was an important part of Anasazi life. Religious services were held in special underground rooms called **kivas** (KEE•vuhs). Chiefs, their faces and bodies painted white, led the people in giving thanks to the Earth Mother, the sun god, and the rain god.

The Anasazi civilization changed by about A.D. 1300. Some archaeologists believe that a 22-year drought in the high mesa lands may have been the reason the Anasazi people left the great pueblos and moved into the valleys of rivers such as the Rio Grande. There they built smaller pueblos or joined other groups in small farming villages.

REVIEW *What materials did the Anasazi use to build pueblos?*

LESSON 3 REVIEW

Check Understanding

1 **Remember the Facts** List three of the earliest civilizations found in the Americas.

2 **Recall the Main Idea** What different ways of life did early peoples of the Americas develop?

Think Critically

3 **Think More About It** In what ways did the environment affect the lives of the Anasazi?

4 **Past to Present** How do ideas spread from one culture to another today?

Show What You Know

Art Activity Imagine that you have written a book about one of the civilizations described in this lesson. Now create a cover for your book. First, choose a title for the book. Then, draw a cover picture that shows the lives of the people you describe. Use your book cover in a bulletin board display.

REVIEW

CONNECT MAIN IDEAS

Use this organizer to show how the environment affected the lives of early peoples. Write three details to support each main idea. A copy of the organizer appears on page 6 of the Activity Book.

The First Americans

Environment

The Search for Early Peoples

The environment affected the ways early peoples moved from place to place.

1. _____
2. _____
3. _____

Ancient Indians

The ancient Indians changed their ways of life as the environment changed.

1. _____
2. _____
3. _____

Early Civilizations

Early peoples living in different parts of the Americas had different ways of life.

1. _____
2. _____
3. _____

WRITE MORE ABOUT IT

Write a Letter Imagine that you are an archaeologist searching for evidence of the first Americans. Write a letter to a friend or family member that tells what it is like to work at a dig. Explain the kinds of artifacts or other evidence you hope to find.

Write a Menu Write a menu that lists the kinds of foods an Ice Age hunter might have eaten on a typical day. Then write a menu for a food gatherer and a menu for an early farmer. How are the three menus different? How are they alike?

USE VOCABULARY

Write the term that correctly matches each definition. Then use each term in a complete sentence.

adobe   band

agriculture   nomad

1. a small group of people who work together to do activities

2. a wanderer who has no settled home

3. farming

4. a mixture of sandy clay and straw that is dried into bricks

CHECK UNDERSTANDING

5. Why did Ice Age hunters move from place to place?

6. What is the name of the land bridge that once linked Asia and the Americas?

7. Why are artifacts from the Meadowcroft Rock Shelter important?

8. How did agriculture change the ways of life of early peoples?

9. What was the most important food crop grown by the first Americans? Why?

10. Why was the Olmec culture so important to the early history of the Americas?

11. What was the greatest mound-building civilization?

12. What was a kiva? What was it used for?

THINK CRITICALLY

13. **Cause and Effect** Why did the oceans become shallow during the last Ice Age?

14. **Personally Speaking** How does the environment affect your life today?

15. **Think More About It** The cultures of the Olmecs, the Mound Builders, and the Anasazi developed in very different ways. Explain how this fact could be used to support the early arrival theory.

APPLY SKILLS

Use a Map to Show Movement
Draw a map of your school. Show places such as your classroom, the cafeteria, the office, and the library. Find out which way is north, and add a compass rose to your map. Now draw a line on your map to show a route from one room to another. Use the compass rose to help you describe which directions the route follows.

Identify Patterns on Time Lines Draw a time line, and label the year A.D. 2000 in the center. Now label the year one decade before A.D. 2000 and the year one decade after it. Label the year one century before A.D. 2000 and one century after it. Label the year one millennium before A.D. 2000 and one millennium after it.

READ MORE ABOUT IT

The Earliest Americans by Helen Roney Sattler. Clarion Books. This book traces the history of the early peoples in America from the earliest known sites until about A.D. 1492.

THE EARLIEST AMERICANS
by HELEN RONEY SATTLER
Illustrated by JEAN DAY ZALLINGER

HARCOURT BRACE

Visit the Internet at
http://www.hbschool.com
for additional resources.

INDIANS OF NORTH AMERICA

"May it be delightful my house;
From my head may it be delightful;
To my feet may it be delightful;
Where I lie may it be delightful;
All above me may it be delightful;
All around me may it be delightful."

A Navajo house blessing

Dora Pino, a Navajo woman
of Magdalena, New Mexico

Northwest Coast

FOCUS

How does living near an ocean affect the lives of people in coastal communities today?

Main Idea Read to find out how living near an ocean affected the lives of the Northwest Coast Indians.

Vocabulary

diversity
cultural region
dugout
pit house
clan
barter
potlatch
totem pole

Over hundreds of years, as old Indian civilizations gave way to new cultures, different tribes with different ways of life slowly settled the continent. North America became a land of great **diversity** , or many differences, among its peoples. By the 1400s people from hundreds of different tribes lived in North America.

Often peoples living in the same area share some ways of life. Such an area is called a **cultural region**. People living in a place with cold weather, for example, wear heavy clothing. Many people living in a place with rich soil farm the land. Yet in North America, there were great differences even among the people of the same cultural region. Think about these differences as you read about the Indians of one cultural region—the Northwest Coast.

The Great Northwest

High in the mountains of the Cascade Range on the border of what are today the states of Washington and Oregon, the Columbia River passes through a narrow gap in the cliffs. For 15 miles (24.1 km) the river thunders through waterfalls and rapids. This area is known as The Dalles (DALZ). For hundreds of years, it was one of the greatest trading centers in North America.

People came to The Dalles from hundreds of miles away. Dozens of tribes, some speaking languages as different from each other as English is from Chinese, took part in the trading through the warm summer months.

The Dalles is part of the area known as the Northwest Coast. The Northwest Coast is a strip of land that stretches 2,000 miles (3,219 km) along the Pacific Ocean from present-day southern Alaska to northern California.

This Makah artifact of a carved figure in a shell is about 500 years old.

71

Early Cultures of North America

ASIA

ARCTIC OCEAN

Legend:
- Arctic
- Subarctic
- Northwest Coast
- Plateau
- California
- Great Basin
- Southwest
- Plains
- Eastern Woodlands
- Middle America
- Caribbean
- —— Present-day border

INUPIAT

YUP'IK

ALEUT

ATHABASKAN

HAN

INUIT

INUIT

INUIT

INUIT

TLINGIT

KASKA

HAIDA

CHIPEWYAN

Hudson Bay

NASKAPI

BEOTHUK

BELLA COOLA

CREE

CREE

CREE

CREE

NOOTKA

PACIFIC OCEAN

MAKAH
CHINOOK

KOOTENAI

BLACKFOOT

CREE

MICMAC

YAKIMA

NEZ PERCÉ

ASSINIBOINE

OJIBWA

OJIBWA

ALGONKIN

PENOBSCOT

CROW

MANDAN

CHIPPEWA

OTTAWA

Great Lakes

HURON

ERIE

IROQUOIS

MASSACHUSET

POMO

PAIUTE

SHOSHONE

CHEYENNE

SIOUX

SIOUX

SAUK
FOX

IROQUOIS LEAGUE
CAYUGA
MOHAWK
ONEIDA
ONONDAGA
SENECA

DELAWARE

SHOSHONE

UTE

PAWNEE

IOWA

MIAMI

PAIUTE

ARAPAHO

ILLINOIS

POWHATAN

YOKUTS

MISSOURI

CHUMASH

KAW

OSAGE

SHAWNEE

CHEROKEE

TUSCARORA

ATLANTIC OCEAN

HOPI
NAVAJO
PUEBLO
ACOMA
ZUNI

APACHE

KIOWA

QUAPAW

YUCHI

CHICKASAW

TOHO'NO-O-OTAM

APACHE

COMANCHE

CADDO

CHOCTAW

NATCHEZ

YAQUI

TIMUCUA

CALUSA

Gulf of Mexico

Tropic of Cancer

COAHUILTEC

CIBONEY

TAINO

ARAWAK

HUICHOL

CIBONEY

Caribbean Sea

TOLTEC
AZTEC

MAYA

MIXTEC
ZAPOTEC

MOSQUITO

SOUTH AMERICA

0   300   600 Miles
0   300   600 Kilometers
Azimuthal Equal-Area Projection

Regions Many of our names for cities, states, rivers, and regions come from Indian languages.

■ *What connections do you see between the names of the Indian cultures on the map and the names of places today?*

The Indians of the Northwest Coast lived between the ocean and rugged mountain ranges, in a land of rivers and forests filled with fish and game. The growing season was short, and the climate was too wet for much agriculture. But there were plenty of fish, especially salmon. There were also plenty of deer, bears, and other animals. There was wood to build houses and make tools. If tribes could not get something by themselves, they could get it by trade.

It might seem surprising that trade was common in an area where travel was so hard. Because mountains made travel by land difficult, people traveled by water. The Columbia River was the "highway" of the Northwest, carrying people from place to place in wooden dugouts. **Dugouts** are boats made from large, hollowed-out logs.

REVIEW *What foods were available to the peoples of the Northwest?*

The Chinooks

The Chinooks (shuh•NUKS) were the best-known traders of the Northwest Coast. This Indian tribe lived near the coast, at the mouth of the Columbia River. Chinook villages were made up of rows of long wooden houses. The houses were built of wooden boards and had no windows. The Chinooks built each house partly over a hole dug in the earth so that some of its rooms were under the ground. Such a house is called a **pit house**.

Several families belonging to the same clan lived in each house. A **clan** is a group of families that are related to one another. Like many other tribes, the Chinooks traced their clans through the mother's line. In other words, the people of the clan had the same mother, grandmother, or great-grandmother. Children belonged to their mother's clan, not to their father's.

Chinook pit houses were made of split wood. These houses usually had no windows and only one door (right). The picture (below) shows the inside of a Chinook house.

The Chinooks controlled the Columbia from the coast all the way to The Dalles. They even made other peoples pay them for the right to travel the river. There were so many peoples speaking different languages that it became difficult to talk at The Dalles. To help solve the problem, the Chinooks developed a language for trading. It was made up of Chinook words and words borrowed from other languages. This trading language made it easier for different peoples to talk to each other and to **barter**, or exchange goods.

And what a lot of different goods there were! People traded dried fish, shells, furs, whale products, seal oil, cedar, dugouts, masks, jewelry, baskets, copper, and even prisoners.

Wealth was very important to the people in the Northwest Coast area. Tribes often attacked one another to gain wealth and, in turn, respect. Prisoners, a sign of wealth, were frequently taken during the many wars. Only very important people could use prisoners as servants.

To show off the things they owned, the Chinooks and other tribes who lived along the coast held **potlatches**. These were special gatherings with feasting and dancing. During a potlatch, the hosts gave away valuable gifts as a sign of their wealth. Members of some clans spent years preparing hundreds of gifts to be given away at the next potlatch.

REVIEW *What role did the Chinooks play in the Northwest Coast trade?*

The Makahs

The waters of the Northwest helped give the peoples who lived there plenty of food. Salmon and other fish, sea otters, and whales were in good supply. Most coastal tribes captured only beached whales, those that had become stranded on shore. The Makahs (mah•KAWZ), however, built canoes to hunt the whales at sea.

Makah whale hunters often spent months preparing for a whale hunt. They fasted and prayed to their gods to favor them. They made new wooden harpoons—long spears with sharp shell points. And they repaired their canoes and paddles. Made of wood, the canoes were 6 feet (1.8 m) wide and carried up to 60 people. They were built for the open ocean. However, they still could be tipped over by an angry whale.

Imagine one group of whale hunters setting out to sea. The chief harpooner leads the hunters. His father and grandfather held the same job before him. After several hours the Makah hunters spot a gray whale. They follow the animal for about 20 miles (32 km) out into the open ocean, slowly closing in. Along the way the chief harpooner shows his respect for the huge animal by singing a special song promising to give it gifts if it allows itself to be killed.

Finally the chief harpooner sees his chance and throws his harpoon. The whale is hit! Sealskin floats tied to the harpoon make it difficult for the whale to dive down into the water. Harpooners from other canoes throw their weapons, too. When the whale dies, the hunters start towing it to shore.

Many Northwest Coast Indians place totem poles outside their houses. Symbols on the pole often tell a family's history. This totem pole was made by a member of the Haida (HY•duh) tribe.

A chief harpooner prepares to throw his weapon at a whale. Whale hunting was important for the Makahs' survival.

After hours of paddling, the Makah hunters are glad to see their village. Wooden houses line the narrow beach between the water and the forest. Outside each house stands a wooden post called a **totem pole**. Each totem pole is beautifully carved with shapes of people and animals. The carvings show each family's history and importance. As the hunters draw near the village, the people on shore rush to greet them.

Little of the prized whale is wasted. The chief harpooner receives the best piece of blubber, or fat. The rest of it is stored for later use. The people will eat the whale's meat and skin. They will make ropes, tools, and bags from different parts of the animal's body. They also will melt some of the blubber for oil to burn as fuel.

REVIEW *How did Makah whalers prepare for a hunt?*

LESSON 1 REVIEW

Check Understanding

1 Remember the Facts What resources were available on the Northwest Coast?

2 Recall the Main Idea How did living near an ocean affect the lives of the Northwest Coast Indians?

Think Critically

3 Think More About It How do you think people from different tribes learned the trading language used at The Dalles?

4 Explore Viewpoints Why were potlatches important to people of the Northwest Coast?

Show What You Know

Art Activity Draw a scene showing part of daily life for one of the tribes of the Northwest Coast. Work with your classmates to put all of your scenes together to form a bulletin board display. Label the display *Lifeways of the Northwest Coast Indians.*

Southwest

FOCUS

What steps do people take today to help themselves live in a dry environment?

Main Idea As you read, think about what the Indians of the Southwest did to help themselves live in a dry environment.

Vocabulary

arid   hogan
kachina   shaman
ceremony

The Southwest is a mostly dry land of rocky mesas, deep canyons, steep cliffs, and beautiful mountains. Fierce heat during the day can be followed by sharp cold at night. Months can go by without a drop of rain. Then a sudden storm can bring so much rain that flash floods race through normally dry canyons.

It is difficult to survive in such a land. But the many peoples of the Southwest found ways not only to survive but to live well.

The Hopis

"Up the ladder and down the ladder." In the Southwest, these words meant "to enter a house." Like their Anasazi ancestors, many peoples of the Southwest lived in pueblos—adobe houses of many rooms built next to or on top of one another. To enter a house or to reach other levels, people climbed ladders. In time all of the tribes who lived in pueblos, peoples such as the Hopis (HOH•peez), the Zunis, and others, became known as the Pueblo peoples.

The name *Hopi* means "Peaceful One." The early Hopis lived in present-day northeastern Arizona, just as many Hopis do today. In early times most of their villages were built on top of high, flat mesas. Steep, narrow trails cut into the rocks led from the mesas down to the fields. There the men grew corn, beans, squash, and cotton. The climate was very dry, or **arid**, so they used water from springs under the ground and from rain showers to water their crops.

While the men worked in the fields, the women ground corn into flour, using flat, smooth stones. Women spent hours

A Hopi dancer performs during a ceremony. The dance is part of the Hopis' religion.

Kachina Figures

Pueblo families taught their children the names and special powers of the kachinas by giving them kachina figures. Fathers and grandfathers carved and painted the wooden figures to look like the different kachinas. By studying the figures, children learned what the spirits stood for. Kachina figures were not for play. They were meant to be treasured and passed on to each child's own children.

each day grinding corn, often singing songs as they worked. Part of every home was filled with jars of corn and flour. Surplus food meant survival during times of drought.

Like other Pueblo peoples, the Hopis believed in gods of the sun, rain, and earth. Spirits called **kachinas** (kuh•CHEE•nuhz) were also an important part of the Hopis' religion. These spirits remain important today. The Hopis believe that kachinas visit the world of living people once a year and enter the bodies of the kachina dancers. The dancers are Hopi men wearing painted masks and dressed to look like the kachinas. Kachina dancers take part in many Hopi **ceremonies**, or special services. Some of these ceremonies are held in kivas underground and others are held in large meeting places outside.

REVIEW *Why was storing extra food important to the Hopis?*

Daily Life

Charlotte and David Yue describe the daily lives of the early Hopis and other Pueblo peoples in their book *The Pueblo.* Read now about how the early Pueblo families lived, worked, and cooperated with each other.

66 Pueblo families lived in one room, but most of their daily activities were out of doors. Their homes were used mainly for sleeping and for being sheltered from bad weather. The terrace was an outdoor kitchen and sitting room. The women went up and down ladders to outside ovens on the terrace or down on the ground. The outdoor drying racks had to be tended, and baskets and pottery were often worked on outside.

The workday began at the first light of dawn. Pueblo people hung up their bedding and everyone washed up. They worked first and ate later. The men would start off to the fields, and the women would sweep the floor and begin preparing the day's food.

Children learned by helping. Boys worked with their fathers and uncles. They would go together to the fields. Younger boys scared away crows or gathered up brush. When a boy was old enough, his father might let him work a plot by himself. Girls worked with their mothers and aunts, grinding beside them at the grinding stones. Even small children would be asked to bring some sticks of firewood. Grandfathers worked on their weaving and often taught the children, giving instruction in what was right and wrong and why. Or the wisdom of their years might entitle them to a ceremonial office or a place in the town council. Grandmothers might still do some of the pottery work. They also gave advice and helped take care of the children.

The men took leftover bread with them to eat in the fields, and the women might have some leftovers for a late morning meal. The workday ended in the late afternoon. The men returned from the fields, and the family sat on the floor and shared the main meal of the day. The evenings were spent talking, laughing, and visiting neighbors. At dark the blankets were again rolled out on the floor for sleeping. 99

REVIEW *In what ways did Pueblo children help with the work of the household?*

LEARNING FROM ILLUSTRATIONS Compare the illustration of the Pueblo with the Navajo shelter shown on page 79. In both shelters a family lived together in a single area. In pueblos, however, more rooms could be added when more space was needed.

■ *What materials do you think were used to build both the pueblo and the Navajo shelter?*

A Pueblo

The wood of Navajo hogans is held together by mud. A hogan is always built so that the doorway faces east.

The Navajos

Not all of the people of the Southwest were Pueblo Indians. Some had different ways of life. Often, however, other tribes learned from the success of the Pueblos and took on some of their lifeways. This was true of the Navajos (NA•vuh•hohz).

The Navajos moved into the Southwest about A.D. 1100. They settled in an area known today as the Four Corners.

This is the place where the corners of the states of Arizona, New Mexico, Utah, and Colorado meet. Many Navajo people still live in the Four Corners area today.

The early Navajos were nomads. They traveled with their clans and did not have a formal chief. They used brushwood, animal skins, and leaves to make new shelters in each place where they stopped to hunt and gather food. Imagine their wonder when they first saw the great pueblos of the Hopis, built high on the mesas and surrounded by fields of corn!

To the Navajos, Hopi villages were filled with treasures—treasures that the Navajos wanted. When items could not be traded, the Navajos sometimes attacked the Hopis and stole baskets, weaving looms, pottery, blankets, and farm tools. In time, however, the Navajos learned Hopi ways. Soon they, too, were growing crops and weaving cotton clothing, as the Hopis did.

The Navajos lived in houses called hogans. A **hogan** (HOH•gahn) is a cone-shaped house built by covering a log frame with mud or grass. Rather than building their hogans

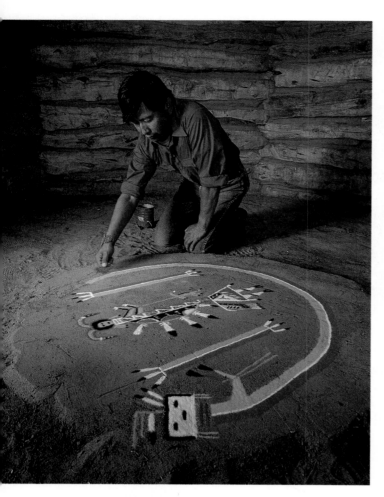

A Navajo shaman creates a sandpainting. The shaman uses charcoal, sandstone, gypsum, and ocher ground up into powders. The powders give the shaman different colors for the painting.

together to form villages, the Navajos built them in small, family-sized groups miles apart from one another.

The Navajos believed in gods they called the Holy People. Some gods, such as the Earth Mother, were kind. Others, such as the sun god, could cause crops to dry up and die. The Navajos believed that they needed to keep praising the gods so that the gods would not use their powers against the people.

As in other Indian cultures, Navajo ceremonies were led by a religious leader and healer called a **shaman** (SHAH•muhn). Shamans called upon the gods to give the people special favors.

Navajo shamans made beautiful sandpaintings, also called dry paintings, that were believed to hold healing powers. First, the shaman created a pattern of religious symbols on the ground, using colored sand. Then, the sick person sat or lay on the sandpainting while the shaman held a special ceremony believed to help him or her feel its healing powers. The painting was always rubbed away after the ceremony.

REVIEW *What lifeways did the Navajos learn from the Hopis?*

LESSON 2 REVIEW

Check Understanding

1 **Remember the Facts**   Why were tribes such as the Hopis known as the Pueblo peoples?

2 **Recall the Main Idea**   What did the Indians of the Southwest do to help themselves live in their dry environment?

Think Critically

3 **Past to Present**   In what ways were early pueblos like present-day apartment buildings? In what ways were they different?

4 **Think More About It**   Why do you think the Navajos decided to end their nomadic way of life and learn some of the Hopi ways?

Show What You Know

Model Activity   Use several small boxes to build a three-dimensional model of a Pueblo village. Use toothpicks, straws, or other things to make ladders, and place the ladders in the model. Display your Pueblo village in the classroom.

Great Plains

Imagine looking out over miles and miles of flat land and gently rolling hills. Tall green grasses move slowly in the breeze. The grassy lands of the Great Plains once fed the buffalo that were the region's most important resource.

At the time of the early Indians, millions of buffalo, or American bison, as scientists call them, roamed the land. These hairy, cowlike beasts moved in huge herds made up of thousands of animals. The herds were so large that they were said to blacken the horizon. These buffalo were an important resource to the Indians of the Great Plains.

The Mandans

Among the Indians of the northern Great Plains were the Mandans. They lived in forests along the Missouri River, in the western part of present-day North Dakota. In their villages the Mandans built circular houses called **lodges**. Each lodge was built over a shallow pit and covered with sod. **Sod** is earth, cut into blocks or mats, that is held together by the grass and its roots. Because Mandan houses were covered with earth, they are often called earth lodges.

The number of earth lodges in a single village ranged from 12 to 100 and each earth lodge was home to several families. Sometimes as many as 60 people, plus their dogs, lived in one lodge. Each family had its own bed or beds next to the outer wall. In the center of the lodge was a shared fireplace under a hole in the roof for letting out smoke. The lodge was warm, and it protected the people during the cold winters.

About twice a year the Mandan villages emptied, as men, women, and children took part in a great buffalo hunt. The people walked for several days from their villages in the river valley forest to the grassy hunting areas of the plains.

FOCUS

How do people in your community use the resources in their environment?

Main Idea Read to learn how the Indians of the Great Plains used the resources in their environment.

Vocabulary

lodge
sod
tepee
travois

The Mandans used buffalo skins to make items such as this shield.

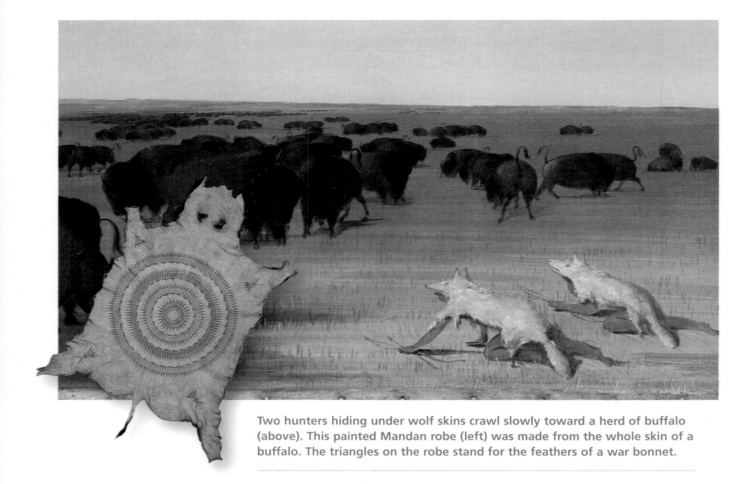

Two hunters hiding under wolf skins crawl slowly toward a herd of buffalo (above). This painted Mandan robe (left) was made from the whole skin of a buffalo. The triangles on the robe stand for the feathers of a war bonnet.

Imagine a Mandan hunting party coming upon a herd. The Mandans do not attack right away. First, the hunters meet to decide exactly what they will do. When each one knows his job, the group is ready.

At dawn the hunt begins. Wearing animal skins as disguises, the hunters creep into position around some of the buffalo. The men move quickly to surround a number of the huge beasts.

At a signal, the hunters shout all together. The frightened buffalo run, and the hunters drive them toward a steep cliff. The buffalo fall over the cliff and are killed.

Most of the women did not take part in the hunt. Their job was to skin the buffalo and prepare them for many uses. The Mandans ate some of the meat right away. The rest they dried and saved to eat when there were no buffalo to hunt. Dried meat, which people today call jerky, can be kept for many months.

The Mandans used every part of the buffalo they hunted. They made clothing, blankets, and moccasins from the skins. They carried water in bags made from the stomachs. They twisted the hair into cord. They made needles, arrowheads, and other tools from the bones. Some Mandans even used the horns of the buffalo to make bows.

The Mandans also farmed. The men of the tribe hunted, and the women grew the crops. Their farms were small, more like gardens. Their crops were mainly beans, corn, squash, and sunflowers.

The Mandans often traded their crops for goods that other tribes brought to them. Their villages became trade centers.

REVIEW *In what two ways did the Mandans get their food?*

The Kiowas

The Kiowas (KY•uh•wahz) of the southern Great Plains did not farm or live in villages. They were nomads, always moving on the vast Plains. This region had no rich river valleys or forests. It was flat grassland. The roots of the short grass were so tough that it was impossible to break the soil with a digging stick. So instead of growing crops, the Kiowas followed the buffalo from place to place.

Although the Kiowas were nomads, they claimed certain areas. Their first known homeland was in what is now western Montana. Later, they migrated eastward over the Rocky Mountains and onto the Great Plains.

The Kiowas followed the known routes of the buffalo herds. Like the Mandans, the Kiowas depended on the buffalo as the most important resource in their way of life. The Kiowas' houses, their clothing, their food, and even the fuel for their fires came from the buffalo. For fuel the Kiowas used dried buffalo droppings, called chips.

Because the Kiowas followed the buffalo herds, they built shelters that were easy to move. One kind was a cone-shaped tent called a **tepee** (TEE•pee). The Kiowas set wooden poles in a circle and tied them together at the top. Then they covered the poles with buffalo skins, leaving a hole at the top to let out the smoke from their fire. The

Kiowas made most of their clothing, such as the moccasins above, out of buffalo skins. Like the Kiowas, the Apaches built shelters that could be easily moved. Dogs were used to help the Indians move their belongings from place to place.

Kiowas also used the buffalo skins for their beds and blankets.

Wood was hard to find because few trees grew on the Great Plains. The Kiowas made double use of their wooden tepee poles by turning them into a kind of carrier called a **travois** (truh•VOY). A travois was made up of two poles fastened to a harness on a dog. Goods were carried on a skin that was tied between the poles. Later, the Kiowas used horses, which they called "big dogs," to drag the poles.

Among the Kiowas each person was equal in the group. No one person was born more important than anyone else. Any man could become chief by proving himself a good hunter and a good leader of people. He became chief because his people chose and trusted him.

The Kiowas who did not follow the ways of the group were free to leave and live on their own. Sometimes a leader and his followers would start a new village. In this way, one tribe often had many subgroups. Each subgroup was made up of families who worked together.

REVIEW *What kind of person did the Kiowas choose as chief?*

Peace

Friend

Trade

LEARNING FROM DIAGRAMS
The Plains Indians often communicated with one another through sign language.
■ *Why do you think the Indians crossed their arms to make the sign for trade?*

LESSON 3 REVIEW

Check Understanding

1 Remember the Facts   In what kinds of shelters did the Mandans and the Kiowas live?

2 Recall the Main Idea   How did the Mandans and the Kiowas use the resources that were found in their environment?

Think Critically

3 Think More About It   Why do you think it was important to carefully plan a buffalo hunt?

4 Personally Speaking   Why do you think it was important for a chief to be a good hunter?

Show What You Know

Poster Activity   Make a poster that shows the many ways the Plains Indians used buffalo. At the top of the poster, draw a buffalo. Then fill your poster with pictures of items the Indians made from different parts of the buffalo. Share your poster with the class.

Eastern Woodlands

FOCUS

How does conflict affect the lives of people today?

Main Idea As you read, think about the ways conflict affected the lives of the peoples of the Eastern Woodlands.

Vocabulary

legend
Iroquois League
confederation
council
longhouse

With this prayer of gratitude, the Haudenosaunee (hoh•dee•noh•SAW•nee), known later as the Iroquois (IR•uh•kwoy), gave thanks for the resources of their land:

> 66 We return thanks to our mother, the earth, which sustains us. We return thanks to the rivers and streams, which supply us with water. We return thanks to all herbs, which furnish medicines for the cure of our diseases. We return thanks to the corn, and to her sisters, the beans and squashes, which give us life. We return thanks to the bushes and trees, which provide us with fruit. . . . 99

The Iroquois lived in what is today the eastern part of the United States. This cultural region was called the Eastern Woodlands. It got its name from the many forests that covered the land. The forests were so thick that in some places sunlight could barely reach the ground.

The Eastern Woodlands was a huge region of great diversity. It had rugged, snow-covered mountains in the north and hot, wet swamps in the south. It also was home to hundreds of different peoples. So many lived there, in fact, that some places became quite crowded, with different tribes often fighting each other for the land.

The Iroquois

The Iroquois lived in the northeastern part of the woodlands. They were among the most powerful peoples of the region. The Iroquois were not one tribe but a group of tribes that lived near

The figures of two people appear at the top part of this Iroquois comb, which was carved out of bone.

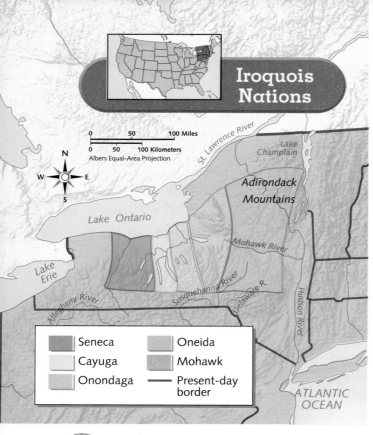

Iroquois Nations

0   50   100 Miles

0   50   100 Kilometers
Albers Equal-Area Projection

St. Lawrence River

Lake Champlain

Adirondack Mountains

Lake Ontario

Mohawk River

Lake Erie

Allegheny River

Susquehanna River

Delaware R.

Hudson River

ATLANTIC OCEAN

- Seneca
- Cayuga
- Onondaga
- Oneida
- Mohawk
- Present-day border

Human-Environment Interactions This map shows the locations of the five tribes that formed the Iroquois League.

■ *How did the locations of the tribes help make working together so important?*

each other and spoke similar languages. These tribes were the Seneca (SEN•uh•kuh), Cayuga (ky•YOO•guh), Onondaga (ah•nuhn•DAHG•uh), Oneida (oh•NY•duh), and Mohawk.

For many years the Iroquois fought with each other and with the neighboring Algonkins (al•GON•kins). The fighting often began over land. Over the years farmers had cleared more and more forest land to raise crops to feed their people. This meant that hunters had to go farther away to find animals, often entering other tribes' lands. But the fighting that began over land continued out of revenge.

Think about this story of a Seneca woman who had lost her son in a battle with the Cayugas. Sad and angry, she asked the men of her clan to attack the Cayugas and pay

them back for her son's death. The Seneca leaders agreed, and their warriors acted quickly. They attacked a Cayuga village, killing many people and taking others prisoner. One of the Cayuga men was given to the Seneca woman in place of her lost son. But now there was likely to be a return attack, and the fighting would go on.

Like many native peoples, the Iroquois often used **legends**, or stories handed down over time, to explain the past. One legend says that a holy man named Dekanawida (deh•kahn•uh•WIH•duh) was one of the first to speak out against all the fighting. He said that the Iroquois must come together "by taking hold of each other's hands so firmly and forming a circle so strong that if a tree should fall upon it, it could not shake nor break it, so that our people and grandchildren shall remain in the circle in security, peace, and happiness."

An Onondaga chief named Hiawatha (hy•uh•WAH•thuh) shared Dekanawida's hopes for peace. Hiawatha visited the Iroquois tribes, asking for an end to the fighting. Tired of war, they finally agreed. They decided to work together in what became known as the **Iroquois League** (LEEG).

In 1570 the members of the Iroquois League agreed to form a **confederation** (kuhn•feh•duh•RAY•shuhn), or loose group of governments. Each tribe governed itself. But matters that were important to all of the groups, such as war and trade, were decided by the Great Council. A **council** is a group that makes laws.

Men from each of the five Iroquois tribes, together called the Five Nations, served on the Great Council. The eldest women of each tribe chose the members of the council. Each member had one vote. All had to agree before anything was done.

The Iroquois said that their confederation was like a big longhouse. A **longhouse** is a long wooden building in which several

Longhouses (left) had no windows, only a door at each end and small holes in the roof to let air in. This computer-generated picture (above) shows the inside of a longhouse.

Iroquois families lived together. It was made of elm bark and had a large door at each end. Just as several families shared a longhouse, the five tribes shared the confederation. They thought of the confederation as a longhouse as big as their land, with the Mohawks guarding the eastern door and the Senecas guarding the western door.

REVIEW *What problems led the Iroquois to form a confederation?*

The Cherokees

Far to the south of the Iroquois lived another people of the Eastern Woodlands—the Cherokees (CHAIR•uh•keez). The Cherokees made their homes in the rich river valleys of the southern Appalachian Mountains. There they grew corn, beans, squash, pumpkins, sunflowers, and tobacco. They gathered wild plants from the forests. They also fished, and they hunted squirrels, rabbits, turkeys, bears, and deer.

Like other tribes of the Southeast, most Cherokee families had two houses. One

house kept them warm in the winter, and the other kept them cool in the summer. Winter houses were small, cone-shaped pit houses made of wooden poles covered with earth. Summer houses were larger box-shaped houses with grass or clay walls and bark roofs. In both winter and summer houses, several families of the same clan lived together.

Cherokee houses—often as many as 300 to 400—were built close together to form villages. At the center of each village was an open square with a temple built high on a flat-topped mound. There the shamans led ceremonies for the community. The most important was the Green Corn Ceremony, held at the end of the summer to give thanks for a good harvest. Shamans also led healing ceremonies. Like other Indian peoples, the Cherokees made many medicines from the plants of the forest.

Leaders called chiefs governed each village, guiding the people on what to do in day-to-day matters. But the villages were also part of a larger Cherokee confederation. From

This painting (above) by George Catlin shows the Choctaws, who, like the Cherokees, played Little War. To control the ball, each player carried two sticks like those shown here (right).

time to time, chiefs from as many as 100 villages came together to discuss important matters—especially matters of war. As in other places in the Eastern Woodlands, wars with neighboring tribes took place often. High wooden fences made of logs were built around each of the villages to keep out enemies.

In most villages the chief in charge of matters of war was also in charge of a game called Little War. It was something like today's game of lacrosse, but it had more players and fewer rules and was much rougher. The object of the game was to throw a small ball between two posts, using a special stick with a net on the end. People came from miles around to watch the game.

REVIEW *Why did the Cherokee chiefs meet as a confederation?*

LESSON 4 REVIEW

Check Understanding

1 Remember the Facts What caused the wars in the Eastern Woodlands?

2 Recall the Main Idea In what ways did conflict affect the lives of the peoples of the Eastern Woodlands?

Think Critically

3 Past to Present How was the Iroquois Confederation like governments today? How was it different?

4 Explore Viewpoints Why did the Iroquois feel that a confederation was like a longhouse?

5 Think More About It Why do you think the Cherokee chief who was in charge of matters of war was also in charge of a ball game?

Show What You Know

Simulation Activity Create a conversation between Hiawatha and members of an Iroquois tribe. In the conversation have Hiawatha try to get the people to join the confederation. With your classmates, put your conversations together to write a scene about the formation of the Iroquois League.

Identify Causes and Effects

1. Why Learn This Skill?

Any action that makes something else happen is a cause. What happens because of that action is an effect. To find the links between events in history, you will need to identify causes and effects. Knowing about causes and effects is also important in your own life. It can help you predict likely outcomes for your actions so that you can make more thoughtful decisions.

2. Remember What You Have Read

Before the Iroquois League was formed, tribes often fought one another. Most of the time the fighting happened because of disagreements over land. As farmers cleared more land to grow crops, hunters had to go farther away to hunt—sometimes into other tribes' lands. The fighting that was first caused by conflicts over land often continued out of revenge.

The Iroquois leaders Dekanawida and Hiawatha feared that all the fighting would destroy their people. They talked to the tribes about peace. The tribes began to work together to form the Iroquois League.

3. Understand the Process

Many events in history have more than one cause and more than one effect. Follow the arrows on this chart to help you identify the causes and the effects that led to the formation of the Iroquois League.

1 What first caused the fighting among the Iroquois tribes?

2 What effect of that fighting caused more fighting?

3 What caused Dekanawida and Hiawatha to work to end the fighting?

4 What was the effect of Dekanawida's and Hiawatha's work?

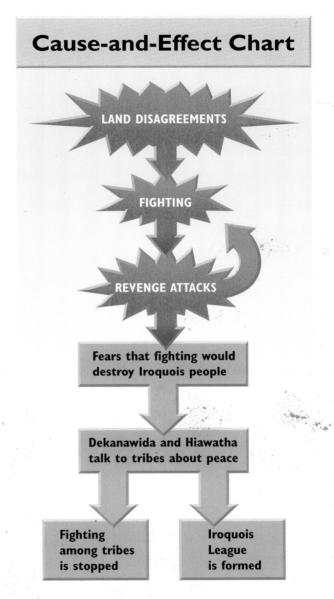

Cause-and-Effect Chart

LAND DISAGREEMENTS

FIGHTING

REVENGE ATTACKS

Fears that fighting would destroy Iroquois people

Dekanawida and Hiawatha talk to tribes about peace

Fighting among tribes is stopped

Iroquois League is formed

4. Think and Apply

Suppose that you are hurrying to school. It is raining, and there are wet leaves on the sidewalk. You slip on the leaves and fall, hurting your leg. As a result, you are late for school and miss an important test. Draw a cause-and-effect chart to show the causes and effects of your fall.

FOCUS

How do people today meet their needs by borrowing ideas from others?

Main Idea Read to learn how Indian peoples of Middle America met their needs by borrowing ideas from other peoples.

Vocabulary

city-state
class
noble
slavery
empire
emperor
tribute

This clay figure shows the clothing and jewelry worn by men of the Mayan upper classes.

Middle America

The cultural region of Middle America includes most of the present-day country of Mexico as well as several countries of Central America. This region was home to one of the oldest civilizations in the Americas—that of the Olmecs. The Indian peoples who came after the Olmecs learned much from this "mother civilization." Two groups who borrowed ideas from the Olmecs and from other peoples of Middle America were the Mayas (MY•uhz) and the Aztecs.

The Mayas

From far off, it looked as if the whole city were made of stone. There were temple pyramids reaching high into the sky. There was a round-topped building where priests studied the stars. There were great palaces, towers that looked over the city, ball courts, and bridges. All of these structures were connected by roads paved with stones. This was Tikal (tih•KAHL), one of the cities built by a people known as the Mayas.

Mayan civilization began to take shape about 500 B.C., during the time of the Olmecs. Building on what the Olmecs had done, the Mayas slowly created their own culture. In time Mayan culture took Olmec ways of life to even greater heights.

The Mayas built more than 100 stone cities in Middle America. Each city had its own ruler and its own government. For this reason, each was called a **city-state**. Tikal, in what is today the country of Guatemala, was the largest. Up to 100,000 people lived there.

Like the Olmecs and some other Indian peoples, the Mayas were divided into social **classes**. These are groups of people treated with different amounts of respect in their society. At the top were the all-powerful priests. Next were the **nobles**, or people from important families. The nobles ruled along with the priests. Below them were traders and craftspeople who worked with wood, stone, leather, gold, and clay. Near the bottom were the farmers, whose corn fed the other classes and made Mayan civilization possible. The only people treated with less respect than the farmers were the slaves.

The Mayas, like some other cultures, enslaved other people. **Slavery** is the practice of holding people against their will and making them carry out orders. Most Mayas who held slaves were nobles. They were thought of as slave owners. The enslaved people were thought of as the owner's property. Most slaves were people accused of crimes. Slavery was their punishment.

The priests and nobles lived in luxury in the cities. But everyday life for most Mayas, who lived in the countryside, meant hard work. Think about the members of one farm family, beginning their day when it is still dark outside. Rising first, the mother lights a fire in the family's small hut, which is made of mud. There are no windows and no furniture. The family eats and sleeps on mats laid on the dirt floor. The mother prepares tortillas (tor•TEE•yahz), or thin corn pancakes. She bakes them over the fire for her husband and son. At dawn both will leave for the fields. It takes hard work to keep the thick jungle from taking over the land where they grow corn, beans, and squash.

When father and son have left, the mother cares for her new baby and begins her own

At Mayan temples priests held religious ceremonies and studied the stars. Most temples looked like this one at Chichén Itzá (chih•CHEHN it•SAH).

Gulf of Mexico

PACIFIC OCEAN

N
W ⊙ E
S

0   100   200 Miles
0   100   200 Kilometers
Azimuthal Equal-Area Projection

•Uxmal   🜂 Cozumel
Yucatán
Peninsula

Tula•
Chapultepec• •Tenochtitlán
            •Cholula
Rio Balsas   •Coxcatlán
                                    Tikal•
Monte Albán•
            •Yagul   •Palenque   Rio Usumacinta
            Bonampak•

•Copán

Maya civilization, A.D. 900
Aztec civilization, A.D. 1500

Regions The Mayas and the Aztecs lived
in parts of what are today Mexico and
Central America.
■ *Why do you think this cultural region is called*
Middle America?

This is a Mayan figure of a woman (right) weaving at
a loom. The loom is fastened to a pole, probably a tree
trunk.

work. Today she will weave cloth and begin
to make extra baskets to store corn. The
harvest this season should be good. There
should be enough corn to feed the family.
They might even have some left over to trade
at the market in the city.

Mayan markets were busy places. Traders
from many miles around bought and sold
honey, cotton cloth, cocoa, feathers, copper
bells, gold dishes, pearls, salt, and dried fish.
All of these goods were carried to and from
the markets on the backs of slaves.

The Mayas believed in gods of the sun,
rain, and many other qualities found in

nature. Mayan priests led religious ceremonies and spent many hours studying the
stars. From watching the movement of the
stars and working out long mathematical
problems, the Mayas made several different
calendars. One of their calendars had 365
days, as our calendar does today. To help
keep track of time, the Mayas used a way of
counting that had the idea of zero—a very
important idea in mathematics. And they
recorded what they learned, using their own
form of picture writing.

REVIEW *How was the Olmec civilization*
important to the Mayas?

The Aztecs

Another culture that developed in Middle America was that of the Mexicas, a tribe later known as the Aztecs. For many years the Aztecs were nomads, moving from place to place in search of food. Then, about A.D. 1200, they began to settle in the Valley of Mexico.

The Aztecs built their capital, Tenochtitlán (tay•nohch•teet•LAHN), on two islands in the middle of Lake Texcoco (tes•KOH•koh). Today Mexico City, the capital of Mexico, stands on this same spot. Legend says that the Aztecs built their capital where they saw a sign from the gods—an eagle with a snake in its mouth, sitting on a cactus. Today the eagle with the snake appears on the Mexican flag.

The Aztecs built a great civilization. By about A.D. 1500 the Aztecs' huge empire included 200,000 square miles (518,000 sq km) and more than 5 million people. An **empire** is a conquered land of many peoples and places governed by one ruler. That ruler is called an **emperor**.

Just as the Mayas had learned from the Olmecs, the Aztecs learned from the Mayas. The Aztecs also borrowed new ways of doing things from peoples they conquered. In this way the Aztec Empire became one of the greatest of the time.

To have more land for farming, the Aztecs built small islands in Lake Texcoco. To do this, they tied large baskets to the lake's bottom and filled them with mud. Then they planted corn and other crops in the new soil. Canals and paved roads connected the many islands to the shore.

In the city's most important square were royal palaces with hundreds of rooms. There were also gardens and a large zoo. The palaces were the homes of the all-powerful Aztec emperor.

Near the emperor's palaces were huge warehouses piled high with tribute. **Tribute** is the name for payments a ruler demands from his or her people. Each year the people had to send goods such as cloth, jewelry, feathers, gold, and corn to Tenochtitlán. If they refused, the emperor would send Aztec soldiers to make them pay.

To protect their empire, the Aztecs had a large army. In wartime, an Aztec leader beat

This drawing tells the story of the Aztecs' search for a place to build their capital. The name Tenochtitlán means "cactus rock." The blue lines in the picture stand for the waters of Lake Texcoco. The symbol of the eagle on the cactus can be seen today on the Mexican flag.

This is the lake city of Tenochtitlán, as painted by Mexican artist Diego Rivera. The city and nearby land were joined by bridges.

the drum on top of the war god's temple to call the army. The soldiers moved at once to prepare for war and join their fighting groups in front of their clan's temple. In 24 hours the Aztec army would be 200,000 strong and ready to fight. Most Aztec soldiers wore special clothing. An Eagle Knight, for example, wore a wooden helmet shaped like an eagle's head. The soldier's quilted cotton armor was covered with eagle feathers.

In the very center of Tenochtitlán, white flat-topped pyramids rose toward the sky. On top of the pyramids stood the great stone temples built to honor the Aztecs' gods.

Past the stone temples was a large, open area where the daily market was held. Each morning canoes crowded the lake, bringing goods from all over the empire and from places outside of it. The people quickly set up their stalls and displayed their goods, eager to do business. More than 60,000 people—from the highest nobles to the lowest farmers—came to the marketplace every day to exchange goods. At the same time they exchanged ideas, often adding new ways of life to the Aztec culture.

REVIEW *From whom did the Aztecs learn many of their lifeways?*

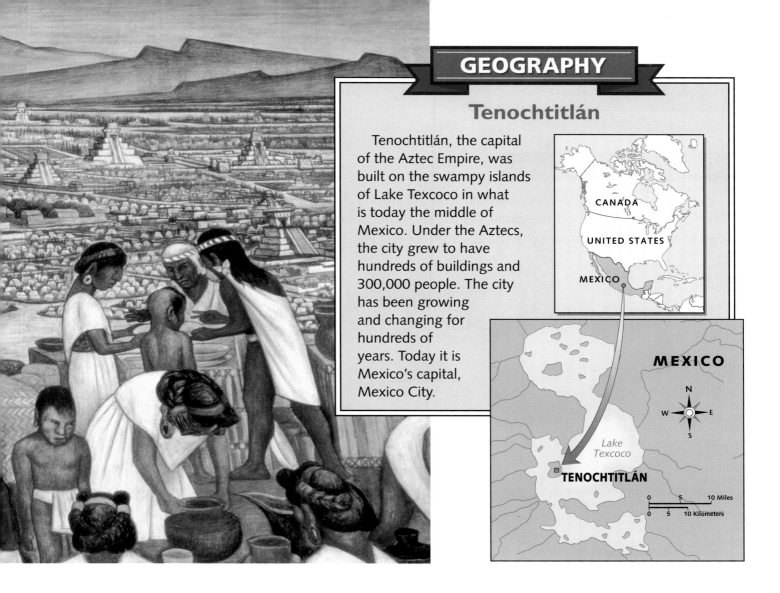

Tenochtitlán

Tenochtitlán, the capital of the Aztec Empire, was built on the swampy islands of Lake Texcoco in what is today the middle of Mexico. Under the Aztecs, the city grew to have hundreds of buildings and 300,000 people. The city has been growing and changing for hundreds of years. Today it is Mexico's capital, Mexico City.

CANADA

UNITED STATES

MEXICO

MEXICO

N
W — E
S

Lake Texcoco

TENOCHTITLÁN

0   5   10 Miles
0   5   10 Kilometers

LESSON 5 REVIEW

Check Understanding

1 Remember the Facts   Why was each city in the Mayan civilization called a city-state?

2 Recall the Main Idea   How did the Indian peoples of Middle America meet their needs by borrowing ideas from other peoples?

Think Critically

3 Think More About It   How were the lives of the Mayan priests and nobles different from the lives of the Mayan farmers?

4 Cause and Effect   How did the Aztecs change their environment when they built the city of Tenochtitlán?

Show What You Know

Art Activity   Create a travel brochure inviting people today to visit the sites of either the Mayan or the Aztec civilization. Your brochure should include a map showing where the civilization was located, as well as a short introduction to the people's history. Include pictures of famous sites. Present your brochure to the class.

CONNECT MAIN IDEAS

Use this organizer to show the diversity of the ways of life of the American Indians. Write three examples for each cultural region. A copy of the organizer appears on page 13 of the Activity Book.

Northwest Coast

1. _____
   _____
2. _____
   _____
3. _____
   _____

Indians of North America

Diversity

Middle America

1. _____
   _____
2. _____
   _____
3. _____
   _____

Southwest

1. _____
   _____
2. _____
   _____
3. _____
   _____

Great Plains

1. _____
   _____
2. _____
   _____
3. _____
   _____

Eastern Woodlands

1. _____
   _____
2. _____
   _____
3. _____
   _____

WRITE MORE ABOUT IT

Write an Invitation Imagine that you are a wealthy Chinook getting ready to hold a potlatch. Write an invitation to a friend, describing your plans for the feast.

Write a Story Write a story entitled *A Day in the Life of an American Indian Family.* Include the conversations of friends and family members in your story.

USE VOCABULARY

Write a term from this list to complete each of the sentences that follow.

barter   shaman

clan   slavery

council   travois

1 A _____ is a group of families that are related to one another.

2 At The Dalles, Indians from many different Northwest Coast tribes met to _____, or exchange goods.

3 A religious leader and healer called a _____ led many Navajo ceremonies.

4 A _____ is a kind of carrier used by the Kiowas to transport goods.

5 A _____ is a group that makes laws.

6 _____ is the practice of holding people against their will and making them carry out orders.

CHECK UNDERSTANDING

7 Why were dugouts especially important to the Indians of the Northwest Coast?

8 What do the carvings on totem poles show?

9 How did Pueblo people prepare for times of drought?

10 What are kachina figures used for?

11 In what ways did the tribes of the Great Plains use the buffalo they hunted?

12 What was the Iroquois League? What was its purpose?

13 What group was in the highest class in Mayan society? What group was in the lowest class?

THINK CRITICALLY

14 **Past to Present** Many Indian clans traced their families through the mother's line. How is that different from the way many people today trace their families?

15 **Think More About It** How were the life-ways of the Makahs and the Kiowas similar, even though they lived in different cultural regions?

16 **Cause and Effect** How did the environment affect the ways the Hopis, Mandans, and Cherokees built their homes?

APPLY SKILLS

Identify Causes and Effects
Think again about the busy trading center at The Dalles. Draw a cause-and-effect chart similar to the chart on page 89. The chart should trace the development of the trading language that was used at The Dalles. Show the causes that led the Indians to make up the language, and show its effects.

READ MORE ABOUT IT

Potlatch: A Tsimshian Celebration by Diane Hoyt-Goldsmith. Holiday House. Text and photographs are used to describe the tradition of the potlatch, which is held by the Tsimshian Indians to celebrate their heritage.

Visit the Internet at
http://www.hbschool.com
for additional resources.

A MULTICULTURAL Country

If a huge quilt could show you what life was like in the Americas in the late 1400s, it would have hundreds of different patches. Their different colors and designs would stand for the many different Indian cultures.

The United States is still a patchwork of many cultures—American Indian, Hispanic, European, African, Asian, Pacific Island, Alaska Native, and others. The people from these many backgrounds are united by being Americans. Yet they also have kept alive their own cultural traditions. This has made the United States a multicultural country—a country of many cultures.

Many people believe that our country's diversity of cultures adds to the richness of American life. Most Americans experience this diversity every day. You hear it in the languages people speak and in the music they play. You see it on signs and in the ways people dress. You taste it in the foods they make. You feel it at times of special celebration.

Think and Apply

BUILDING CITIZENSHIP

Think about the many ways people express their culture. Design a colorful patch that shows a part of your cultural heritage. Then combine your patch with those of your classmates to create a quilt that shows the cultures in your classroom community.

HARCOURT BRACE

Visit the Internet at **http://www.hbschool.com** for additional resources.

CNN Turner Le@rning

Check your media center or classroom video library for the Making Social Studies Relevant videotape of this feature.

UNIT 1 REVIEW

Summarize the Main Ideas
Study the pictures and captions to help you review what you read about in Unit 1.

Illustrate a Scene
Choose one of the Indian peoples described in Unit 1 but not shown here. Draw a picture that shows a scene of daily life for the group you chose. Then write a paragraph that explains the scene. Tell where the scene should be placed in the visual summary.

1 One of the greatest trading centers in North America was located in the Northwest Coast. People from dozens of tribes came in dugout canoes to barter at The Dalles.

3 Many of the peoples of the Southwest lived in pueblos. Drying and storing surplus food helped the people survive during times of drought.

5 The Aztec capital of Tenochtitlán was one of the largest cities of Middle America. The city center had palaces, warehouses, temple pyramids, and a huge market.

2 The peoples of the Great Plains depended on the buffalo. After a buffalo hunt, the people worked to use every part of the animal.

4 To help end the fighting among the peoples of the Eastern Woodlands, the Iroquois formed a confederation. Leaders from each of the five Iroquois tribes served on the Great Council.

USE VOCABULARY

Write a word from this list to complete each of the sentences that follow.

culture   kivas

dugouts   maize

earthworks   origin stories

1 The way of life of a group of people is called its _____.

2 _____ tell of Indian peoples' beliefs about the world and their place in it.

3 _____ was the most important crop grown in the Americas.

4 The mounds built by early peoples for burying their dead or for religious purposes are called _____.

5 The Anasazi held religious services in special underground rooms called _____.

6 The Chinooks traveled the Columbia River in _____, or canoes made from large, hollowed-out logs.

CHECK UNDERSTANDING

7 What is cultural diffusion?

8 What was the religious leader called who led the Navajo ceremonies?

9 In what ways did the Indians of the Great Plains depend on the buffalo?

10 What problems led the Iroquois to form a confederation?

THINK CRITICALLY

11 **Think More About It** What changes in technology brought changes to the lives of early Americans?

12 **Past to Present** Give three examples that show that North America in ancient times was a land of great diversity. Give three examples that show that North America today is a land of great diversity.

APPLY SKILLS

Use a Map to Show Movement
Chaco Canyon, in what is today New Mexico, was a center of Anasazi culture. About 400 miles (644 km) of roads ran between pueblos in the area of Chaco Canyon. Use the map below to answer the questions.

13 In which direction would a person travel to follow the road from Salmon to Pueblo Bonito?

14 In which direction would a person travel to follow the road from Pueblo Pintado to Pueblo Bonito?

Roads of the Anasazi

- ——— Anasazi road
- • Anasazi settlement

REMEMBER

- Share your ideas.
- Cooperate with others to plan your work.
- Take responsibility for your work.
- Help one another.
- Show your group's work to the class.
- Discuss what you learned by working together.

Unit Project Wrap-Up

Create a Map Work with several of your classmates to finish the Unit Project that was described on page 39. First, make sure that your map includes an American Indian group from each of the five cultural regions— the Northwest, the Southwest, the Great Plains, the Eastern Woodlands, and Middle America. Work together to write captions that explain how each Indian group governed itself and met its needs. Display the maps and captions in the classroom or hallway.

ACTIVITY

Make a Cave Wall Painting

Imagine that you and your classmates are Clovis people. You want to draw pictures of a mammoth hunt on a cave wall so your children will learn from your experiences. Tape large pieces of paper to your classroom wall. Form several groups, with each group responsible for a different part of the hunt. Using paint, colored chalk, or markers, draw scenes of the hunt. One scene should show the weapons that were used, including Clovis points and the atlatl. Another scene should show the many ways the people used the mammoth.

ACTIVITY

Draw a Scene of Daily Life

To show how the environment helps shape the way people live, draw a scene from the daily life of an Indian group. Use your textbook and other reference materials to get ideas. Give your scene a title and add it to a classroom display.

103

Unit 1
The Ancient
Americas

Unit
2

Unit 3
Our Colonial
Heritage

Unit 4
The American
Revolution

Unit 5
The New
Nation

EXPLORATIONS AND ENCOUNTERS

For thousands of years the Indian peoples of the Americas developed their own lifeways. They knew little about people in other parts of the world, who knew little or nothing about them. From time to time some adventurous Europeans or Asians or Africans told stories of finding a new, faraway land. But almost all who heard them thought the stories were tall tales. Few people ever dreamed that two other large continents existed. Those unknown continents were North America and South America.

In time all of this was to change. By the late 1400s more and more Europeans were setting out to explore what to them were unknown lands. In the 1500s ship after ship was arriving in the Americas. The lives of the American Indians and the lives of people around the world would never be the same again.

◄ This painting, by H. C. Vroom, is from the 1600s and shows the Dutch fleet returning from the Americas.

UNIT THEMES

- Commonality and Diversity
- Conflict and Cooperation
- Continuity and Change
- Individualism and Interdependence

Unit Project

Make a Globe Complete this project with your classmates as you study this unit. Make a globe by drawing the continents on an inflated balloon. As you read this unit, use different colors to show the routes of at least five explorers, such as Dias, Columbus, and Magellan. You may want to use a string to hang your globe from the classroom ceiling.

NORTH AMERICA

Cahokia

ATLANTIC OCEAN

Tenochtitlán

PACIFIC OCEAN

SOUTH AMERICA

Cuzco

N
W   E
S

0   1,000   2,000 Miles
0   1,000   2,000 Kilometers
Miller Cylindrical Projection

1400   1500

1492
Columbus Lands in America
PAGE 120

1519
Cortés Arrives at Tenochtitlán
PAGE 135

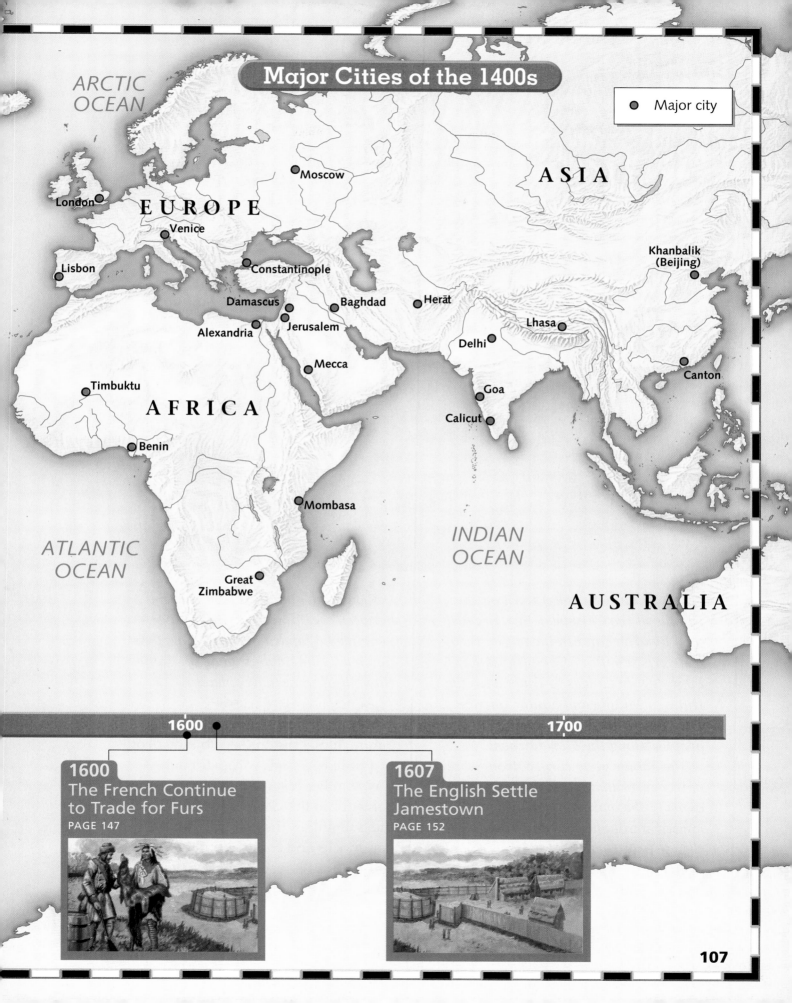

Major Cities of the 1400s

- ● Major city

ARCTIC OCEAN

EUROPE

ASIA

- ● Moscow
- ● London
- ● Venice
- ● Lisbon
- ● Constantinople
- ● Damascus
- ● Baghdad
- ● Herāt
- ● Khanbalik (Beijing)
- ● Jerusalem
- ● Alexandria
- ● Lhasa
- ● Delhi
- ● Mecca
- ● Canton
- ● Timbuktu
- ● Goa
- ● Calicut

AFRICA

- ● Benin

- ● Mombasa

ATLANTIC OCEAN

INDIAN OCEAN

- ● Great Zimbabwe

AUSTRALIA

1600

1700

1600
The French Continue to Trade for Furs
PAGE 147

1607
The English Settle Jamestown
PAGE 152

THE WORLD IN 1492

by Jean Fritz, Katherine Paterson, Patricia McKissack, Fredrick McKissack, Margaret Mahy, and Jamake Highwater
illustrated by John Suh

The Tainos (TY•nohz) lived on the islands of the Caribbean Sea. Because they lived so close to the water, they were expert sailors. They traveled in large dugout canoes to trade with the tribes of Middle and South America. They also traded with North American peoples along the Florida coast.

The Tainos grew corn, cotton, sweet potatoes, peanuts, tobacco, and other crops in the warm climate. They also hunted small animals and birds, and they fished. They lived in houses made from palm trees and slept in swinging beds called hammocks.

Read now about the first meeting between the Tainos and the strange people who landed on their shores. As you read, think about what the Tainos thought of these newcomers.

On that morning of October 12, 1492, a miraculous sight is seen by the people of a little island, now called High Cay, that lies just off the coast of San Salvador in the Caribbean Sea. There in the twilight, as they climb from their hammocks and come out of their palm-leaf-covered houses, they see three moving islands that gradually make their way across the water, coming out of the great unknown and moving ever closer to the astonished people on the shore. In the first light, the floating islands give birth to small rafts that float away from their mothers and drift toward the beach, carrying the most unbelievable of creatures. They look like people made of bright colors. Their faces are covered with bushy hair, as if they are holding squirrels in their mouths.

Despite the strangeness of these creatures, the people are delighted and astounded to see them, and they run toward the water to greet them. At close range, the people realize that the strangers from the sea look like real men, except they have very pale faces covered with bunches of curly hair. They are terribly ugly and have a dreadful smell of spoiled milk. Yet they seem harmless, despite the strange gray and black weapons they carry. The people smile happily when the strangers admire their spears made of reeds and the lovely little ornaments of gold they wear on their ears and nostrils. The people cannot understand why the yellow metal is so fascinating to them.

To make them happy, they bring their strange guests many gifts—green parrots and bundles of precious cotton—in return for which they are given beautiful colored beads and small bells that make a delightful sound. These strangers, who completely hide themselves behind clothing, seem ill at ease with the nakedness of the people of the island, who do not cover their handsome bodies except for lavish painted designs of black, white, and red.

Then a man with a scarlet chest steps forward and tries to talk to the people, though he does not know how to speak properly and can only make strange noises and wave his arms in the air. Despite this strange behavior, the people smile at him respectfully. Hoping to teach him how to speak, they gesture across the landscape, and they tell the scarlet man that their island is called Guanahani. He seems to understand. Then the man points to himself and repeatedly tells the people his name. At this the people of the island begin to laugh. For this stranger has a most peculiar name!
Christopher Columbus.

3

THE **AGE** OF **EXPLORATION**

"I have found a continent, more full of people and animals than our Europe or Asia or Africa."

Amerigo Vespucci, 1503

This portrait of the Italian explorer Amerigo Vespucci was painted by Cristofano dell' Altissimo in the 1500s.

A Legendary Land

FOCUS

In what ways do we learn today about the world around us?

Main Idea As you read, think about ways early Europeans learned about the world around them.

Vocabulary

saga	exploration
knoll	cartographer
encounter	

The Tainos welcomed Christopher Columbus to the island of Guanahani (gwahn•uh•HAHN•ee) in 1492. Like most other Europeans of the time, Columbus knew little about Asia and Africa. He knew nothing about the Americas. Columbus thought he had sailed to Asia. He never knew that he had reached an unknown land.

Stories of an Unknown Land

For a very long time, people had told stories about an unknown land in the ocean between Europe and Asia. The Irish said that a monk named Brendan had sailed to this land in the A.D. 500s. The Chinese told a story about Huishen, a Buddhist monk. He was said to have sailed to this unknown land at about the same time.

No one knows if these stories are true. Sailors from many different places, blown off course by stormy winds, may have been landing on the coast of the Americas for hundreds of years. So many stories were told that it became hard to know what was fact and what was not.

Only one early landing has been proved true. It was made by a people known as the Vikings, who lived in an area in northern Europe that is today the countries of Norway, Sweden, and Denmark. From these lands the Vikings sailed west and built settlements in Iceland and Greenland.

The earliest stories about Vikings visiting an unknown land are found in Viking sagas (SAH•guhz). A **saga** is an adventure story that tells about the brave deeds of people long ago.

Vikings wore bronze helmets like this one, made about A.D. 500, to protect themselves and to frighten their enemies.

A story called the *Greenlanders' Saga* tells of the travels of the Vikings from settlements in Greenland to the Americas. Archaeologists have since found evidence proving that much of the *Greenlanders' Saga* is true.

REVIEW *Who were the first Europeans known to have landed in the Americas?*

The Greenlanders' Saga

About the year A.D. 1000, a Viking named Leif Eriksson (LAYV AIR•ik•suhn) hired a crew and set sail from Greenland, heading west. He was looking for a land he had heard about since he was a boy. It was a land "not mountainous, well-timbered, and with small knolls upon it." A **knoll** is a small, round hill.

The land Eriksson reached was part of what is now Canada. Moving south along the coast, Eriksson soon found a place to spend the winter. The sailors went ashore and built houses of mud and grass. They called the settlement *Vinland,* or "vine land," for the many grapevines that grew there.

Eriksson and his crew returned to Greenland in the spring. During the next several years, the Vikings sailed to Vinland many times. They used it as a base for fishing and hunting.

Leif's brother Thorvald led one trip to Vinland. When the Vikings arrived, they saw what looked like three knolls on the beach. They walked up to them and, instead, found nine people sleeping under boats. The Vikings attacked them. They killed all but one person, who escaped. Later, during that same trip, many boats filled with people came to Vinland and attacked the Vikings. Thorvald was wounded and later died.

Soon after this **encounter**, or meeting, the Vikings ended their trips to North America. The stories of their adventures, however, were kept alive over the years in the *Greenlanders' Saga.*

REVIEW *What and where was Vinland?*

Route of Leif Eriksson

Arctic Circle
GREENLAND
HELLULAND (BAFFIN ISLAND)
80°W
40°
MARKLAND (LABRADOR)
ATLANTIC OCEAN
NORTH AMERICA
VINLAND (NEWFOUNDLAND)
50°N

0   200   400 Miles
0   200   400 Kilometers
Orthographic Projection
70°W
60°W   50°W

→ Leif Eriksson, about A.D.1000

Viking longships could travel on rough, open seas. This longship is about 75 feet (23 m) long and could carry up to 35 people.

Place Eriksson went to places he named Helluland, or "land of flat rocks," and Markland, or "forest land," before settling in Vinland.
■ *What names are used today for these places?*
MAP THEME

Europeans and Exploration

Nearly five hundred years passed before Europeans returned to the Americas. During these years most Europeans did not want to travel to unknown places. They believed the world outside the place they lived was very dangerous. They thought horrible sea monsters waited beneath the ocean, ready to swallow ships whole. They thought the sun was so hot in some places that it made the sea boil.

Another problem was that the Europeans had square-sailed ships that were slow and could sail only with the wind. This would have made a long ocean trip very hard. Even worse, there were not many maps. Those that could be found were so different from one another that no one knew which were correct.

In any case few European rulers were willing to spend their time or money on sailing trips past their borders. Until the 1400s, Europe did not have strong central governments. Instead, it was made up of many small kingdoms and villages. Each was ruled by a noble. These nobles spent too much time fighting one another to care about **exploration**, or searching the unknown.

REVIEW *What kept Europeans from searching for unknown lands?*

The Known World

In 1492, the year the Tainos greeted Christopher Columbus, a group of people in Germany paid Martin Behaim (BAY•hym) an amount equal to $75 to make a new kind of map. The map was in the shape of a ball. It was the first globe ever made in Europe. Behaim called it his "Earth apple." He made it from pieces of leather stitched together.

Behaim's globe showed what he and other European **cartographers**, or makers of maps,

HISTORY

Muslim Mapmakers

Around the 700s the Muslims controlled lands that reached east to the Indus River, west to what is now Spain and Portugal, and south to the Sahara. Over time the Muslims established many trade routes over land and across the Indian Ocean. Years of travel and trade made the Muslims expert geographers. Using the study of stars and the journals of travelers, Muslim mapmakers began to draw highly accurate maps. Many of these maps were used by European explorers.

Al-Idrisi's map shows the known world in 1154. The Arabian peninsula is shown in the center.

thought the Earth was like. Behaim wanted his globe to show the Earth as it really was, but he did not have the facts. Behaim's globe showed the Earth much smaller than it really is. This made it seem as if sailing west from Europe to Asia would be easy. The globe made the trip look as if it would be only about 3,000 miles (4,828 km) long. Today's globes show that the trip is about 10,000 miles (16,093 km) long. More importantly, North and South America block the way. Behaim had no idea that these two continents were there. He did not know about Australia or Antarctica, either. His globe also showed Africa too small and in the wrong shape.

Behaim knew a lot more than other Europeans of his time, though. Some Europeans had heard about the riches in

LEARNING FROM PHOTOGRAPHS This is Martin Behaim's globe seen as both a globe (left) and taken apart and laid flat (above).
■ *Which continents can you identify?*

Asia. But few knew about China's cities, highways, and art. Most Europeans had never heard of the great African empires, such as Mali (MAH•lee) and Songhay (SAHNG•hy). They had no idea that the African city of Timbuktu (tim•buk•TOO) was a center of learning where people studied subjects from mathematics to medicine. And most Europeans knew nothing of the Chinooks, Hopis, Mandans, Cherokees, Mayas, or other Indian cultures of North and South America. They did not know that two other continents lay across the Atlantic Ocean. Even the Atlantic Ocean, which the Europeans called the Ocean Sea or the Green Sea of Darkness, was largely unknown.

REVIEW *What was incorrect on Martin Behaim's globe?*

LESSON I REVIEW

Check Understanding

1 Remember the Facts What did most Europeans know about the Americas in the late 1400s?

2 Recall the Main Idea In what ways did early Europeans learn about the world around them?

Think Critically

3 Personally Speaking Why do you think the Vikings stopped traveling to Vinland?

4 Think More About It Why do you think that Europeans explained the unknown with ideas about monsters living in the seas?

Show What You Know

Mapping Activity Without looking at a map, draw the world and label the continents and oceans. Compare your drawing with the World Map in the Atlas on pages A2–A3. What areas are unknown to you?

Background to European Exploration

FOCUS
What conditions might lead people to explore the unknown today?

Main Idea As you read, think about the conditions that led Europeans to begin exploring the unknown in the 1400s.

Vocabulary
monarch
compass
navigation

Marco Polo liked to tell stories. He often told of adventures to faraway places. Europeans called these places Cathay and the Indies. Marco Polo had been to Cathay, as China was then called, and to the Indies, the islands off the coast of China. He told of meeting Kublai Khan (KOO•bluh KAHN), China's ruler, and seeing amazing things—white bears, black stones that burned, and a place where night lasted all winter and day lasted all summer.

People laughed and called him Marco Millions because he told so many tales. Few Europeans had ever been to Asia, so they could not prove he was wrong. They just thought that the stories he told could not be true. But many were.

Marco Polo

In 1271 Marco Polo left his home in Venice, Italy, to go to Asia with his father and uncle. Niccolò and Maffeo Polo were traders who first heard of the riches of this far-off land from fellow traders. Marco was just 17 years old when they set out.

Four years later, after riding on horses and camels and walking thousands of miles through mountains and deserts, the Polos reached China. There they saw the palace of Kublai Khan. They described it as having walls "all covered with gold and silver and decorated with pictures of dragons and birds and horsemen and . . . scenes of battle." One hall was so big that "a meal might well be served there for more than 6,000 men."

The Polos went on to other places in Asia, such as India and Persia. Marco never reached Japan, but he described it from stories he had heard. In Japan, he said, there was so much gold that whole palaces were built of it.

Marco Polo gave fantastic descriptions of Asia. Many of Polo's stories were about what is today Beijing, China.

Twenty-four years after leaving Venice, Marco Polo returned home with his pockets full of jewels. In time someone wrote down his stories. But it would be nearly 200 years before *The Travels of Marco Polo* appeared as a printed book. When it did, Europeans read it in amazement. Wanting to share in this great wealth, more and more traders took the long land route from Europe to Asia.

REVIEW *What information did Marco Polo bring back to Europe?*

Trade Routes to the East

For hundreds of years, Europeans carried on a busy trade with people from Asia. The goods Europeans wanted most were gold, jewels, silk, perfumes, and especially spices. In the

Kublai Khan, the ruler of China during Marco Polo's visit

days before refrigerators, Europeans prized spices such as pepper, cloves, cinnamon, and nutmeg. They used these spices to make their food taste better and to hide the bad taste of spoiled meat.

For most European traders, however, travel to Asia and back was too hard and took too much time. So instead of going to the Far East, as they then called Asia, most Europeans traveled only part of the way. They went to cities in North Africa and Southwest Asia, which the Europeans called the Middle East. The cities they went to included Alexandria (a•lig•ZAN•dree•uh), Constantinople (kahn•stant•uhn•OH•puhl), Damascus (duh•MAS•kuhs), and Baghdad (BAG•dad). European traders exchanged their goods for

Movement Marco Polo spent 24 years traveling in Asia.
■ *What lands did he visit on his way to China? on his way home to Venice?*

Routes of Marco Polo, 1271–1295

EUROPE
Venice
Constantinople
Black Sea
Trebizond
Ayas
Damascus
Acre
Jerusalem
Alexandria
40°N
Mediterranean Sea
RUSSIA
Caspian Sea
Baghdad
PERSIA
Hormuz
AFRICA
ARABIA
Arabian Sea
Kashgar
ASIA
Kanchow
Shangdu
Khanbalik (Beijing)
Changan
CATHAY (CHINA)
Zaitun
120°E
20°N
PACIFIC OCEAN
INDIA
INDO-CHINA
Pagan
Cochin
South China Sea
Sumatra
Borneo
INDIAN OCEAN
60°E
80°E

→ Route to China
→ Route to Pagan
→ Route to Venice

0   500   1,000 Miles
0   500   1,000 Kilometers
Robinson Projection

N
W   E
S

TECHNOLOGY

The Compass and the Astrolabe

In the 1100s Chinese and European sailors discovered how to make and use a compass. The early compasses were just pieces of magnetic iron floating on straw or cork in a bowl of water. The magnetic iron always pointed north and south, following the direction of the Earth's magnetic field. By the 1400s sailors were using a magnetic needle and had found other ways to make the compass more accurate.

The astrolabe (AS•truh•layb) was used by sailors in the early 1400s. By finding the position of the sun and other known stars, sailors were able to determine their location.

A sailor used the astrobe (left) by positioning the central rod so that it lined up with the sun or the North Star. The compass (right) and the astrolabe (far right) helped sailors determine their direction and position.

goods that traders from the Middle East had gotten in Asia. Then the Europeans made the journey back home, where they sold the Asian goods at the highest prices people were willing to pay. The goods cost a lot. But at least Europeans could get them.

Then suddenly the trade with Asia stopped. In 1453 the Turks, a people from a huge land called the Ottoman Empire, captured the city of Constantinople and took control of the Middle East. This closed the trade routes between Europe and Asia. There would be no more spices or gold or silk unless another way was found to get them.

REVIEW *Why was trade with Asia so important to Europeans?*

Changes in Europe

By the time the city of Constantinople was captured, many changes had taken place in Europe. One of the most important was that the lands ruled by warring nobles had become countries. Portugal, Spain, France, and England were now ruled by **monarchs**, or kings and queens. Most monarchs were strong leaders who kept close watch over their countries and the countries' money.

Over the years Europeans also had made great advances in science and technology. They had learned how to build faster ships. They made a new kind of sail that allowed ships to sail against the wind. They also had made a better compass. A **compass** is an instrument used to find direction. It has a needle that always points north.

All of these changes helped set the stage for European exploration. With Constantinople and the Middle East closed to most traders, Europeans now had a good reason to set out into the unknown to find a new route to Asia and were better able to do so.

REVIEW *What major changes set the stage for European exploration?*

Portugal Leads the Way

Portugal took the lead in the search to find the first water route to Asia. Portugal's monarch, King John, decided to spend as much money as was needed to reach that goal. The trade with Asia was important to him and his people, and they did not want to lose it. King John asked Henry, a prince of Portugal, to direct his country's search.

Prince Henry set up the first European school for training sailors in navigation (na•vuh•GAY•shuhn). **Navigation** is the study of how to plan and control the course of a ship. Because the rewards of being the first to find a water route to Asia would be great, lessons taught at Prince Henry's school were kept secret. Anyone caught taking a map or chart from the school was sentenced to death.

Prince Henry later became known in the English-speaking world as Prince Henry the Navigator. He organized more than 50 voyages of exploration, but he did not go on any of them. For this reason he is sometimes called "the explorer who stayed at home."

Prince Henry (above) led Portugal's search for a water route to Asia. During the late 1400s Europeans used a kind of ship called the caravel (right) for exploration. With three masts and a lateen, or triangular sail, the caravel could sail against the wind.

Prince Henry thought that the most direct way to reach Asia by sea was to go south around Africa and then sail east. Under his direction dozens of Portuguese ships made their way down Africa's west coast. There they found new markets, where they could trade their goods for fruit, gold, and slaves.

Africans and others, such as Native Americans, had been taking prisoners of war as slaves for hundreds of years. Often people sold these slaves to others. European traders quickly saw that they could make money by buying slaves in Africa and taking them to Europe to be sold as servants. By the time of Prince Henry's death in 1460, Portuguese traders were buying about 800 slaves from African traders each year.

At the same time, the search for a water route to Asia went on. Finally, in 1488, Bartholomeu Dias (DEE•ahsh) became the first to sail all the way around the southern tip of Africa—around what is today called the Cape of Good Hope. But fierce storms battered the ship. The sailors grew hungry and sick. Dias wanted to sail on to India, but his sailors made him return to Portugal.

Almost ten years later Vasco da Gama (dah GAH•muh) sailed around the Cape of Good Hope to India. Soon afterward he sailed back to Portugal with his ship full of

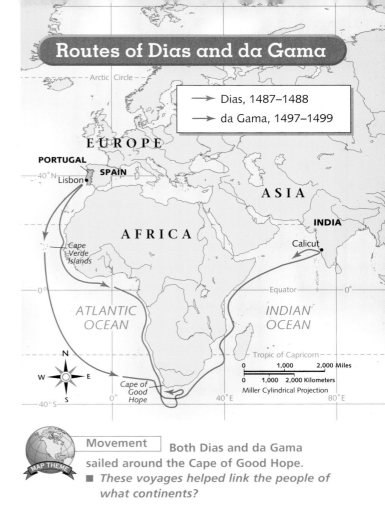

Routes of Dias and da Gama

→ Dias, 1487–1488
→ da Gama, 1497–1499

Movement   Both Dias and da Gama sailed around the Cape of Good Hope.
■ *These voyages helped link the people of what continents?*

spices. Da Gama had finally found a sea route to Asia, showing the way for future explorations.

REVIEW *How did Portugal lead the way in finding a water route to Asia?*

LESSON 2 REVIEW

Check Understanding
1 Remember the Facts   How did the capture of Constantinople affect the Europeans?

2 Recall the Main Idea   What conditions led Europeans to begin exploring the unknown in the 1400s?

Think Critically
3 Cause and Effect   What effects did Marco Polo's travels have on Europeans?

4 Think More About It   Why were strong monarchs important to European exploration?

Show What You Know
Chart Activity   Make a chart with four rows and two columns. Draw a picture of a different spice in each of the four rows of the first column. In the next column, identify the spice and some of its uses. Present your chart to the class.

I, COLUMBUS

MY JOURNAL

1492 - 1493

edited by Peter Roop and Connie Roop

This painting by Peter F. Rothermel, titled *Columbus Before the Queen*, was painted in 1842.

Christopher Columbus had been a sailor almost all his life. Born and raised in Italy, he had sailed all over the known world—to England and the Canary Islands, across the Mediterranean Sea, and along the coast of Africa. He had read **The Travels of Marco Polo** *again and again. He was fascinated by the* stories he had heard of the wealth of Asia—especially the Indies.

For years Columbus had asked Spain's monarchs, King Ferdinand and Queen Isabella, to support his plan to reach Asia by sailing west instead of going around Africa. Columbus believed that sailing west was a quicker, more direct route.

Spain's king and queen, however, were more concerned about life at home. They believed that true unity would come to Spain only if it were a completely Catholic country. For this reason, they drove out the Muslims living in Spain. By 1492 the king and queen had claimed all the land that the Muslims once ruled. That same year they forced the Jews to leave Spain. Spain was then united under one religion and one government.

In 1492 Columbus once again asked Ferdinand and Isabella to support his voyage of exploration. He promised them great wealth and new lands. Columbus also said he would take the Catholic faith to the people of Asia. This time, the king and queen agreed to support his voyage.

On August 3, 1492, Columbus set forth with 89 sailors and three ships—the **Niña** (NEEN•yuh), the **Pinta** (PEEN•tuh), and the **Santa María**. After two months at sea, Columbus made the following entries in his log, or ship's journal. As you read his entries, think about the challenges people face when they are exploring the unknown.

Christopher Columbus was the captain of the *Santa María*. Replicas of the *Niña*, *Pinta,* and *Santa María* (front) were built in Spain.

Wednesday, 10 October, 1492.

Between day and night I made one hundred seventy-seven miles. I told the crew one hundred thirty-two miles, but they could stand it no longer. They grumbled and complained of the long voyage. I told them that, for better or worse, they had to complete the voyage. I cheered them on, telling them of the honors and rewards they would receive. I told them it was useless to complain. I had started to find the Indies and would continue until I had.

Thursday, 11 October, 1492.

I sailed to the west-southwest. The crew of the *Pinta* spotted reeds and a small board. A stick was found that looks man-made, perhaps carved with an iron tool. These made the crew breathe easier; in fact, the men have even become cheerful. A special thanksgiving was offered to God for giving us renewed hope through the many signs of land.

About ten o'clock at night I saw a light to the west. It looked like a wax candle bobbing up and down. It had the same appearance as a light or torch belonging to fishermen or travellers who raised and lowered it. I am the first to admit I was so eager to find land I did not trust my own senses so I called Gutierrez and asked him to watch for the light. After a few moments, he too saw it. I then summoned Rodrigo Sanchez. He saw nothing, nor did any other member of the crew. It was such an uncertain thing I did not feel it was adequate proof of land. Then, at two hours after midnight, the *Pinta* fired a cannon, my signal for the sighting of land.

I now believe the light I saw was truly land. When we caught up with the *Pinta*, I learned Rodrigo de Triana, a seaman, was the first man to sight land. I lay-to till daylight. The land is about six miles to the west.

Friday, 12 October, 1492.

At dawn we saw naked people. I went ashore in the ship's boat,

armed, followed by Martin Pinzon, captain of the *Pinta,* and his brother Vincente Pinzon, captain of the *Niña.* I unfurled the royal banner and the captains brought the flags. After a prayer of thanksgiving, I ordered the captains to witness I was taking possession of this island for the King and Queen. To this island I gave the name San Salvador, in honor of our Blessed Lord. No sooner had we finished taking possession of the island than people came to the beach.

The people call this island Guanahani. Their speech is very fluent, although I do not understand any of it. They are a friendly people who bear no arms except for small spears. They have no iron. I showed one my sword, and through ignorance he grabbed it by the blade and cut himself.

I want the natives to develop a friendly attitude toward us because I know they are a people who can be converted to our Holy Faith more by love than by force. I think they can easily be made Christians, for they seem to have no religion. I will take six of them to Your Highnesses when I

In this painting, titled *Landing of Columbus on the Island of Guanahani*, Columbus claims the new land for the king and queen of Spain.

depart, in order that they may learn our language.

I gave some red caps to some and glass beads to others. They took great pleasure in this and became so friendly it was a marvel. They traded and gave everything they had with good will, but it seems to me that they have very little and are poor in everything. I warned my men to take nothing from the people without giving something in exchange.

This afternoon the people came swimming to our ships and in boats made from one log. They brought parrots, balls of cotton thread, spears, and many other things. We swapped them little glass beads and hawks' bells.

Saturday, 13 October, 1492.

I have tried very hard to find out if there is gold here. I have seen a few natives wear a little piece of gold hanging from a hole made in the nose. By signs, if I interpret them correctly, I learned by going south I can find a king who possesses great containers of gold. I tried to find some natives to take me, but none want to make the journey.

This island is large and very flat. It is green, with many trees. There is a very large lagoon in the middle of the island. There are no mountains. It is a pleasure to gaze upon this place because it is all so green, and the weather is delightful.

In order not to lose time I want to set sail to see if I can find Japan.

One of the rewards Columbus received when he returned to Spain was a personal coat of arms. Notice the pictures of anchors and islands on his coat of arms.

LITERATURE REVIEW

1. What problems did Columbus face on his journey of exploration?

2. What did Columbus first think about the people of Guanahani? Compare this view with the Tainos' view of Columbus, which you read about at the beginning of this unit on pages 108–109.

3. Suppose that you are a sailor on one of Columbus's ships. Write a journal entry for the day you finally see land and encounter new people.

Use Latitude and Longitude

1. Why Learn This Skill?

Just as the numbers of your home address describe where you live in your town, the numbers of your global address tell where your town is located on the Earth. The numbers in a global address stand for lines of latitude and lines of longitude. You can use these lines to help you describe the absolute, or exact, location of any place on the Earth.

2. Lines of Latitude

Mapmakers use a system of imaginary lines to form a grid on maps and globes. The lines that run east and west are the lines of latitude. Lines of latitude are also called **parallels** (PAIR•uh•lelz). This is because they are parallel, or always the same distance from each other. Parallel lines never meet.

Lines of latitude are measured in degrees north and south from the equator, which is labeled 0°, or *zero degrees.* The parallels north of the equator are marked *N* for *north latitude.* This means that they are in the Northern

Hemisphere. The parallels south of the equator are marked *S* for *south latitude.* This means they are in the Southern Hemisphere. The greater the number of degrees marking a parallel, the farther north or south of the equator it is.

3. Lines of Longitude

The lines that run north and south on a map are the lines of longitude, or **meridians**. Each meridian runs from the North Pole to the South Pole. Unlike parallels, which never meet, meridians meet at the poles. Meridians are farthest apart at the equator.

Meridians are numbered in much the same way as parallels are numbered. The meridian marked 0° is called the **prime meridian**. It runs north and south through Greenwich, near the city of London in England. Lines of longitude to the west of the prime meridian are marked *W* for *west longitude.* They are in the Western Hemisphere. The meridians to the east of the prime meridian are marked *E* for *east longitude.* They are in the Eastern Hemisphere.

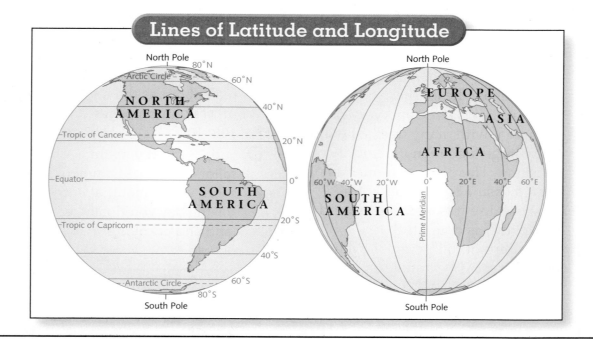

Lines of Latitude and Longitude

Voyages of Columbus

First voyage, 1492–1493
Second voyage, 1493–1496
Third voyage, 1498
Fourth voyage, 1502–1504

ATLANTIC OCEAN

NORTH AMERICA

Bahamas
Cuba
San Salvador
Hispaniola
Jamaica
Puerto Rico
Caribbean Sea
SOUTH AMERICA

EUROPE
PORTUGAL
SPAIN
Lisbon
Palos
Cádiz
Azores
Madeira
Canary Islands

AFRICA

Cape Verde Islands

0   400   800 Miles
0   400   800 Kilometers
Orthographic Projection

4. Understand the Process

The map above shows the four voyages of Christopher Columbus to the Americas. The map has a grid of lines of latitude and longitude drawn over it. The crossing lines of latitude and longitude make it possible to describe absolute location.

Like most maps, this one does not show every parallel and meridian. Every fifteenth parallel is shown from 15°N to 45°N, and every fifteenth meridian is shown from 0° to 90°W.

Now that you know about lines of latitude and longitude, you can use them to find some locations. At the left side of the map, find 30°N. At the top or bottom, find 15°W. Use a finger of each hand to trace these lines to the point where they cross each other. The Canary Islands are not far from this point. So you can say that the location of the Canary Islands is near 30°N, 15°W.

Look for the latitude and longitude that describe the location of Columbus's first landing in the Americas. The closest parallels are 15°N and 30°N. The closest meridian is 75°W. So you can say that the location of the first landing is about 22°N, 75°W.

5. Think and Apply

Think about what you just learned about latitude and longitude. Use the map to answer these questions.

1. What line of latitude is closest to Hispaniola?
2. What line of longitude is closest to the Bahama Islands?
3. What islands are located near 15°N, 30°W?
4. Which location is farther north, 45°N, 60°W or 30°N, 90°W?
5. Which location is farther west, 45°N, 60°W or 30°N, 90°W?

FOCUS

In what ways can new facts change the way we think about events that happened in the past?

Main Idea In what ways did the facts gathered by later explorers change what people thought about the voyages of Columbus?

Vocabulary

conclusion
isthmus
expedition
scurvy

Early Voyages of Exploration

Christopher Columbus never knew that he had not reached Asia. Believing he had reached the Indies, he called the people he met Indians. Until his death in 1506, Columbus kept on saying that he had found a new water route to Asia. Other explorers, however, proved him wrong.

Vespucci Challenges Columbus

News of Columbus's voyages spread quickly through Europe. The news stirred an excitement for adventure not felt since the days of Marco Polo. Soon every monarch in Europe wanted to send ships across the Ocean Sea to find the great riches of the Indies.

In 1497 an Italian named Giovanni Caboto sailed across the Ocean Sea on a voyage paid for by England. Caboto landed in present-day Newfoundland, which is part of Canada. When he returned to England, however, Caboto told everyone that he had found Cathay, the land of the Great Kublai Khan. The English made Caboto a hero. They even gave him an English name, John Cabot.

But not everyone in Europe really believed that Columbus had found the Indies or that Caboto had landed in what is now called China. Amerigo Vespucci (uh•MAIR•ih•goh veh•SPOO•chee) from the Italian city-state of Florence was one of those who did not believe it. In 1499, under orders from the king of Spain, Vespucci sailed to a place south of where Columbus had landed. Two years later the king of Portugal sent Vespucci on another voyage. This time he sailed down the coast of South America from present-day Venezuela to present-day Argentina.

The astrolabe was one of the most important tools used by early explorers. It helped them navigate their ships across unknown seas.

LEARNING FROM MAPS Martin Waldseemüller's map shows Ptolemy (top left) and Vespucci (top right). The Americas are shown (far left) as a long piece of land.
■ *Which continents can you identify?*

On these voyages Vespucci looked for signs that he had reached Asia, as Columbus believed this land to be. Like Columbus, Vespucci had read books by Marco Polo and others who had visited Asia. Yet Vespucci saw nothing that fit what Marco Polo and the others had described. He saw no cities of gold and marble or people wearing cloth of gold.

Something else did not make sense to Vespucci. Years earlier he had studied the work of Ptolemy (TAH•luh•mee), an astronomer in ancient Egypt. From Ptolemy's work, Vespucci had learned that the Earth was larger and Asia was smaller than most people had thought. If Asia were as far east as Columbus claimed, it would cover half the Earth. Vespucci knew that could not be true.

Vespucci also thought about the distance he had traveled. Most sailors of the time could judge how far north or south they had sailed by using instruments such as the cross-staff. The cross-staff was a pole with measurements on it and a sliding crosspiece. Sailors still had trouble, however, measuring how far east or west they had sailed. Vespucci had found a new way of measuring distances east and west. Using his new way, Vespucci figured he had sailed 6,500 miles (10,460 km) from Europe. This figure was more than three times as far as Columbus thought he had sailed.

Based on all the information he now had, Vespucci formed a conclusion. A **conclusion** is a decision or idea reached by thoughtful study. Vespucci concluded that he and Columbus and Caboto had not sailed to Asia. He concluded that the land they had found had to be another continent—the "new world" that some Europeans thought might be there.

Soon a German cartographer named Martin Waldseemüller (VAHLT•zay•mool•er) drew a map of the new continent, using Vespucci's findings. He decided to name the new land for Amerigo Vespucci. In 1507 America appeared on a map for the first time.

REVIEW *What conclusion did Vespucci form?*

A Caravel

Balboa Reaches the Pacific

On September 25, 1513, a group of explorers climbed up a mountain. It was on the west coast of what today is called the Isthmus of Panama. An **isthmus** (IS•muhs) is a narrow strip of land that connects two larger land areas. The Isthmus of Panama connects the continents we know today as North America and South America. The group of explorers, made up of Spanish and African soldiers and Native American guides, had landed on the east coast and walked west until they reached the mountain.

Moving ahead of the rest, Vasco Núñez de Balboa (NOON•yes day bahl•BOH•ah) quickly climbed the last few feet to the mountain peak. Before him lay a huge blue sea. Falling to his knees, Balboa said that the sea—what would later be called the Pacific Ocean— belonged to Spain. A few days later Balboa and the others reached the ocean and explored the coast.

Columbus had believed that Asia stretched from near the eastern edge of Europe all the way around the world. He thought that if he sailed west from Europe across the Atlantic Ocean, he would reach Asia. Now Balboa had come upon a huge ocean on the western side of what Columbus had said was Asia. This proved that Vespucci was right. This also proved that Columbus was wrong. Columbus had not reached Asia but had reached a new continent instead.

REVIEW *What body of water did Balboa reach in 1513?*

Around the World

In September of 1519, five ships and 250 sailors set out from Spain into the Atlantic Ocean. Ferdinand Magellan (muh•JEH•luhn), a Portuguese explorer, led the fleet. The king of Spain had agreed to pay for Magellan's expedition (ek•spuh•DIH•shuhn). An **expedition** is a journey made for a special reason. The reason for Magellan's expedition was to find a way to reach Asia by sailing west around the Americas.

Magellan sailed to what is now Brazil and then south along South America's eastern coast. For months he sailed up rivers into the middle of the continent, hoping to find a river that would go all the way to the ocean on the other side. But he never did, and each time he had to sail the rivers back to the coast. As the ships fought their way through huge, pounding waves and against howling winds, one ship and many of its crew were lost.

Finally, in the fall of 1520, three of Magellan's ships sailed through what is now called the Strait of Magellan, near the southern tip of South America. The sailors found themselves in the same ocean that Balboa had seen. Magellan named it *Pacific*, which means "peaceful," because it seemed so still and quiet compared with the Atlantic.

For more than three months, the ships sailed across the Pacific Ocean. As the months passed, the small amount of food that was left quickly spoiled. There was no

 Movement Vespucci, Balboa, and Magellan all went to places that Europeans had never seen before.
■ *Which explorer's voyage do you think was most important? Why?*

Routes of Vespucci, Balboa, and Magellan

Vespucci, 1499, 1501–1502
Balboa, 1501, 1513
Magellan, 1519–1522

place to stop for fresh food. When the food was gone, the sailors ate rats, sawdust, and leather. Some died of hunger. Other sailors died of **scurvy**, a sickness caused by not getting enough vitamin C, which is found in fresh fruits and vegetables. As the bodies of dead sailors were thrown into the ocean, sharks followed the ships.

In March 1521 the ships reached what are today called the Philippine Islands. Magellan and his crew stayed in the Philippines for several weeks. Then, on April 27, while taking part in a battle between the people of one of the islands, Magellan was killed. His crew soon sailed for home. On September 9, 1522, the 18 starving sailors who were left finally returned to Spain on their one remaining ship.

One of Magellan's ships, the *Victoria*, had sailed around the world. What Columbus had dreamed of was true. Europeans could reach Asia by sailing west. But first they had to sail around the Americas and across the Pacific Ocean in what proved to be a long and dangerous trip.

`REVIEW` *What did Magellan's crew accomplish?*

Magellan used tools for navigation. However, like most explorers of his time, he made mistakes in figuring distances. He and other explorers often found places by accident.

LESSON 4 REVIEW

Check Understanding

1 Remember the Facts   For whom was America named?

2 Recall the Main Idea   In what ways did the facts gathered by Vespucci, Balboa, and Magellan change what people thought about the place where Columbus landed?

Think Critically

3 Think More About It   How do you think the findings of Vespucci, Balboa, and Magellan affected the Europeans' goal of finding a new route to Asia?

4 Cause and Effect   In what ways did food supplies affect early expeditions?

Show What You Know

Mobile Activity   You are responsible for ordering the supplies for a voyage like Magellan's. The ship will be on the ocean for a month, with no refrigeration. Find pictures in magazines of foods and other supplies you would take aboard. Cut out the pictures and paste them on cutouts of a sailing ship. Make a mobile with your pictures. Hang your mobile in the classroom.

Form a Logical Conclusion

1. Why Learn This Skill?

A conclusion is a decision or idea reached by thoughtful study. A logical conclusion is one that is thought out carefully, based on the evidence.

To form a logical conclusion, you must be able to separate facts from opinions. A **fact** is a statement that can be proved true. An **opinion** is a statement that tells what a person thinks or believes. Unlike a fact, an opinion cannot be proved true. To form a logical conclusion, you also must be able to put new facts together with those you already know. This will help you see why things happened in the past, as well as why things happen in your own life today.

2. Remember What You Have Read

You have read that Christopher Columbus formed the conclusion that he had landed in

Amerigo Vespucci, using an astrolabe

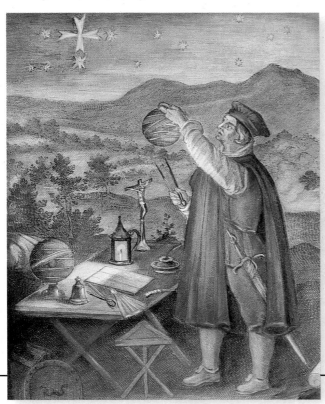

Asia. But Columbus was wrong. When Amerigo Vespucci looked at the facts and gathered new information, he formed a different conclusion—that Columbus had landed on another continent.

Think about the explorers' conclusions as you answer the following questions:

1 Why did Columbus form the conclusion that he had landed in Asia?

2 What evidence did Vespucci have that supported Columbus's conclusion?

3 What evidence did Vespucci have that did not support Columbus's conclusion?

4 How did Vespucci learn about this new information?

5 What conclusion did Vespucci form about where Columbus had landed?

3. Understand the Process

There are many ways to form a conclusion. One way is to follow these steps, as Vespucci might have done.

- Form a question about the subject or the situation.
- Think about evidence you already have that might help you answer the question.
- Gather new evidence that might help you answer the question.
- Form a conclusion based on the strongest evidence.

4. Think and Apply

Write a list of clues that would lead to a certain place in your school, such as the cafeteria, the office, or the library. Read the clues one by one to a partner. Can your partner form a conclusion about where the mystery place is, based on only one or two clues? Why is it important to have as many facts as possible before reaching a logical conclusion?

CHAPTER 3

REVIEW

About 1000
• Leif Eriksson sets
  sail from Greenland

CONNECT MAIN IDEAS

Use this organizer to show how new information helped Europeans gain knowledge and explore the unknown. Write three details for each lesson. A copy of the organizer appears on page 20 of the Activity Book.

The Age of Exploration

A Legendary Land
1. _____
2. _____
3. _____

New Information

Background to European Exploration
1. _____
2. _____
3. _____

New Information

Early Voyages of Exploration
1. _____
2. _____
3. _____

New Information

I, Columbus: My Journal 1492–1493
1. _____
2. _____
3. _____

WRITE MORE ABOUT IT

Write a Report Imagine that you are a Viking who has traveled to a settlement in Vinland. You are living in a base camp for the summer, hunting and fishing. Write a short report about your adventures.

Write an Advertisement Imagine that you are a ship's captain on one of the explorations in this chapter. Write an advertisement calling for sailors. Include in your advertisement places you plan to explore.

1453
• The Turks capture Constantinople

1492
• Columbus sails to the Americas

1522
• Magellan's crew completes their voyage around the world

USE VOCABULARY

Write a term from this list to complete each of the sentences that follow.

cartographer   encounter

compass   isthmus

conclusion   navigation

1 An _____ is a meeting.

2 A _____ is a person who makes maps.

3 A _____ is an instrument used to find direction.

4 _____ is the planning and directing of a ship's course.

5 A _____ is a decision or an idea reached by thoughtful study.

6 An _____ is a narrow strip of land that connects two larger land areas.

CHECK UNDERSTANDING

7 Who was Leif Eriksson?

8 How did Marco Polo's reports about his travels affect people living in Europe?

9 What goods from Asia did Europeans want to buy?

10 What did Columbus hope to find when he began his expedition in 1492?

11 What conclusion did Vespucci form about the lands that he, Columbus, and Caboto had reached?

12 What continents does the Isthmus of Panama connect?

13 Where did Magellan's crew sail?

THINK CRITICALLY

14 **Cause and Effect** How did the capture of Constantinople affect trade between Europe and Asia?

15 **Past to Present** What unknown places might people be interested in exploring today?

APPLY SKILLS

Use Latitude and Longitude Look at the map on page 129. Use the lines of latitude and longitude to describe the following locations: the Cape of Good Hope, the Strait of Magellan, and the part of South America that Vespucci first reached in 1499.

Form a Logical Conclusion Use encyclopedias or other books from the library to find information about the Viking settlement in Vinland. What evidence supports the historians' conclusion that the Vikings were the first Europeans to visit North America?

READ MORE ABOUT IT

If You Were There in 1492 by Barbara Brenner. Bradbury Press. This book looks at life in 1492 from the discovery of America by Columbus to daily life in Europe.

HARCOURT BRACE

Visit the Internet at
http://www.hbschool.com
for additional resources.

4

ENCOUNTERS
IN THE
AMERICAS

"... We have discovered a land rich in gold, pearls, and other things. ... There are in the city many large and beautiful houses ... and many rich citizens. ... And also very pleasant gardens. ..."

Hernando Cortés

A European artist painted this portrait of Motecuhzoma.

Conquest of the Aztecs and Incas

FOCUS

What might cause people of different cultures to fight with one another today?

Main Idea Read to learn what led to fighting between the Spanish and the Aztecs and between the Spanish and the Incas during the 1500s.

Vocabulary

conquistador

civil war

After Columbus, others from Spain—Balboa and Magellan among them—went on to explore the Americas. Driven by their desire for gold and other riches, they pushed deep into North and South America. This was new land to the Spanish. But it was home to the people already living there.

Fall of the Aztecs

The year was 1519, and the Aztec king Motecuhzoma (maw•tay•kwah•SOH•mah) stood in his grand palace at Tenochtitlán, looking out at the night sky. The king watched for signs that would tell him what was to happen.

In the past two years, some odd things had taken place in the Aztec capital. The Earth had shaken. The lake had flooded the city. Comets had been seen in the sky. Aztec priests had studied these natural wonders and decided they were signs that the Aztec Empire was coming to an end.

Then one day people came to the palace bringing news of another strange happening. Men who had white skin and black beards and who rode deer without antlers were coming to Tenochtitlán. The news startled the king. The Aztec people believed that Quetzalcoatl (keht•zahl•koo•WAH•tahl), the light-skinned god, would one day return to rule his people. Could it be that this god of old was coming back?

The person the Aztec Indians thought might be the god Quetzalcoatl was Hernando Cortés (kawr•TEZ). He had been sent by the Spanish government to look for gold. With Cortés were more than 500 soldiers, 14 cannons, 16 horses, and several dogs.

Quetzalcoatl, an Aztec god, was sometimes shown as a snake with feathers. It was believed that he controlled land and sky.

Route of Cortés

NORTH AMERICA

0   400   800 Miles
0   400   800 Kilometers
Azimuthal Equal-Area Projection

ATLANTIC OCEAN

Gulf of Mexico

Tropic of Cancer

Bahamas

Cuba

Tenochtitlán   Veracruz   Yucatán Peninsula   Jamaica   Hispaniola

Caribbean Sea

PACIFIC OCEAN

SOUTH AMERICA

→ Cortés, 1519
Aztec Empire

Location Cortés sailed west from Cuba to what is now Mexico.
■ *How did the location of Tenochtitlán make it difficult for Cortés to conquer the Aztecs?*

Cortés had heard stories about the great wealth of the Aztec Empire. Before setting out, he told his soldiers:

66 We are waging a just and good war which will bring us fame. Almighty God, in whose name it will be waged, will give us victory. I offer you great rewards, although they will be wrapped about with great hardships. . . . I shall make you the richest men who ever crossed the seas. 99

In the spring of 1519, Cortés landed on the east coast of Mexico. He defeated the Indians there and then set out for Tenochtitlán. The journey covered 200 miles (322 km)—from the tropical coast, through snowy mountains, and into the Valley of Mexico.

This painting shows Motecuhzoma (left) meeting with Cortés (right) in Tenochtitlán. Malintzin (next to Cortés) helped translate for the Spanish explorers.

After marching for 83 days, Cortés and his soldiers, joined by large numbers of the Aztecs' Indian enemies, finally reached Tenochtitlán. Thinking that Cortés might be Quetzalcoatl, Motecuhzoma welcomed him, offering housing and gifts of gold. When the Spanish soldiers saw the gold, they were overjoyed.

Cortés soon took Motecuhzoma prisoner. Within two years the Aztec ruler was dead and his capital city was in ruins. Spanish weapons and European diseases, which were new to the Indians, had nearly destroyed the Aztec civilization. By 1521 Cortés had conquered the Aztecs.

Conquering the Aztecs won for Cortés both wealth and glory. He and his soldiers captured the Aztecs' treasures. Among the Europeans, they soon became known as **conquistadors** (kahn•KEES•tah•doors). This Spanish word means "conquerors."

Spain now ruled Mexico. On the ashes of the Aztec capital, the Spanish built Mexico City. Mexico City became the capital of Spain's new empire in the Americas.

REVIEW *How did the Spanish acquire Mexico for their empire?*

Tenochtitlan.

Fall of the Incas

Other conquistadors soon followed Cortés to the Americas. Sixty-year-old Francisco Pizarro (pee•ZAR•oh) was one of them. Pizarro had heard stories of an Indian people whose empire was far richer and more powerful than that of the Aztecs. These people were called the Incas.

In 1531 Pizarro and a group of 180 Spanish and African soldiers sailed from Panama and landed on the west coast of South America. For the next two years, they wandered about the Andes Mountains, stealing gold and riches from the people they found. Then one day they came across a large Inca camp.

One of Pizarro's soldiers described the camp as "beautiful." There were so many tents that the sight filled the Spanish with fear. The soldier said,

66 We never thought the Indians could occupy such a proud position, nor so many tents, so well set up. It filled us . . . with confusion and fear. But we dared not show it. 99

The Spanish would soon learn that the empire of the Incas was even larger and more powerful than they had heard. The empire covered 3,000 miles (4,828 km) of the western coast of South America, including parts of the present-day countries of Peru, Ecuador, Bolivia, Argentina, and Chile. The empire also included over 9 million people.

When Pizarro and his soldiers arrived, the Inca Empire was not at peace. It was being torn in two by a civil war. A **civil war** is a

Route of Pizarro

Movement Pizarro traveled south from Panama to the Inca capital of Cuzco (KOOS•koh). Along the way he found stone-paved roads built by the Incas.

■ *Why do you think these roads were important to the Incas?*

war between people of the same country. The war was being fought between the followers of two brothers, Atahuallpa (ah•tah•WAHL•pah) and Huascar (WAHS•kar). Both said they had the right to the throne. The war finally ended when Atahuallpa killed his brother and became emperor. But the fighting had weakened the empire.

Offering friendship to the new emperor, Pizarro invited

This statue, made of silver and gold, represents an Inca noble. Shells were used to decorate the statue.

Atahuallpa to the Spanish camp. The emperor arrived the next day with several thousand of his people. He was carried on a golden throne lined with parakeet feathers. Around his neck he wore a necklace of giant green emeralds. He wore gold ornaments in his hair.

Pizarro's priest asked Atahuallpa to give up his own religion and accept Christianity. He also asked him to accept the king of Spain as his master.

When Atahuallpa refused, Pizarro took the emperor prisoner. To buy his freedom, Atahuallpa promised Pizarro enough silver and gold to fill a whole room. Atahuallpa's people provided the riches, but Pizarro had Atahuallpa killed anyway.

After Atahuallpa's death in 1533, the Spanish conquered the Inca Empire and made slaves of its people. Inca weapons were no match for Spanish guns and crossbows. For the Spanish, the conquest brought riches and power. But for the Incas, the encounter ended a civilization.

REVIEW *Why did Pizarro order that Atahuallpa be taken prisoner?*

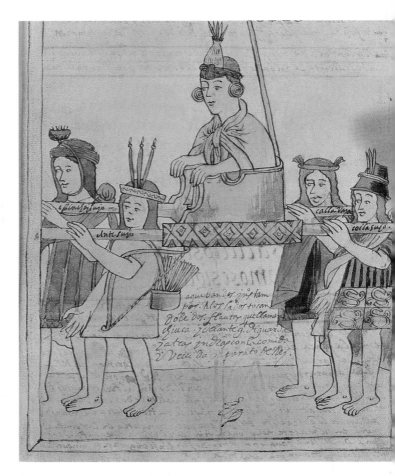

In this drawing the Inca ruler Atahuallpa is being carried to meet Pizarro. Like the Aztecs, some Incas thought their Spanish visitor was a god.

LESSON 1 REVIEW

Check Understanding

1 **Remember the Facts**   What was the goal of Cortés and Pizarro?

2 **Recall the Main Idea**   What was the major reason for the fighting between the Spanish and the Aztecs and between the Spanish and the Incas?

Think Critically

3 **Explore Viewpoints**   Compare the viewpoints of Pizarro and Atahuallpa about who should control land in the Americas. List the reasons each leader might have given to support his ideas.

4 **Past to Present**   Why do some countries today try to conquer other countries? Compare and contrast these reasons with the reasons the Spanish conquistadors had for conquering the Aztecs and the Incas.

Show What You Know

Journal-Writing Activity
Imagine that you are a soldier traveling with Cortés or Pizarro. Write a journal entry that describes what you see as you arrive in the Aztec or Inca Empire. Share your entry with a friend.

The Search for Gold and Riches

FOCUS
What are some reasons people take actions that involve risk and danger?

Main Idea As you read, think about why the Spanish risked the unknown to explore North America in the 1500s.

Vocabulary
grant
mainland
rumor
claim
desertion

Eager to add to their growing empire, Spain's rulers wanted the conquistadors to explore the lands north of Mexico. The Spanish king offered **grants**, or gifts of money, to explorers who would lead expeditions into the northern continent. Believing that North America held riches far greater than the treasures already taken in Middle America and South America, many were quick to accept the offer.

The Spanish Move into Florida

One of the Spanish explorers who received a grant was Juan Ponce de León (PAHN•say day lay•OHN). Ponce de León had sailed with Columbus on his second voyage. He lived for a time on the island of Hispaniola (ees•pah•NYOH•lah), which today is made up of the countries of Haiti and the Dominican Republic. Ponce de León later explored and conquered what has become Puerto Rico and was named governor of the island. There he heard a story about a fountain whose waters were said to make old people young again. This "Fountain of Youth" was supposed to be on an island to the north called Bimini (BIH•muh•nee). Ponce de León set out to find the Fountain of Youth.

He sailed north but did not find Bimini. Instead, in April 1513 he landed on the North American **mainland**, or the main part of the continent, near what is now the city of St. Augustine. He named the mainland *La Florida*, the Spanish word for "filled with flowers." When he tried to start a settlement in Florida, the Calusa Indians, who lived there, attacked. Ponce de León was wounded, and he later died. Though he did not discover a fountain of youth, Ponce de León was the first Spaniard to set foot in what is today the United States.

REVIEW *What was Ponce de León searching for?*

A sixteenth-century Spanish helmet

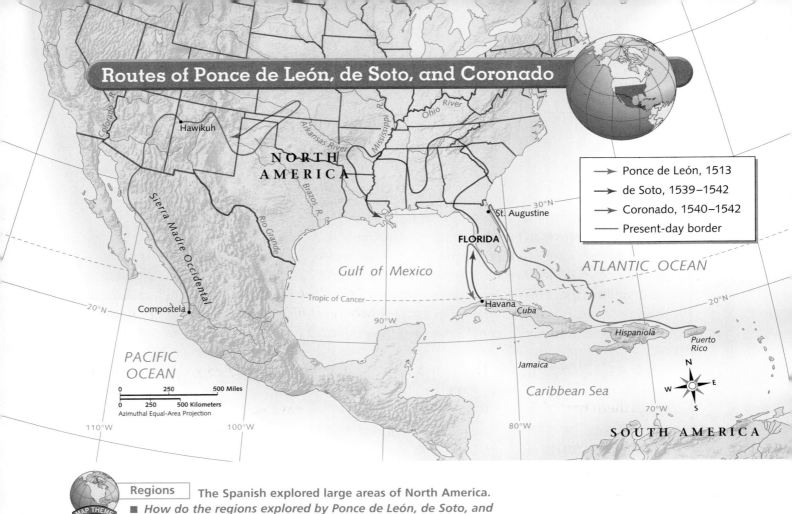

Routes of Ponce de León, de Soto, and Coronado

→ Ponce de León, 1513
→ de Soto, 1539–1542
→ Coronado, 1540–1542
— Present-day border

Regions The Spanish explored large areas of North America.
■ *How do the regions explored by Ponce de León, de Soto, and Coronado reflect the Spanish culture today?*

The Seven Cities of Gold

Stories about treasure sparked more expeditions into the lands north of Mexico. These stories were only **rumors**—stories without proof. But many people believed them. One of the most exciting was about seven cities believed to be built all of gold.

In 1536 four ragged men arrived in Mexico City. They were Álvar Núñez Cabeza de Vaca (kah•BAY•sah day VAH•kuh), two other Spaniards, and a North African named Estéban (ehs•TAY•bahn). They had lived through a shipwreck off the coast of what is today Texas. During their long journey to Mexico, they had heard from the people they met along the way about seven cities rich in gold, silver, and jewels.

The four men told their story to Spanish leaders in Mexico City, who listened carefully. In 1539 the leaders sent Estéban and a priest named Marcos de Niza (day NEE•sah) to see if the rumor was true. During the expedition Estéban was killed by Zuni Indians, who believed he had been sent by an enemy tribe. But Niza returned safely, saying he had seen a golden city.

After hearing Niza's report, Francisco Vásquez de Coronado (kawr•oh•NAH•doh) and more than 1,000 soldiers set out in 1540 to find the seven cities. They moved north out of Mexico and through the present-day states of Arizona, New Mexico, Texas, and Oklahoma into Kansas. They marched through the Zuni village of Hawikuh (hah•wee•KOO) and other Pueblo towns, but nowhere did they find any trace of the Seven

Cities of Gold. Bitter and disappointed, Coronado began the long trip home. The route he took would later become the Santa Fe Trail.

In June 1542 Coronado arrived back in Mexico with only 100 of his soldiers. Some had died. Others had run away. Coronado had not found the Seven Cities of Gold. But he had **claimed** many new lands for Spain, declaring that Spain owned them.

REVIEW *What were the results of Coronado's expedition?*

De Soto Moves Ahead

About the same time Coronado started his expedition, the king of Spain gave Hernando de Soto (day SOH•toh) a grant for an expedition to the northern part of the continent. De Soto put together an army of 600 soldiers and sailed to the west coast of Florida in May 1539. The conquistadors moved north and, by winter, reached what is now Georgia. Finding no gold there, they went on through parts of present-day South Carolina and North Carolina, into the Smoky Mountains of Tennessee, and south into Alabama.

De Soto encountered many Indian peoples during his expedition. These encounters often ended in death for many people. One of the most terrible battles took place in Alabama. There the Spanish fought with some of the descendants of the Mississippian Mound Builders, the Mobile people, who were led by Tascalusa (tuhs•kah•LOO•sah). People who saw the battle wrote later that the number of Indians killed was between 2,500 and 11,000. They had fought, as a Spanish soldier later wrote, "with the desire to die" rather than be defeated. The Spanish lost only

LEARNING FROM PICTURES The bells (right) were brought by de Soto to trade with the Indians. De Soto and his men (below) also brought horses to the Americas.
■ *What might Native Americans have thought when they first saw people riding horses?*

Spanish Explorers

EXPLORER	DATES OF EXPLORATION	AREA EXPLORED
Juan Ponce de León	1513	Puerto Rico and Florida
Hernando Cortés	1519–1536	Eastern and central Mexico and California
Álvar Núñez Cabeza de Vaca	1528–1536	Texas, New Mexico, and Mexico
Francisco Pizarro	1531–1535	The western coast of South America
Hernando de Soto	1539–1542	Southeastern United States and the Mississippi River
Francisco Vásquez de Coronado	1540–1542	Southwestern North America

LEARNING FROM TABLES This table lists several Spaniards who explored North America during the early 1500s.
- *What lands did each person explore? How many years did Pizarro explore South America?*

20 men, but most of their supplies were destroyed in the fighting.

By this time de Soto's army was in poor condition. It had been reduced in size by deaths and **desertions**, in which soldiers ran away from their duties. Yet de Soto and what remained of his army marched on, reaching the banks of the Mississippi River in May 1541. They were the first Europeans to see the great river. The Spanish hurried to build rafts to cross it so they could continue their search for gold on the other side. In what is now Arkansas and Louisiana, the soldiers faced more fights with the Indians they encountered.

For three years the Spanish searched for gold without finding any. Then, in 1542, de Soto died from a fever. "Many of his men did not mourn his passing," one soldier noted, "for he was a stern man." The soldiers buried their leader in the Mississippi River to hide his death from the Indians. Then the Spanish army finally made its way back to Mexico.

Though he found no gold, de Soto claimed much of the land he explored for Spain. The Spanish now claimed all of what is today the southeastern United States.

REVIEW *What lands did de Soto claim for Spain?*

LESSON 2 REVIEW

Check Understanding

1 Remember the Facts Describe what took place when the Spanish explorers encountered different Indian peoples during their travels.

2 Recall the Main Idea Why did the Spanish risk the unknown to explore North America in the 1500s?

Think Critically

3 Personally Speaking How would you react if strangers arrived to explore your community?

4 Think More About It In their battle with the Mobiles, what do you think gave the Spanish an advantage?

Show What You Know

Table Activity Make a table of Spanish explorers and the Indian peoples they encountered. Start with the table on this page. Use reference books or databases to add the names of the Indian groups each explorer met. Add other conquistadors to your table and display it in the classroom.

New People in the Americas

LESSON
3

FOCUS
What brings people to a new place to live?

Main Idea As you read, think about what brought the Spanish and the Africans to the Americas to live.

Vocabulary
missionary
colony
colonist
plantation

The conquistadors changed the history of Spain in the Americas. Up to the time of the Spanish conquests, very few Spanish people had settled in the Americas. Most were either soldiers or missionaries. **Missionaries** are people who teach their religion to others. Spanish soldiers searched for gold. Spanish missionaries taught Christianity to the native peoples.

In time, other people came to the Americas to live. Some came for the wealth they had heard about. Others were made to come as slaves.

Building New Spain

The Spanish government rewarded many of the conquistadors by giving them large areas of conquered land. Most of the land was in Mexico, which the Spaniards called New Spain. It became one of Spain's colonies in the Americas. A **colony** is a settlement ruled by another country. People who live in a colony are called settlers, or **colonists**.

Many colonists worked in gold mines and silver mines. Others set up **plantations**, or huge farms, to grow sugarcane, tobacco, coffee, cocoa, cotton, and other crops to be sold in Spain. The colonists brought with them oxen and plows to work the land and horses to ride. They brought cattle and sheep, fruit trees, grain, and vegetable seeds. Soon the Spanish built new cities, and tens of thousands more colonists came to these cities to live.

The Spanish needed many workers to grow their crops, to mine their gold and silver, and to build and take care of their new cities. So they made the Indian peoples their slaves. They put the enslaved people to work on the plantations and in the mines. The Indians had to work day and night with little food or rest. They had no freedom.

The Indians fought against being enslaved. Many were killed for doing so. Thousands of Indians had already died fighting the Spanish. Now thousands more died from hunger,

Spanish coins like the doubloon were made of pure gold from mines in South America.

Bartolomé de Las Casas (right) was among the first Europeans to call for an end to Indian slavery. He often spoke out against cruelty toward Indian peoples in the Spanish colonies. Under Spanish rule, Indians were forced to mine gold and silver as slaves (above).

overwork, and disease. The Indians had never had the diseases the settlers brought from Europe, such as measles, influenza, smallpox, and scarlet fever. Because of this, their bodies could not fight these diseases. Sometimes whole tribes became ill and died.

Not all of the Spanish colonists believed that the Indians should be enslaved. A friar named Bartolomé de Las Casas (bar•toh•luh•MAY day lahs KAH•sahs), like other Spanish settlers, was given land. He was also given the right to have Indians work on his land as slaves. However, Las Casas spent many years of his life trying to help the Indians. He spoke out so strongly that in 1542 the king of Spain, Charles I, agreed to pass laws to protect the native peoples. These laws, however, were not always carried out.

As the number of Indian workers fell sharply, the Spanish colonists who had depended on slaves faced a problem. Who would work on the plantations and in the mines?

REVIEW *Who did much of the work building New Spain?*

Demand for Labor

For many years people in Europe had been trading goods for slaves with several West African kingdoms. People in the kingdom of Benin (buh•NEEN), for example, carried on a large trade in slaves. They also traded ivory and gold for goods such as tools and guns.

Slavery had been practiced in Africa for a very long time. Most slaves were people who were taken as prisoners in wars. In some parts of Africa slaves could rise to positions of honor and trust. After a time, they could be given their freedom.

At first, enslaved people were treated almost the same in Europe as in Africa. They often worked as house servants. Few owners thought of making slaves do hard work on farms or in mines. Some slaves in Europe became free after a time and worked at jobs they chose. Some even joined European expeditions and armies in the Americas. West African soldiers were with Cortés in Mexico and Pizarro in South America. And 30 Africans were with Balboa when he first saw the Pacific Ocean.

Little by little, however, life for Africans in Europe and in the Americas began to change. One of the most important reasons for this change was that there were not enough workers in the Americas.

As more and more Indians died from disease and overwork, Spanish colonists looked for other workers. In time Africans held as slaves were made to work in the fields and mines. Even Bartolomé de Las Casas, trying to help the Indian peoples, thought that Africans could be used to do this work. It was an idea Las Casas came to regret deeply. For soon Africans were working under the same terrible conditions as the Indians had been working under. Even those Africans who came to the Americas as servants or as free people were made to do the work of slaves. Africans were first used as slaves in large numbers on sugarcane and tobacco plantations on the Caribbean islands. Later they were put to work on the plantations and in the mines on the mainland.

REVIEW *Why did life for Africans in the Americas change?*

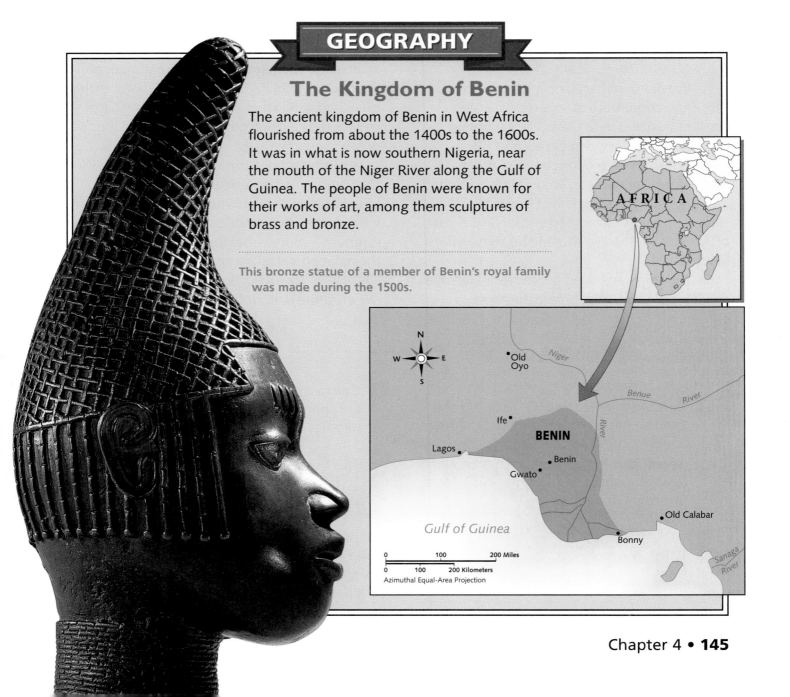

GEOGRAPHY

The Kingdom of Benin

The ancient kingdom of Benin in West Africa flourished from about the 1400s to the 1600s. It was in what is now southern Nigeria, near the mouth of the Niger River along the Gulf of Guinea. The people of Benin were known for their works of art, among them sculptures of brass and bronze.

This bronze statue of a member of Benin's royal family was made during the 1500s.

AFRICA

Old Oyo
Niger
Benue River
Ife
BENIN
River
Lagos
Benin
Gwato
Old Calabar
Gulf of Guinea
Bonny
Sanaga River

0   100   200 Miles
0   100   200 Kilometers
Azimuthal Equal-Area Projection

This painting by Lieutenant Francis Meinell, a British naval officer, was painted in 1846. The painting shows the conditions on slave ships. This ship, the *Abanez*, was Spanish.

The Slave Trade

As the demand for African slaves grew, more and more traders sailed to the west coast of Africa. There the traders emptied their ships of European goods and filled them with slaves. No longer were most slaves prisoners of war. To meet the growing demand, slave traders took people to sell as slaves. So many slaves were traded that part of Africa's west coast became known as the Slave Coast.

On the ships, enslaved people faced terrible conditions. Many died before they even reached the Americas. Some died fighting against the chains and the cruel treatment of the traders. Other Africans died of diseases that quickly passed from person to person on the crowded ships. Still others jumped into the ocean to escape living as slaves.

For those who survived the journey, life in the Americas was difficult. Slaves worked long hours in the fields and in the mines. Their work helped raise money for the Spanish government—money that for a time made Spain the most powerful country in Europe.

REVIEW *How did the slave traders meet the growing demand for African slaves?*

LESSON 3 REVIEW

Check Understanding

1 **Remember the Facts**   How did the Spanish get workers to help build New Spain?

2 **Recall the Main Idea**   What brought Spanish people to the Americas? What brought African people?

Think Critically

3 **Think More About It**   Did the Spanish treat the Indians and the Africans fairly? Give reasons for your answer.

4 **Cause and Effect**   What effects did European diseases have on the Indian peoples?

Show What You Know

Chart Activity   Draw a chart that shows the job descriptions of missionaries, colonists, Indians, and Africans. Use your textbook along with other reference materials to complete your chart. Then share your chart with a classmate.

Encounters with the French and Dutch

FOCUS

How can trade between cultures have both advantages and disadvantages?

Main Idea Read to learn how the fur trade had both advantages and disadvantages for Europeans and Native Americans in North America.

Vocabulary

Northwest Passage
trade network
agent

While the Spanish were growing rich and powerful from their colonies in Middle and South America, the French and the Dutch were making their own claims in North America. They found good fishing waters along the northeast coast, and they began to trade with the Native Americans. In time the trade brought the French and the Dutch new wealth. This was because they traded for an item that was to become nearly as valuable as gold—fur.

The French in North America

When French fishers set up camps on shore to dry their fish, they began to barter for animal furs with Indians who lived nearby. The Indians traded beaver furs and other furs for European goods. The furs the Europeans wanted most were beaver furs, which they made into hats. The goods the Indians wanted most were iron tools, pots, kettles, and guns.

The French and Indian fur trade grew following the voyages of a French explorer named Jacques Cartier (ZHAHK kar•TYAY). Cartier sailed into the Gulf of St. Lawrence in 1534. The next year he sailed up the St. Lawrence River. Cartier thought that by sailing up the river, he might find a water route that cut through North America to Asia. European traders did not know if there was such a route to Asia, which they called the **Northwest Passage**, but they hoped so. Finding the Northwest Passage would mean finding a much faster way to reach Asia.

Jacques Cartier did not find the Northwest Passage, but he did begin to trade with an Indian people known as the Hurons. The Hurons were as eager to have European goods as the French were to get furs.

Jacques Cartier, a French explorer, sailed up the St. Lawrence River searching for a passage through North America to Asia.

Chapter 4 • **147**

Routes of Cartier and Champlain

NORTH AMERICA

Lake Superior

Lake Huron

Lake Ontario

Quebec

Montreal

Lake Champlain

St. Lawrence River

1613–1615

1608–1609

1604–1606

St. Croix

Port Royal

Nova Scotia

Gulf of St. Lawrence

Newfoundland

1607

1603

1604

1534

1535

ATLANTIC OCEAN

50°W

50°N

60°W

0 150 300 Miles
0 150 300 Kilometers
Azimuthal Equal-Area Projection

N W E S

→ Cartier, 1534–1535
→ Champlain, 1603–1615
— Present-day border

Place Jacques Cartier and Samuel de Champlain explored along the waterways in North America.
■ *On which major bodies of water did they travel?*

By 1600 trade with the Indians was very important for many Europeans, especially the French. The business people in France competed with one another to control the trade. The French monarch, King Henry IV, wanted to build colonies in North America. He said that any business in France that wanted to trade with the Indians in North America would first have to start a colony there.

French business people jumped at the chance for riches. Several of them formed a company to start a colony in America. They sent a cartographer there to map the places where beavers were found. The person they sent was Samuel de Champlain (sham•PLAYN). Champlain made his first trip to North America in 1603. At the time no Europeans had settled along the east coast north of the Spanish settlements in Florida.

Champlain spent three months exploring the forests of what is now eastern Canada,

which he called New France. When he returned to Europe, Champlain's reports about the wonderful country across the ocean made many more people want to go to New France. Champlain himself went again, this time as the king's geographer.

For the next five years, Champlain explored the lands along the St. Lawrence River and in what is today Nova Scotia and the state of New York. The search for a place to build a settlement took Champlain back to the St. Lawrence River. There he chose a place that the Hurons called *Kebec*, meaning "the place where the river narrows." In 1608 Kebec became Quebec (kwih•BEK), the first important French settlement in the Americas. About three years later, Champlain founded a trading post at Montreal, where an Indian village called Hochelaga (hahsh•uh•LAG•uh) had once stood.

REVIEW *Why was Samuel de Champlain sent to North America?*

The Struggle for the Fur Trade

The fur trade brought wealth to the French and to their Huron trading partners. Huron traders learned how to use a **trade network**, or system of trading, among the American Indian tribes in eastern Canada. At first the network was good for all the groups that took part in it.

The Hurons acted as **agents**—that is, they did business for other Indian groups. The Hurons traded food for beaver furs with these groups. Then they took the furs to Quebec or Montreal to trade with the French for European goods. The Hurons took home guns, kettles, and metal tools. They then returned to the other Indian tribes to trade some of these goods for more beaver furs.

The Huron trade network lasted until the mid-1600s, when the Iroquois began to trade in the same way as the Hurons. The Iroquois at the time were trading partners with the Dutch. The Dutch had begun building settlements after 1609, when explorer Henry Hudson claimed the land along what is now the Hudson River. New Amsterdam was the capital of the Dutch colony of New Netherland. It was located at the mouth of the Hudson River, where New York City is today. Founded in 1625, New Amsterdam quickly became a center for trade in North America and also for trade with countries around the world.

The Hurons and the Iroquois soon argued over trade with the French and the Dutch. The two Indian groups began to fight for control of the fur trade. Control of the trade would give the winner power over other Indian peoples.

The fighting made both the Hurons and the Iroquois weaker and weaker. The Europeans did nothing to stop the fighting, and sometimes they even tried to keep it

This painting by Paul Kane shows that, in order to survive, many fur trappers lived with Indian tribes (below) and learned their ways of life. Indian snowshoes (right) helped people walk on deep snow.

Trading posts (above) were places to live, as well as places for trading with Indians. The French traded iron goods such as pots and kettles (left) for beaver furs.

going. In time the Europeans were able to take away the weakened Indians' land with all its furs.

The trade and the wars that went with it changed the lives of many Indians of the Eastern Woodlands. The more they wanted European goods, the less they lived in their traditional ways. They changed the ways in which they farmed, hunted, cooked, and even dressed. Many stopped using the skills that had helped them live in the woodlands. Instead, they spent their time hunting for furs and fighting one another over the trade with the Europeans.

REVIEW *How did the fighting between Indian groups help the Europeans?*

LESSON 4 REVIEW

Check Understanding

1. **Remember the Facts**   What groups took part in the fur trade?

2. **Recall the Main Idea**   What were the advantages and disadvantages of the fur trade for the Europeans? for the Native Americans?

Think Critically

3. **Past to Present**   How is trade today both an advantage and a disadvantage for some people?

4. **Cause and Effect**   How did the market for furs in Europe affect the lives of people living in North America?

Show What You Know

Diagram Activity   Create a diagram that shows how the Hurons acted as agents in the fur trade. Your diagram should show who the Hurons traded with and what goods they exchanged. Compare your diagram with those of your classmates.

The English in the Americas

FOCUS

In what ways is cooperation better than conflict?

Main Idea Read to find out how cooperation helped the English colonists at Jamestown and Plymouth.

Vocabulary

armada
profit
pilgrim
compact
Mayflower Compact
interpreter

By the 1600s English people, too, were coming to the Americas. Some came looking for wealth, as many of the Spanish, the French, and the Dutch did. Others came hoping to start a new and better life. Many were nobles and adventurers who had heard rumors of great riches. But most were just ordinary people—men and women, young and old. There were skilled workers, such as carpenters, tailors, and blacksmiths. There were farmers who wanted cheap or free land. And there were people who wanted the freedom to follow their own religion.

The Mystery of Roanoke

English explorers had been sailing across the Atlantic Ocean since the mid-1500s. Sometimes they explored the eastern coast of North America. They also attacked Spanish treasure ships carrying gold and other riches from the Americas to Spain. England's most famous explorer was Francis Drake. During an expedition in 1577, Drake attacked a Spanish ship, stole its treasure, and sailed around the world to escape Spanish warships.

England's monarch, Queen Elizabeth I, encouraged exploration. In 1584 the queen said that Sir Walter Raleigh (RAH•lee), an English noble, could set up England's first colony in North America. In July 1585 Raleigh's colonists landed on an island just off the coast of what is today North Carolina. The Hatteras Indians called the island Roanoke (ROH•uh•nohk). The English called their

Queen Elizabeth I of England encouraged people to start colonies in North America.

Roanoke Island

Roanoke Island is off the coast of North Carolina, south of Albemarle (AL•buh•marl) Sound, between the Outer Banks and the mainland. The island is in what is now Dare County. The county was named for John White's granddaughter, Virginia Dare. Virginia was born August 18, 1587. She was the first child born of English parents in North America. The baby vanished with the other settlers of the Lost Colony.

This painting by John White shows Native Americans who lived near Roanoke Island.

colony Virginia. In less than a year, however, the colony had failed. The colonists did not know how to survive in their new environment. When Francis Drake stopped by the colony in 1586, he found the colonists starving and took them back to England.

In July 1587 Raleigh sent a second group to settle Roanoke Island. Raleigh had chosen John White to lead the new colony. In August, after White helped the colonists get settled, he went back to England for supplies. At this time England needed all its ships for war with Spain, so White could not get back to the people he had left on Roanoke Island.

Three years later, after England had defeated Spain's **armada**, or fleet of warships, John White returned to Roanoke—only to find everyone gone. All that remained were some books with their covers torn off, maps ruined by rain, and weapons covered with rust. White found the letters *CRO* carved on a nearby tree and the word *CROATOAN* carved on a wooden post. White and the people who were with him fired shots into the air. They searched but found nothing. They shouted, but no one answered.

Nothing was ever found of the people of Roanoke Island. Many people believe they went to live with the Croatoan Indians, who later became known as the Lumbee Indians. Many Lumbee Indians today still have the last names of people from the "lost colony."

REVIEW *What happened to the English colony on Roanoke Island?*

Success at Jamestown

On May 24, 1607, three English ships sailed into the deep bay now called the Chesapeake. The ships and the 105 men and boys aboard had been sent to North America by the English business people who formed the Virginia Company of London. The company planned to build a trading post and colony in North America to make a profit. A **profit** is the money left over after everything has been paid for. Despite the company's plans, however, most of the colonists came looking for gold.

The three ships sailed up a river that the men named the James, to honor King James I of England. They landed on a peninsula and decided to start a settlement there. However, the place where they built Jamestown, as they called the settlement, turned out to be a poor choice. The men dug wells, but the water was bad. The land was wet and full of disease-carrying mosquitoes. The way the colonists behaved toward the Indians who lived nearby—taking Indian lands and destroying their crops—also put them in danger of attack.

By the end of the first year, about half of the colonists had died. One colonist later wrote, "Our men were destroyed with cruel diseases, . . . burning fevers, and by wars." They had come to the Americas to get rich.

No one had bothered to plant or gather food for the winter. Many colonists starved.

Life in the colony changed when Captain John Smith became its leader. He probably saved Jamestown from becoming another lost colony. Smith's first act was to make one unbreakable rule: Anyone who did not work did not eat. Soon the colonists were planting gardens, building shelters, and putting up fences to protect the settlement from attack.

More than 30 tribes of Eastern Woodlands Indians lived in Virginia during this time. Most were members of a confederation led by Chief Powhatan (pow•uh•TAN). One day, while exploring the lands around Jamestown, Captain Smith was captured by the Indians. A legend says that the chief's daughter, Pocahontas (poh•kuh•HAHN•tuhs), saved his life. Because of this act Captain Smith made peace with Chief Powhatan. Whether or not this story is true, it is known that fighting continued between the settlers and the Indians of the Eastern Woodlands.

Captain John Smith (below) led the colony of Jamestown and kept its settlers from starving. The colony was located near the Indian Confederation that was led by Chief Powhatan. Chief Powhatan is shown in the upper right corner of the map below.

Despite Jamestown's many troubles, the colony survived and, in time, did well. Five years after the first colonists had sailed up the James River, they found the "gold" that would make the colony rich. It was tobacco. Growing and selling tobacco became a profitable business for the Virginia colonists.

REVIEW *Why did colonists go to Jamestown?*

The Founding of Plymouth Colony

On a cold day late in 1620, a ship called the *Mayflower* set sail from England for the Americas. The 101 colonists on board had agreed to work for the Virginia Company.

The company's owners would pay for the voyage. In return, the settlers would send them furs, fish, and lumber.

Among the colonists on board was a group of families going to the Americas for a special reason. They were Separatists, or people who had separated from the Church of England. At the time, everyone in England had to belong to this church. Those who refused to belong to the Church of England were not safe. So these Separatists decided to go to the Americas, where they hoped to find the freedom to follow their own religion. In time they became known as Pilgrims. A **pilgrim** is a person who makes a journey for a religious reason.

The colonists had planned to settle in the lands governed by the Virginia Company. But

The Mayflower Compact

In the name of God, Amen. We, whose names are underwritten, the Loyal Subjects of our dread Sovereign Lord, King *James*, by the Grace of God, of *Great Britain, France and Ireland*, King, *Defender of the Faith*, etc.

Having undertaken for the Glory of God, and Advancement of the Christian Faith, and the Honour of our King and Country, a voyage to plant the first colony in the northern Parts of Virginia; do by these Presents, solemnly and mutually in the Presence of God and one of another, covenant and combine ourselves together into a civil Body Politick, for our better Ordering and Preservation, and Furtherance of the Ends aforesaid; And by Virtue hereof to enact, constitute, and frame, such just and equal Laws, Ordinances, Acts, Constitutions and Offices, from time to time, as shall be thought most meet and convenient for the General good of the Colony; unto which we promise all due Submission and Obedience.

In Witness whereof we have hereunto subscribed our names at *Cape Cod* the eleventh of *November*, in the Reign of our Sovereign Lord, King *James* of *England, France* and *Ireland*, the eighteenth, and of *Scotland* the fifty-fourth. *Anno Domini, 1620.*

Thanksgiving Day

In the fall of 1621, the Pilgrims gathered their first harvest. William Bradford, governor of Plymouth Colony, decided they should have a celebration so that the people could "rejoice together" to give thanks to God. He invited the neighboring Wampanoag Indians to join the Pilgrims for a festival that lasted for three days. This is what many people today think of as the first Thanksgiving. Thanksgiving celebrations, however, have been held in the Americas for thousands of years. During celebrations such as the Green Corn Ceremony, Indian peoples gave thanks for a good harvest. Some people think the first

European Thanksgiving in the Americas took place in 1598, when Spanish settlers gave thanks for safely reaching the Rio Grande. Thanksgiving became a national holiday in 1863, when President Abraham Lincoln declared the last Thursday in November as "a day of thanksgiving and praise to our beneficent Father."

This painting, titled *The First Thanksgiving,* was painted by Jennie A. Brownscombe. The Pilgrims' Thanksgiving feast included turkeys, fish, clams, oysters, and lobsters.

the *Mayflower* was blown off course by terrible storms and reached the coast of what is today Massachusetts. The settlers were not sure where they were, but they knew that they were not in the lands of the Virginia Company. To help keep order, the 41 men aboard the *Mayflower* signed an agreement, or **compact**. They agreed to make laws for the good of the colony and to obey those laws. Women were expected to follow the laws even though they were not asked to sign the compact. This agreement became known as the **Mayflower Compact**. It is the first example of self-rule by colonists in the Americas.

On December 21, 1620, the Pilgrims landed at a place they called Plymouth, near present-day Cape Cod. The first winter was hard. The weather was cold, there was not enough food, and many settlers became ill. About half of them died.

Help came in the spring. A Native American walked into their village one day and said "Welcome, Englishmen." The Indian was a Wampanoag (wahm•puh•NOH•ag) named Samoset. He had learned English from sailors who fished along the coast. Several days later Samoset returned to the settlement with an Indian who spoke English better than

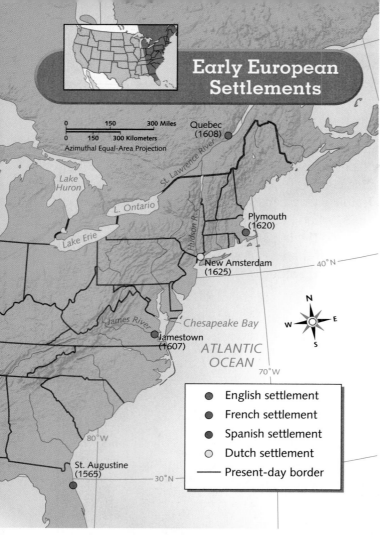

Early European Settlements

0   150   300 Miles
0   150   300 Kilometers
Azimuthal Equal-Area Projection

Quebec (1608)

Lake Huron

L. Ontario

Lake Erie

St. Lawrence River

Hudson R.

Plymouth (1620)

New Amsterdam (1625)

40°N

James River

Chesapeake Bay

Jamestown (1607)

ATLANTIC OCEAN

70°W

N
W — E
S

80°W

St. Augustine (1565)

30°N

● English settlement
● French settlement
● Spanish settlement
○ Dutch settlement
— Present-day border

MAP THEME

Location   Several European countries had established American colonies by 1625.
■ *Why were all the earliest European settlements located near water?*

he did. This man was Tisquantum, or Squanto. Tisquantum had been kidnapped years before and sold as a slave in Spain. He had escaped and spent several years in England before returning to his own land in North America.

Tisquantum stayed with the Pilgrims and became their **interpreter**. He translated the Indians' language and explained their lifeways. He showed the Pilgrims where to fish and how to plant squash, pumpkins, and corn. He helped the Pilgrims survive.

For a time the Pilgrims lived in peace with the Wampanoag Indians, who were led by their chief, Massasoit (ma•suh•SOYT). However, as more English colonists came to settle in Massachusetts, things began to change. The new people were not friendly toward the Indians and settled on more and more of their lands. This caused many quarrels between the Wampanoags and the English colonists that became fights and grew into terrible wars.

During these wars the Wampanoags and other tribes were forced off their lands. Soon very few Native Americans lived along the eastern coast.

REVIEW *How did Tisquantum help the Pilgrims survive in their colony?*

LESSON 5 REVIEW

Check Understanding

1 Remember the Facts   How was life different for the English colonists in Roanoke, Jamestown, and Plymouth?

2 Recall the Main Idea   How did cooperation help the settlers at Jamestown and Plymouth?

Think Critically

3 Think More About It   Why did the Pilgrims think it was important to write the Mayflower Compact?

4 Personally Speaking   Would you rather have been a Jamestown colonist or a Pilgrim at Plymouth? Explain.

Show What You Know

Questioning Activity
Prepare a list of questions you might ask people who wanted to join you in starting a colony. As you write the questions, think about the personal qualities of people you would want to have as your colonists.

Read a Vertical Time Line

1. Why Learn This Skill?

Time lines are an important tool for studying history. By studying a time line, you can find out when certain events happened. You can see the order in which events took place and how one event may have led to another. A time line can also help you see how much time passed between two events.

But not all time lines look the same or are read in the same way. Most time lines run horizontally, or across the page from left to right. But some run vertically, or from top to bottom. To be able to use time lines, it is important to know how to read those that are vertical, as well as those that are horizontal.

2. Understand the Process

Horizontal time lines are read from left to right. The earliest date on a horizontal time line is on the left end, and the most recent date is on the right end. The time line shown on this page is a vertical time line. It is read from top to bottom. The earliest date on a vertical time line is at the top, and the most recent date is at the bottom.

Now use the information on the vertical time line to answer the following questions about European settlement in the Americas.

1. Which European nation was the first to build a settlement in the Americas?
2. In what year was Mexico City founded?
3. How many settlements did the English build on Roanoke Island?
4. Which settlement was built first, Jamestown or New Amsterdam? In what year was each settlement built?
5. When was the first French settlement built in the Americas?
6. How many years passed between the building of Mexico City and the founding of New Amsterdam?

European Settlement in the Americas

1500

1521 • Spanish build Mexico City

1550

1585 • English settle Roanoke Island

1587 • English build a second settlement at Roanoke

1600

1607 • English settle Jamestown

1608 • French settle Quebec

1620 • Pilgrims land at Plymouth

1625 • Dutch settle New Amsterdam

1650

3. Think and Apply

Use some of the events of your school year to make your own vertical time line. These events might include a class field trip, a special program, or a holiday party. After you have finished your time line, share it with a friend or a family member.

REVIEW

1510 • **1540**

1519
• Cortés lands in Mexico

1533
• Pizarro conquers the Incas

1540
• Coronado explores the Southwest

CONNECT MAIN IDEAS

Use this organizer to show how the chapter's main ideas are connected. Write the main idea of each lesson. A copy of the organizer appears on page 28 of the Activity Book.

Encounters in the Americas

Indians

Europeans **Africans**

Conquest of the Aztecs and Incas

_____
_____
_____

The English in the Americas

_____
_____
_____

The Search for Gold and Riches

_____
_____
_____

New People in the Americas

_____
_____
_____

Encounters with the French and Dutch

_____
_____
_____

WRITE MORE ABOUT IT

Write a Script for a Play Write the script for one scene of a play that tells the story of a European settlement in America. Share your script with a classmate.

Write a Classroom Compact Write a classroom compact that lists rules for your class. Explain how this compact will be good for members of your class.

1587
• The English found a second colony at Roanoke

1607
• The English settle Jamestown

1620
• Pilgrims land at Plymouth

1625
• The Dutch found New Amsterdam

USE VOCABULARY

For each group of terms, write a sentence or two that explains how the terms are related.

1. conquistador, claim
2. colony, colonist, plantation
3. trade network, agent
4. pilgrim, Mayflower Compact

CHECK UNDERSTANDING

5. Why did Motecuhzoma welcome Cortés to the Aztec Empire?

6. How did Pizarro conquer the Incas?

7. Who was the first Spaniard to set foot in what is today the United States?

8. What was Coronado searching for on his journey across what is today the southwestern United States? Did he find what he was looking for?

9. Who were the first Europeans to see the Mississippi River?

10. Why did Spanish missionaries come to the Americas?

11. What was the Northwest Passage? How would it help European traders?

12. How did the Hurons run their trade network?

13. Why did the Virginia Company want to build a colony in North America?

14. Why did the Pilgrims want to settle in the Americas?

15. How did the Native Americans help the Pilgrims of Plymouth Colony survive?

THINK CRITICALLY

16. **Think More About It** Why do you think some soldiers exploring the Americas deserted their expeditions?

17. **Explore Viewpoints** How do you think an Indian might have viewed the fighting over control of the fur trade? How might a European settler have viewed it?

APPLY SKILLS

Read a Vertical Time Line Use the time line on page 157 to answer the questions.

18. Did the Pilgrims land at Plymouth before or after the English settled Jamestown?

19. How many years passed between the building of Mexico City and the founding of Quebec?

20. Which European group was the last one to start a settlement in the Americas?

READ MORE ABOUT IT

Stranded at Plimoth Plantation, 1626 by Gary Bowen. HarperCollins. Journal entries tell of one boy's first few months in an English colony.

Visit the Internet at **http://www.hbschool.com** for additional resources.

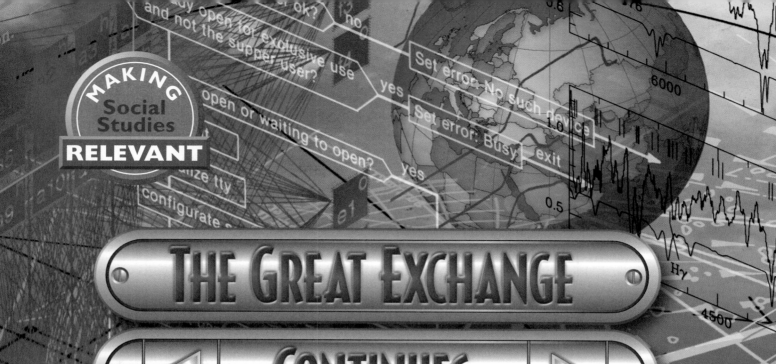

THE GREAT EXCHANGE
◀ CONTINUES ▶

Christopher Columbus's first encounter with the Tainos began a worldwide exchange of plants, animals, people, and ideas that we call the Columbian Exchange or the Great Exchange. In many ways the Great Exchange has never stopped. Products, people, and ideas continue to move all over the world. Today, however, the exchange takes place faster than ever before.

With modern transportation, people and products can reach any location in the world in less than a day. Telephones, fax machines, television, radios, and computers —especially the Internet—have made it possible for people to communicate within minutes or even seconds. The Internet is a network of computers that helps people exchange information from across the country and around the world. News that took months to cross the ocean five centuries ago as the Great Exchange began now takes almost no time at all!

Think and Apply

What benefits does the World Wide Web offer? Do you think it has drawbacks as well? Hold a classroom debate about how electronic communication can change the way we live today.

Visit the Internet at **http://www.hbschool.com** for additional resources.

Check your media center or classroom video library for the Making Social Studies Relevant videotape of this feature.

UNIT 2
REVIEW

VISUAL SUMMARY

Summarize the Main Ideas
Study the pictures and captions to help you review the events you read about in Unit 2.

Write a Diary Entry
Imagine that you are living during the time of an event shown in this visual summary. Write a diary entry that explains what is taking place. Share your work with a classmate.

1 Viking explorers were the first Europeans known to land in the Americas, arriving about A.D. 1000.

3 Christopher Columbus landed in the Americas in 1492. Believing he had reached the Indies, he called the people he met Indians.

5 The demand for workers in the Americas led many colonists to enslave Indians and then Africans.

2 New maps, faster ships, and other advances in technology helped set the stage for European exploration in the late 1400s.

4 Aztec king Motecuhzoma welcomed Hernando Cortés. The Aztecs, like the Incas, were conquered by Spanish conquistadors.

6 By 1600 trade with Indian peoples in the Americas was very important to many Europeans. The fur trade brought wealth to French and Huron traders.

7 Jamestown was settled in 1607. It was the first lasting English settlement in North America.

UNIT 2 REVIEW

USE VOCABULARY

Write the term that matches each definition.

cartographer   expedition

colony   Mayflower Compact

1 a maker of maps

2 a journey taken for a special reason

3 a settlement ruled by another country

4 the first written plan for self-rule by colonists in the Americas

CHECK UNDERSTANDING

5 What was Vinland?

6 What changes in technology helped set the stage for European exploration?

7 What empire did Cortés conquer? What empire did Pizarro conquer?

8 Why were Africans brought to the Spanish colonies?

9 In what ways did the fur trade change the lives of many Indians of the Eastern Woodlands?

10 Who stayed with the Pilgrims and became their interpreter?

THINK CRITICALLY

11 **Cause and Effect** How did the European demand for spices, silk, and other Asian goods lead to the exploration of the Americas?

12 **Personally Speaking** Do you think the voyages of Columbus were more important than the voyages of other explorers? Why or why not?

13 **Think More About It** Why do you think John Smith started a "no work, no food" policy in the Jamestown colony?

APPLY SKILLS

Use Latitude and Longitude
Use the map below to answer the questions.

14 Does the map show an area in the Northern Hemisphere or the Southern Hemisphere? in the Eastern Hemisphere or the Western Hemisphere? How can you tell?

15 Who traveled farther south, Ponce de León or de Soto?

16 What island is located near 20°N, 70°W?

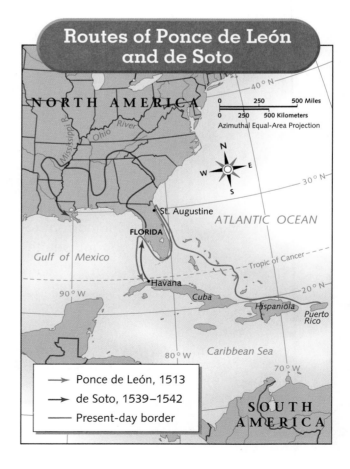

Routes of Ponce de León and de Soto

→ Ponce de León, 1513
→ de Soto, 1539–1542
— Present-day border

REMEMBER

- Share your ideas.
- Cooperate with others to plan your work.
- Take responsibility for your work.
- Help one another.
- Show your group's work to the class.
- Discuss what you learned by working together.

ACTIVITY

Write a
Short Play

Work with other members of your group to write a short play about what you think happened to the settlers of the second colony on Roanoke Island. Include Sir Walter Raleigh and John White as characters. Be sure to explain in your play why you think the settlers carved the word *CROATOAN* on a post.

Unit Project Wrap-Up

Make a Globe With several classmates, finish the Unit Project that was described on page 105. Work together to write a short essay comparing two explorers who sailed for different countries. You may want to list the country each explorer sailed for, the reasons for each expedition, the hardships that each explorer faced, and the results of each expedition. Share your globes and essay with the rest of your classmates.

ACTIVITY

Draw a
Ship

Work together to find out more about one of these ships: the *Santa María*, the *Golden Hind*, or the *Mayflower*. Draw a picture of the ship on a large sheet of paper. Then write a report that gives information about the ship and its history.

OUR COLONIAL HERITAGE

166

The different European colonies were located in separate areas of North America. Few people in New Spain ever saw or spoke with people from New France or from the English colonies. Although all the colonists lived in the Americas, they did not use the word *American* to describe themselves. Most thought of themselves as Spanish, French, Dutch, English, or African, depending on where they came from. They brought to the colonies the languages and customs of their many homelands. Today their traditions—and the traditions of the many Indian peoples—can be seen in the building styles, place names, and languages of the people we call Americans.

◄ The port of Philadelphia, Pennsylvania, in 1752

UNIT THEMES

- Commonality and Diversity
- Continuity and Change
- Individualism and Interdependence

Unit Project

Build a Model Complete this project with your classmates as you study Unit 3. Build a model of either a New England town or a southern plantation. As you read each chapter, make a list of some of the places and types of buildings found in each setting.

167

PACIFIC
OCEAN

Gulf of Alaska

Yukon River

Mackenzie River

Great Bear Lake

Great Slave Lake

Athabasca River

Lake Winnipeg

Columbia River

Missouri

River

Snake R.

Platte River

Colorado River

LOUISIANA

Arkansas R.

○ Santa Fe

Tucson ●

El Paso
del Norte ●

Rio

Grande

Gulf of California

NEW SPAIN

Mexico
City ●

Rio Balsas

	Spanish
	British
	French
	Russian
●	Major city
—	Present-day border

```
0          500        1,000 Miles
0      500      1,000 Kilometers
Modified Azimuthal Equal-Area Projection
```

1500   1550   1600

MID-1500s
**El Camino Real Is
Started**
PAGE 175

1600s
**Plantations Grow
Tobacco**
PAGE 183

North America, 1750

Labrador Sea

Hudson Bay

Lake Superior

Quebec

St. Lawrence River

ACADIA

Montreal

Lake Huron

Lake Michigan

Lake Ontario

Detroit

NEW FRANCE

Lake Erie

Boston

Providence

New York City

Philadelphia

Baltimore

Ohio River

Vincennes

Williamsburg

Jamestown

THE THIRTEEN COLONIES

Mississippi River

Wilmington

Charleston

Savannah

New Orleans

St. Augustine

Gulf of Mexico

Havana

Cuba

Hispaniola

Puerto Rico

Caribbean Sea

ATLANTIC OCEAN

N
W E
S

1650

1700

1630
Puritans Settle Massachusetts
PAGE 185

1682
La Salle Explores the Mississippi River
PAGE 180

GOING TO THE
Colonies

NOVA BRITANNIA.
OFFERING MOST
Excellent fruites by Planting in
VIRGINIA.

Exciting all such as be well affected
to further the same.

LONDON
Printed for SAMVEL MACHAM, and are to besold at
his Shop in Pauls Church-yard, at the
Signe of the Bul-head.
1 6 0 9.

Companies seeking the wealth of the Americas promised colonists good land and riches.

Men used razors like this one to trim or shave their beards.

Few Europeans going to North America as colonists knew what to expect when they arrived. To help them prepare for the experience, one group in England published the following list of things to take when moving to North America. The list was based on the experiences of other colonists. It shows what many colonists brought from Europe to begin their new lives in North America.

*Printed at London for
Fylke Clifton in 1630*

PROPORTION OF PROVISIONS NEEDFUL FOR SUCH AS INTEND TO PLANT themselves in New England, for one whole year.
Collected by the Adventurers, with the advice of the Planters.

Victual
Meal, one Hogshead.
Malt, one Hogshead.
Beef, one hundred weight.
Pork pickled, 100. or Bacon, 74 pound.
Peas, two bushels.
Greates, one bushel.
Butter, two dozen.
Cheese, half a hundred.
Vinegar, two gallons.
Aquavita, one gallon.
Mustard seed, two quarts.
Salt to save fish, half a hogshead.

Apparel

Shoes, six pair.
Boots for men, one pair.
Leather to mend shoes,
    four pound.
Irish stockings, four pair.
Shirts, six.
Handkerchiefs, twelve.
One Sea Cape or Gown, of
    coarse cloth.
Other apparel, as their purses will afford.

Tooles, which may also serve a family of
    four or five persons.
One English Spade.
One steele Shovel. Two Hatchets.
Axes 3. one broad axe, and
    2. felling axes.
One Wood hook.
Hoes 3. one broad of nine inches, and two
    narrow of five or six inches.
One Wimble, with six piercer bits.
One Hammer.
    Other tools as men's several
    occupations require, as Hand saws,
    Whip saws, Thwart saws, Augers,
    Chisels, Frowes, Grind stones, etc.

For Building

Nails of all sorts.
Locks for Door and Chests.
Gimmows for Chests.
Hooks and twists for doors.

Hats made of beaver fur were passed down from older to younger family members. These eyeglasses belonged to Peter Browne, a passenger on the *Mayflower*.

Arms

One Musket, Rest, and Bandeliere.
Powder, ten pound.
Shot, sixteen.
Match, six pound.
One Sword.
One Belt.
One Pistol. With a mold.

For Fishing

Twelve Cod hooks.
Two Lines for fishing.
One Mackerel line,
    and twelve hooks.
28 pound of Lead for
    bullets and fishing
    lead.

This cradle (left) was used by a baby named Peregrine White. The baby was born on the *Mayflower*. Tools like this saw (right) were brought to help build homes in North America.

5

EUROPEANS
SETTLE THROUGHOUT
NORTH AMERICA

"Even if I die on the road, I will not go back, but you can bury me here and I shall very gladly remain among these . . . people if such be the will of God."

Junípero Serra, a Spanish missionary, during a journey to San Diego in 1769

The Spanish Borderlands

LESSON

1

FOCUS
Why might a government today decide to expand its lands?

Main Idea As you read, look for reasons the Spanish government decided to expand its lands in North America.

Vocabulary
buffer
borderlands
presidio
permanent
scarce
hacienda
self-sufficient
mission

The Spanish conquistadors who explored the Americas found what they were looking for—gold and silver. Mining for these treasures became the most important money-making activity in Spain's American colonies. To protect its gold and silver mines from the other European countries that were building colonies in North America, the Spanish created a buffer. A **buffer** is an area of land that serves as a barrier. The buffer north of New Spain protected it from New France, New Netherland, and the English colonies. It came to be known as the Spanish **borderlands**. The borderlands stretched across what are today northern Mexico and the southern United States from Florida to California.

Presidios

Spanish soldiers led the way into the borderlands. Once they found a good place to settle, their first duty was to build a fort, called a **presidio** (pray•SEE•dee•oh), and shelters for the settlers. The largest and most important presidio in the borderlands was named St. Augustine. It was located on the Atlantic coast of Florida on a bay first explored by Juan Ponce de León in 1513.

In 1565 Pedro Menéndez de Avilés (meh•NEN•dehs day ah•vee•LAYS) and 1,500 soldiers and settlers reached the location of present-day St. Augustine. This became the first **permanent**, or long-lasting, European settlement in what is now the United States. St. Augustine was founded 42 years before the English landed at Jamestown and 43 years before the French founded Quebec.

Once the Spanish soldiers landed at St. Augustine, they quickly built small wooden houses and a wooden presidio in which the settlers could seek protection. Fearful of the English pirates and the Indian raiders, the Spanish soon began to strengthen the presidio by building walls of stone around the wooden fort. It took 25 years to finish the presidio Castillo (kah•STEE•yoh) de San Marcos. Even while it was being built,

This glass bottle from St. Augustine is over 400 years old.

Chapter 5 • **173**

St. Augustine

St. Augustine is located in northeastern Florida, near the Atlantic Ocean. Spain built the city and ruled it for more than 200 years. During that time its settlers endured many invasions and attacks. In 1763 the English gained control of St. Augustine. Spain again ruled the settlement from 1783 until 1821, when Florida became part of the United States.

FLORIDA

Castillo de San Marcos

ST. AUGUSTINE

Anastasia Island

ATLANTIC OCEAN

0   5   10 Miles
0   5   10 Kilometers

The Castillo de San Marcos in St. Augustine still stands today and attracts many visitors. It is more than 400 years old.

it was able to protect Spanish settlers from any attackers.

Despite the danger of living in the borderlands, Menéndez felt that the settlement at St. Augustine held great promise. In a letter to the Spanish king, he wrote that Florida could "bring enormous profits from vineyards, sugar, cattle, ship stores, pearls, timber, silk, wheat, and endless supplies of fruit."

St. Augustine never lived up to the hopes of becoming a source of wealth for Spain. But it became important for another reason. It served as Spain's military headquarters in North America. It was one of a line of hundreds of presidios stretching from Florida to California that provided protection for settlers in the borderlands.

REVIEW *Why did Spain build presidios across the borderlands?*

Ranches and Haciendas

The Spanish realized that gold and silver were **scarce**, or not plentiful, in the borderlands. They also knew that in many places the land was so hot and dry "that even the cactus pads appeared to be toasted." But settlers moved there anyway. Most made money by raising livestock and selling the hides and animal fats to markets in the colonies and in Spain. They often traded with Indian tribes for things they needed. They traded with the Pueblos, for example, for corn, pottery, and cotton cloth.

Some ranchers in the borderlands of northern Mexico built large estates called **haciendas** (ah•see•EN•dahs), where they raised cattle and sheep by the thousands.

In what are now Texas and California, cattle were the most important kind of livestock. In the drier climate of what is now New Mexico, settlers raised sheep.

Ranchers who lived on the haciendas raised their own livestock, grew their own crops, and made most of what they needed to live. These **self-sufficient**, or self-supporting, communities developed far from the markets of Mexico City and other large cities.

As they settled throughout the borderlands, the Spanish—and the animals they brought with them—changed life for many of the Indians living there. Horses, long extinct in the Americas, once again roamed the land. The Plains Indians learned to tame horses and use them for transportation, which helped them in hunting and in warfare. In the Southwest, the Navajos learned to raise sheep. They began weaving sheep's wool into colorful clothing and blankets.

REVIEW *How did the horse change the Indians' way of life?*

Missions

Spain's main interests in settling the borderlands were to protect its empire and expand its economy. But the Spanish king also wanted to "bring the people of that land to our Holy Catholic faith." So the Spanish government sent missionaries to the borderlands to persuade the Indians to become Catholics as well as loyal Spanish subjects.

The first successful missionaries in the Spanish borderlands were the Franciscans, a group of Catholic religious workers. The Franciscans built **missions**, or small religious communities, in what are now Georgia, Florida, Texas, New Mexico, Arizona, and California. Their first mission was Nombre de Dios (NOHM•bray day DEE•ohs), or "Name of God," the oldest Spanish mission in the United States. Nombre de Dios was built near St. Augustine in 1565 and was the first in a chain of Spanish missions that would link the Atlantic and Pacific coasts of North America. Father Junípero Serra helped build a string of

Movement Beginning in the late 1500s, the Catholic missionaries traveled throughout the borderlands to build missions. The road system of El Camino Real helped the Spanish protect the missions.

■ *In what other ways could the road have been useful?*

Major Missions of New Spain

New Spain
El Camino Real
Mission

21 missions in California, each "one day's journey" from the next.

When missionaries came to the borderlands, they usually brought with them livestock, fruit trees, and seeds for crops. The missions they built included churches and ranch and farm buildings. Some missions were built near Indian villages. In other places, Indians settled around the missions.

The Spanish and the Indians learned from one another. The Indians taught the Spanish how to build adobe houses and how to use herbs as medicines. The Spanish taught the Indians how to guide a plow instead of using a stick and hoe in the Indian way. The Indians also learned to use other tools and machines the missionaries had brought from Spain.

LEARNING FROM DIAGRAMS The Spanish built missions to spread Christianity.

❶ church
❷ priests' quarters
❸ well
❹ storerooms
❺ candlemaking and weaving
❻ ranch-workers' quarters
❼ workshops
❽ washbasin
❾ Indian village
❿ vegetable garden
⓫ river
⓬ orchards
⓭ vineyard
⓮ tannery

■ *In what ways were missions self-sufficient?*

A Spanish Mission

The coming of the Spanish missions changed the way many American Indians lived and worked. It also changed something more important to the Indians—the way they worshipped. While many Indians kept to their traditional religions, others became Catholics.

At first some American Indians welcomed living at the missions. Like the missionaries, they were learning new ways. And the Spanish missionaries and soldiers protected them from their enemies. But problems soon developed. Many Indians had to give up their religious traditions and had to work on mission farms and ranches against their will. Many missionaries used cruel treatment to control the Indians.

Some Indians fought back. They killed missionaries and

This bowl was found at a Spanish mission. It shows a feathered serpent—a traditional Indian design.

destroyed churches and other mission buildings. To protect its missions, the Spanish government built roads linking them with nearby presidios. El Camino Real (ray•AHL), or "The Royal Road" was started in the middle 1500s. The first part of the road system stretched for more than 600 miles (966 km) from San Diego to Sonoma in what is today California.

The government of New Spain, and later the Mexican government, continued to build new missions in the borderlands until the 1830s. Many cities in the southwestern United States—such as San Antonio, Texas, and San Diego, California—began as missions.

REVIEW *Why did the Spanish government send missionaries to the borderlands?*

LESSON 1 REVIEW

Check Understanding

1 Remember the Facts Name three reasons settlements were established in the Spanish borderlands.

2 Recall the Main Idea Why did the Spanish government decide to expand its lands in North America?

Think Critically

3 Explore Viewpoints How might a Spanish missionary and an Indian mission worker each describe the benefits and problems of living at a Spanish mission?

4 Think More About It What effects did the Spanish have on the Indians living in the borderlands? What effects did the Indians have on the Spanish?

Show What You Know

Letter-Writing Activity Suppose that you are a Spanish soldier protecting forts in the borderlands. Write a letter to your family in Spain telling what you have learned about the presidios, haciendas, and missions you visited as you traveled El Camino Real. Share your letter with a classmate.

FOCUS

What steps do governments take today to protect their interests?

Main Idea Read to find out what steps the French government took to protect its interests in New France.

Vocabulary

royal colony
portage
tributary
proprietary colony
proprietor

The Growth of
New France

In New Spain the Spanish grew wealthy from silver and gold. In New France the French grew wealthy from the fur trade. But unlike the Spanish, most French people were not interested in settling North America. From 1608 to 1763 the French built only two cities in New France—Quebec and Montreal. They also built some small towns across Canada and along the Mississippi River.

A Slow-Growing Empire

The French had been fishing along the eastern coast of North America since the 1500s. In time they moved inland and established a trade in animal furs with the Hurons. The fur trade led to the founding of Quebec in 1608. But by 1625 its population had grown to only about 60 people.

In the early 1600s, civil wars in France kept many people from leaving. Later, under the rule of King Louis XIV, peaceful times returned. The French now had even less reason to leave their country.

Meanwhile, English and Dutch colonists began settling the coastal region south of New France. It was not long before conflicts over the fur trade broke out among the French, the English, and the Dutch, as well as the Iroquois and the Hurons. In time, the Iroquois defeated the Hurons, who were the main trading partners of the French. By the 1660s the French fur trade was nearly destroyed, and the French hold in North America was crumbling.

Hoping to rebuild the French empire in North America, Louis XIV declared New France to be a **royal colony**. The king, rather than business people, would now rule the colony. The king appointed officials to live in New France and help him govern. The head of these officials was called the governor-general.

In 1672 King Louis XIV appointed Count de Frontenac (FRAHN•tuh•nak)

King Louis XIV of France hoped to rebuild New France.

178

governor-general of New France. The governor-general's hot temper and stern ways often got him into trouble with the king. His friendly ways with the Indian peoples, however, helped the colony prosper, or do well.

Europeans used birchbark canoes to explore waterways.

Frontenac encouraged exploration of the West. But the way west was not easy. French ships could not travel very far inland before coming to water that was too shallow or dangerous for sailing. To travel the rivers, the French learned from their American Indian trading partners how to build and use birchbark canoes. These boats could navigate shallow rivers. They also were light enough to be carried around waterfalls and rapids or overland between rivers. The French called this method of transportation **portage** (PAWR•tij).

The Indian peoples often talked with the French about a great river, larger than all the others. The Algonkins called it the Mississippi, which means "Big River." Ever since the days of Jacques Cartier, the French had hoped to find a Northwest Passage through North America to Asia. Frontenac believed that the Mississippi River just might be the route they were looking for.

REVIEW *Why did King Louis XIV declare New France a royal colony?*

Exploring the Mississippi

In 1673 Governor-General de Frontenac sent an expedition to explore the rivers and lakes that he hoped would lead French traders to the Mississippi River and then to Asia. The members of the expedition were Jacques Marquette (ZHAHK mar•KET), a Catholic missionary who knew several Indian languages; Louis Joliet (loo•EE zhohl•YAY), a fur trader; and five others.

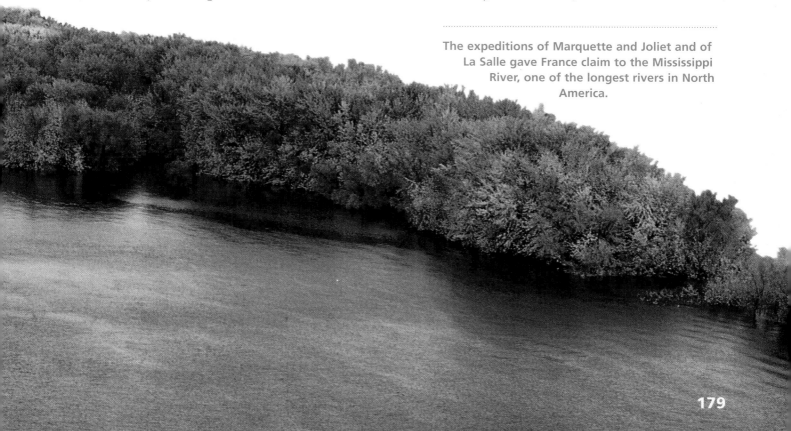

The expeditions of Marquette and Joliet and of La Salle gave France claim to the Mississippi River, one of the longest rivers in North America.

Routes of Marquette and Joliet and La Salle

0   200   400 Miles
0   200   400 Kilometers
Albers Equal-Area Projection

Lake Superior

St. Ignace

Wisconsin R.

Fox R.

Mississippi River

Lake Michigan

Lake Huron

Lake Ontario

St. Lawrence River

Fort Frontenac

Fort Miamis

Lake Erie

Illinois River

Fort Crèvecoeur

Ohio River

NORTH AMERICA

Arkansas River

Mississippi

ATLANTIC OCEAN

Gulf of Mexico

N
W E
S

→ Marquette and Joliet, 1673
→ La Salle, 1679–1682
— Present-day border

Movement Marquette, Joliet, and La Salle traveled on waterways in the interior of North America.

MAP THEME

■ *How far south did Marquette and Joliet travel? How far south did La Salle travel?*

The seven explorers set out in two birch-bark canoes from St. Ignace on Lake Michigan. They crossed the huge lake, entered the Fox River, and then traveled overland to the Wisconsin River. About a month later, at the mouth of the Wisconsin, they saw the Mississippi River for the first time. The explorers followed the big river but soon realized that it could not be the Northwest Passage because the river flowed south.

When the explorers reached the Arkansas River, they met Indians who told them that Europeans lived farther south along the river. The explorers feared that the Europeans might be Spanish or English, so they turned back. In four months Marquette and Joliet traveled about 2,500 miles (4,023 km). Their expedition opened the Mississippi River to trade and settlement by the French. In time, they built trading posts that grew into towns and cities with such French names as St. Louis, Des Moines, and Louisville.

REVIEW *What did Marquette and Joliet find on their expedition?*

Founding Louisiana

After the Marquette and Joliet expedition, another French explorer set out to find the mouth of the Mississippi River. This explorer was René-Robert Cavelier (ka•vuhl•YAY), known as Sieur de La Salle, or "Sir" La Salle (luh•SAL). La Salle and an expedition of 20 French people and about 30 American Indians paddled south from the mouth of the Illinois River on February 6, 1682. Two months later the expedition reached the mouth of the Mississippi. With shouts of "Long live the king!" the explorers fired their guns and claimed the entire Mississippi River valley, including all of its **tributaries**, or branch rivers, for France.

The region La Salle claimed was much larger than he could have imagined. It extended from the Appalachian Mountains in the east to the Rocky Mountains in the west and from the Great Lakes in the north to the Gulf of Mexico in the south. La Salle named the area Louisiana, to honor King Louis XIV.

La Salle tried to establish a settlement in this region. However, hardships led to disagreements, and La Salle was killed by one of his own settlers. The settlement failed.

In 1698 the French king sent another expedition to Louisiana to find La Salle's river and

New France, 1700

NORTH AMERICA

ROCKY MOUNTAINS

LOUISIANA

APPALACHIAN MOUNTAINS

ATLANTIC OCEAN

PACIFIC OCEAN

Gulf of Mexico

Hudson Bay

ACADIA

Quebec
Montreal
Detroit
Des Moines
Vincennes
St. Louis
New Orleans

Lake Superior
Lake Huron
Lake Michigan
Lake Ontario
Lake Erie

Missouri River
Illinois R.
Arkansas River
Mississippi River
Ohio River
Tennessee River
St. Lawrence
Rio Grande

0   300   600 Miles
0   300   600 Kilometers
Azimuthal Equal-Area Projection

New France

Regions This map shows the boundaries of New France in about 1700.
■ *French lands stretched across what major river valleys of North America?*

try again to start a settlement. The leaders of this new expedition were Pierre Le Moyne (luh•MWAHN), known as Sieur d'Iberville (dee•ber•VEEL), and his brother Jean Baptiste (ZHAHN ba•TEEST), known as Sieur de Bienville (byan•VEEL).

In 1699 Iberville and Bienville reached the northern coast of the Gulf of Mexico. Their ships entered the mouth of a great river and sailed upstream. The brothers were not sure they were on the Mississippi until they met Mongoulacha (mahn•goo•LAY•chah), a Taensa (TYN•suh) Indian leader. He was wearing a French-made coat and carrying a letter addressed to La Salle. Mongoulacha told the Europeans his coat was a gift from

Henri de Tonti (ahn•REE duh TOHN•tee). Tonti had stayed in Louisiana after traveling with La Salle several years earlier. Mongoulacha said that Tonti had asked him to give the letter to a white man who would come from the sea. Iberville and Bienville had found La Salle's river.

The brothers soon began to build settlements along the river and, in time, settlers began to arrive. The settlers faced terrible hardships, and many died.

In 1712 the French king made Louisiana a **proprietary colony**. This meant that the king gave ownership to one person, and allowed that person to rule. In 1717 John Law, a Scottish banker, became **proprietor**, or owner,

Chapter 5 • **181**

This drawing shows a French fort at the mouth of the Mississippi in 1700. Iberville is shown standing in a doorway, Bienville is sitting on the riverbank, and Tonti is walking from the riverbank into the fort.

of Louisiana. Law formed a company to build plantations and towns. He brought in thousands of settlers. Finally Louisiana began to grow. In 1722 the town of New Orleans became Louisiana's capital.

Despite Law's efforts, however, the colony still needed workers—especially on the plantations. Many planters began to bring in enslaved Africans to do the work. The French government soon passed laws called the Code Noir (KOHD NWAR), or "Black Code."

These laws restricted the ways in which the Africans in Louisiana could live.

Like the rest of New France, Louisiana failed to attract enough people for it to prosper. By 1763 there were only 80,000 French colonists in the area from Canada to Louisiana. By the same year, and in a much smaller area, there were more than 1,500,000 English colonists in North America.

REVIEW *What lands did La Salle claim?*

LESSON 2 REVIEW

Check Understanding

❶ **Remember the Facts**   Which explorers opened the Mississippi to French trade and settlement?

❷ **Recall the Main Idea**   What steps did the French government take to protect its interests in New France?

Think Critically

❸ **Think More About It**   Why do you think the French people were not interested in settling New France?

❹ **Cause and Effect**   What were the effects of the shortage of workers in Louisiana?

Show What You Know

Newspaper Headline Activity   Write three newspaper headlines about French exploration in North America and the settlement of the Louisiana colony. Compare your headlines with those of your classmates.

Thirteen British Colonies

FOCUS
Why might people today decide to move to a new country to live?

Main Idea As you read, think about why people in Europe decided to move to the colonies of North America during the 1600s and 1700s.

Vocabulary
charter
cash crop
refuge
Puritan
Fundamental Orders
immigrant
indigo
debtor

J amestown and Plymouth were the first of many permanent British settlements in North America. In 1707 England became part of Britain and the English people were then known as the British. By the 1730s the British had settled along the Atlantic coast from present-day Maine to Georgia. In time the area contained not one British colony, but thirteen. Each was formed in its own way and for its own purpose. And in each, the settlers had their own hopes and dreams for their new home.

The Early Southern Colonies

Virginia and Maryland were two of the earliest British colonies. Each was granted a charter by the king, allowing settlement of the Chesapeake Bay region. A **charter** is a document giving a person or group of people official approval to take a certain action.

Virginia began with the settlement of Jamestown in 1607. The Virginia Company of London started Jamestown as a trading post. Five years later, some colonists began growing tobacco as a **cash crop**—a crop that people raise to sell to others rather than to use themselves. The Virginia Company sold its tobacco all over Europe and made huge profits. The use of tobacco became so popular that the company and its colony did well for a time.

At first the British king objected to the sale of tobacco. He thought using it was "a custom loathsome to the eye, hateful to the nose, harmful to the brain, [and] dangerous to the lungs." In 1624 the Virginia Company went out of

The tobacco plant grew well in the warm climate of the southern colonies.

The marketplace at Jamestown, one of the first English settlements in North America

business because of poor management. The king was quick to take back its charter and make Virginia a royal colony. This allowed him to rule Virginia and to keep its tobacco profits for himself.

Tobacco also became an important cash crop for the Maryland colony. Maryland was founded by the Calverts, a family of wealthy business people. The Calverts wanted to build a colony in North America not only to make money but to provide a **refuge**, or safe place, for Catholics. Like other Catholics in England at the time, the Calverts had been treated unfairly because of their religion. The British government approved of only one church—the Church of England.

In 1632 King Charles I chartered the northern Chesapeake Bay region as a proprietary colony. He made Cecilius Calvert, the second Lord Baltimore, its proprietor. One year later the first colonists left England. "I have sent a hopeful colony to Maryland," Calvert wrote. Calvert had named his colony for Queen Henrietta Maria, the king's wife.

From the beginning, Maryland's proprietors welcomed settlers of many religions. Later, in 1649, Maryland passed the first law to guarantee some people religious freedom in North America. The law allowed all Christians to worship as they pleased. Sometimes, however, people of different religions had trouble getting along with one another. In time, disagreements based on religious differences affected life in all 13 British colonies.

REVIEW *What was the most important cash crop in Virginia and Maryland?*

The New England Colonies

Less than ten years after the Pilgrims founded their colony at Plymouth in 1620, another group of religious settlers founded a British colony in North America. These settlers disagreed with many of the practices of the Church of England. They did not separate from the church, as the Pilgrims did, but they wanted to make the church more "pure." For this reason they were called **Puritans**. The Puritans received a charter to start the colony of Massachusetts Bay in the region that British explorers had first called New England.

Beginning in 1630, Puritans built many villages around their chief town, Boston. At the center of each village was a Puritan meetinghouse. And at the center of Puritan life in the Massachusetts Bay colony was religion.

Because religion was so important to the Puritans, newcomers to their colony were expected to follow the Puritans' beliefs. Those who did were given land for farming and a voice in governing their community. Those who did not were not welcomed. Because of disagreements with Puritan

This portrait of a Puritan mother and her baby was painted around 1674.

leaders, some settlers left Massachusetts Bay on their own. Others were sent back to Britain or to other colonies in North America.

In 1636, settlers living in villages along the Connecticut River joined together to form the Connecticut colony. The most well-known of these settlers was a minister—the Reverend Thomas Hooker. Hooker had left his home in Massachusetts Bay because he did not like the way that the colony's Puritan leaders controlled the lives of the colonists.

This drawing shows the Plymouth colony meetinghouse in 1683. The bell above the roof was rung to call people to meetings.

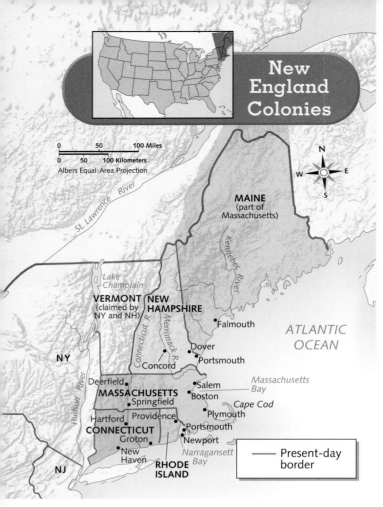

New England Colonies

0 50 100 Miles
0 50 100 Kilometers
Albers Equal-Area Projection

St. Lawrence River

MAINE
(part of Massachusetts)

Kennebec River

Lake Champlain

VERMONT
(claimed by NY and NH)

NEW HAMPSHIRE

Falmouth

Connecticut R.

Merrimack R.

ATLANTIC OCEAN

NY

Concord

Dover

Portsmouth

Hudson River

Deerfield

Salem

Massachusetts Bay

MASSACHUSETTS

Boston

Springfield

Cape Cod

Hartford

Providence

Plymouth

CONNECTICUT

Groton

Portsmouth

New Haven

Newport

RHODE ISLAND

Narragansett Bay

NJ

—— Present-day border

🌐 **Place** New England changes greatly with the seasons.
■ *Which season do you think was hardest for the settlers, considering the climate?*

Hooker thought that a colony's government should be based on what its people wanted, not just on what its leaders wanted. He also believed a colony should be able to elect its leaders. Other settlers in the Connecticut colony agreed with Hooker. In 1639 the colony adopted Hooker's beliefs in the form of the **Fundamental Orders**, the first written system of government in North America. The

Anne Hutchinson was forced to leave Massachusetts Bay.

Fundamental Orders allowed Connecticut's male colonists to elect their government leaders. They were the first colonists in North America to do so.

Roger Williams was another colonist who did not like the way Puritan leaders governed Massachusetts Bay. Williams spoke out time after time, asking for more freedom. Because of his views, Puritan leaders forced Williams to leave the colony. In 1636 Williams and his followers bought land from the Narraganset (nair•uh•GAN•suht) Indians and established the settlement of Providence, in present-day Rhode Island.

Not long after Williams left Massachusetts Bay, the Puritans faced other challenges to their leadership. One such attack came from a colonist named Anne Marbury Hutchinson. Hutchinson disagreed with some of the Puritans' religious teachings. Because of this, the Puritans said she was "a woman not fit for our society." They drove her out, too. Later, Hutchinson, her family, and followers founded a settlement on an island near Providence. In 1647 this settlement and three others were united under a single charter to form the Rhode Island colony.

Some settlers moved out of Massachusetts Bay for reasons other than to find political or religious freedom. Settlers started the town of Strawberry Banke, now known as Portsmouth, New Hampshire, for business reasons. The area had plenty of trees, which the settlers cut down and shipped as lumber back to England. By 1680 the town of Strawberry Banke was granted a charter under the name of the New Hampshire colony.

REVIEW *For what reasons did people establish colonies in New England?*

The Middle Colonies

Not long after the British began setting up colonies in North America, Dutch colonists from the Netherlands began to build settlements in their own colony, called New Netherland. They built their colony along the Hudson River, in parts of what are today New York and New Jersey. The Dutch, along with settlers from French-speaking Belgium, also founded the city of New Amsterdam. Soon colonists expanded New Netherland into what is now New Jersey. In 1638 colonists from Sweden established New Sweden, a string of trading posts in present-day Delaware and southern New Jersey.

The Dutch took over New Sweden in 1655, but in 1664 British forces seized both New Sweden and New Netherland. The British king gave the colonies to his brother James, the Duke of

York. The land was split up and given its present-day names of New York and New Jersey. New York City grew from the Dutch capital of New Amsterdam.

In addition to settling Delaware and southern New Jersey, the Swedish colonists also established trading posts in what is now Pennsylvania. In 1681, after the British had taken control of New Sweden, the British king gave William Penn a charter that made him proprietor of Pennsylvania. William Penn was a member of the Society of Friends, a religious group also known as the

This painting by James Eights shows that many houses in New York were built in the Dutch style, using bricks of different colors. Dutch houses also had a stoop—a wide, high doorstep.

Middle Colonies

0   50   100 Miles
0   50   100 Kilometers
Albers Equal-Area Projection

St. Lawrence River
Lake Champlain
Lake Ontario
Lake Erie
VERMONT (claimed by NY and NH)
NH
Schenectady
NEW YORK
Albany
MA
Connecticut River
Hudson River
CT
RI
PENNSYLVANIA
Delaware River
Susquehanna River
Newark
Morristown
New York City
Long Island
Perth Amboy
Philadelphia
Lancaster
NEW JERSEY
MD
Wilmington
Dover
DELAWARE
Delaware Bay
ATLANTIC OCEAN

N W E S

— Present-day border

Regions The middle colonies were between the New England colonies and the southern colonies.

■ *How do you think the location of the middle colonies affected contact with the other colonies?*

Quakers. British Quakers, like Catholics, often were treated unfairly because of their beliefs. William Penn, like the Calverts of Maryland, wanted to create a refuge where people could worship as they pleased. Quakers and other settlers who wanted religious freedom soon came to Pennsylvania, a name that means "Penn's Woods."

William Penn carefully planned the settlements in his colony. One of them, the town of Philadelphia, was laid out like a checkerboard, with straight streets that formed squares. Philadelphia's location was excellent for shipping and trading since it was located on the Delaware River. The town became the colony's main port for receiving not only goods but also immigrants. **Immigrants** are people who come to live in a country after leaving their home country.

Drawn by Penn's ideas of religious freedom, immigrants moved to Pennsylvania and the other middle colonies from all over Europe. They included Irish Catholics, German Lutherans, and Jews from many countries. Many settled on small farms and raised fruits, vegetables, and wheat. So much wheat was produced in the middle colonies that they were called the "breadbasket" colonies.

REVIEW *What countries built early settlements in the middle colonies?*

This painting (far left) by Edward Hicks shows William Penn signing a treaty with the Indians. Quakers gave American Indians this necklace (left). It was a sign of the strong friendship between the Indians and the colonists of Pennsylvania.

The Southern Colonies

The southern colonies of Virginia and Maryland continued to grow during the 1600s. Then, in 1663, King Charles II granted a charter for another colony in the region. The new colony was south of Virginia, in the lands between Virginia and Spanish Florida. The charter divided the colony, known as Carolina, among eight proprietors.

Even before the charter was granted, colonists from Virginia had been building and farming in the northern part of Carolina. After 1663, colonists from England and the Caribbean, as well as French Protestants called Huguenots (HYOO•guh•nahts), came to settle there.

But the colonists could not survive just by owning land. They needed a cash crop. At first they tried tobacco, silk, grapes, and cotton. Only when they "found out the true way of raising and husking rice" did the colony begin to prosper.

In 1712 the northern two-thirds of the chartered area was divided into two colonies, North Carolina and South Carolina. North Carolina continued to develop as a colony of small farms. In South Carolina, landowners created huge farms in the style of the Spanish plantations of New Spain.

The main cash crop on many of South Carolina's plantations was rice. On land where rice would not grow, landowners found they could grow indigo. **Indigo** is a plant from which blue dye is made.

Indigo became an important cash crop after 17-year-old Eliza Lucas experimented with the plant in the 1740s. Lucas was in charge of three South Carolina plantations owned by her father. Using seeds from the Caribbean, she spent several years growing different kinds of indigo. In 1743 samples of the blue dye made from her plants were found to be of excellent quality. Lucas gave indigo seeds

Location Some southern landowners built huge farms like those in New Spain. ■ *Why do you think most of the settlements in the southern colonies were located in Virginia?*

to her neighbors and friends. Within a few years South Carolina plantation owners were selling a million pounds of indigo a year.

The plantations of South Carolina required many workers. Many landowners filled this need by buying enslaved Africans. The coastal settlement of Charles Towne, later Charleston, South Carolina, became the most important seaport, social center, and slave market in the southern colonies.

The southern one-third of what had originally been Carolina was not settled by the British until 1733. A year earlier James Oglethorpe was given a charter to settle Georgia, a colony named for King George II. Oglethorpe had the idea of bringing over **debtors**, people who had been in prison for

Thirteen British Colonies

New England colonies
Middle colonies
Southern colonies
Present-day border

MAINE
(part of Massachusetts)

VERMONT
(claimed by NY and NH)

St. Lawrence River

Lake Champlain

NEW HAMPSHIRE

NEW YORK

MASSACHUSETTS

Lake Ontario

Hudson River
Connecticut River

RHODE ISLAND
CONNECTICUT

Lake Erie

PENNSYLVANIA

Delaware River
Susquehanna R.

APPALACHIAN MOUNTAINS

NEW JERSEY

MARYLAND   DELAWARE

Potomac River

Ohio River

Chesapeake Bay

VIRGINIA

Roanoke River

NORTH CAROLINA

SOUTH CAROLINA

Savannah River

GEORGIA

ATLANTIC OCEAN

N
W   E
S

0   100   200 Miles
0 100 200 Kilometers
Azimuthal Equal-Area Projection

Location   The 13 British colonies were located along the Atlantic coast.
■ *Why do you think some people think of Maryland as a middle colony while others consider it a southern colony?*

owing money, to settle the colony. Oglethorpe offered each settler 50 acres of land plus a bonus of 50 acres for every debtor the settler brought along to help with the work of these small farms. But his plan did not work, because few people took advantage of Oglethorpe's offer.

The original charter did not allow traders to bring enslaved Africans to the colony, so there were no plantations at first. After 1750, when Georgia law was changed to allow slavery, plantations soon developed.

REVIEW *What three colonies were formed from the lands originally called Carolina?*

LESSON 3 REVIEW

Check Understanding

1 Remember the Facts   How was each of the 13 British colonies established?

2 Recall the Main Idea   Why did people in Europe decide to move to the colonies of North America during the 1600s and 1700s?

Think Critically

3 Think More About It   Do you think most settlers were better off in their new homes or in the places they came from? Explain your answer.

4 Past to Present   What reasons might people have today for coming to the United States to live?

Show What You Know

Planning Activity   Read again the list of items on pages 170–171. Suppose that you are going to a British colony to live. First, select a colony. Then list the ten most important items you would take with you.

Classify Information

1. Why Learn This Skill?

Imagine that you are looking through a drawer full of clothes. The socks, shirts, and jeans are all together in a jumble. It is difficult to find things.

The same problem can happen with information. Like clothing, information is easier to find if it is **classified**, or sorted. Knowing how to classify information can make it easier to find facts.

When you read about the 13 British colonies in the Americas, you were given a lot of information. You learned about where the colonies were built and when they were settled. This and other information can be classified by using a table.

2. Understand the Process

The tables below classify information about the 13 colonies in two different ways.

① In Table A, the colonies are classified according to when they were founded. Which colony was founded first? Which was the last to be founded?

② Table B gives the same information as Table A, but the information is classified differently. In Table B, the colonies are classified according to their location. The New England colonies are listed first, the middle colonies second, and the southern colonies third. Was New York a New England colony or a middle colony? What was the location of Massachusetts? of Virginia?

3. Think and Apply

Make your own table to show information about the Spanish, French, and British colonies. Choose some headings under which to classify the information by topic. Share your table.

Table A: The 13 Colonies

DATE FOUNDED	COLONY	LOCATION
1607	Virginia	Southern colony
1629	Massachusetts	New England colony
1632	Maryland	Southern colony
1636	Connecticut	New England colony
1638	Delaware	Middle colony
1647	Rhode Island	New England colony
1663	North Carolina	Southern colony
1664	New Jersey	Middle colony
1664	New York	Middle colony
1680	New Hampshire	New England colony
1681	Pennsylvania	Middle colony
1712	South Carolina	Southern colony
1733	Georgia	Southern colony

Table B: The 13 Colonies

LOCATION	COLONY	DATE FOUNDED
New England colony	Massachusetts	1629
New England colony	Connecticut	1636
New England colony	Rhode Island	1647
New England colony	New Hampshire	1680
Middle colony	Delaware	1638
Middle colony	New Jersey	1664
Middle colony	New York	1664
Middle colony	Pennsylvania	1681
Southern colony	Virginia	1607
Southern colony	Maryland	1632
Southern colony	North Carolina	1663
Southern colony	South Carolina	1712
Southern colony	Georgia	1733

REVIEW

1560

1565
• The Spanish
  settle
  St. Augustine

1600

1607
• English colonists
  build Jamestown

CONNECT MAIN IDEAS

Use this organizer to show how the chapter's main ideas are connected. Write two examples to support each main idea. A copy of the organizer appears on page 33 of the Activity Book.

Europeans Settle Throughout North America

The Spanish Borderlands

The Spanish government decided to expand its land in North America.

1. _____
2. _____

The Growth of New France

The French government took steps to protect its interests in New France.

1. _____
2. _____

Thirteen British Colonies

The New England Colonies

New England colonists set up different colonies.

1. _____
2. _____

The Middle Colonies

People from different cultures contributed to life in the middle colonies.

1. _____
2. _____

The Southern Colonies

Selling cash crops was important to the people in the southern colonies.

1. _____
2. _____

WRITE MORE ABOUT IT

Write a Travelogue It has been more than 300 years since Marquette and Joliet explored the Mississippi River. Use a map of the United States, your textbook, and other reference materials to describe the route these French explorers followed.

Write "Who Am I?" Questions Choose three of the people who helped build the colonies. For each person, write a question that gives clues about his or her identity and ends with "Who Am I?" Exchange questions with a classmate.

1640	1680	1720	1760

1647
• Colonists settle Connecticut and Rhode Island

1680
• New Hampshire colony is chartered

1681
• Penn founds Pennsylvania

1712
• Carolina is divided into North Carolina and South Carolina

1733
• Georgia colony is settled

USE VOCABULARY

Write the term that correctly matches each definition.

buffer   mission

charter   proprietary colony

immigrant refuge

indigo   royal colony

1 an area of land that serves as a barrier

2 a small religious community

3 a colony ruled by a king

4 a colony owned and ruled by one person who is not the king

5 a document giving a person or group of people the official approval to take a certain action

6 a safe place

7 a person who comes to live in a country from his or her home country

8 a plant from which a blue dye is made

CHECK UNDERSTANDING

9 What was the first permanent European settlement in North America?

10 How did conflicts over the fur trade change the way New France was ruled?

11 What cash crop was important to the early southern colonies? Why?

12 Who were the Puritans, and where did they first settle?

13 What were the Fundamental Orders?

14 What city grew from the Dutch capital of New Amsterdam?

THINK CRITICALLY

15 **Explore Viewpoints** What reasons did the Spanish king give for wanting to build missions in the borderlands? How might the Indians have viewed those reasons?

16 **Past to Present** Why do some cities in the Middle West region of the United States have French names?

APPLY SKILLS

Classify Information The following figures give the estimated population for each of the 13 British colonies in 1750. Use this information to make a table that shows which colonies had more than 100,000 people and which ones had fewer than 100,000 people.

Connecticut 111,280
Delaware 28,704
Georgia 5,200
Maryland 141,073
Massachusetts 188,000
New Hampshire 27,505
New Jersey 71,393
New York 76,696
North Carolina . . . 72,984
Pennsylvania 119,666
Rhode Island 33,226
South Carolina . . . 64,000
Virginia 231,033

READ MORE ABOUT IT

Jacques Marquette and Louis Jolliet by Zachary Kent. Childrens Press. This book, from The World's Great Explorers series, tells about the exploration of the Mississippi River.

Visit the Internet at **http://www.hbschool.com** for additional resources.

LIFE IN THE BRITISH COLONIES

"Such a medley! Such a mixed multitude of all classes and complexions."

Charles Woodmason, a minister, describing the people of a Carolina settlement in the 1760s

John Singleton Copley painted this portrait of a British colonist in the 1770s.

Life in Towns and Cities

FOCUS

What different kinds of towns and cities are found in the United States today?

Main Idea As you read, think about the different kinds of towns and cities found in the British colonies.

Vocabulary

town meeting
common
militia
farm produce
import
Conestoga
county seat
county
export
triangular trade route
apprentice

During the late 1600s and early 1700s, more and more immigrants arrived in the British colonies. In time, some of the early settlements grew into towns and cities. Life in the towns and cities varied from place to place, depending on where they were built and on who settled there.

New England Towns

Many settlers in the New England colonies lived in towns where, as one settler wrote, "every man . . . lives in a tidy warm house, has plenty of good food and fuel, with whole clothes from head to foot, [made by] his family." Most New England towns were self-sufficient communities in which the people grew or made most of what they needed.

The earliest New England towns were built on a narrow road. Each of the town's families had a house on this lane. Families had their own gardens and planted rows of fruit trees. They also had pens for cows, sheep, chickens, or pigs. In the fields near the town, the people grew crops to sell to others and to use for themselves.

A meetinghouse stood at the center of most New England towns. In many places people came to the meetinghouse several times a week to worship together. The meetinghouse was also used for town meetings. At a **town meeting** male landowners could take part in government. They voted on laws and chose workers for the town.

Two of the most important town workers were the herder and the constable. The herder was the person who took care of the animals on the town's **common**, an open area where sheep and cattle grazed. The constable was a police officer who made sure people obeyed the town's laws. Another important worker was the leader of the town's **militia**, or volunteer army. At least once a year, the men and boys of the town gathered on the common to train and drill.

REVIEW *What was the meetinghouse used for?*

This picture, titled *Colonial Days*, was painted by E. L. Henry.

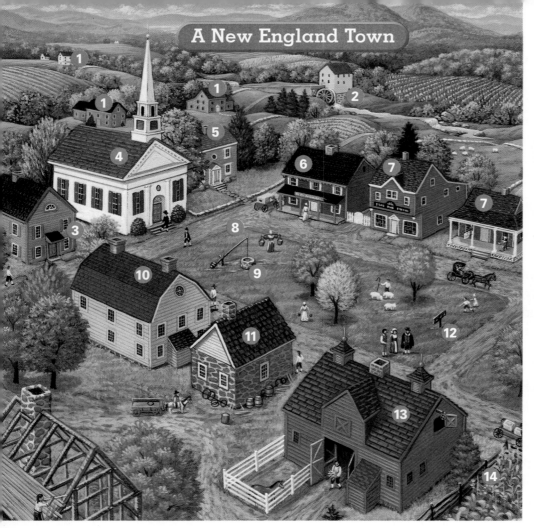

A New England Town

LEARNING FROM DIAGRAMS
The most important building in most New England towns was the meetinghouse. There also were shops for skilled workers and a general store. People who were punished were sometimes made to stand in the stocks on the common.

❶ houses
❷ mill
❸ school —
❹ meetinghouse
❺ minister's house
❻ general store
❼ shops
❽ common
❾ well
❿ cobbler
⓫ cooper
⓬ stocks
⓭ blacksmith
⓮ garden
■ *What else was the town common used for?*

Market Towns

Another kind of town developed in many places, especially in the middle colonies. This was the market town. Farmers traveled to market towns to trade their **farm produce**—grains, fruits, and vegetables—for goods and services.

In most market towns a general store sold **imports**, or goods brought into the colonies from other countries. The imports included tea, sugar, spices, cloth, shoes, stockings, and buttons. Near the general store was the shop of a cobbler, who made and repaired shoes. There was often a blacksmith's shop, where iron was made into horseshoes, hinges, and nails. Most market towns also had a gristmill, where grain was made into flour and meal, and a sawmill, where logs were sawed into lumber.

Market towns often had more than one church. A Lutheran church might be a block away from a Quaker meetinghouse or just down the street from a Methodist church.

To carry their produce to market towns, many Pennsylvania farmers used big covered wagons called **Conestogas**. Conestogas were much larger than regular wagons. When a visitor from Europe first saw them, he called them "huge moving houses."

When market towns grew along rivers, farmers carried their produce to the towns by boat instead of by wagon. It was easier and cheaper to ship heavy goods by water. After unloading their produce, farmers returned home, their boats filled with goods from the general store.

REVIEW *What kinds of goods were bought and sold in market towns?*

County Seats

In the colonies that depended on cash crops, especially the southern colonies, there were few towns. But several times a year, plantation families would pack their bags, dress in their finest clothes, and travel to the **county seat**. This was the main town for each **county**, or large part of a colony. People went to church, held dances, and traded crops for goods at the county seat. Some plantation owners bought and sold slaves there. Along with a church and a general store, most county seats had a courthouse and a jail.

White men who owned land and other property met at the county seat to make laws and vote for government leaders. This meant, however, that women, American Indians, and Africans had no voice in how the colony was run.

REVIEW *Why was the county seat important for people living on plantations?*

Cities

By the middle of the 1700s, several towns along the Atlantic coast had grown into cities. Among these cities were New York City, Philadelphia, and Charleston. They all had good harbors, and they grew because of trade. Ships arrived at these cities, carrying new settlers and imported goods. After a few weeks in port, the ships sailed away loaded with **exports**, or goods to be sold in other countries. Exports from the colonies included raw materials such as furs, lumber, and dried fish, as well as cash crops.

Many ships followed a direct trade route between Britain and the 13 colonies. This was because the British government wanted the colonies to send their exports only to Britain or to other British colonies. The government also wanted the colonists to buy manufactured goods only from Britain.

Some ships followed what came to be known as **triangular trade routes**. These routes linked Britain, the British colonies, and Africa as the three points of a great triangle on the Atlantic Ocean. Traders carried manufactured goods from Britain and raw materials from the 13 colonies and the West Indies. They also carried enslaved people from Africa. Their trip across the Atlantic Ocean is called the Middle Passage.

Most coastal cities grew because of trade. However, people in the cities also worked in other kinds of businesses. Many people made their living from the sea—by fishing, whaling, or shipbuilding. Others sold goods

This harbor scene shows the city of Charleston, South Carolina, in the 1730s. Charleston was one of the busiest port cities in colonial America.

Colonial Trade Routes

Tobacco, furs, lumber, rice
Manufactured goods
Slaves, sugar, molasses, coffee
Grain, meat, fish
Sugar, molasses, fruit, coffee
Rum, iron products
Slaves
Iron products, silver

BRITAIN
EUROPE
NORTH AMERICA
Boston
New York City
Philadelphia
Norfolk
Charleston
ATLANTIC OCEAN
WEST INDIES
Caribbean Sea
SOUTH AMERICA
AFRICA

45°W 30°W 15°W
0 1,000 2,000 Miles
0 1,000 2,000 Kilometers
Miller Cylindrical Projection

45°N
30°N
Tropic of Cancer
15°N
15°W
0° Equator

90°W
75°W 60°W
45°W 30°W

The 13 colonies
Trade route

N
W   E
S

Movement Some traders followed triangular routes between Britain, Africa, and the British colonies.
■ *What was traded at each point of the triangular trade route?*

that they made by using special skills. There were hatmakers, tailors, printers, and many other skilled workers. Young people often learned such jobs by becoming apprentices. An **apprentice** was a person who moved in with the family of a skilled worker and helped in the family's business for several years.

REVIEW *Why were the first colonial cities located along the Atlantic coast?*

LESSON I REVIEW

Check Understanding

1 Remember the Facts In colonial times, where were the different kinds of towns and cities located?

2 Recall the Main Idea In what ways were colonial towns different from one another? How were the towns different from the cities?

Think Critically

3 Think More About It What needs of the colonists did towns and cities meet?

4 Past to Present Town meetings are still held in many towns in the New England states today. Why do you think this tradition continues?

Show What You Know
Diorama Activity Work with a group of classmates to make a diorama. Create a scene showing everyday life in a colonial town or city. Display your diorama in the classroom.

Read a Circle Graph

1. Why Learn This Skill?

Suppose you are writing a report on the British colonies. You want to show in a simple, clear way that the population of the colonies was made up of people from many different places. One way to show the information is by making a graph. Graphs make it easier to see and compare information.

2. Circle Graph

One kind of graph is a circle graph. A circle graph is often called a pie graph because it is round and divided into pieces, or parts, like a pie. A circle graph compares amounts and makes it easy to see how much each part is in relation to the whole.

The circle graph on this page shows the population of the 13 British colonies in 1775. The graph's parts are the many different ethnic groups that made up the population at that time.

You will see that a percent, shown by the symbol % in the graph, is given in each part of the graph. Suppose you cut a giant pie into 100 pieces. Those 100 pieces together equal the whole pie, or 100 percent of it. Fifty pieces would be one-half of the pie, or 50 percent of it. Ten pieces would be one-tenth of the pie, or 10 percent of it.

3. Understand the Process

Find *English* on the graph. The English made up about 49 percent of the population of the 13 British colonies in 1775. That "slice" is almost 50 percent, or one-half, of the "pie."

Like other graphs, a circle graph can help you make comparisons. You can compare the parts to one another or to the whole.

Use the circle graph to answer the following questions.

❶ What percent of the population did the Germans make up?

❷ What percent of the population was made up of Swedish colonists?

❸ Which group made up 3 percent of the population?

❹ Were there more Scottish and Swedish colonists or German and French colonists?

4. Think and Apply

Use information from the circle graph on this page to write a paragraph about the people of the 13 British colonies. First, compare the sizes of the different ethnic groups. Then, use the information to form a conclusion about the languages that may have been spoken in the British colonies. Compare your conclusion with the conclusions formed by your classmates. How are the conclusions similar? How are they different?

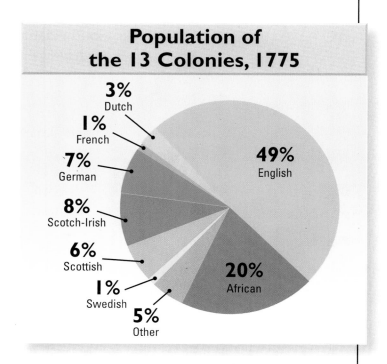

Population of the 13 Colonies, 1775

- 3% Dutch
- 1% French
- 7% German
- 8% Scotch-Irish
- 6% Scottish
- 1% Swedish
- 5% Other
- 49% English
- 20% African

FOCUS

How do societies today separate people into different groups?

Main Idea Read to learn about the ways that plantation life separated people into different groups.

Vocabulary

broker
indentured servant
auction

Life on Plantations

As towns and cities grew in many of the British colonies, plantations also grew—especially in the southern colonies. Settlements in Virginia, Maryland, the Carolinas, and Georgia became successful because the plantations there were able to grow more and more cash crops. Plantation owners were known as planters. Many planters bought as much land as they could. With bigger plantations, they could grow more crops to sell.

Plantations needed many hands to do the work. Most planters hired farm workers as well as servants to help out. Before long they added other workers—enslaved Africans. Over time, slaves had a major impact on life in the southern colonies.

A Southern Plantation

From the time the Jamestown settlers began growing tobacco, plantations became important to the economy of the South. Planters soon learned to grow other cash crops as well, such as rice and indigo, and plantations spread to other southern colonies.

The earliest plantations were usually built along waterways. The main building was the planter's house. Servants and slaves lived in small buildings nearby. Because of the danger of fire, kitchens were in a separate building. There were sheds for storing crops and barns for livestock. There also might be a carpenter's shop, a blacksmith's shop, and a laundry. If the plantation was on a river, it most likely had its own dock. Plantations that were not on a waterway were connected by roads to another planter's dock.

Money was rarely used in the plantation economy. Instead, crops were used to trade. Crop buyers would travel up and down southern waterways, their boats filled with British-made goods such as shoes, lace, thread, farm tools, and dishes. The planters traded tobacco, rice, and indigo for these goods.

Rice was an important cash crop in the southern colonies.

A Southern Plantation

LEARNING FROM DIAGRAMS Like a Spanish hacienda, a plantation was mostly self-sufficient. Planters grew food, and skilled workers produced many needed goods. Goods that could not be made on a plantation were brought in through trade.

1. brickmaker
2. cattle pen
3. slave cabins
4. overseer's house
5. stable
6. tobacco barn
7. tobacco fields
8. kitchen
9. main house
10. carpenter
11. laundry
12. warehouse
13. dock

■ *Why were many plantations built near waterways?*

Owners of the largest plantations most often sold their crops through a British broker. A **broker** is a person who is paid to buy and sell for someone else. Planters sent their crops to Britain with a list of things they wanted the broker to buy for them. The broker then sold the crops, bought what the planter wanted, and sent the goods back to the colonies.

REVIEW *What was used instead of money in the plantation economy?*

Servants and Slaves

On small plantations, everyone in the planter's family worked. As plantations grew, planters added more workers. In time, the main job of the planter's family was to help watch over the work of others—both servants and slaves.

Many of the earliest workers in the Americas came as indentured servants. An **indentured servant** was a person who agreed to work for another person without pay for a certain length of time. Many indentured servants were Europeans who had wanted to move to the colonies but had no money. A planter or other business owner paid for the trip, and the person agreed to work without pay for anywhere from two to seven years. Once this time was over, the indentured servant was free.

Not all indentured servants had come willingly to the British colonies. Some were sent by British courts to work in the colonies as punishment to pay for their crimes. Other indentured servants were people who had been kidnapped and then sold in the colonies.

Among the first indentured servants to be sold in the British colonies were kidnapped Africans. By the middle 1600s, however, traders were bringing thousands of Africans to the British colonies not as indentured servants but as slaves. Unlike indentured servants, slaves were not given their freedom after a certain length of time. They were enslaved for life. In time, laws were passed saying that the children of enslaved people were slaves, too.

Olaudah Equiano (OHL•uh•dah ek•wee•AHN•oh) was 11 years old when he was taken from his village in Africa. He described what happened this way:

66 One day, when all our people were gone to the fields to work, and only I and my dear sister were left to mind the house, two men and a woman got over our walls. In a moment they seized us both, and without giving us time to cry out, they stopped our mouths and ran off with us into the nearest woods. 99

Equiano was soon parted from his sister and sold at an **auction**, or public sale. Like other enslaved Africans, he had no choices about his future.

REVIEW *What kinds of workers were there on plantations?*

Plantation Duties

Plantations in the southern colonies were often far from one another and far from any towns. Weeks or months could go by without visitors and without news about the latest happenings. For this reason visitors were always welcome.

Although slaves did most of the work, planters had many responsibilities. A planter had to see that the crops were planted, harvested, stored, and shipped. Careful records had to be kept in order to run the plantation as a successful business.

One of the most famous early Virginia planters was William Byrd II. We know much about him because he kept a diary. Byrd's diary shows how difficult life on plantations could be. Many of his diary entries are about sickness and death. Some are about financial worries. More than once Byrd learned that the ships carrying his cash crops to Britain had sunk at sea. Even his neighbors gave him problems. "In the evening I took a walk about the plantation and found that some of my good neighbors had dug down the bank of my ditch to let their hogs into my pasture, for which I was out of humor."

A planter's wife had the same responsibilities as other colonial women caring for a household. She had to clothe and feed her family. Her household—family, servants, and slaves—sometimes numbered in the hundreds. It was up to her to see that all these people had food, clothing, and medical care.

Advertisements for enslaved people (far left) were given out before auctions. Slaves who were sick were often forced to hide their illnesses long enough to be sold. Olaudah Equiano (left) was freed from slavery and later wrote a book about his life.

Most plantation owners and their families lived in large houses filled with expensive furnishings. Many had ballrooms, music rooms, and libraries.

There were few schools in the southern colonies because people lived so far apart. Large plantations had their own small schools for children to learn basic reading and writing. Planters often hired teachers from Europe for their children. When they were about 12 or 13 years old, the young people might attend special town schools. After that, boys often went to college either in Britain or in the colonies. By age 12 or 13, girls stopped going to school. Planters' daughters were supposed to learn only the basic skills and "to read and sew with their needle."

There were no schools for servants or for the African slaves on the plantations. Laws in the colonies did not allow slaves to learn to read and write. By the age of 10, most young Africans were working alongside the adults.

Enslaved people were expected to spend their days working. At any time, they could be whipped for falling behind in their work. But at night, when their work was finished, the Africans often told stories and sang songs about their homeland. The Africans found ways to keep their heritage alive.

REVIEW *Why were there so few schools in the southern colonies?*

LESSON 2 REVIEW

Check Understanding

1 Remember the Facts Describe life on a typical plantation in the southern colonies.

2 Recall the Main Idea In what ways were people on southern plantations separated into different groups?

Think Critically

3 Think More About It Describe the differences between being an indentured servant and being a slave.

4 Explore Viewpoints How do you think Olaudah Equiano and William Byrd II each viewed life on the plantations?

Show What You Know

Diary Activity Suppose that you are living on a plantation in colonial times. Take on a role, and write an entry in a diary to show what a day on the plantation is like. Share your entry with a classmate.

FOCUS

How do people today meet the challenges in their lives?

Main Idea As you read, look for ways the settlers met the challenges of living on the frontier.

Vocabulary

backcountry
fall line
loft
coureur de bois

Life on the Frontier

T he history of the British colonies, like the history of all of the United States, is the story of people on the move. People left settled areas along the Atlantic coast and pushed farther inland to claim what they saw as open land. Settlers hoped to make a piece of this frontier land into a farm, where they could build a house and raise a family. They felt that moving to the frontier would give them a chance for a better life.

The Great Wagon Road

In the early 1700s most of the cities, towns, plantations, and farms in the British colonies were located in the Coastal Plain region of the present-day United States. Few colonists had settled in the **backcountry**, which was the land between the Coastal Plain and the Appalachian Mountains. People called this region the frontier or the backcountry because it was beyond, or "in back of," the settled area.

The lack of roads and the waterfalls in the rivers along the Fall Line made travel to the backcountry difficult. A **fall line** is a place where the land drops sharply, causing rivers to form waterfalls. Settlers who went into the backcountry had to carry their boats and supplies around the waterfalls.

By the middle 1700s large numbers of German and Scotch-Irish immigrants had begun moving from Pennsylvania into the backcountry of western Virginia and the Carolinas. To get there, the settlers followed an old Indian trail. As more settlers used the trail, it became wider, until finally wagons could travel on it. This trail became known as the Great Wagon Road.

From Pennsylvania the Great Wagon Road passed through the Shenandoah Valley of Virginia and along the eastern side of the Blue Ridge Mountains. The land there was hilly, and travel on the road was difficult. "[In places] it was so slippery the horses could not keep their footing but fell . . . to their knees," wrote one traveler. However, the Great Wagon

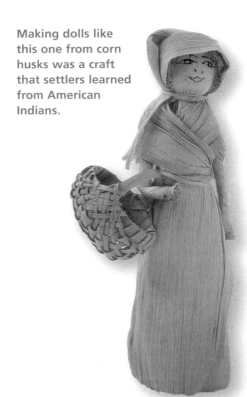

Making dolls like this one from corn husks was a craft that settlers learned from American Indians.

British Colonists Move West

MAINE
(part of Massachusetts)

VERMONT
(claimed by NY and NH)

NEW HAMPSHIRE
• Falmouth
• Portsmouth

MASSACHUSETTS
• Boston • Plymouth
Albany • • Providence
• Newport

NEW YORK
New Haven •
RHODE ISLAND
CONNECTICUT

New York City •

PENNSYLVANIA
NEW JERSEY
Lancaster • • Philadelphia
• Wilmington

MARYLAND
• Baltimore
DELAWARE

VIRGINIA
• Williamsburg
Jamestown • • Norfolk

NORTH CAROLINA
New Bern •

SOUTH CAROLINA
• Wilmington

ATLANTIC OCEAN

Augusta •
• Charleston

GEORGIA
Savannah

St. Lawrence River
Lake Champlain
Connecticut River
Mohawk R.
Hudson River
Lake Ontario
Lake Erie
Ohio River
APPALACHIAN MOUNTAINS
Potomac River
James River
Savannah River

Legend:
- Settled by 1660
- Settled by 1700
- Settled by 1760
- — Great Wagon Road
- - - - Fall Line
- — Present-day border

0   100   200 Miles
0   100   200 Kilometers
Azimuthal Equal-Area Projection

Road was the only way to get wagons loaded with household goods to the backcountry.

Among the thousands of people who chose to follow the Great Wagon Road from Pennsylvania was a young man named Daniel Boone. Later, Boone would make new roads that took settlers even farther west. Boone's roads led through the Appalachian Mountains into what are now Kentucky and Tennessee.

REVIEW *Why was the Great Wagon Road important to the settlement of the backcountry?*

Living in the Backcountry

Most of the people who settled the back-country, including the Boone family, lived simply. Their homes were no more than log huts with chimneys made of sticks and mud. Most houses had one room with a dirt floor and no windows. Light came through the open door in the daytime and from the fire-place at night. Families burned wood in the fireplace to cook their food and to keep their homes warm.

As time went on, families made their homes more comfortable. Some added win-dows. Others covered their dirt floors with wooden boards.

At night the adults in a family spread their blankets over piles of dry leaves on the floor. The children slept in the **loft**, a part of the house between the ceiling and the roof. To get up to the loft, they climbed a ladder, which was often just wooden pegs driven into the wall.

Movement   Although colonies had claimed land beyond the Fall Line, few settlers had moved into this area.

■ *By what year had settlers from the 13 colonies moved past the Fall Line?*

A settler named Oliver Johnson remembered sleeping in a loft when he was a child growing up on the frontier. He wrote,

66 If you slept in the loft, you pulled your head under the covers during a storm. When you got up in the mornin[g], you [would] shake the snow off the covers, grab your shirt and britches [pants] and hop down the ladder to the fireplace, where it was good and warm. 99

People on the frontier worked hard for their food, hunting in the forests and farming in the clearings. They farmed in the Indian way, planting corn, beans, and squash all in the same mound of soil. The cornstalks provided a stake for the bean plants to climb, and the squash vines spread out on the ground between the mounds.

Frontier families made almost everything they needed. They churned their own butter, dyed their own cloth, and made their own soap and candles. There were no butchers, carpenters, candlemakers, or soapmakers. Those who could not do things for themselves, a frontier minister observed in 1711, would "have but a bad time of it; for help is not to be had at any rate."

Life on the frontier was full of dangers. Families had to protect themselves not only from wild animals but also from human enemies. The settlers had to meet these dangers with little or no help from others.

REVIEW *How did families living in the backcountry get the food and household goods they needed?*

LEARNING FROM DIAGRAMS Life was hard and often lonely for early settlers in the backcountry. Families had to work together to protect themselves and to provide all the items they might need.

❶ candlemaking
❷ farming
❸ cleared land
❹ chopping wood
❺ fire used for cooking and warmth
❻ sewing
❼ children's loft
❽ butter churn

■ *In what ways is this frontier family self-sufficient?*

Frontier Life

The Ohio River Valley

Always wanting more land, people on the frontier moved farther and farther west. By the middle 1700s, British fur traders had crossed the Appalachian Mountains into the Ohio River valley. They moved into land claimed by several British colonies as well as by France.

France claimed the huge region but had settled very little of the land. The French **coureurs de bois** (koo•RUR duh BWAH), or "runners of the woods," traded with American Indians for furs. The furs were bought by trading companies, which sold them in Europe at a profit. Many coureurs de bois had good relations with the Indians of the area.

British fur traders moved into the Ohio River

The beaver was hunted for its valuable fur.

valley to take the fur trade away from the French. To do this, the British offered the Indians more goods for fewer furs. The tribes had to decide whether they would trade with the British or the French. The French had been friends to the Indians for many years. But the British gave the Indians more of the goods they wanted at a lower price. In time the French lost many of their Indian trading partners to the British.

In 1753, British settlers began arriving in the Ohio River valley. Even though there were only a few British colonists who settled west of the Appalachian Mountains, the French were upset. In order to protect their lands from the British, they built a line of forts in what is now western Pennsylvania. It was not long before the bad feelings between the British and the French turned into a war on the frontier.

REVIEW *Why did the British and the French want to settle the Ohio River valley?*

LESSON 3 REVIEW

Check Understanding

1 Recall the Facts Why did the French lose many of their Indian trading partners to the British?

2 Remember the Main Idea In what ways did the settlers meet the challenges of living on the frontier?

Think Critically

3 Think More About It What skills did the settlers need to survive on the frontier? Which skills do you think they learned from the Indians?

4 Personally Speaking If you had been a settler in frontier days, do you think you would have enjoyed life in the backcountry? Why or why not?

Show What You Know

Writing Activity Imagine that you are a settler who has moved to the frontier in the early 1700s. Write a journal entry in which you describe your journey to the backcountry and the building of your new home. Share your journal entry with a classmate.

Use a Product Map

1. Why Learn This Skill?

Symbols provide people with helpful information every day. If you see the symbol of a telephone receiver on a sign, for example, you know that a telephone is nearby. Map symbols also provide helpful information. They tell you such things as what cities are state capitals or where state borders are located.

Like other maps, product maps can help give you an overall, or general, picture of a place. Symbols for products tell you where certain products are made or grown. This can help you understand more about the kinds of work people in those places do. This, in turn, can help you to better understand the economic activities of a place.

This general picture of a place can help you make generalizations. A **generalization** is a statement based on facts. It is used to summarize groups of facts and show relationships between them. A generalization tells what is true most of the time. It may contain words such as *often, many, most, generally,* or *usually.*

2. Map Symbols

Notice that this map of colonial products has two map keys. The map key in the lower right part of the map uses colors as symbols. The one in the upper left part of the map uses pictures.

The map key that uses colors shows the division of the 13 British colonies into three regions. These regions are identified as the New England colonies, the middle colonies, and the southern colonies. The colonies within each region are shown in the same color. This map key also tells you that the borders shown on the map are those of the present-day states, not those of the colonies.

In the other map key, pictures stand for the important goods produced in the colonies.

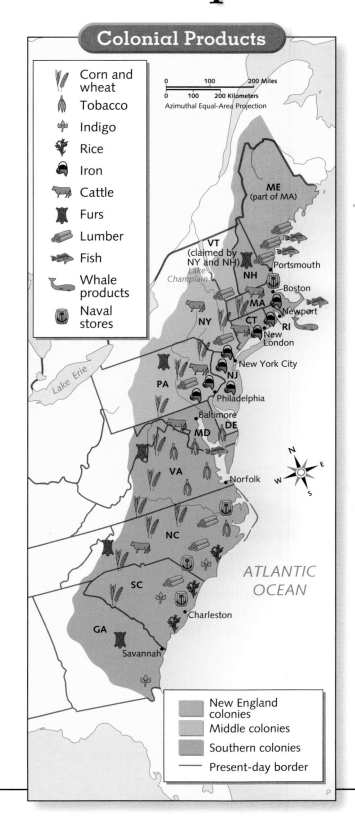

Colonial Products

Corn and wheat
Tobacco
Indigo
Rice
Iron
Cattle
Furs
Lumber
Fish
Whale products
Naval stores

0   100   200 Miles
0   100   200 Kilometers
Azimuthal Equal-Area Projection

ME (part of MA)
VT (claimed by NY and NH)
Lake Champlain
NH
Portsmouth
Boston
MA
Newport
NY
CT
RI
New London
Lake Erie
New York City
PA
NJ
Philadelphia
Baltimore
MD
DE
VA
Norfolk
NC
SC
Charleston
GA
Savannah
ATLANTIC OCEAN

New England colonies
Middle colonies
Southern colonies
Present-day border

The New England Colonies	The Middle Colonies	The Southern Colonies
Connecticut	Delaware	Georgia
Massachusetts	New Jersey	Maryland
New Hampshire	New York	North Carolina
Rhode Island	Pennsylvania	South Carolina
		Virginia

These goods were important not only because they were sold in the colonies, but also because they were exported for sale in Britain. The map shows only some of the most important goods that were produced in the colonies.

Some of the map symbols stand for certain products and raw materials, such as tobacco, indigo, iron, and lumber. Others stand for groups of products. Naval stores, for example, are products such as tar and rope that are used to build and repair ships. Whale products include the oils used for making lamp fuel and candles.

3. Understand the Process

Now that you know more about the symbols in the map keys, you can use these questions as a guide for making generalizations about the colonial economy.

1. What color is used to show the New England colonies? the middle colonies? the southern colonies?

2. What products appear most often on the map in the New England colonies?

3. What generalization can you make about the kinds of work most people did in the New England colonies?

4. What generalization can you make about the economy of the New England colonies?

5. What products appear most often on the map in the middle colonies?

6. What generalization can you make about the kinds of work most people did in the middle colonies?

7. What generalization can you make about the economy of the middle colonies?

8. What products appear most often on the map in the southern colonies?

9. What generalization can you make about the kinds of work most people did in the southern colonies?

10. What generalization can you make about the economy of the southern colonies?

11. What generalization can you make about the kinds of work most people did in all 13 colonies?

12. What generalization can you make about the economy of the 13 colonies?

4. Think and Apply

Draw a product map of your state. Use an encyclopedia, atlas, or almanac to gather the information you will need. Use colors to show the different regions of your state, and then use pictures to show the products that are important there. Also include labels for cities and nearby states. Then invite a classmate to use your map to make some generalizations about the economy of your state.

CONNECT MAIN IDEAS

Use this organizer to compare the ways of life of the early colonists. Write three examples for each place. A copy of the organizer appears on page 39 of the Activity Book.

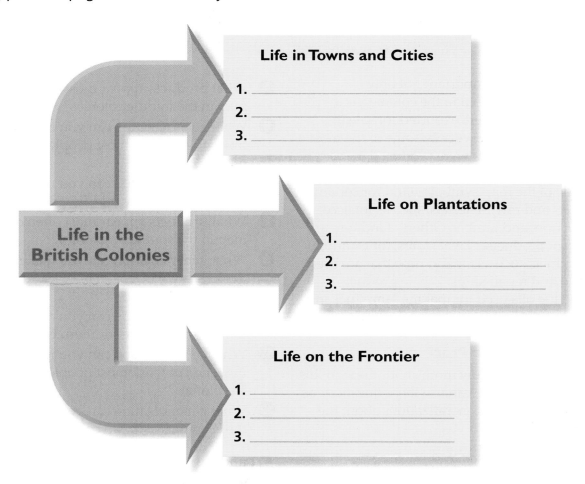

Life in the British Colonies

Life in Towns and Cities

1. _____
2. _____
3. _____

Life on Plantations

1. _____
2. _____
3. _____

Life on the Frontier

1. _____
2. _____
3. _____

WRITE MORE ABOUT IT

Write a Description The people who lived in market towns depended on one another for different goods and products. Imagine that you are visiting a colonial market town for the first time. Describe the sights, sounds, and smells around you.

Write a Conversation Write a conversation that might have taken place between two settlers who lived in the backcountry. The two settlers should discuss the work they did during the day and their hopes for their families in the future.

USE VOCABULARY

For each pair of terms, write a sentence or two that explains how the terms are related.

1. town meeting, common
2. import, export
3. county seat, county
4. apprentice, indentured servant
5. backcountry, fall line

CHECK UNDERSTANDING

6. What were the uses of the meetinghouse in most New England towns?
7. Who made the laws and voted for government leaders in the colonies?
8. What kinds of goods did general stores sell?
9. What were the triangular trade routes?
10. What effect did trade have on coastal cities?
11. How did planters get their indentured servants?
12. How were indentured servants different from slaves?
13. What was the main job of the planter's family?
14. Why did the British move into the Ohio River valley?

THINK CRITICALLY

15. **Past to Present** People in New England gathered at the meetinghouse for town meetings. Where do you think town meetings are held today?
16. **Explore Viewpoints** How would living on a plantation have been different from living in or near a town?

17. **Cause and Effect** What effect did the triangular trade routes have on the people of the British colonies?
18. **Think More About It** How were southern waterways important to plantation life?
19. **Personally Speaking** Would you have been willing to become an indentured servant in order to move to the colonies? Explain your answer.

APPLY SKILLS

Read a Circle Graph Use the circle graph on page 199 to answer these questions.

20. Who made up the second-largest group of people in the 13 colonies?
21. Were there more German or more French settlers in the 13 colonies?

Use a Product Map Use the product map on page 208 to list the major products of the southern colonies. Then write a generalization about which products were related to the rise of slavery.

READ MORE ABOUT IT

Colonial Places by Sarah Howarth. Millbrook. Through art and text, the author discusses the importance of 13 places around which life centered in a colonial community.

Visit the Internet at
http://www.hbschool.com
for additional resources.

Life in Colonial
WILLIAMSBURG

Many students think of history as something that happened to other people in other times. It may not seem real to them. It might even seem like a fantasy. At a living history museum, however, history comes alive. You can see it. You can hear it. You can smell it. You can even act it out.

Colonial Williamsburg is the restored capital of eighteenth-century Virginia. On a visit there you can experience the sights, sounds, and smells of colonial life in the 1700s. You can see the homes and other buildings. You can talk with the shop owners and the craftspeople. You can smell food cooking at the inn. You can also try activities such as churning butter, dipping candles, and playing colonial games.

History is more than just names and dates. It is the story of people just like you who lived in another time.

Dressed in colonial-style clothing, this woman makes a basket as people did over 200 years ago.

Before the capital of Virginia was moved from Williamsburg to Richmond in 1780, Virginia governors lived in the Governor's Palace (background). Lenses for glasses were prepared by hand in the colonies (above). In colonial times weavers at large looms (right) made fabric by using linen and wool yarns.

VISUAL SUMMARY

Summarize the Main Ideas
Study the pictures and captions to help you review the events you read about in Unit 3.

Write a Story
Imagine that you are one of the people in a picture on this visual summary. Write a story about yourself. Tell who you are and where you came from or where you are going. Describe where you live. Tell about a problem you had. How did the problem get solved?

1 The Spanish built many missions in their borderlands.

2 The French grew wealthy by trading with Indian peoples for furs.

5 Roads such as El Camino Real connected the Spanish missions and presidios.

7 In the borderlands north of Mexico, Spanish settlers raised large herds of livestock.

3 People who moved west from the British colonies lived on the frontier.

4 The British had 13 colonies along the Atlantic coast. Most New England towns had a meetinghouse for town meetings and for worship.

6 Many immigrants came to the middle colonies and made a living by working on small farms.

9 On plantations in the southern British colonies, planters grew cash crops such as tobacco and indigo.

8 La Salle claimed the Mississippi River valley for France.

USE VOCABULARY

Use each term in a sentence that will help explain its meaning.

1 presidio   5 debtor

2 permanent   6 militia

3 tributary   7 broker

4 charter   8 auction

CHECK UNDERSTANDING

9 What was the most important money-making activity in Spain's American colonies?

10 Why did the Spanish government build roads linking Spanish missions to presidios?

11 What convinced Iberville and Bienville that they had found La Salle's river?

12 What attracted European immigrants to the middle colonies?

13 What different groups of people worked on southern plantations? What work did each group do?

14 What route did many people follow as they traveled to the backcountry?

THINK CRITICALLY

15 **Cause and Effect** How did the beliefs of the Puritans lead to the founding of other colonies in New England?

16 **Past to Present** Describe how religious freedom affects people in the United States today.

17 **Personally Speaking** Would you rather have been a planter or a planter's broker? Explain your answer.

APPLY SKILLS

Use a Product Map The map below shows some colonial industries. Which industries were important to all three regions? What generalizations can you make about the ironworks industry?

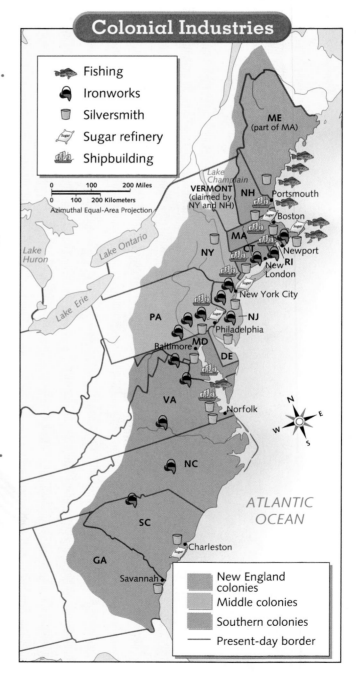

Colonial Industries

Legend:
- Fishing
- Ironworks
- Silversmith
- Sugar refinery
- Shipbuilding

0   100   200 Miles
0 100 200 Kilometers
Azimuthal Equal-Area Projection

- New England colonies
- Middle colonies
- Southern colonies
- Present-day border

REMEMBER

- Share your ideas.
- Cooperate with others to plan your work.
- Take responsibility for your work.
- Help one another.
- Show your group's work to the class.
- Discuss what you learned by working together.

ACTIVITY Draw a
Product Map

Work in a group to draw an outline map of the 13 British colonies on a large sheet of paper. Maps in your textbook and in encyclopedias can help you. Label the colonies and their largest cities. Also label large bodies of water. Then draw symbols to show each colony's major products. Point out places and products as you present the map to the class.

ACTIVITY Plan a
Presentation

Enslaved Africans found ways to keep their traditions alive. Some told stories and sang songs they remembered from Africa. Work in a group, using reference books, to find a traditional African story or song. As a group, decide how you will present the story or song to your classmates and invited guests. You may want to perform a story as a play or do a dramatic reading of it. You may want to sing a song as a group or invite the whole class to take part.

ACTIVITY Make a
Poster

You have learned about the ways in which Spanish settlers changed the lives of Indians in the borderlands. Work in a group to make a poster that shows at least three of these ways. Display the poster in your classroom.

Unit Project Wrap-Up

Build a Model Work in a group to finish the Unit Project described on page 167. Use small boxes, construction paper, and other materials to build your model. The town should have a common, a general store, a blacksmith's shop, a mill, a meetinghouse, and a school. The plantation should include the planter's house, a kitchen, barns, buildings for servants and slaves, and fields.

217

THE AMERICAN REVOLUTION

The colonists who moved to North America continued to be citizens of the European lands they came from. Over the years many British colonists grew unhappy with British rule. They had little voice in a government that was thousands of miles away. In time the British colonies in North America decided to break away from their homeland. They won their freedom, but only after a long and bitter fight.

◄ The Battle of Princeton, 1777

UNIT THEMES

- Conflict and Cooperation
- Continuity and Change
- Individualism and Interdependence
- Interaction Within Different Environments

Unit Project

Create a Book Complete this project as you study Unit 4. With your classmates, you will create a book about the American Revolution. As you read, make a list of the key events, people, and places you learn about. Your list will help you decide which items to include in your book.

CANADA

PACIFIC
OCEAN

YAKIMA

Columbia River

CHINOOK

NEZ
PERCE

Snake

River

MODOC

PAIUTE

Great Salt
Lake

POMO

San Francisco ○

MIWOK

YOKUTS

Missouri River

KIOWA

MANDAN

CROW

SIOUX

CHEYENNE

Platte River

PAWNEE

ARAPAHO

UTE

Colorado River

PAIUTE

HOPI   NAVAJO

○ Santa Fe

CAHUILLA

APACHE   COMANCHE

○ San Diego

MEXICO

○ Tucson

PIMA

Rio Grande

0   200   400 Miles
0   200   400 Kilometers
Albers Equal-Area Projection

▨	The 13 colonies
●	Major British colonial town
○	Major Spanish colonial town
●	Major French colonial town
SIOUX	Name of Indian tribe
───	Present-day national border

1765   1770   1775

1765
The Stamp Act
PAGE 233

1773
Boston Tea Party
PAGE 239

1775
The American
Revolution Begins
PAGE 241

Colonial America, 1770s

ABNAKI

MAINE (part of MA)

OTTAWA ALGONKIN

Montreal

Lake Superior

SIOUX

Mississippi River

FOX

SAC

OTTAWA

Lake Michigan

Lake Huron

Detroit

Lake Erie

Lake Ontario

IROQUOIS

NH

Portsmouth

Boston

NEW YORK

MA

Providence

Hartford

RI

Newport

CT

New London

New York City

KICKAPOO

MIAMI

WYANDOT

DELAWARE

PENNSYLVANIA

NEW JERSEY

Philadelphia

IOWA

ILLINOIS

Baltimore

DELAWARE

MD

MISSOURI

SHAWNEE

VIRGINIA

Williamsburg

Norfolk

KAW

St. Louis

Vincennes

Ohio River

ATLANTIC OCEAN

OSAGE

Arkansas River

Tennessee River

NORTH CAROLINA

Mississippi River

CHEROKEE

SOUTH CAROLINA

Wilmington

WICHITA

CHICKASAW

GEORGIA

Charleston

CADDO

CREEK

NATCHEZ

Savannah

CHOCTAW

St. Augustine

New Orleans

Gulf of Mexico

AIS

SEMINOLE

CALUSA

N E W S

1780

1785

1776
The Declaration of Independence
PAGE 252

1783
The American Revolution Ends
PAGE 268

G·U·N·S
for
GENERAL WASHINGTON

by Seymour Reit
illustrated by Paul Bachem

Crack! Crack! Crack!

The sound of musket fire cut through the stillness of the sleeping camp. Colonial soldiers, bleary-eyed, tumbled out of their shelters with their weapons ready and raced toward the palisade.[1] One of these men was a trooper named William Knox, who had been hoping to see action. Excited, he joined the others on the firing line and peered into the gray mist.

The news spread quickly among the waiting men. Hidden by morning fog, a British patrol had slipped across Mill Creek in an attempt to probe the rebel defenses. But an alert sentinel had spotted them in the marshes and opened fire. Others had joined in and the redcoats, giving up, had raced to their barge and escaped. The immediate crisis was over.

With shrugs and yawns, the soldiers trudged back to their warm beds. But Will Knox was too keyed up to go back to sleep. Unloading his musket, he walked across the drill grounds and climbed a rise called Prospect Hill. From here he could see his beloved Boston, locked in the hands of

[1]**palisade:** fence of wooden stakes

the enemy to the southeast. The city was only a few miles away, but it could well have been a thousand; the British had thrown a tight blockade around the city, and nobody could get in or out.

On this frosty morning in October of 1775, a sharp wind was blowing, but William was warmly dressed. Some weeks earlier a regiment of Pennsylvania frontiersmen had come marching into camp. Tough, hardy men, they wore long homespun shirts of butternut brown, fringed leather tunics, leggins, and Indian-style moccasins. Will had traded his best hunting knife, plus half a pound of sugar, for a long shirt and tunic. He'd also fancied one of the fine coonskin caps worn by the Pennsylvania men, but those were scarce, so he had to make do with an ordinary militia tricorn.[2]

Now, sitting with his back against a log rampart,[3] the trooper studied the sweeping view. From where he sat the city looked like an island; it was entirely surrounded by water, except for a narrow causeway called Boston Neck. This strip of land was fortified and guarded by British redcoats. The rest of the area, lying in Boston Harbor, was patrolled by the powerful frigates[4] of the Royal Navy.

Will had just turned nineteen and had joined the Continental Army after the fighting at Lexington and Concord. He'd been born in Boston on Sea Street and had lived there with his parents, brothers, and sisters. When Will was only three, his father had gone off to the West Indies to seek his fortune. He died while away and Will's older brother, Henry, became the head of the little family. Henry Knox was now twenty-five and a trusted officer on General Washington's staff. In Will's admiring eyes, Henry was a true hero—at least, William felt, he *would* be a hero if there were only something to be heroic *about*.

Many people at the time of the American Revolution believed that it was heroic to fight for their freedom. In this unit you will read the story of the American Revolution. You will learn about the causes of the war and about the colonists who, like Will and Henry Knox, fought to win their freedom from the British government.

[2]**tricorn:** three-cornered hat
[3]**rampart:** protective barrier
[4]**frigate:** kind of warship

DIFFERENCES DIVIDE
BRITAIN
AND ITS
COLONIES

"The Revolution was effected before the war commenced. The Revolution was in the minds and hearts of the people . . ."

John Adams, leader from the colony of Massachusetts

Government in the Colonies

LESSON

1

Main Idea As you read, look for reasons the British colonists became unhappy with British rule.

Vocabulary
Parliament
self-government
democracy
legislature
ally
tax
authority

During colonial times, Spain, France, and Britain were ruled in different ways. So, too, were their colonies. New Spain and New France were ruled by monarchs in Europe. Sometimes the king or queen asked advisers to help make laws. More often the monarch ruled alone. In the 13 British colonies, however, the government ruled in a different way.

British Rule

The British monarch made some of the laws. Some British citizens also took part in deciding what laws were made. The people in Britain elected leaders to speak for them in the part of the government called **Parliament**. The members of Parliament passed the laws for all British people.

The monarch and Parliament governed not only Britain but also the British colonies in North America. But the people living in the colonies were not allowed to vote in British elections. So, unlike other British citizens, the colonists could not elect lawmakers to speak and act for them in Parliament.

Some of the American colonists thought they should have **self-government**. That is, they thought they should be able to make their own laws. The colonists felt that people in Britain did not understand life in the colonies. After all, the colonies were more than 3,000 miles (4,828 km) away from London, Britain's capital city. What worked for Britain did not always work for the colonies, where ways of life were different.

As the colonies developed in the 1600s and 1700s, the monarch and Parliament let the colonists make some of the laws that affected them. Government in the British colonies became more like a **democracy**, a government in which the people take part. But Parliament was quick to remind the colonists that they were British subjects. Parliament had to approve the laws the colonists made. And the colonists still had to follow the laws made by Parliament.

The British colonists welcomed the chance for self-government. In New England, towns had been making

The British flag in 1750

North America in 1750

NORTH AMERICA

PACIFIC OCEAN

Hudson Bay

NEW FRANCE

LOUISIANA

ATLANTIC OCEAN

BRITISH COLONIES

FLORIDA

NEW SPAIN

Gulf of Mexico

Caribbean Sea

140°W

50°N

50°W

30°N

30°N

10°N

80°W

N W E S

British
French
Spanish
Russian
Disputed

0   600   1,200 Miles
0   600   1,200 Kilometers
Azimuthal Equal-Area Projection

Regions This map shows the lands in North America that were claimed by Europeans in 1750. Notice that the British claimed much of the Atlantic coast.

■ *What advantages did the British gain by having control of the coast?*

laws from the beginning. Soon every colony began making its own laws. People serving in **legislatures**, which were like small, local Parliaments, made most of the decisions. The first of these colonial legislatures was known as the House of Burgesses. It was established in the Virginia colony in 1619.

The 13 colonial legislatures were made up of wealthy male property owners. People were elected to the legislatures by the property owners in each

colony. The legislatures made laws for ruling their own colonies and set up local militias for protection.

Besides its legislature, each colony had a governor. The king chose the governor of a royal colony. In proprietary colonies, the proprietor named the governor. The governor made sure that the laws the colonial legislatures made were ones the British government would agree to. The governor also made sure that the colonists obeyed the laws passed in Britain.

REVIEW *How were laws made for governing the British colonies?*

The French and Indian War

British colonists ruled themselves without problems for many years. Then, little by little, things began to change. In 1753 the French in Canada began building forts on lands in the Ohio River valley claimed by both France and Britain. The British colonists viewed this move as an attack.

In the fighting that followed, both the French and the British colonists were helped by their Indian **allies**, or friends in war. The British colonists, however, could not fight off the French and their Indian allies with just the help of their own Indian allies. The British government sent its army to help the colonists fight what came to be called the French and Indian War. With the help of the British army and of their Indian allies, especially the Iroquois, the British colonists defeated the French and their Indian allies in 1763.

This horn, used to carry gunpowder, was given to a British officer during the French and Indian War. It is engraved with a map showing some of the areas where the heaviest fighting took place.

The French and Indian War, 1754–1763

NEW FRANCE

Quebec

St. Lawrence R.

Ft. Beauséjour

Ft. Louisbourg

Lake Huron

Montreal

Lake Champlain

MAINE (part of Mass.)

Ft. Frontenac

Lake Ontario

Ft. Crown Point

Ft. Ticonderoga

Ft. William Henry

Ft. Niagara

Ft. Oswego

Ft. Edward

NEW HAMPSHIRE

ATLANTIC OCEAN

Ft. Presqu' Isle

NEW YORK

MASSACHUSETTS

Boston

Lake Erie

Ft. Le Boeuf

CONNECTICUT

RHODE ISLAND

Ft. Duquesne

PENNSYLVANIA

New York City

Ft. Necessity

Ft. Ligonier

Philadelphia

Ohio River

Ft. Cumberland

MARYLAND

NEW JERSEY

Baltimore

DELAWARE

VIRGINIA

0   100   200 Miles
0   100   200 Kilometers
Azimuthal Equal-Area Projection

N W E S

British territory — British fort
French territory — French fort
Disputed territory — Major battle
Present-day border

Human-Environment Interactions Both France and Britain built forts to protect the lands they claimed in North America.
■ *Where were most of the major battles of the French and Indian War fought?*

MAP THEME

After the French and Indian War, French Canada became a British colony. The British also gained French lands in North America between the Appalachian Mountains and the Mississippi River. Many British colonists were eager to settle these new western lands.

The British had won more land, but the French and Indian War had cost a lot of money. Keeping British soldiers in North America to protect the newly won land cost even more. Someone had to pay for the armies needed to make and keep the peace.

The people in Britain were already paying heavy **taxes**, or money paid to a government to run the country. They refused to pay more

to take care of what seemed to be a colonial problem. So King George III and Parliament decided that the colonists would have to pay for part of the cost of the war. They would also have to pay for the cost of keeping British soldiers in North America.

The colonists agreed to this plan, but many were angry about it. The colonial legislatures had been making their own tax laws. Now Parliament was telling them what taxes to pay. Then the British king took two more steps that angered the colonists.

First, he gave an order stating that the colonists were to stop settling the western lands just won from France. Settlers already

This scene from 1704 shows an early conflict between France's Indian allies and American colonists in the town of Deerfield, Massachusetts. Why do you think the Indians fought on different sides?

living in the area were to leave immediately. This order was called the Proclamation of 1763. It reserved these lands for the Native Americans as their "hunting grounds." The king hoped this order would prevent more wars between the colonists and the Indians. But the colonists became furious.

Then, to make matters worse, the king gave his colonial governors greater **authority**, or control, over the colonies. The colonists were allowed to keep their legislatures. However, the governor could order the legislatures to change any laws he did not like.

The colonists did not expect these changes. They had hoped to gain more authority to govern themselves. Now the colonists were reminded that they had to obey laws made in London. The colonists felt that the king knew little or nothing about their lives in North America. But what could they do?

REVIEW *How did the lives of the British colonists change after the French and Indian War?*

LESSON I REVIEW

Check Understanding

1 Remember the Facts What were the causes of the French and Indian War?

2 Recall the Main Idea Why did the colonists become unhappy with British rule after the French and Indian War?

Think Critically

3 Think More About It Why do you think only wealthy male property owners were allowed to serve in colonial legislatures?

4 Explore Viewpoints Explain how each of the following people might have felt about the Proclamation of 1763: a member of Parliament, a colonist, and a Native American.

Show What You Know

Speech Activity Plan a speech in favor of colonial self-government to give to the British Parliament. Present your speech to the class.

Use a Historical Map

1. Why Learn This Skill?

A historical map gives information about a place as it was in the past. It can show where past events took place. It can also show what features cities and countries had at a particular time. Knowing how to use a historical map can help you gather information about the past.

2. Understand the Process

Many atlases and history books contain historical maps. The title of a historical map usually tells you the subject of the map and the time period the map shows. The map on this page shows North America in 1763, at the end of the French and Indian War.

North America in 1763

British

British (reserved for Indians)

French

Spanish

Russian

Disputed

Proclamation Line of 1763

PACIFIC OCEAN

NORTH AMERICA

NEW SPAIN

LOUISIANA

13 COLONIES

FLORIDA

Hudson Bay

ATLANTIC OCEAN

Gulf of Mexico

Caribbean Sea

SOUTH AMERICA

50°N

140°W

30°N

70°N

50°W

50°N

30°N

80°W

10°N

0   600   1,200 Miles

0   600   1,200 Kilometers

Azimuthal Equal-Area Projection

Look at the map key to learn what each symbol means. Then use these questions to guide you in gathering information.

1. What color shows the land controlled by the Russians in 1763? by the French? by the Spanish?

2. What land did the Russians control in North America at this time?

3. Which country controlled more land in North America in 1763, Britain or France?

4. Which country claimed Florida in 1763?

One of the symbols in the map key has a pattern of diagonal stripes, called **hatch lines**. Hatch lines are often used on historical maps to indicate land that was claimed by more than one country or land that had a special purpose. The map key on this page tells you that land shown by hatch lines was controlled by the British—that is why one of the colors of the hatch lines is the same as the color used for the British. It also tells you that the British reserved this land for another group—the Native Americans.

In 1763 the British drew an imaginary line through North America called the Proclamation Line of 1763. Find the line on the map. The Proclamation Line of 1763 served as the border between the land of the 13 colonies and the land that the British reserved for the Native Americans.

3. Think and Apply

Look at the map on page 226 showing North America in 1750. Then write a paragraph that tells what the map shows and why historical maps are useful. What time period is shown? What symbols are used to show information? How was the United States different then from the way it is today? Share your paragraph with a classmate.

MAP SKILLS

Self-Government or

After the French and Indian War, Britain and the colonies began to disagree on matters of government. People had different ideas about what colonies were for and who should govern them. Here are five opinions on British rule and colonial self-government.

Joseph Fish

Joseph Fish was a minister in Connecticut. Like many colonists, he did not talk much about public affairs. But in this case he had very strong feelings. In a letter to his daughter Mary, he wrote:

66 They [the British] seem determined to distress us to the last degree, if not to destroy us, unless we submit to the yoke of slavery they have prepared for us. 99

John Appleton

John Appleton was a merchant in Charleston, South Carolina. He traded tobacco, rice, and lumber for tea from China and cloth from India. This was his opinion:

66 We were doing fine here in the colonies when they [the king and Parliament] left us alone. Now I find taxes on everything I bring into the colonies to sell. It is bound to hurt business. 99

British Leader

In a letter to a friend, a member of Parliament told how he felt about the colonies. Here is part of his letter:

66 Certainly, you don't think we are going to let all these colonies make whatever rules they want. English authority must be obeyed wherever the English flag flies. 99

The idea of self-government was important to many families living in the colonies.

British Rule?

Parliament

A committee of Parliament wrote a report on the purpose of the colonies. This is what part of the report said:

&6 We must remind all members of Parliament that colonies were set up for the good of England, not for the good of the colonists. These settlements can provide us with many needed things—tobacco, lumber, whale oil, fish, grain, and furs. And, they also provide England with a place to sell our manufactured goods. 99

Prime Minister

In a speech to the members of Parliament, Prime Minister George Grenville explained why new rules were being made for the colonies. Here is part of what he said:

&6 So it is only right and just that the colonists help to pay for the protection we are giving them. Clearly, Parliament and the King have authority over the colonies. It is in the name of that authority that we suggest new rules which will make the colonists pay taxes to the English government. 99

Compare Viewpoints

1. What views about government did each person or group hold?
2. Why do you think each person or group held those views?

Think and Apply

People often hold different views about issues because of their jobs or backgrounds or the places where they live. Choose an issue about which the people in your class or community have different ideas. Find out what people think about the issue.

Many people in Britain had strong opinions about colonial rule.

FOCUS

How do individuals and groups today work to make changes in their government?

Main Idea Read to learn how individuals and groups in the British colonies worked to make changes in their government.

Vocabulary

tariff	repeal
Loyalist	massacre
representation	
treason	
public opinion	
petition	
liberty	
boycott	
congress	

Quarrels and Conflicts

The people in the 13 British colonies had to buy many goods they could not grow or make themselves. They bought sugar, molasses, paper, glass, lead, paint, and tea from Britain, the British colonies in the Caribbean, and other countries. To pay for these goods, the colonists sold furs, fish, wood, tobacco, rice, wheat, corn, cattle, and other products to the British and people in other countries. Quarrels over these imports and exports were among the first to come between the colonists and their British rulers.

New Taxes for the Colonists

When Parliament decided that the colonists should help pay the cost of the French and Indian War, it also decided how the payment would be made. In 1764 Parliament passed a law that came to be known as the Sugar Act. This law said the colonists must pay a tax on many goods coming to the colonies from other places. When colonists bought a pound of sugar, for example, they had to pay an extra amount in addition to the item's price. The extra money they paid was a **tariff**, a tax on goods brought into a country.

This tariff angered many colonists. What bothered these colonists the most was that they had had no part in making this tax law. The king and Parliament had taxed the colonists without their consent.

Two of the first colonists to speak out against the new taxes were Mercy Otis Warren and her brother, James Otis, of Massachusetts. She called the British "greedy," while he called the tariff "unjust" and "a burden."

But not all the colonists agreed with Warren and Otis. Some held the British view. These people were called **Loyalists** or Tories. Loyalist Martin Howard of Rhode Island felt that the colonists should be more grateful to the king and Parliament than they were. After all, he and other Loyalists argued, without British help, France or even Spain

Barrels like this one were used to ship goods during colonial times.

Under the Stamp Act, colonists had to pay for stamps (left) to be attached to printed goods of all kinds. The tax money collected for the stamps was sent to the British government. Some colonists made cartoon stamps (right) to show how they felt about the Stamp Act.

might have ruled the colonists. As Howard said, "Yet for a moment I wish that those unworthy subjects of Britain could feel the iron rod of a Spanish inquisitor or a French tax agent. This would indeed be a punishment suited to their ungrateful feelings."

REVIEW *What did the colonists think of the new taxes on sugar and other goods?*

The Stamp Act

Less than a year after the Sugar Act went into effect, Parliament made another tax law. This one angered the colonists more than the first had. It was called the Stamp Act. Almost everything written or printed on paper in the colonies—from newspapers to playing cards—had to have a special stamp on it to show that a tax had been paid.

In the case of the Stamp Act, as with the other tariffs, the money was not the issue that the colonists minded most. What really bothered them was that they had not agreed to

the taxes. They had no **representation** in Parliament—no one acting or speaking for them.

James Otis asked his fellow colonists not to buy paper goods that had been stamped. Otis told a crowd in Boston that they should refuse to pay the taxes. Many colonists began repeating Otis's words,

66 no taxation without
representation. 99

Other colonists also dared to speak out against the Stamp Act. In Virginia, Patrick Henry told the members of the House of Burgesses that they alone should decide what taxes were placed. Henry said that Parliament did not represent the colonies. The colonies had their own legislatures to represent them.

Some Loyalist Virginia lawmakers shouted "Treason!" By accusing Patrick Henry of **treason**, they were saying that he was working against the government. "If this

Chapter 7 • 233

be treason, make the most of it," Henry answered.

What James Otis and Patrick Henry had said about the Stamp Act influenced **public opinion**, or what people thought, in the colonies. The Virginia legislature listened to Patrick Henry. It voted against paying any new taxes the monarch or Parliament made unless the colonists agreed to them. More and more people decided not to buy goods that had been stamped. Everywhere people were repeating the words *no taxation without representation*.

REVIEW *Why were many colonists angry at the British government about the Stamp Act?*

People Protest in Different Ways

Word of the colonists' anger over the Stamp Act soon reached King George III and the British Parliament. Some members of Parliament said that James Otis and Patrick Henry should be thrown in prison for speaking out against the government. But no harm came to the two men.

Some colonists wrote letters to Parliament about the law. Others held public meetings and sent long **petitions**—requests for action signed by many people—asking King George III to change the Stamp Act. But the king paid little attention to the colonists.

Throughout the 13 colonies, people met in groups to talk and act against the new taxes. In the Massachusetts colony, they called themselves the Sons of Liberty and the Daughters of Liberty. *Liberty* was the word heard over and over again. To most colonists, **liberty** meant freedom to make their own laws.

Members of these groups told other colonists that they should stop buying the stamped goods. They even asked the people to **boycott**, or refuse to buy, any British goods. In Boston the Daughters of Liberty knitted, wove cloth, and spun thread so that

Crowds often gathered to hear Patrick Henry's fiery speeches. Henry, shown here arguing a court case, was a lawyer and a member of the House of Burgesses.

colonists could boycott British-made cloth. People sang this song:

" Young ladies in town and those that live 'round,
Wear none but your own country linen,
Of economy [saving money] boast, let your pride be the most,
To show clothes of your own make and spinning. "

Some of the Sons of Liberty protested in more violent ways. They attacked the homes of tax collectors and other royal officials, breaking their windows and stealing their property. They beat some tax collectors and chased several out of the Massachusetts colony.

Other colonists tried peaceful ways of protest. They decided to talk directly to the British lawmakers. The Pennsylvania legislature sent representatives to ask Parliament to think about the colonists' wish for representation. Among those sent was Benjamin Franklin of Philadelphia.

Over the course of 50 years he had helped change Philadelphia from a simple colonial town to one of the best-planned cities in North America. He had organized the volunteer fire department, started Philadelphia's first hospital, and directed street lighting and paving projects. He also had organized the town watch, a group of volunteers that protected Philadelphia's citizens. Benjamin Franklin was the city's and the colony's most respected scientist, business leader, and citizen.

Franklin warned the British lawmakers that the colonists would fight if Parliament sent the British army to make them pay the new taxes. He said, "The seeds of liberty are universally sown there [in Pennsylvania], and nothing can eradicate [destroy] them." But British leaders did not listen to Franklin's warning.

REVIEW *In what different ways did colonists act against the new taxes?*

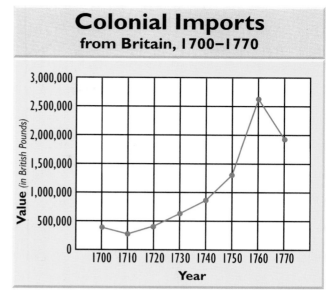

Colonial Imports
from Britain, 1700–1770

LEARNING FROM GRAPHS This graph shows the value of the goods imported from Britain to the 13 colonies between 1700 and 1770. The values are shown in British pounds, the money used in both Britain and the colonies.

■ *Between which years did colonial imports increase the most?*

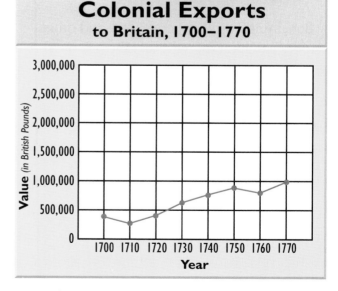

Colonial Exports
to Britain, 1700–1770

LEARNING FROM GRAPHS This graph shows the value of the goods exported from the 13 colonies to Britain between 1700 and 1770.

■ *Why do you think that in many years the colonists imported more goods than they exported?*

Benjamin Franklin was an inventor and a scientist as well as a colonial leader. Among his inventions were the bifocal reading glasses (above) and the lightning rod.

The Stamp Act Congress

Benjamin Franklin, James Otis, and other leaders had long thought that the colonies should work together instead of acting separately. In 1765 people who felt this way held a meeting in New York City called the Stamp Act Congress. A **congress** is a meeting of representatives who have the authority to make decisions. Nine colonies sent representatives to the Stamp Act Congress. They discussed the problems that the new tax laws had caused. The congress decided to ask people in all the colonies to refuse to buy stamped goods.

When Parliament heard about the Stamp Act Congress and the anger of the colonists, it **repealed** the Stamp Act. This meant that the Stamp Act was no longer a law. Although Parliament repealed this law, in 1767 it added some new ones, called the Townshend Acts,

that affected trade in the colonies. By passing these new laws, the British government wanted to show that it still could make laws for the colonists.

To prove its authority over the colonists, Parliament sent more soldiers to North America. By 1770 there were more than 9,000 British soldiers in the 13 colonies. The colonists were told that the soldiers were there to protect the far-off western lands won in the French and Indian War. But the soldiers were in the cities along the eastern coast!

Having British soldiers in their cities angered many of the colonists. The soldiers seemed like a police force that the colonists did not need. Sometimes this anger led to rock-throwing and name-calling. The colonists called the British soldiers "redcoats" and "bloodybacks," making fun of their red uniforms. The British soldiers paid them back by destroying colonial property and doing

This engraving (far left) by Paul Revere shows his view of the Boston Massacre. Crispus Attucks (left) and four others were killed. The drawing below appeared on protest posters and contained the initials of the five people who were killed.

other damage—by riding their horses through churches and other buildings, for example.

As the anger between the British soldiers and the colonists grew stronger, fights broke out more and more often. Some of the worst fighting took place in Boston on March 5, 1770. In the evening a crowd gathered near several British soldiers. Some colonists in the crowd shouted insults at the soldiers and began to throw rocks and snowballs. As the crowd moved forward, the soldiers opened fire. Three colonists were killed, and two died

later. Among the dead was a 47-year-old runaway slave named Crispus Attucks (AT•uhks). Attucks had led the charge against the soldiers. He was the first person to be killed for American independence.

The events of that day have become known as the Boston Massacre. A **massacre** is the killing of a number of people who cannot defend themselves. Soon after the Boston Massacre took place, an uneasy calm settled over the 13 colonies.

REVIEW *What was the purpose of the Stamp Act Congress?*

LESSON 2 REVIEW

Check Understanding

1. **Remember the Facts** Why did the Sugar Act anger the colonists?

2. **Recall the Main Idea** How did the colonists work to make changes in the British government?

Think Critically

3. **Past to Present** How do you think people would feel today if they were taxed without representation?

4. **Think More About It** Why do you think the British government wanted to show its authority over the colonies?

5. **Cause and Effect** Why did the British want to make new tax laws for the colonies? What happened when they did?

Show What You Know

Writing Activity Imagine that you are a reporter who has just interviewed a colonist protesting British rule. Write a newspaper article that describes this person's opinion on British taxation or the representation the colonists have. In the article, tell whether or not you share the opinion.

FOCUS

What brings people together in difficult times?

Main Idea As you read, think about what brought the colonists together as they protested British rule.

Vocabulary

Committee of
  Correspondence
consequence
blockade
quarter
Continental Congress
right
Minuteman
Patriot

Colonists Unite

In the months following the Boston Massacre, King George III received report after report of continued fighting and boycotts in the 13 British colonies. Petitions, too, poured in to the king from the colonists. When the king chose not to act on them, the colonists decided to act on their own.

The Committees of Correspondence

The Stamp Act Congress had shown that the colonists could work together. But when their representatives were not meeting, it was not as easy for them to work together or even to communicate from day to day. This was because news traveled slowly. It could take weeks for people in one colony to find out what was happening in the other colonies.

In November 1772, Samuel Adams of Massachusetts found an answer to this problem. Adams was one of his colony's leaders. He had spoken out many times against British rule.

Adams's answer was to set up a Committee of Correspondence in Boston. Just three months later, 80 committees had been organized in the Massachusetts colony. Samuel Adams then got cities and towns in other colonies to do the same.

These **Committees of Correspondence** corresponded with, or wrote letters to, one another. Writers told what was being done in their colonies to protest the latest British laws. The letters were then delivered by riders on horseback. In this way anything that happened in one colony quickly became known in all the others.

Quill pens used during colonial times were made from feathers. The person using a pen dipped the tip in a small bottle of ink.

REVIEW *Why were the Committees of Correspondence set up?*

The Boston Tea Party

In 1773 Parliament passed another new law. This law allowed a British company to sell tea in the colonies for a very low price. This would hurt colonial merchants, and the colonists would still have to pay a tax on tea!

People in every colony soon decided to boycott British tea. In Pennsylvania and New York, colonists did not allow ships carrying British tea to enter their ports. In Massachusetts, however, ships' captains refused to be turned away. Angry colonists showed their feelings in what later became known as the Boston Tea Party.

British ships carrying tea arrived in Boston Harbor in December 1773. Late one night, members of the Sons of Liberty, disguised as Mohawk Indians, boarded the ships, broke open all the chests of tea, and dumped the tea into the harbor. As they threw the tea overboard, they sang:

> 66 Rally, Mohawks! bring out your
> axes,
> And tell King George we'll pay no
> taxes. 99

The colonists knew that their actions could have very serious **consequences** (KAHN•suh•kwens•ihz), or results. After hearing about the Boston Tea Party, Parliament decided to punish the colony of Massachusetts. A law was passed saying that no ship carrying colonial goods could leave Boston Harbor until the colonists paid for all the tea that had been destroyed. To enforce the new law,

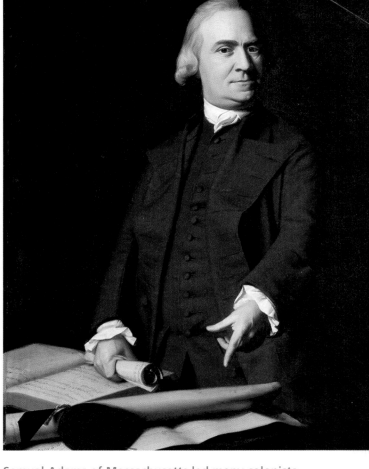

Samuel Adams of Massachusetts led many colonists in protesting British rule. He helped form the Sons of Liberty and organized the Committees of Correspondence.

More than 300 chests of tea were dumped into Boston Harbor during the Boston Tea Party. Legend says that this chest washed ashore the next morning.

Parliament ordered the Royal Navy to blockade Boston Harbor. To **blockade** is to use warships to prevent other ships from entering or leaving a harbor. The British government wanted to show the colonists that they had to obey its laws.

To further prove its authority, the British government ordered the colonists to **quarter** British soldiers, or pay for their housing. The colonists had to feed the soldiers and give them a place to sleep. The king also made General Thomas Gage the new

This painting shows one artist's idea of what happened at the Boston Tea Party. One colonist remembered, "In about three hours from the time we went on board, we had thus broken and thrown overboard every tea chest to be found."

colonial governor of Massachusetts. Gage was head of the British army in North America. In response to the new laws, colonists shouted, "Intolerable acts!" These new laws soon became known as the Intolerable Acts.

People acted against the tax on tea in other colonies, too. In Edenton, North Carolina, a colonist named Penelope Barker led 51 women in a "tea party" of their own. They agreed to do everything they could to help with the tea boycott. They declared that they could not "be indifferent to whatever affected the peace and happiness of the country." The Edenton Tea Party has been called by one historian "the earliest known instance of political activity on the part of women in the American colonies."

REVIEW *Why did colonists hold the Boston and Edenton tea parties?*

The Continental Congress

Many of the colonists believed that the British government would do anything, even use its army, to make them obey the laws. So the Committees of Correspondence called a meeting of representatives of all the colonies to decide what to do. The meeting took place in Philadelphia in September 1774. Because it was the first meeting of its kind on the North American continent, the colonists called it the **Continental Congress**. Representatives from every colony except Georgia came to the meeting.

Members of the Continental Congress agreed to stop all trade with Britain. The Congress also said that the colonies would no longer obey British laws when the laws took away their liberty as citizens. The colonists told Parliament, "We are *for the present* only resolved to pursue . . . peaceable measures." The Congress agreed that if the demands for colonial **rights**, or freedoms, were not met, it would meet again in May 1775 to decide what to do next.

In Virginia the House of Burgesses suggested that colonists start preparing for war. Others strongly opposed the idea. In March of 1775, Patrick Henry gave the most famous speech of his career. Americans have long remembered its final words:

> 66 I know not what course others may take; but as for me, give me liberty or give me death! 99

REVIEW *Why did the Continental Congress meet?*

Fighting at Lexington and Concord

By the end of the Continental Congress, anger against the British government had turned Massachusetts into an armed camp. Members of the colony's militia companies became **Minutemen**, fighters who could be ready in a minute to defend Massachusetts. The British, too, kept their soldiers and their weapons ready.

The colonists who were against the British now called themselves **Patriots**. In April 1775 British General Thomas Gage, the new governor of Massachusetts, heard that the Patriots were storing weapons

"One if by land, two if by sea." Two lanterns hanging in a church tower signaled that the British were coming to Concord by boat across the Charles River.

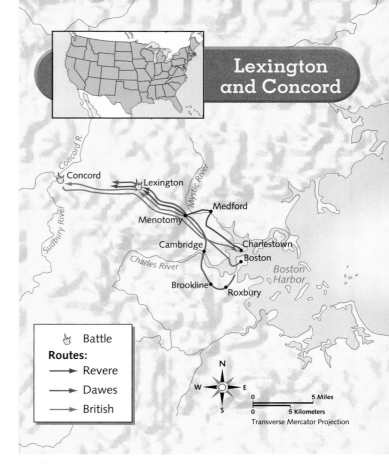

Lexington and Concord

Battle
Routes:
→ Revere
→ Dawes
→ British

Movement   The battles at Lexington and Concord were the first of the Revolutionary War.

■ *What cities did Revere and Dawes ride through to warn of the British approach?*

in the town of Concord near Boston. Gage also heard that John Hancock and Samuel Adams, two leaders of the Sons of Liberty, were staying nearby, in the village of Lexington. The general sent 700 British soldiers to find the weapons and arrest the Patriot leaders.

But Paul Revere and William Dawes, members of the Sons of Liberty, rode out on the night of April 18 to warn Hancock and Adams that British soldiers were on their way. When the British arrived in Lexington on April 19, they found Minutemen waiting for them. The Minutemen were of all

Paul Revere
1735–1818

Paul Revere was one of the few people in Boston to own a horse. He kept one because he liked to spend his free time galloping through the countryside. Revere was a silversmith. As a Son of Liberty, Revere often carried messages from the Boston Committee of Correspondence to committees in other towns. In 1773 he rode to Philadelphia with news of the Boston Tea Party. But his most famous ride was the one he made to Lexington on the night of April 18, 1775, carrying the news "the British are coming!"

ages. Many owned property. Some were workingmen. At least five were Africans. Several of them were slaves. Shots were fired, and eight of the Minutemen were killed. Several others were wounded.

The British marched on to Concord, but the weapons they expected to find had been moved. As they marched back to Boston, they were shot at by Minutemen from the woods and fields beside the road. British losses for the day were 73 killed and 174 wounded. Of the 4,000 Minutemen at Lexington and Concord, 93 were killed or wounded in the fighting.

To honor the event, poet Ralph Waldo Emerson wrote a poem called the "Concord Hymn," which begins,

> 66 By the rude bridge that arched the
>   flood,
>   Their flag to April's breeze unfurled,
>   Here once the embattled farmers
>   stood,
>   And fired the shot heard round the
>   world. 99

The shots fired at Lexington and Concord marked the beginning of a long, bitter war between Britain and its American colonies.

REVIEW *Why did the British go to Lexington and Concord?*

LESSON 3 REVIEW

Check Understanding

1 **Remember the Facts** How did the Committees of Correspondence help bring the colonies together?

2 **Recall the Main Idea** What brought the colonists together as they protested British rule?

Think Critically

3 **Explore Viewpoints** Describe how people in each of these groups might have viewed the Boston Tea Party: Parliament, Loyalists, Patriots.

4 **Personally Speaking** Do you think the Minutemen had any advantages over the British soldiers? Explain your answer.

Show What You Know
Letter-Writing Activity
Imagine that it is the spring of 1775, and you are a member of the Committee of Correspondence in Boston. Write a letter to a member of the committee in Philadelphia, telling what is taking place in your city.

Make Economic Choices

1. Why Learn This Skill?

When you buy something at the store or decide what to order at a restaurant, you are making an economic choice. Sometimes making an economic choice is difficult. In order to buy or do one thing, you have to give up buying or doing something else. This is called a **trade-off**. What you give up is the **opportunity cost** of what you get. Knowing about trade-offs and opportunity costs can help you make thoughtful economic choices.

2. Remember What You Have Read

Like people today, the colonists had to make many economic choices. They, too, faced tradeoffs and opportunity costs. Their economic choices, however, were made even more difficult by the continuing protests against British rule.

You have read that in 1773 Parliament passed a new law that affected the tea trade in the colonies. How did many colonists show their anger over the new law?

3. Understand the Process

Imagine that you are a colonist living in Annapolis, Maryland, in 1774. Like many other colonists, you like to drink tea. You have to make a choice. Should you buy British tea? Or should you buy the local tea, sassafras?

❶ Think about the trade-offs. To do this, you must balance the advantages and disadvantages of your choices. British tea tastes much better than sassafras, but you would have to pay a tax. And by buying British tea, you would not be taking part in the boycott. Sassafras tea does not cost as much, but it tastes spicy. Buying sassafras tea, however, would show that you support the boycott.

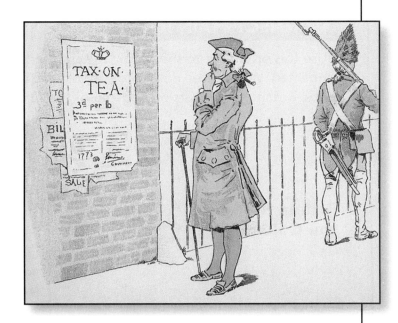

A colonist in Boston reads a notice about the tea tax.

❷ Think about the opportunity costs. You do not have enough money to buy both teas, so you have to give up one. If you buy the British tea, you give up extra money to pay the tax. You also give up taking part in the boycott. If you show support for the boycott by buying the sassafras, you give up the good taste of the British tea. What choice would you make?

4. Think and Apply

Imagine that a family member has given you $25 for your birthday, and you are trying to decide how to spend it. You may want to buy two compact discs or take some friends out for pizza. You do not have to spend all your money on one thing. You can choose some of one thing and some of another. Explain to a partner the trade-offs and opportunity costs of your choices.

1750   1755

1754
• The French
and Indian
War begins

CONNECT MAIN IDEAS

Use this organizer to show how the chapter's main ideas are connected. Write three details to support each main idea. A copy of the organizer appears on page 45 of the Activity Book.

Britain Rules the Colonies

Differences Divide Britain and Its Colonies

Britain and the Colonies Go to War

Government in the Colonies

The British colonists became unhappy with British rule.

1. _____
2. _____
3. _____

Quarrels and Conflicts

Individuals and groups in the British colonies worked to make changes in their government.

1. _____
2. _____
3. _____

Colonists Unite

The colonists came together as they protested British rule.

1. _____
2. _____
3. _____

WRITE MORE ABOUT IT

Write a Persuasive Letter Imagine that you are living in one of the British colonies in 1770. Write a letter in which you try to persuade a member of Parliament to help American colonists gain self-government.

Write a Report Choose one of the colonists you read about in this chapter. Then write a report on his or her life. Explain the person's role in the events leading to the American Revolution.

1763
• The French and Indian War ends

1765
• The Stamp Act Congress

1767
• The Townshend Acts

1770
• The Boston Massacre

1773
• The Boston Tea Party

1775
• Fighting at Lexington and Concord

USE VOCABULARY

For each group of terms, write a sentence or two that explains how the terms are related.

1 self-government, democracy

2 tax, tariff

3 Parliament, congress

4 Loyalist, Patriot

5 boycott, petition

6 liberty, right

CHECK UNDERSTANDING

7 How were laws made for the British colonies?

8 What was the purpose of the Proclamation of 1763? How did most colonists react to it?

9 Why were some colonists unhappy with the Sugar Act?

10 Why was the Stamp Act repealed?

11 What was the purpose of the Committees of Correspondence?

12 Why did the Intolerable Acts make the colonists so angry?

13 Who were the Minutemen?

14 What was the effect of the fighting at Lexington and Concord?

THINK CRITICALLY

15 **Personally Speaking** Do you think it was the colonists' responsibility to help pay for the French and Indian War? Explain your answer.

16 **Explore Viewpoints** What do you think members of Parliament thought about the idea of taxation without representation?

17 **Cause and Effect** What were some of the causes and effects of the Boston Tea Party?

18 **Think More About It** How do you think the Committees of Correspondence affected decisions made by colonial leaders?

APPLY SKILLS

Use a Historical Map Compare the map on page 229 with a present-day political map of the United States. What states have been formed from the land that the British reserved for Indians in 1763.

Make Economic Choices Imagine that you need to choose between buying a video game or a pair of soccer shoes. How would you make this economic choice? Identify the trade-offs and opportunity costs.

READ MORE ABOUT IT

The Boston Tea Party by Laurie A. O'Neill. Millbrook Press. Diaries, letters, and biographies bring to life the Boston Tea Party.

HARCOURT BRACE

Visit the Internet at
http://www.hbschool.com
for additional resources.

CHAPTER 8

THE WAR FOR INDEPENDENCE

"In Freedom we're born, and like Sons of the brave, Will never surrender, . . ."

Mercy Otis Warren, American writer

246

At War with the Homeland

LESSON
1

FOCUS
What might give one side an advantage over the other in a war today?

Main Idea As you read, think about what gave the British army an advantage over the Continental army as the war began.

Vocabulary
olive branch
Continental
mercenary
enlist

The Committees of Correspondence quickly spread the news of the fighting at Lexington and Concord. A second Continental Congress was called, and it met in Philadelphia in May 1775. Some of the most important colonial leaders went to the meeting to decide what to do now that a battle had been fought. Pennsylvania sent Benjamin Franklin. Massachusetts sent John Hancock, Samuel Adams, and John Adams. Virginia sent George Washington and the fiery Patrick Henry.

The Second Continental Congress

The Second Continental Congress moved carefully. The Patriots sent a letter called the Olive Branch Petition to King George III, telling him of their desire for peace and asking him to repeal the Intolerable Acts. An **olive branch** has stood for peace since ancient times. But in case the king refused to repeal the laws, the Second Continental Congress decided to form a colonial army.

The Congress asked all the colonies to send soldiers to Massachusetts. It chose George Washington of Virginia to lead this new Continental army. Washington, who had fought in the French and Indian War, came to the meeting in uniform to show that he would like to be the army's general. But it was Washington's understanding of soldiers and war that caused the Congress to choose him instead of such leaders as Artemas Ward, Charles Lee, or John Hancock.

The Second Continental Congress asked each colony to give money to support the new army. The money was needed to pay full-time soldiers and to buy guns, bullets, food, and uniforms. The Congress also voted to print its own paper money, which came to be known as Continental currency.

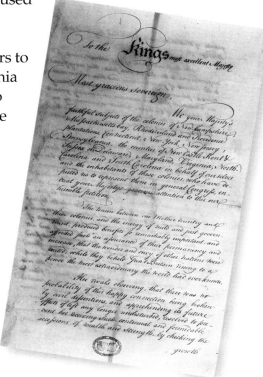

The Patriots sent the king the Olive Branch Petition to ask him to repeal unfair laws.

Philadelphia

Philadelphia calls itself "The Most Historic City in America"—and with good reason. It first earned its place in history in 1774, when the First Continental Congress met in Carpenters' Hall, in the city's center. Over the next 30 years, many of the most important events in American history took place in Philadelphia.

This scene of colonial Philadelphia shows the intersection of Second and Market.

In everything it did, the Congress wanted to believe the words of Patrick Henry:

66 The distinctions between Virginians, Pennsylvanians, New Yorkers are no more. I am not a Virginian but an American. 99

The Second Continental Congress came to stand for the new unity of the 13 colonies.

REVIEW *Why did colonial leaders call a second meeting of the Continental Congress?*

The Continental Army

George Washington left Philadelphia right away to take charge of his army, which had already fought its first major battle. The Battle of Bunker Hill, which took place in Boston on June 17, 1775, was one of the fiercest battles of the whole war. It was so fierce that to save bullets, the colonists were ordered, "Don't fire until you see the whites of their eyes." The colonists drove the British back twice before running out of bullets.

General George Washington arrived in Massachusetts to meet his army less than three weeks after this battle. The 14,500 soldiers, mostly from the northern colonies, wore no uniforms—only their ordinary clothes. Those who had guns carried flintlock muskets, which could not be used to shoot very far. Many of the soldiers had no guns at all. Instead, they carried spears and axes as weapons.

Some of Washington's soldiers had fought on the frontier and in the French and Indian War. The soldiers had learned to fight the way the Native Americans did—in irregular lines and from hiding places. They did not fight the way a European army would—side by side in straight lines. In fact, they had never fought as an army. Washington made rules for his soldiers and trained them. Slowly, Washington created the beginning of an army whose soldiers were proud to be called **Continentals**. The Continentals made up the first colonial army.

With little money and not much training, the Continentals went to war against the most powerful army in the world. Later, an officer would report, "It is incredible that soldiers composed of men of every age, even children of fifteen, of whites and blacks, almost naked, unpaid, and rather poorly fed, can march so well and withstand fire so steadfastly."

REVIEW *What was the Continental army like when Washington took charge?*

The British Advantage

Unlike George Washington's army of mostly first-time soldiers, the British army was made up of professional soldiers. They had the best training, the most experienced officers, and the newest weapons. They also had help. The British used **mercenaries** (MER•suhn•air•eez), or hired soldiers, to fight on their side. Some of these soldiers were Hessians, from the Hesse region of Germany. The British also had Native American allies. Many tribes hated the colonists because settlers had taken over Indian lands.

But the British had problems, too. It was hard to fight a war that was 3,000 miles (4,828 km) from home. They had trouble getting supplies across the Atlantic Ocean.

The artist and soldier Charles Willson Peale painted this portrait of George Washington. The poster below called for young men to join Washington's Continental army to defend the American colonies from enemies.

This scene at the Battle of Bunker Hill in 1775 was painted by Howard Pyle. Although the British eventually took the hill, their way of marching in straight lines during an attack caused more than 1,000 British soldiers to be killed or wounded.

In the early days of the war, the British used their greater numbers and experience as fighters to take the advantage over the Continental army. While the British had 50,000 soldiers, General Washington usually had no more than 10,000 soldiers in his army at any one time. Most of the Americans **enlisted** in, or joined, the army for one year at a time. They might stay that long or longer, or they might not. When harvesttime came, some of the Continentals would go home to their farms. If they did not get their pay as soldiers, they would not stay in the army. Washington did his best to keep his army together.

REVIEW *How was the British army different from the Continental army?*

LESSON 1 REVIEW

Check Understanding

① **Remember the Facts**   What actions did the Second Continental Congress take?

② **Recall the Main Idea**   What gave the British army an advantage over the Continental army as the war began?

Think Critically

③ **Personally Speaking**   What do you think might have happened if the British king had accepted the Olive Branch Petition?

④ **Think More About It**   George Washington overcame many problems in leading his soldiers against the British army. What qualities should a good leader have?

Show What You Know

Simulation Activity   Role-play a conversation in which you tell a partner why he or she should join the Continental army. Try to make each side of the conversation as real as you can. Discuss your conversation with classmates.

Read a Political Cartoon

1. Why Learn This Skill?

Cartoons that express opinions about politics or about government are called **political cartoons**. Political cartoons are most often found in newspapers and magazines. Knowing how to read a political cartoon will help you understand its humor and its meaning.

2. Study an American Political Cartoon

Benjamin Franklin drew the cartoon shown on this page. It may have been the first American political cartoon. It appeared in the *Pennsylvania Gazette* in 1754. Franklin was representing the Pennsylvania colony at the Albany Congress in New York. At this meeting he presented a "Plan of Union" for the colonies. He hoped his cartoon would make colonial leaders want to unite.

Franklin used his cartoon to urge colonists to support his plan for a union. The snake in the cartoon stands for most of the colonies. Each piece of the snake represents one or more of the colonies. The saying "Join, or Die" was based on an old tale about snakes. According to this story, a snake that was cut into pieces would come to life again if it was put back together before sunset. Franklin wanted the pieces of the snake—the colonies—to come together to survive.

3. Understand the Process

In his cartoon, Benjamin Franklin used the snake as a symbol. Symbols are a good way to show ideas that are sometimes hard to draw in a picture—ideas such as unity among the colonies. The use of symbols can make the message of a political cartoon easier to understand.

Animals are often used as symbols for ideas in political cartoons. The eagle is often used to represent the idea of freedom. The dove stands for the idea of peace. The hawk stands for war. The snail is used as a symbol of slowness.

To understand the meaning of a political cartoon, you first need to identify the symbols that are used. Then you need to think about the ideas that the symbols stand for.

4. Think and Apply

Begin a collection of political cartoons. Cut political cartoons out of old newspapers or magazines. Then write short captions to help explain the meaning of each cartoon. Make up a political cartoon of your own to add to the collection.

Franklin hoped this cartoon would help unite the colonies. It represents all the colonies except Delaware and Georgia.

FOCUS

Why is it important for leaders today to explain the reasons for their decisions?

Main Idea Read to learn why it was important for colonial leaders to explain their decision to break free from British rule.

Vocabulary

revolution
independence
allegiance
declaration
grievance

The Decision for Independence

Although they were already at war, many colonists still believed that their problems with the British government could be settled without more fighting. They hoped the king and Parliament would let them take part in making the laws. By 1776 that thinking began to change, and the colonists prepared for a longer war.

The First Steps

One of the Patriots who did the most to change public opinion in the colonies was Thomas Paine. In January 1776 Paine published a pamphlet he called *Common Sense*. In it he attacked King George III as a bully and questioned the idea of one person having all the authority to rule. Thomas Paine felt that people should rule themselves. He called for a sudden, complete change of government—a **revolution** (reh•vuh•LOO•shuhn). The colonies should cut their ties with the British government, he said, and set up their own government.

People throughout the colonies talked about *Common Sense*. After nearly a year of war, the idea of **independence**, or freedom to govern on their own, sounded good to many colonists. It also sounded good to many members of the Second Continental Congress. The time to act had come.

On June 7, 1776, Richard Henry Lee of Virginia gave a speech to Congress. He said,

66 these United Colonies are and of right ought to be free and independent States. 99

He went on to say that the colonies no longer owed **allegiance** (uh•LEE•juhnts), or loyalty, to the king.

In Britain, Thomas Paine lost his job as a tax collector after asking for a raise. Benjamin Franklin, who was in London at the time, suggested that Paine go to America.

Benjamin Franklin, John Adams, and Thomas Jefferson (above) included in the Declaration the idea that a government gets its power from the consent of the people. This early copy (above right) shows some of the many changes Jefferson made as he wrote the Declaration of Independence. Jefferson's travel desk (right) holds the first draft of the Declaration of Independence.

The Congress waited almost a month before voting on the idea of cutting ties with the British government. Not all of the colonies were ready for independence. They needed more time to decide before taking such a dangerous step. The leaders of the Congress hoped that a month's wait would help all 13 colonies decide in favor of independence. In the meantime, they formed a committee to draw up a **declaration**, or official statement, of independence.

The members of the committee were Benjamin Franklin of Pennsylvania, John Adams of Massachusetts, Robert R. Livingston of New York, Roger Sherman of Connecticut, and Thomas Jefferson of Virginia. Each member added ideas about what the Declaration should say. Thomas Jefferson did most of the writing.

Only 33 years old, Thomas Jefferson was a leader of the Patriots in Virginia. He was a lawyer, he had studied government, and he had already written about the problems with British rule. Two years before, he had written *A Summary View of the Rights of British America,* in which he had listed for the First Continental Congress the changes the colonies wanted in their government. When the Declaration committee was selected, Jefferson began work at once. Every evening for the next 17 days, Jefferson wrote—and rewrote—the document that would become the Declaration of Independence.

REVIEW *Why did Congress wait before voting on independence?*

Writing the Declaration

Thomas Jefferson wanted his words to help the colonists win their war for freedom. He wrote very carefully. He had to state the facts so that people would agree that the cause for independence was right and that it was worth fighting for.

Jefferson planned the Declaration in several parts. In the introduction, he stated why the Declaration was needed. He said that sometimes a group of people must cut themselves off from the country they once belonged to. They find they have no choice but to form a new nation with the same authority as other independent countries. Jefferson said that when people do this, they must have good reasons. And, he said, they must explain their reasons so there is no doubt about why such a step is taken.

In the second part of the Declaration, Jefferson listed the colonists' main ideas about government. The words he wrote in 1776 are among the most famous in American history. Jefferson said:

66 We hold these truths to be self-evident, that all men are created equal, that they are endowed [provided] by their Creator with certain unalienable Rights, that among these are Life, Liberty and the pursuit of Happiness. 99

In the third and longest part of the Declaration, Jefferson listed the colonists' **grievances** (GREE•vuhns•ez), or complaints, about the unfair practices of the king and Parliament. He also listed the ways the colonists had tried to settle their differences with the British government peacefully. But, he noted, the king had refused to listen to the colonists. Such a king, Jefferson wrote, was "unfit to be the ruler of a free people."

John Trumbull's painting of the signing of the Declaration of Independence shows 48 members of the Second Continental Congress. The delegates met in Pennsylvania's State House, known today as Independence Hall. Those who signed the Declaration did so knowing that they were risking their lives and property.

Then, in the last part of the Declaration, Jefferson wrote that for all of the reasons he had described, the 13 colonies were no longer a part of Britain.

66 We, therefore, . . . in the Name, and by Authority of the good People of these Colonies, solemnly publish and declare, That these United Colonies are, and of Right ought to be Free and Independent States. . . . 99

When he finished writing, Jefferson gave the Declaration to Congress, and on June 28 it was read aloud. Then the members returned to Richard Henry Lee's idea of cutting ties with Britain. On the morning of July 2, 1776, Lee's idea was approved without a single "no" vote. The Congress spent the next two days talking about the Declaration. After several small changes were made, it was approved on July 4, 1776. The 13 colonies had declared independence.

REVIEW *What did Jefferson describe in the longest part of the Declaration of Independence?*

Independence Day

On July 4, 1776, the Second Continental Congress approved the Declaration of Independence. After the vote, the president of the Congress, John Hancock, signed his name to the document in large, bold writing. John Adams, writing home to his wife, Abigail, said that the event should be remembered with shows, games, sports, guns, bells, bonfires, and fireworks "from this time forward for evermore." Americans have celebrated the Fourth of July, or Independence Day, as a national holiday ever since.

On July 8, 1776, Patriots rang the Liberty Bell in Philadelphia's State House to celebrate the adoption of the Declaration of Independence. The bell was rung each year after that until it cracked in 1835. The words written on the bell, "Proclaim Liberty throughout all the land unto all the inhabitants thereof," are from the Bible.

LESSON 2 REVIEW

Check Understanding

1 **Remember the Facts** What was the purpose of each part of the Declaration of Independence?

2 **Recall the Main Idea** Why was it important for colonial leaders to explain their decision to break free from British rule?

Think Critically

3 **Think More About It** Why do you think colonial leaders asked Thomas Jefferson to write the Declaration of Independence?

4 **Personally Speaking** What do you think Jefferson meant when he wrote "all men are created equal"?

5 **Past to Present** Why do you think the Declaration is still important today?

Show What You Know

Art Activity With a partner, create an advertisement for Thomas Paine's pamphlet *Common Sense*. Include in your advertisement at least one of the ideas the colonists will read about. Share your advertisement with the class.

FOCUS

How do people's experiences affect the decisions they make?

Main Idea As you read, think about how people's experiences affected their decision to take sides in the American Revolution.

Vocabulary

neutral
pacifist
movement
encroach
regiment

Americans Take Sides

After the Declaration of Independence was signed, people had to decide if they would support the rebelling colonies or the British king. Some chose to be **neutral** (NOO•truhl), taking neither side. Those who were neutral were willing to accept the outcome of the revolution, whichever way it went.

About a third of the colonists were Loyalists, and another third were Patriots. The last third chose to remain neutral. Friends, neighbors, and families were sometimes torn apart by the need to choose sides. The fighting became as much a civil war as it was a war with the British.

Churches and the War

Many factors affected people's views on independence. One was religion. "There is a time to pray and a time to fight," Peter Muhlenberg, a young Lutheran minister, told his followers. Then, before their eyes, he tore off his church robes to show the uniform of a Patriot militia officer. His father, the colonies' Lutheran leader, was shocked—he himself was a Loyalist. The Lutherans, like the people of other church groups, were divided between Patriots and Loyalists.

Taking sides was especially hard for Anglican Church members. The British king was the head of the Anglican Church, as the Church of England was called in the colonies. Many Anglicans in the northern and middle colonies supported the king, while many of those in the southern colonies worked for independence.

Most Congregationalists, members of the largest church group in the colonies, worked for independence, as did many northern Presbyterians and Baptists. Many southern Presbyterians, however, were Loyalists.

Members of the Society of Friends, also called Quakers, would not fight in the war for independence.

Button molds were used to make metal buttons for Continental army uniforms.

Mary Ludwig Hays earned the name Molly Pitcher by bringing water to the troops during the long, hot Battle of Monmouth, fought in June 1778.

Quakers are against all wars, because they believe that violence for any reason is wrong. These **pacifists**, or believers in peaceful settlement of differences, published pamphlets calling for an end to the war. Loyalists and Patriots both saw pacifists as their enemies.

REVIEW *How did some people's religious beliefs affect the way they felt about independence?*

Women and War

Many women in the colonies took part in the **movement**, or effort by many people, to gain freedom. When Patriot leaders asked the colonists to boycott British-made goods, women in Boston and other colonial towns banded together to make their own goods. Many women worked for independence in other ways.

Some women formed groups to raise money for the war and collect clothing for the soldiers. In Lancaster, Pennsylvania, women formed a group that was called the Unmarried Ladies of America. Each member promised that she would never give her hand in marriage to any gentleman until he had first proved himself a Patriot.

Women also took part in the fighting. Like some women, Mary Ludwig Hays traveled with her husband after he enlisted in the Continental army. When her husband fell during the Battle of Monmouth, Hays took over the firing of his cannon. Mary Slocumb rode through thick forests at night to join her husband and other members of the North Carolina militia. She fought with them in the Battle of Moores Creek Bridge.

In Boston, Phillis Wheatley wrote poems that were praised by George Washington. She used her mind to champion the independence movement. So did Mercy Otis Warren. She wrote a play that made fun of the British and supported the Patriots.

Patriot Abigail Adams wanted to be sure that independence would be good for women as well as men. She wrote to her husband, John, "If particular care and attention are not paid to the ladies we are determined to foment [start] a rebellion and will not hold ourselves bound to obey any laws in which we have no voice or representation." Not all women were Patriots. There were Loyalist women in every colony. Some of them fought for the British. Many others brought the British food and supplies.

REVIEW *How did women on both sides take part in the Revolution?*

Native Americans and the War

An Oneida chief is said to have told a Patriot, "We have heard of the unhappy differences and great contention betwixt you and Old England. We cannot meddle in this dispute between two brothers. . . . Should the great king of England apply to us for aid, we shall decline him; if the colonies apply to us, we shall refuse."

Over the years Native Americans had grown angry with both the American colonists and the British. Settlers from both sides continued to **encroach** on traditional Indian lands, moving onto them without asking. By 1776 the land between the Appalachian Mountains and the Mississippi River was being taken over by Europeans, despite the Proclamation of 1763, which forbade settlement there.

Yet many Native Americans had come to depend on Europeans as trading partners. For this reason the Patriots hoped that the Indians would at least stay out of the war, even if they would not fight for them. The British, however, promised to give the Indians guns and other European goods if they agreed to help the British army. Many tribes in the Ohio River valley, so often at war with each other, made peace in order "to assist His Majesty's troops." Other tribes, however, were divided. In the Hudson River valley, some of the Iroquois fought for the Patriots. Others decided to fight for the British.

Most Indians, however, stayed out of the fighting. When asked to take sides, one Cherokee chief is said to have told both the colonists and the British that the Great Spirit "has given you many advantages, but he has not created us to be your slaves. We are a separate people!"

REVIEW *What view did most Indians take about the fighting?*

Africans and the War

At the start of the war, free Africans were as quick to take sides as their European neighbors. Peter Salem was among at least five Africans who fought at Concord with the Minutemen. A few weeks later he and other Africans, both free and enslaved, fought at the Battle of Bunker Hill in Boston, Massachusetts. About 5,000 Africans fought in the Continental army during the Revolutionary War.

Enslaved Africans who enlisted in the Continental army were promised freedom after the war as a reward. Many were so filled with ideas of freedom and liberty that they changed their names. Among the names listed in army records are Cuff Freedom, Dick Freedom, Ned Freedom, Peter Freeman, Cuff Liberty, Jeffrey Liberty, and Pomp Liberty.

BIOGRAPHY

Phillis Wheatley
1753?–1784

When she was only five or six years old, a young African girl, probably born in the country of Senegal, was kidnapped and enslaved. She was taken to Boston and sold to John Wheatley in 1761. Unlike many other slave owners, Wheatley educated the young girl and then freed her. Phillis Wheatley, who took the last name of her owner, was one of the earliest American poets.

Francis Marion, known as the Swamp Fox, led Continental soldiers through southern swamps as they defended the South against the British.

The royal governor of Virginia, John Murray, Earl of Dunmore, also promised to give enslaved Africans their freedom if they ran away from their owners and were "able and willing to bear arms" for the British government. In a few weeks nearly 300 runaway slaves were enlisted in the Ethiopian Regiment of the British army. A **regiment** is a large group of soldiers. These soldiers wore uniforms that had patches reading *Liberty to Slaves*.

REVIEW *What promise caused some enslaved Africans to take sides in the American Revolution?*

LESSON 3 REVIEW

Check Understanding

1 Remember the Facts Why did the American Revolution become as much a civil war as it was a war with Britain?

2 Recall the Main Idea How did people's experiences affect their decision to take sides in the American Revolution?

Think Critically

3 Past to Present How might people who are pacifists view conflicts that sometimes take place around the world today?

4 Explore Viewpoints Imagine that you are a Native American or an African during the American Revolution. List the important reasons you might have to choose one side over the other.

Show What You Know

Chart Activity Draw a chart showing the colonial groups that worked for independence and the groups that remained loyal to the British government. Do some research to find out why each group chose the side it did.

SAMUEL'S CHOICE

by RICHARD BERLETH
illustrated by BILL MAUGHAN

Taking the side of the Patriots was a difficult decision for many people, but especially difficult for enslaved Africans. The Declaration of Independence stated that "all men are created equal." Yet many Patriot leaders owned slaves. Even if the Patriots won their freedom from Britain, enslaved people knew that they probably would not win freedom from slavery.

Read now about the choice made by a 14-year-old boy named Samuel Abraham, who was held as a slave in Brooklyn, New York. Samuel, his friend Sana, and other slaves worked on the farm of a Loyalist named Isaac van Ditmas.

In the summer of 1776, General George Washington and the Continental army were forced to retreat from Brooklyn as the British approached. In the fighting that followed, Samuel chose to help the Patriots, carrying dozens of Patriots to safety in his boat. One of the people he helped was Major Mordecai Gist.

When I tied the boat to the dock below the Heights, Major Gist clapped his hands on my shoulders and looked me in the eyes. "Samuel," he said, "out in that creek you did more than many a free man for your country. I'd take it as a privilege if you'd consent to be my orderly and march beside me. And General Washington may need handy boatmen like you soon enough."

The next day it rained and rained. A thick sea fog covered the land. I looked everywhere for Sana. Many soldiers crowded into the camp, but they could tell me nothing. Alone and frightened, I mended the holes in my sail, pushing the big needle through the canvas, drawing it back again. Then, I heard voices nearby.

Major Gist stood there with an officer in a fine blue uniform. They asked me how deep the water was at this point between Brooklyn and Manhattan. They wanted to know if a British ship could sail between the two places. I told them that most ships could. Only the fog was keeping the British men-of-war from trapping Washington's army on Long Island.

The officer in the blue uniform thanked me. He and Major Gist walked away, looking thoughtful.

The next day the heavy rains continued. I spread the sail over the boat and slept snug and dry. Then I heard the voice I missed more than any in the world calling, "Samuel, Samuel Abraham!" Sana had found me! It was not a dream. "You chose, Samuel," she said. "You did it right. You chose our new country." From under her cloak she took a hot, steaming loaf wrapped in a napkin—her freedom bread, the sweetest I ever tasted. While we ate, she told me that Toby and Nathaniel were safe.

But this new country was in danger. Major Gist came to me again and explained that every boat was needed to carry Washington's army from Brooklyn to Manhattan. The army had to retreat that night. I was going to help save the army with Farmer Isaac's boat. Wouldn't he be surprised?

On the night that General Washington's army left Brooklyn, the worst storm I'd ever seen blew in from the Northeast. The wind howled. It drove the rain, stinging, into our eyes. It shook buildings and knocked down chimneys. And it whipped the water at Brooklyn Ferry into a sea of foam.

Down from the Heights in file marched Washington's army. The men entered the boats Major Gist and others had gathered at the ferry landing.

"What we need is a rope to cling to," someone said in the dark. "A rope stretching from here to Manhattan to guide us against the wind and current."

"There's rope here in the shipyard," a soldier

remembered. "Buoys to float the rope across, too. But who can cross this flood in the dark?"

"Can you do it, Samuel?" Major Gist asked. "Can you get across with the rope?"

"I can do it, Major," I shouted, the wind tearing the words out of my mouth. But I wasn't sure. Even if the rope were fed out from shore slowly, the sail might split or the rope might tear down the mast. But the British ships were sure to force their way between Brooklyn and Manhattan. I had to try.

When the rope was ready, I tied it to the foot of the mast. Sana jumped into the boat. I shouted at her to stay behind, but she wouldn't move. There was no time to lose. I shoved off into the swirling current.

My only hope was to let the shore current carry me out into midstream, and then, as the wind and tide thrust the boat toward the other shore, raise the sail and race for the Manhattan landing.

Fighting the rudder, I heard Sana's voice in my ear. "Will we make it, Samuel?" Water crashed over the side. Sana was bailing as fast as she could. "I can't swim, Samuel!" she cried into the wind. We were halfway across to Manhattan, and the boat was filling with sea. The gale was spinning us around. The rope was pulling us backward. I heaved at the sail, praying the mending wouldn't tear.

Then, as the sail filled, the boom swung around with a crack, and we were darting forward at last. On the Manhattan landing, by lantern light, we could see people waiting. Over the roar of the storm, we heard them cheering us on. But Isaac's boat was sinking. The rope was tearing the mast out of the bottom. With a terrible crash, the mast broke and was carried over the side. A second later the bow smashed into the side of a wharf, and I found myself in the water swimming with one arm, clinging to Sana with the other.

We stumbled ashore on Manhattan Island, where kind people wrapped us in blankets. They were smiling—the rope was across! The boats full of Washington's soldiers would follow. We had done it, together.

All through the night Washington's men followed that rope, boat after boat, across the water. In the stormy darkness, every soldier escaped from Long Island.

And so the fight for freedom would go on. It would take many long years before we would beat the British king, but never again did I wonder what freedom was, or what it cost. It was people pulling together. It was strong hands helping. It was one person caring about another.

And where was Washington? Many times that night Sana and I hoped to see him.

"Why, Samuel," Major Gist told us later, "he was that officer in the blue coat who asked you how deep the water was between Brooklyn and Manhattan. Last night the general arrested a farmer in Brooklyn

for helping the British. That farmer, Isaac van Ditmas, turned all of his property over to the Army of the Continental Congress in exchange for his freedom. It seems now that you and Sana have no master."

From that day forward, we and Isaac's other slaves were to be citizens of a new nation.

LITERATURE REVIEW

1. How did Samuel help the Continental army?
2. Why do you think Samuel chose to help the Patriots?
3. Write a conversation that could have taken place as Samuel and other slaves on Isaac's farm decided what to do when they learned they no longer had a master.

FOCUS

How do people meet difficult challenges today?

Main Idea   As you read, look for ways Americans met the challenges of their war for independence.

Vocabulary

siege
treaty
negotiate

Victory and Independence

After General Washington's retreat following the Battle of Long Island, Continental troops moved into New Jersey. There, they won important battles at Trenton and Princeton. But victory was still far from certain. In December 1777 General Washington set up headquarters at Valley Forge, Pennsylvania, near Philadelphia. That winter his ragged army was almost destroyed by cold and hunger. By Washington's own count, 2,898 of his men had no boots. Many were ill, and many died. The Patriots had declared their independence, but would their army be strong enough to win it?

Help from Other Lands

The Patriots received some help from soldiers of other countries. Among these soldiers were two Polish officers, Casimir Pulaski (puh•LAS•kee) and Thaddeus Kosciuszko (kawsh•CHUSH•koh). Later Kosciuszko returned to Poland to lead a revolution there. Among others who came from Europe were the German soldiers Johann de Kalb and Friedrich von Steuben (vahn SHTOY•buhn). The Marquis de Lafayette (lah•fee•ET), a 20-year-old French noble, came from France to fight along with the Americans.

At Valley Forge during the winter of 1777, von Steuben reported to Washington and took on the job of drilling the Continental army so that the soldiers would be ready to move quickly. By the spring of 1778 the soldiers had been trained and were marching well.

In the meantime, the Continental Congress had sent Benjamin Franklin to Paris to ask the French to join the war. The French were eager to see the American colonies win the war and weaken their longtime enemy, the British. But the French felt that the colonists did not have much of a chance of winning.

The Badge of Merit was designed by George Washington and given to soldiers who showed special bravery. Today this award is known as the Purple Heart.

Major Battles of the Revolution

Lake Superior

Lake Huron

Lake Michigan

Lake Ontario

Lake Erie

MAINE
(part of Mass.)

St. Lawrence River

Mohawk River

Saratoga 1777

Bennington 1777

NH

Boston 1775

NEW YORK

Concord 1775

Lexington 1775

MA

CT

RI

Hudson River

West Point
New York City

Allegheny R.

PENNSYLVANIA

NJ

Long Island 1776

Maumee River

Susquehanna River

Delaware R.

Princeton 1777

Valley Forge

Trenton 1776

Wabash River

Brandywine 1777

Germantown 1777

Philadelphia

MARYLAND

Potomac River

Baltimore

DELAWARE

Mississippi River

VIRGINIA

ATLANTIC OCEAN

Cahokia 1778

Vincennes 1779

James River

Richmond

Yorktown 1781

Chesapeake Bay

Kaskaskia 1778

River

Roanoke River

Ohio River

LOUISIANA

Cumberland River

Guilford Courthouse 1781

NORTH CAROLINA

Cape Fear R.

Charlotte

Tennessee River

Kings Mountain 1780

Cowpens 1781

Savannah River

Camden 1780

Wilmington

SOUTH CAROLINA

Ocmulgee River

GEORGIA

Charleston 1780

Savannah 1779

Altamaha River

Gulf of Mexico

	American colonies
	British territory
	Spanish territory
⚜	American victory
⚜	British victory
—	Present-day border

N
W E
S

40°N
70°W
35°N
30°N

80°W
95°W
75°W

0   100   200 Miles
0   100   200 Kilometers
Albers Equal-Area Projection

Regions This map shows the major battles of the Revolutionary War.
■ *In which region did most of the early battles take place? In which region did the later battles take place?*

Franklin talked with the French leaders for months. Then came news of the colonists' great victory at Saratoga in New York. More than 5,000 British soldiers under General John Burgoyne (ber•GOYN) had moved south from Canada, hoping to cut the colonies in two. Instead, on October 17, 1777, the British lost to Continental soldiers led by General Horatio Gates.

The colonists' great victory at Saratoga showed the French that the colonists stood a chance of winning the war. The French sent guns, ships, and soldiers. With the help of the French soldiers, the colonists fought more battles, including the siege of Savannah in 1779. A **siege** is a long-lasting attack. At the siege of Savannah, more than 800 Haitians, 80 of them slaves, fought alongside the French and Continental soldiers. Haiti was a French colony in the Caribbean.

After the victory at Saratoga, some other countries helped the colonists, too. In 1779 Bernardo de Gálvez (GAHL•ves), the Spanish governor of Louisiana, sent guns, food, and money to the Patriots. Later he led his own soldiers in taking a British fort in Florida. One Spanish-born soldier, Jorge Farragut (HAWR•hay FAIR•uh•guht), fought in both the Continental army and navy.

REVIEW *Why did the French decide to help the Patriots in their war for independence?*

LEARNING FROM DIAGRAMS The American and French troops surround the British at Yorktown.

❶ French soldiers
❷ British soldiers
❸ American soldiers
❹ French navy
❺ Chesapeake Bay

■ *Why were the British at a disadvantage in the Battle of Yorktown?*

Battle of Yorktown

Victory at Yorktown

When the British government learned that France was helping the Americans, British army leaders moved their attack from the northern colonies to the southern colonies. The British hoped that the greater Loyalist support in the South would help defeat the Patriots once and for all. With the help of the Loyalists, the British army captured Charleston, South Carolina, in 1780. Pushing north from South Carolina, the British then charged through North Carolina and into Virginia.

During 1781 the fighting centered in Virginia. For several weeks Benedict Arnold, a former Continental army officer, attacked colonial towns in Virginia for the British.

Arnold was a traitor—he acted against his country. Earlier, he had turned over the plans to the American fort at West Point, New York, in exchange for money and a high rank in the British army.

By late summer of 1781, British General Charles Cornwallis had set up at Yorktown, a small Virginia town on Chesapeake Bay, where it was easy for British ships to land supplies. The French and the Continentals moved quickly to defeat the British at Yorktown. The French joined forces with the Continentals near New York City, and the two armies marched to Virginia and surrounded Yorktown. At the same time, the French navy took control of Chesapeake Bay. Now the British navy could not get supplies to the British army at Yorktown. The British army was trapped.

In John Trumbull's painting (below) of the surrender at Yorktown, American General Benjamin Lincoln (center, on the white horse) receives the surrender from an aide to British General Cornwallis. George Washington is in front of the American flag.

In late September Cornwallis sent word to his commander in the north. "If you cannot relieve me very soon," he said, "you must be prepared to hear the worst."

The worst happened. Surrounded and under siege for two weeks from both land and sea, Cornwallis had to give up. A person who was there wrote, "At two o'clock in the evening Oct. 19th, 1781, the British army, led by General O'Hara, marched out of its lines, with colors cased [flags folded] and drums beating a British march." When the French and American soldiers heard the drums, they stopped their fire. The British and Hessian soldiers then marched out of Yorktown and laid down their weapons in a field.

Though fighting dragged on in some places for more than two years, it was clear that victory had been decided at Yorktown in 1781. The Patriots had won after a long and hard fight.

REVIEW *How did the French help the Americans win the Battle of Yorktown?*

The Treaty of Paris

The Battle of Yorktown did not end the Revolutionary War. The Treaty of Paris did that. A **treaty** is an agreement between countries.

Work on the treaty began in April 1782 when the British sent Richard Oswald, a wealthy merchant, to Paris to talk with Benjamin Franklin. Franklin gave Oswald the American terms—that is, what the Americans wanted in the treaty. One of the terms was that the British monarch and Parliament had to accept American independence and remove British soldiers from American soil. Franklin told Oswald that Americans might feel better toward the British if Parliament paid those whose towns had been destroyed in the war.

In return, the British asked that all of the Loyalists who remained in the United States be treated fairly. Many Loyalists fled to Nova Scotia, New Brunswick, and other parts of Canada, and to the Bahamas. Those who returned to Britain were sorry they did. Most

HISTORY

1775–1783

The American Revolution took place mainly on the east coast of North America. During that time, however, other events were happening on the western part of the continent. Spanish-speaking people were settling American Indian lands in the area that stretched from the Mississippi River to the Pacific Ocean—the present-day Southwest. They were building towns and giving names to places that later would become part of the United States. In Hawaii, whaling ships from all over the world were stopping for supplies. In Alaska, Russian fur traders were setting up trading posts.

LEARNING FROM TIME LINES This time line lists key battles and other important events of the American Revolution.

■ *How long after the war began was independence declared?*

Key Events of the Revolution

1775		1780		1785

1775
• Battles of Lexington, Concord, and Bunker Hill

1776
• Declaration of Independence

1777
• Battle of Saratoga

1777–1778
• Winter at Valley Forge

1781
• Battle of Yorktown

1783
• Treaty of Paris

could not find jobs and soon became very poor. Instead of being grateful for their support, the British government ignored them.

The British and Americans **negotiated**, or talked with one another to work out an agreement. After more than a year of such talks, the Treaty of Paris was signed by British and American representatives on September 3, 1783.

The Treaty of Paris named the United States of America as a new nation and described its borders. The United States would reach to Florida in the south. The northern border would be an imaginary line through the Great Lakes. The Mississippi River formed the western border. The fact that much of the land between the Appalachian Mountains and the Mississippi River was the home of many American Indian tribes was of little or no interest to the leaders who signed the treaty.

The Treaty of Paris was just as much a victory as winning at Yorktown had been. Independence was now a fact. But the Americans faced many problems. They had formed a new country, yet the 3 million people in the 13 new states were far from united.

REVIEW *What were the effects of the Treaty of Paris?*

North America in 1783

United States
British
French
Spanish
Russian
Claimed by Britain, Spain, and Russia

Regions This map shows North America in 1783, following the Treaty of Paris.
■ *What were the boundaries of the new nation called the United States?*

LESSON 5 REVIEW

Check Understanding

1 Remember the Facts How was help from Europeans important to the colonists in winning the war?

2 Recall the Main Idea How did the colonists meet the challenges of their war for independence?

Think Critically

3 Think More About It Why do you think the colonists did not give up when it looked as if they would not win the war?

4 Past to Present What can Americans today learn from the Patriots?

Show What You Know

Research Activity Because the Revolution was so important, many places are named after people who fought on the Patriots' side. Use an atlas to locate as many places as you can that are named for Washington, Franklin, Gálvez, Lafayette, and others. Compare your list with that of a classmate.

1775

1775
• Second Continental Congress

1776
• The Declaration of Independence

1777
• Battle of Saratoga
• Winter at Valley Forge

CONNECT MAIN IDEAS

Use this organizer to show how the chapter's main ideas are connected. Write the main idea of each lesson. A copy of the organizer appears on page 52 of the Activity Book.

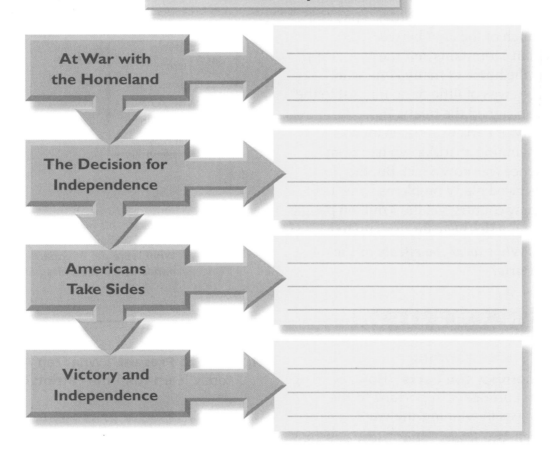

The War for Independence

At War with the Homeland

The Decision for Independence

Americans Take Sides

Victory and Independence

WRITE MORE ABOUT IT

Write a Pamphlet Take the role of a Loyalist or a Patriot. Write a short pamphlet that explains your point of view about British rule. Explain why you have chosen that side.

Write a Newspaper Article Imagine that you are a reporter who witnessed the British surrender at Yorktown. Write a newspaper article describing what you saw.

USE VOCABULARY

Use each term in a sentence that helps explain its meaning.

1. olive branch
2. enlist
3. allegiance
4. declaration
5. grievance
6. neutral
7. pacifist
8. negotiate

CHECK UNDERSTANDING

9. How did the Second Continental Congress try to make peace with Britain?

10. What were some of the advantages that the British army had over the Continental army?

11. What did the Declaration of Independence tell the world?

12. How did Patriots who did not fight in the war show their support for independence?

13. How was help from other countries important to the American victory?

14. What was the most important result of the Battle of Saratoga?

15. Put these events in the proper order: the Treaty of Paris, the Declaration of Independence, Valley Forge, the Battle of Bunker Hill, and the Battle of Yorktown.

THINK CRITICALLY

16. **Think More About It** Many leaders of the Revolution, such as George Washington and Thomas Jefferson, were successful and wealthy. Why would they risk everything they had to take part in a revolution?

17. **Cause and Effect** How did the military training of Continental soldiers affect the war?

18. **Personally Speaking** Imagine that you are a delegate to the Second Continental Congress. Do you think you would sign the Declaration of Independence? Explain your answer.

19. **Past to Present** How do American citizens today let their government know about their grievances?

20. **Explore Viewpoints** Explain how Patriots and Loyalists viewed the American Revolution.

APPLY SKILLS

Read a Political Cartoon Look through newspapers and magazines for a political cartoon about a subject that interests you. Cut out the cartoon and paste it on a sheet of paper. Below the cartoon, write a brief paragraph that explains its meaning.

READ MORE ABOUT IT

If You Were There in 1776 by Barbara Brenner. Macmillan. This book tells how daily life during the late eighteenth century shaped the ideas in the Declaration of Independence.

If You Were There in 1776 by Barbara Brenner

HARCOURT BRACE

Visit the Internet at
http://www.hbschool.com
for additional resources.

Tiananmen

In 1776 the American Patriots struggled for freedom. Today people in some parts of the world are doing the same. In April 1989, college students in China wanted their country to be more like a democracy. The college students gathered at Tiananmen (TYAHN•AHN•MEN) Square in the center of Beijing (BAY•JING), the capital city, to express their views.

Thousands of people, young and old, went to the square every day to show their support for the students. One group made its own Statue of Liberty out of plastic foam. Other people made posters. One poster quoted the Declaration of Independence, calling for "life, liberty and the pursuit of happiness" for all Chinese people. Another recalled Patrick Henry's famous words "give me liberty or give me death."

The demonstration in Tiananmen Square ended violently on June 4, 1989. That morning, hundreds of Chinese soldiers poured into the square, killing many of the demonstrators.

Shen Tong, a Beijing University student speaking at an Independence Day celebration in Boston on July 4, 1989, compared the Tiananmen Square massacre with the Boston Massacre. "People died," Shen said of the Boston Massacre, "but it sparked the American struggle for independence. I do not believe that the Tiananmen Square massacre was the end of the democracy movement in China. It was the beginning." Today many people in China continue the struggle for freedom.

Beijing

Square

Think and Apply

Think about what happened at Tiananmen Square. Find examples of people struggling today for freedom or independence. Select the example that interests you the most. Use a Venn diagram to compare and contrast the present-day struggles and events with those of the American Revolution. Share your findings with a classmate.

HARCOURT BRACE

Visit the Internet at **http://www.hbschool.com** for additional resources.

CNN Turner Le@rning

Check your media center or classroom video library for the Making Social Studies Relevant videotape of this feature.

中华人民共和国万岁

UNIT 4 REVIEW

Summarize the Main Ideas
Study the pictures and captions shown in this visual summary to help you review Unit 4.

Show More of the Story
Draw pictures and write captions that describe more about the American Revolution. Label the pictures, and tell where they should go on the visual summary.

1 The colonists were forced to pay taxes to Britain. They especially hated the tax law called the Stamp Act.

4 Minutemen faced British soldiers at Lexington and Concord in April 1775. This was the start of the War for Independence.

6 Support from the colonists helped the soldiers in the Continental army face many hardships.

3 Paul Revere and William Dawes went on a night ride to warn of approaching British soldiers.

2 At the Boston Tea Party, colonists dumped tea from British ships into Boston Harbor.

5 On July 4, 1776, the Declaration of Independence was approved by members of the Continental Congress.

7 The American victory at Yorktown forced the British to surrender. In 1783 the Treaty of Paris named the United States as a new nation.

USE VOCABULARY

Write the term that matches each definition.

Continental	**tax**
self-government	**treaty**

1. making one's own laws

2. money paid to a government for running it

3. a soldier in George Washington's army

4. an agreement between countries

CHECK UNDERSTANDING

5. What actions by the British king angered the colonists?

6. How did the actions of Thomas Paine, Crispus Attucks, and Paul Revere affect the outcome of the American Revolution?

7. Why did some enslaved Africans join the British side, while others fought on the side of the colonies?

8. What battle made the French believe the colonists could really defeat the British?

THINK CRITICALLY

9. **Past to Present** What does the Declaration of Independence mean to Americans today?

10. **Explore Viewpoints** People in the British colonies were divided in their views about self-government and independence. What were these different views? Why did people hold them?

11. **Personally Speaking** What person who took part in the American Revolution do you admire most? Why?

APPLY SKILLS

Use a Historical Map The Treaty of Paris described the borders of the new country. However, there remained land disputes between former colonies. The United States and Britain also continued to dispute land in the new country. Use the map below to answer the questions.

12. What year does this map show?

13. How are disputed lands shown on the map?

14. Which two former colonies claimed the same land in 1784?

15. Describe the location of the land claimed by both the United States and Britain.

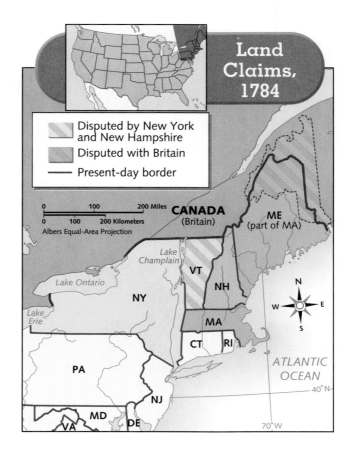

Land Claims, 1784

Disputed by New York and New Hampshire
Disputed with Britain
Present-day border

0   100   200 Miles
0   100   200 Kilometers
Albers Equal-Area Projection

CANADA (Britain)
ME (part of MA)
Lake Champlain
VT
Lake Ontario
NH
NY
Lake Erie
MA
CT   RI
ATLANTIC OCEAN
PA
40°N
NJ
MD   DE
VA
70°W

REMEMBER
- Share your ideas.
- Cooperate with others to plan your work.
- Take responsibility for your work.
- Help one another.
- Show your group's work to the class.
- Discuss what you learned by working together.

ACTIVITY
Present a
Dramatic Reading

After the Declaration of Independence was signed in 1776, copies of it were sent to all the colonies. In many towns the Declaration was read aloud at public meetings. The readers showed the importance of the document by adding drama to their reading. Your class should work in four groups, each responsible for preparing a dramatic reading of one part of the Declaration of Independence. Each group member should help read his or her group's part.

ACTIVITY
Make a
Time Line

Work with three or four classmates. Make a time line showing the important events of the American Revolution. Begin with the Stamp Act, and end with the signing of the Treaty of Paris. Be sure to label the date of each key event on the time line.

ACTIVITY
Make a
Model

Imagine that you are taking part in a Fourth of July celebration. With three or four of your classmates, build a model for a parade float that shows an important event of the American Revolution. Display your model in the classroom.

Unit Project Wrap-Up

Create a Book Work with classmates to finish the Unit Project that was described on page 219. Choose a few items from your lists to include in a book about the American Revolution. Then write a description of each item. Work together to illustrate your book with either drawings or pictures cut out of magazines. Write captions describing the illustrations, and give your book a title. Invite students from other classes for a reading.

THE NEW NATION

When the American people won their independence from Britain, they had to decide what kind of government they should form. Should the former colonies have a single government? Should the colonies become 13 separate states with no central government? One thing was certain. The newly independent country had to give its people some authority over the new government.

◄ *Signing the Constitution*, a painting by Howard Chandler Christy

UNIT THEMES

- Conflict and Cooperation
- Individualism and Interdependence

Unit Project

Draw a Poster Complete this project as you study Unit 5. As you read, write a list of details about each event described in the unit. Choose one of the events to illustrate on a poster. Use your list to remind you of details you may add to your drawing. Give your poster a title, and share it with your classmates.

CANADA

ROCKY MOUNTAINS

GREAT PLAINS

OREGON COUNTRY

River

Columbia

Snake River

PACIFIC OCEAN

Missouri

Platte River

GREAT BASIN

LOUISIANA

Colorado River

Arkansas River

San Francisco

Mojave Desert

Los Angeles

San Diego

NEW SPAIN

Santa Fe

El Paso del Norte

Rio Grande

San Antonio

Laredo

United States

British

Spanish

Claimed by Britain, Spain, and Russia

● City or settlement

1786

1788

JAN. 1787
Shays's Rebellion
PAGE 286

MAY 1787
Delegates Meet in Philadelphia
PAGE 291

North America, 1790s

CANADA

Quebec
Montreal

MAINE
(part of MA)

VT
(claimed by
NY and NH)

NH

Portsmouth

Albany

Boston

MA

Providence

NEW YORK

CT

RI

New Haven

Lake Superior

Lake Huron

Lake Michigan

Lake Ontario

Lake Erie

Mississippi River

Allegheny River

New York City

Princeton

NJ

Western
Reserve

PA

Pittsburgh

Philadelphia

Wilmington

NORTHWEST
TERRITORY

MD

DE

Annapolis

Washington, D.C.

UNITED
STATES

Vincennes

River

Richmond

Norfolk

ATLANTIC
OCEAN

St. Louis

Ohio River

VIRGINIA

KENTUCKY

APPALACHIAN MOUNTAINS

NORTH
CAROLINA

New Bern

TENNESSEE

River

SOUTH
CAROLINA

Tennessee

N

W   E

S

Mississippi

TERRITORY SOUTH
OF THE OHIO RIVER
(claimed by GA)

GEORGIA

Charleston

Savannah

MISSISSIPPI
TERRITORY

Natchez

St. Augustine

New Orleans

FLORIDA

Gulf of Mexico

0   200   400 Miles
0   200   400 Kilometers
Albers Equal-Area Projection

1790

1792

SEPT. 1787
Signing the
Constitution
PAGE 315

APR. 1789
Washington's Oath
PAGE 325

DEC. 1791
The Bill of Rights
PAGE 322

We the People

Shh!

We're Writing the Constitution

by Jean Fritz
pictures by Tomie dePaola

The job of turning the 13 former British colonies into a single country was not easy. The biggest problem was getting people to think of themselves as citizens of a new country—the United States of America. Until this time most people thought of themselves as citizens of their states rather than of one country.

After the Revolutionary War most people in America were glad that they were no longer British. Still, they were not ready to call themselves Americans. The last thing they wanted was to become a nation. They were citizens of their own separate states, just as they had always been: each state different, each state proud of its own character, each state quick to poke fun at other states. To Southerners, New Englanders might be "no-account Yankees." To New Englanders, Pennsylvanians might be "lousy Buckskins." But to everyone the states themselves were all important. "Sovereign states," they called them. They loved the sound of "sovereign" because it meant that they were their own bosses.

George Washington, however, scoffed at the idea of "sovereign states." He knew that the states could not be truly independent for long and survive. Ever since the Declaration of Independence had been signed, people had referred to the country as the United States of America. It was about time, he thought, for them to act and feel united.

Once during the war Washington had decided it would be a good idea if his troops swore allegiance to the United States. As a start, he lined up some troops from New Jersey and asked them to take such an oath. They looked at Washington as if he'd taken leave of his senses. How could they do that? they cried. New Jersey was their country!

So Washington dropped the idea. In time, he hoped, the states would see that they needed to become one nation, united under a strong central government.

But that time would be long in coming.

9

THE CONSTITUTION

"In the new code of laws, which I suppose it will be necessary for you to make, I desire you would remember the ladies, and be more generous and favorable to them than [were] your ancestors."

Abigail Adams, in a letter to her husband, John, March 31, 1776

The Articles of Confederation

FOCUS
What problems might be caused by a weak government?

Main Idea As you read, look for problems that were caused by the weaknesses of the United States government under the Articles of Confederation.

Vocabulary

constitution	territory
republic	township
ambassador	ordinance
inflation	

Before the war with Britain had ended, the Continental Congress decided to set up a national government for the 13 former colonies. The newly independent states had already started to write their own **constitutions**, or plans of government. But leaders believed that the country also needed a national government with its own constitution. Then all 13 states could act together as one nation.

"A Firm League of Friendship"

Most people did not want a powerful national government for the country. After all, they had just fought a war to get rid of one. They were afraid that a strong national government would make laws for their states just as the British king and Parliament had made laws for the colonies. Now that they finally had won their independence, they did not want to give it away to a national government.

In 1781 the states accepted the plan for a central government approved by the Continental Congress. The plan, written mostly by representative John Dickinson, united the states in a confederation. The confederation would be something like the Iroquois League, which brought together different Indian tribes. The Confederation of the United States of America would bring together 13 independent states in "a firm league of friendship." This first plan of government for the new country was called the Articles of Confederation.

Some people thought that the country should be run by a single leader, such as George Washington.

John Dickinson headed the committee that wrote the first draft of the Articles of Confederation.

Instead, the Articles of Confederation created a **republic**, a form of government in which people elect representatives to run the country. Under the Articles, voters of each state elected leaders who, in turn, chose representatives. These representatives met in a Congress, or national legislature, where each state had one vote. Congress could do only certain things. Most important, it could declare war, make treaties, and settle serious disagreements between states.

For Congress to make a law or decide on important questions, at least 9 of the 13 states had to agree. However, the states seldom agreed on anything. Each wanted its own way. No state wanted to be under the control of the other states.

No state wanted to be under the rule of one person, either. That is why the Articles did not allow a single leader to control the government. The states were afraid of giving one person too much authority. That person might become like a monarch. So a committee of representatives kept the government running when Congress was not meeting.

The Articles also did not plan for a national court system. Congress acted as a court for settling disagreements between states. But most often the states did not obey Congress anyway. People who had disagreements with their state governments had no national court where they could settle their differences.

REVIEW *What could Congress do under the Articles of Confederation?*

This staff was used to list the members of the League of the Haudenosaunee, a confederation of five Iroquois tribes. The pegs in the staff stood for each tribe's representatives. How was the early government of the United States like the Iroquois League?

Problems from the Start

Under the Articles of Confederation, the national government did not work well. It was, as George Washington called it, "a half-starved, limping government."

Often there were not enough representatives present to allow Congress to meet. Even when there were, the legislature had no place of its own to hold meetings. Congress met sometimes in Philadelphia and sometimes in Annapolis, Maryland. It also met in Princeton or in Trenton, New Jersey. Most Americans did not know where or when Congress was meeting. Foreign **ambassadors**, representatives from one country to another, did not know either. When the first Dutch ambassador arrived in the United States, he spent ten days looking for Congress. He finally found Congress in Princeton, where it had been chased by soldiers demanding their pay for fighting in the Revolutionary War.

Even when Congress met, however, it could do only what the Articles of Confederation allowed. The Articles did not allow Congress to raise a national army without the states' permission. State leaders were afraid the national government would use such an army to make them obey national laws. This rule let the states keep their authority, but it also meant there would be no army to defend the nation if Spanish troops should attack from Florida or British troops should attack from Canada.

The Articles did not allow Congress to make laws about trade or about taxes. To get the money needed to run the national government, Congress had to ask each state to pay its share. But Congress did not have the authority to make the states pay what they owed. For three years Congress did not even have enough money to pay its members!

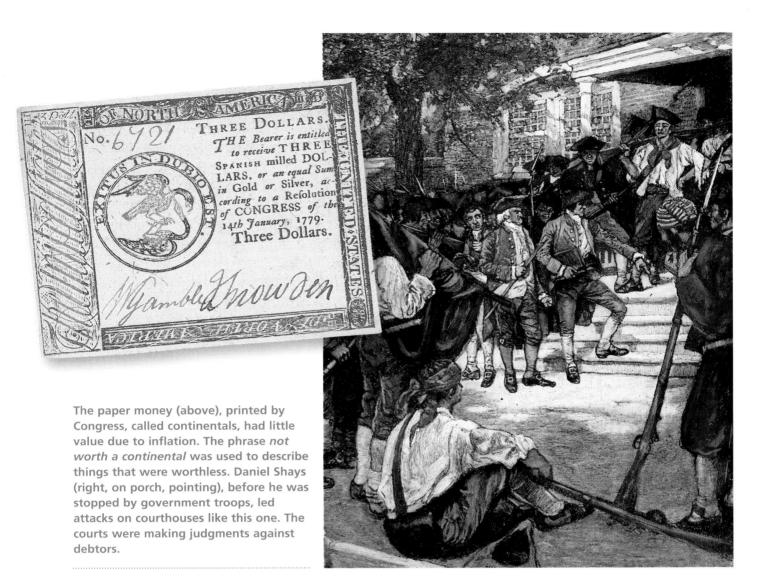

The paper money (above), printed by Congress, called continentals, had little value due to inflation. The phrase *not worth a continental* was used to describe things that were worthless. Daniel Shays (right, on porch, pointing), before he was stopped by government troops, led attacks on courthouses like this one. The courts were making judgments against debtors.

Congress did have the authority to print and to coin money. But when it tried to pay its debts from the war, it printed too much and caused terrible inflation. When there is **inflation**, more and more money is needed to buy the same goods. During this time, for example, goods that used to cost two cents would cost twenty dollars.

Many people, such as the soldiers who had not been paid, soon had money problems. Most of these people were farmers. They already had to pay state taxes—taxes they thought were too high. But they also had to buy tools and seeds for planting. Many went into debt because they had to borrow money. Some states made debtors

pay back what they owed right away. If they did not, the state could take away their land or send them to prison. Many farmers protested to their state governments. Some protests, such as Shays's Rebellion, became violent.

In the fall of 1786, Daniel Shays, a former captain in the Continental army, and about 1,200 other poor farmers wanted to show their anger toward their state, Massachusetts. In January 1787 they attacked a building used for storing weapons in the western part of the state. The weapons belonged to the national government, not to Massachusetts, but Shays and the protesters did not care. "That crowd [the members of Congress] is too weak to act!" said Shays. But the governor of Massachusetts was not. He called out the state militia to end the rebellion. Four protesters died in the fighting.

Shays's Rebellion was quickly put down, but it showed that people were not happy with their government. Under the Articles of Confederation, Congress could do little to help them. Congress did not even have the money or the authority to defend national property—like the weapons in western Massachusetts. Many people feared that unrest would spread to other states.

REVIEW *What problems did people face under the Articles of Confederation?*

The Western Lands

Under the Articles of Confederation, Congress did make some important decisions on how to divide and govern the country's western lands. These lands stretched from the Appalachian Mountains to the Mississippi River.

After the French and Indian War, Britain had refused to allow new settlement west of the Proclamation Line of 1763, near the Appalachian Mountains. This land was reserved for the Native Americans. Once the new United States was independent, however, it opened the frontier to settlement. Settlers poured into the Ohio River valley.

Regions This map shows the system used to divide the Northwest Territory into townships and sections.

■ *In what ways do you think this system could be useful?*

The Northwest Territory, 1785

0   100   200 Miles
0   100   200 Kilometers
Albers Equal-Area Projection

CANADA (Britain)

Lake Superior
Lake Michigan
Lake Huron
Lake Ontario
Lake Erie

MINNESOTA
WISCONSIN
MICHIGAN
IOWA
ILLINOIS
INDIANA
OHIO
MISSOURI
KENTUCKY
WEST VIRGINIA
VIRGINIA
PENNSYLVANIA
NEW YORK
NJ
MD
DE
ATLANTIC OCEAN

Mississippi River
Missouri River
Ohio River

Sections in One Township

1 mile

36	30	24	18	12	6
35	29	23	17	11	5
34	28	22	16	10	4
33	27	21	15	9	3
32	26	20	14	8	2
31	25	19	13	7	1

6 miles

Northwest Territory
Present-day border
Present-day names of states are used.

George Washington was once a surveyor. He owned this bronze compass.

The land north of the Ohio River was called the Northwest Territory. A **territory** is land that belongs to a national government but is not a state.

In 1785 Congress set up a system to survey, or measure, the western lands. The land was divided into squares called **townships**. Each side of a township measured 6 miles (9.7 km). Each township, in turn, was divided into 36 squares, or sections. This system of surveying by townships and sections can still be seen in parts of the United States.

In 1787 Congress passed the Northwest Ordinance. The **ordinance**, or set of laws, established governments in the Northwest Territory and described the steps by which new states would be formed from the lands. The Northwest Ordinance also set other conditions. It did not allow people to keep slaves in the Northwest Territory. It said that Native Americans should be treated fairly. And it encouraged townships to help build schools.

The Northwest Ordinance was a good plan for the growth of the United States. It showed what could be done when members of Congress worked together. But since this did not happen often, many people thought that Congress was not important.

REVIEW *What did the Northwest Ordinance accomplish?*

LESSON I REVIEW

Check Understanding

❶ Remember the Facts What was the first plan for governing the 13 states after the Revolutionary War?

❷ Recall the Main Idea What problems were caused by the weaknesses of the United States government under the Articles of Confederation?

Think Critically

❸ Think More About It Why were the former colonists afraid of a strong national government?

❹ Explore Viewpoints What do you think the Native Americans living in the western lands would have said about the Northwest Ordinance? Explain your answer.

Show What You Know

Speech Activity With a partner, plan a speech explaining how the 13 former colonies could solve the problems of the Articles of Confederation. Practice your speech with your partner, and then deliver it to the class.

FOCUS

How can people cooperate to make changes in their nation?

Main Idea
Read to learn how American leaders worked together to change the government of the United States.

Vocabulary

convention
delegate
Preamble

A New Plan of Government

Just after the Revolutionary War, the former colonists had been afraid of a national government that was too strong. Now the people had a government that was too weak to work well. The confederation was really 13 separate and independent states rather than one nation. The country was not really united. The British, in fact, called it the "Disunited States."

"A Rope of Sand"

James Madison was a member of Congress under the Articles of Confederation. In 1779 Madison had been elected to represent Virginia. Jemmy, as his friends called him, was 29 years old and the youngest member of Congress. He was to spend most of his life in public service. Madison became a student of government. He read everything he could find about ancient and modern ways of governing.

Madison was worried about the weaknesses of the Articles of Confederation. Congress had little authority over the states. Madison said he was afraid that Congress had become "a rope of sand," or not strong.

Such leaders as George Washington, Thomas Jefferson, and John Adams agreed with Madison. Once, while traveling in Britain, John Adams had been asked, "Do you represent one nation or thirteen?" Madison and the other leaders began to argue for a stronger national government. Only a strong national government could keep the confederation from breaking apart, Madison said.

Others did not agree. Patrick Henry of Virginia was one of many who supported the Articles of Confederation. These leaders were afraid of a strong national government. A rope of sand, they said, was better than a rod of iron.

REVIEW *Why did James Madison say that Congress had become "a rope of sand"?*

This United States flag was made in 1781. How is today's flag different?

Agreeing to Work Together

The states argued and argued among themselves over such things as borders and trade. Maryland and Virginia fought over who had the right to control travel on the Potomac River, which ran between them. Both states wanted to control the middle of the river because it was a good, deep shipping lane.

The states argued about money, too. Each state printed its own paper money in addition to the money printed by the national government. States fought over whose money would be used when people from one state bought goods in another state. Some states even placed a tax on goods brought in from other states.

Things became so difficult that a **convention**, or an important meeting, was held in Annapolis, Maryland, in September 1786. Alexander Hamilton of New York and James Madison of Virginia called the meeting to give the states a chance to talk out their problems. However, representatives from only five states—New York, New Jersey, Pennsylvania, Delaware, and Virginia—attended. The representatives, or **delegates**, talked for days before deciding that the country needed a stronger national government. This meant that the Articles of Confederation had to be changed.

Led by Hamilton and Madison, the delegates to the Annapolis Convention sent a letter to Congress asking it to call a second convention. Delegates from all the states could meet there to discuss their problems and decide whether changing the Articles might help solve the problems.

At first Congress did not want to call a convention, but after Shays's Rebellion it agreed to do so. Each state was asked to send delegates to a convention to be held in Philadelphia in the spring of 1787. Only Rhode Island refused the invitation.

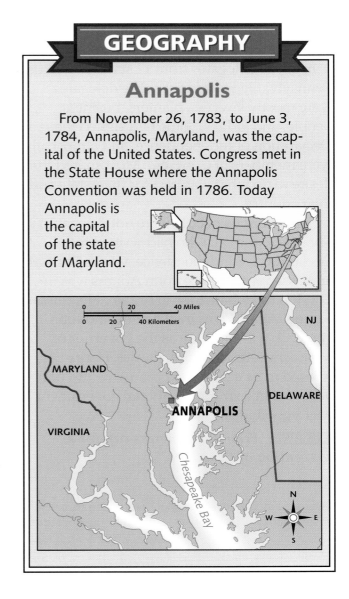

GEOGRAPHY

Annapolis

From November 26, 1783, to June 3, 1784, Annapolis, Maryland, was the capital of the United States. Congress met in the State House where the Annapolis Convention was held in 1786. Today Annapolis is the capital of the state of Maryland.

The delegates to the convention began to gather in Philadelphia in May 1787. When Thomas Jefferson saw the list of those attending, he wrote to John Adams, "It really is an assembly of demigods [heroes]."

One of the first to arrive was George Washington of Virginia. In 1787 Washington was 55 years old and the most honored hero of the American Revolution. The first thing the delegates did was elect Washington president of the convention.

The most colorful arrival was made by Benjamin Franklin, then 81 years old and governor of Pennsylvania. Unable to walk far or to ride in a bumpy carriage, Franklin arrived in a Chinese sedan chair carried by prisoners from the Philadelphia jail.

In all, 55 delegates from 12 states met in the Pennsylvania State House. The delegates were mostly lawyers, planters, business people, and judges. Some had signed the Declaration of Independence, and almost all were members of Congress. Most shared the desire to do what was best for their state and their country.

Some famous people were not delegates. Thomas Jefferson, who had written the Declaration of Independence, was in Paris as ambassador to France. John Adams was in London as ambassador to Britain. His cousin Samuel Adams was in ill health, and John Hancock was too busy as the governor of Massachusetts to attend. Patrick Henry refused to be a delegate because he did not believe that a stronger national government was a good idea.

REVIEW *Why did Congress call for a convention of the states?*

The Convention Begins

From the beginning the delegates agreed to hold a secret meeting. They believed this would help them make the best decisions. They covered the windows and sealed them shut. Guards watched the doors and hallways.

As the meeting was called to order, many of the delegates offered ideas they thought would make the Articles of Confederation better. But they soon saw that there was no way to simply fix up the old plan of government. Only a new plan—a new constitution—would do. They agreed to unite the nation under a strong central government instead of through a "firm league of friendship."

The delegates to this Constitutional Convention wrote the new rules of government with great care. They called these new rules the Constitution of the United States of

Delegates at the Constitutional Convention (bottom) decided on the new rules of government that were written down in the Constitution (below).

America. Gouverneur (guh•vuh•NIR) Morris of Pennsylvania spent long hours working out each sentence. The delegates gave Morris the job of writing down all the ideas that had been approved during the convention.

In the **Preamble**, or introduction to the Constitution, Morris began with the words *We the people of the United States. . . .* Morris had originally written *We the people of the States of New Hampshire, Massachusetts, ...* But he changed the words because he wanted the American people to know that the Constitution would make them citizens of a nation first and citizens of separate states second.

Morris went on to explain in the Preamble that the purpose of the Constitution was to create a better plan of government. This government would work toward justice and peace. It would allow the nation to defend itself against any enemies. It would promote the country's well-being. And it would provide "the blessings of liberty" for the American people.

REVIEW *What was the purpose of the Constitution?*

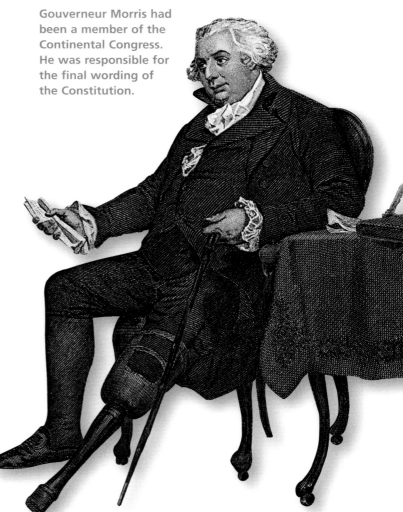

Gouverneur Morris had been a member of the Continental Congress. He was responsible for the final wording of the Constitution.

LESSON 2 REVIEW

Check Understanding

1 Remember the Facts For what reason did Gouverneur Morris change the opening of the Constitution's Preamble?

2 Recall the Main Idea In what ways did American leaders work together to change the government of the United States?

Think Critically

3 Personally Speaking Would you have wanted to go to the Constitutional Convention? Explain your answer.

4 Cause and Effect What caused some states to argue among themselves?

5 Explore Viewpoints How might Patrick Henry have felt about the way Gouverneur Morris wrote the Constitution's Preamble?

Show What You Know

Research Activity Use the Internet, encyclopedias, and biographies to gather information about a convention delegate. Write a report and share it with your classmates.

Figure Travel Time and Distance

1. Why Learn This Skill?

When planning any trip, it is important to know the travel time, or how long the trip will take to complete. Travel time can be affected by many things, including the weather in a place or the speed you are traveling. But the two most important things that affect travel time are the distance you will travel and the method of transportation you will use. As you know, traveling by jet airplane is much faster than traveling by car or train.

2. Understand the Process

In the 1700s, however, there were no cars, trains, or airplanes. Roads were sometimes little more than dirt paths winding across the countryside. This made travel much slower and more difficult than it is today.

Imagine that you are a delegate planning your trip to the Constitutional Convention in Philadelphia, Pennsylvania. You will start your trip in Charleston, South Carolina, in a horse-drawn carriage. You have been told that the

Routes to the Constitutional Convention, 1787

Colonial road

ATLANTIC OCEAN

Albers Equal-Area Projection

roads are bad north of New Bern, North Carolina, so you will continue from there on horseback. To save money, you will travel from Annapolis, Maryland, on foot. How long will it take you to get from Charleston to Philadelphia? To answer this question, you will need to figure out the distances between the cities. You will also need to know the travel time for the different forms of transportation used in the late 1700s.

The map on page 294 shows the routes that some of the delegates to the Constitutional Convention might have taken to reach Philadelphia in 1787. The map scale can help you figure out the distances on these routes. The map scale shows distance in both miles and kilometers. In this skill lesson, you will use only miles to measure distance.

Use a ruler to measure the map scale. What length on the ruler equals 200 miles? To measure a curving route, you can use a string. Hold the string on the map, and use a pencil or pen to make a mark on the string at the starting point. Then lay the string along the route. Make another mark on the string at the ending point. Place the string against the map scale. You can measure the distance by making a mark at every length of 200 miles.

The chart on this page shows travel time for different forms of transportation. People at the time of the convention often traveled in horse-drawn carriages. Horse-drawn carriages could go about 110 miles a day. How many days did it take to get from Providence, Rhode Island, to Philadelphia by carriage? To figure this out, divide the number of miles by the travel time. The total number of miles between Providence and Philadelphia is about 240. If you divide that number by 110, you get 2 with a remainder of 20. So it took about 2 days to get from Providence to Philadelphia by carriage.

Now use the map and the chart to answer the questions that follow.

Travel Time

Transportation
Miles Traveled Per Day

Walking — 36

Horseback — 70

Horse-drawn carriage — 110

1. About how many miles is it from Pittsburgh, Pennsylvania, to Philadelphia?

2. How long might it have taken a delegate traveling in a horse-drawn carriage to get from Pittsburgh to the convention in Philadelphia?

3. How long might it have taken a delegate from New York, such as Alexander Hamilton, to travel on horseback from New York City to Philadelphia?

4. How long might it have taken a delegate from Wilmington, Delaware, to walk from Wilmington to Philadelphia?

3. Think and Apply

Measure the distance between two cities on a present-day highway map, using the map scale. Find the shortest highway distance between the two cities. Then, using a travel rate of 55 miles per hour, figure out how long it would take to travel by car between those two cities.

MAP SKILLS

FOCUS

How can people with different ideas reach agreement?

Main Idea   Read to learn how delegates to the Constitutional Convention reached agreement on a new plan of government.

Vocabulary

compromise   debate
federal system   Union
bill

Debates and Compromises

The delegates to the Constitutional Convention often did not agree with one another. The Constitution came into being only because the delegates were willing to compromise. To **compromise** means to give up some of what you want in order to reach an agreement. As compromises were made, decisions were written down and the Constitution took shape.

A Federal System of Government

The convention delegates first talked about the relationship between the states and the new national government. Few of the delegates agreed with George Read of Delaware, who thought that the states should be done away with altogether. Even those who wanted a strong national government said that getting rid of the states would be going too far.

But the delegates knew that the Articles of Confederation—with strong state governments and a weak national government—must be changed. So they agreed to create a **federal system** in which the authority to govern would be shared. The states would keep some authority, give away some authority, and share some authority with the national, or federal, government.

The states would keep authority over their own affairs. They would set up schools and local governments, for example. They would make laws for businesses and set rules for state and local elections.

The national government would keep all authority over matters that affected the country as a whole. The states would no longer print money, raise armies and navies, or make treaties with other countries, for example. Under the Articles of Confederation, each state had done these things as if it were a separate country.

The states would share authority with the national government, too. Both would be able to set up their own court

The sketch (top) shows the original design for the Great Seal of the United States. The Great Seal (above) is still used on important government documents today.

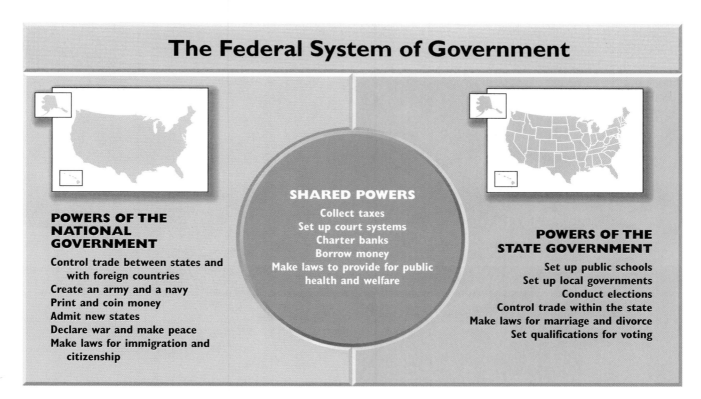

The Federal System of Government

POWERS OF THE NATIONAL GOVERNMENT

Control trade between states and with foreign countries
Create an army and a navy
Print and coin money
Admit new states
Declare war and make peace
Make laws for immigration and citizenship

SHARED POWERS

Collect taxes
Set up court systems
Charter banks
Borrow money
Make laws to provide for public health and welfare

POWERS OF THE STATE GOVERNMENT

Set up public schools
Set up local governments
Conduct elections
Control trade within the state
Make laws for marriage and divorce
Set qualifications for voting

LEARNING FROM DIAGRAMS Under a federal system, some powers are given to the national government, some are given to the states, and others are shared.
■ *Which level of government can print money?*

system and raise money by taxing citizens, for example.

The states and the national government might not always agree, however. In that case the national government would have authority over the state governments. The delegates made it clear that under this new federal system, the Constitution would be "the supreme law of the land."

REVIEW *How is a federal system of government different from a confederation?*

The Great Compromise

One of the first important disagreements among the delegates to the Constitutional Convention was about how each state would be represented in Congress, the new national legislature. Most delegates agreed that the Congress should have two parts, or houses. But they disagreed about how representatives should be chosen.

Edmund Randolph and the other Virginia delegates, including James Madison, thought the number of representatives a state would have in Congress should be based on the number of people living in that state. Under this plan, called the Virginia Plan, more people in a state would mean more representatives and more votes in Congress. This plan would help the large states, such as Virginia, Pennsylvania, and New York, which had large populations.

"Not fair!" shouted delegates from the small states. William Paterson of New Jersey said he "had rather submit to a monarch, to a despot [strict ruler], than to such a fate." Paterson offered his own plan for representation, called the New Jersey Plan. Under the New Jersey Plan, the new Congress would have one house rather than two. Each state would have one vote. This plan would help the small states by giving them the same amount of representation as the large states.

Edmund Randolph wrote the Virginia Plan, which called for representation to be based on population.

The delegates argued for weeks about representation. Which plan would be more fair? The larger states wanted the Virginia Plan. The smaller states wanted the New Jersey Plan. Neither side would give in. "We are now at full stop," said Roger Sherman of Connecticut.

As president of the convention, George Washington chose a committee with one member from each state to work out a compromise. Roger Sherman, a member of the committee, offered a new plan, based on the idea of a two-house Congress. In one house, representation would be based on the number of people in each state, as in the Virginia Plan. In the other house, each state would have an equal vote, as in the New Jersey Plan. Either house could present a **bill**, or an idea for a new law. But the other house would have to agree to it before it could become a law.

Large-state delegates on the committee did not like Sherman's plan because they felt it gave too much authority to the small states. So the committee added another idea. The house in which representation was based on the number of people in each state would have the authority to tax. Bills having to do with money could come only from this house. The house in which each state had an equal vote could then agree to the bill or not.

The committee presented its compromise plan to the whole convention. The delegates **debated**, or argued, the good and bad points of the compromise. At first, supporters of the Virginia and New Jersey plans held firm. But they came to understand that if they did not compromise, they would not have a new government. Because Sherman's compromise kept the plan for the Constitution alive, some people called it the Great Compromise of the convention.

REVIEW *What was the Great Compromise?*

The Three-fifths Compromise

More compromises were made before the convention was over. One had to do with a problem that had long divided the northern and southern states—slavery. Delegates from the two regions argued about whether enslaved Africans should be counted in determining how many representatives a state should have.

At the time of the convention, nearly 4 million people lived in the United States. Almost 2 million lived in the southern states. Of that number, about 667,000 were slaves.

Because the northern states had fewer enslaved Africans than the southern states, the northern states did not want slaves to be counted for representation. After all, the delegates argued, slaves were not citizens under the Articles of Confederation and they would not become citizens under the Constitution. Delegates from the southern states wanted slaves to be counted. That way the southern states could count more people and get more representatives, and therefore more votes, in Congress.

The delegates also debated how much each state should pay in taxes to support the national government. They agreed that each state's share should be based on the number of people in the state. For taxes, the delegates from the southern states did not want slaves counted, while the delegates from the northern states did.

Once again, the delegates reached a compromise. Three-fifths of the total number of slaves would be counted when figuring both representation and taxes. For every five slaves, a state could count three.

The delegates agreed to the Three-fifths Compromise to move closer to forming a new government. But there were still problems to solve and more compromises to make before the delegates' work was done.

REVIEW *What was the Three-fifths Compromise?*

Slavery and the Constitution

The delegates did not find it easy to compromise on every subject they debated. The subject of slavery nearly broke up the convention—and the United States of America. Some of the delegates believed that slavery was wrong and that it should be ended. Others, especially those from the southern states, believed that the economy in their region depended on slavery.

More than one-fourth of the delegates owned slaves. These men decided not to use the word *slave* in the Constitution. Instead, they described enslaved people as "such persons" or "all other persons." The words

George Washington met with his advisers to discuss issues related to the new government of the United States of America.

person held to service or labor came closest to describing slaves. But even though the delegates did not use the word *slave,* they could not get around the problem of slavery. If the Constitution was to stand for liberty, how could it allow slavery?

The subject of slavery came up most often in the debate over the authority of Congress to control trade with other countries. Some delegates from both northern and southern states did not want Congress to have the authority to end the slave trade. But other delegates from both regions wanted the slave trade stopped.

George Mason of Virginia, an owner of more than 200 slaves, tried to end the trade of enslaved people. "I hold it essential," said Mason, "that the general government should have power to prevent the increase of slavery." He believed that over time, all slaves should be set free.

John Rutledge of South Carolina did not agree. Plantation owners in his state and other southern states depended on enslaved workers to grow their cash crops. The slave problem was so important to Rutledge that

he questioned "whether the Southern states shall or shall not be parties to the Union" if the slave trade were stopped.

Fearing that the southern states would break away from the **Union**—the United States of America—the delegates compromised. They gave Congress the authority to make laws controlling trade. But Congress could not stop the slave trade for at least 20 years. In the meantime, the delegates at the convention took no steps to end slavery in the states.

REVIEW *What compromise did the delegates reach on the slave trade?*

LESSON 3 REVIEW

Check Understanding

1. **Remember the Facts** What debates almost ended the Constitutional Convention?

2. **Recall the Main Idea** How did the delegates at the Constitutional Convention reach agreement on a new plan of government?

Think Critically

3. **Personally Speaking** Why do you think it is important that government leaders today compromise to reach agreement?

4. **Cause and Effect** How might the southern states have been affected if the Constitution had put an end to the slave trade?

Show What You Know

Simulation Activity
With a partner, role-play a debate between delegates at the Constitutional Convention. One delegate should represent a large state and the other should represent a small state. Tell what you think of the Virginia Plan and the New Jersey Plan.

Compromise to Resolve Conflicts

1. Why Learn This Skill?

There are many ways to handle a disagreement. You can walk away and let the strong feelings fade over time. You can talk about it and explain your thoughts about a disagreement. You also can compromise. Knowing how to compromise gives you another way to resolve, or settle, conflicts.

2. Remember What You Have Read

Many people believe that if the delegates to the Constitutional Convention had not been willing to compromise, the Constitution would never have been written. You have read that one of the most serious disagreements at the convention was over representation in the new legislature. Delegates from the large states wanted representation in Congress to be based on population. This would give the large states more representatives—and more votes— than the small states. Delegates from the small states wanted each state to have one representative. This would give all the states equal representation.

Roger Sherman

Roger Sherman helped resolve this disagreement by suggesting what later became known as the Great Compromise. Congress would be made up of two houses. In one house, representation would be based on population. In the other house, each state would have two representatives and two votes. Both sides got some of what they wanted, but both sides also had to give up other things they wanted.

3. Understand the Process

To resolve a conflict through compromise, you can follow steps similar to the ones below.

1. Before you begin to talk with the person you disagree with, be aware that you may have to give up some of the things you would like.
2. Tell the other person clearly what you want.
3. Decide which of the things you want are most important to you.
4. Present a plan for a possible compromise. Let the other person present his or her plan.
5. Talk about any differences in the two plans.
6. Present another plan for a compromise, this time giving up one of the things that is not most important to you. Continue talking until the two of you agree on a compromise plan.
7. If either of you becomes angry, take a break and calm down before you go on talking.
8. If there are many people on each side of the disagreement, each side should choose one or two people to do most of the talking.

4. Think and Apply

With your classmates, choose an issue that you do not all agree on. Form sides to discuss the issue, using the steps in Understand the Process.

FOCUS

How can people make
sure that no branch of
the government holds
too much authority?

Main Idea As you
read, look for ways the
delegates made sure
that no branch of the
United States govern-
ment would have too
much authority.

Vocabulary

legislative branch
executive branch
judicial branch
separation of powers
majority
census
electoral college
veto
impeach
justice
override
unconstitutional
checks and balances

This early
gavel, used in
the Senate to
open and close
meetings, had no
handle.

A Government of Three Branches

Under the Articles of Confederation, Congress made the laws, approved the laws, and acted as a court to settle disagreements between the states. But having only one branch of government had created problems. So the delegates to the Constitutional Convention decided there would be three branches of government instead of one. Each would have its own authority. A **legislative branch** would make the laws. An **executive branch** would carry out the laws. A **judicial branch** would settle differences about the meaning of the laws. Once the delegates agreed to this **separation of powers**, or division of the national government, they had to decide how the three branches would work together.

Legislative Branch

Like the Congress under the Articles of Confederation, the Congress under the Constitution would make laws. But the new Congress was to have more authority than the old one. The new Congress, for example, could make laws to raise taxes, control trade with other countries, print and coin money, raise an army and a navy, and declare war.

The new Congress would have two houses, the House of Representatives and the Senate. Either house could propose most bills. For a bill to become a law, the **majority**, or the greater part, of each house would have to vote for it.

The number of members each state sent to the House of Representatives would depend on the state's population. A **census**, or population count, would be taken every ten years to determine the number of people in each state. Today the number of members in the House of Representatives is limited to 435. In the Senate, each state has two senators, as originally planned.

James Madison thought that the members of both houses of Congress should be elected by the voters of each state. Other delegates, however, disagreed. Many felt that most people were not educated enough or

How a Bill Becomes a Law

A member of the House or Senate introduces a bill.

COMMITTEES

The bill is reviewed by committees.

The House and Senate vote to approve the bill.

The bill goes to the President.

VETO

If the President vetoes the bill, it returns to Congress.

SIGN

If the President signs the bill, it becomes a law.

LAW

If the bill gets a two-thirds majority vote in Congress, it becomes a law.

LEARNING FROM DIAGRAMS Under the Constitution, a bill must follow the steps shown in this diagram to become a law.
■ *When does the President receive the bill?*

informed enough to have a say in government. After a long debate, a compromise was worked out. The delegates agreed that citizens should vote directly for members of the House of Representatives. Senators would be elected by their state legislatures. Today, however, citizens vote directly for members of both houses of Congress, as Madison wanted.

The delegates also decided on other rules for Congress that are still in effect. Members of the House of Representatives serve for two years. Senators serve for six years. To qualify, members of the House of Representatives must be at least 25 years old, must have been citizens of the United States for at least seven years, and must live in the state they represent. Senators must be at least 30 years old, must have been citizens of the United States for nine years, and must live in the state they represent.

REVIEW *What are the duties of Congress?*

Executive Branch

Once Congress makes the laws, it is the job of the executive branch to carry them out. In doing so, the executive branch runs the day-to-day business of government.

The delegates had many long debates about the executive branch. One of the most heated was about whether it should be headed by one person or by a group of people. James Wilson of Pennsylvania felt that one person should be the chief executive, or leader. He thought that a single executive would govern more effectively than a committee. Even though some delegates feared that a single executive would be too much like a monarch, most agreed with Wilson. They decided on a single chief executive, called the President. The President serves for four years.

It was also Wilson's idea to have citizens vote for electors, who, in turn, would vote for the President. This group of electors is called the **electoral college**.

The delegates also had long debates about how much authority the President should have. Many thought the President should be able to **veto**, or reject, bills passed by Congress.

George Mason of Virginia disagreed. Such authority, he thought, was too much like that held by a king or queen. But most of the other delegates were willing to take a chance on a strong executive. The delegates counted on the other branches to keep the executive branch under control.

The debates went on and on, but finally the executive branch began to take shape. It was decided that the President would represent the nation in dealing with other countries and would head the nation's military forces. To run for President, a person must be at least 35 years old and must have been born in the United States. The President's chief responsibility would be to "take care that the laws be faithfully executed." If these duties were not carried out, Congress could **impeach** the President. This means that it could accuse the President of wrongdoing. The President could then be tried and removed from office if found guilty.

REVIEW *What are the duties of the President?*

Judicial Branch

Once laws are made and carried out, someone must decide if they are working fairly. This is the job of the judicial branch, or court system. The states had always had their own courts. But the delegates to the Constitutional Convention agreed on the need for a national, or federal, court system. The courts in this system would decide cases having to do with national laws, treaties, or the Constitution. They would also decide cases between states or between citizens of different states.

The delegates did not plan the judicial branch in great detail. They made the most decisions about the highest court in the United States—which they called the Supreme Court.

Edmund Randolph wanted Congress to choose the **justices**, or judges, for the Supreme Court. James Wilson wanted the President to have this authority. A compromise was worked out. The President would name the justices, and the Senate would vote on them. It was decided that a justice would stay in office for life. In this way, justices could reach decisions fairly without worrying about losing their jobs.

No decision was made at the Constitutional Convention as to how many justices would be on the Supreme Court. Congress decided on that number later. At first there were six justices on the court. Today there are nine.

REVIEW *What are the duties of the judicial branch?*

The scales of justice stand for fair treatment.

Checks and Balances

EXECUTIVE BRANCH

THE PRESIDENT
- Manages the government
- Proposes new laws
- Makes treaties
- Heads the armed forces

Can veto a bill passed by Congress

Can override a President's veto

Can rule a President's actions unconstitutional

Appoints Supreme Court justices

LEGISLATIVE BRANCH

THE CONGRESS
- Passes taxes
- Makes laws
- Approves treaties
- Approves appointments

Approves appointments of Supreme Court justices

Can rule that a law is unconstitutional

JUDICIAL BRANCH

THE SUPREME COURT AND OTHER FEDERAL COURTS
- Decides whether or not laws are constitutional
- Explains the meanings of treaties

LEARNING FROM DIAGRAMS This diagram shows the checks and balances among the three branches of government.
- ■ *How can the President check the authority of Congress? How can Congress check the authority of the Supreme Court?*

Working Together

None of the delegates wanted any one branch of government to have too much authority. So they gave each branch some ways to check, or limit, the authority of the others.

Congress, for example, can check the authority of the President by overriding the President's veto. To **override** a veto means to vote to cancel it. The Supreme Court can check the authority of Congress by ruling that a law is **unconstitutional**, or does not follow the Constitution. The President can check the authority of the Supreme Court by choosing its justices.

The delegates set up these checks to keep a balance of authority among the three branches. The system of **checks and balances** keeps any one branch of government from using its authority wrongly. It helps the branches work together as equal partners.

REVIEW *What is the purpose of checks and balances among the three branches of the United States government?*

LESSON 4 REVIEW

Check Understanding

1 **Remember the Facts** What are the duties of each branch of the national government?

2 **Recall the Main Idea** How did the delegates to the Constitutional Convention make sure that no branch of the government would have too much authority?

Think Critically

3 **Cause and Effect** What might happen if one branch of the government became too powerful?

Show What You Know
Diagram Activity Make a diagram that shows the separation of powers and the checks and balances.

1787

by Joan Anderson
illustrated by Teresa Fasolino

During the hot and humid summer of 1787, the 55 delegates to the Constitutional Convention worked at writing a new plan of government. In the seven parts, or Articles, of their plan, they described the duties of each branch of government and the relations among the states. They also wrote rules for making changes to the Constitution. Finally the time came for the delegates to sign their names to show they agreed with what had been written.

Read now about the last day of the convention in this story of historical fiction. Jared Mifflin, the boy who tells the story, is James Madison's helper. As Jared listens to the delegates debate, he wonders if the Constitution will ever be signed.

WE, THE PEOPLE OF THE UNITED STATES,

*in order to form
a more perfect Union,
Establish Justice,
insure domestic Tranquillity,
provide for the common defense,
promote the general Welfare,
and secure the
Blessings of Liberty
to ourselves and our Posterity,
do ordain and establish
this Constitution for the
United States of America . . .*

As Secretary Jackson continued to read, Jared stood in the back of the East Room gazing upon the delegates, none of whom moved a hair as they listened to the words they had labored so hard to formulate[1] into a sturdy document. *Another hour or so, and the whole thing will be over,* Jared thought, a tinge of sadness stirring his soul as he realized his unique experience was coming to an end.

The windows of the East Room had finally been opened, allowing an unfamiliar cool breeze to descend upon the delegates at this, their last official meeting. . . .

---

[1] **formulate:** state in an exact way

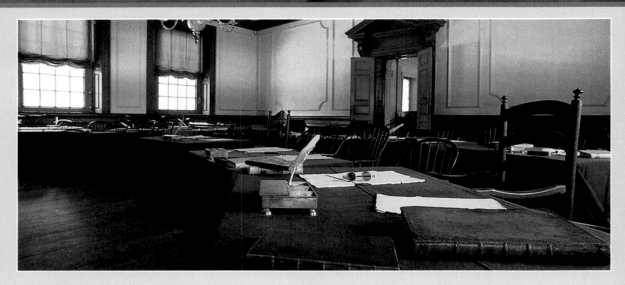

The delegates to the Constitutional Convention met inside the Pennsylvania State House, now known as Independence Hall.

"And so, let it be Done," General Jackson began the final phrase that now was familiar to Jared because he had read and reread Uncle Thomas's first draft, ". . . in convention by the unanimous[2] consent of the states present, the seventeenth day of September in the year of our Lord, One Thousand Seven Hundred and Eighty Seven and of the Independence of the United States of America the Twelfth. In witness whereof we have hereunto subscribed[3] our names."

Jared gazed about the room, wondering what would happen next. He focused on General Washington, assuming that he would make the next move. There were some stirrings from the Virginians. *They're probably thinking up last-minute suggestions,*

Jared surmised.[4] Suddenly, George Mason asked for the floor. Everyone was sitting on the edge of their chairs.

"Gentlemen," he said in a strong, bold tone, "after much soul-searching I must inform you that since this Constitution does not yet contain a Bill of Rights I cannot, in all good conscience, subscribe to the document that lays waiting."

Jared was stunned. Mr. Mason's attendance during the summer had been almost perfect, and he'd sat on many committees. How could he not sign? No sooner had he taken his seat than Virginia's Governor Randolph rose—to agree with George Mason. "I will gladly present this Constitution to the legislature in Virginia but cannot, at this time, find it in my heart to put name to paper."

[2]**unanimous:** in complete agreement
[3]**subscribed:** signed below

[4]**surmised:** guessed

Now the room was full of rumblings. Governor Randolph had been one of the early arrivals and the first to speak at the opening of the Convention. He was the one who presented the Virginia Plan, Jared recalled—the paper on which the new Constitution drew some of its ideas! The various states were now huddled together in discussion and General Washington had to bang the gavel several times to bring order to the room. *How many others would follow suit?* Jared wondered.

"I must inform my colleagues that I, too, will not sign this Constitution in its present form," Elbridge Gerry of Massachusetts announced from his seat at the back of the room.

Here we go, Jared thought. *Divisiveness spreading once again from state to state.*

"Mr. President," the voice of Alexander Hamilton rose from the other side of the room. "May I speak?"

Washington nodded, not a trace of emotion on his stoic[5] face.

Jared turned to look at Mr. Hamilton, the man responsible for calling the

HAMILTON

meeting at Annapolis, where the writing of a Constitution was first discussed. More than anyone else, it seemed that Alexander Hamilton cared about nationhood. He had written numerous articles and papers advocating[6] a strong federal government. Ironically he'd had to endure a delegation that completely disagreed with him throughout this Convention.

"I must express my deepest anxiety that every member should sign," he said with an urgency in his voice. "If a few characters of consequence refuse to sign, their actions could do infinite mischief by kindling latent sparks which lurk under the general enthusiasm for this Constitution." He sat down, but did not take his eyes off Governor Randolph, to whom he was obviously delivering these brief but firmly stated remarks.

There was momentary silence. Jared wished that General Washington would rise and simply commence the signing. Instead, yet another delegate took the floor. *Oh no,* Jared thought, *another Massachusetts man. Will he also dissent?*

---

[5] **stoic:** calm

[6] **advocating:** speaking for

Nathaniel Gorham instead moved that the stipulation for representation in the House be changed from one representative per forty thousand citizens to one per thirty thousand. *How could they change anything now?* Jared wondered, as he gazed over at the beautifully printed pieces of parchment that were spread out on the table. *With this latest diversion, the Convention will surely trail on for days*, he sighed. Knowing how meticulously[7] these men had worked over this document, clause by clause, article by article, Jared resigned himself to the delay and took a seat on the stool provided for him by the door.

Rufus King seconded the motion, and Jared got set to watch yet another debate on representation. But instead, General Washington rose from his seat to make a statement. "Being the presiding member," he informed the group, "I know I am not at liberty to comment one way or another and have not done so until this moment. However, I must agree with my colleagues," he continued. "It has always appeared to me that an

exceptional plan would be to have one representative for every thirty thousand citizens, and it would give me much satisfaction to see it adopted."

That did it. Everyone agreed to vote with the man considered to be the foremost of all Americans. With the representation issue finally put to rest and no one else jumping up with final objections, Dr. Franklin asked for the floor.

Finally! Jared said to himself. *Not many men here are going to disagree with Benjamin Franklin, no matter what he says.*

"Due to a weakened voice, gentlemen," he began, "I have asked my friend James Wilson to read you my sentiments on this momentous day." He nodded for Wilson to begin:

"Mr. President, I confess that there are several parts of this Constitution which I do not at present approve, but I am not sure I shall ever approve them. For having lived a long time, I have experienced many instances of being obliged by better information or fuller consideration to change opinions even on important subjects which I once thought right, but found to be otherwise.

WASHINGTON

----

[7]**meticulously:** very carefully

It is, therefore, that the older I grow, the more apt I am to doubt my own judgment, and to pay more respect to the judgment of others.

In these sentiments, sir, I agree to this Constitution with all its faults, if they are such. . . . I doubt, too, whether any other convention we can obtain, may be able to make a better Constitution.

For when you assemble a number of men to have the advantage of their joint wisdom, you inevitably assemble with those men all their prejudices, their passions, their errors of opinion, their local interest, and their selfish views. From such an assembly can a perfect production be expected?

It, therefore, astonishes me, sir, to find this system approaching so near to perfection as it does; and I think it will astonish our enemies. . . .

Thus I consent, sir. I cannot help expressing a wish that every member of the Convention who may still have objections to it, would with me, on this occasion, doubt a little of his own infallibility,[8] and to make manifest our unanimity, put his name to this instrument."

FRANKLIN

When Franklin's speech was over, the signing began. George Washington was first to write on the cream-colored parchment. Delegates from each state followed. In the end, all but 16 of the 55 delegates signed the new United States Constitution on September 17, 1787. Mason, Randolph, and Gerry did not sign. The 13 others had already left the convention and returned home.

As Benjamin Franklin left the convention hall, he was asked by the wife of Philadelphia's mayor what kind of government the new nation would have. "A republic," he told her, "if you can keep it." Franklin's words were meant for all the people of the United States.

---

[8]**infallibility:** inability to make a mistake

LITERATURE REVIEW

1. Why did the delegates decide to stop debating and sign the Constitution?
2. Why do you think Benjamin Franklin believed that a "perfect" Constitution was not possible?
3. Write a short scene about the closing of the Constitutional Convention. With classmates, act out your scene for the class.

1780   •   1782

1781
• The Articles of
Confederation
are approved

CONNECT MAIN IDEAS

Use this organizer to show how the chapter's main ideas are connected. Write the main idea of each lesson, and list the three branches of government. A copy of the organizer appears on page 60 of the Activity Book.

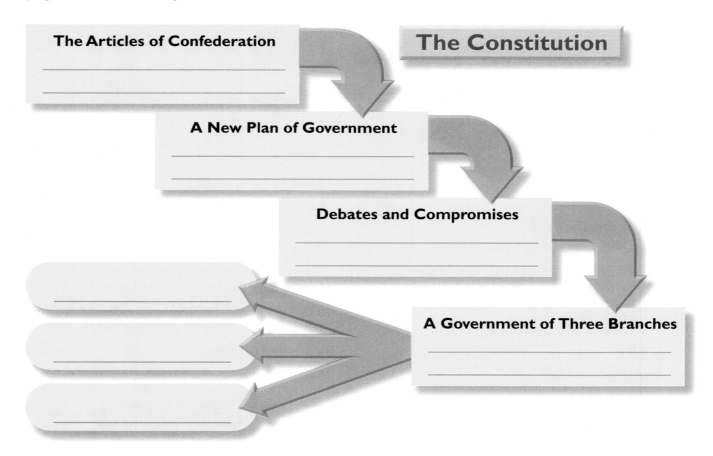

The Articles of Confederation

The Constitution

A New Plan of Government

Debates and Compromises

A Government of Three Branches

WRITE MORE ABOUT IT

Write a Persuasive Letter Imagine that you are living during the time delegates were meeting to discuss the Articles of Confederation. Write a letter telling why you think the Articles of Confederation should or should not be changed.

Report a News Event Suppose that you are a newspaper reporter who has been asked to cover the Constitutional Convention. Write a short newspaper article in which you explain the Great Compromise. Be sure to tell how it will affect the outcome of the convention.

1784   1786   1788

1786
• The Annapolis
  Convention is held

1787
• The Constitutional
  Convention is held
• The Constitution is written

USE VOCABULARY

Write one or two sentences for each pair of terms to explain how the terms are related.

1. territory, township
2. convention, delegate
3. compromise, debate
4. veto, override

CHECK UNDERSTANDING

5. How was the United States under the Articles of Confederation like the Iroquois League?

6. What powers did Congress have under the Articles of Confederation? What powers did it not have?

7. When and where was the Constitutional Convention held?

8. How is authority shared in a federal system of government?

9. What were the differences between the New Jersey Plan and the Virginia Plan?

10. What are the three branches of the United States government? Describe the duties of each branch.

11. How are justices on the Supreme Court chosen? How long do they serve?

THINK CRITICALLY

12. **Explore Viewpoints** Most delegates to the Constitutional Convention thought the chief executive should be paid. Benjamin Franklin thought the President should serve without pay. Which view would you have supported? Why?

13. **Think More About It** How did the Three-fifths Compromise settle one of the disagreements between the northern and southern states?

APPLY SKILLS

Figure Travel Time and Distance
Use the map on page 294 and the chart on page 295 to answer these questions.

14. How many days might it have taken to travel on horseback from Charleston to Philadelphia?

15. How many days might it have taken to walk from New York City to Philadelphia?

16. How many days might it have taken to get from Boston to Philadelphia by carriage?

Compromise to Resolve Conflicts
Think of something that you and a friend disagree about. Then list the steps that you might follow to resolve your conflict.

READ MORE ABOUT IT

The Great Little Madison by Jean Fritz. G. P. Putnam's Sons. This biography, which traces the life of James Madison, tells how he grew from a sickly child to become the fourth President of the United States.

Visit the Internet at
http://www.hbschool.com
for additional resources.

Chapter 9 • **313**

10

A NEW GOVERNMENT BEGINS

"The basis of our political systems is the right of the people to make and to alter their constitutions of government."

George Washington, in his farewell speech as President, 1796

A portrait of George Washington by Gilbert Stuart

Approving the Constitution

FOCUS
What would make the people of a country want to support its plan of government?

Main Idea As you read, think about what made the people of the United States want to support the Constitution.

Vocabulary
ratify
Federalist
Anti-Federalist

James Madison had taken careful notes all through the Constitutional Convention. The day his fellow delegates signed their approval for the new plan of government, Madison wrote in his notebook,

“ Whilst the last members were signing it Doctor Franklin looking towards the President's Chair, at the back of which a rising sun happened to be painted, observed to a few members near him, that Painters had found it difficult to distinguish in their art a rising from a setting sun. I have, said he, often and often in the course of the Session . . . looked at that behind the President without being able to tell whether it was rising or setting: But now at length I have the happiness to know that it is a rising and not a setting Sun. ”

Despite Franklin's words, the new plan of government that he and the other delegates had approved was not yet the law of the land. According to Article VII of the Constitution, 9 of the 13 states had to **ratify**, or agree to, the Constitution before it would become law.

State Ratifying Conventions

Once the delegates signed the Constitution on September 17, 1787, George Washington ordered that it be sent to Congress. Congress, in turn, sent copies to the states. To decide about the new plan of government, the states held their own ratifying conventions. In each state, the people elected delegates to go to the state convention and vote for or against the Constitution.

This ink stand was used by the signers of the Declaration of Independence and of the Constitution.

315

The chair (far left) that was used during the Constitutional Convention is still on display inside Independence Hall in Philadelphia. The top part of the chair (left) shows the "rising sun."

At the state conventions, debate began all over again. Some delegates, such as Patrick Henry in Virginia and George Clinton in New York, told their conventions that the new national government was too strong. Samuel Adams told delegates in Massachusetts that he did not like the way the Preamble began with *We the People*. He thought it should say *We the States*.

There was one point, however, on which the delegates to just about every state convention agreed. They felt the Constitution needed to list the things the government could *not* do. This would protect the rights of the states and the people.

The state delegates wanted to protect freedoms such as the right to tell the government if it was doing something wrong. They remembered that Patrick Henry and James Otis had almost been sent to prison for speaking out against the British government. The delegates did not want the new national government to have the authority to take the same action.

The delegates to the state ratifying conventions said they would be more willing to agree to the Constitution if a list of rights was added to it. So supporters of the Constitution promised that after it was ratified, a bill of rights would be added.

REVIEW *Why were many delegates not willing at first to agree to the new Constitution?*

This political cartoon celebrated the ratification of the Constitution by 11 of the 13 states. It expressed the hope that North Carolina and Rhode Island would also ratify the Constitution.

Ratification of the Constitution

Legend:
- United States
- 1787 Year of ratification
- Present-day border

Scale:
0 — 100 — 200 Miles
0 — 100 — 200 Kilometers
Albers Equal-Area Projection

CANADA (Britain)

Lake Ontario

Lake Erie

MAINE (part of MA)

VERMONT (claimed by NY and NH)

NEW HAMPSHIRE 1788

NEW YORK 1788

MASSACHUSETTS 1788

RHODE ISLAND 1790

CONNECTICUT 1788

PENNSYLVANIA 1787

NEW JERSEY 1787

DELAWARE 1787

MARYLAND 1788

VIRGINIA 1788

NORTH CAROLINA 1789

SOUTH CAROLINA 1788

GEORGIA 1788

FLORIDA (Spain)

ATLANTIC OCEAN

Gulf of Mexico

The Vote

The first state to call for a vote on the Constitution was Delaware. On December 7, 1787, all the state delegates voted to ratify. Later that month, delegates in Pennsylvania and New Jersey also voted to ratify. In January 1788, delegates in Georgia and Connecticut voted to ratify. But several states still had not voted. Among those were the states of New York and Virginia. People wondered how the new government could possibly work if the country's largest states voted against it.

From January to June 1788, people who were for the new Constitution and people who were against it both tried to get the support of people in the states that had not voted. Those citizens who wanted the Constitution

STATE	DATE	VOTES FOR	VOTES AGAINST
Delaware	December 7, 1787	30	0
Pennsylvania	December 12, 1787	46	23
New Jersey	December 18, 1787	38	0
Georgia	January 2, 1788	26	0
Connecticut	January 9, 1788	128	40
Massachusetts	February 6, 1788	187	168
Maryland	April 28, 1788	63	11
South Carolina	May 23, 1788	149	73
New Hampshire	June 21, 1788	57	47
Virginia	June 25, 1788	89	79
New York	July 26, 1788	30	27
North Carolina	November 21, 1789	194	77
Rhode Island	May 29, 1790	34	32

Place The map and table show when the Constitution was ratified in each of the 13 states. The table also lists the number of votes for and against the ratification.

■ Which states ratified the Constitution in 1787? What state was the last to ratify the Constitution? In which state was the vote closest to being a tie?

came to be called **Federalists**. Those citizens who did not want it became known as **Anti-Federalists**. Federalists wanted the plan's strong national government. Anti-Federalists did not want a strong national government unless a bill of rights was added to the plan.

In New York, Federalists and Anti-Federalists used the newspapers to tell how they felt and why. Alexander Hamilton, James Madison, and John Jay wrote letters to the newspapers, defending the Constitution. These letters were later published together as a book called *The Federalist*.

Those who could read followed the debate in the newspapers. Others listened to the arguments at community meetings and even at church services. Some people saw the new Constitution as the work of "lawyers, and men of learning, and moneyed men that talk so finely . . . to make us poor, illiterate people swallow down the pill." But others thought that having a government with three branches and a Congress with two houses was a good idea. They also liked the promise of a bill of rights.

No one was sure how all the arguing would affect the ratifying conventions. In Massachusetts, however, the promise of a bill of rights changed the minds of some very important people. Samuel Adams and John Hancock went to the ratifying convention as

The banner (below right) was carried by members of the Society of Pewterers in a parade held to celebrate New York's ratification of the Constitution. Pewterers were people who made plates and other items out of a metal called pewter. Alexander Hamilton wrote most of the letters published in *The Federalist* (below left). Many people believe that this book provides the best description of the ideas behind the Constitution.

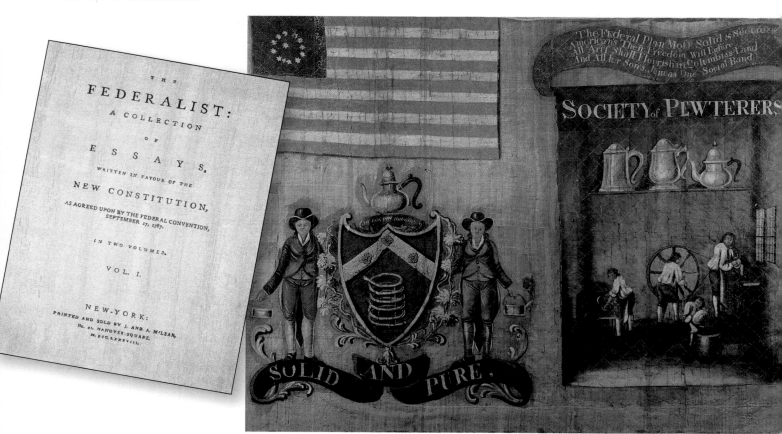

1789

The new government of the United States went to work early in 1789. That same year, in France, another change in government began—the French Revolution. This was a long, terrible conflict that took many lives. But when the revolution was over, the French had overthrown their monarchy.

In many ways, what was important to the Americans during the American Revolution was also important to the French. The leaders of the French Revolution believed in democratic ideas such as liberty. Even the colors of the French Revolution were red, white, and blue, like those of the United States flag.

The present-day French flag also shares the same colors with the United States flag.

firm Anti-Federalists. They returned home as Federalists. Massachusetts easily ratified the Constitution in February 1788.

Maryland and South Carolina soon followed Massachusetts. Then, on June 21, 1788, New Hampshire became the ninth state to ratify the United States Constitution. That was enough for the new plan of government to become law. That summer, Virginia and New York voted for the Constitution. By early 1789 the new government was at work. North Carolina ratified later that year. The last state to ratify the Constitution, Rhode Island, finally gave its approval in 1790.

REVIEW *What was* **The Federalist?**

LESSON 1 REVIEW

Check Understanding

1 **Remember the Facts**   Who were the Federalists and the Anti-Federalists?

2 **Recall the Main Idea**   What made the people of the United States want to support the Constitution?

Think Critically

3 **Think More About It**   Why do you think winning ratification in large states such as New York and Virginia was so important?

4 **Cause and Effect**   What effect did the promise of a bill of rights have on the debate over ratification?

Show What You Know

Cartoon Activity   Choose one side in the debate over the ratification of the Constitution. Draw a political cartoon, showing your point of view. Ask a family member or a classmate to interpret the meaning of your political cartoon.

For or Against a

James Madison

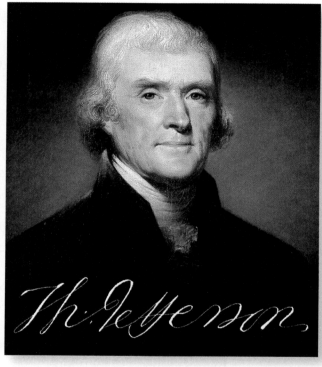

Thomas Jefferson

James Madison and Thomas Jefferson liked and respected one another. Both men were important leaders who were born and grew up in Virginia. Both served in Virginia's legislature. Jefferson took part in writing the Declaration of Independence, and Madison helped write the Constitution. But Jefferson and Madison disagreed about many things, such as the need for a bill of rights to be added to the Constitution.

Shortly after the Constitutional Convention ended, Madison sent Jefferson a copy of the Constitution along with a long letter about the convention. Jefferson wrote back, explaining why he felt a bill of rights was needed. At first, Madison saw little need for a bill of rights and felt that any changes to the Constitution would just prolong the debate and threaten ratification. Read the following parts of Jefferson's and Madison's letters.

Bill of Rights?

Jefferson to Madison—December 20, 1787

❝Let me add that a bill of rights is what the people are entitled to against every government on earth, general or particular, and what no just government should refuse . . .❞

Madison to Jefferson—April 22, 1788

❝Should this [the demand for a bill of rights] be carried in the affirmative, . . . I think the Constitution, and the Union will be both endangered.❞

Jefferson to Madison—July 31, 1788

❝I hope therefore a bill of rights will be formed to guard the peoples against the federal government, as they are already guarded against their state governments in most instances.❞

Madison to Jefferson—October 17, 1788

❝I have never thought the omission [of a bill of rights] a material defect, nor been anxious to supply it even by subsequent amendment . . . A bill of rights will be good ground for an appeal to the sense of the community. . . .❞

Jefferson to Madison—March 15, 1789

❝I am much pleased with the prospect that a declaration of rights will be added: and hope it will be done in that way which will not endanger the whole frame of the government, or any essential part of it.❞

Compare Viewpoints

1. What viewpoint about the Bill of Rights did Jefferson hold?

2. What viewpoint about the Bill of Rights did Madison hold at first?

3. How did Madison's viewpoint change over time?

Think and Apply

People often change their views about things over time. You have read that James Madison changed his view about the need for a bill of rights. Can you think of times when you changed your views on a subject? What caused you to change your views? Was it talks with friends, some new information you learned, or something else?

FOCUS

Why do citizens have responsibilities to their nation as well as individual rights?

Main Idea Read to learn about individual rights that come from the Constitution and about American citizens' responsibilities.

Vocabulary

amendment
Bill of Rights
due process of law
human rights
jury
patriotism

Rights and Responsibilities

As promised, not long after the states had ratified the United States Constitution, it was changed. Ten **amendments**, or changes, were added to protect the rights of the people. These ten amendments, called the **Bill of Rights**, describe freedoms that the government cannot take away and list actions that the government is not allowed to take.

The British had long had a Bill of Rights. But the British monarch and Parliament could ignore it or change it any time they wanted. The American Bill of Rights became part of the Constitution in December of 1791. There is only one way it can be changed—by another amendment.

The Bill of Rights

The First Amendment in the Bill of Rights is perhaps the most famous because the freedoms it guarantees are so much a part of our daily lives. The First Amendment says that people have the freedom to follow any religion they want, or no religion at all. It protects freedom of speech and freedom of the press. It also says that people can hold meetings to discuss problems and that they can ask the government to hear their complaints.

The Second Amendment protects people's right to carry arms, or weapons. It says, "A well-regulated militia being necessary to the security of a free State, the right of the people to keep and bear arms shall not be infringed."

The Third Amendment says that the government cannot force citizens to pay for quartering, or housing, soldiers. Before the Revolutionary War, many colonists had to spend their own money to house and feed British soldiers. Under the Fourth Amendment, the government cannot order that a person's home be searched or property taken away without there being a good reason.

The Fifth through Eighth Amendments have to do with **due process of law**. This means that people have the right to a fair public trial. They do not have to speak against themselves.

On this American coin from 1795, Lady Liberty wears the type of cap that former slaves in ancient Rome wore to show they had been freed.

The painting (above) shows Benjamin Franklin in a print shop holding a freshly printed page. During the late 1700s, the printing press (right) was the main tool for spreading news and opinions. Why do you think the Bill of Rights includes freedom of the press?

They have the right to have a lawyer speak for them in court. They cannot be put on trial twice for the same crime or be given "cruel or unusual" punishment.

The Ninth Amendment says that people have many other rights that are not listed in detail in the Constitution. Among these are **human rights**—the freedoms that all people should have. The Declaration of Independence calls them "unalienable rights" and lists them as "Life, Liberty, and the pursuit of Happiness."

As a final protection for citizens, the Tenth Amendment says that the national government can do only those things listed in the Constitution. All other authority belongs to the states or to the people.

REVIEW *Why is the Bill of Rights an important part of the Constitution?*

Citizens' Responsibilities

With the first ten amendments, the American people made it clear that their rights were important. Government must protect these rights. But the people also have a role to play. Certain responsibilities go along with the rights of citizens. For the United States to remain free and strong, its citizens have to take an active part in its government.

The responsibilities of citizens are not written in the Constitution. They are implied, or suggested. The Constitution says, for example, that the laws of the United States are the highest laws in the nation. This implies that citizens should respect and obey the laws. The Constitution gives citizens the right to elect representatives to govern them. This implies that citizens should take part in government by voting in elections.

The Constitution gives Congress the authority to raise an army. This means that citizens should be ready to defend the country. The Constitution says that every person that is charged with a crime will be judged by a **jury**—a group of citizens who decide a case in court. So citizens must be willing to be members of juries when they are asked. The Constitution also gives Congress the authority to raise money to run the country. Citizens must be willing to pay taxes if the country is to run smoothly.

REVIEW *Why should citizens take an active part in government?*

Toward a New Plan of Government

| 1780 | 1782 | 1784 | 1786 | 1788 | 1790 | 1792 |

1781
• The Articles of Confederation are ratified

1783
• The Revolutionary War ends

1787
• Shays's Rebellion
• Delegates sign the Constitution

1788
• The Constitution is ratified

1791
• The Bill of Rights is added to the Constitution

LEARNING FROM TIME LINES This time line lists the key events leading toward the ratification of the Constitution and the addition of the Bill of Rights.
■ *For how many years were the Articles of Confederation in effect?*

Love of Country

The writers of the Constitution were not sure that their new government would last. They looked to other countries and other times in history. No other nation had a government quite like the one described by the Constitution. No other people had the kinds of freedoms that American citizens now enjoyed. But would the people be able to keep their government going and protect their freedoms over time?

This would depend on having good citizens, or as the writers of the Constitution described them—"a virtuous citizenry." Past republics, like that of ancient Rome, broke up when the people grew greedy and selfish. To stay strong, the American people had to keep alive the spirit that had given the country its independence and its Constitution. The writers of the Constitution felt that a love of country is important because it helps keep this spirit alive. But **patriotism**, or love of country, is more than simply waving the American flag at special times. Americans have to be virtuous citizens all the time.

REVIEW *Why is love of country important?*

LESSON 2 REVIEW

Check Understanding
1 Remember the Facts What important freedoms are protected by the Bill of Rights?

2 Recall the Main Idea What are the main rights and responsibilities of American citizens?

Think Critically
3 Think More About It Can American citizens have rights without responsibilities? Why or why not?

4 Personally Speaking What do you think is the most important right described in the Bill of Rights? Explain your answer.

Show What You Know
Art Activity Make a collage by cutting out drawings, photographs, and cartoons that show one or more of the rights listed in the Bill of Rights. Share your collage with your classmates.

Putting the New Government to Work

LESSON

3

FOCUS

Why must a nation's leaders be willing to work together for government to work well?

Main Idea As you read, look for ways the nation's leaders worked together to carry out the new plan of government.

Vocabulary

Cabinet
political party
campaign

In early 1789, elections were held for the first time under the new government. Property-owning male citizens all over the country elected the first members of the House of Representatives. Legislatures of the 13 states each chose two senators. The electoral college chose the nation's first President.

New Leaders

Fourteen years after members of Congress had chosen George Washington to lead the Continental army, the electoral college elected him as the nation's first President. John Adams, the runner-up to Washington in the voting, became the first Vice President. His job was to help President Washington with his presidential duties.

On April 30, 1789, George Washington stood on the balcony of Federal Hall in New York City, where the new Congress was to meet for the first time. There he recited the President's oath of office:

> 66 I do solemnly swear (or affirm) that I will faithfully execute the office of President of the United States, and will to the best of my ability preserve, protect, and defend the Constitution of the United States. 99

The new President and the first Congress helped the government make a good start. Congress decided on the number of justices who would serve on the Supreme Court. The President named John Jay as the first chief justice. Washington chose new leaders, too, for important jobs in the executive branch. These were the secretaries, or heads, of the departments of state, the treasury, and war. These departments would carry out the main responsibilities of the executive branch.

This pitcher from 1789 marks the election of George Washington as the nation's first President.

President Washington asked Thomas Jefferson, who had served as ambassador to France, to help him deal with other countries. He made Jefferson the nation's first secretary of state. Jefferson worked to set up ties with the leading world powers of that day— Spain, France, and the former enemy of the United States, Britain.

Alexander Hamilton was given the important job of secretary of the treasury. The national government badly needed money. Hamilton worked with Congress to set up a new banking system and pass new tax laws. He also ordered the printing and coining of money.

George Washington chose Henry Knox, who had been a general in the Revolutionary War, as secretary of war. Knox had helped the Continental army defeat the British at the Battle of Yorktown. Knox began building a national army of 1,000 soldiers to defend the nation's western border.

Edmund Randolph became the President's chief law officer and legal adviser, now called the attorney general. He told the President what the Constitution and the nation's other laws would and would not allow him to do.

Jefferson, Hamilton, Knox, and Randolph together were known as the **Cabinet**, a group of the President's most important advisers. Every President since Washington has relied on a Cabinet for help in carrying out the duties of the executive branch. Under later Presidents, the number of Cabinet members grew as the executive branch took on more responsibilities.

REVIEW *How did George Washington divide the responsibilities of the executive branch?*

Washington rode from Virginia to New York, where he recited the oath of office. This painting shows children giving him flowers as he passes through New Jersey.

Presidents' Day

Pins like this one were worn to celebrate Washington's election.

George Washington's birthday was first celebrated as a holiday in the late 1700s. Washington was born on February 22, 1732, according to the calendar we use today. However, by the calendar used during Washington's time, he was born on February 11. For this reason the holiday was celebrated on different days by different people.

Another great President, Abraham Lincoln, was born on February 12, 1809. His birthday is also celebrated. Starting in the 1970s some states combined the birthday celebrations for Washington and Lincoln on a holiday called Presidents' Day. This day is the third Monday of February each year.

New Disagreements

Almost as soon as the new government got started, President Washington's two top advisers began to quarrel. Thomas Jefferson and Alexander Hamilton disagreed on almost every problem facing the new nation.

One of the main disagreements between the two leaders had to do with the authority of the states and the national government. Jefferson worked for the rights of the states. He did not trust a strong national government. Hamilton wanted a strong national government and did not trust the states to act on their own.

Jefferson and Hamilton also disagreed about what some parts of the Constitution meant. Jefferson said the national government had only the authority described in the Constitution. He said that all other authority belonged to the states. Hamilton said that the Constitution allowed the national government far greater authority over many more areas than those it listed. He felt that the government should be active in all parts of American life.

There were other differences. Jefferson wanted Americans across the country to spread out and live on farms. "When we get piled upon one another in large cities," Jefferson argued, "we shall become corrupt." Hamilton wanted the United States to be a nation of cities. He thought the national government should build ports and factories.

Jefferson thought the United States should have close ties with France. After all, France had been an ally of the nation in the Revolutionary War. Hamilton wanted the United States to become friendlier with Britain to make use of Britain's trading network, which covered much of the world.

REVIEW *What were the main disagreements between Jefferson and Hamilton?*

The First Political Parties

Representatives and senators in Congress began to take sides in the Jefferson-Hamilton quarrel. They even started voting together as groups. These groups formed the nation's first **political parties**. Party members tried to get others to agree with their ideas and chose leaders who shared the party's point of view.

Hamilton's followers formed what became known as the Federalist party. The party's members were some of the same people who had supported the Constitution during the state ratifying conventions. John Adams, John Jay, and Henry Knox all became members of the Federalist party.

Many Anti-Federalists took Jefferson's side in the quarrel. Patrick Henry, George Clinton, and others formed the Democratic-Republican party. They were also called simply Republicans. Jefferson's Republican party was not today's Republican party, which was formed much later. In fact, it was the beginning of the present-day Democratic party.

Most often Federalists and Republicans had to compromise so that laws could get passed. In one compromise, they agreed that a national capital would be built as a permanent home for the new government. But the capital would not be part of any one state. Maryland and Virginia would both give up some of their land to create the District of Columbia (D.C.). George Washington himself chose the location for the capital city that came to carry his name.

REVIEW *What were the main differences between Federalists and Republicans?*

A Peaceful Change in Leadership

In 1792 the electoral college chose George Washington as President, just as it had done in 1789. Many people hoped that Washington would remain President even longer than eight years. They felt that two 4-year terms were not enough—the country needed his leadership. In 1796, however, Washington turned down the chance to run again and went home to Mount Vernon, his plantation

Alexander Hamilton (left) and Thomas Jefferson (right) disagreed over how much authority they believed the Constitution gave to the national government. Hamilton favored a strong national government. Jefferson supported the power of the states.

in Virginia. In leaving after two terms, Washington set an example that many other Presidents would follow. Later the Constitution would be changed so that no President could serve more than two terms in office.

But by 1796 the growth of political parties had changed the way the electoral college chose the President. Instead of making its own list of people to choose from, the electoral college was given lists made by each party's leaders. The electoral college chose from these lists when it voted for the President.

When George Washington left office, the Federalist party backed John Adams, Washington's Vice President. Thomas Jefferson was the Republicans' choice.

As they had done with their quarrel over the Constitution, the Federalists and the Republicans took their fight to the people through the newspapers. This fight was less polite, though. Instead of arguing about problems, the political parties called one another names.

The **campaign**, or race for office, was bitter. Yet the election was peaceful. In the end John Adams won by three electoral votes over Jefferson, who became the Vice President.

On March 4, 1797, John Adams took the President's oath of office in Philadelphia's Congress Hall, next door to the more famous Independence Hall. This was an important day in history. It marked one of the first times in the history of the world that a nation had changed leaders by means of a peaceful election.

John Adams started his term as President in Philadelphia, where Congress met. By the end of his term, in November 1800, the government had moved to the District of Columbia. When John Adams and his family moved to the new capital city, they lived in a special house built for the President. It has had several names, among them the President's House, the Executive Mansion, and the White House—the name by which it is best known today.

Abigail Adams, the President's wife, was impressed by her new home. She wrote to her daughter in Massachusetts that the house was "built for ages to come." Could the same be said for the nation's new government and its Constitution?

REVIEW *What was important about the way John Adams became President?*

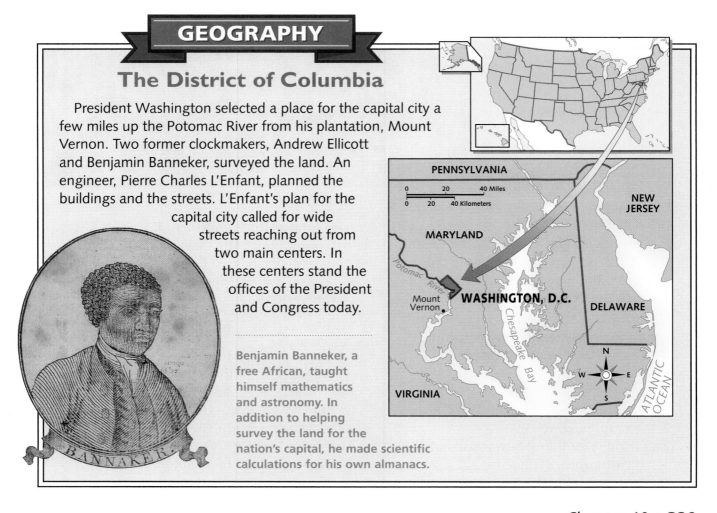

GEOGRAPHY

The District of Columbia

President Washington selected a place for the capital city a few miles up the Potomac River from his plantation, Mount Vernon. Two former clockmakers, Andrew Ellicott and Benjamin Banneker, surveyed the land. An engineer, Pierre Charles L'Enfant, planned the buildings and the streets. L'Enfant's plan for the capital city called for wide streets reaching out from two main centers. In these centers stand the offices of the President and Congress today.

Benjamin Banneker, a free African, taught himself mathematics and astronomy. In addition to helping survey the land for the nation's capital, he made scientific calculations for his own almanacs.

BANNAKER.

PENNSYLVANIA

0   20   40 Miles
0   20   40 Kilometers

NEW JERSEY

MARYLAND

Potomac River

Mount Vernon

WASHINGTON, D.C.

DELAWARE

Chesapeake Bay

VIRGINIA

ATLANTIC OCEAN

N W E S

Washington, D.C.

LEARNING FROM DIAGRAMS

Washington, D.C., today reflects Pierre Charles L'Enfant's original plan.

❶ United States Capitol
❷ Independence Avenue
❸ Pennsylvania Avenue
❹ National Gallery of Art
❺ The Mall
❻ National Air and Space Museum
❼ Hirshhorn Museum and Sculpture Garden
❽ National Museum of Natural History
❾ Smithsonian Institution Building (Smithsonian Museums 4, 6, 7, 8, 10, 13, 14)
❿ Freer Gallery of Art
⑪ Smithsonian Arts & Industries Building
⑫ White House
⑬ Constitution Avenue
⑭ National Museum of American History
⑮ Department of Agriculture
⑯ Washington Monument
⑰ 17th Street
⑱ Reflecting Pool
⑲ Vietnam Veterans Memorial
⑳ Lincoln Memorial

■ *Which buildings play an important role in the United States government?*

LESSON 3 REVIEW

Check Understanding

❶ **Remember the Facts** What caused political parties to form? How did they change the way the electoral college chose the President?

❷ **Recall the Main Idea** How did the nation's early leaders work together to carry out the new plan of government?

Think Critically

❸ **Past to Present** Why is the President's Cabinet larger today than in Washington's time?

❹ **Personally Speaking** If you had been a member of the electoral college in 1796, which leader would you have chosen as President? Explain your answer.

Show What You Know

Newspaper Activity
Imagine a problem George Washington is facing as the first President of the United States. Then write a newspaper article comparing how Alexander Hamilton and Thomas Jefferson might feel about the problem.

Learn from a Document

Skills

1. Why Learn This Skill?

You have already studied many documents that are important to American history, such as the Mayflower Compact and the Declaration of Independence. In the study of history, a document is any photograph, recording, or written or printed paper that gives information. Maps, letters, drawings, and journals are all documents. So are some kinds of money, such as the paper money shown below.

Historical documents are primary sources that give information about the past. They tell us information that many books cannot tell us. Knowing how to gather information from a historical document can help you learn more about life in the past.

2. Understand the Process

In 1790 Secretary of the Treasury Alexander Hamilton asked Congress to set up the Bank of the United States. The bank would be a safe place to store the money the government collected in taxes. It would also lend money to merchants and manufacturers, which would speed the growth of business. One way the bank would lend money would be by printing paper money called banknotes.

In 1798 the Bank of the United States printed the banknote shown below. This is an important document because it gives information about the time in which it was printed.

Sometimes you have to look hard to find information on a document. Study the document by using these questions as a guide:

1. How do you know this banknote was printed by the Bank of the United States?
2. What tells you how much the banknote is worth?
3. The name of the holder and the date have been written by hand on the banknote. What might this tell you about how this banknote was used?

3. Think and Apply

With a partner, compare the 1798 banknote with a dollar bill of today. What can you learn from each one that you cannot learn from the other? Share your observations with classmates.

CHAPTER ◀ **10**
REVIEW

1785

1787
• Delegates sign
the Constitution

CONNECT MAIN IDEAS

Use this organizer to show how the chapter's main ideas are connected. Write a sentence or two describing how each idea shown below helped to build a new government. A copy of the organizer appears on page 65 of the Activity Book.

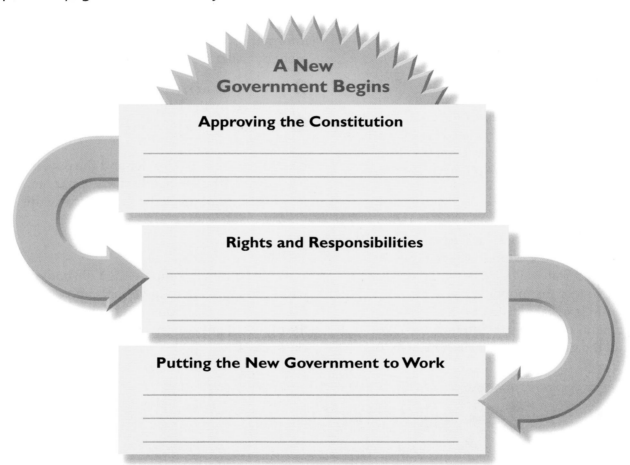

A New Government Begins

Approving the Constitution
_____
_____
_____

Rights and Responsibilities
_____
_____
_____

Putting the New Government to Work
_____
_____
_____

WRITE MORE ABOUT IT

Write a Persuasive Letter Suppose that you are either an Anti-Federalist or a Federalist. Write a letter describing your views about the ratification of the Constitution. Tell in the letter why you think a bill of rights should or should not be added.

Write an Explanation Imagine that you are an adviser to President Washington. He asks you to explain the differences that divide Thomas Jefferson and Alexander Hamilton. Write what you will tell the President about the leaders' disagreements.

1790   1795   1800

1789
• Government under the new Constitution begins
• George Washington becomes the first President of the United States

1797
• John Adams becomes the second President of the United States

USE VOCABULARY

For each group of underlined words, write the term from the list below that has the same meaning.

amendments	**jury**
Cabinet	**patriotism**
campaign	**ratify**

1 Nine of the 13 states had to <u>agree to</u> the Constitution before it would become law.

2 Ten <u>changes</u> were added to the Constitution.

3 A person charged with a crime is judged by a <u>group of citizens who decide a case in court</u>.

4 The writers of the Constitution felt that <u>love of country</u> was very important.

5 President Washington relied on a <u>group of the President's most important advisers</u>.

6 The <u>race for office</u> between Adams and Jefferson was bitter.

CHECK UNDERSTANDING

7 What collection of letters defended the Constitution?

8 What rights are granted under the First Amendment in the Bill of Rights?

9 What leaders were members of the first Cabinet? What office did each member hold?

10 What were the first two political parties?

11 Who was the second President of the United States? Who was his Vice President?

THINK CRITICALLY

12 **Cause and Effect** What promise helped persuade states to ratify the Constitution?

13 **Personally Speaking** The First Amendment protects freedom of speech and freedom of the press. Can you think of any examples in which these rights should be limited? Explain your answer.

APPLY SKILLS

Learn from a Document Use the banner on page 318 to answer these questions.

14 Who carried this banner?

15 Why do you think they chose to include the American flag on their banner?

16 What do the words *solid* and *pure* on the banner tell you?

17 What does the banner tell you about the work of a pewterer?

READ MORE ABOUT IT

A More Perfect Union: The Story of Our Constitution by Betsy and Giulio Maestro. Mulberry. This book presents an account of how the Constitution of the United States was drafted and ratified.

Visit the Internet at **http://www.hbschool.com** for additional resources.

★★★★ WHO ★★★★ *Can* *Vote?*

In 1787, at the time of the Constitutional Convention, only certain citizens could vote. In order to vote, a person had to own something of value, such as land. And in most places, a person had to be white, male, and at least 21 years old. The Constitution that became the American plan of government in 1789 did not change that.

In 1870, the Fifteenth Amendment gave African American men the right to vote. Women gained the right to vote in 1920, when the Nineteenth Amendment was ratified. In 1924 Congress passed a law giving Native Americans the right to vote. And in 1971 the Twenty-Sixth Amendment set 18 as the voting age for all United States citizens.

Today more people than ever before in our country's history have the right to vote. Yet not everyone takes advantage of this right. Only about 55 percent of Americans who can vote actually do so. It is important that all Americans vote. Taking part in choosing our leaders is one way that American citizens can help keep the United States running smoothly.

Campaign buttons and pins for many Democratic candidates are shown on this page. Those featured on the next page show support for Republicans.

Think and Apply

Think about why it is important for American citizens to vote. Then write a persuasive letter that explains why citizens need to take part in government by voting. Share your letter with the class.

HARCOURT BRACE

Visit the Internet at **http://www.hbschool.com** for additional resources.

CNN
Turner Le@rning

Check your media center or classroom video library for the Making Social Studies Relevant videotape of this feature.

Summarize the Main Ideas
Study the pictures and captions to help you review the events you read about in Unit 5.

Write a Journal
Imagine that you are a delegate to the Constitutional Convention. Write several journal entries that tell what you think about the events shown in this visual summary.

1 Under the Articles of Confederation, the national government had little authority. In the late 1780s Daniel Shays led a rebellion in Massachusetts.

4 On September 17, 1787, the United States Constitution was signed at the convention. It was later ratified by all 13 states.

5 The Constitution says that the President is the head of the executive branch. George Washington, the first President, took the oath of office on April 30, 1789.

3 The delegates met at the Pennsylvania State House. They decided that a new plan of government was needed and described it in the Constitution.

2 Delegates from the states went to a convention in Philadelphia to discuss their problems.

6 Many people wanted the Constitution to protect their rights. Ten amendments were added to the Constitution—they form the Bill of Rights.

USE VOCABULARY

Write the term that correctly matches each definition.

ambassador	**human rights**
census	**majority**

1. a representative from one country to another country
2. the greater part
3. a population count
4. the freedoms that all people should have

CHECK UNDERSTANDING

5. What problems caused the delegates to the Constitutional Convention to disagree? How were the problems settled?

6. What was considered by many people to be a major problem with the Constitution after it was written? How was that problem finally solved?

7. How were Thomas Jefferson's and Alexander Hamilton's views about the role of government different?

THINK CRITICALLY

8. **Explore Viewpoints** James Madison said he was afraid Congress had become "a rope of sand" under the Articles of Confederation. Others, like Patrick Henry, argued that a rope of sand was better than a rod of iron. What did these two leaders mean?

9. **Think More About It** Imagine that you are a member of the House of Representatives and have just written a new bill. Describe the process your bill will take on its way to becoming a law.

APPLY SKILLS

Figure Travel Time and Distance

The map below shows George Washington's route from his home, Mount Vernon, to New York City, where he took the oath of office as the first President. Washington rode his horse on the journey. Use the map to answer the questions, figuring that Washington traveled about 70 miles a day.

10. How long would it have taken George Washington to ride from Mount Vernon, in Virginia, to Wilmington, Delaware?

11. How long would it have taken George Washington to ride from Philadelphia to New York City?

12. How long would Washington's entire journey from Mount Vernon to New York City have taken?

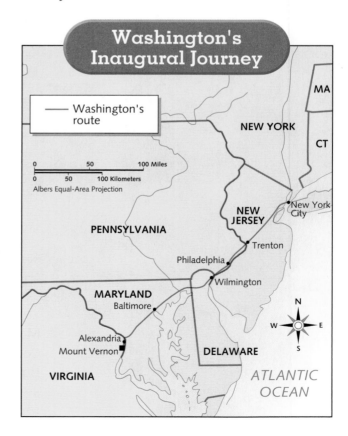

Washington's Inaugural Journey

— Washington's route

REMEMBER

- Share your ideas.
- Cooperate with others to plan your work.
- Take responsibility for your work.
- Help one another.
- Show your group's work to the class.
- Discuss what you learned by working together.

ACTIVITY Make a Book

Work in a group to write and design a book about the Bill of Rights. Your book should summarize each of the amendments in the Bill of Rights and explain how each is important to people today. To illustrate your book, draw pictures or cut out pictures from magazines and newspapers. Give your book a title, and display it where others in your school can read it.

ACTIVITY Write and Perform a Class Play

Write and perform a play about the conflicts and cooperation that led to the ratification of the Constitution. As a class, decide on the people and events you want to include in your play. Give your play a title. Then form small groups. Each group will write one scene. Decide on roles and other responsibilities, such as making costumes and sets, and have at least one rehearsal. Then perform the play for invited guests from your school or community.

ACTIVITY Draw a Map

Work in a group to draw a map that shows the United States at the time the Constitution was ratified. Include the 13 states, the state capitals, and the Northwest Territory. Color each state to show the year it ratified the Constitution. Use blue for 1787, red for 1788, yellow for 1789, and green for 1790. Make a key for your map. Then use the map to help explain to your classmates how the Constitution was ratified.

Unit Project Wrap-Up

Draw a Poster Work with several classmates to display your posters. Arrange the posters to show the order in which the events happened. Each group member should choose one of the events shown and write a short report. Use encyclopedias, biographies, and the Internet to find additional information. Present your posters and reports to the class.

OUR NATION GROWS

The United States grew rapidly in the 50 years after the War for Independence. As more people came to live in the new country, many began to leave the 13 states to find more land. At first, the settlers went only as far as the Appalachian Mountains. Later they traveled to the Mississippi River. By the 1840s they had crossed the continent and were building new settlements on the Pacific coast and in the Southwest.

During those same 50 years, the United States became more important among the countries of the world. The young nation fought another war with Britain and showed itself to be a leader among the countries in the Americas. While the United States built a strong industrial economy, more and more of its people demanded their rights as citizens.

◄ This scene of pioneers moving west was painted by Albert Bierstadt in 1867.

UNIT THEMES

■ Conflict and Cooperation

■ Continuity and Change

■ Individualism and Interdependence

■ Interaction Within Different Environments

Unit Project

Make a Diorama Complete this project as you study Unit 6. Make a diorama that shows pioneer life on the frontier. As you read, sketch pictures that illustrate the lives of the pioneers. Use your sketches to help you plan what you are going to show in your diorama.

341

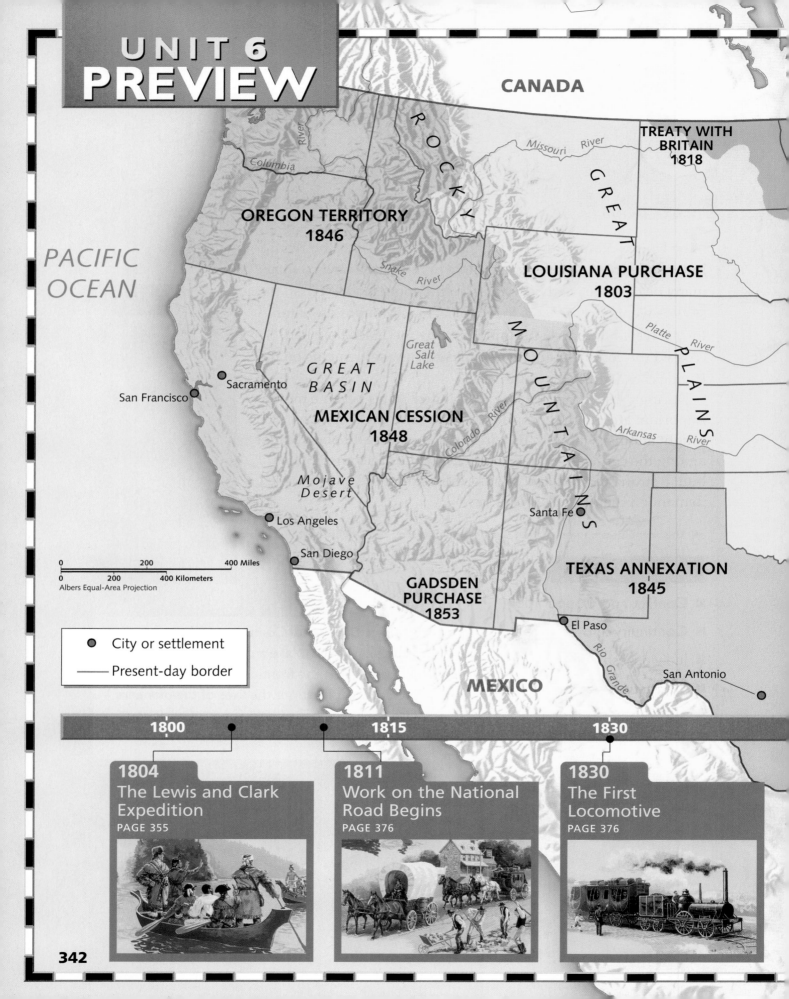

CANADA

TREATY WITH BRITAIN 1818

Missouri River

ROCKY

GREAT

Columbia River

OREGON TERRITORY 1846

Snake River

LOUISIANA PURCHASE 1803

PACIFIC OCEAN

M O U N T A I N S

Platte River

P L A I N S

Great Salt Lake

GREAT BASIN

San Francisco

Sacramento

MEXICAN CESSION 1848

Colorado River

Arkansas River

Mojave Desert

Los Angeles

San Diego

Santa Fe

TEXAS ANNEXATION 1845

GADSDEN PURCHASE 1853

El Paso

Rio Grande

MEXICO

San Antonio

	200		400 Miles
0			
0	200	400 Kilometers	

Albers Equal-Area Projection

● City or settlement

── Present-day border

	1800		1815		1830

1804
The Lewis and Clark Expedition
PAGE 355

1811
Work on the National Road Begins
PAGE 376

1830
The First Locomotive
PAGE 376

The United States, 1783–1853

TREATY WITH BRITAIN 1842

CANADA

Lake Superior

Lake Huron

Lake Michigan

Lake Ontario

Lake Erie

Mississippi River

Milwaukee

Detroit

Chicago

Cleveland

Pittsburgh

Allegheny River

Buffalo

Troy

Albany

Portland

Portsmouth

Boston

Providence

Hartford

New York City

Philadelphia

Wilmington

Baltimore

Annapolis

Washington, D.C.

Indianapolis

UNITED STATES 1783

Ohio River

Missouri River

St. Louis

Louisville

Richmond

Norfolk

ATLANTIC OCEAN

APPALACHIAN MOUNTAINS

Tennessee River

Nashville

New Bern

Wilmington

Atlanta

Charleston

Birmingham

Mississippi River

Savannah

Dallas

Natchez

1810

1813

Jacksonville

St. Augustine

Houston

1812

New Orleans

FLORIDA 1819

Gulf of Mexico

N
E
W
S

1845

1860

MID-1800s
Abolitionist Movement

PAGE 393

343

CASSIE'S JOURNEY

by Brett Harvey
illustrated by Ed Martinez

The people who settled the West came from many different places. Most came from the first 13 states, but some came from as far away as Europe and Asia. Almost everyone had read about the American West in newspapers, magazines, books, or letters. Many had heard about it in songs.

The West promised a new life to people like Cassie and her family, whom you will meet in this story. But getting to the West to enjoy its benefits was not easy. People traveling in wagon trains faced long, hard journeys. Sometimes food ran out, or water or firewood could not be found. People moving to the West faced these problems and more.

It's been raining for two days and everything is wet, wet, wet—our clothes, our bedding, even our food. Last night the rain was so heavy and the wind was blowing so hard that we couldn't make a fire. We had cold coffee and soggy bread for supper. This morning Mama cooked our breakfast under an umbrella. Today it's raining in sheets of gray so we have to stay in the wagon with the flaps tied down tight. I hate riding in the wagon—its swaying motion and the screeching noise of the wheels make me feel seasick. Mama is drilling us in our multiplication tables. I wonder if we'll ever be dry again.

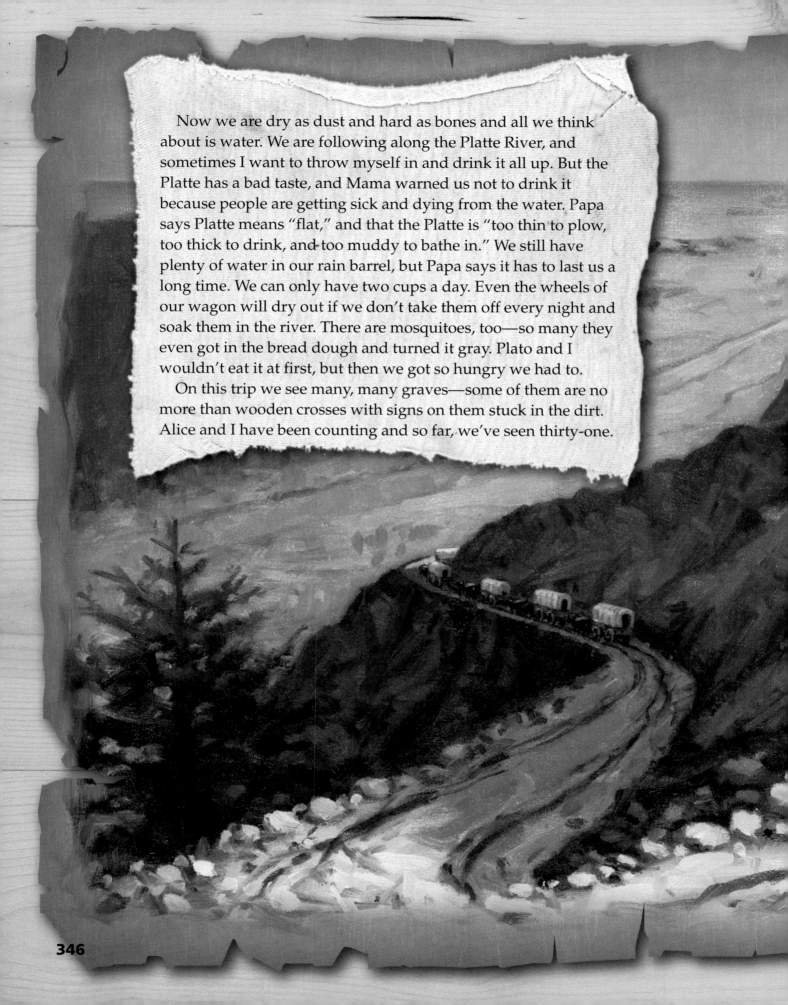

Now we are dry as dust and hard as bones and all we think about is water. We are following along the Platte River, and sometimes I want to throw myself in and drink it all up. But the Platte has a bad taste, and Mama warned us not to drink it because people are getting sick and dying from the water. Papa says Platte means "flat," and that the Platte is "too thin to plow, too thick to drink, and too muddy to bathe in." We still have plenty of water in our rain barrel, but Papa says it has to last us a long time. We can only have two cups a day. Even the wheels of our wagon will dry out if we don't take them off every night and soak them in the river. There are mosquitoes, too—so many they even got in the bread dough and turned it gray. Plato and I wouldn't eat it at first, but then we got so hungry we had to.

On this trip we see many, many graves—some of them are no more than wooden crosses with signs on them stuck in the dirt. Alice and I have been counting and so far, we've seen thirty-one.

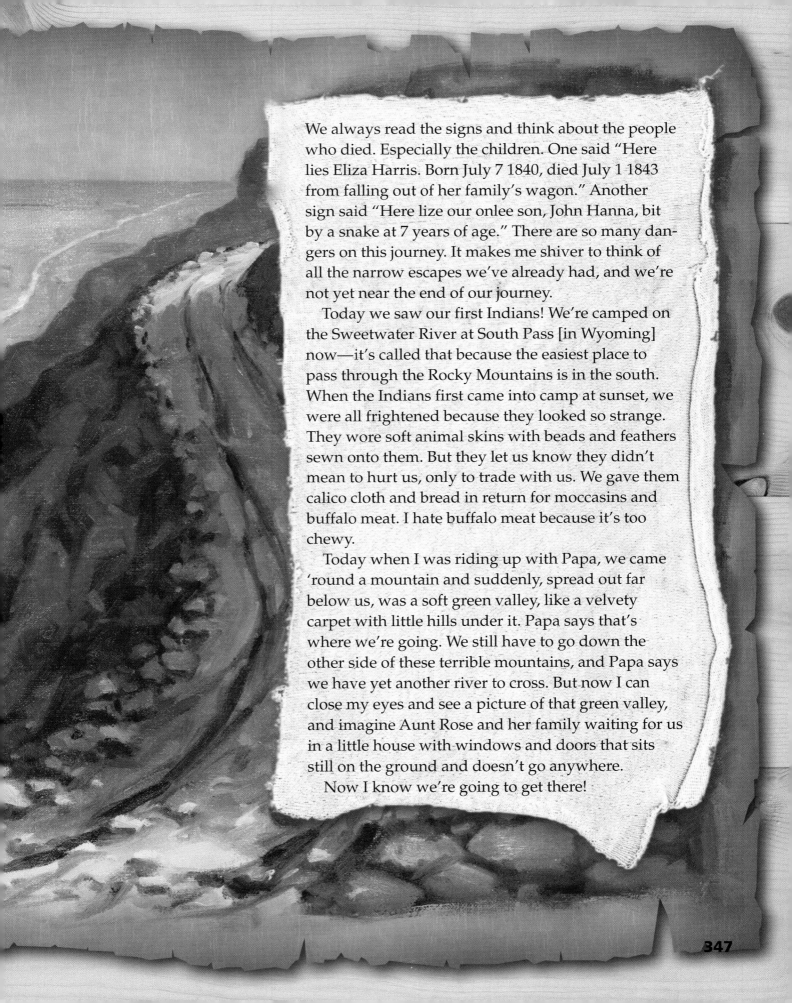

We always read the signs and think about the people who died. Especially the children. One said "Here lies Eliza Harris. Born July 7 1840, died July 1 1843 from falling out of her family's wagon." Another sign said "Here lize our onlee son, John Hanna, bit by a snake at 7 years of age." There are so many dangers on this journey. It makes me shiver to think of all the narrow escapes we've already had, and we're not yet near the end of our journey.

Today we saw our first Indians! We're camped on the Sweetwater River at South Pass [in Wyoming] now—it's called that because the easiest place to pass through the Rocky Mountains is in the south. When the Indians first came into camp at sunset, we were all frightened because they looked so strange. They wore soft animal skins with beads and feathers sewn onto them. But they let us know they didn't mean to hurt us, only to trade with us. We gave them calico cloth and bread in return for moccasins and buffalo meat. I hate buffalo meat because it's too chewy.

Today when I was riding up with Papa, we came 'round a mountain and suddenly, spread out far below us, was a soft green valley, like a velvety carpet with little hills under it. Papa says that's where we're going. We still have to go down the other side of these terrible mountains, and Papa says we have yet another river to cross. But now I can close my eyes and see a picture of that green valley, and imagine Aunt Rose and her family waiting for us in a little house with windows and doors that sits still on the ground and doesn't go anywhere.

Now I know we're going to get there!

ON THE MOVE

"The ax has cut the forest down, The laboring ox has smoothed all clear, Apples now grow where pine trees stood, And slow cows graze instead of deer."

From the poem "The Wilderness Is Tamed" by Elizabeth Coatsworth

Mary Prosser, a pioneer woman

Across the Appalachians

LESSON

1

FOCUS
What problems might a person face in moving to a new place today?

Main Idea As you read, look for some of the problems the early settlers faced when they crossed the Appalachian Mountains.

Vocabulary
pioneer

In 1783 the Treaty of Paris, which ended the War for Independence, set the Mississippi River as the new nation's western border. When people talked about the West in those days, they meant all of the land between the Appalachian Mountains and the Mississippi River. This was the American frontier.

Daniel Boone

Even before the Treaty of Paris, American pioneers were pushing the frontier west. A **pioneer** is a person who first settles a new place. Daniel Boone was one of the earliest and best-known American pioneers to cross the Appalachians.

Boone was born in Pennsylvania. He was 16 years old when his family moved to the Yadkin Valley of North Carolina. Boone came to love living in the woods and hunting.

During the French and Indian War, Boone served in the army. There he met John Finley, a fur trader. Boone later remembered the stories Finley told about a wonderful land west of the Appalachian Mountains. There, Finley said, green forests and meadows stretched for miles.

After the war Boone tried to find this land, now known as Kentucky. But he could not find a way over the mountains. He looked for the Warrior's Path, an Indian trail Finley had described that crossed the mountains, but he could not find it.

Soon after Boone returned home, a peddler, or seller, came to the door of the Boone house in North Carolina. The peddler was John Finley! With Finley's help, Boone again tried to find Kentucky. This time he found the Warrior's Path and followed it across the Appalachian Mountains through what was called the Cumberland Gap. Boone later told a friend what he had seen on the other side.

66 Thousands of Buffalo roamed the Kentucky hills and the land looked as if it never would become poor. 99

Pioneer leader Daniel Boone was dedicated to exploring and settling the American frontier.

349

Both the Cherokees and Shawnees lived in settlements throughout Kentucky. Several times the Shawnees captured Boone during his visits there. Each time they let him go with a warning not to come back. But Boone did not listen. He returned again and again to Kentucky to explore and to hunt. Stories of Boone's adventures and Kentucky's rich land soon spread, making people want to settle there.

REVIEW *What did Daniel Boone find when he reached Kentucky?*

Settling Kentucky

As word spread about Kentucky, several families tried to make their way over the mountains. But the Cherokees and Shawnees did not want to give up their land. They fought the pioneers, who had to turn back. Finally, in 1774, the Virginia militia fought a battle with the Indians and won. Virginia leaders made Indian leaders sign a treaty giving up their lands in Kentucky.

As soon as the treaty was signed, a land developer hired Daniel Boone to clear a road to Kentucky. In March 1775 Boone led a group through the Cumberland Gap. Cutting down trees and bushes to make way for wagons, the workers cleared a path through

Human-Environment Interactions
This map shows the different routes people used to travel to Kentucky. In the painting by George Caleb Bingham (above left) Daniel Boone leads pioneers through the Cumberland Gap.
■ *What route did Boone follow through the Appalachian Mountains?*

the wilderness. This path came to be known as the Wilderness Road.

Once in Kentucky, Boone built a fort and named it Boonesborough. He then returned to North Carolina to lead a group of settlers to Kentucky. In August he set out with his family and some neighbors for the new land. It was a slow, hard trip over the mountains. Getting a cow to walk 300 miles (483 km) was not easy. Sometimes wild animals scared the horses so much, they ran off in all directions. The Cherokees and Shawnees made surprise attacks, hoping to scare off the pioneers. But the settlers pushed on to Boonesborough, joining others at Kentucky's first pioneer settlement.

Over the next few years, thousands of pioneers took the Wilderness Road to the rich valleys beyond the Appalachian Mountains. Many more settlements were built in Kentucky and in Tennessee to the south. By 1800, American and European settlers had moved as far west as the Mississippi River. Kentucky and Tennessee had become states. Farmers in these states shipped their crops and animals on flatboats down the Mississippi River to the port of New Orleans, then controlled by Spain. From New Orleans the goods went by ship to markets on the east coast of the United States.

REVIEW *How did Daniel Boone help settle the West?*

Pioneer Life

Life on the western frontier was hard for pioneer families like the Boones. After they bought their land from a land developer, they had to clear thick forest in order to build their homes and farms. Most pioneers had little food to last until their first crops were ready. One pioneer told how poor his family was when they first settled in Kentucky.

66 My Wife and I had neither spoon, dish, knife, or any thing to do with when we began life. 99

Pioneer families had to become self-sufficient very quickly, or they did not survive on the frontier. They built their own homes, grew their own food, and made their own clothes and tools. They bartered with the

HISTORY

Log Cabins

Most pioneers in Kentucky lived in log cabins because such homes were quick and easy to build. First, a number of straight trees, all about the same size around, were chosen. Then, the trees were cut down and trimmed to the right length. The logs were pulled by horses or dragged by hand to where the cabin was to be built. Notches were cut at the ends so that the logs would fit together. Next, the logs were lifted into place. The spaces between the logs were "chinked," or filled with mud, clay, or moss. Finally, a roof and a fireplace were added. Following this plan, two people could build a log cabin in about two weeks.

Settlers Move West, 1790–1850

WA, OR, MT, ND, ID, WY, SD, NE, CA, NV, UT, CO, KS, AZ, NM, OK, TX

CANADA

ME, NY, VT, NH, Portland, Albany, MA, Boston, CT, RI, Providence, PA, New York City, NJ, Philadelphia, MD, DE, Washington, D.C., WV, VA, Richmond, OH, IN, IL, MI, WI, MN, IA, MO, KY, TN, NC, SC, GA, AR, MS, AL, LA, FL

Lake Superior, Lake Michigan, Lake Huron, Lake Ontario, Lake Erie, Milwaukee, Detroit, Buffalo, Chicago, Cleveland, Pittsburgh, St. Louis, Louisville, Nashville, Birmingham, Charleston, Jacksonville, New Orleans, Houston, Dallas, Santa Fe

APPALACHIAN MTS., Mississippi R., Ohio River, Missouri R.

PACIFIC OCEAN

ATLANTIC OCEAN

MEXICO

Gulf of Mexico

N E W S

0   200   400 Miles
0   200   400 Kilometers
Albers Equal-Area Projection

Settled by 1790
Settled by 1820
Settled by 1850
— Present-day border

MAP THEME

Regions This map shows the westward settlement of American pioneers at different times.
■ *What areas did pioneers settle from 1790 to 1820?*

Indian peoples, who traded furs, tobacco, cotton, and corn for cloth and other useful goods.

As pioneers continued moving onto Indian lands, many banded together in forts to protect themselves. In some settlements they built their log houses close together with a high log fence all around.

REVIEW *How did pioneer families become self-sufficient?*

LESSON 1 REVIEW

Check Understanding

1 Remember the Facts Why did pioneers push west into the frontier?

2 Recall the Main Idea What problems did the early settlers face when they crossed the Appalachian Mountains?

Think Critically

3 Cause and Effect How did Daniel Boone's Wilderness Road help the settlement of Kentucky and the West?

4 Think More About It Do you think the Indians and the pioneers could have lived peacefully together in the American West? Explain your answer.

Show What You Know

Poster Activity It is 1775, and you own a general store in North Carolina. Create a poster with pictures of some of the supplies you think a pioneer would need to take west. Display your poster in the classroom.

The Louisiana Purchase

FOCUS
What might people today learn from the examples set by people in the past?

Main Idea As you read, look for things that American pioneers learned from the explorers who traveled west before them.

Vocabulary
purchase
pathfinder

In time some of the pioneers who had settled between the Appalachians and the Mississippi began to look beyond the mighty river. Spain and France claimed these rich lands, although it was mostly Indian peoples who lived there. In one of the largest land sales in history, the United States bought part of this region from France in 1803. The way was now open for settlers to move even farther west.

The Incredible Purchase

Shortly before noon on March 4, 1801, Thomas Jefferson walked through the muddy streets of Washington, D.C., to the Capitol building. The writer of the Declaration of Independence was about to become the third President of the young nation. His simple clothes seemed right for the new capital, which was only half built.

After he took the President's oath of office, Jefferson spoke of his hopes for the country. He called the United States "a rising nation, spread over a wide and fruitful land." He knew, however, that the country faced a big problem. Spain had closed the port of New Orleans to western farmers, hoping to stop the United States frontier from moving farther west.

Spain had taken over all of Louisiana, including New Orleans, after France lost the French and Indian War. The French had given this huge area to Spain to keep the British from getting control of it. In 1802 President Jefferson learned that Spain had secretly given Louisiana back to France. Now, Jefferson thought, was the time to act.

Jefferson had two representatives ask the French leader, Napoleon Bonaparte (nuh•POH•lee•uhn BOH•nuh•part), to sell part of Louisiana, including New Orleans, to the United States. Jefferson was willing to offer

Thomas Jefferson became the third President of the United States.

The Louisiana Purchase

United States
Louisiana Purchase, 1803
Oregon Country
→ Route of Lewis and Clark, 1804–1806
→ Route of Pike, 1806–1807

0   200   400 Miles
0   200   400 Kilometers
Albers Equal-Area Projection

Place The huge territory of the Louisiana Purchase was later divided among 15 states.
■ *What natural features of the territory made it easier to explore?*

$10 million. But Bonaparte had other problems on his mind. France was preparing for war with Britain. And people in the French colony of St. Domingue (SEN daw•MENG) in the Caribbean had rebelled against France. Needing money to pay for two wars, Bonaparte offered to sell *all* of Louisiana to the United States. To the surprise of the Americans, the price was $15 million— for more than 800,000 square miles (2,071,840 sq km)!

On April 30, 1803, the United States agreed to **purchase**, or to buy, the huge territory, reaching from the Mississippi River west to the Rocky Mountains and from New Orleans north to Canada. The territory became known as the Louisiana Purchase. With it the United States doubled in size and became one of the largest countries in the world.

REVIEW *How did the Louisiana Purchase change the United States?*

BIOGRAPHY

Toussaint-Louverture 1743–1803

In 1791 Pierre Dominique Toussaint-Louverture (TOO•san LOO•ver•tur) helped lead a slave revolt in St. Domingue. Peace returned only after France agreed to end slavery in its colonies. An experienced soldier, Toussaint held several military positions on the island and soon became its most important leader. In 1802 the French tried to take back St. Domingue, and Toussaint was arrested. He died in prison, but the French could not defeat the rebels. On January 1, 1804, St. Domingue became the independent country of Haiti.

The Lewis and Clark Expedition

Few people in the United States knew much about the lands of the Louisiana Purchase. It was an area that Americans had never explored. President Jefferson asked Meriwether Lewis to lead an expedition to learn all he could about the new land. Lewis was to be a **pathfinder**, someone who finds a way through an unknown region.

Lewis had been an army officer in the wilderness of the Northwest Territory. He chose William Clark, a good friend, to help him lead the expedition. Clark was an excellent cartographer. Lewis and Clark put together a group of about 30 men, most of them frontier soldiers. One member of the group was York, William Clark's African slave. York contributed to the mission through his skill in hunting and fishing.

The leaders called their group the Corps of Discovery. On a spring morning in May 1804, the group left St. Louis and traveled up the Missouri River. The pathfinders spent the summer and fall pushing deep into the Louisiana Purchase. When they reached present-day North Dakota, they built a winter camp near a Mandan village.

While there, Lewis and Clark hired a French fur trader to translate some Indian languages for them. The fur trader was married to a Shoshone (shoh•SHOH•nee) woman who was named Sacagawea (sak•uh•juh•WEE•uh). Sacagawea agreed to serve as a translator when the Corps of Discovery reached the land of the Shoshones.

In the spring of 1805, the Lewis and Clark expedition again moved up the Missouri River by boat. But they would need horses in order to cross the Rocky Mountains. They put their hope in Sacagawea and the Shoshones.

This picture shows Sacagawea (below) using sign language to communicate with the Chinooks during the Lewis and Clark expedition. This page from William Clark's journal (right) shows a drawing he made during the journey.

"If we do not find them or some other nation who have horses, I fear the successful issue of our voyage will be very doubtful," Lewis wrote in his journal.

At last the expedition reached the lands of the Shoshones. Sacagawea's brother, Cameahwait (kah•MEE•ah•wayt), was now the chief. He gave the expedition horses, and the pathfinders continued their journey over the Rockies.

BIOGRAPHY

Sacagawea
1786?–1812?

Sacagawea, whose name in Shoshone means "Bird Woman," helped the members of the Lewis and Clark expedition survive. With her help the pathfinders completed their journey to the Pacific Ocean and back. In 1809 Clark brought Sacagawea, her husband, and her young son to St. Louis, where they settled on a farm. Little more is known about Sacagawea. One story says that she died on the Missouri River as early as 1812. Other stories say she died and was buried on the Wind River Reservation in Wyoming in 1884.

Once over the mountains, they built more boats. They went down the Snake River to the Columbia River and on to the Pacific Ocean. In November 1805, after traveling for more than a year and more than 3,000 miles (4,828 km), Clark wrote in his journal,

66 Great joy in camp. We are in view of the . . . great Pacific Octean which we have been so long anxious to see, and the roreing or noise made by the waves brakeing on the rockey shores (as I may suppose) may be heard distinctly. 99

The Corps of Discovery returned to St. Louis in September 1806. Lewis and Clark brought back seeds, plants, and even living animals. Among these were many birds. Lewis and Clark were able to report much about the land and its people. The expedition also brought back maps showing the major rivers and mountains. Clark had carefully mapped important passes through the Rockies. In later years these maps helped pioneers on their way to the Pacific coast.

REVIEW *What did Lewis and Clark learn from their expedition?*

Pikes Peak (below) was named after Zebulon Pike, who tried to climb to the top but failed.

Journey to the Southwest

A few weeks before Lewis and Clark returned to St. Louis, another expedition set out from Missouri to explore the southwestern part of the Louisiana Purchase. A small group of pathfinders led by Captain Zebulon Pike followed the Arkansas River through the middle part of the new lands.

By the winter of 1806, Pike had reached a great prairie in present-day Kansas. He saw with wonder that the prairie was covered with thousands of buffalo.

As the expedition traveled farther west, Pike saw what he described as a "blue mountain" in the distance. Today that blue mountain is called Pikes Peak, for the explorer. It is part of the Rocky Mountain range.

Pike's expedition followed the mountains south. The explorers built a small fort beside what Pike thought was the Red River. It was really the northern part of the Rio

Zebulon Pike became a general in the War of 1812 and was killed in battle.

Grande. The expedition had wandered out of the Louisiana Purchase and onto Spanish land!

Spanish soldiers soon arrived and took Pike and the other explorers to Santa Fe, the capital of the Spanish colony of New Mexico. The explorers were put in jail for being on Spanish land. In Santa Fe the Spanish governor asked Pike if the United States was getting ready to invade the Spanish lands. Pike said no, but in fact the expedition did lead to an "invasion" of another kind.

When he was set free several months later, Pike described the route to the Spanish lands. He reported that the people of Santa Fe needed manufactured goods. Soon American traders were heading for New Mexico as part of a great economic invasion.

REVIEW *How did Pike help start an economic invasion of the West?*

LESSON 2 REVIEW

Check Understanding

1 Remember the Facts What were the boundaries of the Louisiana Purchase?

2 Recall the Main Idea What did American pioneers learn from those who traveled west before them?

Think Critically

3 Think More About It Why do you think President Jefferson thought it was important for Lewis and Clark to explore the Louisiana Purchase?

4 Explore Viewpoints Why did the Spanish fear Pike's entry into their lands? What might Pike have thought of their viewpoint?

Show What You Know

Simulation Activity Imagine that you are planning an expedition into an unknown land. List the things you hope to learn during your travels. Share your list with a classmate.

FOCUS

What do you think
makes people feel
proud of their country?

Main Idea Read to
learn how the War of
1812 helped make
Americans proud of
their country.

Vocabulary

impressment
nationalism
annex
doctrine

A Second War with Britain

T he exciting stories of pathfinders such as Meriwether Lewis, William Clark, and Zebulon Pike made many people want to move to the West. But American Indians still fought with American pioneers, trying to turn them back. In the Northwest Territory, the British helped the Indians by selling them guns. Before long, trouble in the Northwest Territory helped push the United States into a second war with Britain.

Tecumseh and the Prophet

As more and more pioneers moved to the Northwest Territory, many Indians grew angry that so much of their land was being lost. The leader of these Indians was a Shawnee named Tecumseh (tuh•KUHM•suh). Tecumseh dreamed of forming a strong Indian confederation. He went from one tribe to another with his brother, Tenskwatawa (ten•SKWAHT•uh•wah), whom people called the Prophet, talking about his plan. Tecumseh called on the tribes to stop fighting one another and to unite against the Americans settling their land.

Prophetstown was the Shawnee town where Tecumseh had his headquarters. It was just below the mouth of the Tippecanoe River, near where Lafayette, Indiana, is today.

In 1809, by signing the Treaty of Fort Wayne, a group of Indian tribes agreed to sell 3 million acres of land to the United States government. Upon hearing the news, Tecumseh cried, "Sell a country! Why not sell the air, the clouds, and the great sea?"

Tecumseh said that no one tribe had the right to sell land. He warned the Americans that the Indians would fight if they were made to give up any more of their land. The Indians led by Tecumseh were eager for battle, but Tecumseh would not let them fight unless they were attacked first.

The Prophet was a well-known religious leader of the Shawnee people.

The Shawnee chief Tecumseh (left) wanted the United States to stop forcing Indians from their homelands. A computer drawing (above) shows what Prophetstown may have looked like before it was attacked.

In 1811 Tecumseh decided to talk with the Creeks and other Indian tribes living in Kentucky and Tennessee about his plan for a confederation. Before he left, he told the Prophet to keep the peace until he returned.

REVIEW *What plan did Tecumseh have for the Indian tribes?*

Battle of Tippecanoe

William Henry Harrison was governor of the Indiana Territory in 1811. Knowing that Tecumseh was away from Prophetstown, Harrison sent 1,000 soldiers to the Shawnee town. They camped nearby on the night of November 6, 1811. The Prophet feared that the soldiers would soon attack, so he ordered the Indians to attack first. The morning of November 7, the terrible Battle of Tippecanoe took place.

Neither side clearly won the battle. The Americans destroyed Prophetstown, but the Indians went through the Northwest Territory, attacking settlers.

Many people blamed the Indian attacks on Britain. They said the British were giving guns to the Indians and talking against American settlers. People in the Northwest Territory thought the answer was simple— take over Canada and drive the British out of North America.

REVIEW *What were the results of the Battle of Tippecanoe?*

War Fever

People in the South, too, were angry with Britain. To stop Americans from trading with the French and other Europeans, the British stopped American ships at sea. They even

Key Events of the War of 1812

1811   1812   1813   1814   1815

November
• Battle of Tippecanoe

June
• War declared

September
• Battle of Lake Erie

October
• Battle of The Thames

August
• Attack on Washington, D.C.

September
• Attack on Fort McHenry

December
• Peace treaty signed

January
• Battle of New Orleans

LEARNING FROM TIME LINES This time line shows the key events of the War of 1812.
■ *What do the last two dates on the time line tell you about communication in the early 1800s?*

took sailors off American ships and put them to work on British ships. Taking workers this way is called **impressment**.

People in the West and the South called on the United States government to declare war on Britain. Those who spoke up the most were known as War Hawks. The War Hawks blamed the British in Canada for encouraging the Indians to fight against settlers in the West. They blamed the British government for stopping trade in the South. Eager for more land, the War Hawks even hoped to take Canada from Britain.

Not everyone wanted war, however. Northern merchants had made a lot of money trading with the British. They did not want a war that would end their trade. Yet the desire for war was so great all over the rest of the country that Congress voted to declare war on Britain in 1812. It seemed as if a "war fever" had swept the nation.

REVIEW *Which regions of the United States wanted war with Britain?*

Regions Both sides won major battles during the War of 1812.
■ *How many battles were fought near the Great Lakes?*

The War of 1812

As the fighting began, Britain had the strongest navy in the world. Yet the small United States Navy, with only 16 ships, won an important battle on Lake Erie that became

Major Battles of the War of 1812

American victory
British victory

a turning point in the war. Ships commanded by American Captain Oliver Hazard Perry defeated the British on September 10, 1813. After the battle, Perry sent a message to General William Henry Harrison saying, "We have met the enemy and they are ours."

With British control weakened on the Great Lakes, General Harrison was able to lead American soldiers across Lake Erie into Canada. At the Battle of The Thames (TEMZ) on October 5, 1813, the American forces led by Harrison defeated the British and their Indian allies. Among the dead was Tecumseh, who was fighting on the British side.

Tecumseh's plan for a strong Indian confederation died with him. From that time on, settlers in the Northwest Territory were free from attacks by Indians.

REVIEW *What was a turning point in the War of 1812?*

During the war the British burned several buildings in Washington, D.C.—the White House, the Capitol, the Treasury, and some private homes. Dolley Madison (above left) was able to save just a few things from the White House before she was forced to flee from British troops.

British Raids

In August 1814, British troops marched on Washington, D.C.—a city of only 8,000 people. As the cracking of rifles and the booming of cannons filled the air, President James Madison rode to the battle 7 miles (11.3 km) away. First Lady Dolley Madison stayed behind, racing through the White House to save what she could from the British soldiers. She narrowly escaped. When the British arrived, they set fire to the White House, the Capitol, and other buildings.

With Washington in flames, the British sailed up Chesapeake Bay to Baltimore. But Baltimore was protected by Fort McHenry. Although British ships bombed the fort for hours, the Americans refused to surrender.

Unable to defeat the American forces at Baltimore, the British sailed south to New Orleans. But American soldiers under General Andrew Jackson were waiting for them.

The British laid siege to New Orleans for ten days. Fierce fighting from Jackson's soldiers finally made the British leave the city. Americans would later learn that the Battle of New Orleans had not been necessary. On December 24, 1814—two weeks before the battle—the British and Americans had signed a peace treaty in Europe. Word that the war was over had not reached New Orleans in time.

REVIEW *What were the results of British attacks on American cities?*

Birth of the Monroe Doctrine, a painting by Clyde DeLand, shows President Monroe (standing) discussing his doctrine with members of his Cabinet.

The Era of Good Feelings

After the War of 1812, Americans were proud that the United States had proved itself equal to a great European nation. A wave of **nationalism**, or pride in the country, swept the land. People began to feel for the first time that they were Americans, not Ohioans, Virginians, or New Yorkers. For this reason the years from 1817 to 1825 have been called the Era of Good Feelings.

National pride could be seen in the government's strong dealings with other countries. President James Monroe set a new border between the United States and British Canada. He also convinced Spain to give up claims in West Florida, which had been **annexed**, or added on, earlier, and to give East Florida to the United States.

President Monroe knew that if the United States wanted to keep growing, it had to stop the growth of the Spanish, French, and British colonies in the Americas. So on December 2, 1823, the President announced a **doctrine**, or government plan of action, that came to be called the Monroe Doctrine. The Monroe Doctrine declared that the United States was willing to go to war to stop European countries from expanding their American empires.

REVIEW *How did the War of 1812 affect the United States and its people?*

LESSON 3 REVIEW

Check Understanding

1 **Remember the Facts**   What did Tecumseh hope to accomplish by talking to other Indian tribes in the Northwest Territory?

2 **Recall the Main Idea**   How did the War of 1812 help make Americans proud of their country?

Think Critically

3 **Explore Viewpoints**   Why did people from the North, the South, and the West feel differently about going to war with Britain?

4 **Past to Present**   Many Americans who took part in the War of 1812 became national heroes. Who are some heroes of today? What actions helped them become known as heroes?

Show What You Know

Research Activity   Use the Internet or encyclopedias to find out more about the navy's battles in the War of 1812. Write a report about one battle. Draw a picture to illustrate your report. Present your findings to the class.

Predict a Likely Outcome

1. Why Learn This Skill?

People often make **predictions**. This means that they look at the way things are and decide what they think will most likely happen next. When people make predictions, they are not guessing about what will happen in the future. They are using information and past experiences to predict a probable, or likely, outcome.

2. Understand the Process

You have read about the War of 1812. The British lost the Battle of The Thames. The Indian leader Tecumseh died during the battle, and Indian attacks on settlers in the Northwest Territory soon ended.

You can use this information to predict what probably happened next in the westward movement of settlers after the War of 1812. Follow these steps:

① Think about what you already know about the loss of Indian lands as settlers moved west during the early years of the United States. Look for patterns in the events that took place.

② Review the new information you learned about Tecumseh and the War of 1812.

③ Make a prediction about the westward movement of settlers following the war.

④ As you read or gather more information, ask yourself whether you still think your prediction is correct.

⑤ If necessary, go through the steps again to form a new prediction.

After going through these steps, you should have been able to predict that pioneers would continue to move west, building settlements on Indian lands.

3. Think and Apply

In 1823 the Monroe Doctrine was announced. Follow the steps listed above to predict how the Monroe Doctrine would affect the growth of the United States. As you read the next chapter, see whether the new information you learn supports your prediction.

This painting, by German American artist Emanuel G. Leutze, shows one person's view of the westward movement of settlers.

By the Dawn's Early Light

The Story of The Star-Spangled Banner

by Steven Kroll

illustrated by Dan Andreasen

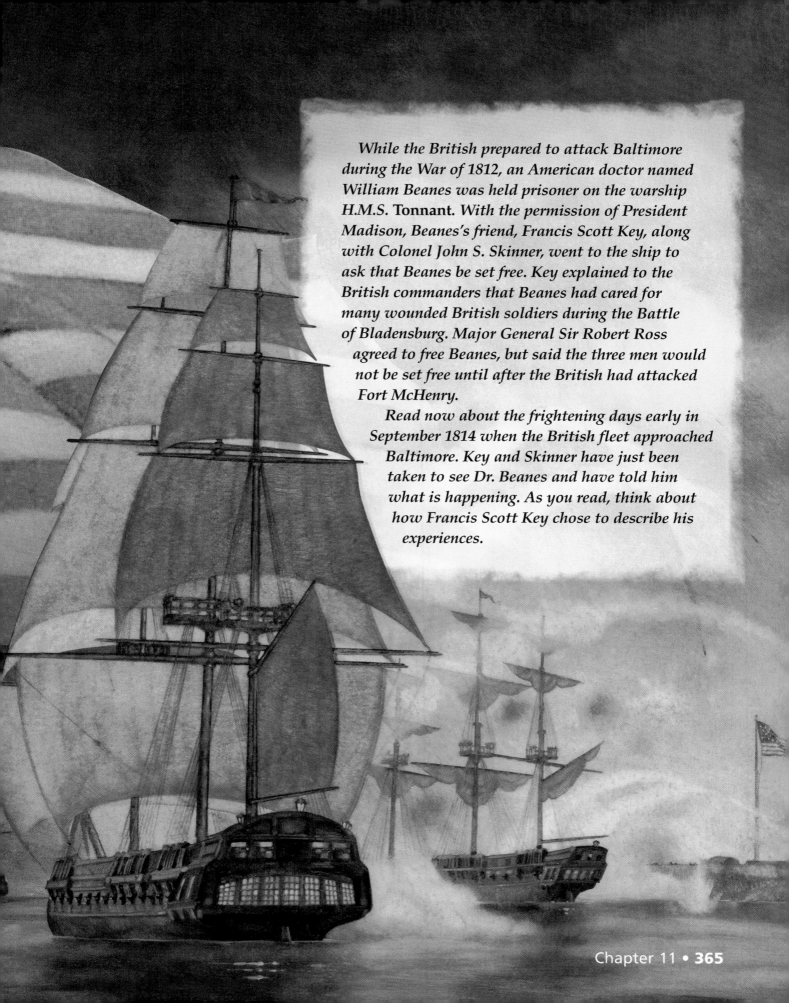

While the British prepared to attack Baltimore during the War of 1812, an American doctor named William Beanes was held prisoner on the warship H.M.S. Tonnant. With the permission of President Madison, Beanes's friend, Francis Scott Key, along with Colonel John S. Skinner, went to the ship to ask that Beanes be set free. Key explained to the British commanders that Beanes had cared for many wounded British soldiers during the Battle of Bladensburg. Major General Sir Robert Ross agreed to free Beanes, but said the three men would not be set free until after the British had attacked Fort McHenry.

Read now about the frightening days early in September 1814 when the British fleet approached Baltimore. Key and Skinner have just been taken to see Dr. Beanes and have told him what is happening. As you read, think about how Francis Scott Key chose to describe his experiences.

"And we must sit and watch while our country is attacked?" Beanes exclaimed.

"I'm afraid so," Colonel Skinner replied.

The three Americans were put up on the frigate *Surprise*, and for three days the British fleet crept up Chesapeake Bay.

Meanwhile, Baltimore was getting ready. Though inexperienced, the militia was on call. The city was ringed by trenches and ramparts[1] built by citizens. At star-shaped Fort McHenry, out on Whetstone Point overlooking the Patapsco River, a thousand troops were under the command of Major George Armistead. They had thrown up barriers outside the moat, placed sandbags around the powder magazine,[2] and sunk many small ships and barges in the north channel of the river to slow enemy progress.

They had also stationed a half-dozen small gunboats between the sunken hulls and the city.

There was a bold, new flag flying over the fort. Forty-two by thirty feet, fifteen stars and fifteen stripes, it was the work of Mary Pickersgill and her daughter, Caroline.

On Saturday, September 10th, the British fleet anchored off North Point at the mouth of the Patapsco River. Francis, Colonel Skinner, and Dr. Beanes were hustled from the *Surprise* back to their own small boat. Admiral Cochrane had decided to take personal command of the bombardment. He wanted the smaller, faster frigate as his flagship.

Sunday morning, Baltimore's church bells called the militia to arms. Monday, boats filled with British soldiers in scarlet uniforms began leaving for shore. Francis watched grimly. Things did not look good for the Americans.

With the troops underway on land, the fleet began moving upriver. As the ships came within view of Fort McHenry, the Stars and Stripes were waving overhead.

Later that afternoon, word came from shore. The Americans had retreated to positions outside the city. General Ross had been killed.

---

[1]**rampart:** protective barrier
[2]**powder magazine:** storage area for gunpowder

A silence seemed to fall over the fleet, but preparations continued. Francis, Dr. Beanes, and Colonel Skinner spent a restless night as sixteen smaller British ships moved into the shallower water closer to the fort.

At dawn the bombardment began. The noise was so great and the smell of burning powder so strong that the three hostages were forced to take refuge in their cabin. When the response from the fort seemed to die away for a moment, it became clear that the Americans' thirty-six-pound shells were not reaching the ships. But then the heavy shelling and rocketing began again and went on hour after hour.

At dusk Francis crawled out onto the deck. "Can you see the flag?" Dr. Beanes called after him.

Francis squinted through the smoke and the din and the glow of the setting sun. "The flag is flying," he replied.

Soon after, it began to rain.

Thunder and lightning joined the booming of the guns. Very late that night, Francis struggled out on deck again. Though he could not know it, at that moment the British were trying to land a thousand men at Ferry Branch. An American sentry discovered them and Fort McHenry began to fire. As the barges fled, every available American gun pursued them.

The rainy night sky was suddenly lit up, and in that moment Francis could see the flag again. It was soaked now and drooping from its staff, but it was there, still there.

By dawn the rain had stopped and the fight was over. Peering through the clouds, Francis, Dr. Beanes, and Colonel Skinner strained to see what flag was flying over the fort. Had the British triumphed in the night? But no, there it was, unfurling in the breeze, the Stars and Stripes!

All his life, Francis had written poetry. He reached into his pocket and found an old letter. With the tune to the song, "To Anacreon[3] in Heaven" in mind, he scribbled *O say can you see* and then *by the dawn's early light.*

He wrote a few more lines, crossed out a few, but there wasn't much time.

---

[3]**Anacreon:** a Greek poet

Already redcoats were leaving for the ships. The fleet was abandoning the assault!

The sails of the little cartel boat[4] were returned to the members of its American crew. By afternoon, Francis, Dr. Beanes, and Colonel Skinner were back in Baltimore.

Cheering crowds were everywhere. The three men went straight to the Indian Queen Hotel on Baltimore Street, rested and had supper, but later that night, Francis finished the four stanzas[5] of his poem.

The next day he went to visit his brother-in-law, Judge Joseph Nicholson, who had been at Fort McHenry. Judge Nicholson loved the new poem. "Let's get it printed," he insisted.

The judge rushed over to the *Baltimore American*, but the printers weren't back from defending the fort. A young apprentice, Samuel Sands, agreed to set the verses in type and run off the handbills. Because Francis hadn't thought of a title, Judge Nicholson came up with "The Defense of Fort McHenry," but it wasn't long before everyone was singing what had come to be known as "The Star-Spangled Banner."

---

[4]**cartel boat:** cargo boat
[5]**stanza:** section of a poem

The Star-Spangled Banner

Words by
Francis Scott Key
(1779-1843)

Music by
J. Stafford Smith
(1750-1836)

Oh— say can you see by the dawn's ear - ly light What so proud - ly we hail'd at the twi - light's last gleam - ing whose broad stripes and bright stars through the per - il - ous fight O'er the ram - parts we watch'd were so gal - lant - ly stream - ing? And the rock - ets' red glare the bombs burst - ing in air, Gave proof through the night that our flag was still there. Oh, say does that— star - span - gled ban - ner yet— wave—— O'er the land—— of the free and the home of the brave?

1. How did Francis Scott Key describe his experiences during the Battle of Baltimore?

2. How did ordinary citizens help Baltimore survive the British bombing?

3. Imagine that you were part of the Baltimore militia during the British bombing. Write a letter to a friend, telling how you feel about Francis Scott Key's poem.

1775   1785

1775
• Daniel Boone
  settles Kentucky

CONNECT MAIN IDEAS

Use this organizer to show how the chapter's main ideas are connected. Write one or two sentences to tell about each person or pair of people or to summarize each event or idea. A copy of the organizer appears on page 71 of the Activity Book.

On the Move

Across the Appalachians	The Louisiana Purchase	A Second War with Britain
Daniel Boone _____	The Purchase _____	Tecumseh and the Prophet _____
Settling Kentucky _____	Lewis and Clark _____	The War of 1812 _____
Pioneer Life _____	Zebulon Pike _____	The Era of Good Feelings _____

WRITE MORE ABOUT IT

Express an Opinion Suppose that President Jefferson has asked for your opinion on whether or not the United States should purchase the Louisiana Territory. Write what you would tell him.

Write a Newspaper Article Imagine that you are a writer for a Baltimore newspaper. Write a headline and a short article about Francis Scott Key and the exciting events at Fort McHenry.

| 1795 | 1805 | 1815 | 1825 |

1801
• Thomas Jefferson becomes the third President

1804
• Lewis and Clark expedition begins

1812
• The War of 1812 begins

1823
• The Monroe Doctrine is announced

USE VOCABULARY

Use the terms from the list to complete the paragraphs that follow. Use each term once.

annex   pathfinders

impressment   pioneers

nationalism   purchase

When the American Revolution ended, **①** settled the western frontier. Then, in 1803, the United States decided to **②** land west of the Mississippi River. **③** soon found ways through this unknown region.

The United States found itself at war with Britain. Americans were upset over the **④** of sailors. Although neither side was clearly the winner, a wave of **⑤** swept the land. The United States decided to **⑥** Spanish West Florida.

CHECK UNDERSTANDING

⑦ What was the Wilderness Road?

⑧ Why did pioneers often band together in forts?

⑨ What did Spain hope to do by closing the port of New Orleans to western farmers?

⑩ What did Lewis and Clark accomplish? How did Sacagawea help them?

⑪ Why did many Americans blame the British for Indian attacks on settlers?

⑫ Why were many northern merchants against the idea of declaring war on Britain?

⑬ What was the Era of Good Feelings?

⑭ Who was Francis Scott Key?

THINK CRITICALLY

⑮ Think More About It What do you think Tecumseh meant when he said that no one tribe had the right to sell land?

⑯ Personally Speaking Why do you think so many pioneers chose to risk their lives to settle in Kentucky and Tennessee? Would you have made the same choice? Explain.

⑰ Explore Viewpoints How do you think Americans viewed the Monroe Doctrine? How do you think Europeans viewed the Monroe Doctrine?

APPLY SKILLS

Predict a Likely Outcome Think about the events that usually take place in school on each day of the week. Predict the events that are likely to take place next week. What steps might you follow to make these predictions?

READ MORE ABOUT IT

A Pioneer Sampler: The Daily Life of a Pioneer Family in 1840 by Barbara Greenwood. Houghton Mifflin. This book tells about daily pioneer life and contains many activities for readers to enjoy.

Visit the Internet at **http://www.hbschool.com** for additional resources.

12

THE WAY WEST

"I am determined to sustain myself as long as possible & die like a soldier who never forgets what is due to his own honor & that of his country— victory or death."

The words of William Travis, describing the determination of those fighting for Texas independence

Juan Seguín, fighter for Texas independence

The Industrial Revolution

FOCUS

How might a new technology change a person's life today?

Main Idea As you read, look for ways new technology changed life in the United States in the 1800s.

Vocabulary

Industrial Revolution
textile mill
mass production
interchangeable part
transport
canal
locomotive

Before the War of 1812, the economy of the United States had been growing. This growth increased after the war. New inventions changed the way goods were made. People began using machines instead of hand tools. New transportation routes were built. This **Industrial Revolution** brought great changes in the ways people lived, worked, and traveled.

Industry Comes to the United States

In a factory in Britain, a young worker named Samuel Slater carefully studied the new spinning machine until he could remember exactly how each iron gear and wooden spool worked. This invention made large textile mills possible. **Textile mills** are factories where fibers such as cotton and wool are woven into cloth, or textiles. In 1789 Britain was the only country in the world that had this technology.

The British kept new inventions, such as those in the British textile mills, closely guarded secrets. Anyone caught leaving Britain with machine designs was put in jail. Samuel Slater was about to break British law.

Slater took his knowledge to the United States. Remembering each part he had studied, he made a spinning machine for a business person named Moses Brown. In 1790 Brown and Slater built a textile mill at Pawtucket, Rhode Island. It was America's first factory. Samuel Slater had brought the Industrial Revolution to the United States.

REVIEW *What technology did Samuel Slater bring to the United States?*

Born in Britain, Samuel Slater came to the United States in 1789.

Samuel Slater built America's first textile mill (above). The machines in the mill, such as this wooden spinning machine (right), ran on waterpower and made yarn quickly at low cost.

Mass Production

Another idea changed American manufacturing forever. An inventor named Eli Whitney thought of a new way of manufacturing that could produce large amounts of goods at one time. His idea came to be called mass production.

Before this time, one craftworker made each product from start to finish. Muskets, for example, were made by hand, one at a time. Because each craftworker had his or her own way of making parts and putting them together, no two muskets were exactly the same. To repair a broken musket, a craftworker had to make a new part to fit it.

Whitney thought of a way workers could make more muskets. He built machines that made identical copies of each part. Such interchangeable parts could be used to make or repair any musket. Whitney also made machines to put the parts together quickly.

Mass production made it possible to use untrained workers in factories. No longer were craftworkers needed to make most products. Anyone could put together machine-made parts. Using interchangeable parts, factory workers could manufacture more goods much more quickly than craftworkers could.

REVIEW *How did the idea of mass production change manufacturing?*

The Lowell System

From 1810 to 1812 Francis Cabot Lowell of Massachusetts visited textile mills and factories in Britain. As Samuel Slater had done earlier, Lowell studied the way the machines worked. He took care to remember the way the separate spinning, dyeing, and weaving mills were planned.

When Lowell returned to the United States, he started his own textile mill at Waltham, Massachusetts. He put spinning, dyeing, and weaving together under one roof. This was a change from having a different factory for each step. In Lowell's textile mill, raw cotton went into the factory and finished cloth came out. Nothing like that had ever been done before. Other manufacturers began following Lowell's lead as they built factories.

Young women and children came to work in Lowell's textile mills. When a girl named Harriet Hanson was ten years old, she began work as a "doffer." From five o'clock in the morning until seven in the evening, Harriet changed spools of thread on the spinning machines. She "wanted to earn money like the other little girls."

The hours were long, but Harriet did not think the work was hard. She had time to read, sew, and sometimes play. She enjoyed living in a boardinghouse where meals and rooms were provided for mill workers.

Lowell took care to set up good living conditions for his workers. Other manufacturers did not show the same care. As the demand for many manufactured goods grew, more factories—and more factory workers—were needed. Many workers, both young and old, soon were working long hours in dangerous conditions.

By the 1840s thousands of immigrants were coming to the United States each year to take jobs in the new factories. The populations of manufacturing cities like New York, Boston, Philadelphia, and Baltimore grew quickly. Almost half of the immigrants were from Ireland. Others came from Germany, Poland, and other parts of northern and central Europe.

REVIEW *Why were immigrants coming to the United States in the 1840s?*

The Erie Canal

The new factories turned out many products. But factory owners had a problem. How could they **transport**, or carry, their products from the factories to their customers, many of whom lived in the West? The people in the West, too, needed to transport their farm products to the cities in the East.

To help solve this problem, the New York legislature voted in 1817 to build a **canal**, or human-made waterway. The Erie Canal would link Buffalo on Lake Erie with Troy on the Hudson River. It would be 363 miles (584 km) long—the longest canal in the world.

Most of the Erie Canal was dug by hand by some 3,000 Irish immigrants. The workers were paid 80 cents a day and were given meals and housing. These wages were three times what the immigrants could earn in Ireland. The high wages acted like a magnet to attract thousands of Europeans to the United States.

Bells rang to tell Lowell's workers (right) when it was mealtime and when it was time to start work. The picture (below) shows a young girl packing cotton into containers.

When the Erie Canal was finished in 1825, it opened a transportation route to the heart of the young nation. The opening of this route helped make New York City the leading trade city in the United States.

REVIEW *Why was the Erie Canal built?*

The National Road

During the early years of the nation, Americans lacked a good system of roads. Most roads were just dirt paths that were full of tree stumps and holes. The roads turned into rivers of mud when it rained.

Just before Ohio became a state in 1803, Congress voted to build a road from the Atlantic coast to Ohio. The road would be used to transport goods and help settlers travel to the new state. This route became known as the National Road.

Work on the National Road began on November 20, 1811. The road was built using the best technology of the day. It was wide and level, and it was paved with stones and tar. It was opened for traffic in 1818, when it stretched from Maryland to what would become West Virginia. It was then built through Ohio and Indiana and was finished in Vandalia, Illinois, in 1841. The National Road became the land route that linked the East with the West.

REVIEW *Why was the National Road built?*

Steamboats and Railroads

At about the same time that the National Road and the Erie Canal were being built, Americans were inventing new forms of travel. Steamboats took the place of flat-bottom barges as the main form of river

LEARNING FROM DIAGRAMS Lake Erie is 572 feet (174 m) higher than the Hudson River. To move between the lake and the river, boats must go uphill or downhill on the Erie Canal. They do this by using locks, similar to the one shown here.

A lock is a short part of a canal with a gate at each end. After a boat enters the lock, both gates are shut and the water level is raised or lowered. When the water level matches the level beyond the lock, the gate at the far end opens and the boat goes on its way.

❶ lower water lock chamber
❷ gates controlled by balance beam
❸ watertight gates
❹ towing rope
❺ canal towpath
❻ water level in lock chamber is raised to higher level
❼ lock gates opening
❽ higher water lock chamber
■ *How were the boats moved through the locks?*

A Canal Lock

Movement These maps show major transportation links that had been built in the United States by 1850.

■ *Why do you think few links had been built west of the Mississippi River?*

transportation. Railroads changed the way people and goods moved on land.

In 1807 Robert Fulton amazed watchers when his steamboat, the *Clermont,* chugged up the Hudson River. The steamboat was powered by a steam engine, which had been invented in Britain in the 1700s. In 1811 the *New Orleans* made the first steamboat voyage from Pittsburgh to New Orleans. By the 1820s great paddle-wheel steamboats could be seen on most large rivers and lakes in the United States. Trips that once took months by flatboat now took only a few days.

Transportation in the East, 1850

Major road

Major canal

Major railroad

The *Tom Thumb* was made famous in a race with a horse. The locomotive was small, but powerful for its day. The first locomotives went about 10 miles (16.1 km) per hour.

Railroads had a slower start. At first many people had fears about traveling by train. Some did not think the trains would stay on the tracks. Some thought that fast speeds would cause human blood to boil!

One of the first **locomotives**, or railroad engines, made in the United States was the *Tom Thumb*. A manufacturer named Peter Cooper built it in 1830 for the Baltimore and Ohio Railroad. The company had been using railroad cars pulled by horses for its 13-mile (21-km) service between Baltimore and Ellicott's Mills, Maryland. To prove a steam engine could pull a heavy load faster than a horse, Cooper raced his *Tom Thumb* against a railroad car pulled by a horse. The locomotive broke down before the finish line and lost the race. Even so, it was clear that the steam locomotive had better pulling power than a horse.

The number of railroads grew quickly after 1830. By 1850 about 9,000 miles (14,484 km) of track had been laid, mostly near the Atlantic coast. Railroads made it easier to move raw materials and manufactured goods to all regions of the country. As the railroads grew, so did manufacturing in the United States.

REVIEW *What inventions improved transportation in the early 1800s?*

LESSON 1 REVIEW

Check Understanding

1 **Remember the Facts** Who brought the Industrial Revolution to the United States?

2 **Recall the Main Idea** How did new technology change the way people lived in the United States in the 1800s?

Think Critically

3 **Cause and Effect** How did more factories lead to better transportation? How did better transportation lead to more factories?

4 **Past to Present** What kinds of transportation connect the regions of the United States today?

Show What You Know

Writing Activity Imagine that you work at a Lowell textile mill or another early factory. Write a letter to a friend, telling what you like and do not like about working in the factory. Share your letter with a classmate.

The Age of Jackson

FOCUS
What problems might divide people living in a country today?

Main Idea Read to learn about the problems that divided the American people in the early 1800s.

Vocabulary
sectionalism
states' rights
secede
ruling

On July 4, 1826, the United States was 50 years old. Americans everywhere celebrated with parades, speeches, and parties. Many hoped that the two old patriots John Adams and Thomas Jefferson would live to see the celebration. Both men did live to greet that Fourth of July, but they both died before sunset. In Philadelphia the Liberty Bell tolled at their passing. The deep sound of the bell marked the end of an age that had brought the American people independence and a new nation. But as the old age ended, a new age dawned with new leaders and new challenges for the United States.

"Old Hickory"

On March 4, 1829, Andrew Jackson took the oath of office as the seventh President of the United States. The Union he was to lead had grown from the original 13 states to 24 states. Vermont, Maine, Kentucky, and Tennessee had become states. The states of Ohio, Illinois, and Indiana had been carved from the Northwest Territory. The states of Louisiana and Missouri had been formed from the Louisiana Purchase territory. Alabama became a state after the Creeks were forced off their land. The state of Mississippi and the Territory of Florida had been created from land once claimed by Spain.

The Presidents before Jackson had all been property owners from either Massachusetts or Virginia. They also had all been well educated. Jackson had a different background. He had been born on the frontier of South Carolina to a poor family living in a log cabin. Tough and stubborn, he taught himself law and became a judge. As a soldier he earned the nickname Old Hickory, hickory being a very hard wood. "He's tough," said his soldiers. "Tough as hickory." As a general he had become a hero during the War of 1812.

The election that made Jackson President was the first in which all white American men could vote.

President Andrew Jackson

Voter Participation, 1824–1840

Percent of Eligible Voters Who Voted

Election Year

LEARNING FROM GRAPHS This graph shows the percent of eligible voters who voted between 1824 and 1840.

■ *About what percent of eligible voters voted in the election of 1828?*

Before that time, voting had been only for men who owned property. The change came about partly because of the new western states. There the vote was given to all white men, not just property owners. By the election of 1828, the eastern states were following this example. Many of the new voters chose Jackson because they felt he was a "common man," like them.

REVIEW *What change in voting helped Andrew Jackson become President?*

Regional Disagreements

As President, Jackson went right on being both tough and stubborn. He vetoed a bank bill that would have helped the rich factory owners in the North. Government should not help the rich get richer, he said. The government should instead "shower its favors alike on the high and the low, the rich and the poor."

Many of President Jackson's decisions were based on his background of living on the western frontier. People from the North and the South were more interested in helping their own section, or region, rather than the country as a whole. This regional loyalty is called **sectionalism**.

Sectionalism became a problem in 1828 when Congress set a high tariff on imports. The tariff was supposed to help northern factory owners sell their manufactured goods because it made European goods cost more. However, the tariff also raised the prices southerners had to pay for goods they could get only from Europe.

Jackson's Vice President, John C. Calhoun of South Carolina, was loyal to the South. He argued against the tariff. Calhoun believed in **states' rights**, or the idea that the states have final authority over the national government. No one knew how President Jackson felt about states' rights until he spoke at a dinner in honor of the late Thomas Jefferson. Jackson looked straight at Calhoun and said,

66 Our Union—It must be preserved [kept]. 99

Calhoun answered, "The Union—next to our liberty most dear." Calhoun also believed that the Union was important. But he still felt that the rights of individual states were more important than the Union. This was the beginning of a deep split between Jackson and Calhoun. Calhoun soon resigned as Jackson's Vice President.

The debate over states' rights went on. In 1832 Congress passed another tariff. South Carolina said it would **secede**, or leave the Union, because of it. President Jackson warned South Carolina's leaders that leaving the Union was treason. South Carolina's leaders backed down, but sectionalism only grew stronger in the years to come.

REVIEW *What leader spoke out for states' rights? Who spoke against it?*

Indian Removal

Pathfinders had reported that the plains west of the Mississippi were of no use to the settlers. At that time people believed that soil was good only where trees grew. They began to think that the Indians should move west to those treeless lands. Jackson put the idea into action.

In 1830 Congress passed the Indian Removal Act. This act said that all Indians east of the Mississippi must leave their land and move west. Once this bill became a law, President Jackson ordered the Choctaws, Creeks, Seminoles, Chickasaws, Cherokees, and other tribes to live in the Indian Territory, which is today the state of Oklahoma.

Many tribes fought against removal. Among them were the Seminoles of Florida, led by Chief Osceola. Many runaway slaves helped the Seminoles in their fight. But, like other tribes, most of the Seminoles were either killed or forced to leave their homes.

The 15,000 Cherokees made up one of the richest tribes in the United States. They had many towns and villages throughout the Southeast. Many Cherokees owned small farms, and a few had large plantations where Africans were enslaved. The Cherokees had their own government, a republic with a constitution and elected leaders who met at their capital of New Echota (ih•KOHT•uh) in Georgia.

In 1791 the United States government had agreed to the independence of the Cherokee nation by signing a treaty. However, in 1828 lawmakers in Georgia said that Cherokee laws were no longer in effect. In 1829, when gold was discovered on Cherokee lands, settlers poured in to stake their claims.

The Cherokee nation, led by Chief John Ross, fought back in the United States courts, and their case went all the way to the United

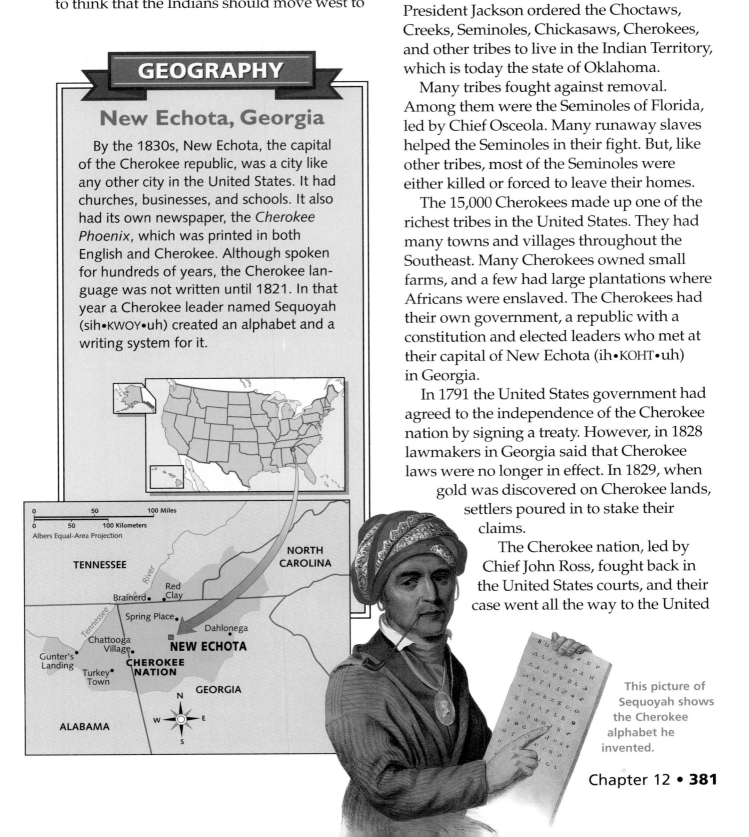

GEOGRAPHY

New Echota, Georgia

By the 1830s, New Echota, the capital of the Cherokee republic, was a city like any other city in the United States. It had churches, businesses, and schools. It also had its own newspaper, the *Cherokee Phoenix*, which was printed in both English and Cherokee. Although spoken for hundreds of years, the Cherokee language was not written until 1821. In that year a Cherokee leader named Sequoyah (sih•KWOY•uh) created an alphabet and a writing system for it.

0   50   100 Miles
0   50   100 Kilometers
Albers Equal-Area Projection

TENNESSEE

NORTH CAROLINA

River

Red Clay

Brainerd

Tennessee

Spring Place

Dahlonega

Chattooga Village

NEW ECHOTA

Gunter's Landing

CHEROKEE NATION

Turkey Town

GEORGIA

N W E S

ALABAMA

This picture of Sequoyah shows the Cherokee alphabet he invented.

This painting, called *The Choctaw Removal,* was created by the Choctaw artist Valjean Hessing. The Choctaw were one of the many Indian tribes that were forced to leave their homes. What feelings does the artist show in the painting?

States Supreme Court. In 1832 the Chief Justice of the Supreme Court, John Marshall, gave the Court's **ruling**, or decision. He said that the United States should protect the Cherokees and their lands in Georgia. Yet, instead of supporting the court ruling, President Jackson ignored it.

By late 1838, soldiers had forced the last large group of Cherokees to leave their lands and travel more than 800 miles (1,287 km) to the Indian Territory. Their long, painful journey came to be called the Trail of Tears. It ended on March 26, 1839, after more than 4,000 Cherokees had died of cold, disease, and lack of food. John G. Burnett, a soldier who was there, said, "The trail was a trail of death."

REVIEW *What was the Trail of Tears?*

LESSON 2 REVIEW

Check Understanding

1 Remember the Facts What group of people helped Andrew Jackson win the election of 1828?

2 Recall the Main Idea What problems divided the American people in the early 1800s?

Think Critically

3 Explore Viewpoints How would the Cherokees have viewed the Indian Removal Act? How would Georgia's settlers have viewed it?

4 Think More About It How do you think life on the frontier encouraged the growth of democracy?

Show What You Know

Writing Activity Make a list of the qualities that helped Andrew Jackson get elected President. Then write phrases that he might have used as campaign slogans for his elections in 1828 and 1832. Copy your slogans onto large sheets of paper and display them in the classroom.

Westward Ho!

In the early 1800s Americans began to move beyond their country's borders. With the rallying cry "Westward Ho!," they looked to the Spanish colony of Texas, the Oregon Country in the Pacific Northwest, and other western lands. The idea of the lands in the West being set aside for Indian peoples was soon forgotten. In 1845 the words *manifest destiny* were heard for the first time. The **Manifest Destiny** was the belief shared by many Americans that it was the certain future of the United States to stretch from the Atlantic Ocean to the Pacific Ocean.

FOCUS
How might a country today expand its territory?

Main Idea   Read to learn how the United States expanded its territory in the 1800s.

Vocabulary
Manifest Destiny
dictator
forty-niner

Americans in Texas

Since the earliest years of European settlement, Spain had built missions and presidios all over Texas. Yet few settlers lived on this open borderland. In 1820 Moses Austin, a Missouri banker, asked Spanish leaders if he might start a colony of Americans in Texas. The Spanish agreed, but Austin died before he could carry out his plan.

Stephen F. Austin, Moses Austin's son, took up his father's work and started the colony. He chose land between the Brazos and Colorado rivers. In 1821 the first colonists began to settle there. That same year, Mexico won its independence from Spain. Texas now belonged to Mexico.

Austin and the American settlers worked hard, and they soon did well in raising cotton, corn, and cattle. Encouraged by their success, the Mexican government decided to let more people settle in Texas. At first the Mexican government left the Americans in Texas alone. But in time Mexico's leaders became worried about the growing number of Americans on their land.

In 1830 the Mexican government passed a law that said no more American settlers could come to Texas. The Mexican government also said that settlers already in Texas had to obey Mexico's laws and pay more taxes. These changes angered Texans.

Stephen F. Austin began a settlement in Texas. Present-day Austin, Texas, was named for him.

Then, in 1834, another change took place. General Antonio López de Santa Anna took over the Mexican government and made himself **dictator**, a leader who has total authority. When Santa Anna sent soldiers to Texas to enforce Mexican laws, fighting broke out.

REVIEW *Why did Americans first come to Texas?*

The Texas Revolution

Working together, a force of Americans and Mexicans living in Texas attacked the town of San Antonio on December 5, 1835. After four days of fighting, Mexican troops were driven from the center of the town. They surrendered on December 11. The defeat angered General Santa Anna. He marched on San Antonio with thousands of soldiers, planning to take back the city.

Church bells rang out a warning as the huge Mexican army came close to the city in February 1836. Texas rebels in San Antonio took shelter behind the walls of the Alamo, an old Spanish mission church. Among them were American volunteers willing to help the Texas rebels in their fight for freedom. They included James Bowie, Davy Crockett, and William B. Travis, who served as commander. Juan Seguín and several other Texans also arrived to help. Some fighters were joined by their wives and children.

For 13 days the Mexican soldiers attacked the Alamo. The defenders fought to the end. Finally, on March 6, 1836, the Alamo fell. The force of about 189 Texans had been killed. Santa Anna spared the lives of the women and children.

During the attack at the Alamo, Texas leaders met. On March 2, 1836, they declared

At the Alamo fewer than 200 Texans faced more than 2,000 Mexican soldiers. In this painting Davy Crockett swings his rifle at the enemy after having run out of ammunition. The Alamo was one of the most well-known battles of the Texas revolution.

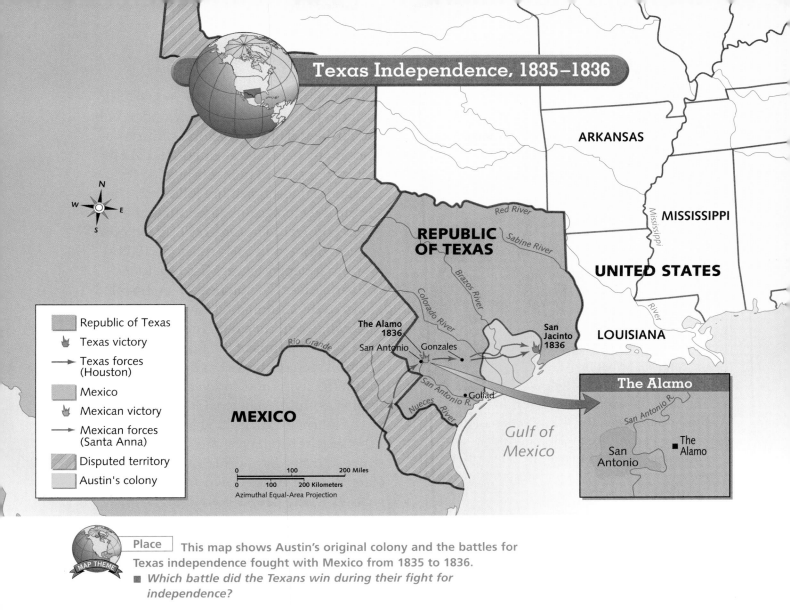

Texas Independence, 1835–1836

Legend:
- Republic of Texas
- Texas victory
- Texas forces (Houston)
- Mexico
- Mexican victory
- Mexican forces (Santa Anna)
- Disputed territory
- Austin's colony

ARKANSAS

MISSISSIPPI

UNITED STATES

REPUBLIC OF TEXAS

Red River

Sabine River

Brazos River

Colorado River

The Alamo 1836

San Antonio

Gonzales

Rio Grande

San Jacinto 1836

LOUISIANA

Mississippi River

River

San Antonio R.

Nueces River

Goliad

MEXICO

Gulf of Mexico

0   100   200 Miles
0   100   200 Kilometers
Azimuthal Equal-Area Projection

The Alamo

San Antonio R.

San Antonio

■ The Alamo

Place This map shows Austin's original colony and the battles for Texas independence fought with Mexico from 1835 to 1836.
■ *Which battle did the Texans win during their fight for independence?*

independence from Mexico and set up the Republic of Texas. They chose David G. Burnet as president and Sam Houston as commander of the army.

After the fall of the Alamo, Santa Anna moved quickly to end the Texas revolution. On March 27 he ordered more than 300 prisoners killed at Goliad. But other Texans fought on, yelling "Remember the Alamo!" and "Remember Goliad!"

On April 21 Houston's army took the Mexicans by surprise at the Battle of San Jacinto (juh•SINT•oh) and captured Santa Anna. Houston offered to let Santa Anna live

in return for Texas's independence. Santa Anna agreed, and his army returned to Mexico. Texas remained an independent republic until it became a state of the United States in 1845. Sam Houston served twice as president of the republic and later as governor of the state of Texas.

The Texas flag, adopted in 1839, has a single white star and red, white, and blue bars. For this reason Texas was known as the Lone Star Republic. Today it is known as the Lone Star State.

REVIEW *When did Texas become a republic?*

John C. Frémont
1813–1890

In the early 1800s the United States government decided that maps of the West needed to be made. These maps would help traveling settlers decide which routes to take and where to settle. John C. Frémont, a surveyor, was chosen to lead the expedition. In 1842, 1843, and 1844 he explored much of the land between the Rocky Mountains and the Pacific Ocean. His detailed written accounts of the land, bodies of water, and climate helped thousands of Americans settle the West.

The Oregon Country

American pioneers continued to push west. In 1834, Christian missionaries journeyed to the Oregon Country. This region was made up of present-day Oregon, Washington, and Idaho, and parts of Montana and Wyoming. In 1836 Marcus and Narcissa Whitman and Henry and Eliza Spalding set up missions near the Walla Walla Valley. They hoped to teach Christianity to the Indians.

The missionaries' letters to people back East told of the green valleys, wooded hills, and fertile soil of the Oregon Country—a place many began to dream of. In 1842 the first large group of pioneers headed for Oregon. Thousands more followed. The route they took came to be called the Oregon Trail. The Oregon Trail led northwest more than 2,000 miles (3,219 km) from Independence, Missouri, to the Platte River. The pioneers then traveled across the Continental Divide, an imaginary line that runs north and south along the highest points of the Rocky Mountains. The trail then continued to the Snake and Columbia rivers and ended at the Willamette (wuh•LA•muht) Valley of Oregon.

The journey took as long as six months. What a hard trip it was! Fresh water was scarce, but sudden storms soaked the travelers. Wagons broke down. Rivers had to be crossed. Many people died along the way. Yet many reached Oregon, and the settlements there grew quickly.

To protect its settlements, the United States wanted a clear dividing line between its Oregon territory and nearby British land. In 1846 President James K. Polk signed a treaty with Britain fixing the 49th parallel of latitude as the boundary between the United States and the British territory in Canada. The treaty gave the United States the lands now known as Oregon, Washington, Idaho, western Montana, and Wyoming.

REVIEW *How did people in the East learn about the Oregon Country?*

This quilt was signed by people traveling together in a wagon train.

The Mormons in Utah

In the 1840s the Mormons, or members of the Church of Jesus Christ of Latter-day Saints, joined the pioneers moving west. Under their first leader, Joseph Smith, the Mormons had settled in Nauvoo (naw•VOO), Illinois. But their beliefs caused problems with other settlers, and in 1844 an angry crowd killed Joseph Smith.

When Brigham Young became the new leader of the Mormons, he decided that they should move to a place where no one would bother them. In 1846 Young and the first group of Mormons to head west set out for the Rocky Mountains.

In July 1847 the Mormons reached the Great Salt Lake valley in the Great Basin. Young chose this harsh land to settle in because he thought that no other settlers would want it. He used words from the Bible to tell his followers, "We will make this desert blossom as the rose."

One of the first things the Mormons did was build irrigation canals. The canals brought water from the mountains to turn the dry land into farmland.

The Mormons did make the land blossom with crops of grain, fruit, and vegetables. The region grew rapidly, and soon it became the Utah Territory. Brigham Young became its first governor.

REVIEW *Why did the Mormons move to present-day Utah?*

War with Mexico

The land the Mormons settled in the Great Basin belonged to Mexico. In 1848, only a few months later, that land became part of the United States.

James K. Polk was President then, and he wanted to see the United States reach to the Pacific Ocean. He thought that all the lands west of Texas should be part of the United States.

Mormon pioneers get ready to move out from what is today Omaha, Nebraska. They stayed there for the winter before completing their journey westward.

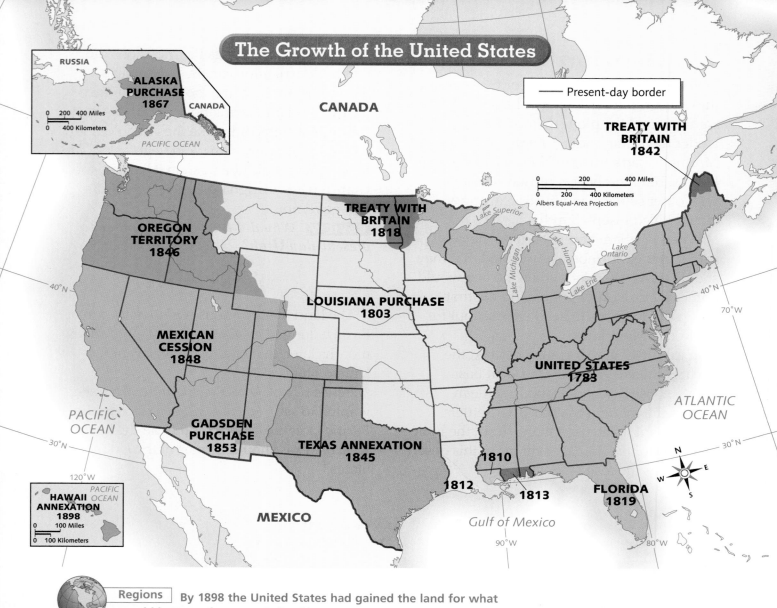

The Growth of the United States

— Present-day border

RUSSIA

ALASKA PURCHASE 1867

CANADA

0 200 400 Miles
0 400 Kilometers

PACIFIC OCEAN

CANADA

TREATY WITH BRITAIN 1842

TREATY WITH BRITAIN 1818

Lake Superior
Lake Michigan
Lake Huron
Lake Ontario
Lake Erie

OREGON TERRITORY 1846

LOUISIANA PURCHASE 1803

40°N

40°N

70°W

MEXICAN CESSION 1848

UNITED STATES 1783

ATLANTIC OCEAN

PACIFIC OCEAN

GADSDEN PURCHASE 1853

TEXAS ANNEXATION 1845

30°N

30°N

120°W

1810

1812

1813

FLORIDA 1819

HAWAII ANNEXATION 1898
PACIFIC OCEAN

0 100 Miles
0 100 Kilometers

MEXICO

Gulf of Mexico

90°W

80°W

N
W E
S

0 200 400 Miles
0 200 400 Kilometers
Albers Equal-Area Projection

Regions By 1898 the United States had gained the land for what would become the present-day 50 states.
■ *When did the United States first gain land on the Pacific coast?*

In January 1846 President Polk sent American soldiers into lands in southern Texas that were disputed between the United States and Mexico. In April Mexican troops crossed the Rio Grande and attacked an American patrol. Polk then asked Congress to declare war on Mexico.

In 1847 the United States invaded Mexico by sea. American soldiers led by General Winfield Scott marched from Veracruz to Mexico City. After a year of fighting, the war was over. In 1848 Mexico and the United States signed the Treaty of Guadalupe

Hidalgo (gwah•dah•LOO•pay ee•DAHL•goh). In the treaty, the United States agreed to pay $15 million for California and the land that now makes up Utah, Nevada, and parts of Arizona, New Mexico, Colorado, and Wyoming. Then in 1853, the United States purchased more land from Mexico in the Gadsden Purchase. This brought the part of the country between Canada and Mexico to its present size. This area, made up of 48 states, is known as the Continental United States.

REVIEW *What did the United States agree to purchase in its treaty with Mexico?*

The California Gold Rush

Just a few days before the treaty with Mexico was signed, gold was found in California. In January 1848 James Marshall and his workers were building a waterwheel for John Sutter's new sawmill near Sacramento. Something in the water glittered. Marshall picked it up. He held a shiny stone that was half the size of a pea. Then he and his workers saw another and another. The news soon reached the eastern states. Gold had been discovered!

Less than a year later, more than 80,000 gold seekers came to California. They were called **forty-niners** because they arrived in the year 1849. Most had made their way west on the Oregon Trail, cutting south across the Nevada desert to California. The easier but much more expensive way was to travel around Cape Horn, the tip of South America, by clipper ship. Clipper ships were the fastest ships to sail the oceans. For gold seekers in a hurry to reach California and willing to pay extra to get there fast, the journey around Cape Horn took from three to four months.

These forty-niners are trying to find gold among stones in a riverbed. Looking for gold was hard work, and the chances of finding any were slim.

The gold rush quickly filled California with new people. They came from Europe and Asia as well as from the United States. In 1850, only two years after Marshall's discovery at Sutter's Mill, California became a state.

REVIEW *Why did thousands of people travel to California in 1849?*

LESSON 3 REVIEW

Check Understanding

1 Remember the Facts Why did American settlers move west into Texas, Oregon, Utah, and California?

2 Recall the Main Idea How did the United States expand its territory in the 1800s?

Think Critically

3 Personally Speaking What qualities do you think a pioneer needed in order to settle on the frontier? Why would those qualities be important?

4 Past to Present Are there still pioneers and frontiers today? Explain your answer.

Show What You Know

Art Activity Make a picture map of the growth of the western United States. On your map, show the Alamo, the Whitman and Spalding missions, travelers on the Oregon Trail, Mormon settlers, and forty-niners. Share your map with family members.

Use Relief and Elevation Maps

1. Why Learn This Skill?

When we think of traveling long distances today, we think of going by airplane, car, or train. Early pioneers, however, had to travel long distances by walking or by riding in wagons. They had to cross steep mountains and wade across wide rivers.

Relief maps and elevation maps can help you better understand how difficult the journeys of the pioneers must have been. Both types of maps show how high or how low the land is.

2. Relief and Elevation

A relief map helps you picture the physical features of the land. **Relief** (rih•LEEF), or the differences in height of an area of land, is often shown by shading. Heavily shaded areas on a relief map show high relief, or sharp rises and drops in the land. Lightly shaded areas show low relief, where the land gently rises or falls. Areas with no shading show land that is mostly flat.

Look at the relief map showing trails to the West. You will see that there is heavy shading in the western lands—showing areas of high relief, such as the Rocky Mountains and the Cascade Range. In the eastern lands, there is little shading—showing land that has low relief, such as the Great Plains, which is mostly flat land.

Relief Map: Trails to the West

Legend:
- → California Trail
- → Mormon Trail
- → Old Spanish Trail
- → Oregon Trail
- → Santa Fe Trail
- ····· Continental Divide
- ■ Fort
- ⌂ Mission
- — Present-day border

This picture was taken of pioneers traveling in Kansas. Using the relief map that shows trails to the West, how would you describe the land in Kansas?

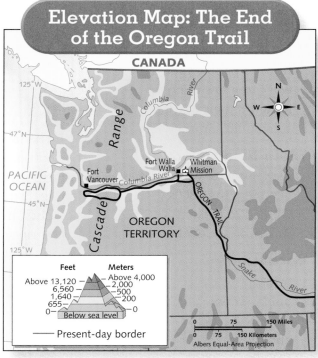

Elevation Map: The End of the Oregon Trail

CANADA

PACIFIC OCEAN

Cascade Range

Columbia River

Fort Vancouver

Fort Walla Walla

Whitman Mission

OREGON TERRITORY

OREGON TRAIL

Snake River

Feet	Meters
Above 13,120	Above 4,000
6,560	2,000
1,640	500
655	200
0	0

Below sea level

—— Present-day border

0   75   150 Miles
0   75   150 Kilometers
Albers Equal-Area Projection

A relief map, however, does not tell you the elevation (eh•luh•VAY•shuhn) of the land. **Elevation** is the height of the land. Land that is level with the surface of the ocean is said to be at sea level. Its elevation is zero. The elevation of all other land is measured from sea level, up or down, in feet or meters. To find the elevation of a place, you must look at an elevation map.

Most elevation maps use color to show elevation. Look at the elevation map showing the end of the Oregon Trail. The map key tells you which colors are used to show different elevations. Green is used for the lowest land shown on this map, which is between sea level and 655 feet (200 m). Purple is used for the highest land, which is above 13,120 feet (4,000 m).

3. Understand the Process

Use the questions that follow as a guide to help you learn how to use relief maps and elevation maps.

1 What is the difference between a relief map and an elevation map?

2 To find the elevation at Fort Walla Walla, should you use a relief map or an elevation map?

3 Will a relief map tell you whether western Oregon is flat or mountainous?

4 How high are the highest areas in Oregon?

5 Where are the lowest areas in Oregon?

6 What is the elevation of the land at Fort Vancouver?

4. Think and Apply

Imagine that you are a pioneer on the Oregon Trail. On the relief map, use your finger to trace the route of the trail from Independence to Fort Vancouver. Describe the landforms you pass along the way. Once you reach Oregon, use the elevation map to describe in greater detail the final days of your journey.

MAP SKILLS

FOCUS
How do people today work to make things better in their school, community, or country?

Main Idea As you read, look for ways people in the 1800s worked to make American society better.

Vocabulary
reform
public school
abolish
abolitionist
equality

An Age of Reform

The fast growth of the United States in the first half of the 1800s made many Americans hopeful. They saw how the nation's growth in manufacturing and in size helped many people. But they also saw the need to **reform**, or change for the better, many parts of American life.

America's growth caused some problems, too. So many Americans were concerned about these problems that the 1830s through the 1850s became an age of reform. During this time many Americans worked to improve life for others.

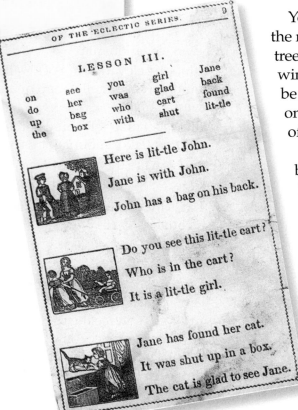

OF THE ECLECTIC SERIES.   9

LESSON III.

on	see	you	girl	Jane
do	her	was	glad	back
up	bag	who	cart	found
the	box	with	shut	lit-tle

Here is lit-tle John.

Jane is with John.

John has a bag on his back.

Do you see this lit-tle cart?

Who is in the cart?

It is a lit-tle girl.

Jane has found her cat.

It was shut up in a box.

The cat is glad to see Jane.

Better Schools

Young Horace Mann was excited to see the red leaves falling from the oak and maple trees in Massachusetts. He knew that when winter put an end to farm work, he would be able to go to school. Horace's school had only one room and one teacher for children of all ages. And there were very few books.

When Horace Mann grew up, he became a reformer in education. In 1837 Mann was made secretary of the Massachusetts Board of Education. He worked to improve the state's **public schools**, the schools paid for by taxes and open to all children.

Horace Mann wanted more specific laws requiring children to go to school. He called for special schools to train teachers. In Mann's day most teachers worked only

This spelling book was used in some schools during the early 1800s. How is this similar to spelling books used today?

part-time. They were often students of law or of religion. Mann wanted full-time, well-trained teachers. He also wanted new schools built. Before this time most public-school classes were held in stores or in people's homes.

By 1850 many of Horace Mann's ideas were being used in the North and the West. Most white children received an elementary school education and sometimes a high-school education. Free African children, however, had to go to separate schools. In the South, most boys who were white went to private schools. Girls had few chances for education. Enslaved children had none.

REVIEW *What reforms in education did Horace Mann try to bring about?*

The Fight Against Slavery

While Horace Mann worked to improve education during the age of reform, other reformers worked to **abolish**, or end, slavery. Since the early days of the country's history, some Americans had been deeply troubled by slavery. Soon they started working together to help enslaved people gain their freedom. Among the first to speak out were members of a religious group called the Quakers. In 1775 the Quakers formed the first group to work against slavery—an antislavery society.

Abolitionists (a•buh•LIH•shuhn•ists), or people who wanted to abolish slavery, worked to end slavery in different ways. Some abolitionists used the written word to spread their message. In 1827 Samuel Cornish and John Russwurm started a newspaper that called for **equality**, or the same

rights, for all Americans. The newspaper, *Freedom's Journal*, was the first to be owned and written by Africans in the United States. "Too long," Cornish and Russwurm wrote, "have others spoken for us."

A few years later another abolitionist, William Lloyd Garrison, founded a news-paper called *The Liberator*. In it he called for a complete end to slavery at once.

> 66 On this subject I do not wish to think, or speak, or write with moderation. I will not retreat a single inch—AND I WILL BE HEARD. 99

In 1852 a novel by abolitionist Harriet Beecher Stowe turned many people against slavery. The book, called *Uncle Tom's Cabin*, told the heartbreaking story of slaves being mistreated by a cruel slave owner. The book

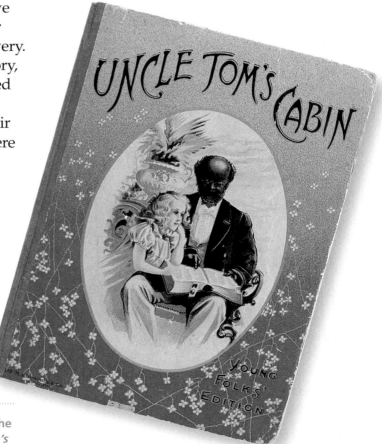

Millions of people around the world read about the cruel conditions of slavery in the novel *Uncle Tom's Cabin*.

The Webb family (above) were abolitionists who read the novel *Uncle Tom's Cabin* to audiences in the North. Large crowds came to hear Sojourner Truth (right). She spoke against slavery and in favor of women's rights.

FREE LECTURE!

SOJOURNER TRUTH,

Who has been a slave in the State of New York, and who has been a Lecturer for the last twenty-three years, whose characteristics have been so vividly portrayed by Mrs. Harriet Beecher Stowe, as the African Sybil, will deliver a lecture upon the present issues of the day,

At   On

And will give her experience as a Slave mother and religious woman. She comes highly recommended as a public speaker, having the approval of many thousands who have heard her earnest appeals, among whom are Wendell Phillips, Wm. Lloyd Garrison, and other distinguished men of the nation.

☞ At the close of her discourse she will offer for sale her photograph and a few of her choice songs.

quickly became a best-seller and was made into a play.

While some abolitionists were writing, other abolitionists were giving speeches. One of the speakers was Frederick Douglass, a runaway slave. William Lloyd Garrison had asked him to speak at an abolitionist meeting. Douglass slowly rose and walked up to the stage. He shared from the heart how it felt to be free. Douglass also told his listeners the story of his daring escape from slavery.

When Douglass finished speaking, everyone cheered. Before long, he had become the leading abolitionist speaker. His speeches made many people agree that slavery had to be stopped.

Like Douglass, Sojourner Truth traveled the country speaking out against slavery. Sojourner Truth was a former slave named Isabella. She believed that God had called her to "travel up and down the land" to preach. She decided to change her name to Sojourner, which means "traveler." She chose Truth as a last name.

Sojourner Truth believed that slavery could be ended peacefully. Frederick Douglass argued in his speeches that only rebellion would end it.

In the end, Douglass was proved right. The nation that grew large and strong in the 1800s would soon be divided by civil war.

REVIEW *How did abolitionists work to end slavery?*

Rights for Women

In 1840 Elizabeth Cady Stanton and Lucretia Mott went to a convention of abolitionists in London, Britain. However, they were not allowed to speak because they were women. Stanton and Mott were so angry that they decided to hold their own convention— for women's rights.

The first women's rights convention met on July 19 and 20, 1848, at Seneca Falls, New York. Those who attended the convention wanted women to have the same political, social, and economic rights as men. They wrote a statement saying that women should have "all the rights and privileges which belong to them as citizens of the United States." The statement called for women to be able to own property, to keep the wages that they earned, and to be given **suffrage**, or the right to vote.

The reformers began to get some support. In 1850 Susan B. Anthony of New York worked for women teachers to have the same pay as men teachers and for women to have the same property rights as men. She later became a leader of the women's suffrage movement.

GEOGRAPHY

Seneca Falls, New York

Seneca Falls is a small town in the middle of New York State, between Rochester and Syracuse. Seneca Falls was the home of Elizabeth Cady Stanton. With Lucretia Mott, Stanton planned the first women's rights convention in the summer of 1848. Those attending the Seneca Falls Convention called for women to work together to win their rights as citizens. Today Seneca Falls has a Women's Hall of Fame.

Elizabeth Cady Stanton (left) spoke at the first women's rights convention and wrote a document called the Declaration of Sentiments. The document describes women's rights by using words from the Declaration of Independence. But Stanton added some words, as in "all men *and women* are created equal."

Susan Brownell Anthony 1820–1906

For most of her life, Susan B. Anthony worked to get women the right to vote. She was once arrested and fined $100 for breaking the law by voting in an election for President. Anthony also started a weekly newspaper and wrote books to spread her message. Susan B. Anthony died 14 years before the Nineteenth Amendment to the Constitution became law. From 1979 to 1981, the United States government honored her work for women's rights by minting one-dollar coins with her picture on them. Susan B. Anthony was the first woman to have her picture on a coin in the United States.

Sojourner Truth used her speaking skills to help. In 1851 Truth was at a women's rights convention in Ohio. When a man said, "Women are weak," she answered,

66 The man over there says women need to be helped into carriages and lifted over ditches and puddles, and have the best place everywhere. Nobody helps me into carriages and over puddles, or gives me the best place— and ain't I a woman? 99

Women won a few rights during this time. A few states gave women control of the money they earned and of the property they owned. Some places, like Wyoming Territory, allowed women to vote. Wyoming Territory was the first place in the United States and in the world to grant women the right to vote. However, it would not be until 1920 that the Nineteenth Amendment gave all women in the United States this right.

REVIEW *What reforms did Elizabeth Cady Stanton and others work for?*

LESSON 4 REVIEW

Check Understanding

1 Remember the Facts What did reformers want to change about American society?

2 Recall the Main Idea How did reformers in the 1800s work to improve American society?

Think Critically

3 Cause and Effect How might public schools today be different if Horace Mann had not worked to reform education in the early 1800s?

4 Personally Speaking Why do you think so many people wanted to hear Frederick Douglass tell his story?

Show What You Know

Writing Activity Imagine that you are a reformer in the 1800s. Write a letter in which you try to persuade a member of the school board to make a change in the public schools. Be sure to give the reason the change is needed. Collect the letters in a binder for classroom display.

Use a Double-Bar Graph

1. Why Learn This Skill?

People often make comparisons and look at how things have changed over time. Some parents mark their children's heights on a wall to keep a record of how much the children have grown each year. If records are kept for two children, the parents can compare how much each has grown over the years and how much each has grown compared with the other. A good way to compare such information is by making a double-bar graph. A double-bar graph allows you to compare information quickly and to see changes over time.

2. Understand the Process

Between 1790 and 1850 both the urban and rural populations of the United States grew at a steady pace. The double-bar graph on this page shows the differences in urban and rural populations for these years. It also shows how urban and rural populations have changed over time.

1 Look at the words and numbers along the top, bottom, and left-hand side of the graph. Years are listed along the bottom, and numbers of people are listed along the left-hand side.

2 Notice that the information on this graph is shown only for every tenth year from 1790 to 1850.

3 Notice how different colors—blue and red—are used to show the urban population and the rural population.

4 Read the graph by running your finger up to the top of each bar and then left to the population number. If the top of the bar is between numbered lines, estimate the population by selecting a number between those two numbers.

5 Compare the heights of the blue bars with one another. Then compare the heights

Urban and Rural Population, 1790–1850

with the red bars. How did the urban population change over time? How did the rural population change over time?

6 Now compare the heights of the blue bar and the red bar for each year shown. This allows you to compare urban growth with rural growth over time. How does the double-bar graph help you understand how the population of the United States grew between 1790 and 1850?

3. Think and Apply

Make a double-bar graph of your test scores in social studies and in another subject. Label the bottom of your graph by grading periods. Along the left-hand side of your graph, list possible test scores. For example, you could mark 0 percent on the bottom and go up in 10-percent units, reaching 100 percent at the top. Each period, make a bar to represent your test scores in each subject. Remember to use a different color for each subject.

1820   1830

1829
• Andrew Jackson becomes
  the President of the United States

1830
• Steam
  locomotives

CONNECT MAIN IDEAS

Use this organizer to show how the chapter's main ideas are connected. Write three details to support each main idea. A copy of the organizer appears on page 79 of the Activity Book.

The Industrial Revolution
New technology changed life
in the United States in the 1800s.

1. _____
2. _____
3. _____

The Age of Jackson
Problems divided the American
people in the early 1800s.

1. _____
2. _____
3. _____

The Way West   N
                   W ✴ E
                      S

Westward Ho!
The United States expanded
its territory in the 1800s.

1. _____
2. _____
3. _____

An Age of Reform
People in the 1800s worked to
make American society better.

1. _____
2. _____
3. _____

WRITE MORE ABOUT IT

Write a Conversation Write a conversation that could have taken place between Eli Whitney and a factory owner. Whitney and the factory owner should discuss how mass production will affect Americans.

Write a Letter Imagine that you witnessed the race between the *Tom Thumb* locomotive and the railroad car pulled by a horse. Write a letter to a friend describing the excitement of the event.

1840   1850   1860

1838
• Cherokees are forced
  from their land

1848
• Gold is found
  in California

1853
• Continental United States
  is formed

USE VOCABULARY

Write a term from this list to complete each of the sentences that follow.

equality   **secede**

Manifest Destiny   **transport**

1 Factories needed to _____ their products to their customers.

2 South Carolina threatened to _____ in 1832 because Congress passed another tariff.

3 In 1845 the term _____ was first used to describe the idea that the United States would one day stretch from the Atlantic Ocean to the Pacific Ocean.

4 Some reformers called for _____, or the same rights, for all Americans.

CHECK UNDERSTANDING

5 How was Francis Cabot Lowell's textile mill different from earlier ones?

6 How was the National Road important to the country's growth?

7 Why did sectionalism become a problem in 1828?

8 What was the Trail of Tears?

9 What group settled the Utah Territory? Why did they go there?

10 What lands did the United States purchase after the war with Mexico?

11 Who were Frederick Douglass and Sojourner Truth? How did they spread their messages?

12 Why was the first women's rights convention held?

THINK CRITICALLY

13 **Explore Viewpoints** How did Vice President Calhoun's view of states' rights differ from the one held by President Jackson?

14 **Cause and Effect** What effect did the California gold rush have on the growth of the United States?

APPLY SKILLS

Use Relief and Elevation Maps
Use the maps on pages 390 and 391 to answer these questions.

15 What is the elevation of the land at the Whitman Mission?

16 How would you describe the land near Fort Laramie?

Use a Double-Bar Graph Make a double-bar graph showing the high and low temperatures over the next five days. Each day, make bars for the high and low temperatures. Use different colors for the two temperatures.

READ MORE ABOUT IT

Erie Canal: Canoeing America's Great Waterway by Peter Lourie. Boyds Mills Press. Enjoy a historical canoe tour of the Erie Canal.

Visit the Internet at
http://www.hbschool.com
for additional resources.

TODAY'S PATHFINDERS

Two hundred years ago much of North America was still unknown to people living in the United States. It lay beyond the frontier—the edge of settled regions. Today most places on the continent have been explored, and those that can be lived in have been settled. People today are exploring new kinds of frontiers.

Two of today's new frontiers are space and the deep ocean. Instead of traveling by horse or by wagon, present-day pathfinders explore in special vehicles that can travel great distances above the Earth or deep within the ocean waters. Instead of clothes made from animal furs to protect them from cold weather, today's explorers wear special suits to protect them from the harsh environments of space or the ocean floor.

Like those of the past, today's pathfinders are leading the way for others who will follow. Space stations and underwater laboratories already have been built where pathfinders can live and work for a period of time. Their success may lead to the building of permanent settlements in the future. One day people may live their whole lives in space or in the ocean waters.

The space suit (left) allows a space explorer to breathe while in space, where there is no air. The special suit for exploring the ocean (right) protects the wearer from the crushing pressures of the deep ocean waters.

The *Deepstar 4000* (bottom left) was one of the first vehicles used to explore the depths of the ocean. The *Nautile* (below) was used to explore the sunken ship *Titanic* that lies 12,300 feet (3,750 m) below the ocean's surface. Space explorers (bottom right) perform tasks outside the space shuttle far above the Earth.

Think and Apply

BUILDING CITIZENSHIP

Think about ways the work of present-day pathfinders could change the way people live. Create a poster that shows what life might be like in the future because of the exploration taking place today. Share your poster with classmates.

HARCOURT BRACE

Visit the Internet at **http://www.hbschool.com** for additional resources.

CNN Turner Le@rning

Check your media center or classroom video library for the Making Social Studies Relevant videotape of this feature.

UNIT 6 REVIEW

Summarize the Main Ideas
Study the pictures and captions to help you review the events you read about in Unit 6.

Create a Visual Summary
Choose a topic that is discussed in this unit. Then create your own visual summary about that topic. Draw simple pictures, and label each one. Remember to add a title.

1 The Industrial Revolution brought great changes to the United States. The nation's first factory was built in 1790.

4 In 1811 work began on the National Road. It became the main land route between the East and the West.

6 By the mid-1800s, the nation had gained Texas, the Oregon Country, and other western lands. At the Alamo in 1836, Texans had fought for independence from Mexico.

2 In 1803 the Louisiana Purchase doubled the nation's size. Lewis and Clark explored the new territory with help from Sacagawea.

3 In the early 1800s, steamboats made travel by river much faster.

5 The first locomotive in the nation was built in 1830. Railroads grew quickly after that.

7 The Indian Removal Act of 1830 forced American Indians to leave their homes and make difficult journeys to the West.

ABOLISH SLAVERY

8 Many Americans saw the need for reform. People such as Sojourner Truth spoke out against slavery.

UNIT 6 REVIEW

USE VOCABULARY

Use each term in a sentence that will help explain its meaning.

1. purchase
2. doctrine
3. Industrial Revolution
4. textile mill
5. canal
6. forty-niners
7. reform
8. abolitionist

CHECK UNDERSTANDING

9. How was the Cumberland Gap important to Daniel Boone, the development of the Wilderness Road, and the settlement of the American frontier?

10. How did Thomas Jefferson help double the size of the United States?

11. What was the purpose of the Lewis and Clark expedition?

12. What is mass production? Who first put this idea for producing goods into practice?

13. Why was the Erie Canal built?

14. What was the result of the Indian Removal Act of 1830?

15. What physical features first attracted pioneers to the Oregon Country?

THINK CRITICALLY

16. **Past to Present** Technology changed life for Americans in the 1800s. How does technology change life for Americans today?

17. **Personally Speaking** If you had been alive in 1849, would you have gone to California in search of gold? Explain your answer.

18. **Think More About It** What do you think helped make Frederick Douglass such an effective abolitionist speaker?

APPLY SKILLS

Use Relief and Elevation Maps
Use the map below to answer the questions.

19. Where did the Trail of Tears lead to?

20. Which part of the Trail of Tears passed through mountains? How do you know?

21. What is the elevation of the land near Murfreesboro? near Springfield?

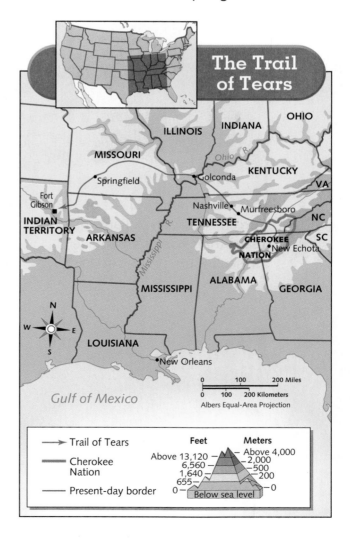

COOPERATIVE LEARNING WORKSHOP

REMEMBER
- Share your ideas.
- Cooperate with others to plan your work.
- Take responsibility for your work.
- Help one another.
- Show your group's work to the class.
- Discuss what you learned by working together.

 Write and Perform a
Scene for a Play

Work with members of a group to write a scene for a play about a typical workday at an early textile mill. The scene should tell something about the workers and the working conditions at the mill. Decide who the characters in the scene will be, and write dialogue for them. Then choose roles, practice the scene, and perform it for your class.

 Draw a
Map

Work together to draw a map showing how the United States grew in the first half of the 1800s. Maps in your textbook and in atlases can help you. First, draw an outline map of the country, and label major landforms and bodies of water. Then, color the boundaries of the United States in 1783, following the American Revolution. Use different colors to show the Louisiana Purchase, Florida, Texas, the Oregon Country, and the land that the United States purchased following its war with Mexico. Add a map key to your map.

 Make a
Time Line

Work in a group to draw a time line on a large sheet of paper. Show the years from 1770 to 1850, using ten-year periods. Then label the time line with events from this unit. Draw pictures to illustrate the events.

Unit Project Wrap-Up

Make a Diorama Finish the Unit Project from page 341. Then work in groups to discuss the scenes shown in each diorama. Discuss how important it was for the pioneers to cooperate with each other if they were to survive. Work together to write descriptions for each scene shown. Be sure to include examples of how pioneers helped one another. Share your dioramas and descriptions with the class.

405

WAR DIVIDES THE NATION

During the early 1800s the United States grew and changed. New towns sprang up across the land. Many Americans moved west to explore and settle distant places.

Yet all was not well in the young country. Problems divided the people of the United States. In 1861 the problems dividing Americans led to war. The war split the country in two, with people living in the North fighting people living in the South.

The United States was not the same after this terrible war. The war brought some good changes, but it left bitter feelings among the country's people for many years to come.

◀ This painting by James Hope shows a scene at the Battle of Antietam in Maryland in 1862.

UNIT THEMES

- Conflict and Cooperation
- Continuity and Change
- Individualism and Interdependence

Unit Project

Make a Time Line Complete this project as you study Unit 7. Use a long piece of paper to make a time line. Label 1790 as the first date on the time line and 1880 as the last date. As you read about events relating to the Civil War, add them to the time line. Draw pictures to illustrate the events. Display your finished time line in the classroom or hallway.

407

CANADA

WASHINGTON
TERRITORY

Columbia *River*

OREGON

Snake *River*

R O C K Y

Missouri *River*

DAKOTA
TERRITORY

G R E A T

P L A I N S

PACIFIC
OCEAN

NEVADA
TERRITORY

*GREAT
BASIN*

Sacramento

San Francisco

CALIFORNIA

N
W E
S

*Mojave
Desert*

Los Angeles

San Diego

*Great
Salt
Lake*

UTAH
TERRITORY

NEBRASKA
TERRITORY

Platte *River*

M
O
U
N
T
A
I
N
S

COLORADO
TERRITORY

Arkansas *River*

KANSAS

Colorado River

NEW MEXICO
TERRITORY

Santa Fe

TEXAS

El Paso

Rio *Grande*

MEXICO

0   200   400 Miles
0   200   400 Kilometers
Albers Equal-Area Projection

| 1860 | | 1862 | 1864 |

1860
Lincoln Is Elected President
PAGE 431

1861
Civil War Begins
PAGE 432

The Nation Divided, 1861

MAINE

CANADA

MINNESOTA

Lake Superior

WISCONSIN

MICHIGAN

Lake Huron

Lake Michigan

VT

NH

Portland

Troy

Boston

Albany

MA

Providence

Lake Ontario

NEW YORK

CT

Buffalo

RI

Milwaukee

Detroit

Lake Erie

New York City

Mississippi River

Cedar Rapids

Chicago

Cleveland

PA

Gettysburg

NEW JERSEY

Philadelphia

IOWA

Pittsburgh

Baltimore

ILLINOIS

INDIANA

OHIO

MD

DE

Annapolis

Cincinnati

River

WEST VIRGINIA (1863)

Washington, D.C.

VIRGINIA

Missouri River

St. Louis

Louisville

Ohio

Richmond

Norfolk

Perryville

MISSOURI

KENTUCKY

APPALACHIAN MOUNTAINS

Appomattox Courthouse

MApS

Paducah

Nashville

Tennessee River

Raleigh

INDIAN TERRITORY

Memphis

TENNESSEE

NORTH CAROLINA

Mississippi River

Wilmington

ARKANSAS

ALABAMA

SOUTH CAROLINA

Atlanta

MISSISSIPPI

Montgomery

GEORGIA

Charleston

Dallas

Vicksburg

Jackson

Savannah

LOUISIANA

Mobile

Pensacola

Jacksonville

St. Augustine

Port Hudson

New Orleans

FLORIDA

Gulf of Mexico

ATLANTIC OCEAN

Legend:
- Union state
- Border state
- Confederate state
- Territory
- ● Major city

1866

1865
Lee Surrenders

PAGE 458

1865
Freedmen's Bureau

PAGE 464

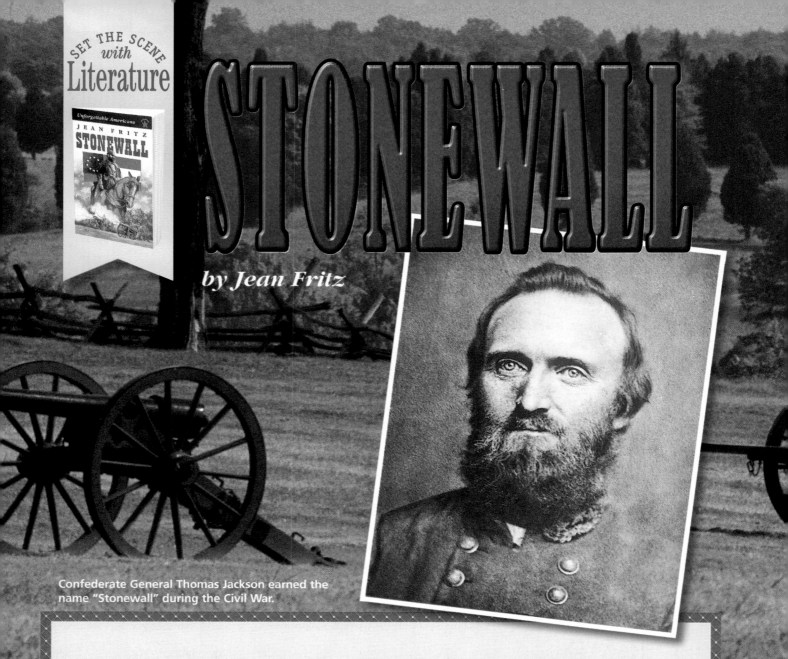

SET THE SCENE with **Literature**

STONEWALL

by Jean Fritz

Confederate General Thomas Jackson earned the name "Stonewall" during the Civil War.

In towns and cities across the country, thousands of excited young men signed up to join the army. It was 1861, and the country was at war. Northerners and Southerners alike signed up, but not to fight on the same side. They signed up to fight each other.

Most people said that it would be a quick and easy war. It would be over, they said, after only one or two battles.

Most people also said that their side would win.

Read now about the war's first major battle, which took place near the small Virginia town of Manassas Junction, not far from Washington, D.C. Imagine Northern soldiers, called Yankees, lining up for the first time against Southern soldiers, called Confederates or Rebels, as crowds looked on.

This building, known as the "Stone House," was used as a hospital by Confederate and Union soldiers during the Battle of Bull Run.

As the participants gathered at Manassas, excitement mounted. At last! This was it! The war was starting! Victory was in the air as if nothing else could possibly exist. The Confederates, obviously outnumbered, were lined up in a defensive position beside a small stream known as Bull Run, but if they worried, they didn't show it. Hadn't they always believed that one rebel could beat five Yankees? As for the Yankees, they straggled down to Manassas, stopping to pick blackberries—in no hurry, for hadn't they been told that the Rebs would run once they saw how bold the Yanks were? Even the civilians in Washington, high-ranking officials and their wives, were so sure of a Union victory that they planned to picnic on the outskirts of Manassas on the Big Day. They would drink champagne and toast the army and cry "Bravo! Bravo!" What could be nicer?

Although there had been several days of initial skirmishing, the Big Day turned out to be Sunday, July 21st. A beautiful sunny day—perfect for a picnic. Carriages were drawn up on a hill overlooking Bull Run; ladies rustled under parasols; gentlemen adjusted field glasses; couriers galloped up with the latest news. Good news, all of it. Yankee advances. Confederate confusion. So it went for the first six hours.

Yet not all the Confederates had been heard from. The Army of the Shenandoah that was supposed to be held in the hills by the Union watchdog forces had eluded their enemy on July 18th and had left for Manassas. At first they'd been slow. The men didn't know where they were going or why and saw no reason to rush just because their officers told them to. Finally General Thomas Jackson, whose brigade led the march, stopped them and read an official statement. "Our gallant army under General Beauregard is now attacked by overwhelming numbers," Jackson read. He asked the troops if they would not "step out like men and make a forced march to save the country."

A battle! The men yelled their approval—a special rebel yell. . . . It was a fierce sound that a Yankee soldier once said sent a corkscrew sensation down the spine. Woh-who-ey. The yell rose to a pitch on the *who* and held there, trembling and drawn out, then fell with a thud on the *ey*. The men quickened their pace. Woh-who-ey. For eighteen hours they marched until at last, having waded waist deep through the green Shenandoah River, they dropped, exhausted. They marched and they rode a train for a few hours, and then they marched again. But they were there now. The question was: Were they in time?

By noon on the 21st it was clear that Beauregard had positioned the major part of his army in the wrong place. While the enemy was concentrating its forces on the left, the Confederates were wasting their time on the right. In the general scramble to change positions, Jackson and his brigade found themselves in the thick of the activity. Union men were in the distance but steadily advancing; the Confederates were retreating. As one officer passed Jackson, he shook his head. "The day is going against us," he said.

"If you think so, sir," Jackson replied, "don't say anything about it."

Jackson did not plunge forward to meet the enemy, as his men might have expected. Looking over the field, he saw a plateau which he recognized as the best possible position for making a stand. Here he placed his men and artillery and when the enemy fire closed in, Jackson stood before his brigade, his blue eyes blazing, the old battle fever upon him. Walking back and forth, indifferent to bullets, he was lifted out of himself, possessed with a power he'd known only once before, in Mexico. He understood exactly how to get the most out of every man and every gun and he *willed* victory into the day. "The fight," as one officer put it, "was just then hot enough to make [Jackson] feel well." Shot in the hand as he held it up, Jackson wrapped a handkerchief around the wound and went on as if nothing had happened.

In another part of the field, General Bee, a West Point classmate of Jackson's, was desperately trying to stop a retreat. "Look yonder!" he cried to his men. "There's Jackson standing like a stone wall."

General Bee was killed almost as soon as he'd finished speaking, but retreating Confederates did see how well Jackson's line was holding and gradually they began to rally around it. The last reinforcements from Shenandoah army, which had just arrived, were rushed to the scene. And the tide of the battle began to turn.

Men were supposed to be at least 18 years old to join the army, but some boys much younger—like the two shown here—still signed up. Most boys were not allowed to fight. Instead they tended horses, drove wagons, or served as drummer boys.

What started out for many as an exciting adventure ended in fear, injury, and death at the Battle of Bull Run (above). One Union soldier, staggering from the battlefield, told an onlooker, "I've had enough fighting to last my lifetime." During the battle, Private A. P. Hubbard's pocket-sized Bible (right) saved his life, protecting him from a bullet that ripped the book apart.

When the center of the Union line was in plain sight, General Beauregard ordered a charge. Jackson relayed the order.

"Reserve your fire till they come within fifty yards," he shouted, "then fire and give them the bayonet. And when you charge, yell like furies."

The orders were carried out precisely.

Woh-who-ey!

Woh-who-ey!

Suddenly the entire Union army was falling back, then turning around and hurrying off the field. A huge, confused mob mixed with panic-stricken picnickers headed pell-mell back to Washington.

The battle was over and with it some of the innocent glory was gone. For the fields were strewn with bodies—young men who only the day before had been laughing and making jokes. Two thousand Confederates killed or wounded; three thousand Union men. Stopped right in the midst of doing something. In the middle of a sentence perhaps, in mid-step, in the act of raising a rifle, at the beginning of a smile. Struck down, blown apart as if they weren't *people*. As if they weren't *young*. How could inexperienced men have imagined what death would be like on a battlefield?

In one day soldiers on both sides became veterans, but of course the victors felt better than the losers. If they could win a battle, southerners said, they could win a war.

CHAPTER 13

BACKGROUND TO THE CONFLICT

"I appear this evening as a thief and robber. I stole this head, these limbs, this body from my master, and ran off with them."

Frederick Douglass, a runaway slave and abolitionist, about 1842

This photograph of Frederick Douglass was taken in 1856.

414

Differences Divide North and South

FOCUS
What might cause people living in different regions to disagree today?

Main Idea As you read, look for the reasons that caused people in the North and the South to disagree during the middle 1800s.

Vocabulary
cotton gin

Differences among Americans help make the nation strong. Sometimes, however, differences come between people. In the mid-1800s differences became disagreements between Americans living in two regions—the North and the South. These disagreements threatened to tear the country apart.

Regional Differences

Many of the differences between the North and the South developed over time, as people in each region found different ways of making a living. In the mid-1800s most Americans still lived and worked on farms. For many people, however, life was changing.

In the North, factories seemed to be springing up everywhere, making all kinds of goods. Many people were moving from their farms to towns and cities, where they hoped to work in the factories. People even came from other countries to find jobs.

Life in the South was not changing as quickly. Factories were being built and cities were growing, yet farming remained the most common way to earn a living. The biggest farms were plantations along the Coastal Plain and near the Mississippi River. Planters there raised acres and acres of cash crops, such as cotton, rice, tobacco, and sugarcane, to sell at market.

Wealthy plantation owners were among the South's leaders. Many white Southerners copied the ways of these planters and dreamed about owning their own plantations someday. Yet few ever did. Most lived on small farms, where they raised cattle, cut lumber, and grew only enough food to feed their families.

Cotton was an important cash crop in the South. Many Southerners depended on cotton to make a living.

Many people in the North were moving to cities to find work. This painting (top) shows a busy street scene in New York City. In the South farming continued to be the center of life. This scene (below) shows a cotton plantation along the Mississippi River.

Partly because of the differences in work opportunities between the two regions, many more people lived in the North than in the South. By 1860 the population of the North had grown to more than 19 million. Only 11 million people lived in the South. Of those 11 million people, nearly 4 million were Africans held as slaves.

REVIEW *How was the North different from the South?*

The Slave Economy

Slavery had been a part of American life since colonial days. In many places, however, slavery did not last. Some people thought that slavery was wrong. Others could not make money using enslaved workers. The cost of feeding, clothing, and housing slaves was too great.

Yet slavery continued in the South, where owners had come to depend on the work of

Southern Slaveholders, 1860

75% owned no slaves

3% owned 20 or more slaves

5% owned 1 slave

4% owned 10–19 slaves

13% owned 2–9 slaves

LEARNING FROM GRAPHS Most Northerners once thought that all Southerners owned slaves. Look at the circle graph to tell if this is true.
■ *What percent of Southerners owned no slaves at all in 1860? What percent did own slaves?*

enslaved people. Slaves were made to work as miners, carpenters, factory workers, and house servants. Most, however, were taken to large plantations. There they worked in the fields, raising acres of cash crops for the planters to sell at market.

Not every white Southerner owned slaves. In fact, most did not. By 1860 only one white Southern family in four owned slaves. Many of these families lived on small farms with one or two slaves. Only a few wealthy slaveholders lived on large plantations with many slaves. These planters together owned more than half of the population of slaves in the South.

REVIEW *Why was slavery important in the Southern states?*

"King Cotton"

In the early years of settlement in the South, few planters grew cotton—the plant from which soft, cool cotton cloth is made. Cotton was in great demand. But before it could be sold, workers had to separate the small seeds from the white cotton fibers. This was a slow, tiring job that took too many people too much time. Inventor Eli Whitney changed this.

In 1793 Whitney invented a machine called the cotton gin, or engine. The **cotton gin** removed the seeds from the cotton fibers much faster than workers could. This one change in technology led to many other changes.

BIOGRAPHY

Eli Whitney
1765–1825

Eli Whitney taught school and studied law. He also liked to fix things. While visiting a friend's Georgia plantation, he learned how difficult it was to remove the seeds from cotton. Whitney invented a machine that could take care of the problem. Soon so many people wanted cotton gins that he could not make enough to keep up with the demand. Other people began to make and sell copies of his invention. Whitney had to pay lawyers to stop others from copying his work. This used up most of the money he made from inventing the cotton gin.

Cotton: From Plantation to Mill

LEARNING FROM DIAGRAMS Turning raw cotton into cloth was a long process that led from farms and plantations to textile mills. The steps shown here are ❶ harvesting the cotton on the plantation; ❷ removing the seeds and cleaning the cotton with the cotton gin; ❸ shipping the cleaned cotton; and ❹ spinning the fibers into threads at the textile mill.

■ *What inventions helped speed up the process of turning raw cotton into cloth?*

With Whitney's cotton gin, cotton could be cleaned and prepared for market in less time. Planters could then sell more cotton and make more money. They sold the cotton to textile mills in the North and in Europe.

Worldwide demand for cotton made both Southern planters and Northern textile-mill owners rich. It also created a demand for more enslaved workers. Planters needed slaves to plant the seeds, weed the fields, pick the cotton, and run the cotton gins. "Cotton is King," said Senator James Henry Hammond of South Carolina, "and the African must be a slave, or there's an end of all things, and soon."

REVIEW *How did the cotton gin help speed up cotton production?*

North and South Disagree

By the mid-1800s some Southerners did not like the way growth was booming in the North. As a writer for one Alabama newspaper described it,

66 The North fattens and grows rich upon the South. We depend upon it for our entire supplies. . . . The slaveholder dresses in Northern goods, rides in a Northern saddle. . . . His land is cleared with a Northern axe, and a Yankee clock sits upon his mantel-piece. . . . 99

Bad feelings over growth were not the worst of the troubles between the North and the South. Far worse was the disagreement over states' rights and slavery. Northerners and Southerners had argued since colonial days about whether states should allow slavery. The argument flared up again with the rapid settlement of the western frontier.

Over the years pioneers and soldiers had pushed many of the Indian peoples off their lands. This made it possible for more settlers to move west. The settlers took with them their own ways of life. For settlers from the North, this meant a way of life without slaves. For some settlers from the South, however, this meant taking their enslaved workers with them.

It was not long before the question of the spread of slavery to the frontier became one of the most argued issues in the country. Most white Northerners thought that slavery should go no farther than where it already was—in the South. Most white Southerners believed that slave owners had the right to take their slaves wherever they wanted, including to the West.

The disagreement over slavery led to fierce arguments. Even so, the number of people held as slaves in the South continued to grow. So did the number of enslaved people who were taken west.

REVIEW *Why did the settlement of the western frontier bring about new arguments over slavery?*

LESSON 1 REVIEW

Check Understanding

1 Remember the Facts In what ways were the North and the South different?

2 Recall the Main Idea What caused people living in the North and the South to disagree during the middle 1800s?

Think Critically

3 Think More About It How did the differences between the North and the South affect the ways of life in the two regions?

4 Cause and Effect How did the invention of the cotton gin affect Northern textile-mill owners?

Show What You Know

Art Activity Think about how the cotton gin changed life in the 1800s. Create an advertisement for the people of that time that explains how the cotton gin affects those who make and buy cotton and cotton products. Then present your advertisement to the class.

Use Graphs to Identify Trends

1. Why Learn This Skill?

Some graphs show information that can help you see patterns of change over time. These patterns are called **trends**. A graph showing the number of people living in the United States since 1800 would show that the number has gone up steadily over the years. The trend, then, has been for the population of the United States to increase.

Graphs can show trends that go upward, go downward, or hold steady. Some graphs show trends that change. For example, a graph could show a downward trend for a time and then an upward trend.

2. Understand the Process

Follow the numbered steps to identify the trends shown by the two graphs on this page. The first is a line graph that shows the amount of cotton produced in the United States from 1800 to 1860. The second is a bar graph that shows the number of people enslaved in the United States from 1800 to 1860.

1 Look at the line graph. About how much cotton was produced in 1800? About how much cotton was produced in 1830? About how much cotton was produced in 1860? You can see that the amount of cotton produced from 1800 to 1860 went up. The trend, then, was for cotton production to go up during this period of time.

2 Look at the bar graph. About how many people were enslaved in 1800? About how many people were enslaved in 1830? About how many people were enslaved in 1860? What trend does the bar graph show?

3. Think and Apply

Think about the trends that are shown in these graphs. Write a paragraph that describes what the trends tell you about the connection between cotton production and slavery between 1800 and 1860. Share your paragraph with a classmate.

Cotton Production, 1800–1860

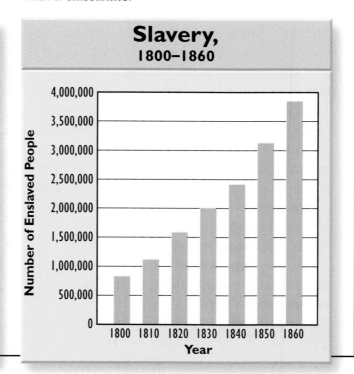

Slavery, 1800–1860

Africans in Slavery and Freedom

FOCUS
In what ways do people today protest against unfair treatment?

Main Idea   As you read, look for ways enslaved people protested against being held in slavery.

Vocabulary

slave code
overseer
spiritual
resist
Underground Railroad

In 1800 there were nearly 900,000 slaves in the United States. By 1860 there were nearly 4 million. Some Africans—both in the North and in the South—were free. In fact, by 1860 nearly 500,000 free Africans were living in the United States. Yet they did not have the rights of full citizenship. Despite the hardships, most Africans found ways to survive. Some also found ways to fight back.

Life Under Slavery

Most Southern states had laws that shaped the day-to-day lives of enslaved people. These laws were called **slave codes**. Under these codes slaves were not allowed to leave their owners' land, to meet in groups, or to buy or sell goods. Most were not allowed to learn to read and write. They were treated as property, and few were given any special privileges.

Some slave owners hired people called **overseers** to watch the slaves as they worked and to punish them if they fell behind. Slave owners broke up families by selling husbands without their wives, and children without their parents. They punished enslaved people harshly for disobeying.

"No day ever dawns for the slave, nor is it looked for," one African of the time wrote. "For the slave it is all night—all night, forever."

To help themselves survive, many enslaved people formed close-knit communities. Families, friends, and neighbors helped one another, giving comfort and support. They talked of what they remembered about Africa or what they had heard about it from others. They tried to keep their traditions alive.

Religious beliefs gave many enslaved people the strength they needed to handle the hardships of life under slavery.

Many slaves had to wear identification badges sewn to their clothing.

Enslaved people were sold, usually one at a time, at auctions. Families were often separated because relatives could be bought by different slave owners.

Some slaves expressed their beliefs by singing spirituals. **Spirituals** (SPIR•ih•chuh•wuhlz) are religious songs based on Bible stories. One spiritual told the deepest feelings of those who were enslaved.

❝ If I had my way,
If I had my way,
If I had my way,
I'd tear this building down. ❞

REVIEW *How did people in slave communities help one another?*

Fighting Back

Most enslaved Africans did whatever they could to **resist**, or act against, slavery. Some resisted in quiet ways, secretly damaging the plantation. They broke tools, making the damage look like an accident. They left gates open so that farm animals could escape. They let boats drift away. They hid household goods.

Such actions were dangerous, and slaves had to be careful to escape punishment. Some acted as if they did not understand what they had been told. They said they were sorry and would try to do better. "Got one mind for the boss to see," one slave song went. "Got another mind for what I know is me."

Other slaves chose a more violent way to resist—they rebelled. One rebellion took place in Southampton County, Virginia, on a hot August night in 1831. An enslaved African named Nat Turner led an attack that killed 57 people, among them Turner's owner and the owner's family. Slave owners trying to end the rebellion killed more than 100 slaves. Turner and the other leaders were caught, put on trial, and hanged.

Despite the dangers, the rebellions went on. On the night of October 16, 1859, a white abolitionist named John Brown and a group of followers seized a government storehouse in Harpers Ferry, in what is now West Virginia. The storehouse was filled with guns. Brown planned to give the guns to slaves so they could fight for their freedom. Like Turner, Brown was caught, put on trial, and hanged.

Such rebellions frightened many white Southerners. As one visitor to the South reported, "I have known times here when not a single planter had a calm night's rest. They never lie down to sleep without . . . loaded pistols at their sides."

REVIEW *In what ways did enslaved people resist slavery?*

Running Away

Over the years, thousands of slaves chose another way to resist slavery. They tried to gain their freedom by running away.

Some slaves ran away alone. Others tried to escape with their families or friends. Some planned their escape carefully, slowly gathering what they would need. Others saw a sudden chance and decided quickly—they ran.

Once away from their owners' land, runaways had to find safe places to hide. Many were helped along the way by other slaves. Some were taken in by Indian peoples. Other slaves hid in forests, swamps, or mountains—sometimes for years. One former slave from Virginia remembered,

66 Father got beat up so much that after a while he ran away and lived in the woods. Mama used to send John, my oldest brother, out to the woods with food for Father. . . . Father wasn't the only one hiding in the woods. There was his cousin, Gabriel, that was hiding and a man named Charlie. 99

Some runaways stayed in hiding, but others went on with their journey until they

$150 REWARD

RANAWAY from the subscriber, on the night of the 2d instant, a negro man, who calls himself *Henry May*, about 22 years old, 5 feet 6 or 8 inches high, ordinary color, rather chunky built, bushy head, and has it divided mostly on one side, and keeps it very nicely combed; has been raised in the house, and is a first rate dining-room servant, and was in a tavern in Louisville for 18 months. I expect he is now in Louisville trying to make his escape to a free state, (in all probability to Cincinnati, Ohio.) Perhaps he may try to get employment on a steamboat. He is a good cook, and is handy in any capacity as a house servant. Had on when he left, a dark cassinett coatee, and dark striped cassinett pantaloons, new—he had other clothing. I will give $50 reward if taken in Louisville; 100 dollars if taken one hundred miles from Louisville in this State, and 150 dollars if taken out of this State, and delivered to me, or secured in any jail so that I can get him again.
Bardstown, Ky., September 3d, 1838. WILLIAM BURKE.

Slave owners often sent out posters (above) offering rewards for the return of runaway slaves. This painting by Eastman Johnson (left) shows one family's escape. The painting is called *A Ride for Liberty—The Fugitive Slaves.*

reached free land in the Northern states or in Canada or Mexico. They traveled for weeks or months, some guided only by the North Star. Others found helping hands to lead the way—the brave men and women of the Underground Railroad.

The Underground Railroad was not under the ground, and it was not a real railroad. The **Underground Railroad** was a system of escape routes leading to freedom. Most routes led from the South to the Northern states and to Canada. Some led to Mexico and to the Caribbean.

Members of the Underground Railroad were called conductors. Working at night, conductors led runaways from one hiding place to the next along the routes. These hiding places—barns, attics, secret rooms— were called stations. There the runaways could rest and eat, preparing for the next night's journey to the next station on the route.

Most conductors of the Underground Railroad were either free Africans or white Northerners who opposed slavery. Harriet Tubman, who had escaped from slavery herself, was one of the best-known conductors of the Underground Railroad. During the 1850s Tubman returned to the South 20 times and guided about 300 people to freedom. She proudly claimed, "I never lost a single passenger."

REVIEW *How did the Underground Railroad help slaves escape?*

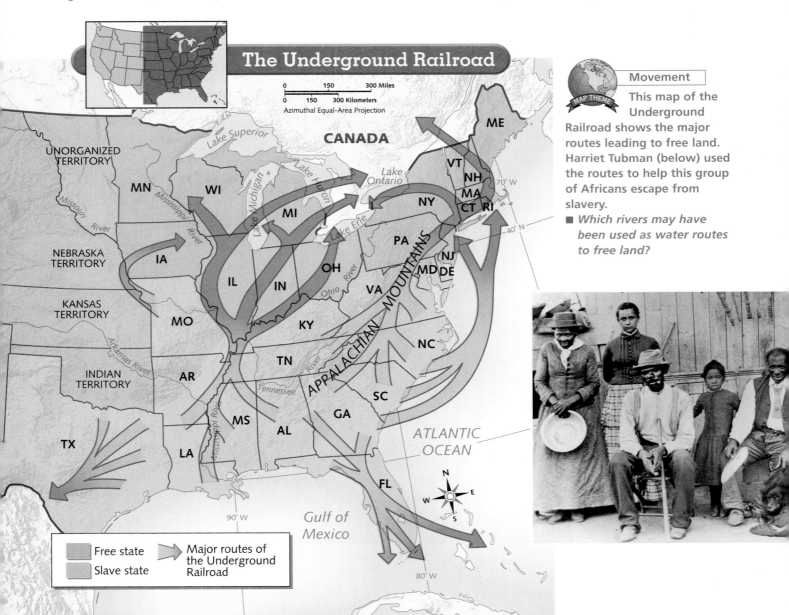

The Underground Railroad

0   150   300 Miles
0   150   300 Kilometers
Azimuthal Equal-Area Projection

CANADA

UNORGANIZED TERRITORY

Lake Superior
Lake Michigan
Lake Huron
Lake Ontario
Lake Erie

ME
VT
NH
MA
CT RI
NY
PA
NJ
MD DE
VA

MN
WI
MI
IA
IL
IN
OH
Missouri River
Mississippi River
Ohio River

NEBRASKA TERRITORY

KANSAS TERRITORY

INDIAN TERRITORY

Arkansas River

MO
KY
TN
Tennessee River
APPALACHIAN MOUNTAINS
NC
SC
GA
AR
MS
AL
Mississippi River
TX
LA
FL

ATLANTIC OCEAN

Gulf of Mexico

70° W
40° N
90° W
80° W

N
E
W
S

Movement
This map of the Underground Railroad shows the major routes leading to free land. Harriet Tubman (below) used the routes to help this group of Africans escape from slavery.
■ *Which rivers may have been used as water routes to free land?*

Free state
Slave state

Major routes of the Underground Railroad

Free Africans

Not all Africans of the time were enslaved. By 1860 nearly half a million free Africans lived in the United States. A few were members of families that had been free since colonial times, or at least since the American Revolution. Some were former slaves who had been freed by their owners. Others had bought their freedom or had become free by running away.

Many free Africans lived in cities, where they had a better chance of finding a job. They worked in many different professions. Some were carpenters, tailors, blacksmiths, and shopkeepers. Others became ministers, doctors, nurses, and teachers.

Some free Africans became quite wealthy. Jehu Jones, for example, owned and ran one of South Carolina's best hotels. James Forten ran a busy sail factory in Philadelphia, where many ships were built. Thomy Lafon made a fortune from his businesses in New Orleans.

For most Africans, however, life was hard no matter where they lived. They were unwelcome in many places and often were treated unfairly. State laws in both the North and the South gave them little freedom. Most were not allowed to vote or to meet in groups. They

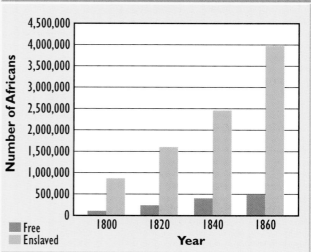

Africans in the United States, 1800–1860

LEARNING FROM GRAPHS This graph shows the numbers of free and enslaved Africans in the United States from 1800 to 1860.
■ *What trends does the graph show?*

could not attend certain schools or hold certain jobs. Some free Africans were wrongly accused of being runaways. Others were taken and sold into slavery. The danger of losing the little freedom they had was very real.

REVIEW *What was life like for most free Africans in the early 1800s?*

LESSON 2 REVIEW

Check Understanding

1 Remember the Facts What was the Underground Railroad?

2 Recall the Main Idea In what ways did enslaved people protest against being held in slavery?

Think Critically

3 Personally Speaking Why do you think many enslaved people were willing to risk their lives to resist being held as slaves? Explain your answer.

4 Past to Present In what ways do people today protest if they are denied freedom?

Show What You Know

Poster Activity Think about some symbols of freedom. Look through old magazines and newspapers for pictures that express the meaning of freedom. Cut out the pictures, and use them to create a poster that shows the idea of freedom. Add your poster to a class display titled *Freedom*.

FOCUS

In what ways do people today try to settle disagreements?

Main Idea Read to learn about the ways Northerners and Southerners tried to settle their disagreements during the early 1800s.

Vocabulary

free state
slave state

Facing a National Problem

A s time passed, more and more Northerners wanted an end to slavery, while more and more slave owners grew angry and bitter. Americans began to understand that slavery was not just a problem between the people of two regions. It had become a problem for the whole country.

New Compromises

One leader who worked hard to help settle the differences dividing the country was Henry Clay of Kentucky. As a member of Congress, Clay often found himself in the middle of heated arguments about slavery.

The worst arguments broke out over the spread of slavery to the West. Each time groups of settlers asked to join the Union as a new state, the same question arose. Would the new state be a free state or a slave state? A **free state** did not allow slavery. A **slave state** did.

For a time there were as many free states as slave states. This kept a balance between the North and the South. Then, in 1819, settlers in the Missouri Territory, a part of the Louisiana Purchase, asked to join the Union as a slave state. If this happened, slave states would outnumber free states.

The Missouri question became a heated debate that dragged on for months. Henry Clay worked day and night to help solve the problem. Clay himself owned slaves. But he did not want to see the question of slavery tear the country apart. Finally, in 1820, he persuaded Congress to agree to a compromise—the Missouri Compromise.

Under this plan Missouri would be allowed to join the Union as a slave state. Maine would join as a free state. This would keep the balance between free states and slave states. Then an imaginary line would be drawn through the rest of the lands gained in the Louisiana Purchase. Slavery would be allowed south of the line. Places north of the line would be free.

Henry Clay became known as the Great Compromiser because of his work to help settle the differences between the North and the South.

The Missouri Compromise, 1820

Legend:
- Free state
- Free territory
- Admitted as a free state
- Slave state
- Slave territory
- Admitted as a slave state
- Missouri Compromise line

0 200 400 Miles
0 200 400 Kilometers
Albers Equal-Area Projection

Regions The Missouri Compromise line divided lands that could join the Union as free states from lands that could join as slave states.

■ *Which two states were admitted to the Union as part of the compromise? Were they admitted as free states or as slave states?*

The Missouri Compromise kept the peace for nearly 30 years. During this time six new states joined the Union, but the number of free states and slave states remained equal.

Then, in 1848, the United States gained new lands after winning the war with Mexico. Settlers in California, a part of these new lands, soon asked to join the Union as a free state.

Henry Clay once again found himself in the middle of an argument in Congress over slavery. Once again he worked toward a compromise. This plan became known as the Compromise of 1850.

Under this compromise California joined the Union as a free state. The rest of the lands won from Mexico were divided into two territories—New Mexico and Utah. The people

there would decide for their territory whether or not to allow slavery.

The Compromise of 1850 also had a new law dealing with runaway slaves. Under the Fugitive Slave Law, anyone caught helping slaves to escape would be punished. People who found runaway slaves—even runaways who had reached the North—had to return them to the South.

Henry Clay, who became known as the Great Compromiser, died in 1852. He never gave up hope that the country would find a peaceful way to settle its differences. On a marker by his grave in Lexington, Kentucky, are the words *I know no North—no South—no East—no West.*

REVIEW *What two compromises on the spread of slavery did Congress reach?*

In 1857 the Supreme Court decided that Dred Scott (far left) should not be given his freedom. Chief Justice Roger Taney (left) spoke for the Court.

Hopes for Peace Fade

Even with the compromises, bad feelings grew between the North and the South. In 1854 harsh words turned to violence.

The problem began when Congress passed the Kansas-Nebraska Act. This new law changed the rules of the Missouri Compromise. Under the compromise, slavery would not have been allowed in the territories of Kansas and Nebraska. Under the Kansas-Nebraska Act, people living in those lands were now given the chance to decide for themselves whether to allow slavery. They would decide by voting.

Kansas quickly became the center of attention. People for and against slavery rushed into the territory, hoping to help decide the vote. It was not long before fighting broke out between the two sides. More than 200 people were killed in the dispute that came to be known as Bleeding Kansas.

While fighting went on in Kansas, those against slavery suffered another defeat. In 1857 the Supreme Court decided the case of an enslaved African named Dred Scott. Scott had asked the Court for his freedom. The Court said no.

Scott argued that he should be free because he had once lived on free land.

Scott's owner had often moved from place to place. When he moved, Scott went with him. For a time they lived in Illinois, a free state. Then they lived in the Wisconsin Territory, a free territory under the Missouri Compromise.

After Scott's owner died, Scott took his case to court. The case moved from judge to judge until it landed in the Supreme Court. There Scott lost his fight for freedom. Chief Justice Roger B. Taney (TAW•nee) said that Scott had "none of the rights and privileges" of American citizens. He was a slave, Taney said. Living on free land did not change that.

Taney had more to say. He declared that Congress had no right to outlaw slavery in the Wisconsin Territory to begin with. The Constitution protects people's right to own property. Slaves, he said, were property. He believed that the Missouri Compromise was keeping people in some places from owning property. This, he said, went against the Constitution.

Many people had hoped that the Dred Scott decision would settle the battle over slavery once and for all. Instead, it made the problem worse.

REVIEW *Why did the Supreme Court deny freedom to Dred Scott?*

Abraham Lincoln Works for Change

The Kansas-Nebraska Act and the Dred Scott decision caused violence and anger that caught the attention of Americans across the country. Soon new leaders began to speak out. One of these leaders was Abraham Lincoln.

Abraham Lincoln had grown up on the frontier in Kentucky and Indiana. Like other pioneers, he had had a hard life. He worked so many hours on the family farm that he often could not go to school. But he borrowed books and read all he could.

When Lincoln was a young man, he moved with his family to Illinois. There he held several jobs before serving in the state legislature. He studied law, and in time he became a lawyer. In the late 1840s he served a term in Congress. During these years the matter of the spread of slavery to the West became an important question.

Lincoln was against the spread of slavery. He did not think the government had the right to end all slavery in the country. But he hoped that if slavery were not allowed to spread, it would one day die out.

Lincoln joined a new political party that was formed to fight the spread of slavery. This party was called the Republican party. He even thought about running again for

This ticket was to a fair held in 1858 where money was raised to fight slavery.

government office. The Kansas-Nebraska Act and the Dred Scott decision helped him make up his mind. In 1858 Lincoln entered a race for the United States Senate. He ran against Stephen A. Douglas, who had written the Kansas-Nebraska Act.

REVIEW *Why did Abraham Lincoln join the Republican party?*

The Lincoln-Douglas Debates

Few people could have been more different from each other than Lincoln and Douglas. Abraham Lincoln was a tall, thin man from the frontier. His thick, black hair looked uncombed. He wore plain, dark clothes that were a bit rumpled. He was not well known around the country. In fact, few people outside of Illinois had heard of him.

Stephen Douglas was heavy and a full foot shorter than Lincoln. He was well educated and wore fine clothes—a ruffled shirt, tailored suit, and polished boots. He was already serving in the Senate, and many Americans across the country knew of him. People called him the Little Giant.

In one way, though, Lincoln and Douglas were very much alike. They were both powerful public speakers. In the summer of 1858, the two men traveled around Illinois and debated questions that were important to voters. Huge crowds turned out to listen. Everyone wanted to hear Lincoln and Douglas debate about whether slavery should be allowed in the West.

Stephen Douglas argued that each new state should decide the slavery question for itself. That was what the country's founders had allowed, he said, and that was what the new Kansas-Nebraska Act allowed.

Abraham Lincoln disagreed. He said that "the framers of the Constitution intended and expected" slavery to end. The problem, he pointed out, was more than a question of

Stephen Douglas and Abraham Lincoln held seven debates in 1858. This painting shows Lincoln (standing) and Douglas (to Lincoln's right) debating in Charleston, Illinois.

what each state wanted. It was a question of right and wrong. Slavery should not spread to the West, he said, because slavery was wrong. Lincoln said,

66 That is the real issue. That is the issue that will continue in this country when these poor tongues of Judge Douglas and myself shall be silent. It

is the eternal struggle between these two principles—right and wrong—throughout the world. 99

Stephen Douglas won the race for the Senate. But people around the country now knew who Abraham Lincoln was.

REVIEW *How did Lincoln's views differ from those of Douglas?*

LESSON 3 REVIEW

Check Understanding

① **Remember the Facts** What events led Abraham Lincoln to speak out against slavery?

② **Recall the Main Idea** In what ways did the Northerners and the Southerners try to settle their disagreements during the early 1800s?

Think Critically

③ **Think More About It** How was the Missouri Compromise changed by the Kansas-Nebraska Act and the Dred Scott decision?

④ **Past to Present** Do you think it is still important for leaders today to hold debates before elections? Explain your answer.

Show What You Know

Simulation Activity Imagine that you have been asked to interview Henry Clay, Dred Scott, Stephen Douglas, or Abraham Lincoln. Write the questions you would ask and the answers the person might give. With a classmate, practice role-playing your interview. Present your interview to the class.

A Time for Hard Decisions

FOCUS
When must people today make difficult decisions in their lives?

Main Idea   Read to learn about the difficult decisions Americans had to make in 1860 and 1861.

Vocabulary
Confederacy

In 1860 Americans prepared to choose a new President. They listened to speeches. They read newspapers. They watched parades. They also worried. Anger and bitterness were driving the North and the South farther apart than ever. Could a new President hold the country together?

The Election of 1860

The question of the spread of slavery to the West seemed to be all that people talked about during the election of 1860. Stephen Douglas ran as a member of the Democratic party. He argued that western settlers should decide for themselves whether to allow slavery. However, many Democrats in the South backed another leader—John Breckinridge of Kentucky. Breckinridge thought that the government should allow slavery everywhere in the West.

Abraham Lincoln ran as a member of the Republican party. He spoke out strongly against the spread of slavery. He promised not to stop slavery in the South, where it was already practiced. But he said that he hoped it would one day end there, too.

Many white Southerners worried about what would happen if Lincoln became President. They thought that the problem was far greater than the question of slavery. They believed that their whole way of life was being attacked. Some said that their states would secede from the Union if Lincoln was elected.

On election day, November 6, 1860, Lincoln won the Presidency. Southern leaders did not wait long before carrying out their threat. On December 20, South Carolina's leaders declared that

66 . . . the United States of America is hereby dissolved. 99

With these words South Carolina seceded from the Union. The state refused to have a President who was against slavery.

A supporter of Stephen Douglas wore this campaign button during the election of 1860.

There were six other states—Mississippi, Florida, Alabama, Georgia, Louisiana, and Texas—that soon followed South Carolina's example.

Together these seven states formed a new country. They called the new country the Confederate States of America, or the **Confederacy** (kuhn•FEH•duh•ruh•see). They elected a Mississippi senator, Jefferson Davis, as president. The United States was now split in two.

REVIEW *What did seven Southern states decide to do after Lincoln was elected President?*

This poster (above) urged people to vote for Lincoln and his running mate, Hannibal Hamlin. The gold ax (right) was a campaign pin worn by Lincoln's supporters. The "WIDE AWAKE" on the handle meant that his supporters were "wide awake" to dangers that might affect the Union.

Fort Sumter

Abraham Lincoln had little time to celebrate winning the election. He wanted to save the Union—to keep the country together. Yet seven states had said that they were no longer part of the Union. What would he do about those states?

Some people told Lincoln to let the seven states go. Others said that he should give in on the slavery question and hope that the Southern states would return. Still others felt that Lincoln should use the army to end the revolt.

Lincoln thought a great deal about his choices. He hoped to prevent a war. "We are not enemies, but friends," Lincoln told Southerners after taking the oath of office as President of the United States on March 4, 1861. "We must not be enemies." The very next day, however, Lincoln received an important message. When he read it, he knew that time was running out. The message was from Major Robert Anderson. Anderson was the commander of Fort Sumter.

When the Southern states seceded, they had taken over post offices, forts, and other federal government property. Fort Sumter, which was located on an island off the coast of South Carolina, near Charleston, was one of the few forts in the Confederate States of America that remained in Union hands. The message from Major Anderson said that supplies at the fort were almost gone. If new supplies were not sent soon, Anderson would have to surrender the fort to the Confederacy.

Lincoln knew that he had an important decision to make. His goal was to keep Fort Sumter under Union control. But several problems stood in the way. The most important problem was that the fort was running out of supplies.

Lincoln thought very carefully about his choices. Each one had its own possible consequences. He could send supplies to the fort. If he did, the Southerners might attack. He could send troops to the fort. If he did, the Southerners would surely attack. He could choose to do nothing at all. By doing nothing, he would really be giving the fort to the Confederacy because Major Anderson would have to surrender.

Finally, President Lincoln made the choice he thought was the best. He decided that he would send supply ships to the fort. Then he waited to see how the Southerners would react.

Now Confederate president Jefferson Davis had to make a decision. His goal was to take control of Fort Sumter for the Confederate states. His problem was that Union troops held the fort. President Lincoln

This scene shows the Confederate attack on Fort Sumter.

GEOGRAPHY

Fort Sumter

Fort Sumter was one of several forts built to protect American coastlines following the War of 1812. Building the fort was a long, difficult job. Workers first had to build the island on which the fort would stand. Then they built the fort itself, with walls 5 to 10 feet (1.5–3 m) thick and nearly 40 feet (12 m) high. Today Fort Sumter is part of the national park system.

SOUTH CAROLINA

N
W E
S

Charleston

Charleston Harbor

FORT SUMTER

ATLANTIC OCEAN

0   1   2 Miles
0   1   2 Kilometers

The Union Breaks Apart

November 1860	December 1860	January 1861	February 1861	March 1861	April 1861	May 1861
Lincoln is elected President	South Carolina secedes	Mississippi, Florida, Alabama, Georgia, and Louisiana secede	Texas secedes	Lincoln is inaugurated President	Southern troops attack Fort Sumter Virginia secedes	Arkansas, Tennessee, and North Carolina secede

LEARNING FROM TIME LINES This time line shows when each of 11 Southern states seceded from the Union.
- *Which state was the first to secede from the Union? Which states were the last to secede?*

was now sending supply ships to help those troops.

Like Abraham Lincoln, Jefferson Davis thought carefully about his choices and their possible consequences. Then he made what he thought was the best choice, even though he knew that one possible result was war. Davis decided to attack the fort before the Union supply ships arrived. On April 12, 1861, Confederate soldiers fired on Fort Sumter. The next day Major Anderson and his men ran out of ammunition and had to give up.

Davis had met his goal. Lincoln had not. Lincoln quickly called for Americans to join an army to stop the rebellion. Fearing that Northern armies would march into the South, the states of Virginia, Arkansas, Tennessee, and North Carolina joined the seven states already in the Confederacy. Now the country was even more divided. The Civil War had begun.

REVIEW *What did Davis decide to do when Lincoln said he would send supplies to Fort Sumter?*

LESSON 4 REVIEW

Check Understanding
1. **Remember the Facts**   What event led South Carolina's leaders to secede from the Union?
2. **Recall the Main Idea**   What difficult decisions did Americans make in 1860 and 1861?

Think Critically
3. **Personally Speaking**   Do you think Abraham Lincoln made the right decision when he decided to send supplies to Fort Sumter? Explain your answer.

4. **Think More About It**   Why do you think Fort Sumter was important to both Abraham Lincoln and Jefferson Davis?

Show What You Know

Writing Activity   Write two headlines that could have appeared in newspapers following the attack on Fort Sumter. The first should be a headline for a newspaper in the North. The second should be a headline for a newspaper in the South. Present the headlines to your classmates.

Make a Thoughtful Decision

1. Why Learn This Skill?

Did you have to make a decision today? Did you have to decide whether to go somewhere with your friends? Did you have to decide how to settle a disagreement with someone?

You make many decisions every day. Some decisions are easy. Other decisions are more difficult. The difficult ones may require more thought because your choices may have lasting consequences.

2. Remember What You Have Read

You have read about the difficult decisions Abraham Lincoln and Jefferson Davis had to make as supplies ran out at Fort Sumter in South Carolina. The ways in which these leaders came to their decisions show how a thoughtful decision can be made. Think again about what happened.

1 What goal did each leader have?
2 What steps did each leader follow in making a decision?
3 What choice did each leader make?
4 What were the consequences of Lincoln's choice? of Davis's choice?

3. Understand the Process

You can use similar steps to help make a thoughtful decision.

- Identify your goal.
- Think about problems that may keep you from reaching your goal.
- Identify the actions that you could take to reach your goal.
- Think about the possible consequences of each action.
- List your choices for action. Begin with those that might have the best results, and end with those that might have the worst results.
- Make the choice that seems best.
- Put your choice into action.
- Think about whether your choice helped you reach your goal.

4. Think and Apply

Think about a decision you made at school. What steps did you follow? What choice did you make? What were the consequences? Do you think you made a thoughtful decision? Explain your answers.

Abraham Lincoln
(far left)
Jefferson Davis
(left)

Union or Secession?

The Union flag as it looked in 1861

An early Confederate flag

At the news of Abraham Lincoln's election as President, Americans in both the North and the South got ready for what some called the Revolution of 1860. Some hoped that the South would not carry out its threat to secede. Lincoln himself said, "The people of the South have too much sense to attempt the ruin of the government." But he and others did not understand how badly many Southerners wanted their independence.

Not all Southerners agreed about seceding, though. Some were against it. Others thought that the South should first give Lincoln a chance. They would be willing to secede only if nothing else worked. Still others wanted to secede right away.

Two Southerners who made their feelings clear were Edmund Ruffin of Virginia and Sam Houston, the governor of Texas. The words of the two men show how they felt about secession, or seceding from the Union.

Edmund Ruffin

❦I will be out of Virginia before Lincoln's inauguration, and so . . . avoid being, as a Virginian, under his government even for an hour. I, at least, will become a citizen of the seceded Confederate States, and will not again reside in my native state, nor enter it except to make visits to my children, until Virginia shall also secede. . . . This result . . . cannot be delayed long.

The bloodshed of South Carolinians defending their soil and their rights, or maintaining the possession of their harbor . . . will stir doubly fast the sluggish blood of the more backward Southern States into secession.❧

Sam Houston

❦Let me tell you what is coming. . . . Your fathers and husbands, your sons and brothers, will be herded at the point of the bayonet. . . . You may, after the sacrifice of countless millions of treasure and hundreds of thousands of lives, as a bare possibility, win Southern independence. . . . But I doubt it. I tell you that, while I believe with you in the doctrine of States' Rights, the North is determined to preserve this Union. They are not a fiery, impulsive people as you are, for they live in colder climates. But when they begin to move in a given direction . . . they move with the steady momentum and perseverance of a mighty avalanche.❧

Compare Viewpoints

1. What viewpoint about seceding did Ruffin hold? How do you know?
2. What viewpoint about seceding did Houston hold? How do you know?
3. What other viewpoints might Southerners have held on the matter of secession? Governor Thomas H. Hicks of Maryland said, "The only safety of Maryland lies in preserving a neutral position between our brethren of the North and of the South." What view did the governor hold?

Think and Apply

You have read that three Southerners—Ruffin, Houston, and Hicks—each had a different view about secession. At what other times in history have people from the same region held different views about something?

1820

1830

1820
• The Missouri
  Compromise

1831
• Nat Turner's
  rebellion

CONNECT MAIN IDEAS

Use this organizer to show how the chapter's main ideas are connected. Write three details to support each main idea. A copy of the
organizer appears on page 86 of the Activity Book.

Differences Divide North and South
People in the North and the South
disagreed during the middle 1800s.

1. _____
2. _____
3. _____

Africans in Slavery and Freedom
Enslaved people protested against
being held in slavery.

1. _____
2. _____
3. _____

Background
to the
Conflict

Facing a National Problem
Northerners and Southerners tried to
settle disagreements during the 1800s.

1. _____
2. _____
3. _____

A Time for Hard Decisions
Americans had to make important
decisions in 1860 and 1861.

1. _____
2. _____
3. _____

WRITE MORE ABOUT IT

Write Your Opinion Tell whether or not you
think agreeing to a compromise is always a
good way to settle differences. Explain your
answer.

Compare Viewpoints Write a paragraph
that compares Stephen Douglas's and
Abraham Lincoln's points of view on how
the slavery question should be settled.

1850
• The Compromise of 1850

1861
• Confederate soldiers attack Fort Sumter

USE VOCABULARY

For each pair of terms, write a sentence or two that explains how the terms are related.

1. slave code, overseer
2. resist, spiritual
3. free state, slave state

CHECK UNDERSTANDING

4. How was life in the North changing in the middle 1800s?
5. Why did Southern planters feel they needed enslaved workers?
6. How did the invention of the cotton gin affect cotton production?
7. How did the settlement of the West add to the argument over slavery?
8. What kinds of laws affected the everyday lives of slaves?
9. What role did religion play in the lives of many enslaved people?
10. Why was the North Star important to some runaway slaves?
11. How did the Compromise of 1850 help satisfy the demands of slaveholders?
12. Why did the Kansas-Nebraska Act lead to fighting?
13. What major decisions led to the start of the Civil War?

THINK CRITICALLY

14. **Personally Speaking** What kind of person do you think a conductor on the Underground Railroad needed to be?

15. **Cause and Effect** Why did compromises fail to settle disagreements over the issue of slavery?
16. **Explore Viewpoints** How do you think Henry Clay would have felt about the Dred Scott decision?
17. **Think More About It** How did the Lincoln-Douglas debates affect Lincoln's political career?

APPLY SKILLS

Use Graphs to Identify Trends Look in newspapers or magazines for a bar graph or a line graph that shows a trend. Cut out the graph and tape it to a sheet of paper. Below the graph, identify the trend shown. How does the trend change over time?

Make a Thoughtful Decision Imagine that a friend has asked you to allow your home to be used as a station on the Underground Railroad. What steps might you follow to come to a decision?

READ MORE ABOUT IT

Lincoln: In His Own Words by Milton Meltzer. Harcourt Brace. In this book, read about Lincoln's life, thoughts, and actions through his own words.

HARCOURT BRACE

Visit the Internet at **http://www.hbschool.com** for additional resources.

Chapter 13 • **439**

CHAPTER 14

CIVIL WAR
AND
RECONSTRUCTION

"I put in many hours of weary work and soon thought myself quite a soldier. . . . I was elected First Sergeant, much to my surprise. Just what a First Sergeant's duties might be, I had no idea."

Elisha Rhodes,
Pawtucket,
Rhode Island, 1861

Confederate private Edwin Jennison, killed at the Seven Days' Battles in 1862

The Fighting Begins

LESSON

1

FOCUS

Why is it sometimes difficult to choose sides in a disagreement?

Main Idea   As you read, think about why it was difficult for many Americans to choose sides during the Civil War.

Vocabulary

border state
Emancipation
   Proclamation

W hen Confederate soldiers fired on Fort Sumter, hopes for peace between the North and the South ended. Now Americans had to make some difficult decisions.

Taking Sides

In the weeks following the attack on Fort Sumter, many people thought that the war would be short and easy. For most, the choice of which side to support was clear.

Most Northerners supported the Union. They believed that it was wrong that the Southern states had broken away from the Union. They were willing to go to war to save their flag and all that it stood for. "If it is necessary that I should fall on the battlefield for my country," wrote a soldier from New England, "I am ready. . . . I am willing—perfectly willing—to lay down all my joys in this life, to help maintain this government."

Most white Southerners supported the Confederacy. They were willing to go to war to win their independence. Whether they owned slaves or not, many felt that the North was trying to change the South. They thought that the government was taking away their rights. The only way to get those rights back, they believed, was to secede.

The need to defend their land also led many Southerners to join the fight. One young soldier, caught early in the war by Union troops, told his captors, "I'm fighting because you're down here."

For some Americans, however, the choice between the Union and the Confederacy was not an easy one. People in Missouri, Kentucky, Maryland, and Delaware were torn between the two sides. These **border states** were between the North and South. Although they

In some of the early battles, soldiers wore the clothes they had brought from home. Later, Northern soldiers would wear blue uniforms (above), and Southerners would wear gray uniforms (left).

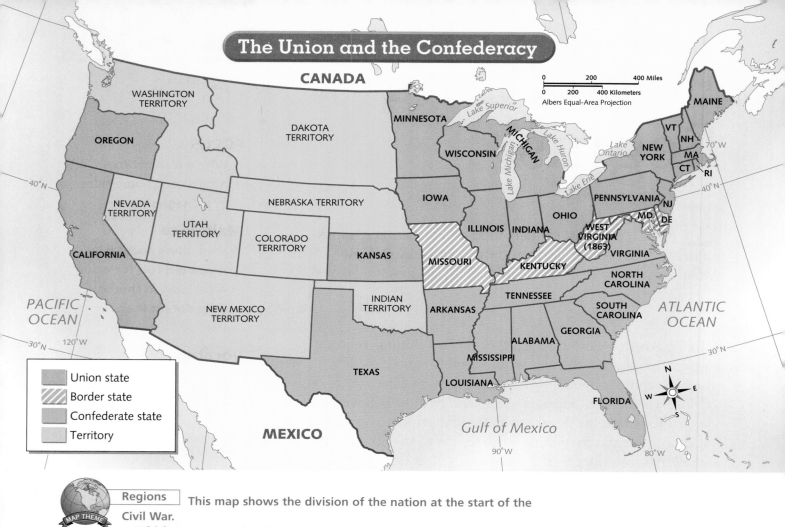

The Union and the Confederacy

CANADA

MAINE

WASHINGTON TERRITORY

OREGON

DAKOTA TERRITORY

MINNESOTA

Lake Superior

WISCONSIN

MICHIGAN

Lake Huron

Lake Ontario

VT

NH

NEW YORK

MA

CT

RI

70°W

40°N

NEVADA TERRITORY

UTAH TERRITORY

NEBRASKA TERRITORY

IOWA

ILLINOIS

INDIANA

OHIO

Lake Erie

PENNSYLVANIA

NJ

MD

DE

WEST VIRGINIA (1863)

40°N

CALIFORNIA

COLORADO TERRITORY

KANSAS

MISSOURI

KENTUCKY

VIRGINIA

PACIFIC OCEAN

NEW MEXICO TERRITORY

INDIAN TERRITORY

ARKANSAS

TENNESSEE

NORTH CAROLINA

SOUTH CAROLINA

ATLANTIC OCEAN

30°N

120°W

GEORGIA

ALABAMA

MISSISSIPPI

TEXAS

LOUISIANA

FLORIDA

30°N

Union state
Border state
Confederate state
Territory

MEXICO

Gulf of Mexico

90°W

80°W

0   200   400 Miles
0   200   400 Kilometers
Albers Equal-Area Projection

N
W   E
S

Regions This map shows the division of the nation at the start of the Civil War.
■ *Which states were border states?*

allowed slavery, they had remained a part of the Union. When the time came for people in the border states to choose sides, some fought for the North. Others fought for the South.

Taking sides was also hard for people living in some parts of the South. In the mountains of eastern Tennessee and northern Alabama, there was very little slavery. Many people there sided with the North. In western Virginia, feelings for the Union were so strong that the people voted to break away from Virginia and form a new state. West Virginia joined the Union in 1863.

Taking sides was also hard for many in the Indian nations. By the time of the war, the Cherokee, Creek, Seminole, Choctaw, and Chickasaw peoples had been driven from their lands to the Indian Territory, which is

today Oklahoma. When it came time to choose sides, most people in these five tribes had little reason to like either the North or the South. In the end the Choctaws and the Chickasaws fought for the South. The Creeks, Seminoles, and Cherokees were divided between the Union and the Confederacy.

The decisions people had to make in these early days of the war divided families and friends. When war finally came, four of Henry Clay's grandsons decided to join the Confederacy. Three others fought for the Union. Even President Lincoln's own family was divided. Mary Todd Lincoln, his wife, had been born in Kentucky. Four of her brothers fought for the South.

REVIEW *Why was taking sides hard for people in the border states?*

Lee Joins the Confederacy

On April 19, 1861—a week after the attack on Fort Sumter—Robert E. Lee paced his bedroom floor. It was nearly midnight. Lee was a United States Army colonel. The day before, President Lincoln had asked him to take command of a Union army. Just hours later Lee had learned that his home state of Virginia had seceded.

Lee loved his country. He was a graduate of the United States Military Academy at West Point, New York. He had fought in the war with Mexico and had served his country for 32 years. Yet Lee also loved Virginia. Could he lead an army that would fight his family and neighbors?

The next morning Lee told Mary, his wife, what he had decided. He turned down Lincoln's offer and quit the Union army. A few days later he took command of Virginia's troops. Lee knew he would be fighting old friends who were fighting for the Union. Even so, he decided to serve Virginia. "I cannot raise my hand against my birthplace, my home, my children," he said.

REVIEW *Why was it difficult for Robert E. Lee to choose sides in the war?*

Battle Plans

Three months after the attack on Fort Sumter, two armies of eager young men prepared for the first major battle of the war. The battle took place at Bull Run, a stream near the town of Manassas Junction, Virginia.

After hours of fighting, the South won the battle. The defeat shocked the Union. Northerners had entered the war feeling very strong. The North had nearly twice as many people as the South. It had more factories to make weapons and supplies. It had more railroads to get those supplies to the troops.

But the South had proved more powerful than most Northerners had expected. Southerners fighting to defend their own land had a very strong will to win. Stories were already being told about the bravery of officers such as "Stonewall" Jackson.

Robert E. Lee led the Confederate troops throughout the war. These gloves (left) protected Lee's hands when he was in battle.

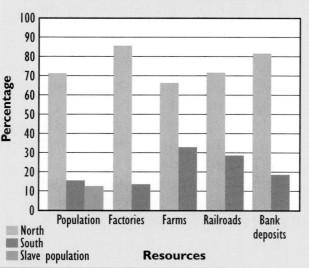

Resources of the North and South, 1860

Percentage

Population · Factories · Farms · Railroads · Bank deposits

Resources

- North
- South
- Slave population

LEARNING FROM GRAPHS This graph compares the resources of the North and the South at the beginning of the Civil War.

■ *Which side had more resources?*

Lincoln quickly began to look for new officers of his own. He called for more soldiers. He also called for new battle plans.

An early Northern plan to win the war had to do with trade. The South depended on trade with the North and with other countries to buy such goods as cloth, shoes, and guns. The North hoped to cut off trade by setting up a blockade. Northern warships would stop trading ships from leaving or entering Southern ports. Without trade, the South would slowly become weaker.

Not everyone in the North liked the idea of a blockade. Some made fun of it, calling it the Anaconda (a•nuh•KAHN•duh) Plan. An anaconda is a large snake that squeezes its prey to death. Although this plan would slowly weaken the South, many people in the North wanted quicker action. They said the government should send the army to enter the South by force—to invade. "On to Richmond!" they

cried. Richmond, Virginia, had become the capital of the Confederacy.

At first the most important fighting plan of the Confederate leaders was simply to protect their lands. Some Southerners compared their situation with the way things were for George Washington and the Patriots during the Revolutionary War. Southerners hoped to defend their homes against invaders and slowly wear down their enemy, just as the Patriots had worn down the British.

But many Southerners, just like many Northerners, were impatient. Cries of "On to Washington!" were soon answered with plans to invade the North.

Southerners also hoped that some countries in Europe would help them win the war. Britain and France depended on cotton to keep their textile mills running. Many thought that these countries would help the South as soon as their supplies of cotton ran low.

In both the North and the South, only men were allowed to join the army. Women, however, found many ways to help. They took over factory, business, and farm jobs that men left behind. They sent food to the troops, made bandages, and collected supplies. Many women, such as Clara Barton and Sally Tompkins, worked as nurses. A few served as spies, and some even dressed as men, joined the army, and fought in battles.

REVIEW *What were the strengths of the North? of the South?*

The War and Slavery

As the fighting dragged on into 1862, Northern plans seemed to be working. The blockade brought trade to a halt, and supplies ran very low in the South. Plantations and shops were destroyed.

Even so, the North had not won yet. Thousands of Union soldiers were dying in battle.

Clara Barton
1821–1912

"While our soldiers stand and fight, I can stand and feed and nurse them." Clara Barton followed the fighting from battle to battle, caring for sick and wounded Union soldiers. Barton had always tried to help people in need. She taught school for a time and then worked as a government clerk. When the Civil War broke out, she wanted to help. Her work is still carried on by the American Red Cross. Barton founded the American branch of this world organization in 1881.

President Lincoln knew he had to find a way to push the North to victory.

To Lincoln, the purpose of the war was to keep the country together—to save the Union. Yet he knew that slavery was the issue that had divided the country. He realized that writing an order to free the slaves would greatly help the North. The loss of millions of enslaved workers would be a blow to the South. Freeing the slaves would also help in another way. It would turn the British, who needed cotton but were against slavery, toward the Union.

Abraham Lincoln held back on declaring an **Emancipation Proclamation**, an order freeing the slaves. He feared that such a step might turn people in the border states, as well as some states in the North, against the Union. Lincoln's waiting made the abolitionists angry. William Lloyd Garrison wrote that Lincoln was "nothing better than a wet rag."

As the war went on, Lincoln thought more and more about the question of slavery. Had the time come to write an Emancipation Proclamation? What would be the consequences if he made such a decision?

REVIEW *Why did Lincoln think that an Emancipation Proclamation would help the North?*

LESSON 1 REVIEW

Check Understanding

❶ **Remember the Facts** What were the battle plans of the North and the South?

❷ **Recall the Main Idea** Why was it difficult for many Americans to choose sides during the Civil War?

Think Critically

❸ **Explore Viewpoints** Why might a person in a border state have joined the Union army or the Confederate army?

❹ **Past to Present** During the war many people told President Lincoln how they felt about slavery. How do government leaders learn about people's opinions today?

Show What You Know

Writing Activity Imagine that you are living in the South during the Civil War. Write a diary entry describing how the Union's blockade is changing your life.

The *Signature That Changed America*

by Harold Holzer

In 1862 Abraham Lincoln faced one of his hardest decisions as President. He wanted to save the Union, but the fighting seemed to go on and on between Union and Confederate troops. Lincoln knew that an order to free the slaves could help the North. Abolitionists wanted him to sign such an order. But Lincoln also knew that an Emancipation Proclamation would make some people in both the North and the South angry.

Read now about the days when Lincoln made a decision about slavery and took action. As you read, think about why it is important for leaders to consider many points of view before making a decision.

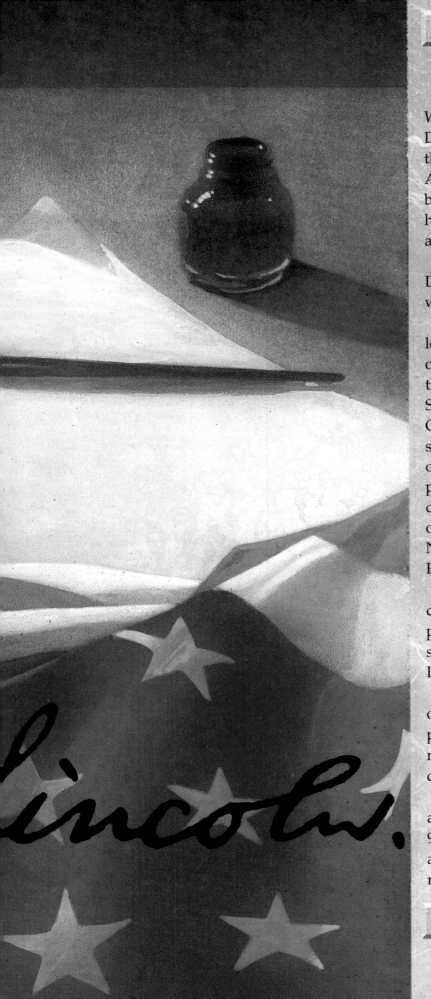

It was January 1, 1863. The Civil War was still raging, but in Washington, D.C., this was a day of celebration. At the White House, President and Mrs. Abraham Lincoln welcomed the new year by hosting a party. For hours they greeted hundreds of visitors, just as Presidents and First Ladies had done for years.

But this was no ordinary New Year's Day at the White House. Today history would be made.

In mid-afternoon the President quietly left the party and walked upstairs to his office on the second floor. Waiting for him there were Secretary of State William H. Seward and members of Lincoln's staff. On a large table in the center of the room sat an official-looking document, written out in beautiful handwriting by a professional "engrosser." Lincoln sat down at the table, the document spread out before him. The moment was at hand. Now, at last, the President would sign the Emancipation Proclamation.

Abraham Lincoln took pen in hand, dipped it in ink, and then, unexpectedly, paused and put the pen down. To his surprise—and to everyone else's—Lincoln's hand was trembling.

It was not, Lincoln later said, "because of any uncertainty or hesitation on my part." As he put it, "I never in my life felt more certain that I am doing right than I do in signing this paper."

But greeting so many guests had taken a toll. "I have been shaking hands since 9 o'clock this morning, and my hand is almost paralyzed," Lincoln explained. "If my name ever goes into history it will be for this act, and my whole soul is in it. If my hand trembles when I sign the proclamation, all who examine the document hereafter will say, 'He hesitated.'"

After a few moments Lincoln again took pen in hand. The room was quiet except for the muffled sounds of laughter and music drifting upstairs from the party below. Slowly but firmly he wrote "Abraham Lincoln" at the bottom of the document that declared all slaves in the Confederacy "forever free."

With that, Lincoln glanced at his signature, looked up, smiled, and modestly said, "That will do."

What Lincoln's proclamation did—and did not do—has been debated ever since. Some argue that the Emancipation Proclamation did little. After all, it ordered slaves freed only in the states of the Confederacy—the states where Lincoln had no authority. But in the words of one contemporary, the document struck like a second Declaration of Independence. In truth, nothing so revolutionary had happened since the Revolutionary War itself. Perhaps that is why Lincoln worried so long before finally doing what some thought he should have done the moment he became President.

Lincoln had been against slavery all his life. Seeing slaves in chains for the first time in New Orleans, he vowed: "If I ever get a chance to hit this thing, I'll hit it hard." As a young legislator in Illinois, he had been one of the few lawmakers to sign a resolution against slavery. Years later he spoke angrily against the idea that slavery should be allowed to spread to the western territories.

Abraham Lincoln (right) wrote this draft (below) of the Emancipation Proclamation.

True, Lincoln did not then believe in equality for Africans living in the United States. He did not yet think they should be permitted to vote or sit on juries. But he differed with most citizens of the day by declaring, "In the right to eat the bread which his own hands earn," a black man "is my equal and . . . the equal of every living man."

When Lincoln was elected President in 1860, he promised to do nothing to interfere with slavery in the slave states. He still believed that slavery was wrong, but he felt that personal belief did not give him the right to act. After a year of war, however, Lincoln decided that the only way to put the Union back together was to fight not only against Confederate armies but also against slavery itself. "We must free the slaves," he confided, "or ourselves be subdued."

Then why did he not order slaves freed immediately? Lincoln believed that the country was simply not ready for it. "It is my conviction," he said, "that had the proclamation been issued even six months earlier than it was, public sentiment would not have sustained it." The President worried that if he acted against slavery too soon, he would lose support in the important border states, which he wanted so much to keep in the Union. Lincoln could not afford to lose the slave state of Maryland, for example. If Maryland seceded, then Washington, D.C., would become a capital city inside an enemy country! Lincoln worried, too, that Northern voters might turn against Republicans and elect a new Congress unwilling to continue the war. So he waited.

Not until July 1862 did Lincoln finally decide that he could safely act. "Things had gone on from bad to worse," he said, "until I felt that we had reached the end of our rope . . . that we had about played our last card and must change our tactics, or lose the game."

On July 22, a blisteringly hot summer day, Lincoln called a meeting of the Cabinet and told the members he had an important decision to announce. He warned them that he would listen to no arguments. He had already made up his mind. Then he unfolded some papers and slowly read aloud his first draft of the proclamation. No one present dared speak against it, but Secretary of State Seward expressed a reasonable concern. With the war going so badly, wouldn't the announcement be taken by most Americans as "a cry for help— our last shriek on the retreat?" Seward wanted the President to postpone the proclamation until the Union could win a victory on the battlefield. Lincoln agreed.

Over the next two months, emancipation was the best-kept secret in America. Then, on September 17, 1862, Union troops finally gave Lincoln a victory. The North defeated the South at the Battle of Antietam in Maryland. Five days later Abraham Lincoln announced the Emancipation Proclamation.

Just as Lincoln had feared, the emancipation was immediately and bitterly attacked. Some newspapers warned that it would set off riots. Union soldiers began deserting in greater

Abraham Lincoln meets with members of his cabinet to discuss the Emancipation Proclamation (left). William H. Seward is sitting across from Lincoln. To celebrate the Emancipation Proclamation, the document was reprinted on this poster (below).

numbers than ever. That fall, Lincoln's Republican party suffered losses in elections for Congress.

But Lincoln did not back down. On January 1—with his trembling hand steadied—he signed the final proclamation. He even added his hope that former slaves would now join Union armies to fight for the freedom the emancipation promised. Everyone knew that, for all its good intentions, the Emancipation Proclamation would do nothing unless Union armies could win victories in Rebel states. That is exactly what happened. The Emancipation Proclamation freed 200,000 slaves as Union troops marched farther and farther into the Confederacy.

By the stroke of his pen, Lincoln had launched a second American Revolution. He not only had helped end the shame of human bondage in America but had guaranteed the survival of American democracy. As he put it, "By giving freedom to the slave, we assure freedom to the free."

LITERATURE REVIEW

1 Why was it important for Lincoln to think about all points of view before deciding to write the Emancipation Proclamation?

2 Why did some people think the Emancipation Proclamation did very little?

3 Lincoln said, "By giving freedom to the slave, we assure freedom to the free." Rewrite Lincoln's words in your own words to show classmates what you think he meant.

FOCUS

What actions might help bring a difficult conflict to an end?

Main Idea As you read, think about the events that helped bring the Civil War to an end.

Vocabulary

Gettysburg Address
assassination

The Long Road to a Union Victory

The Emancipation Proclamation did not give enslaved people instant freedom. The order was only for the states that had left the Union—not the four border states. And until Union troops were sent to the Confederate states to see that the Emancipation Proclamation was carried out, many people there remained enslaved. Still, it gave new hope to Africans and new spirit to the North.

In the months that followed, the North seemed to be winning the war. Yet terrible battles lay ahead, and many more soldiers would die before the war's end.

African Regiments

Africans had fought to defend the United States since the Revolutionary War. Over the years, however, many had been kept from joining the army. By the start of the Civil War, they were not allowed to serve in the army.

As the war went on, many Africans decided to form their own regiments to fight for the Union. While they trained, their leaders asked Congress to let them enlist. Finally, in 1862, with no end to the war in sight and fewer white soldiers joining the army, Congress agreed. More than 186,000 Africans signed up. They formed 166 regiments of artillery, cavalry, infantry, and engineers.

At first African soldiers were not paid as much as white soldiers. They were given poor equipment, and they often ran out of supplies. To make things worse, Confederate soldiers said that they would enslave or kill any African soldiers they captured.

Even with the hardships and the dangers, African soldiers soon proved themselves in battle. They led raids behind Confederate lines and served as spies and scouts. They fought in almost every battle,

Like many other Africans in the United States, this soldier, Andrew Scott, fought for the Union.

African troops played a key role in support of the Union. This photograph shows members of an artillery unit completing cannon drills.

facing some of the worst fighting of the war. More than 38,000 African soldiers lost their lives defending the Union.

REVIEW *How did African regiments help the Union war effort?*

Grant Leads the Union

Another boost for the North came when President Lincoln finally found a general as good as Confederate general Robert E. Lee. His name was Ulysses S. Grant.

Like Lee, Grant had been educated at West Point and had fought in the war with Mexico. When the Civil War began, Grant offered his services to the Union army. His quick decisions in battles soon led to Union victories. After one battle, when the Confederates asked for the terms of surrender, Grant replied, "No terms except an unconditional and immediate surrender can be accepted." After that, Northerners liked to say that Grant's initials, *U. S.*, stood for *Unconditional Surrender.*

One of Grant's most important battles began in May 1863 at Vicksburg, Mississippi. After two attacks Grant decided to surround and lay siege to the city. For weeks Union guns pounded Vicksburg. Grant and his soldiers cut off all supplies to the city. The trapped Confederates, both soldiers and townspeople, soon ran out of food. They had to tear down houses for firewood and dig caves in hillsides for shelter. Finally, on the Fourth of July, the starving people of Vicksburg gave in.

Vicksburg proved to be a key victory. It gave the Union control of the Mississippi River. This, in turn, helped weaken the Confederacy by cutting it into two parts. As one Union soldier wrote from Vicksburg, "This was the most glorious Fourth I ever spent." President Lincoln was overjoyed when he heard about the victory. Before long he gave Grant command of all Union troops.

REVIEW *Why was Grant's victory at Vicksburg important?*

Gettysburg

At about the same time that Grant won Vicksburg, other Union troops were facing the invading army of Robert E. Lee in the small town of Gettysburg, Pennsylvania. The Battle of Gettysburg ended in one of the most important Union victories of the war. But more than 3,000 Union soldiers and nearly 4,000 Confederates were killed. More than 20,000 on each side were wounded or reported missing.

The fate of the Fourteenth Tennessee Regiment tells the story. When the battle began, there were 365 men in the unit. When the battle ended, there were only 3.

On November 19, 1863, President Lincoln went to Gettysburg to dedicate a cemetery for those who had died there. A crowd of nearly 6,000 people gathered for the ceremony.

Lincoln gave a short speech that day. In fact, he spoke for less than three minutes. A photographer who was there hoped to take a picture of the President as he gave his speech. But by the time the photographer had set up his heavy camera, Lincoln had already sat down!

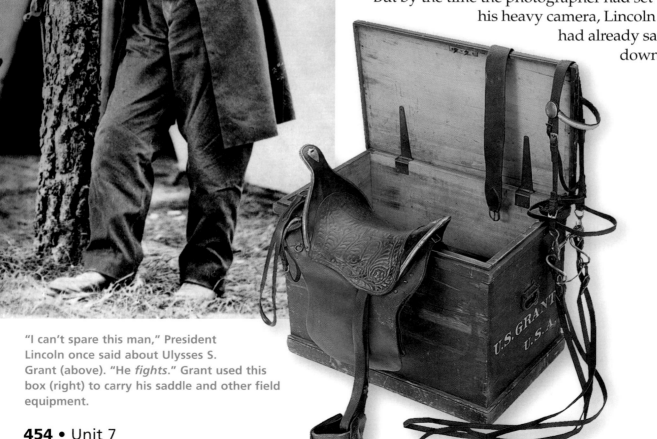

"I can't spare this man," President Lincoln once said about Ulysses S. Grant (above). "He *fights*." Grant used this box (right) to carry his saddle and other field equipment.

THE GETTYSBURG ADDRESS

Four score and seven years ago our fathers brought forth on this continent, a new nation, conceived in Liberty, and dedicated to the proposition that all men are created equal.

Now we are engaged in a great civil war, testing whether that nation, or any nation so conceived and so dedicated, can long endure. We are met on a great battlefield of that war. We have come to dedicate a portion of that field, as a final resting place for those who here gave their lives that that nation might live. It is altogether fitting and proper that we should do this.

But, in a larger sense, we can not dedicate—we can not consecrate—we can not hallow—this ground. The brave men, living and dead, who struggled here, have consecrated it, far above our poor power to add or detract. The world will little note, nor long remember what we say here, but it can never forget what they did here. It is for us the living, rather, to be dedicated here to the unfinished work which they who fought here have thus far so nobly advanced. It is rather for us to be here dedicated to the great task remaining before us—that from these honored dead we take increased devotion to that cause for which they gave the last full measure of devotion—that we here highly resolve that these dead shall not have died in vain—that this nation, under God, shall have a new birth of freedom—and that government of the people, by the people, for the people, shall not perish from the earth.

Lincoln's speech at Gettysburg was so short that many people in the crowd were disappointed. Lincoln himself called it "a flat failure." But people soon realized that this short speech, later known as the **Gettysburg Address**, was one of the most inspiring ever given by an American leader.

In the Gettysburg Address, Lincoln spoke to the heart of the war-weary North. He spoke of the ideals of liberty and equality on which the country had been founded. He honored the soldiers who had died defending those ideals. And he called on Americans to try even harder to win the struggle those soldiers had died for—to save the "government of the people, by the people, for the people" so that the Union would be preserved.

REVIEW *What did President Lincoln ask Americans to do in his speech at Gettysburg?*

This photograph shows a home that was damaged in Atlanta, Georgia, during the Union army's March to the Sea.

The March to the Sea

More Union victories followed those at Vicksburg and Gettysburg. Then came one of the worst times for the South—the invasion of Georgia.

In 1864 Union General William Tecumseh Sherman led his army south from Tennessee into Georgia. Through heavy fighting Sherman pushed to Atlanta, the railroad center of the South. As he took the city, much of it burned to the ground.

From Atlanta, Sherman's troops headed toward Savannah, on the Atlantic coast. Their march has become known as the March to the Sea. The goal of this march was to destroy everything that could help the South in the war. Sherman hoped that this would break the South's will to fight. "We cannot change the hearts of those people of the South," Sherman said, "but we can make war so terrible . . . make them so sick of war that generations would pass away before they would again appeal to it." Cutting a path of destruction 60 miles (97 km) wide and 300 miles (483 km) long, Union troops burned homes and stores, destroyed crops, wrecked bridges, and tore up railroad tracks.

On December 22, 1864, Savannah fell to Union troops. That night Sherman sent a message to President Lincoln. "I beg to present you as a Christmas gift the city of Savannah." Sherman then turned north and marched through South Carolina, destroying even more than he had in Georgia.

REVIEW *What was the purpose of Sherman's March to the Sea?*

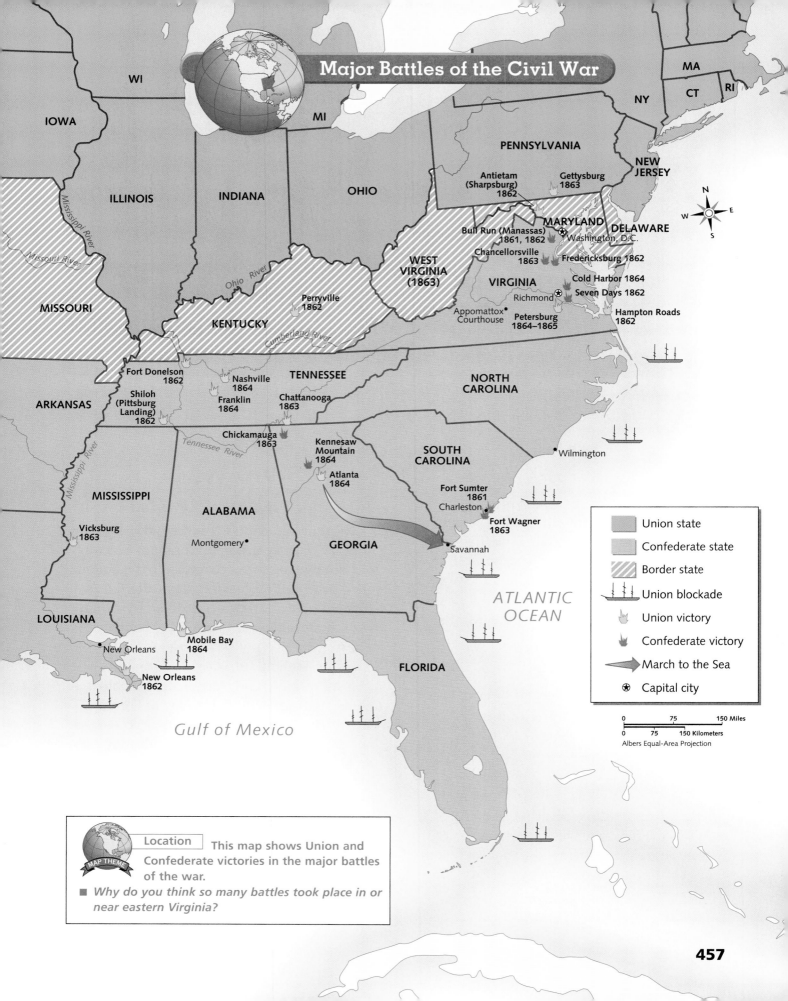

Major Battles of the Civil War

WI

MI

MA

CT

RI

NY

NEW JERSEY

PENNSYLVANIA

IOWA

ILLINOIS

INDIANA

OHIO

Antietam (Sharpsburg) 1862

Gettysburg 1863

MARYLAND

DELAWARE

Washington, D.C.

Bull Run (Manassas) 1861, 1862

Chancellorsville 1863

Fredericksburg 1862

MISSOURI

KENTUCKY

Perryville 1862

WEST VIRGINIA (1863)

VIRGINIA

Richmond

Cold Harbor 1864

Seven Days 1862

Appomattox Courthouse

Petersburg 1864–1865

Hampton Roads 1862

Ohio River

Cumberland River

Fort Donelson 1862

Nashville 1864

TENNESSEE

NORTH CAROLINA

ARKANSAS

Shiloh (Pittsburg Landing) 1862

Franklin 1864

Chattanooga 1863

Tennessee River

Chickamauga 1863

Kennesaw Mountain 1864

SOUTH CAROLINA

Wilmington

MISSISSIPPI

ALABAMA

Atlanta 1864

Fort Sumter 1861

Charleston

Vicksburg 1863

GEORGIA

Fort Wagner 1863

Montgomery

Savannah

ATLANTIC OCEAN

LOUISIANA

New Orleans

Mobile Bay 1864

New Orleans 1862

FLORIDA

Gulf of Mexico

N
W E
S

Mississippi River

Missouri River

Legend

	Union state
	Confederate state
	Border state
	Union blockade
	Union victory
	Confederate victory
	March to the Sea
✪	Capital city

0   75   150 Miles
0   75   150 Kilometers
Albers Equal-Area Projection

Location This map shows Union and Confederate victories in the major battles of the war.

■ *Why do you think so many battles took place in or near eastern Virginia?*

457

Robert E. Lee (seated at left) surrendered to Ulysses S. Grant (seated at right) at the home of Wilmer McLean in Appomattox Courthouse, Virginia.

Lee Surrenders

In April 1865 Grant's Union army met Lee's Confederate army in Virginia. Lee's troops were starving, and their clothes were in rags. Grant's soldiers, who were well armed and well fed, kept pushing the Confederate troops.

Finally, Lee and his troops were trapped. Lee could neither fight nor retreat. He decided to surrender. Lee said,

66 There is nothing left for me to do but to go and see General Grant, and I would rather die a thousand deaths. 99

Lee surrendered his army to Grant at the town of Appomattox Courthouse on April 9, 1865. In the next few weeks, as word of Lee's surrender reached them, other Southern generals surrendered, too. The war was over.

REVIEW *What problems led to Lee's surrender?*

One More Tragic Death

The war had ended, but there was still another tragedy to come. Abraham Lincoln did not live to see peace return to the Union. On April 14, 1865, just five days after Lee's surrender, Lincoln was murdered by a man who thought he was helping the South. The murder of a political leader is called an **assassination** (uh•sa•suhn•AY•shuhn).

The President and Mary Todd Lincoln, his wife, had been watching a play at Ford's Theater in Washington, D.C. It was there that an actor named John Wilkes Booth shot the President and ran. Booth died later, during his escape.

Lincoln's assassination shocked both the North and the South. Northerners had lost the leader who had guided the Union to victory. Many gathered in the streets when they heard the news. Some cried openly. Others marched silently. People hung black cloth everywhere—on buildings, fences, and trees.

Memorial Day

On May 5, 1866, people in Waterloo, New York, honored those who died in the Civil War. The people closed businesses for the day and decorated soldiers' graves with flowers. This was the beginning of the holiday known as Memorial Day, or Decoration Day. On this day Americans remember those who gave their lives for their country. At the Arlington National Cemetery, a wreath is placed on the Tomb of the Unknowns. Three unknown American soldiers who were killed in war are buried there. Today most states observe Memorial Day on the last Monday in May.

The Tomb of the Unknowns at Arlington National Cemetery is guarded 24 hours a day, 365 days a year, by the United States Army.

Many Southerners were also saddened by the death of the President. Lincoln had said he would treat the South fairly in defeat. He had promised to bring the country together again "with malice toward none, with charity for all." What would happen now that the President was dead?

Mary Chesnut feared the worst. When she learned of the assassination, Chesnut wrote in her diary, "Lincoln—old Abe Lincoln—killed . . . I know this foul murder will bring down worse miseries on us."

REVIEW *Why was Lincoln's death a shock to both the North and the South?*

LESSON 3 REVIEW

Check Understanding

1. **Remember the Facts** What is the Gettysburg Address?
2. **Recall the Main Idea** What events helped bring the Civil War to an end?

Think Critically

3. **Think More About It** In what ways did individual Americans make a difference during the war?
4. **Past to Present** Why do you think people today still find meaning in the words of Abraham Lincoln's Gettysburg Address?

5. **Explore Viewpoints** If you had lived in the North during the Civil War, how might you have felt about General Sherman's March to the Sea? How might you have felt about it if you had lived in the South?

Show What You Know

Diorama Activity Make a diorama of one of the events described in this lesson. Your diorama should show either conflict or cooperation. Share your diorama with your classmates.

Compare Maps with Different Scales

1. Why Learn This Skill?

A map scale compares a distance on a map to a distance in the real world. It helps you find the real distance between places. Map scales are different depending on how much area is shown. Knowing about different map scales can help you choose the best map for gathering the information you need.

2. Map Scales

Look at the map below and the map on page 461. They show the same area around Gettysburg, Pennsylvania, but with different scales. On Map A, Gettysburg looks smaller. For that reason the scale is said to be smaller. On Map B, Gettysburg appears larger, and the scale is said to be larger.

When the map scale is larger, more details can be shown. For example, note the details of the woods on Map B. Also note that Map B is a larger map. It takes a larger piece of paper to show a place on a map with a large scale than to show it on a map with a smaller scale. Although they have different scales, Maps A and B can both be used to measure the distance between the same two places.

3. Understand the Process

On July 2, 1863, the second day of the Battle of Gettysburg, the Union line stretched from Spangler's Spring north to Culp's Hill, on to Cemetery Hill, south along Cemetery Ridge to the hill called Little Round Top, and beyond. What was the real distance in miles between Cemetery Hill and Little Round Top? To find out, follow the steps below:

1 On Map A, use a ruler to measure the exact length of the scale, or use a pencil to mark off the length on a sheet of paper. How long is the line that stands for one mile?

Map A: Gettysburg, July 1–3, 1863

Herr Ridge
McPherson Ridge
Gettysburg
0   0.5   1 Mile
0   0.5   1 Kilometer
Willoughby Run
Seminary Ridge
Cemetery Hill
Culp's Hill
Spangler's Spring
The Angle
Cemetery Ridge
Copse of Trees
N W E S
Peach Orchard
The Wheatfield
Rock Creek
Devil's Den
Plum Run
Little Round Top

Orchard
▲ Hilltop
● Spring
— Road

2 Still using Map A, find Cemetery Hill and Little Round Top. Using the ruler or the sheet of paper you marked, measure the distance between these two hills. How many times can you fit the scale length end to end between the two hills? Multiply the number of scale lengths between the hills by the distance that the scale length represents. What is the real distance in miles between Cemetery Hill and Little Round Top?

3 Now go through the same steps for Map B. How long is the scale length that stands for one mile? Use that scale length to measure the distance between Cemetery Hill and Little Round Top on the map. What is the real distance in miles? Are the real distances you found on the two maps the same? You should see that even when map scales are different, the real distances shown on the maps are the same.

4 Now measure the distance between the Confederate line at the Peach Orchard and the Union line at Little Round Top. What is the real distance between the Confederate line and the Union line? Which map did you use to find the distance? Explain why you chose that map.

4. Think and Apply

Think about how you use maps when you travel. Find two road maps with different scales—perhaps a road map of your state and a road map of a large city within your state. Compare the real distances in miles between two places that are on both maps. How far apart are the two places? Are the distances the same on both maps? When would it be more helpful to use the state map, with the smaller scale? When would it be more helpful to use the city map, with the larger scale? Share your answers with a classmate.

Map B: Gettysburg, July 2, 1863

FOCUS

How can new laws affect the lives of citizens?

Main Idea Read to learn about how new laws affected the lives of Americans in the years following the Civil War.

Vocabulary

sharecropping
Reconstruction
scalawag
carpetbagger
segregation

Life After the War

When the Civil War finally ended, it was clear that peace had not come easily. More than 600,000 soldiers had died. Many others had returned home wounded. Much of the South was destroyed. And now the President was dead. As one Southerner remembered, "All the talk was of burning homes, houses knocked to pieces . . . famine, murder, desolation."

The years following the war were hard ones. However, the end of the war brought new hope to at least one group of people—the former slaves.

A Free People

With the Union victory, 4 million enslaved people were freed. Most slaves were already free by the time the Civil War ended in 1865. In December of that year, the Thirteenth Amendment to the Constitution ended slavery in the United States forever. "I felt like a bird out of a cage," one former slave remembered, looking back on the day he was set free. "I could hardly ask to feel any better than I did that day."

Free Africans quickly began to form new communities. They built churches and schools. They opened stores. They formed groups to help people find jobs and to take care of people who were sick. In 1866, only one year after the war ended, one African leader proudly said, "We have progressed a century in a year."

As soon as they could, many former slaves began to search for family members who had been sold and sent away under slavery. Newspapers were filled with advertisements asking for help in finding loved ones. This ad appeared in a newspaper in Nashville, Tennessee. "During the year 1849, Thomas Sample carried away from this city, as his slaves, our daughter, Polly, and son,

By making slavery against the law, the Thirteenth Amendment ended slavery in the United States forever.

In this painting a preacher visits a family of former slaves. Many African families had been split up because of slavery.

George. . . . We will give $100 each for them to any person who will assist them, or . . . get word to us of their whereabouts."

Many families never found their missing loved ones. But for those that did, it was a time of great joy. "I wish you could see this people as they step from slavery into freedom," one Union soldier wrote to his wife. "Families which had been for a long time broken up are united and oh! such happiness."

Former slaves worked hard to build new lives. Yet life remained difficult. Often it was hard just to find food, clothing, and shelter. Many began to look to the United States government for help.

REVIEW *How did free Africans help one another after the war?*

HERITAGE

Juneteenth

Abraham Lincoln signed the Emancipation Proclamation on January 1, 1863. But because Union troops did not control Texas at the time, the order had little effect there. On June 19, 1865, Union soldiers landed at Galveston, Texas. On that day Union General Gordon Granger read an order declaring that all slaves in Texas were free. Today people in Texas and across the country celebrate June 19, or Juneteenth, as a day of freedom. It is a holiday marked by picnics, parades, and family gatherings.

This photograph shows people going to a Juneteenth celebration.

Many former slaves, like those shown outside of this Freedmen's Bureau school, were eager to learn to read and write.

The Freedmen's Bureau

In 1865 Congress set up an organization to help former slaves. This group was called the Bureau of Refugees, Freedmen, and Abandoned Lands—or the Freedmen's Bureau.

The Freedmen's Bureau gave food and other supplies to freed slaves. It also helped some white farmers rebuild their farms. The most important work of the Freedmen's Bureau, however, was education. Newly freed slaves were eager to learn to read and write. To help meet this need, the Freedmen's Bureau built more than 4,000 schools and hired thousands of teachers.

The Freedmen's Bureau also wanted to help former slaves earn a living by giving them land to farm. This plan, however, did not work out. The land was to have come from the plantations taken during the war. But the government decided to give the plantations back to their original owners. In the end, most former slaves were not given land. Without money to buy land of their own, they had to find work where they could.

REVIEW *What was the purpose of the Freedmen's Bureau?*

Sharecropping

In their search for jobs, some former slaves went back to work on plantations. Many planters welcomed them. Fields needed to be plowed, and crops needed to be planted. Now, however, planters had to pay Africans for their work.

In the days following the war, there was not much money. Instead of paying workers in cash, many landowners paid them in shares. Under this system, known as **sharecropping**, a landowner gave a worker a cabin, mules, tools, and seed. The worker then farmed the land. At harvesttime the landowner took part of the crops, plus enough to cover the cost of the worker's rent and supplies. What was left was the worker's share.

Sharecropping gave landowners the help they needed to work the fields. It also gave former slaves work for pay. Yet few people got ahead through sharecropping. When crops failed, both landowners and workers suffered. Even in good times, most workers' shares were very little, if anything at all.

REVIEW *Why did landowners pay workers in shares rather than in cash?*

As sharecroppers, former slaves were paid for their work. But sharecropping was a hard way to make a living, and it put many families in debt.

A New President

As Americans were getting used to their new lives after the war, government leaders began making plans for bringing the country back together. This time of rebuilding was called **Reconstruction**.

After Lincoln's death the Vice President, Andrew Johnson, became the new President. Johnson tried to carry out Lincoln's promise to be fair to the South in defeat. He pardoned most Confederates who promised loyalty to the United States. They were then given back the rights of citizenship and were allowed to vote. Their states held elections, and state governments went back to work.

Johnson also said that the Confederate states must abolish slavery. This requirement was met when the Thirteenth Amendment was passed late in 1865. Johnson then said that the last of the Confederate states could return to the Union.

Such easy terms, however, made some people angry. Many Northerners felt that the Confederates were not being punished at all. White Southerners were being elected to office and taking over state governments just as they always had. Yet no one talked about the rights of former slaves. What would happen to them?

It was not long before laws were passed in the South to limit the rights of former slaves. These laws were called black codes. The black codes differed from state to state. In most states Africans were not allowed to vote. In some they were not allowed to travel freely. They could not own certain kinds of property or work in certain businesses. They could be made to work in the fields without pay if they could not find another job.

Many, however, faced an even worse problem. Shortly after the war ended, secret groups formed in the South that tried to keep Africans from having their rights as free persons. Most of those who joined these groups were upset about their war losses and angry about the new rights of former slaves.

One such group was the Ku Klux Klan, or the KKK. Dressed in white robes and hoods, its members delivered nighttime messages of hate. Klan members broke into homes and attacked and killed Africans. They burned African schools and churches. They punished anyone who helped former slaves. It was a time of terror for many people.

REVIEW *What did Andrew Johnson try to carry out when he became President?*

Congress Takes Action

Many leaders of Congress were alarmed about the way former slaves in some Southern states were being treated. They believed that President Johnson's Reconstruction plan was not working. So they voted to change to a plan of their own—a plan that was much tougher on white Southerners.

First, Congress did away with the new state governments and put the Southern states under the army's rule. Union soldiers kept order, and army officers were made governors. Before each Southern state could reestablish its government, it had to write a new state constitution giving all men, both black and white, the right to vote. To return to the Union, a state also had to pass the Fourteenth Amendment. This amendment gave citizenship to all people born in the United States—including former slaves.

Johnson was very angry about this plan and about other laws that Congress passed to cut back his authority. Believing that these laws were unconstitutional, Johnson refused to carry them out. Then, in 1868, the House of Representatives voted to impeach the President, or charge him with a crime. He was put on trial in the Senate. There, in a very close vote, he was found not guilty. Although he stayed in office, Johnson was no longer a strong leader.

The Southern states began to write new state constitutions and pass the Fourteenth Amendment. State elections were held once again. For the first time, African Americans from the South were elected to Congress. They also served in state governments that took over the job of rebuilding the South.

REVIEW *Why did Congress vote to change Johnson's Reconstruction plan?*

Reconstruction Ends

The new state governments made many important changes. They did away with the black codes. They approved the Fifteenth Amendment, which said that no citizen could be kept from voting because of race. They built hospitals and schools and repaired roads, bridges, and railroads.

Yet the work of the state governments did not make everyone happy. To pay for their Reconstruction projects, state leaders placed high taxes on land. These taxes hurt landowners, who were trying to get their farms and plantations working again. Some were forced to sell their land because they could not pay the taxes.

Many white Southerners soon grew angry with their state leaders. They did not like the fact that African Americans were voting and

The disagreements between Congress and Andrew Johnson (far left) led to his impeachment. Johnson's trial in the Senate drew crowds of people, and tickets (left) were scarce.

taking part in government. They did not like the white Southerners who supported the government. They called them **scalawags** (SKA•lih•wagz)—people who support something for their own gain. They also did not like being told what to do by Northerners. Under military rule Northern soldiers guarded their streets. Other Northerners went to the South to try to help with Reconstruction or to make a profit by buying land or opening businesses. White Southerners called them **carpetbaggers** because many of them arrived carrying

The first African Americans to serve in the United States Congress were elected during Reconstruction.

their belongings in suitcases made of carpet pieces.

Some white Southerners tried again to take the authority away from their state leaders. One way they did this was to control the way people voted. Groups such as the Ku Klux Klan used violence to keep African Americans from voting or to make sure that they voted as they were told. Sometimes the votes of African Americans simply were not counted.

In time white Southerners once again took control of their state governments. New state laws were passed that made it very hard, if not impossible, for African Americans to vote. African Americans had to go to separate schools and churches and sit in separate railroad cars. Such laws led to the **segregation**, or separation, of black people and white people.

Reconstruction was over by 1877. In that year the last of the Union troops left the South. The rights and freedoms African Americans had just won were again taken away in the South.

REVIEW *How did white Southerners take authority back from their state leaders as Reconstruction ended?*

LESSON 4 REVIEW

Check Understanding

1 Remember the Facts In what ways did the government try to help former slaves?

2 Recall the Main Idea How did new laws affect the lives of Americans in the years following the Civil War?

Think Critically

3 Think More About It In what ways did life change for former slaves who became sharecroppers?

4 Explore Viewpoints Why do you think Lincoln wanted to be fair to the South in defeat?

Show What You Know

Writing Activity Imagine that you are a news reporter. Write an interview with a former slave, a Southern landowner, a Union soldier in the South, or a carpetbagger. Provide both questions and answers.

1860   1865

1863
- The Emancipation Proclamation is signed
- Abraham Lincoln delivers the Gettysburg Address

1865
- The Civil War ends
- Abraham Lincoln is assassinated

CONNECT MAIN IDEAS

Use this organizer to show how the chapter's main ideas are connected. Write a sentence or two telling how each event or idea affected the lives of Americans during the Civil War and Reconstruction. A copy of the organizer appears on page 92 of the Activity Book.

Choosing Sides

_____

_____

_____

Emancipation Proclamation

_____

_____

_____

Civil War and Reconstruction

Union Victories

_____

_____

_____

Rebuilding America

_____

_____

_____

WRITE MORE ABOUT IT

Write a Diary Entry Imagine that you are living in one of the border states at the beginning of the Civil War. Write a diary entry in which you tell why you think some members of your family have chosen to fight for the North while others have chosen to fight for the South.

Write a News Story Imagine that you are a newspaper reporter covering the White House in 1863. Write an article for your newspaper in which you tell readers what the Emancipation Proclamation will do, why President Lincoln has decided to issue it, and how it will affect the war.

1868
• The House of Representatives votes to impeach President Johnson

1877
• Reconstruction ends

USE VOCABULARY

Use each term in a complete sentence that will help explain its meaning.

1. border state
2. Emancipation Proclamation
3. assassination
4. sharecropping
5. carpetbagger
6. segregation

CHECK UNDERSTANDING

7. Why did the Confederacy hope to receive help from Britain and France?

8. Why did Lincoln finally decide to issue the Emancipation Proclamation?

9. How did African soldiers help the North?

10. Why were some Southerners sad about Lincoln's death?

11. What was the purpose of the Freedmen's Bureau?

12. How did the black codes help bring about the end of President Johnson's Reconstruction plan?

THINK CRITICALLY

13. **Personally Speaking** If you had been in Robert E. Lee's place, would you have made the decision to join the Confederacy? Why or why not?

14. **Explore Viewpoints** Mary Chesnut wrote, "I know this foul murder will bring down worse miseries on us." What do you think she meant? Explain your answer.

15. **Think More About It** The most important work of the Freedmen's Bureau was education. Why is education important to people in a free country?

16. **Past to Present** Government leaders raised taxes to pay for rebuilding the South. Today government leaders sometimes increase taxes to help pay for new projects. How can taxes both help and hurt people?

APPLY SKILLS

Compare Maps with Different Scales The maps on pages 460 and 461 show the area around Gettysburg. You can visit this area today at the Gettysburg National Military Park in Pennsylvania. Use either map to answer the questions.

17. How far would you have to walk to go from the battle sites of Devil's Den to the Wheatfield?

18. Which map did you use to answer this question? Why did you choose that map?

READ MORE ABOUT IT

A House Divided: The Lives of Ulysses S. Grant and Robert E. Lee by Jules Archer. Scholastic. This book tells about two well-known military leaders in the Civil War.

HARCOURT BRACE

Visit the Internet at
http://www.hbschool.com
for additional resources.

The Fight For FREEDOM Goes On

The Civil War changed forever the way most Americans thought about one another. People who had been friends had fought as enemies. People who had been enslaved were now free. Those who had been thought of as property were now citizens of the United States.

Yet the rights that African Americans had fought so long for were still kept out of reach. In the years following the Civil War, many African Americans were kept from voting and holding office. They were made to live their lives apart from other citizens, in separate neighborhoods and schools. It would be 100 years after the Civil War before African Americans would gain the full rights of United States citizenship.

In the 1950s and 1960s, Americans across the country began to take part in the Civil Rights movement. This was a movement to gain the rights promised to all people in the Constitution. One of the greatest leaders of the Civil Rights movement was Dr. Martin Luther King, Jr. In 1963 King gave a speech about his hopes for the future. He said that he dreamed of a time when all the unfair ways of the past would end. He dreamed of a day when "the sons of former slaves and the sons of former slave owners will be able to sit down together at the table of brotherhood." On that day, King said, all Americans will finally be able to sing together the words of an old spiritual,

> " Free at last!
> Free at last!
> Thank God Almighty,
> We are free at last! "

Think and Apply

Think about people today who are working for equal rights. Identify an individual or a group working to protect people's rights and freedoms. Gather information about the person or group, and prepare a report for the class.

BUILDING CITIZENSHIP

HARCOURT BRACE

Visit the Internet at **http://www.hbschool.com** for additional resources.

CNN
Turner Le@rning

Check your media center or classroom video library for the Making Social Studies Relevant videotape of this feature.

UNIT 7 REVIEW

VISUAL SUMMARY

Summarize the Main Ideas
Study the pictures and captions to help you review the events you read about in Unit 7.

Dramatize the Story
Choose any of the people shown in this visual summary, and invent a conversation they might have with us today describing their experiences. Act out the conversation with a classmate.

1 As slavery continued in the South, more and more enslaved people tried to escape by running away.

3 During the Civil War thousands of people in both the North and the South joined the war effort.

6 During Reconstruction the Freedmen's Bureau opened schools for former slaves.

2 After Abraham Lincoln was elected President in 1860, Southern states seceded from the Union.

4 The war dragged on for four long years, destroying property and lives on both sides.

5 Robert E. Lee surrendered his Confederate forces to Union General Ulysses S. Grant in Appomattox Courthouse in 1865.

7 After the war, life was difficult for former slaves, even though they were now free. Many tried to build new lives as sharecroppers.

473

UNIT 7
REVIEW

USE VOCABULARY

Write the term that correctly matches each definition. Then use each term in a complete sentence.

Confederacy   Reconstruction

Gettysburg Address   spiritual

1 a religious song based on a Bible story

2 the new country formed by the Southern states after they seceded from the Union

3 a famous speech given by Abraham Lincoln

4 a time of rebuilding

CHECK UNDERSTANDING

5 In what ways had the South come to depend on the work of enslaved people?

6 How did the Underground Railroad help enslaved Africans?

7 What was the Missouri Compromise? What was the Kansas-Nebraska Act?

8 How did the Emancipation Proclamation affect the war?

9 What problems led Congress to change President Andrew Johnson's Reconstruction plan?

THINK CRITICALLY

10 **Explore Viewpoints** Lincoln once was called "the miserable tool of traitors and rebels." Today he is thought of as a great leader. Why might someone at the time have been so critical of him?

11 **Past to Present** Why is it important for Presidents today to consider different viewpoints before making a decision?

APPLY SKILLS

Compare Maps with Different Scales The Battle of Gettysburg ended when Pickett's Charge—led by Confederate General George Pickett—was stopped at the Angle and the Copse of Trees. Use the map below and the maps on pages 460–461 to answer the questions.

12 Compare the map on this page to Map A on page 460. Which would more clearly show Pickett's Charge or other troop movements over small distances? Explain.

Gettysburg, July 3, 1863

Orchard
Hilltop
Woods
Union troops
Confederate troops
Pickett's Charge
Road

0   0.25   0.5 Mile
0   0.25   0.5 Kilometer

Gettysburg

Culp's Hill

Cemetery Hill

Seminary Ridge

The Angle

Cemetery Ridge

Copse of Trees

Peach Orchard

Plum Run

The Wheatfield

Devil's Den

Plum Run

Little Round Top

REMEMBER

- Share your ideas.
- Cooperate with others to plan your work.
- Take responsibility for your work.
- Help one another.
- Show your group's work to the class.
- Discuss what you learned by working together.

 ACTIVITY

Draw a Map

Work together to draw a map of the United States at the time of the Civil War. Use different colors for the states of the Union and the states of the Confederacy. Write the date on which each Southern state seceded. Draw diagonal lines on the border states. Label the capitals of the North and the South and the major battle sites. Use your map to tell your classmates about one event of the Civil War.

 ACTIVITY Publish a

Class Magazine

You and your classmates have decided to put together a magazine about the Civil War. First, plan your magazine by preparing a table of contents. Decide what articles and illustrations you would like to include. Give your magazine a title. Then form several small groups, with each group working on a different part of the magazine. Once all the groups have finished, put the parts together. Ask permission to display the magazine in the school library.

 ACTIVITY Honor Your

Hero

Choose someone you admire from the Civil War as the subject of a poster for a display called *Heroes of the Civil War*. Work together to find or draw a picture of the person or a picture of a scene showing the person in action. Then add words or phrases around the picture that tell what made that person a hero. Present your poster to the class.

Unit Project Wrap-Up

Make a Time Line Work with a partner to finish the Unit Project that was described on page 407. First, make a list of the major events of the Civil War. Then exchange lists with your partner to make sure that you have included the most important events on your time line. Write captions describing any illustrations that you have drawn for the time line. Share your time lines with the class.

INVENTION AND CHANGE

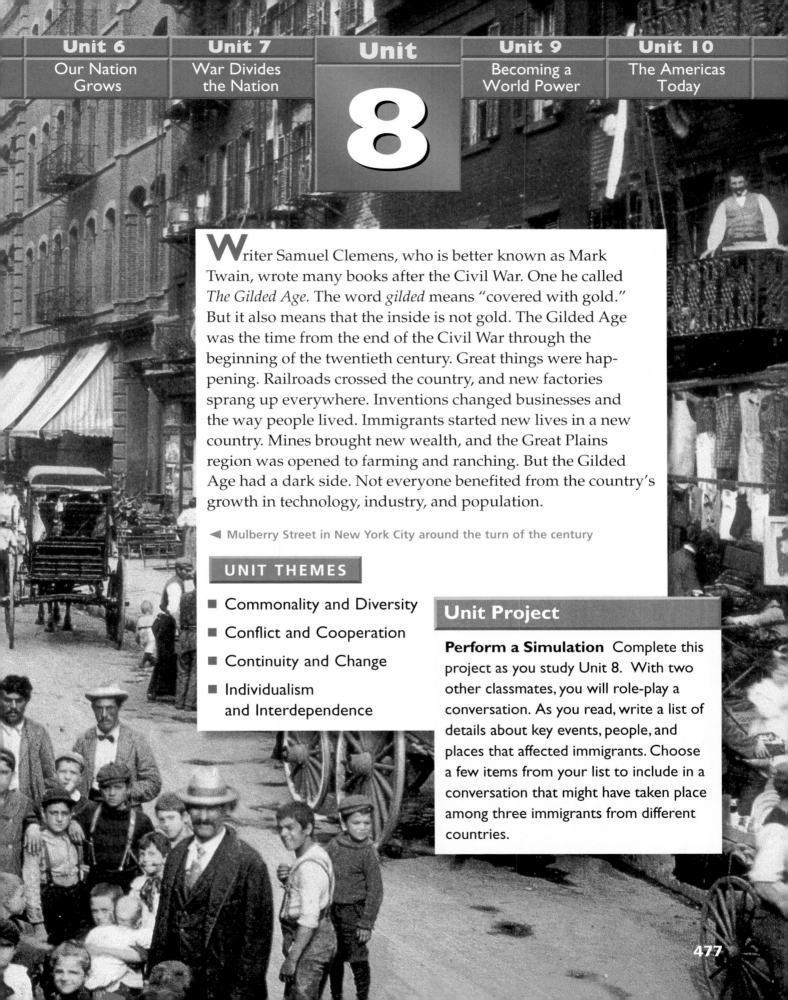

Writer Samuel Clemens, who is better known as Mark Twain, wrote many books after the Civil War. One he called *The Gilded Age.* The word *gilded* means "covered with gold." But it also means that the inside is not gold. The Gilded Age was the time from the end of the Civil War through the beginning of the twentieth century. Great things were happening. Railroads crossed the country, and new factories sprang up everywhere. Inventions changed businesses and the way people lived. Immigrants started new lives in a new country. Mines brought new wealth, and the Great Plains region was opened to farming and ranching. But the Gilded Age had a dark side. Not everyone benefited from the country's growth in technology, industry, and population.

◄ Mulberry Street in New York City around the turn of the century

UNIT THEMES

- Commonality and Diversity
- Conflict and Cooperation
- Continuity and Change
- Individualism and Interdependence

Unit Project

Perform a Simulation Complete this project as you study Unit 8. With two other classmates, you will role-play a conversation. As you read, write a list of details about key events, people, and places that affected immigrants. Choose a few items from your list to include in a conversation that might have taken place among three immigrants from different countries.

477

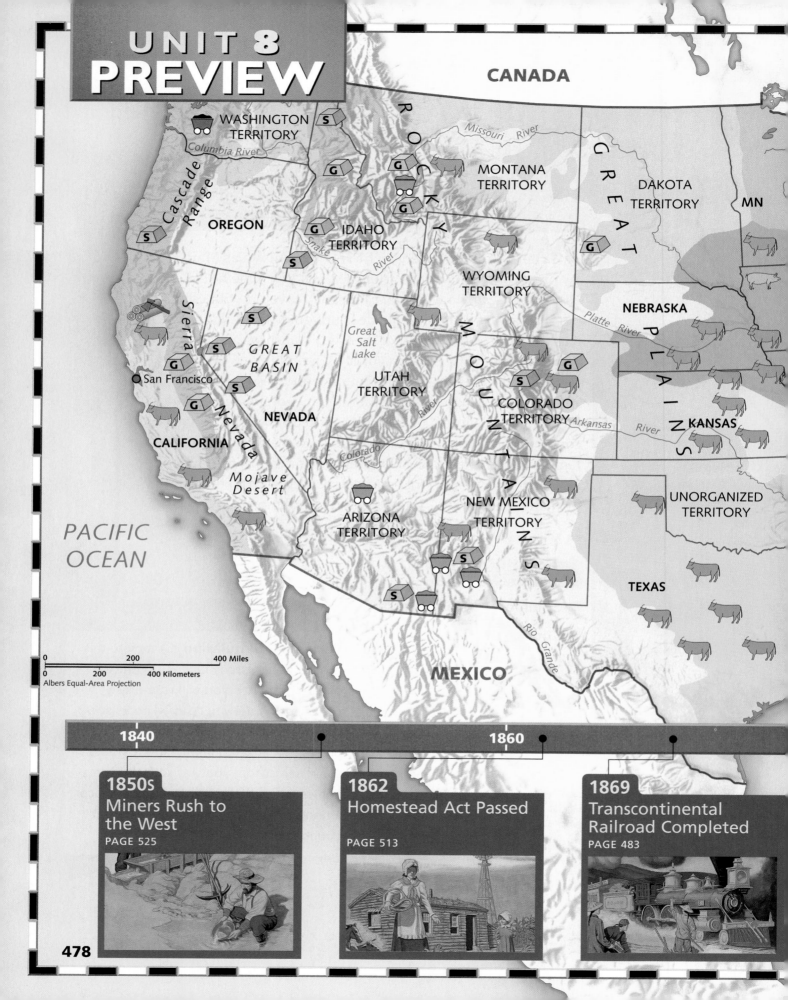

UNIT 8 PREVIEW

CANADA

WASHINGTON TERRITORY

Columbia River

Cascade Range

OREGON

ROCKY

Missouri River

MONTANA TERRITORY

GREAT

DAKOTA TERRITORY

MN

IDAHO TERRITORY

Snake River

WYOMING TERRITORY

NEBRASKA

Platte River

Sierra Nevada

San Francisco

GREAT BASIN

Great Salt Lake

UTAH TERRITORY

M
O
U
N
T
A
I
N
S

COLORADO TERRITORY

Arkansas River

P
L
A
I
N
S

KANSAS

NEVADA

CALIFORNIA

Mojave Desert

Colorado

ARIZONA TERRITORY

NEW MEXICO TERRITORY

UNORGANIZED TERRITORY

PACIFIC OCEAN

TEXAS

Rio Grande

MEXICO

0   200   400 Miles
0   200   400 Kilometers
Albers Equal-Area Projection

1840   1860

1850s
Miners Rush to the West
PAGE 525

1862
Homestead Act Passed
PAGE 513

1869
Transcontinental Railroad Completed
PAGE 483

478

United States Land Use and Resources, 1870

CANADA

MAINE

VT NH

MICHIGAN

WISCONSIN

Lake Superior

Lake Huron

Lake Michigan

MA Boston

NEW YORK

Buffalo

Lake Ontario

Lake Erie

RHODE ISLAND

CT

New York City

Newark

PA

NEW JERSEY

Philadelphia

IOWA

Chicago

ILLINOIS

OHIO

Cincinnati

MD Baltimore

DE

Washington, D.C.

WV

VIRGINIA

INDIANA

St. Louis

Louisville

Ohio River

KY

NORTH CAROLINA

MISSOURI

APPALACHIAN MOUNTAINS

Tennessee River

TENNESSEE

SOUTH CAROLINA

ARKANSAS

G

G

ALABAMA

GEORGIA

Mississippi River

MISSISSIPPI

LOUISIANA

New Orleans

FLORIDA

Gulf of Mexico

ATLANTIC OCEAN

N E W S

Legend

Corn and winter wheat	Beef cattle
Corn	Hogs
Wheat	Timber
Dairy cattle and hay	Copper
Tobacco	Coal
Cotton	Iron and steel works
Fruits and vegetables	S Silver
Little-used land	G Gold
	Oil

● City with more than 100,000 people

1880

1900

Late 1800s
New Immigrants Come to the United States
PAGE 495

Late 1800s
Plains Indians Fight for Their Homelands
PAGE 529

The Story of Thomas Alva Edison
by Margaret Cousins

Thomas Alva Edison may have been the greatest inventor of all time. He invented the phonograph, the movie camera, and the microphone. But his most important invention was the electric lightbulb. Can you imagine a world without electric lights?

The first electric lightbulbs were called filament bulbs or incandescent bulbs because of the way they worked. Electricity flowed through a thin piece of carbon—the filament—inside a glass bulb. This filament became so hot that it was incandescent, or glowed with a white light.

After many failures and more than a few explosions, Edison finally had an electric light-bulb that worked. The first public demonstration of the amazing invention was at Edison's workshop in Menlo Park, New Jersey. It was a night of great excitement.

After the news of the electric lamp was published, people swarmed to Menlo Park. Edison then announced a demonstration of the incandescent lamp for New Year's Eve. This was one of the most unusual New Year's Eve parties ever given. The Pennsylvania Railroad transported more than three thousand persons to Menlo Park on the cold, snowy last night of the year 1879. They came from both New York and Philadelphia.

Edison had put some of his lamps along two wires strung between the leafless trees on the road leading from the railway station to his laboratory. As the trains began to pull in in the winter darkness, he pulled the switch and the electric lamps glowed like golden flowers, illuminating the road with a flood of light and casting long rays across the snow.

It is hard for us to imagine how exciting this was to people who had never seen an electric light. Many of them were sophisticated city people, dressed in their New Year's Eve party clothes; but they all gasped. It was the most beautiful sight they had ever seen. It was fairyland!

Edison stood in the power house, watching the dynamo turn steam power into the electric current to light the lamps. He was wearing an old gray shirt, a flannel coat full of acid holes and some chalk-stained, dusty trousers. A broad-brimmed black felt hat sat on the back of his head. Some people took him for a coal stoker[1], so he had a good chance to listen to what they were saying.

"It's a miracle!"

"Did you ever see anything so beautiful?"

"He's a wizard! A wizard!"

Suddenly there was a scream and a commotion. A young lady was standing near the generators with her hair down her back.

"I'm sorry," Edison said. "The generators magnetized her hairpins and pulled them all out of her hair!" He apologized to the lady and gave her a silk kerchief to put on her head. "Maybe this will help," he said, but she fled back to the train.

The success of the New Year's Eve demonstration at Menlo Park created excitement all over the world. Cables, letters, telegrams and gifts descended on Edison. He was no longer just a hero, but the "American Wizard."

Thomas Edison was not the only inventor making important discoveries in the years after the Civil War. Alexander Graham Bell invented the telephone in 1876, and a revolution in communication began. The first automobiles came into use, and transportation changed forever. This growth of technology sparked the growth of industry that marks the period of history in the United States from 1865 to 1920.

---

[1] **coal stoker:** person who shovels coal into a furnace

INDUSTRY
AND
IMMIGRATION

"When we set foot on these shores, . . . we were bewildered and lost. We did not know where to turn for shelter or food. Fortunately, there were enough of us so that some set to putting up these houses while others looked for food."

The leader of an Asian miners' organization, addressing a group of newly arrived immigrants

Many immigrants, like this Asian woman, came to the United States in the late 1800s and early 1900s.

Big Business and Industrial Cities

FOCUS

How have new inventions changed your life?

Main Idea Read to learn how new inventions changed life in the United States in the years after the Civil War.

Vocabulary

free enterprise
transcontinental railroad
capital resource
invest
stock
corporation
entrepreneur
consolidate
refinery
monopoly
hub

The Industrial Revolution came to the United States in the early 1800s. During this time, machines started to replace hand tools, and factories began to replace craft shops. After the Civil War, even greater changes took place in American industry. Inventors developed new technologies, and business owners had more freedom to run their businesses in new ways. It was an important time for **free enterprise**—an economic system in which people are able to start and run their own businesses with little control by the government.

Railroads

When Abraham Lincoln ran for President in 1860, the Republican party promised to build a **transcontinental railroad**. This was to be a railroad that went across the continent, linking the Atlantic and Pacific coasts. When Lincoln was elected, he kept his party's promise. In 1862 Congress gave two companies the right to build the railroad. The government gave them land and lent them money. Railroads already had been built from the Atlantic coast west to Nebraska. The Union Pacific built west from Omaha, Nebraska. The Central Pacific built east from Sacramento, California. On May 10, 1869, the two railroads met at Promontory, Utah.

The Union Pacific–Central Pacific was not the only railroad across the West for long. By the 1890s four more railroads had been built from midwestern cities to the Pacific coast. Railroads in the East added to their systems, too. In 1860 the United States had just over 30,000 miles (48,000 km) of track. By 1900 it had more than 193,000 miles (311,000 km) of track.

One reason for the growth of railroads was the development of new inventions that improved rail transportation. George Westinghouse's air brake made trains safer by stopping the locomotive and all the cars at the same time. Inventor Granville T. Woods improved the air brake and developed a telegraph system that let trains and stations communicate with one another.

A golden spike with a prayer written on it was used to complete the first transcontinental railroad.

The Telegraph

Just as railroad tracks carried people and goods across the country, the telegraph began carrying messages. An American inventor, Samuel F. B. Morse, experimented with sending electricity along iron wires during the 1830s. To send messages along the wires, Morse invented a code system in which dots and dashes stand for letters of the alphabet. The railroads quickly saw how useful Morse code and the telegraph would be, and telegraph lines were soon strung from pole to pole along railroad tracks. The telegraph helped railroads send messages ahead to warn of dangers and to tell people when trains were late. It also carried news to every part of the country in minutes. For the first time, news could travel faster than people.

By tapping out messages on the telegraph, people could communicate over long distances.

As the railroads grew, their owners faced many problems. The railroad companies had to buy more locomotives, cars, and tracks. They had to pay the workers who laid and repaired the tracks, as well as the workers who ran the trains. To do all this, they needed **capital resources**, or money to run their businesses. Railroad owners, including Cornelius Vanderbilt and James J. Hill, received millions of dollars from the government, but they needed more. They got the money they needed from people who invested in the railroads. To **invest** is to buy shares of a business in the hope of earning a profit. These shares are called **stocks**.

As the railroads grew, many people bought stock in railroad companies. Buying stock let them own part of the railroad. When the railroad company made money, stock owners received part of the profit. Businesses that sell shares of stock to investors are called **corporations**.

Although people who bought stock were part owners of businesses, they did not run them. A board of directors ran each corporation. Managers took care of the day-to-day activities. Many railroad businesses became corporations in the late 1800s.

REVIEW *Why did people invest money in railroads?*

The Steel Industry

In the early part of the Industrial Revolution, iron was used to build bridges, buildings, and railroads. In fact, the early growth of railroads depended on iron tracks. As locomotives got bigger and heavier, however, iron tracks were no longer strong enough. Many lasted only about three years.

Steel tracks were harder and lasted longer, but steel cost a great deal to make. Steel is made from iron with small amounts of other metals added. Because of its cost, steel was used only for small items, such as knives and swords.

By the 1850s inventors in both Britain and the United States had developed ways to make steel more cheaply and easily. The British way was named after the British inventor Henry Bessemer, who came up with the new process of making steel. The Bessemer process melted iron ore and other metals together in a new kind of furnace. The higher heat of this "blast furnace" made the steel stronger.

During the 1860s an American entrepreneur (ahn•truh•pruh•NER) named Andrew Carnegie visited Britain and saw the Bessemer process for the first time. An **entrepreneur** is a person who sets up a new business, taking a chance on making or losing money. After returning to the United States, Carnegie looked for investors to help him build a small steel mill near Pittsburgh, Pennsylvania. By the early 1870s business was good for Carnegie. With his profits he built more steel mills and made even larger profits.

Carnegie bought mines to supply his steel mills with coal and iron. He then bought ships to carry these natural resources to his mills. With his mines and ships, he could make more steel at a lower cost than other mills could. He could then afford to lower the price of his steel.

Other steel mills were not able to compete with the low prices that Carnegie could offer. Soon Carnegie bought these other mills and **consolidated**, or joined, their businesses with his. In 1899 he formed a large new corporation called the Carnegie Steel Company. This company became one of the largest steel businesses in the United States, and Andrew Carnegie became one of the richest people in the world.

REVIEW *How was Carnegie able to make more steel for less money?*

The Oil Industry

Just as Andrew Carnegie did, John D. Rockefeller saw that he could become rich in business. Rockefeller was 24 years old in 1863 when he set up an oil refinery near Cleveland, Ohio. A **refinery** is a factory where crude, or raw, oil is made into usable products. The first products made by Rockefeller's refinery

LEARNING FROM GRAPHS Andrew Carnegie (left) helped the steel industry grow in the United States.
■ *Between which years did steel production increase the most?*

LEARNING FROM GRAPHS John D. Rockefeller (right) controlled most of the oil business in the United States.
■ *About how many barrels of oil were produced in 1890?*

Steel Production,
1865–1900

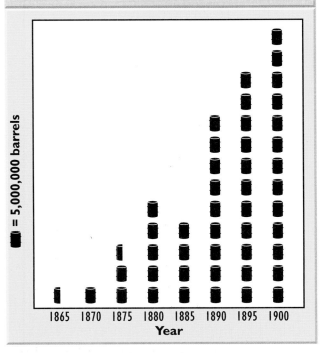

Oil Production,
1865–1900

were grease and kerosene for lamps. Electricity was not yet in use.

Many business people were building refineries because oil had been found in Ohio, Pennsylvania, and West Virginia. The Rockefeller refinery was one of 30 in the Cleveland area. Within a few years, Rockefeller had bought most of the other refineries. In 1870 he consolidated them into one business, which he called the Standard Oil Company.

Rather than let other companies make a profit from his business, Rockefeller did something similar to what Carnegie had done. He bought forests to get his own lumber. He bought a barrel factory to make his own barrels. He bought ships and railroad cars to carry his products. Soon other companies could not match Rockefeller's low prices for oil products. Before long, Rockefeller had a **monopoly**, or almost complete control, of the oil business. By 1899 the Standard Oil Company controlled about 90 percent of the country's oil refining business.

After the invention of the gasoline engine, automobiles came into use, and Rockefeller's oil refineries produced gasoline and engine oil. Standard Oil's yearly profits zoomed to more than $45 million.

REVIEW *How did Rockefeller get a monopoly in the oil business?*

The New Industrial Cities

Before the Civil War the most important cities in the United States were those on good harbors near the oceans. But with the growth of railroads and industries such as steel and oil after the Civil War, new industrial cities developed inland, far from the coast. Some were built close to the resources needed by their mills and factories. Others depended on railroads to bring these materials from great distances.

The region west of the Appalachians and east of the Mississippi had many important resources. Because western Pennsylvania had iron ore, coal, and limestone—the resources needed for making iron and steel—places such as Pittsburgh were among the first iron and steel centers in the North. Birmingham, Alabama, in the South, was close to iron and coal deposits, and also became an iron and steel center.

Iron ore deposits also were found in the hills of the Mesabi Range near Lake Superior. The ore was taken by barge across Lake Superior and on to Chicago and other cities on the Great Lakes. Trains brought coal from the Appalachian region to the same cities. With these resources, cities such as Chicago, Illinois; Gary, Indiana; Cleveland, Ohio; and Detroit, Michigan, became industrial cities.

Most of the new industrial cities were far from harbors. They depended on trains to bring in raw materials and to carry out finished products.

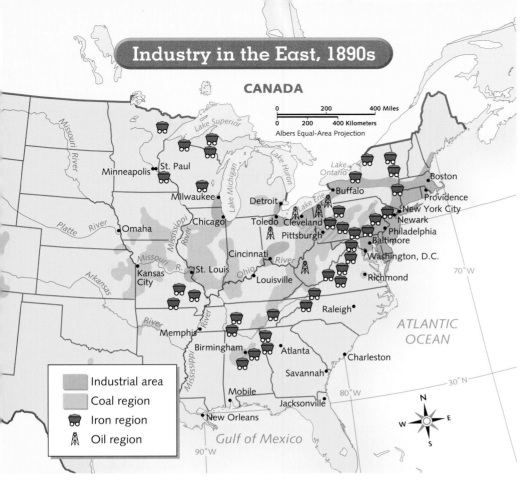

Industry in the East, 1890s

CANADA

0   200   400 Miles
0   200   400 Kilometers
Albers Equal-Area Projection

Lake Superior
Lake Michigan
Lake Huron
Lake Ontario
Lake Erie

Minneapolis   St. Paul
Milwaukee
Detroit   Buffalo
Chicago   Toledo   Cleveland
Omaha   Pittsburgh
Kansas City   St. Louis
               Cincinnati
               Louisville
Memphis
Birmingham   Atlanta
Mobile
New Orleans   Jacksonville

Boston
Providence
New York City
Newark
Philadelphia
Baltimore
Washington, D.C.
Richmond
Raleigh
Charleston
Savannah

Missouri River
Platte River
Arkansas River
Mississippi River
Missouri R.
Ohio River

ATLANTIC OCEAN

Gulf of Mexico

70°W
80°W
90°W
30°N

N S E W

Industrial area
Coal region
Iron region
Oil region

MAP THEME

Human-Environment Interactions

This map shows industrial areas and resource regions in the eastern part of the United States in the 1890s.

■ *If you were going to build an oil refinery in 1890, where would you put it? Where would you build a steel mill?*

Because of the railroads, businesses that used iron and steel to make their products built factories near iron and steel centers. Railroads brought in raw materials to the factories and carried out finished products to deliver to customers. Cities such as Chicago, Cleveland, and Pittsburgh, as well as Atlanta, Georgia, became railroad hubs. A **hub** is a city where many trains make stops on their way to different destinations.

REVIEW *Why did inland cities become important in the late 1800s?*

LESSON 1 REVIEW

Check Understanding

❶ **Remember the Facts** Who were the important business leaders in the steel and oil industries?

❷ **Recall the Main Idea** How did new inventions change life in the United States in the years after the Civil War?

Think Critically

❸ **Past to Present** What kinds of businesses do you think are the most important today?

❹ **Explore Viewpoints** How do you think other oil refinery owners felt about Rockefeller's monopoly of the oil business?

Show What You Know

Table Activity Make a table comparing information about Andrew Carnegie and John D. Rockefeller. Be sure to include information about their businesses. Share your table with a classmate.

Use a Time Zone Map

1. Why Learn This Skill?

People have always used sun time, basing the time of day on the sun's position. According to sun time, noon is the hour when the sun reaches its highest position in the sky. By this rule, you know it is noon when the sun is directly overhead. But when it is noon where you are, the sun is not at its highest point at other places. Because of the Earth's rotation, the sun has not yet reached its highest point at places west of you. And the sun is past its highest point at places east of you. So according to sun time, these other places have different times.

Telling time by the sun was not a problem until people began to travel long distances. When railroads began to cross the United States and Canada, no one knew what time to use to follow train schedules. So a new time system was developed. Knowing how to use this system is just as important today as it was during the 1800s.

2. Time Zones

As the railroad industry grew, managers set schedules of times that trains would arrive at and depart from places along their routes. But setting schedules was difficult because of the many time differences from place to place. No one knew whose time to use. Most railroads set their own times. They called it "railroad time." By the 1880s there were about 100 different railroad times. This was very confusing.

Finally, two men had an idea to solve the problem. Charles Dowd of the United States and Sandford Fleming of Canada divided the world into time zones. A **time zone** is a region in which a single time is used.

Fleming and Dowd divided the world into 24 time zones. A new time zone begins at every fifteenth meridian, starting at the prime meridian and moving west. In each new time zone to the west, the time is one hour earlier than in the time zone before it. All parts of a time zone use the same time. In the 1880s the railroads began to use this system. Today most of the countries in the world follow it.

The United States has six time zones. From east to west, they are the eastern, central, mountain, Pacific, Alaska, and Hawaii-Aleutian time zones.

3. Understand the Process

How can you figure out what time it is in different time zones? Following the steps in the examples below can help you.

1 Find Maryland on the map. It is in the eastern time zone.

An accurate pocket watch was important to the engineer on a train. Time zones solved the problem of how to set the watch.

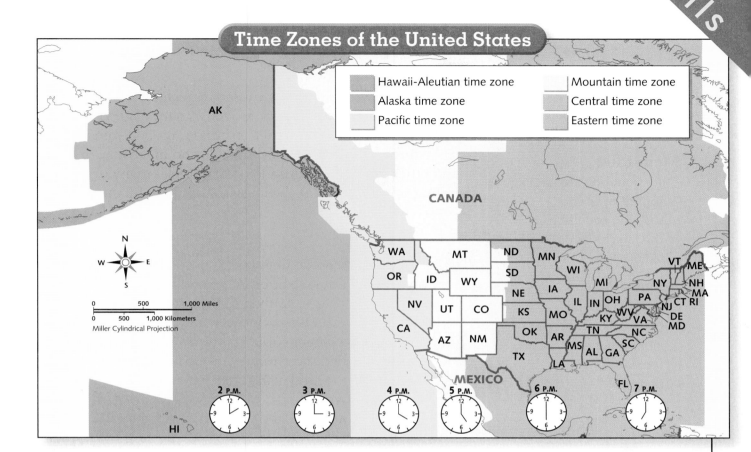

Time Zones of the United States

Hawaii-Aleutian time zone	Mountain time zone
Alaska time zone	Central time zone
Pacific time zone	Eastern time zone

2 P.M. 3 P.M. 4 P.M. 5 P.M. 6 P.M. 7 P.M.

2 Now find Arkansas. It is in the central time zone, which is just west of the eastern time zone. The time in the central time zone is one hour earlier than in the eastern time zone. To find the time in Arkansas, subtract one hour from the time in Maryland.

3 Find Colorado on the map. It is in the mountain time zone. The time is two hours earlier in Colorado than in Maryland. To find the time in Colorado, subtract two hours from the time in Maryland.

4 Now look to the west on the map to find California. It is in the Pacific time zone. The time is three hours earlier in California than in Maryland. To find the time in California, subtract three hours from the time in Maryland.

5 Locate the largest part of Alaska, in the Alaska time zone. The time there is four

hours earlier than in Maryland. To find the time in this part of Alaska, subtract four hours from the time in Maryland.

6 Find Hawaii on the map. It is in the Hawaii-Aleutian time zone. The time is five hours earlier in Hawaii than in Maryland. To find the time in Hawaii, subtract five hours from the time in Maryland.

4. Think and Apply

Use an almanac or atlas to find a world time zone map. Suppose it is 9:00 A.M. where you live. Find the time in each of these cities: London, England; Tokyo, Japan; and Cairo, Egypt. Help other students understand time zones by describing how you figured out the time for each of these cities. Then explain when it would be helpful to know the time in different places.

FOCUS

How do people today improve their working conditions?

Main Idea   Read to find out how people fought for better working conditions in the late 1800s and early 1900s.

Vocabulary

human resource
strike
labor union
federation
regulate

Growing Pains

The growth of industry caused a greater need for **human resources**, or workers, as well as natural and capital resources. People were needed to build railroads, mine coal, stoke furnaces in steel mills, refine oil, and make machines and other products. Thousands of workers—many of them immigrants—moved to the industrial cities to fill these jobs.

Work in the Factories

Because there were so many people looking for work, factory owners were able to hire people willing to work for little pay, or low wages. As the years passed, the number of workers went up and wages went down. Soon many factory workers could no longer support their families on the low wages. They needed more money just to buy food and pay rent. To bring in the money they needed, many parents sent their children to work.

Between 1890 and 1910 the number of working children between the ages of 10 and 15 went from 1.5 million to 2 million. By 1910, almost one-fifth of the workers in the United States were children.

Many children no longer had time for school. They worked in factories all day or, in some cases, all night. In 1906 John

This photo shows men and women working in a clothing shop in New York City. People often had to work long hours for little pay.

Spargo, a reporter, described what he saw in one glassmaking factory.

66 The hours of labor for the 'night shift' were from 5:30 P.M. to 3:30 A.M. . . . Then began the work of . . . the 'carrying-in boys,' sometimes called 'carrier pigeons,' [who] took the red-hot bottles from the benches, three or four at a time. . . . The work of these 'carrying-in boys,' several of whom were less than twelve years old, was by far the hardest of all. They were kept on a slow run all the time from the benches to the annealing [finishing] oven . . . [the trip] was one hundred feet, and the boys made seventy-two trips per hour, making the distance traveled in eight hours nearly twenty-two miles. Over half of this distance the boys were carrying their hot loads to the oven. The pay of these boys varies from sixty cents to a dollar for eight hours' work. 99

Workers of all ages had another problem, too—machines that were unsafe. Hundreds of workers were killed each year in factory accidents, and thousands more were badly hurt.

REVIEW *What problems did working children face?*

Owners Against Workers

Some workers complained about their working conditions. Others went on **strike**, or stopped work, as a way to get factory owners to listen to them. Few factory owners did. They just fired the people who complained and hired new workers. Plenty of people were still looking for jobs.

An employer saved money by hiring children because they could be paid much less than adults. The children shown in this photograph are working in a textile mill.

As conditions grew worse, some workers started to fight back. By themselves they could do little against the powerful factory owners. So they joined together to form labor unions. A **labor union** is a group of workers who take action to improve their working conditions.

One early labor union leader was Samuel Gompers. When Gompers was 13 years old, he went to work in a cigarmakers' shop. The cigarmakers often worked from sunrise until sunset. Most were paid only pennies an hour. Gompers joined a cigarmakers' union, and soon he was the union leader in his shop. In 1877 Gompers helped bring all of the cigarmakers' unions together to form one large union. Members of the union went on strike because they wanted a shorter workday and better wages. The strike failed. The people who owned the cigarmakers' shops also owned many of the apartment buildings where workers lived. They fired the striking workers and put them out of their apartments.

After this experience Gompers decided that cigarmakers needed the support of other workers to make the labor union stronger. So he asked other workers to join his union. He believed that only skilled workers should be in this group. If skilled workers went on strike, it would be hard to replace them. A strike might then have a better chance of success. Gompers and other leaders organized groups of carpenters, plumbers, and bricklayers to join with the cigarmakers in one large federation. A **federation** is an organization made up of many related groups.

In 1886 Samuel Gompers helped form the American Federation of Labor, or AFL. As the AFL got larger, business leaders began to listen to its representatives. The AFL asked for higher wages and a shorter workday. Workers sang,

> 66 Eight hours for work,
>   eight hours for rest,
>   eight hours for what we will. 99

The AFL also wanted better working conditions, accident insurance, and an end to child labor. The insurance would pay the wages and medical bills for workers who were hurt on the job.

REVIEW *What were the goals of the American Federation of Labor?*

Labor Unions and Strikes

Going on strike became the labor unions' most important way to be heard by the factory owners. Sometimes, however, strikes became violent. Violence did not help the unions. In fact, some labor unions lost their power as a result.

In 1886, workers belonging to a labor union known as the Knights of Labor went on strike against the McCormick Harvesting Machine Company. The union demanded higher wages and an eight-hour workday. During one protest meeting, strikers clashed with police at Haymarket Square in Chicago. When someone threw a bomb, seven police officers were killed and many other people were hurt. The police did not find out who threw the bomb, but people blamed the labor union. The Knights of Labor soon lost many of its members.

One of the most violent strikes during this time took place in 1892 at a Carnegie steel mill in Homestead, Pennsylvania, near Pittsburgh. While Andrew Carnegie was in Scotland, one of his managers, Henry Clay Frick, announced a pay cut. In June the workers went on strike. Frick fought back. He shut down the mill and hired private police

Labor Union
Membership, 1898–1920

LEARNING FROM GRAPHS
Samuel Gompers (right) helped form the American Federation of Labor. The graph (above) shows the number of workers who joined unions from 1898 to 1920.

■ *How did union membership change during this time?*

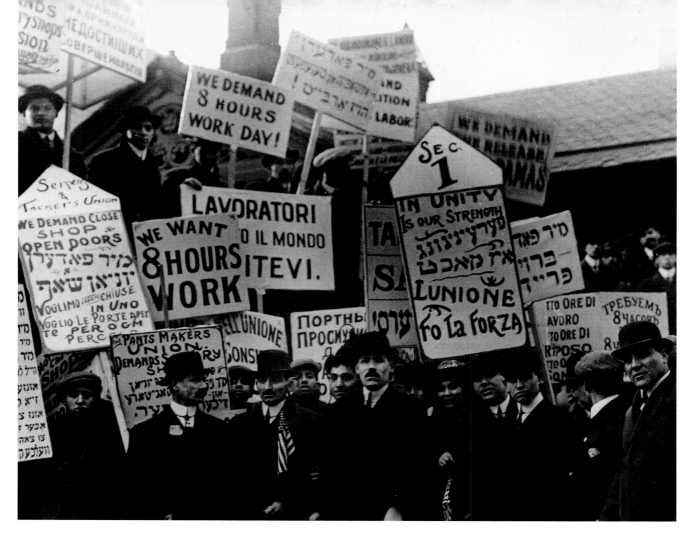

One of the demands of these New York City clothing workers was an eight-hour workday. Many of the workers in this photograph were immigrants and carried signs in their own languages, including Italian, Yiddish, and Russian.

from the Pinkerton National Detective Agency to protect it.

When 300 Pinkertons, as Pinkerton agents were called, arrived in Homestead, they were met by hundreds of angry union workers. A fight broke out, and 7 Pinkertons and 9 strikers were killed. The governor of Pennsylvania sent in soldiers from the National Guard to keep order.

The Homestead strike went on for more than four months. Finally the union gave up. Frick won, but many people began to think that factory owners should listen to labor unions' demands.

REVIEW *What caused the Homestead strike?*

Government and Business

Workers went on strike in the hope of making their lives and working conditions better. But pay was still low, and many children still had to work. More and more workers were hurt in accidents every year. Workers hoped that the government would help, but many government leaders took the side of the factory owners.

Government leaders believed that business people helped make the country's economy strong by producing goods and creating new jobs. The leaders felt that government should leave factory owners and

Labor Day

In New York City on September 5, 1882, Americans held the first Labor Day parade. Matthew Maguire, a machine worker, and Peter McGuire, a carpenter and a founder of an early labor union, came up with the idea of Labor Day. It is a day to honor working people and to recognize their importance to the United States. In 1894 Congress made Labor Day a legal holiday. Today the United States and Canada celebrate Labor Day on the first Monday in September. Many other countries also honor workers with labor celebrations.

A Labor Day parade in the early 1900s

their businesses alone. For industry to grow, they said, businesses had to be free to produce goods in the ways that were best for them.

Business leaders also felt that the government should leave their companies alone. They did not want government leaders telling them how to run their own businesses. They feared that the government would then **regulate** their businesses, or control them by law. Business owners wanted to be controlled by as few laws as possible.

REVIEW *Why did the government choose to leave business owners alone?*

LESSON 2 REVIEW

Check Understanding

1 **Remember the Facts** What were conditions like for factory workers during the late 1800s and early 1900s?

2 **Recall the Main Idea** How did people fight for better working conditions in the late 1800s and early 1900s?

Think Critically

3 **Explore Viewpoints** How do you think workers in the late 1800s felt about going on strike? How do you think business owners felt about strikes?

4 **Personally Speaking** Suppose you had been one of the young workers in the glassmaking factory that the reporter John Spargo described. How do you think you might have felt about your job?

Show What You Know

Art Activity Think about the problems factory workers faced in the late 1800s. Draw a poster that a labor union might have used to get people to join. Display your poster in the classroom.

New Immigrants

FOCUS
What problems do immigrants to the United States face today?

Main Idea Read to learn about some of the problems that immigrants to the United States faced in the past.

Vocabulary
prejudice
barrio
tenement
naturalization

About three of every four workers in the Carnegie steel mills had been born outside the United States. Carnegie himself had been born in Scotland. When he was 12 years old, he had moved to the United States with his father. Between 1860 and 1910, about 23 million immigrants arrived in the United States. Those from Asia and Latin America settled mostly in the West and Southwest. Latin America is made up of all the countries in the Americas south of the United States. Those from Europe settled mostly in the cities in the East and in the growing industrial cities of the Middle West. Immigrants from all over the world played an important part in the growth of industry and agriculture in the United States.

Asian Immigrants

Chinese people came to the United States in great numbers after the California gold rush of 1849. By 1852 about 25,000 Chinese people had arrived in San Francisco and were working in the goldfields.

Like other immigrant groups, the Chinese faced prejudice from some Americans. **Prejudice** is a negative feeling some people have toward others because of their race or culture. The Chinese had to pay a tax to pan for gold that no one else had to pay. Some Americans tried to force the Chinese out of the goldfields.

As less and less gold was found in the goldfields, the Chinese looked for other work. Because they wanted to stay in the United States, they worked for low wages. Some Chinese immigrants worked in mining and agriculture. Thousands worked for the Central Pacific Railroad to build the transcontinental railroad.

By the 1870s many Americans wanted to stop the Chinese from coming to the United States. They also wanted Chinese people who were already in the United States to go back to China. The Americans worried that the

Thousands of Asians entered the United States through Angel Island in San Francisco.

Some Mexican American families had lived in the United States for many years. This photograph shows five generations of the Aguilar family in Texas in 1902.

immigrants would take their jobs. California and other western states passed laws that made life harder for the Chinese. Chinese people could not get state jobs, and they had to pay higher state taxes. State courts would not hear lawsuits brought by Chinese people. Finally, in 1882, Congress passed a law that stopped all immigration by Chinese people for ten years. By this time there were about 75,000 Chinese immigrants living in the United States.

Japanese and other Asian people were still allowed to come to the United States. Most found jobs in agriculture. Many bought small farms in California and in other parts of the Southwest. But in time they, too, met with prejudice. By the early 1900s many Americans were calling for a stop to all immigration from Asia. But instead of putting a stop to it, the United States government passed laws to limit the number of immigrants from Asia.

REVIEW *Why did many Americans want to stop Asian immigration?*

Latin American Immigrants

During the late 1800s, immigrants from Latin America moved to many places in the United States to find work. By 1900 about 80,000 Mexican immigrants had settled in Texas, New Mexico, Arizona, and southern California. Some immigrants from Cuba came to the United States to find work in cigarmakers' shops. During the 1860s people from Chile and Peru settled in the western United States to mine for gold and silver. By 1900 more than 14,000 people from Central and South America had moved to the United States. Mexicans made up the largest group of immigrants that came from Latin America at this time.

Some Mexicans had lived in the southwestern part of the United States for years. Many lived in places that had been part of Mexico before the Treaty of Guadalupe Hidalgo, which ended the war between the United States and Mexico in 1848. By the late

1800s, newcomers from Mexico began to settle in the United States.

Like most other new immigrants to the United States, few Mexicans spoke English or knew people in the United States. Imagine how these immigrants must have felt when they first met people from their homeland already living in the United States. Just to be able to talk with people in their own language made them feel more at home.

Soon barrios sprang up in most cities in the Southwest. A **barrio** is a neighborhood of Spanish-speaking people. People in the barrios helped one another. The immigrants who had been in the Southwest longer helped the newcomers find homes and jobs. Many Mexican immigrants found jobs on farms. They spent up to 14 hours a day planting, weeding, and picking lettuce, tomatoes, and grapes. Others found factory jobs in the cities.

Like other immigrants, those from Mexico met with prejudice. Some people tried to make them go back to Mexico. In 1910 a writer for a Mexican newspaper wondered what made "our workingmen, so attached to the land, . . . abandon the country [Mexico], even at the risk of the Yankee contempt [lack of respect] with which they are treated on the other side of the Bravo [Rio Grande]."

REVIEW *How did living in the barrios help immigrants from Mexico?*

European Immigrants

European immigrants were by far the largest group to come to the United States. Between 1890 and 1920, nearly 16 million immigrants arrived from countries in Europe.

Before 1890 most European immigrants had come from northern and western Europe. They had come from countries such as Britain, Ireland, Scotland, Germany, Norway, and Sweden. These were the immigrants who had helped build the Erie Canal and who had taken part in the great westward movement.

LEARNING FROM GRAPHS The number of immigrants to the United States is shown on this graph for four different periods of time. Many immigrants, like this family (below right), came from Europe.

■ *When were there more immigrants from eastern Europe than from northwestern Europe?*

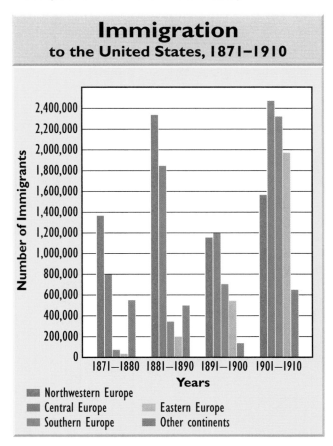

Immigration
to the United States, 1871–1910

Number of Immigrants

2,400,000
2,200,000
2,000,000
1,800,000
1,600,000
1,400,000
1,200,000
1,000,000
800,000
600,000
400,000
200,000
0

1871–1880 1881–1890 1891–1900 1901–1910
Years

■ Northwestern Europe
■ Central Europe   ■ Eastern Europe
■ Southern Europe   ■ Other continents

Around 1890 a new period of immigration began. Some people still came from the countries of northern and western Europe, but now many came from countries in southern and eastern Europe. They came from Italy, Greece, Poland, Austria, Hungary, Armenia, and Russia. Many of these people were poor and unhappy in their homelands. Often they did not have enough to eat. They came to the United States hoping for a better life.

Most of the ships that brought European immigrants to the United States landed at Ellis Island in New York Bay. Many immigrants stayed in New York City. After a while some moved to the new industrial cities, where they hoped to find factory jobs. Many immigrants had lived on small farms in Europe, and they had hoped to buy land in the United States. But few had enough money to do that. Most lived with relatives or friends. Many lived crowded together in poorly built apartment houses called **tenements**. Wages were so low that everyone in the family, even young children, had to work just to earn enough money for food.

Like other immigrants, the Europeans often met with prejudice. Posters about jobs sometimes said things like "Irish need not apply." Some newcomers were even treated badly by immigrants who had arrived earlier. Immigrants who were already living and working in the United States worried that the new immigrants would take away their jobs.

REVIEW *From what parts of Europe did many immigrants come before 1890?*

GEOGRAPHY

Angel Island and Ellis Island

In the late 1800s and early 1900s, Angel Island in San Francisco Bay and Ellis Island in New York Bay were the places where ships carrying immigrants landed in the United States. At the immigration stations on both islands, immigrants were checked for health problems. Anyone with a serious illness was sent back to his or her country. Immigrants also had to tell about themselves, their families, and their job skills. Sometimes the names of immigrants were changed by mistake because the workers filling out papers could not understand different languages.

Immigrant children came from many different cultures. This diversity is shown by these children who were living in Gary, Indiana.

Becoming a Citizen

No matter how hard their lives were, many immigrants felt that becoming an American citizen was very important. Being a citizen meant taking part in the government, voting, and serving on juries. To many immigrants, these rights were something new.

Immigrants could become American citizens through a process called **naturalization**. They had to live in the United States for five years and then pass a test. The test asked questions about the government and history of the United States, such as *Who makes the laws in the United States?* and *Who was the first President?*

The questions on the test had to be answered in English. Thousands of immigrants went to school after work so they could learn English to take the test. Those who passed the test pledged allegiance, or loyalty, to the United States.

66 I pledge allegiance to the Flag of the United States of America, and to the Republic for which it stands, one Nation under God, indivisible, with liberty and justice for all. 99

REVIEW *How did an immigrant become a citizen of the United States?*

LESSON 3 REVIEW

Check Understanding

1 **Remember the Facts**   What were some of the reasons immigrants came to the United States?

2 **Recall the Main Idea**   What were some of the problems that immigrants to the United States faced in the past?

Think Critically

3 **Personally Speaking**   How might you feel if someone showed prejudice toward you?

4 **Think More About It**   Why was becoming a United States citizen important to many immigrants?

Show What You Know

Writing Activity   Imagine that it is the late 1800s and you are an immigrant who has just arrived in the United States. You are looking for a job. Use the information in this lesson to write a journal entry about what you might see and do. Share your writing with a classmate.

THE GREAT MIGRATION

AN AMERICAN STORY

*story and paintings
by Jacob Lawrence*

Even as immigrants were moving to the United States from other countries, people within the United States were moving from place to place. This was true of many different groups of Americans, including African Americans.

After the Civil War, most African Americans in the South found jobs as workers on farms or as sharecroppers on plantations. Few moved into the cities. But between 1916 and 1919, many decided to move to the industrial cities in the North— to New York, Chicago, Detroit, Pittsburgh,

Cleveland, and St. Louis. During these years workers were needed to take over the factory jobs of those who had left to fight in a war in Europe. The war would later be called World War I. When African Americans left their farms to become factory workers, their lives changed forever.

Jacob Lawrence's family took part in this great migration from the South. Read his story to learn more about the migration and about the problems African Americans shared with other newcomers to northern cities in the early 1900s.

Around the time I was born, many African-Americans from the South left home and traveled to cities in the North in search of a better life. My family was part of this great migration.

There was a shortage of workers in northern factories because many had left their jobs to fight in the First World War.

The factory owners had to find new workers to replace those who were marching off to war.

Northern industries offered southern blacks jobs as workers and lent them money, to be repaid later, for their railroad tickets. The northbound trains were packed with recruits.

Nature had ravaged the South. Floods ruined farms. The boll weevil destroyed cotton crops.

The war had doubled the cost of food, making life even harder for the poor.

Railroad stations were so crowded with migrants that guards were called in to keep order.

The flood of migrants northward left crops back home to dry and spoil.

For African-Americans the South was barren in many ways. There was no justice for them in the courts, and their lives were often in danger.

Although slavery had long been abolished, white landowners treated the black tenant farmers harshly and unfairly.

And so the migration grew.

Segregation divided the South.

The black newspapers told of better housing and jobs in the North.

Families would arrive very early at railroad stations to make sure they could get on the northbound trains.

Early arrival was not easy, because African-Americans found on the streets could be arrested for no reason.

And the migrants kept coming.

In the South there was little opportunity for education, and children labored in the fields. These were more reasons for people to move north, leaving some communities deserted.

There was much excitement and discussion about the great migration.

Agents from northern factories flocked into southern counties and towns, looking for laborers.

Families often gathered to discuss whether to go north or to stay south. The promise of better housing in the North could not be ignored.

The railroad stations were crowded with migrants.

Letters from relatives in the North and articles in the black press portrayed a better life outside the South.

Many migrants arrived in Chicago.

In Chicago and other cities they labored in the steel mills . . . and on the railroads.

And the migrants kept coming.

Southern landowners, stripped of cheap labor, tried to stop the migration by jailing the labor agents and the migrants. Sometimes the agents disguised themselves to avoid arrest, but the migrants were often taken from railroad stations and jailed until the trains departed.

Black and white southern leaders met to discuss ways to improve conditions to stop the flow of workers north.

Although life in the North was better, it was not ideal.

Many migrants moved to Pittsburgh, which was a great industrial center at the time.

Although they were promised better housing in the North, some families were forced to live in overcrowded and unhealthy quarters.

The migrants soon learned that segregation was not confined to the South.

Many northern workers were angry because they had to compete with the migrants for housing and jobs. There were riots.

Longtime African-American residents living in the North did not welcome the newcomers from the South and often treated them with disdain.

The migrants had to rely on each other. The storefront church was a welcoming place and the center of their lives, in joy and in sorrow.

Black professionals, such as doctors and lawyers, soon followed their patients and clients north. Female workers were among the last to leave.

Life in the North brought many challenges, but the migrants' lives had changed for the better. The children were able to go to school, and their parents gained the freedom to vote.

And the migrants kept coming.

Theirs is a story of African-American strength and courage. I share it now as my parents told it to me, because their struggles and triumphs ring true today. People all over the world are still on the move, trying to build better lives for themselves and for their families.

LITERATURE REVIEW

1 What events and problems caused Jacob Lawrence's family to move to the North?

2 What problems did African Americans share with other newcomers to northern cities in the early 1900s?

3 Imagine that you are an African American who has moved to the North during the time of World War I. Write a letter to Jacob Lawrence's family describing how life in the North is different from life in the South.

The Growth of Cities

By the beginning of the twentieth century, cities in the United States were growing fast. Some people thought they were growing too fast. No one had expected such growth, and no one had planned for it. Millions of people were moving to American cities from farms, and millions more were coming from other countries. There were just too many people in one place. As cities grew, so did their problems.

City Problems

One problem was that of overcrowded tenements. When one person in a tenement became ill, disease spread through the tenement quickly. In one overcrowded Chicago tenement, three out of every five children born in 1900 died before they were three years old. A newspaper reporter named Jacob Riis (REES) described the same kind of poor living conditions in New York City tenements.

Riis saw that when someone died in a tenement, a ribbon tied into a bow was hung on the tenement door—black for an adult and white for a child. Riis wrote,

> 66 Listen! That short hacking cough, that tiny, helpless wail—what do they mean? They mean that the soiled bow of white you saw on the door downstairs will have another story to tell—Oh! a sadly familiar story—before the day is at an end. The child is dying with measles. With half a chance it might have lived; but it had none. 99

Jacob Riis was a Danish immigrant whose photographs and newspaper articles helped improve living conditions in the cities.

Insects and rats in the garbage spread the germs of illness. With so many people in the cities, garbage piled up. At this time there was no regular garbage collection. Even in the largest cities, garbage was eaten by pigs in the streets.

The danger of fire became greater as new buildings went up. Most were made partly of wood. Terrible fires burned down whole city blocks. The Great Chicago

This photograph of a family living in a crowded tenement apartment was taken by Jessie Tarbox Beals, the first woman to work as a news photographer.

Fire of 1871 was one of the worst. It burned for 24 hours, killing at least 300 people and leaving more than 90,000 people homeless. Few cities at that time had full-time fire departments.

Crime was another problem in cities. Because of the crowds, it was hard for the police to find lawbreakers. Sometimes a gang would take over an entire city neighborhood, and even the police would be afraid to go into it.

REVIEW *What problems faced many people who were living in cities?*

Help for the Cities' Poor

Some people who lived in cities tried to solve the problems they saw around them. Jane Addams was one of these people. Addams came from a wealthy family and had gone to college, something few women at that time were able to do. She worried about the growing problems of the tenements in Chicago.

While traveling in Britain, Addams had visited a place called Toynbee Hall. It was a settlement house, a community center where

people could learn new skills. Addams took the idea back to Chicago.

66 It is hard to tell just when the very simple plan . . . began. . . . But I gradually became convinced that it would be a good thing to rent a house in a part of the city where many . . . needs are found. 99

In 1889 Addams started Hull House in Chicago with Ellen Gates Starr. The workers in Hull House ran a kindergarten for children whose mothers worked. They taught classes in sewing, cooking, and the English language. Later they worked to improve living conditions in tenements and health and safety conditions in the mills and factories. They also tried to get laws passed to regulate child labor.

Hull House became a model for other community centers. In 1890 African American teacher Janie Porter Barrett founded a settlement house in Hampton, Virginia. Three years later, Lillian Wald started the Henry Street Settlement in New York City. By 1900 almost 100 settlement houses had opened.

REVIEW *Why were settlement houses important in the cities?*

The Changing City

Even with their many problems, cities came to stand for all that was good in industrial America. Besides factories, stores, and tenements, cities had parks, theaters, and zoos that people could enjoy when they had free time. Cities also had schools, railroad stations, and tall office buildings.

Before this time buildings could not be taller than four or five stories because their walls were made only of bricks. The bricks on the bottom had to hold up the weight of all the bricks above them. In the 1880s an engineer named William Jenney found a way to build taller buildings. Jenney used steel frames to hold up a building the way a skeleton holds up a body. In 1885 Jenney finished building the ten-story Home Insurance Company Building in Chicago. It was the world's first tall steel-frame building, or **skyscraper**.

As buildings were made taller and taller— 20 stories, then 50 stories, then 100 stories—fast, safe elevators were needed. The first electric elevator was put into a skyscraper in New York City in 1889.

As cities grew upward, they also grew outward. When the first cities were built in the United States, people walked to and from work. As people began moving away from the center of the city, transportation was needed to help them get to their jobs.

In 1865 most cities had streetcars pulled by horses. Horses could go only about 6 miles (9.7 km) an hour on flat ground, and each horse cost about $200—about the price of a car in today's money. In San Francisco the

A Skyscraper

LEARNING FROM DIAGRAMS This diagram shows an early skyscraper being built. Electric elevators like the one below were first put into skyscrapers.

■ *Why do you think skyscrapers need elevators?*

Streetcars were an important form of transportation in many cities. This streetcar had open sides that made it easy to board.

horses had to pull the cars up very steep hills. This was hard for the horses and slow for the passengers. An inventor named Andrew S. Hallidie worked on the problem. In 1871 he invented the cable car. Cable cars ran on tracks and were attached to a steam-powered cable, or strong wire, that ran in a slot in the street. The cable pulled the cars at about 9 miles (14.5 km) an hour up and down steep hills. Fifteen cities put in cable cars. Chicago had 710 cable cars!

Then, in the late 1880s, inventor Frank Sprague built an electric streetcar that was first used in Richmond, Virginia. Sprague's streetcar also ran on tracks, but it was powered by electricity rather than by steam. A small wheel on a trolley pole on top of the car rode along an overhead electric wire. The new streetcar was called a trolley car. By 1890 more than 50 cities had trolley transportation systems.

As more tracks were laid, people moved farther and farther from the center of the city. They could ride trolley cars to work or shop in the city and live away from the inner city's problems.

REVIEW *What inventions helped cities grow upward and outward during the late 1800s?*

LESSON 5 REVIEW

Check Understanding

1 **Remember the Facts**   How did cities change in the late 1800s?

2 **Recall the Main Idea**   What problems did people face as cities grew larger, and how did some people work to solve them?

Think Critically

3 **Think More About It**   In what ways do you think Jane Addams was like the labor union leader Samuel Gompers? How were they different?

4 **Cause and Effect**   How did the inventions you read about in this lesson affect the way people lived in cities?

Show What You Know

TV Report Activity   With several classmates, prepare an outline for a TV program on life in the cities in the late 1800s. Write down topics for your program. Then list ideas for interviews, pictures, maps, charts, and graphs. Present your outline to your classmates.

Solve a Problem

1. Why Learn This Skill?

People everywhere face problems at one time or another. Many people face more than one problem at the same time. Think about a problem you have faced recently. How did you know you had a problem? Were you able to solve it? Did you wish you could have found a better way to solve the problem? Knowing how to solve problems is a skill that you will use all your life.

2. Remember What You Have Read

You have read about the many problems that made city life difficult in the late 1800s and early 1900s. Overcrowding, disease, fire, and crime were among the problems that people faced. Jane Addams was one person who tried to help. Think again about the problems Addams saw and the way she tried to solve them.

1 What problems did Jane Addams see in Chicago?

2 What solution did Addams learn about when she visited Toynbee Hall?

3 What did Addams decide was a good way to solve the problems in Chicago?

4 How did Addams carry out her solution?

5 How did Addams's solution help solve the problems of city life?

3. Understand the Process

You can use similar steps to help solve problems.

- Identify the problem.
- Think of possible solutions.
- Compare the solutions, and choose the best one.
- Plan how to carry out the solution.
- Try your solution, and think about how well it helps solve the problem.

4. Think and Apply

Identify a problem in your community or school. Write a plan for solving the problem. What steps did you follow? What solution did you choose? Do you think that your solution will help solve the problem? Explain your answer.

Jane Addams started Hull House (far left) to help Chicago's immigrants. Addams (left, with a child at Hull House) was one of the country's best-known reformers.

CHAPTER 15

REVIEW

| 1865 | 1875 | 1885 |

1869
• Transcontinental railroad completed

1886
• Samuel Gompers helps form the AFL

CONNECT MAIN IDEAS

Use this graphic organizer to show how the chapter's main ideas are connected. Write three details to support each main idea. A copy of the organizer appears on page 101 of the Activity Book.

New inventions changed life in the United States.
1. _____
2. _____
3. _____

People worked to solve problems in the cities.
1. _____
2. _____
3. _____

Industry and Immigration

People fought for better working conditions.
1. _____
2. _____
3. _____

Immigrants to the United States faced problems.
1. _____
2. _____
3. _____

African Americans shared problems with other newcomers to cities.
1. _____
2. _____
3. _____

WRITE MORE ABOUT IT

Write a Magazine Article Imagine that you have been asked to write a magazine article about working conditions in the United States in the early 1900s. As part of your research, you visit several factories. Describe what you see there.

Write a Letter Imagine that it is the early 1900s and you and your family have just moved from a farm to a big city. Write a letter to a friend. Describe how your new life in the city is different from your old life on the farm.

Late 1800s
• Immigrants from Asia, Latin America, and Europe come to the United States

1916
• Many African Americans from the South begin moving to industrial cities in the North

USE VOCABULARY

For each group of underlined words in the sentences, write the term from the list below that has the same meaning.

corporation	labor union
invest	prejudice

1 Some people <u>buy shares of a business</u> in the hope of making money.

2 People can own part of a <u>business that sells shares of stock to investors.</u>

3 Workers sometimes form a <u>group that tries to improve their working conditions.</u>

4 Immigrants sometimes face <u>a negative feeling some people have toward others because of their race or culture.</u>

CHECK UNDERSTANDING

5 What was the transcontinental railroad?

6 What did immigrants have to do to become citizens of the United States?

7 Why did many African Americans move to industrial cities in the North?

8 How did settlement houses improve life for people in the cities?

THINK CRITICALLY

9 **Personally Speaking** How would your life be different if the electric lightbulb had not been invented?

10 **Explore Viewpoints** How do you think workers' views of labor unions differed from the views held by the factory owners?

11 **Think More About It** Why do you think some factory owners in the early 1900s treated their workers badly?

12 **Cause and Effect** How did railroads affect the growth of cities?

APPLY SKILLS

Use a Time Zone Map Use the time zone map on page 489 to answer these questions:

13 If it is 5:00 P.M. in Georgia, what time is it in California?

14 If it is 10:00 A.M. in Illinois, what time is it in Ohio?

15 If it is 3:00 A.M. in North Carolina, what time is it in Colorado?

Solve a Problem Identify a problem faced by a person you read about in this chapter. Use the steps listed on page 509 to write a plan that you think might help solve the problem.

READ MORE ABOUT IT

Immigrant Kids by Russell Freedman. Puffin. Read about the everyday lives of immigrant children during the late 1800s and early 1900s.

HARCOURT BRACE

Visit the Internet at **http://www.hbschool.com** for additional resources.

Chapter 15 • **511**

THE LAST FRONTIER

"Most of the time we were solitary adventurers in a great land as fresh and new as a spring morning, and we were free and full of the zest of darers."

Charles Goodnight, Texas cattle driver and rancher

Cowhands like the one in this photograph worked on ranches throughout the West.

Farming the Great Plains

The explorers of the early 1800s who crossed the Great Plains described the region as a desert. By the late 1800s, however, farmers were turning the plains into fields of wheat. The Great Plains would become the "breadbasket" of the United States and the greatest wheat-growing region in the world.

Settling the Plains

In 1862, while the Civil War was being fought in the East, Congress passed the Homestead Act. This law opened the Great Plains to settlers by giving 160 acres of land to any head of a family who was over 21 years of age and who would live on it for five years. Between 1862 and 1900 about 80 million acres of government land on the Great Plains was settled. The government lands were called homesteads, and the people who settled them were known as **homesteaders**.

Thousands of other settlers bought western land at low prices from the railroads. Over the years the government had given the railroads millions of acres of land on the Great Plains. Railroad owners used the land to build new railroad lines. But they also wanted people to settle the Plains because settlers would bring more business. Settlers would use the railroads for travel. Farmers would use the railroads to send their products to the cities in the Middle West and in the East.

The railroads placed advertisements for land sales in newspapers all over the United States and in other countries. Many Americans jumped at the chance to buy land in the West. Most wanted to start farms or ranches. Some planned to open businesses. More than 100,000 immigrants moved to the West from northern and western Europe.

LESSON

1

FOCUS
How do people today change their ways of life to suit their environments?

Main Idea As you read, look for changes farmers made in order to live on the Great Plains.

Vocabulary
homesteader
bonanza farm

This poster (below) advertised land for sale in northern Missouri. The price of the land was often less than $10 an acre. Farmers raised millions of tons of wheat (bottom) on the Great Plains.

By 1890 there were 5 million people living on the Great Plains.

The best lands on the Great Plains were quickly taken. In the Oklahoma land rush of 1889, thousands of homesteaders raced one another to claim land. By 1890 most of the territories in the Great Plains had enough people to become states. North Dakota, South Dakota, and Montana joined the Union in 1889. Wyoming joined in 1890. Oklahoma followed in 1907.

REVIEW *How did settlers get land on the Great Plains?*

Life on the Family Farm

Living on the Great Plains was very different from living in most other places in the United States. Trees for building homes were scarce, but there was plenty of sod. Many settlers used sod to build their houses. Sod houses were cool in summer and warm in winter, but keeping them clean was a problem. Dirt often fell from the sod ceiling onto the furniture. Sometimes snakes did, too! Leaky roofs were common. "There was

Movement This map shows the areas of the United States that were settled by 1870 and by 1890.

■ *As settlers moved west, what happened to the frontier?*

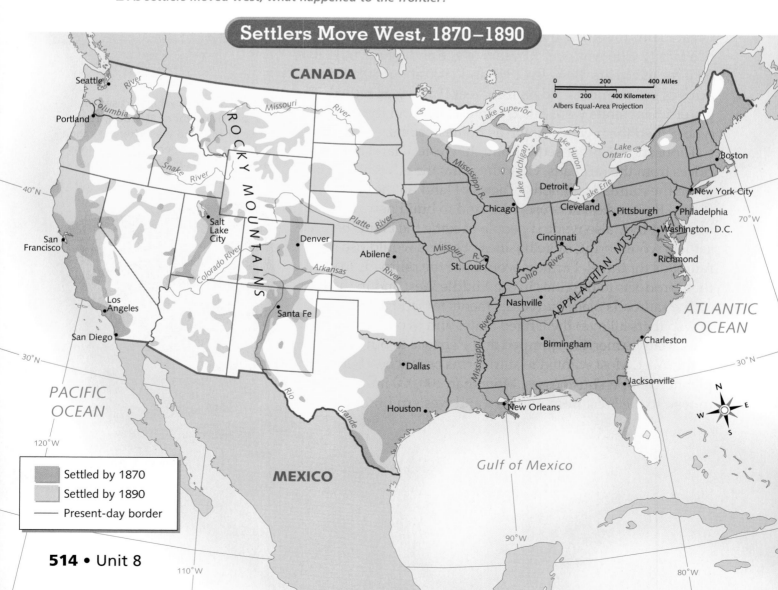

Settlers Move West, 1870–1890

Settled by 1870
Settled by 1890
Present-day border

Because few trees grew on the Great Plains, many families lived in houses made of sod. Windmills were used to pump water from wells dug in the ground.

running water in our sod house," joked one Kansas girl. "It ran through the roof."

Farm families on the Great Plains faced other problems. In summer, sun baked the soil into dust. In winter, snow and bitter temperatures froze the region. In years of drought nothing grew. When crops did grow, farmers worried about prairie fires and hailstorms. One settler on the Plains, Susan Orcutt, wrote that they would have had plenty to eat "if the hail hadn't cut our rye down and ruined our corn and potatoes."

Insects, too, were a problem on the Plains. Grasshoppers attacked in 1874. They came by the millions, turning the sky black and eating anything that was green. Adelheit Viets was wearing a white dress with green stripes the day the grasshoppers came. "The grasshoppers settled on me and ate up every bit of green stripe in the dress before anything could be done about it," she exaggerated.

Changes in technology helped many farm families survive tough times on the Great Plains. New models of windmills let farmers pump water from hundreds of feet below the ground. A stronger plow, invented by James Oliver of Indiana, helped homesteaders cut through the thick sod. And harvesting machines made farm work easier.

Sometimes the hardships became so great that some people left their farms. But most stayed. They built churches and schools, starting towns and cities all over the Great Plains.

REVIEW *What hardships did the early Plains farmers face?*

"Bonanza Farms"

Using the new technology and the railroads, some companies started large farms on the Great Plains. People in the East invested money in these **bonanza farms**. A bonanza is something that brings a good profit or other reward.

The first bonanza farms on the Great Plains grew wheat in the Red River valley of present-day North Dakota and Minnesota. By 1890 there were about 300 of these farms, each one spreading over thousands of acres.

Bonanza farms were run just like factories. Managers ran the farms. Farm workers had specialized jobs, and everything was done by machines. When the wheat crop was ripe, workers used 30-horse teams to pull harvesting machines across the fields. Tons of wheat from bonanza farms were sent by railroad to feed millions of people in the cities of the Middle West and the East.

Bonanza farms could raise crops cheaply, and their investors made very large profits. Managers bought seed and equipment in large amounts, so they paid lower prices. But in times of drought and when wheat prices were low, profits fell. When profits fell, many bonanza farms on the Great Plains went out of business. This left many managers and farm workers without jobs.

REVIEW *How was a bonanza farm like a factory?*

Regions This map shows the areas where American farm products were raised during the late 1800s.

■ *If you had lived on the Great Plains during this time, what crops would you probably have grown?*

Agriculture in the Late 1800s

Legend:
- Corn and winter wheat
- Corn
- Wheat
- Dairy cattle and hay
- Tobacco
- Cotton
- Fruits and vegetables
- Little-used land
- Beef cattle
- Hogs
- Present-day border

TECHNOLOGY

The Reaper

For hundreds of years, farmers harvested crops such as wheat by using a scythe (SYTH), a long, curved knife with a handle. Using a scythe was very hard work. In 1831 an inventor named Cyrus McCormick built a harvesting machine called a reaper. Farmers could cut as much wheat in one day with McCormick's reaper as they could cut in two weeks with a scythe. In 1847 McCormick started a reaper factory in Chicago. Many of the reapers used on farms on the Great Plains were built by the McCormick Harvesting Machine Company.

In the late 1800s some farmers began to use combines (above). Combines are both reapers that cut the crops and threshers that separate the grain from the straw.

LESSON I REVIEW

Check Understanding

1 Remember the Facts What hardships did the homesteaders face?

2 Recall the Main Idea What changes did farmers have to make in order to live on the Great Plains?

Think Critically

3 Think More About It Why do you think people stayed on the Great Plains despite the hardships?

4 Personally Speaking How do you think you would have liked living on the Great Plains during this time? Explain your answer.

Show What You Know

Art Activity Draw a picture of a settlement on the Great Plains. Include a house and farm equipment. Share your picture with classmates or a family member.

Understand a Climograph

1. Why Learn This Skill?

In the late 1800s, many Americans who moved from eastern cities to the Great Plains were surprised by much of what they found there. Nothing surprised them more than the constant wind and the extremes of temperature and precipitation. Suppose that you and your family were moving to another part of the country or another part of the world. You probably would want to know more about the climate before you moved there.

2. Understand the Process

One way to learn about the climate of a place is to study a climograph, or climate graph. A **climograph** shows the average monthly temperature and the average monthly precipitation for a place. Both temperature and precipitation information are shown on the same graph. The temperatures are shown as a line graph. The amounts of precipitation are shown as a bar graph. The months are listed along the bottom of a climograph, from January to December.

Study the climographs on page 519. Along the left-hand side of each climograph is a Fahrenheit scale for temperature. A point is shown on the climograph for the average temperature for each month. These points are connected with a red line. By studying the line, you can see which months are hotter and which are colder.

Along the right-hand side of each climograph is a scale for precipitation. The average monthly amounts of precipitation are shown in inches. By studying the heights of the green bars, you can see which months are usually dry and which are usually wet.

These two climographs show weather averages for Omaha, Nebraska, and Philadelphia, Pennsylvania. Omaha is on the Great Plains, and Philadelphia is near the Atlantic coast. By comparing the climographs, you can see the differences in temperature and precipitation between these two places. This might help you understand why many early settlers on the Great Plains were surprised by new climates. Use the climographs to answer the questions on page 519.

Many pioneers experienced blizzards in the northern part of the Great Plains. A blizzard is a dangerous snowstorm with winds of 35 miles (56 km) per hour or more.

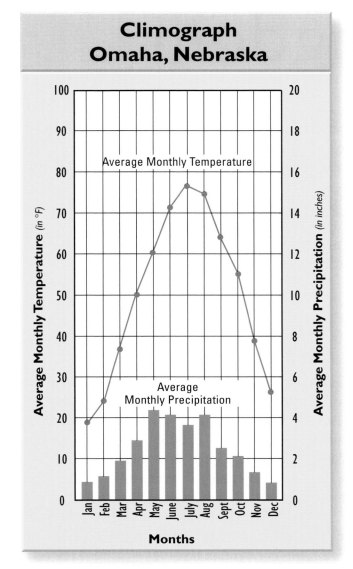

Climograph
Omaha, Nebraska

Average Monthly Temperature (in °F)

Average Monthly Precipitation (in inches)

Average Monthly Temperature

Average Monthly Precipitation

Jan Feb Mar Apr May June July Aug Sept Oct Nov Dec

Months

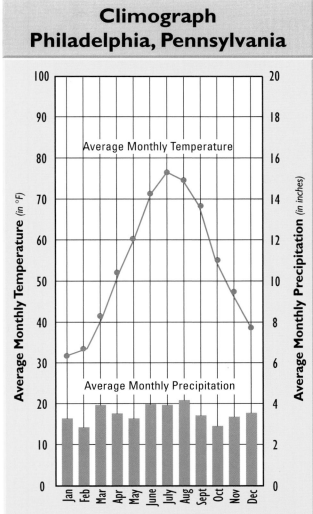

Climograph
Philadelphia, Pennsylvania

Average Monthly Temperature (in °F)

Average Monthly Precipitation (in inches)

Average Monthly Temperature

Average Monthly Precipitation

Jan Feb Mar Apr May June July Aug Sept Oct Nov Dec

Months

1 Which is the warmest month in each of the cities?

2 Which is the coldest month in each place?

3 What are the wettest months in each city?

4 What are the driest months in each city?

5 Which city receives more precipitation during the year?

6 What is the average temperature for each place in January?

7 How much precipitation falls during January in each place?

3. Think and Apply

Use an almanac or encyclopedia to create a climograph for your city or for a city close to where you live. Compare your climograph with the ones shown on this page. Which place shows the greatest changes in temperature and precipitation? Share your findings with a family member or friend. Then discuss the importance of this information. When might people need to know this information? What does it tell you about the place where you live?

FOCUS

How do people build businesses today?

Main Idea As you read, find out how ranchers built the Cattle Kingdom.

Vocabulary

long drive
open range
vaquero
barbed wire
range war

The Cattle Kingdom

Ranching in the American West began in the 1700s in what is now Texas, when that area was a Spanish colony. The first ranches were started with cattle brought from Spain. By the early 1800s, settlers from the United States and Mexico had moved to Texas. Many of these settlers started ranches. After the Civil War, cattle ranches spread throughout the Great Plains. Parts of the region came to be known as the Cattle Kingdom. In the Cattle Kingdom, ranching became a way of life.

The Rise of the Cattle Industry

Before the Civil War, there was not much money to be made from raising cattle in Texas. There, cattle sold for only about $4 each. Early ranchers raised cattle for leather and for tallow, or fat, which they used for making candles and soap. After the Civil War, however, there was a great demand for beef in northern cities. Cattle sold there for 10 times as much as they did in Texas. It was clear that ranchers could make a lot more money if they could get their cattle to northern markets.

Railroad lines were the answer. Joseph McCoy, a cattle trader, built large cattle pens called stockyards near some

Cowhands today continue to take care of cattle on ranches.

railroad tracks in Abilene, Kansas. Then he sent word to ranchers in Texas that he would buy whole herds of cattle. In 1867 Texas ranchers started moving huge herds of cattle north to Abilene. Later, as the railroad was built farther west, other cities also became important "cow towns," or places where stockyards were located. These were Dodge City, Kansas; Ogallala, Nebraska; and Cheyenne, Wyoming.

A cattle drive was the best way to get cattle to the cow towns. On a cattle drive, ranch workers on horseback would drive the cattle, or make them move to another place. Between 1867 and 1890, Texas ranchers drove about 10 million head of cattle north. These trips were called **long drives**.

Each long drive took about three months. During the drive a trail boss managed a crew of 10 to 12 cowhands, who were all skilled ranch workers. During a long drive a crew could move as many as 3,000 cattle.

The long drives followed several trails. One of these was the Chisholm (CHIZ•uhm) Trail. It started in southern Texas and ran all the way to Abilene. When the herds reached Abilene, the cattle were loaded onto freight cars and sent to Chicago, where they were prepared for market. Their meat was then sent in refrigerated freight cars to northern markets. The invention of the refrigerated freight car also allowed farmers from as far away as California to send fruits and vegetables across the country without spoiling.

REVIEW *What were the long drives?*

Cattle Trails

Movement This map shows four of the major cattle trails used during the 1880s.
■ *Why did the trails run north and south?*

The Open Range

Cattle ranchers soon started letting their herds graze on the huge open grasslands of the Great Plains. The cattle ranchers did not own the grasslands, but they used millions of acres of this government land for their herds of cattle. The government allowed the ranchers to use this land as **open range**, or free grazing land.

Many of the early ranches were owned and run by families. One of the best-known ranches was started by Richard King in Texas in the 1850s. The King Ranch covered more than 1 million acres.

While few ranches were as large as King's, most still covered thousands of acres. The ranches had to be large because the cattle needed a lot of grazing land to get enough to eat. They also needed water. Rivers, lakes, and streams often determined the size and location of ranches. "Wherever there is any water, there is a ranch," said one cattle rancher.

By the 1880s large companies owned many ranches. They used land offered by the government and money from investors to set up huge ranches. About 20 companies invested $12 million in Wyoming ranches alone.

REVIEW *Why were open range lands important to ranchers?*

Ranch Life

Living on a ranch meant hard work for everyone. Women often cooked for all the cowhands and did other chores. Even children did adults' jobs, such as caring for the horses and herding cattle.

One of the most important events in ranch life was the roundup. Each spring and fall ranchers and hired cowhands rounded up the cattle and drove them from the open range to a stockyard. There they marked the cattle with a brand. A brand is a small piece of iron with a long handle. The piece of iron is heated and pressed against the animal's hide to leave a mark. Each rancher's brand had a special shape, so it was easy to tell from the brand who owned which cattle.

Cowhands learned many of their skills from Mexican **vaqueros** (bah•KAY•rohs), the first cowhands. About one-fourth of all early cowhands in the United States were Mexican.

BIOGRAPHY

Bill Pickett 1870?–1932

A ranch boss once described African American cowhand Bill Pickett as "the greatest sweat and dirt cowhand that ever lived—bar none." Pickett worked for much of his life on the 101 Ranch in what is now Oklahoma. He also was part of the 101 Ranch Wild West Show. Pickett, a rodeo rider, was said to have started bulldogging, or steer wrestling. In 1971 Pickett was elected to the National Cowboy Hall of Fame and Western Heritage Center. He was the first African American to receive that honor.

Cowhands like Bill Pickett used braided ropes to round up cattle.

This photograph shows mealtime in a cowhand camp.

Many familiar cowhand words, such as *lariat*, or rope, and *chaps*, or leather trousers, come from Spanish words. The word *rodeo* is the Spanish word for "roundup."

The cowhand has become a legend of the American West. People picture a rider wearing boots with pointed toes, wide-brimmed hat, and leather chaps. But real cowhands had hard lives. They made little money and sometimes worked under poor weather conditions. The long drives and the roundups also kept them away from their families for long periods of time. Most worked as cowhands for only a few years before they settled in towns or on farms. A popular song of this time ended with these words:

> 66 Good-by, old trail boss, I wish
>   you no harm;
> I'm quittin' this business to go
>   on the farm.
> I'll sell my old saddle and buy me
>   a plow;
> And never, no never, will I rope
>   another cow. 99

REVIEW *What work did cowhands do?*

End of the Cattle Kingdom

The cattle industry continued to grow throughout the late 1800s. At its peak, the Cattle Kingdom stretched all the way from Texas to Montana. But it was not long before a number of different problems began to affect cattle ranching.

It was difficult for farmers to grow crops in the same areas where cattle ranchers kept their herds. The cattle wandered into the farmers' fields and trampled or ate the crops. To keep the cattle out, farmers built fences. Some ranchers also built fences to keep cattle from wandering off the ranches.

In 1874 Joseph Glidden invented a new kind of wire that could be used to make fences. Glidden twisted two strands of steel wire together. Then he placed sharp points, or barbs, every few inches along the wire. This new kind of wire became known as **barbed wire**. A farmer or rancher could fence in fields by using wooden posts with this wire strung between them. A barbed-wire fence was easier and cheaper to build than one made of rock or wood.

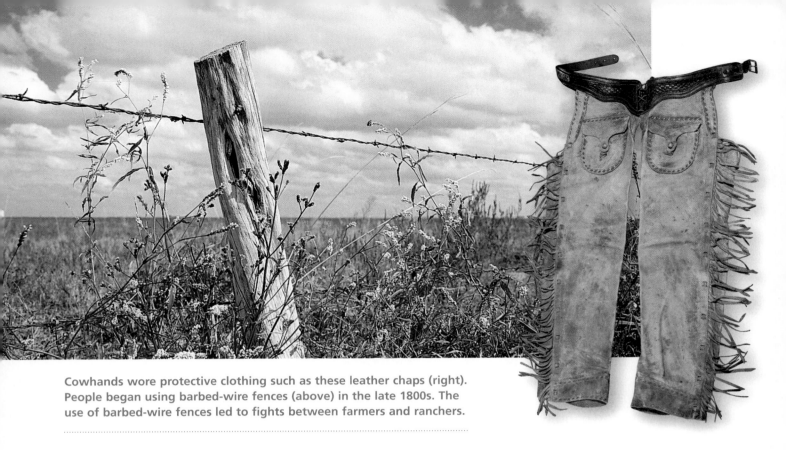

Cowhands wore protective clothing such as these leather chaps (right). People began using barbed-wire fences (above) in the late 1800s. The use of barbed-wire fences led to fights between farmers and ranchers.

Not all farmers and ranchers on the Great Plains wanted fences built on open range land. Farmers did not like having the barbed-wire fences of large cattle ranches near their land. And ranchers did not like fences that kept their cattle from getting to water. Angry farmers and ranchers soon were cutting one another's barbed-wire fences. People even started shooting one another. These fights, called **range wars**, went on through the 1880s.

Finally the ranchers were told they had to move their cattle off government land or buy it. Later, farmers began raising cattle themselves. Before long, the days of the open range and the Cattle Kingdom were over.

REVIEW *How did fences affect the Cattle Kingdom?*

LESSON 2 REVIEW

Check Understanding

❶ **Remember the Facts** How did ranchers in Texas get their cattle to markets in the North?

❷ **Recall the Main Idea** How did ranchers build the Cattle Kingdom?

Think Critically

❸ **Think More About It** Why was it important for cowhands to work together on the long drives?

❹ **Cause and Effect** How did new inventions affect the Cattle Kingdom?

Show What You Know

Diorama Activity Think about the activities that would take place on a ranch. Use pictures, models, or computer visuals to make a diorama of a ranch scene. Display your diorama for the class.

Mining in the West

While homesteaders farmed the Great Plains and cowhands worked on ranches, miners rushed to the West to get rich. After the California gold rush of 1849, there were other finds. Thousands hurried to the Colorado Territory after gold was found near Pikes Peak in 1858. Wagons with the words "Pikes Peak or Bust" painted on their sides crowded the western trails. In 1859 silver was found in the Virginia City area of present-day Nevada. Later, finds in what are now Arizona, Idaho, Montana, and Alaska started a mining boom in the West.

FOCUS
How do individuals and groups play important roles in history?

Main Idea   Read to learn how individual miners and mining companies helped settle the West.

Vocabulary
prospector
boom
bust
vigilance

Mining Booms and Busts

Many of the early **prospectors**—people who searched for gold, silver, or other mineral resources—worked alone. They roamed the West, leading their packhorses loaded with gear and mining tools. With luck they might find $25 worth of gold or silver—a lot of money in those days— by scooping gravel in a stream.

In most places, the minerals above the ground were taken out in just a few years. The land was then said to have been "worked out." To get to the minerals below the ground, mines had to be dug. It became harder for prospectors working alone to find and dig out the minerals. Only large companies could afford to buy heavy equipment and to pay workers to dig mines deep underground.

Towns soon grew up around the mines. Some sprang up almost overnight. Miners at first made shelters out of whatever materials they could find, such as blankets, old shirts, and even potato sacks.

Some miners panned for gold. They used a pan to sift through gravel in a stream.

Chapter 16 • 525

As the towns grew, refineries were built to process the minerals. Stores and other businesses moved in as the mines and refineries hired more workers. Many of these workers came from cities in the East. Others were immigrants from Asia, Europe, and Latin America.

Some mining towns grew quickly. During the mining **boom**, or time of quick economic growth, towns such as Denver, Colorado, and Boise, Idaho, became centers of industry and transportation as well as mining. Other mining towns were just as quickly abandoned. During a **bust**, or time of quick economic decline, people left these towns as soon as all of the gold, silver, or other valuable minerals ran out. Some of these deserted towns, called ghost towns, can still be seen in the West today.

REVIEW *What is the difference between a boom and a bust?*

Life in Mining Communities

Mining towns usually started as mining camps made up of prospectors looking for minerals in the same place. Unlike farmers and ranchers, most prospectors did not take their families with them. Fights often broke out among prospectors, and mining camps were not safe places.

Mining brought many different groups of people to the West in the late 1800s. Prospectors from Mexico, the United States, Chile, and Peru each formed their own settlements. In other mining regions, the settlers were a mix of Americans born in the United States and immigrants from Europe and Asia.

Many Asian immigrants, like those in this photograph (left), came to the United States to work in mining towns. Prospectors weighed gold with a balance (above) to find out how much the gold was worth.

Mining in the West, 1848–1898

ARCTIC OCEAN

170° W

Nome

ALASKA

Fairbanks

160° W

70° N

150° W

Dawson
Klondike

Juneau

CANADA

50° N

140° W

PACIFIC OCEAN

Seattle
Spokane

40° N

Helena
Butte

Boise

Deadwood
Black Hills

Sacramento
San Francisco

Virginia City
Comstock Lode

UNITED STATES

Denver
Leadville
Pikes Peak

130° W

Los Angeles
San Diego

120° W

Tucson
Tombstone

Silver City

30° N

110° W

MEXICO

Tropic of Cancer

Gold
Silver
Copper
▲ Mountain peak
— Present-day border

0   250   500 Miles
0   250   500 Kilometers
Azimuthal Equal-Area Projection

Place During the late 1800s, hundreds of thousands of people hoped to get rich by mining in the West. This map shows many of the places that had deposits of gold, silver, and copper.

■ *What mineral had the largest deposits? Where was it found?*

Irish and Chinese workers who came to work on the transcontinental railroad stayed to work in the mines when the railroad was completed.

As mining camps grew into towns, some families arrived. But there was no law and little order. The towns had no organized governments, and there were no sheriffs. "Street fights were frequent," one writer reported, "and . . . everyone was on his guard against a random shot."

In some mining communities, groups of people would form Vigilance Committees. **Vigilance** means watching over something or someone. Vigilance Committees watched over towns to maintain law and order. As more families arrived, many mining towns set up governments and started schools, hospitals, and churches.

REVIEW *What was a Vigilance Committee?*

LESSON 3 REVIEW

Check Understanding

1 **Remember the Facts** What cities of today started as mining communities?

2 **Recall the Main Idea** How did individual miners and mining companies help settle the West?

Think Critically

3 **Cause and Effect** What caused some mining communities to become ghost towns?

4 **Think More About It** Why do you think early mining communities were dangerous places to live?

Show What You Know

Brainstorming Activity
Think about the problems in mining communities. Work with a partner to prepare a list of five laws you might make in starting a new government in a mining community.

Chapter 16 • **527**

FOCUS

In what ways do people today work to keep their traditions?

Main Idea As you read, find out how Native Americans in the late 1800s worked to keep their ways of life.

Vocabulary

reservation

Conflict in the West

The native peoples of the Great Plains thought the western lands would be theirs forever. The United States government had promised them the lands in a treaty in 1830. At first miners and traders just crossed Indian lands on their way to California and Oregon. By 1862, however, homesteaders and ranchers were settling the Great Plains. Railroad workers arrived, too. The newcomers began killing the Plains Indians' most important resource—the buffalo.

Railroads and the Buffalo

The railroads made it easier for settlers to live in the West. Railroads carried people and supplies to farms, ranches, and mining towns. They took grain, beef, and minerals from the West to cities in the East. But the railroads that made things easy for the settlers caused great problems for the Indians of the Plains.

The problems began when hunters working for the railroads started killing large numbers of buffalo. Hunters shot buffalo to feed the workers who were laying track. William "Buffalo Bill" Cody, a well-known buffalo hunter and army scout, killed enough buffalo to feed 1,000 workers for more than a year.

After the railroads were built, the killing continued. Many buffalo were shot by settlers for their hides, which were sold to make coats. The Plains Indians believed this hunting was wasteful because only the animals' hides were used. When they hunted, the Plains Indians used almost every part of the buffalo to meet their needs.

In the 1860s about 15 million buffalo lived on the Great Plains. Within 20 years, fewer than 1,000 were left. Without the buffalo for food, clothing, and shelter, the traditional way of life of the Plains Indians came to an end.

REVIEW *Why did the buffalo disappear from the Plains?*

In this scene from the 1870s, railroad workers shoot at buffalo blocking the tracks.

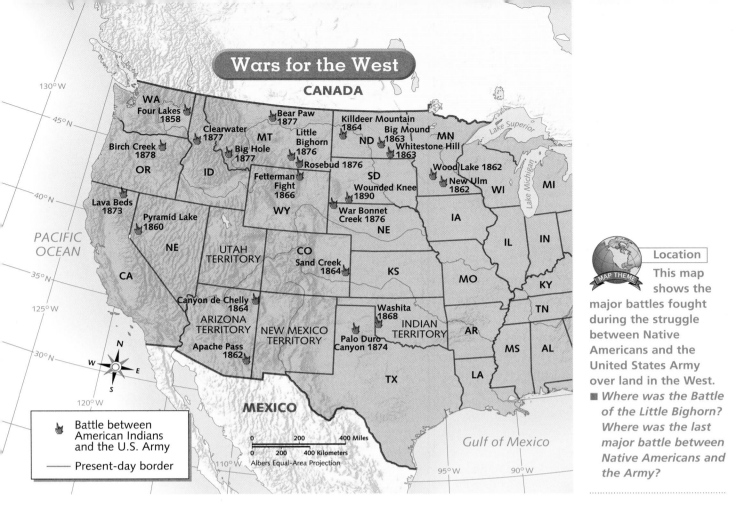

Wars for the West

CANADA

130°W
45°N
40°N
35°N
30°N
125°W
120°W
110°W

WA
Four Lakes 1858
Clearwater 1877
Birch Creek 1878
OR
Big Hole 1877
ID
MT
Little Bighorn 1876
Fetterman Fight 1866
WY
Lava Beds 1873
Pyramid Lake 1860
NE
UTAH TERRITORY
CO
Sand Creek 1864
Canyon de Chelly 1864
ARIZONA TERRITORY
NEW MEXICO TERRITORY
Apache Pass 1862
Palo Duro Canyon 1874
Washita 1868
INDIAN TERRITORY
CA
KS
TX
MEXICO

Bear Paw 1877
Killdeer Mountain 1864
Big Mound 1863
ND
Whitestone Hill 1863
MN
Rosebud 1876
SD
Wood Lake 1862
New Ulm 1862
WI
Wounded Knee 1890
War Bonnet Creek 1876
NE
IA
Lake Superior
Lake Michigan
MI
IL
IN
MO
KY
TN
AR
MS
AL
LA
Gulf of Mexico

PACIFIC OCEAN

N
W   E
S

Battle between American Indians and the U.S. Army
——— Present-day border

0   200   400 Miles
0   200   400 Kilometers
Albers Equal-Area Projection

Location

This map shows the major battles fought during the struggle between Native Americans and the United States Army over land in the West.

■ *Where was the Battle of the Little Bighorn? Where was the last major battle between Native Americans and the Army?*

Fighting Back

The Sioux (SOO) were a powerful tribe of the northern Plains. In the mid-1800s miners and settlers began appearing on Sioux land. To protect these people, in 1865 the United States Army began guarding a road that passed through Sioux land and led to the gold mines of Montana. For three years the Sioux, led by Chief Red Cloud, fought miners and soldiers as they traveled through Indian lands.

Finally, in 1868, the United States government signed a treaty with the Sioux. In the treaty, the government leaders promised that the Indians would have a reservation west of the Missouri River in the Black Hills of the Dakota Territory. A **reservation** is an area of land set aside by the government as a home for Native Americans. In the treaty, the government promised that this land would belong to the Sioux forever.

The treaty did not last long, however. In 1875 gold was discovered on the Great Sioux Reservation. Thousands of miners paid no attention to the treaty and went looking for gold in the Black Hills. The government tried to buy back the land from the Sioux, but the Sioux would not sell it. In 1876 United States soldiers marched in to take the land.

Lieutenant Colonel George Custer led some of the soldiers. Two of the chiefs leading the Sioux were Sitting Bull and Crazy Horse. Custer attacked the Sioux and their Cheyenne allies at the Little Bighorn River. His soldiers were quickly surrounded by 2,500 Indians. In the battle that followed, Custer and all the soldiers he led into the battle were killed.

After the Battle of the Little Bighorn, the government sent more soldiers into the Black Hills. The Sioux were made to return to their reservation, which was now much smaller than the one the government originally had promised.

In 1890 a terrible massacre took place at Wounded Knee Creek in South Dakota. About 300 Sioux were killed. It was the last battle between the Sioux and the United States Army.

REVIEW *Why did Custer attack the Sioux?*

The Nez Perces

The United States government used force against other Indian tribes, including the Nez Perces (NES PER•suhz). The Nez Perces lived on the Columbia Plateau in Oregon. In 1877 the government told the tribe it had to move to a small reservation in Idaho. The Nez Perce leader, Chief Joseph, said no.

During the summer of 1877, Chief Joseph and 800 men, women, and children tried to escape to Canada. They traveled for 15 weeks through the present-day states of Idaho, Wyoming, and Montana. Less than 40 miles (64 km) from the Canadian border, the group was caught by United States soldiers. Telling his people to give up, Chief Joseph said,

66 I am tired of fighting. Our chiefs are killed. . . . It is cold and we have no blankets. Our little children are freezing to death. . . . My heart is sick and sad. From where the sun now stands, I will fight no more forever. 99

REVIEW *Why did Chief Joseph surrender?*

Movement This map shows when Indian tribes lost their lands to the United States government. Some lands were bought through treaties. Others were taken. Some lands were never officially given up.

■ *In what direction were lands lost over time? How does this relate to the movement of settlers?*

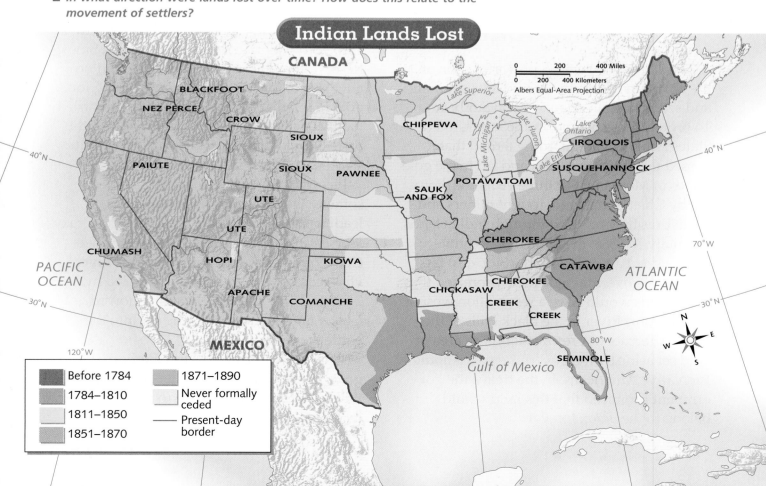

Indian Lands Lost

Legend:
- Before 1784
- 1784–1810
- 1811–1850
- 1851–1870
- 1871–1890
- Never formally ceded
- Present-day border

The Apaches

By 1880 almost all the Indians in the United States had been made to move onto reservations. Among the last to give up were the Apaches (uh•PACH•eez), who were led by a chief named Geronimo. The Apaches fought one of the longest of the many wars between Native Americans and the United States.

The war began in the 1850s when miners and settlers started moving onto the Apache lands of present-day New Mexico and Arizona. Fear and hate grew as each side attacked the other. In 1877 the United States government made the Apaches move to the San Carlos Reservation in Arizona.

On the hot, dry reservation land, it was hard to grow food. Food that the government gave to the reservation was often spoiled. In 1881 the government found out that the Apaches planned to rebel. Soldiers were sent onto the reservation. Afraid that the army would attack, Geronimo and about 75 of his people went to the Sierra Madre of Mexico. From these mountains, they attacked Arizona settlers.

The Indians escaped capture for the next five years. Then, in 1886, an Apache scout working for the United States Army led the soldiers to Geronimo's hiding place. Geronimo told the soldiers, "Once I moved about like the wind. Now I surrender to you and that is all."

Geronimo's surrender ended years of war between American Indians and the government. Although there was still some fighting, most Indians had been made to leave their lands and move onto reservations. Once the Indians were on reservations, the government tried to change the Indians' traditional ways of life. The Indians would not accept this. By the 1920s government officials realized that their efforts to change the Indians were not working. In 1924 Congress granted citizenship to all American Indians and later gave control of reservation lands to the Indians that lived on them.

REVIEW *Why did the Apaches plan to rebel?*

Geronimo's Apache name, Goyaale, means "the smart one." The Mexicans gave him the name Geronimo, which means "Jerome" in Spanish.

LESSON 4 REVIEW

Check Understanding

1 Remember the Facts What was the most important resource for the Plains Indians?

2 Recall the Main Idea How did Native Americans in the late 1800s work to keep their ways of life?

Think Critically

3 Personally Speaking How do you think you might feel if you were made to change your way of life?

4 Think More About It How could the government have ended the conflict with the Plains Indians peacefully? Explain your answer.

Show What You Know

Time Line Activity With a partner, draw and illustrate a time line for the major events in this lesson. Display your time line in the classroom.

CHAPTER 16
REVIEW

| 1840 | 1855 | 1870 |

1849
• California gold rush begins

1862
• Homestead Act passed

CONNECT MAIN IDEAS

Use this graphic organizer to show how the chapter's main ideas are connected. Write the main idea of each lesson. A copy of the organizer appears on page 107 of the Activity Book.

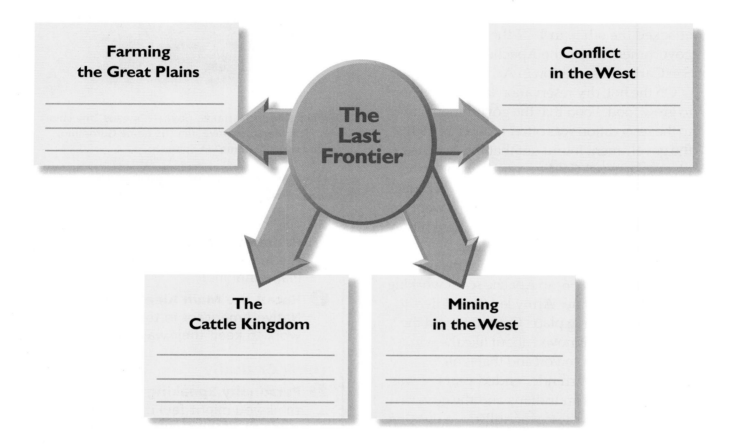

Farming the Great Plains

Conflict in the West

The Last Frontier

The Cattle Kingdom

Mining in the West

WRITE MORE ABOUT IT

Write an Advertisement To attract easterners to the Great Plains, the railroads placed advertisements in newspapers, offering low-cost land to settlers. Write an advertisement describing the benefits of living in the Great Plains region that would encourage people to move there.

Write a Conversation Write a conversation that could have taken place between Chief Joseph and other leaders of the Nez Perces as they tried to escape to Canada in 1877. The conversation should describe the Indians' experiences as they fled from the United States Army soldiers.

| 1885 | • | 1900 | 1915 | • | 1930 |

Late 1800s
• The Cattle Kingdom comes to an end

1924
• U.S. citizenship granted to all American Indians

USE VOCABULARY

Choose a term from this list to complete each of the sentences that follow.

homesteader   **reservation**

open range   **vigilance**

prospector

1. The government allowed ranchers on the Great Plains to use the land as _____.

2. A _____ searched for gold, silver, or other mineral resources.

3. A _____ was a person who settled government land.

4. _____ means watching over someone or something.

5. When gold was discovered on the Sioux _____ , thousands of miners went there to look for gold.

CHECK UNDERSTANDING

6. Why did railroad owners want people to settle on the Great Plains?

7. Who invented a stronger plow that helped farmers cut through the thick sod?

8. How were railroads important to early cow towns?

9. What new invention caused the range wars in the Plains?

10. Who brought law and order to mining towns?

11. What was the last battle between the Sioux and the United States Army?

12. How did the government try to change the way Indians lived?

THINK CRITICALLY

13. **Past to Present** When the buffalo disappeared, the Plains Indians lost a resource that was very important to them. Name some natural resources that, if lost today, would greatly change the way we live.

14. **Personally Speaking** Would you have chosen to be a homesteader, a cowhand, or a prospector? Explain your answer.

APPLY SKILLS

Understand a Climograph Use the climographs on page 519 to answer the questions.

15. Which city has about the same amount of precipitation every month?

16. Which city has a warmer average temperature in March?

17. What conclusion can be made about the average temperatures in June, July, and August for both cities?

READ MORE ABOUT IT

Pioneer Girl by Andrea Warren. Morrow Junior Books. This book tells the true story of Grace McCance, a young pioneer who lived on a Nebraska homestead with her family.

Visit the Internet at **http://www.hbschool.com** for additional resources.

"Give me your tired, your poor, Your huddled masses yearning to breathe free..."

Coming to the United States Today

Since colonial times, people from all over the world have come to the Americas, many of them to the United States. Some chose to come to start new lives, sometimes because of hard times in their homelands.

In 1883 an American named Emma Lazarus wrote "The New Colossus," a poem that helped welcome the hundreds of thousands of people who were immigrating to the United States each year. The poem is written on the base of the Statue of Liberty, which stands in New York Bay. Part of it says

> ❝ Give me your tired, your poor,
> Your huddled masses yearning to
> breathe free . . . ❞

The Statue of Liberty and Lazarus's words continue to welcome the large numbers of immigrants who come to the United States today. The United States still attracts people from all over the world who hope to find better lives and greater freedom. The Statue of Liberty has become a well-known symbol of this freedom.

Think and Apply

Think about why people come to the United States today. Collect magazine and newspaper articles about present-day immigrants. Compare their reasons for moving with those of immigrants of the early twentieth century. Report your findings to the class.

HARCOURT BRACE

Visit the Internet at **http://www.hbschool.com** for additional resources.

CNN Turner Le@rning

Check your media center or classroom video library for the Making Social Studies Relevant videotape of this feature.

UNIT 8
REVIEW

Summarize the Main Ideas
Study the pictures and captions to help you review the events you read about in Unit 8.

Illustrate a Story
Make your own visual summary for one of the following: 1) the growth of hub cities, 2) the migration of African Americans to northern cities, 3) the building of skyscrapers, or 4) the working conditions for factory workers during the late 1800s.

1 After the Civil War, American industry grew and changed. Asian immigrants worked on the transcontinental railroad, which linked the Atlantic and Pacific coasts.

3 During the late 1800s and early 1900s, millions of immigrants came to the United States hoping to find better lives.

4 Offers of free and low-cost land brought many settlers to the Great Plains.

6 Mining towns developed, as prospectors moved to the West in the hope of finding gold.

2 Inventions helped industry grow. A new process allowed steel to be produced more cheaply. The inventions of the lightbulb and the telephone changed everyday life.

5 Ranchers on the Great Plains raised cattle. Cowhands worked hard, especially on cattle drives and roundups.

7 Indians on the Great Plains fought for their homelands against United States soldiers. But by 1890, most Indians in the United States had been forced onto reservations.

UNIT 8
REVIEW

USE VOCABULARY

Write the term that correctly matches each definition below.

boom	**refinery**
monopoly	**regulate**
naturalization	**vaquero**

1. a factory where crude oil is made into usable products

2. almost complete control of an industry

3. to control by law

4. the process through which immigrants become citizens

5. a Mexican cowhand

6. a time of quick economic growth

CHECK UNDERSTANDING

7. Where did new industrial cities develop in the late 1800s and early 1900s?

8. How did workers try to improve their working conditions in the late 1800s?

9. Why was it important for ranchers to get their cattle to northern cities?

10. Who led United States soldiers into the Battle of the Little Bighorn? What caused this battle?

THINK CRITICALLY

11. **Past to Present** How are industries in the United States today like industries in the late 1800s? How are they different?

12. **Think More About It** Why do you think immigrants often moved to neighborhoods made up of other immigrants from the same country?

13. **Personally Speaking** Suppose you were a worker in the late 1800s. How might you feel about people who thought that government should leave factory owners and their businesses alone? Explain your answer.

14. **Cause and Effect** What effect did the American Federation of Labor have on the treatment of workers by business leaders?

APPLY SKILLS

Use a Time Zone Map Suppose you live in Nevada and you have a friend who lives in Utah. Use the map below to answer the questions.

15. When you are getting ready for school at 7:00 A.M., what time is it in Utah?

16. When your friend gets home from school at 3:00 P.M. in Utah, what time is it in Nevada?

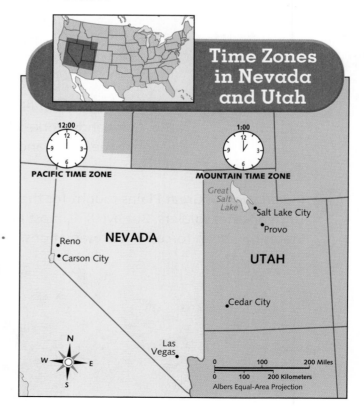

Time Zones in Nevada and Utah

538 • Unit 8

REMEMBER

- Share your ideas.
- Cooperate with others to plan your work.
- Take responsibility for your work.
- Help one another.
- Show your group's work to the class.
- Discuss what you learned by working together.

ACTIVITY

Make a Diorama

With some classmates, make a diorama that shows a ranch, a homestead, an Indian village, or a mining camp. Include a scene that shows how the people lived and the work they did. Display your diorama in the classroom.

ACTIVITY

Paint a Mural

Work with a group of classmates to paint a mural that shows how cities were changing in the late 1800s and early 1900s. Show both the problems that cities faced and the opportunities they offered. Display the mural in your classroom.

ACTIVITY

Hold a Debate

Hold a debate on the need for labor unions in the late 1800s and early 1900s. To prepare for the debate, work in groups. With the other members of your group, make a list of the issues that concern factory owners. Then make a list of the issues that concern workers. Your class should decide which groups will represent each side in the debate. During the debate, group members should take turns speaking.

Unit Project Wrap-Up

Perform a Simulation Work with two of your classmates to complete the Unit Project on page 477. Write a conversation that might have taken place among three immigrants from different countries. From your lists, you and your partners should decide on which details to include in your conversation. You should also decide which country each member of your group will represent. Write the conversation with your partners, and perform it for your classmates. While role-playing the conversation, each member of your group should hold the flag from the country he or she is representing.

BECOMING A WORLD POWER

By the end of the 1890s, the United States had entered a new time in its history. Until then the nation had worked mostly to develop its own resources, away from the rest of the world. Now the United States was looking beyond its national borders. It was ready to become a world leader.

◄ Navy battleships return home after the American victory in the Spanish-American War.

UNIT THEMES

■ Conflict and Cooperation

■ Commonality and Diversity

■ Individualism and Interdependence

■ Continuity and Change

Unit Project

Make a Class Mural Complete this project as you study Unit 9. As you read, write a list of details about events described in the unit. Choose several of the events to illustrate in a mural. Give your mural a title, and share it with your classmates.

CANADA

Seattle
Range
River
WASHINGTON

Portland
Columbia

MONTANA

RUSSIA
ARCTIC OCEAN

ALASKA TERRITORY
CANADA

Bering Sea

0   400 Miles
0   400 Kilometers

PACIFIC OCEAN

Cascade

OREGON

Pacific

IDAHO

Great
Northern
Missouri
River
Northern
Pacific

ROCKY

WYOMING

Snake
River

Union   Pacific

Ogden
Great
Salt
Lake
Salt Lake
City

Cheyenne

○ City with more than 100,000 people

• Other important city

Major railroad

United States

United States territory

Sierra Nevada

Southern

Central

Pacific

GREAT
BASIN

UTAH

MOUNTAINS

Denver ○
COLORADO

Sacramento

○ San Francisco

NEVADA

Colorado
River

CALIFORNIA

Mojave
Desert

Atlantic   and   Pacific

Albuquerque

Topeka   and   Santa Fe

Los Angeles

ARIZONA
TERRITORY

NEW MEXICO
TERRITORY

HAWAII
TERRITORY

PACIFIC
OCEAN

0   100 Miles
0   100 Kilometers

PACIFIC
OCEAN

Southern

Pacific

El Paso

Rio Grande

MEXICO

0   200   400 Miles
0   200   400 Kilometers
Albers Equal-Area Projection

1870   1890   1910

1898
Spanish-American War
PAGE 548

1917
U.S. Enters World War I
PAGE 560

The United States, 1890s

CANADA

MAINE
• Augusta

NORTH DAKOTA
• Fargo

MINNESOTA
• Duluth
Minneapolis ○○ St. Paul

SOUTH DAKOTA

WISCONSIN
Milwaukee ○
Chicago ○

MICHIGAN
Detroit ○

Lake Superior
Lake Huron
Lake Michigan
Lake Erie
Lake Ontario

NEW YORK
VT   NH
Albany •   Boston ○
New York Central   Providence ○
Buffalo ○   Rochester •   MA
CT
RHODE ISLAND

Jersey City ○○ New York City
Newark
NEW JERSEY
Philadelphia

IOWA
NEBRASKA
Omaha •
Platte R.

Ft. Wayne •
INDIANA
Indianapolis •

OHIO
Columbus •
Cleveland ○
PA
Pittsburgh •
Pennsylvania
B&O
MD ○ Baltimore
DE
Washington, D.C.

ILLINOIS
Union Pacific
Missouri River
Illinois Central

Kansas City ○
Kansas Pacific
KANSAS

MISSOURI
St. Louis ○
Mississippi River

Cincinnati •
Pennsylvania River
WEST VIRGINIA
Louisville •
Ohio River

KENTUCKY

VIRGINIA
APPALACHIAN MOUNTAINS

OKLAHOMA TERRITORY
Arkansas River

ARKANSAS
Little Rock •

TENNESSEE
Tennessee R.
Southern Rail

NORTH CAROLINA

SOUTH CAROLINA
Columbia •

INDIAN TERRITORY

TEXAS
Texas and Pacific
Dallas •

MISSISSIPPI
Montgomery •
ALABAMA

Atlanta •
GEORGIA
Savannah •

Southern Pacific
Houston •

LOUISIANA
New Orleans ○

Jacksonville •

FLORIDA

Gulf of Mexico

ATLANTIC OCEAN

N
W   E
S

1930   1950

1929
Great Depression Begins
PAGE 575

1941
U.S. Enters World War II
PAGE 585

THIS MAN'S WAR

by CHARLES F. MINDER

When the United States took part in events in other parts of the world, it was more than a government taking action. Individual Americans had an important part in each story. In the first half of the twentieth century, the United States fought in two world wars. More than 4 million American soldiers fought in the first war, which the United States entered against Germany in 1917. Read now from a letter written by one of those young soldiers to his mother. In it Charles Minder, from New York, describes how he felt about fighting in a war.

Thursday, August 15, 1918

Dear Mother,

. . . I felt a couple of bullets cut the long grass over my head. If I told you I wasn't scared, I would be a liar. I felt like a dumb animal cornered and that my end was near. As soon as it stopped a little, I said, "Come on, men!" and led the way back. It was starting to get light and we had to make the top of the hill and get back into the town, or we would be out of luck. We double-timed[1] up the hill gladly, with all our equipment. Just near the top, we passed a well, and the bullets started to pick up the dirt all around us.

_____

[1] **double-timed:** moved quickly

Some German machine gunner had spotted us. We all knelt on the other side of the well and, one by one, managed to crawl just a little farther, where we got behind a cement wall. It was almost daylight. . . . I looked at my watch and it was five o'clock. We were all dead tired and fell asleep and didn't wake up until nine this morning. We were hungry and opened up a couple of cans of corned-beef and hardtack[2] and, with some water in our canteens, that was our breakfast.

We saw some signs showing we were in a town called Fismes[3]. It sure had been wrecked by artillery[4] fire. I don't remember seeing one house that wasn't hit, and all being deserted, it was a very mysterious looking town. Marching back thru the town, we saw hundreds of dead Germans and Americans lying where they fell. It was the most gruesome sight I have seen yet, and made me realize more than ever, how ridiculous and unnecessary this business of war is.

I figured that the rest of the company must have returned to the next town over, Villersávoye, where we started out from yesterday afternoon. I was right, and when we got back there at noon today, they were all surprised to see me and my squad. They thought that we had been killed last night.

Three of the men in my squad, who were with me last night, went to the hospital this afternoon, Purcell, Kujawa and Stadler. My squad is shot to pieces, yet we are going back again tonight, when it gets dark, to where we started for yesterday.

We could smell some very beautiful lilacs last night while we were on the way up and took deep whiffs of their perfume in the dark, thinking that there was a lilac bush near by. We found out today that the smell was gas. Our Captain and Lieutenant Krell were gassed, and a lot of men in the other two platoons. My throat is raw and my eyes have been watering all afternoon, but outside of that I am all right.

We just had a good meal at four o'clock, and everybody has been resting and cleaning up this afternoon, as we go up again tonight to relieve the other machine-gun company that is in the line. I found out this afternoon that the place where we were last night is called the "Valley of Death." It is such a terrible position, because the Germans are on top of the hill on the other side and can shoot down on top of us and across the valley into the town of Fismes. It is one hot spot. So it looks like we are in for a little excitement. As soon as it gets dark, we start, so will close, Mother Dear. I wish I was home now.

Charles

---

[2] **hardtack:** biscuits baked hard to last a long time

[3] **Fismes:** (FEEM)
[4] **artillery:** large guns on wheels

17

THE UNITED STATES AND THE WORLD

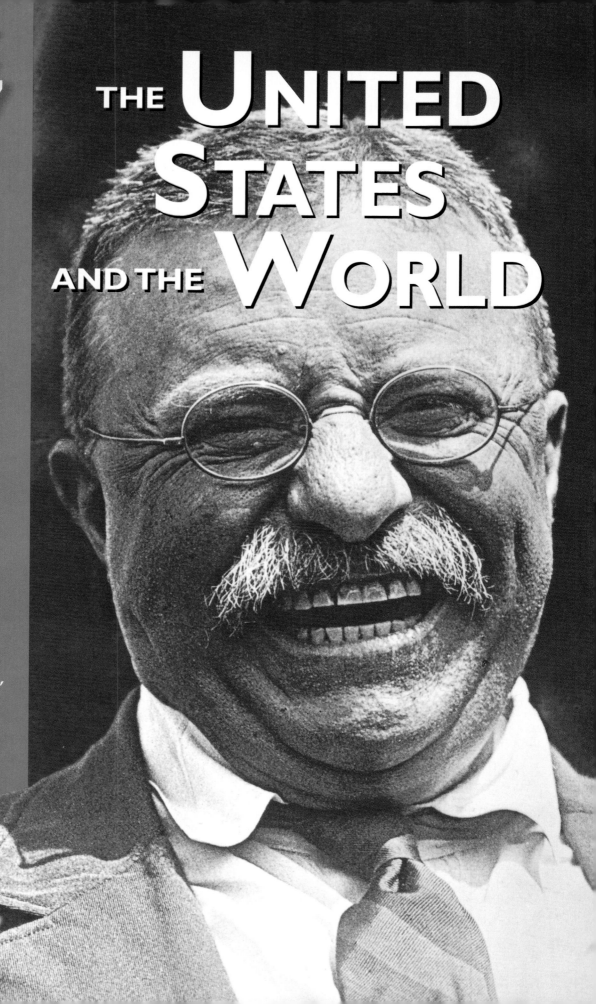

"I have always been fond of the West African proverb: Speak softly and carry a big stick, you will go far."

Theodore Roosevelt, Governor of New York and later President of the United States, 1900

Building an Empire

By the late 1800s, the United States led the world in industry and agriculture. Like many European nations at that time, the United States wanted to stretch its borders and set up colonies. Now that the western frontier had been settled, many Americans were ready to find new frontiers. American leaders also felt that new lands would bring new sources of raw materials and new markets for the nation's goods. The time seemed right for the United States to become a world power.

FOCUS

Why might a country today decide to take a more active part in what is going on in the world?

Main Idea As you read, find out why the United States decided at the end of the 1800s to add to its territory and power around the world.

Vocabulary

imperialism
armistice

Alaska

In 1867 the United States bought Alaska from Russia for $7.2 million—about two cents an acre. Most Americans knew little about Alaska or its peoples. Many thought it was foolish of the United States to buy a piece of land so far north. Some called it the "Polar Bear Garden."

Then, in 1896, prospectors found gold in the Klondike region. The Klondike was in Canada's Yukon Territory, near its border with Alaska. The discovery started a gold rush like the one in California in 1849. From 1897 to 1899 more than 100,000 people raced to Alaska hoping to get rich. Some did find gold. But conditions were harsh, and thousands died.

Alaska brought new wealth to the United States. The land was full of natural resources, such as fish, timber, coal, and copper. Because buying Alaska turned out to be so profitable, many Americans soon thought the United States should try to get more new lands across the seas.

REVIEW *What caused people to become interested in Alaska?*

The discovery of gold brought many prospectors to Alaska with hopes of getting rich.

The Hawaiian Islands

The Hawaiian Islands are about 2,400 miles (3,862 km) southwest of California, in the Pacific Ocean. Polynesian people in the Pacific migrated to Hawaii by the eighth century, and the islands were ruled by Polynesian kings and queens. By the 1800s many Americans had settled there.

Among the first Americans to arrive in Hawaii were Christian missionaries. They began to settle in the islands about 1820. Soon after, American business people started cattle ranches and sugar plantations there. By the 1870s American missionaries and sugar planters controlled much of the land and trade in Hawaii.

In 1887 the Hawaiian king, Kalakaua (kah•lah•KAH•ooh•ah), tried to keep the Americans from taking over the islands. The Americans then decided to take away the king's authority. They wanted the United States to annex Hawaii. The Americans made Kalakaua sign a new constitution that left the Hawaiian monarchy without authority.

In 1893 the new Hawaiian ruler, Queen Liliuokalani (lih•lee•uh•woh•kuh•LAH•nee), tried to bring back the monarchy's authority. Liliuokalani promised to make "Hawaii for Hawaiians" once again. But the Americans made her give up her throne. They took over the government and set up a republic. In 1898 Congress decided to annex Hawaii to the United States.

REVIEW *How did Hawaii become a part of the United States?*

War with Spain

After the United States took control of Alaska and Hawaii, some people accused the country's leaders of **imperialism**, or empire building. This brought the United States into conflict with European nations that had also spread beyond their borders—especially Spain.

By the end of the 1800s, Cuba and Puerto Rico were the only two colonies Spain had left in the Western Hemisphere. Many Cubans wanted their island to be independent from Spain. Twice, in 1868 and in 1895, they had rebelled against Spanish rule, but the rebellions failed.

Lydia Liliuokalani became queen of Hawaii in 1891. Queen Lil', as she was called, wrote the well-known song "Aloha Oe," or "Farewell to Thee." The Hawaiian Islands (below) are beautiful volcanic lands.

Nearly one-fourth of the United States soldiers who fought in Cuba were African Americans. The soldiers in this photograph served in the United States Cavalry. All soldiers who had fought in the war were given a medal like the one shown here.

Many Americans supported the Cubans' fight for independence, including Americans who had moved there to start businesses. Newspapers in the United States were full of stories about Spain's harsh rule of the island. As the fighting continued, President William McKinley ordered the battleship *Maine* to Havana, Cuba, to protect the lives and property of Americans living there. On February 15, 1898, the *Maine* exploded in Havana's harbor. More than 200 sailors were killed. It was not clear why the ship blew up. The United States, however, blamed Spain. "Remember the *Maine!*" Americans cried, calling for action. On April 25, the United States declared war on Spain.

The first battles of the Spanish-American War were not fought in Cuba. They were fought halfway around the world. Less

The Spanish-American War: Caribbean, 1898

→ American forces
→ Spanish forces
♨ Battle

FLORIDA
Tampa
Gulf of Mexico
Key West
Bahamas
ATLANTIC OCEAN
64°W
24°N
Tropic of Cancer
Maine exploded — Havana
Cuba
San Juan Hill — Santiago
HAITI DOMINICAN REPUBLIC
San Juan
Jamaica
Guánica
Puerto Rico
16°N
Caribbean Sea
72°W
80°W

0   150   300 Miles
0   150   300 Kilometers
Albers Equal-Area Projection

Movement This map shows the main movements of Spanish and American forces around Cuba.

■ *About how many miles from Tampa is the place where the* Maine *exploded?*

than two weeks after war was declared, the United States Navy was sent to the Philippine Islands. Led by Commodore George Dewey, the navy destroyed the Spanish fleet and captured Manila Bay.

In the United States, many thousands of Americans volunteered to fight in the war. The army grew from about 30,000 soldiers to more than 274,000. Among those who volunteered was Theodore Roosevelt, who had been assistant secretary of the navy. He had quit his job to form a fighting company made up mostly of cowhands and college athletes. In Cuba, the Rough Riders, as they were called, took part in the Battle of San Juan Hill and the siege of Santiago. The siege ended on July 17, 1898, and the Spanish in Santiago soon signed an armistice. An **armistice** is an agreement to stop fighting a war.

The Spanish-American War lasted less than four months. More than 5,000 American soldiers died, most from diseases such as malaria and yellow fever. But the war helped the United States become a stronger world power. Under the peace treaty, Spain agreed to give the United States control of Cuba, Puerto Rico, Guam, and the Philippine Islands. Cuba became an independent country in 1901. The Philippine Islands gained independence in 1946. Puerto Rico and Guam remain territories of the United States today.

REVIEW *Why did the United States go to war with Spain?*

Theodore Roosevelt

Theodore Roosevelt returned from Cuba well known and well liked. He was soon elected governor of New York. Two years later he was Vice President, serving under President William McKinley. On September 6, 1901, President McKinley was shot in Buffalo, New York, by a person who was against the government. McKinley died eight days later, and Roosevelt became President.

Roosevelt was a man of action. He believed that the United States should actively use its power to shape events in the world. He believed that what happened in the rest of the world affected the United States.

When Russia and Japan were at war with one another in 1904 and 1905, President Roosevelt helped the two nations work out a peace agreement. Because of his work, Roosevelt became the first American to receive the Nobel Peace Prize. The Nobel Peace Prize is awarded each year to a person or an organization that helps bring peace to the world.

In 1907 President Roosevelt, the peacemaker, decided to remind other countries that he was also the leader of a powerful military force. He sent a fleet of warships, painted a dazzling white, on a world cruise. According to Roosevelt, the Great White Fleet

BIOGRAPHY

José Martí
1853–1895

José Martí (mar•TEE), a leader of the Cuban revolution, is a national hero in Cuba today. He was a writer who spoke out against Spanish rule in the late 1800s. Many of Martí's poems, articles, and speeches were printed in newspapers in the United States. They helped tell the Cubans' story. Martí died three years before the Spanish-American War. Even so, many people feel he did more than any other Cuban leader to win Cuba's freedom from Spain.

United States Possessions, 1900

0   1,000   2,000 Miles
0   1,000   2,000 Kilometers
Scale accurate at equator
Miller Cylindrical Projection

RUSSIA

ASIA

CHINA

JAPAN

PACIFIC   OCEAN

ALASKA
1867

CANADA

NORTH
AMERICA

UNITED STATES

ATLANTIC
OCEAN

ALEUTIAN ISLANDS
1867

MIDWAY
ISLANDS
1867

40°N

Tropic of Cancer

CUBA
1898

PUERTO
RICO
1898

WAKE ISLAND
1898

JOHNSTON
ISLAND
1858

HAWAIIAN
ISLANDS
1898

MEXICO

PHILIPPINE
ISLANDS
1898

GUAM
1898

HOWLAND ISLAND
1857

KINGMAN REEF   1858

PALMYRA ISLAND   1898

N
W   E
S

BAKER ISLAND
1857

JARVIS ISLAND   1857

Equator   0°

100°W

140°E

AMERICAN
SAMOA
1899

SOUTH
AMERICA

AUSTRALIA

180°

140°W

U.S. possession
1857   Date acquired

Location   This map shows when the United States gained lands in different places around the world.

■ *In what year did the United States acquire the lands that would become the state of Alaska? When did it acquire the lands that would become the state of Hawaii?*

showed the world that now "the Pacific was as much our home as the Atlantic."

REVIEW *Why did Roosevelt believe the United States should use its power to shape events in the world?*

The Panama Canal

One of President Roosevelt's goals was to build a canal in Panama, in Central America. The canal would link the Atlantic and Pacific oceans. This, in turn, would link American territories in the Atlantic with those in the Pacific. "I wish to see the United States the dominant power on the shores of the Pacific Ocean," Roosevelt said.

For years people had talked about building a canal in Panama. Such a canal would cut across the isthmus that joined North America and South America. A French company had tried to build such a canal in the 1880s but had given up because of the thick jungle and the diseases that killed many of the workers.

In 1902 Congress voted to build the canal. But the Isthmus of Panama did not belong to the United States. It belonged to Colombia, a South American country. The United States offered Colombia $10 million for the right to build the canal. But Colombia would not agree to sell.

Roosevelt then spread the word that he would welcome a revolution in Panama to end Colombian rule. He sent the United States Navy to protect the isthmus. If a revolution began, the navy was to keep Colombian troops from landing on shore.

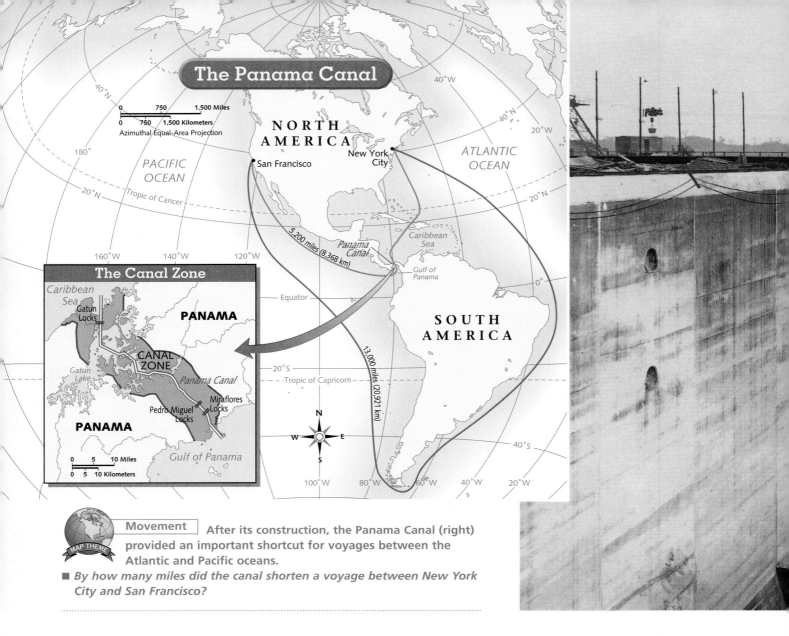

The Panama Canal

750   1,500 Miles
0   750   1,500 Kilometers
Azimuthal Equal-Area Projection

NORTH AMERICA

PACIFIC OCEAN

ATLANTIC OCEAN

New York City

San Francisco

5,200 miles (8,368 km)

Panama Canal

Caribbean Sea

Gulf of Panama

Equator

SOUTH AMERICA

13,000 miles (20,921 km)

Tropic of Capricorn

The Canal Zone

Caribbean Sea

PANAMA

Gatun Locks

CANAL ZONE

Gatun Lake

Panama Canal

Pedro Miguel Locks

Miraflores Locks

PANAMA

Gulf of Panama

0   5   10 Miles
0   5   10 Kilometers

Movement After its construction, the Panama Canal (right) provided an important shortcut for voyages between the Atlantic and Pacific oceans.

■ *By how many miles did the canal shorten a voyage between New York City and San Francisco?*

Within three months such a revolution took place, and the people of Panama formed a new nation. Panama's new leaders then gave the United States the right to build the canal. The United States would control the canal and an area 5 miles (8 km) wide on each side of it.

Work on the canal began in 1904. Workers guided huge earth-moving machines to cut down the trees and thick growth of jungle. Engineers designed huge canal locks to help ships move through the waterway.

Unlike the French workers who had first tried to build the canal, American workers were able to stay healthy. Doctors now knew

that malaria and yellow fever, the diseases that had stopped the French, were carried by mosquitoes. The Americans learned to control the mosquitoes by draining all of the swamps where the insects lived.

Building the canal took ten years and cost about $380 million. In 1906 Roosevelt visited the canal site. It was the first time a President had left the United States while in office. The first ship passed through the Panama Canal on August 15, 1914. Today the canal helps move people and goods around the world.

REVIEW *Why did the United States want to build the Panama Canal?*

Check Understanding

1 Remember the Facts What lands did the United States gain in the 1800s?

2 Recall the Main Idea Why did the United States decide at the end of the 1800s to add to its territory and power around the world?

Think Critically

3 Explore Viewpoints What do you think Queen Liliuokalani meant by the phrase, "Hawaii for Hawaiians"?

4 Past to Present Do you think the Panama Canal is as important today as it was when it opened? Why or why not?

Show What You Know

Globe Activity Work with a partner to trace water routes around the world. Use your finger to follow the routes a ship might follow from the east coast to the west coast of the United States before and after the opening of the Panama Canal.

Compare Map Projections

1. Why Learn This Skill?

Because the Earth is round and maps are flat, maps cannot represent the Earth's shape exactly. Only a globe, which is round, can do that. To show the round Earth on a flat piece of paper, cartographers must change the shape of the globe, splitting or stretching it to make it flat. As a result, every map has **distortions**, or areas that are not accurate.

Over the years, cartographers have found different ways of showing the Earth on flat paper. These different views are called **projections**. All map projections have distortions, but different kinds of projections have different kinds of distortions. Identifying areas on a map that are distorted will help you understand how different kinds of maps can best be used.

2. Understand the Process

Map A and Map B both show the same area of the Earth, but they are different projections. Map A is an equal-area projection. Equal-area projections show the sizes of regions in correct relation to one another, but they distort, or change, their shapes. There are many kinds of equal-area projections. The azimuthal (a•zuh•MUH•thul) equal-area projection on

Map A: Empire Building, 1914

Legend:
- Belgian
- British
- Dutch
- French
- German
- Italian
- Japanese
- Portuguese
- Spanish
- American

0   1,000   2,000 Miles
0   1,000   2,000 Kilometers
Azimuthal Equal-Area Projection

Map B: Empire Building, 1914

Legend:
- Belgian
- British
- Dutch
- French
- German
- Italian
- Japanese
- Portuguese
- Spanish
- American

0   1,000   2,000 Miles
0   1,000   2,000 Kilometers
Miller Cylindrical Projection

Map A is one kind. Another is the Albers equal-area projection.

Map B is a conformal projection. Notice that the meridians are all an equal distance apart. On a globe, however, these lines get closer together as they approach the poles. Notice also that the parallels closer to the poles are farther apart than those near the equator. On a globe the parallels are all equal distances apart. Conformal projections show directions correctly, but they distort sizes, especially of the places near the poles. The Miller cylindrical projection used on Map B is just one example of a conformal projection. Another is the orthographic (or•thuh•GRAF•ihk) projection.

Use Map A and Map B to answer the following questions.

1 On which parts of Maps A and B do the shapes of the land areas appear to be the same?

2 On which map does Africa appear to be larger? On which map is the size of Africa more accurate?

3 On which map do the meridians get closer together toward the poles?

4 On which map does the space between the parallels get greater toward the poles?

3. Think and Apply

Look at the maps in the Atlas on pages A2–A15 to see other map projections. Write a paragraph about the advantages and disadvantages of using equal-area and conformal projections.

FOCUS

How do people today work to improve life in the United States?

Main Idea As you read, look for ways people worked to improve life in the United States in the early 1900s.

Vocabulary

progressive
commission
conservation
merit system
political boss
civil rights

Progressives and Reform

President Theodore Roosevelt used the authority of his office in many ways. He added to American power in the world. He also worked to bring about needed reform at home. Roosevelt and his supporters were called **progressives** because they wanted to improve government and make life better. For some people, this is what progress meant.

The Square Deal

Roosevelt believed it was the job of the federal government to help citizens as much as possible. He started a program called the Square Deal. Under this program, everyone was to be given the same opportunities to succeed.

To make sure that people could get fair treatment, Roosevelt wanted the federal government to make rules for businesses. He set up or increased the authority of special committees called **commissions**. One of these was the Interstate Commerce Commission. Part of its job was to study railroad fares. When the commission decided fares were too high, it made railroad owners lower them.

Roosevelt asked Congress to give the government the authority to see that foods and medicines were safe. In 1906 Congress passed the Pure Food and Drug Act. The act said that all foods and medicines had to meet government safety standards. Congress also passed the Meat Inspection Act. This act said that inspectors would go to all plants that packaged meat to make sure the meat was handled safely.

Roosevelt also was interested in conservation. **Conservation** is a way to protect the environment by keeping natural resources from being wasted or destroyed. Roosevelt set aside millions of acres of land in different parts of the country as national parks. Among these were the Grand Canyon, Mesa Verde, and Glacier national parks.

REVIEW *What was the Square Deal?*

The explorer and writer John Muir helped persuade Congress to establish Yosemite (yoh•SEH•muh•tee) National Park in 1890. Muir (right) met there with Theodore Roosevelt (left) in 1903.

State and City Reforms

Progressives also worked in state governments. In Wisconsin, Governor Robert La Follette did for his state what Roosevelt was doing for the nation. La Follette made so many reforms that Roosevelt called Wisconsin a "laboratory of democracy."

Elected officials in many states had been giving government jobs to people who did favors for them. To keep this from happening in Wisconsin, Robert La Follette started a **merit system** to make sure that people were qualified for their jobs. Each person applying for a government job was given a test. The person who got the highest score on the test got the job.

La Follette wanted to help workers. He asked the state legislature to pass a law saying that a workday must be no more than ten hours. A second law was passed listing jobs for which children could not be hired. A third law said that the state would pay workers who were hurt on their jobs. To provide the money to do this, factory owners had to make payments to the state.

People in other states called what La Follette was doing the Wisconsin Idea. Many states copied his changes. By 1918, 20 of the 48 states had passed progressive laws like those in Wisconsin.

Many progressive reforms affected city governments, which were often run by political bosses. Some city leaders—especially mayors—were called **political bosses** because they controlled the city government. Most of these bosses had dishonest people working for them. Some of these people gave money to voters so they would vote for the boss. Sometimes they cheated in elections by counting the votes of people who were not citizens or of people who had died. In this way, political bosses often were elected to office again and again.

THE "BRAINS"
THAT ACHIEVED THE TAMMANY VICTORY AT THE ROCHESTER DEMOCRATIC CONVENTION.

This political cartoon by Thomas Nast suggests that money was used to influence political decision making in New York City. Nast's political cartoons helped bring an end to William Tweed's boss rule in the city.

One of the best-known political bosses was William Tweed. Boss Tweed, as he was called, ran New York City for years and robbed it of millions of dollars. He protected himself by controlling the city police department.

Progressives wanted to end boss rule. One way to do this was to change the form of city government. To keep one person—the mayor—from having all the authority, some city governments set up commissions made up of several people. Each commission member took care of one part of the government, such as the police department, the fire department, or water services. Before long, more than 400 cities had set up commission governments.

REVIEW *What reforms were made by states and cities?*

Civil Rights

Progressive leaders showed what governments could do to make life better for many of the nation's people. However, they did little about the problems of prejudice. So

Booker T. Washington
1856–1915

Booker T. Washington was born into slavery. Freed after the Civil War, he worked his way through school as a janitor. After graduating he became a teacher. During Reconstruction, he had seen how hard it was for African American people to fight prejudice. He believed that African Americans could get fair treatment only by becoming skilled workers. Washington led an effort to provide African Americans with more opportunities for education and training. In 1881 he helped found Tuskegee Institute, a trade school for African Americans, in Alabama.

W. E. B. Du Bois
1868–1963

W. E. B. Du Bois strongly disagreed with Washington's point of view. He wanted African Americans to improve their situation by fighting for equal rights. Du Bois graduated from Fisk University and received a doctorate from Harvard. A gifted speaker, teacher, and writer, he devoted his career to improving life for African Americans. In the later years of his life, Du Bois believed that prejudice in the United States would never be broken down. He decided to leave the United States in 1961 and spent the rest of his life in the West African country of Ghana (GAH•nuh).

African American leaders used progressive ideas to try to solve the problem.

One important African American leader of this time was W. E. B. Du Bois (doo•BOYS). In 1909 Du Bois and other progressive leaders formed the National Association for the Advancement of Colored People (NAACP). Members of the NAACP worked to change state laws that did not give full civil rights to African Americans. **Civil rights** are the rights guaranteed to all citizens by the Constitution.

The National Urban League, founded in 1910, also worked for equal rights. It worked to find jobs and homes for African Americans living in cities.

REVIEW *How did people try to fight prejudice in the early 1900s?*

LESSON 2 REVIEW

Check Understanding

❶ **Remember the Facts**   Who were the leading progressives in the United States in the early 1900s?

❷ **Recall the Main Idea**   How did people work to improve life in the United States in the early 1900s?

Think Critically

❸ **Past to Present**   How do people work for civil rights today?

❹ **Think More About It**   How were the reforms of the Wisconsin Idea examples of progressive thinking?

Show What You Know

Simulation Activity   Imagine that you are a progressive reformer from the early 1900s. Think about one of the problems you read about in this lesson. State your view about the problem to the class.

The Great War

FOCUS
Why do people today sometimes decide to take part in other people's disagreements?

Main Idea As you read, find out why the leaders of the United States decided to enter World War I.

Vocabulary
alliance
military draft
no-man's-land
isolation

The United States entered the twentieth century as a strong nation. When conflict among the nations of Europe exploded into war in 1914, the United States hoped to stay out of the fighting. In time, however, the nation's leaders decided to enter what was then known as the Great War. Later it would be called World War I.

Dangerous Alliances

On one side in the war were the Allied Powers, or Allies—including Russia, France, Britain, and Italy. On the other side were the Central Powers—Germany, Austria-Hungary, the Ottoman Empire, and Bulgaria.

The European countries had formed these **alliances**, or partnerships, to protect themselves. In each alliance the members promised to help one another if they were attacked by another country. They hoped that this would prevent war. But it had the opposite effect.

Serbia, a country in southern Europe, bordered Austria-Hungary. Many Serbs lived in the southern part of Austria-Hungary and longed to be a part of their Serbian homeland. On June 28, 1914, a Serb rebel shot and killed two members of Austria-Hungary's royal family in the city of Sarajevo (sar•uh•YAY•voh). Austria-Hungary soon declared war on Serbia. Because of their alliances, the European nations were drawn one by one into the conflict.

At first the United States did not join an alliance. President Woodrow Wilson asked Americans to be "impartial in thought as well as in action." He and many other Americans wanted the country to be neutral in the war.

But Americans were soon drawn into the conflict. Prowling the seas were German submarines, called *Unterseeboots*, or U-boats. On May 7, 1915, a U-boat sank the British passenger ship *Lusitania*. Almost 1,200 people were killed. Among the dead were 128 Americans. People

This 1917 poster of "Uncle Sam" was used to bring people into the United States Army.

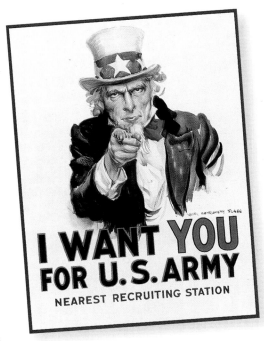

Chapter 17 • **559**

in the United States were angry at Germany. Some began to believe the United States should enter the war on the side of the Allies. But President Wilson still hoped to keep the United States neutral. In 1916 he was again elected President. His campaign slogan was "He kept us out of war."

REVIEW *Which countries were the Allied Powers and which were the Central Powers?*

The United States Enters the War

In early 1917 German leaders said that U-boats would attack all ships in British waters. U-boats then sank three American merchant ships, killing many Americans aboard. President Wilson had finally had enough. On April 2, 1917, he asked the United States Congress to declare war on Germany, saying, "The world must be made safe for democracy." Four days later, the United States joined the Allied Powers.

The United States was not ready for war. Its army was small, and it did not have many weapons. To make the army larger, Congress passed the Selective Service Act. The new law provided for a **military draft**, a way of bringing people into the army. All men between the ages of 21 and 30 had to sign up with special committees called draft boards. Soldiers were then chosen from the list of names. A year later the draft age range was changed to include men between the ages of 18 and 45.

Many Americans thought the draft was a good idea since it would bring together soldiers of different backgrounds. However, many Native Americans, Mexican Americans, African Americans, and immigrants faced the same prejudices in the military as they did at home. They were kept in separate units and were not allowed to do certain jobs. Yet all American soldiers, no matter what their backgrounds, faced the same dangers.

REVIEW *What was the purpose of the draft?*

The *Lusitania,* shown in port, was a passenger ship. Before the ship was attacked, a warning (right) was printed in newspapers. It said that the German government might destroy British ships and that passengers traveled at their own risk.

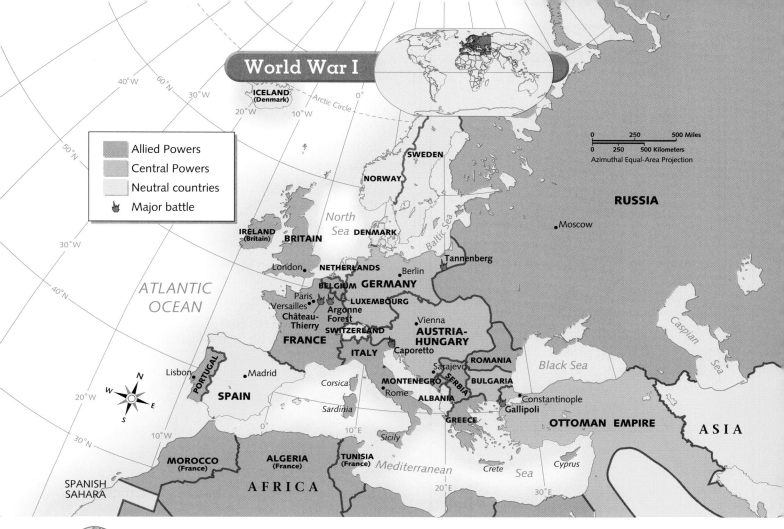

World War I

Legend:
- Allied Powers
- Central Powers
- Neutral countries
- 🔥 Major battle

0 250 500 Miles
0 250 500 Kilometers
Azimuthal Equal-Area Projection

Regions This map shows regions controlled by the Central Powers, the Allied Powers, and neutral countries in Europe during World War I.
■ *What problems do you think Germany had because of Allied Powers on both its eastern and western borders?*

New Weapons

When American soldiers arrived in Europe during the summer of 1917, many were sent to France, where most of the fighting took place. In France, most soldiers fought one another from trenches, or ditches, dug in the ground. The trenches of the two opposing sides were separated by a **no-man's-land**. This was land not held by either side but filled with barbed wire and land mines, or bombs buried in the ground.

Soldiers in the trenches faced terrible new weapons. The Germans had developed a machine gun that fired hundreds of bullets each minute. To fight against the machine gun, the British developed the tank. Tanks could cross the no-man's-land, crushing the barbed wire. Machine gun bullets could not go through the tank walls. Against the tank, the Germans used poison gas, the most feared of the new weapons. It killed soldiers—even those in tanks—by making them unable to breathe. While battles raged on the ground, dozens of airplane pilots fought overhead in air battles called dogfights.

During the summer of 1918, the war went on with neither side gaining much ground. The number of Americans in the trenches grew from 27,000 in early June to 500,000 by

1917

While World War I was taking place in Europe, revolutions were taking place in other parts of the world. In 1910 Francisco Madero led a revolution in Mexico against President Porfirio Díaz, who ruled as a dictator. Several leaders fought for power in Mexico in the years that followed. In 1917 a new constitution was written. It is the basis of government in Mexico today.

A revolution also took place in Russia, where life for many was hard. In 1917 a group of revolutionaries led by Vladimir Illyich Lenin took control. Russia's monarch, Nicholas II, was killed. Life for the Russians became even worse when harsh new rulers came to power.

Women in the War

The United States government did not let women fight in the war. Instead, many women took over jobs left by men who had gone to fight in the war. Some women became mechanics or farm workers. Others became police officers. Some women worked in weapons factories. Some went to Europe as nurses or ambulance drivers. Thousands more joined the army and the navy as clerks and telegraph operators.

Katherine Stinson of San Antonio, Texas, wanted to become a fighter pilot in the war. Stinson and her mother opened a flying school in 1913. The army, however, would not let her fly in battle. So she flew across the United States, raising money for the Red Cross. Then she went to Europe and served as an ambulance driver.

Women's wartime work helped bring one very important change after the war. The Nineteenth Amendment to the Constitution was passed in 1920. This amendment gave women the right to vote. Carrie Chapman Catt, a women's suffrage leader, later called the Nineteenth Amendment "the greatest thing that came out of the war."

REVIEW *How did women help in wartime?*

the end of August. Before the war ended, about 53,000 Americans were killed. Another 230,000 were wounded. More than 8 million people from countries around the world died in the war.

REVIEW *What new weapons were used in the war?*

LEARNING FROM TIME LINES This time line shows some of the key events of World War I. During the war some American women served as ambulance drivers.

■ *For how many years after the beginning of World War I did the United States remain neutral?*

World War I

1913	1916	1919
1914 • World War I begins	1915 • *Lusitania* is attacked	1918 • World War I ends
1913 • Wilson becomes President		1917 • The United States enters World War I

This painting by John Christen Johansen shows Allied leaders at the signing of the Treaty of Versailles.

The War Ends

Americans made an important difference in the Great War. Soldiers gave military help. Shiploads of American wheat, canned foods, and guns helped supply the Allied armies. Working together, the Allies began to push back the German army. Finally, on November 11, 1918, the Germans surrendered. On that day they signed an armistice that ended the fighting.

The Great War was over, and American soldiers came home. Leaders of the Allies gathered to make peace terms. During these talks President Wilson described his idea for a League of Nations, to which all nations could belong. Wilson hoped the organization would help find peaceful ways to solve problems among nations.

The Treaty of Versailles (ver•SY), which had ended the war, set up the League of Nations. But the United States did not join. The United States Senate must vote to approve treaties. It voted not to approve the Treaty of Versailles because many senators did not want the United States to belong to the League of Nations. They believed that the United States should stay out of other countries' problems. They felt that the nation should adopt a policy of **isolation**—remaining separate from other countries.

REVIEW *What was the League of Nations?*

LESSON 3 REVIEW

Check Understanding

1 Remember the Facts Why did European countries form alliances in the early 1900s?

2 Recall the Main Idea Why did the leaders of the United States decide to enter World War I?

Think Critically

3 Think More About It Could the United States have avoided entering the war? Explain.

4 Past to Present How does the United States use its power to affect what happens in the world today?

Show What You Know

Journal-Writing Activity
Imagine that you are a soldier in a trench in 1918. Write a journal entry that describes what you see and hear. Include a description of how you spend your days. Share your work with a family member.

Recognize Propaganda

1. Why Learn This Skill?

Propaganda is information or ideas designed to help or harm a cause. It is used by people to persuade others to share their views. Being able to recognize propaganda will help you make thoughtful and informed decisions.

2. Remember What You Have Read

Each side in a war often uses propaganda to help win support for its cause. Think about what you have read about World War I. The United States remained neutral during the early years of the war. Then, after German U-boats began to sink American ships, the United States joined the Allied Powers and declared war on Germany.

One week after war was declared, President Wilson set up the Committee on Public Information, headed by George Creel. Creel's job was to "sell the war to the American people." To do this, Creel hired artists and writers to wage a propaganda campaign in support of the war. The committee printed millions of leaflets and posters praising American soldiers for fighting for democracy. At the same time, they accused the German government of carrying out terrible crimes in their effort to take over the world.

Posters, like those shown below, were designed to help gather support for United States troops during World War I. Poster A encouraged Americans to enlist in the army. Poster B encouraged Americans not to waste food, which was needed to support United States troops. The troops needed plenty of food to keep their strength in battle.

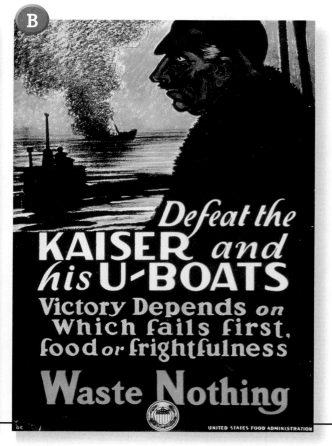

To the American soldiers of German descent.

You say in your loose leaf that you serve in an honorable way in the U. S. Army. Do you think it honorable to fight the country that has given birth to your fathers or forefathers? . . . We are fighting for everything dear to us, for our homes, our very existence. What are you fighting for, why did you come over here, four thousand miles away from your own home? Did Germany do you any harm, did it ever threaten you? Your leaders are Misleaders, they have lied to you that we were slaves of a tyrant, and you are guilty of gross ignorance if you believe one word of it. . . . There is more freedom in Germany indeed than in the land of Dictator Wilson. We do not try to deceive you, we do not promise you a farm, but we assure you that every honest man willing to work has infinitely better chances in Germany where we do not suffer corrupt politicians, deceiving land speculators, nor cheating contractors. Lay down your gun, your innermost soul is not in this fight. Come to us, you will not regret it.

The German government waged a propaganda campaign of its own during the war. German soldiers dropped leaflets like the one shown above from airplanes or hot-air balloons. The leaflets were dropped near where American troops were stationed. Some leaflets were packed in artillery shells and shot across the trenches to the Americans.

3. Understand the Process

Study the posters on page 564 and read the leaflet above. Then answer the following questions to help you learn about these primary-source documents.

❶ To whom are the posters addressed? To whom is the leaflet addressed?

❷ What points are being made on the posters? What points are being made in the leaflet?

❸ Do you think the posters would persuade you to support the American troops?

❹ What facts does the writer of the leaflet give? What opinions does the writer give?

❺ If you were a German American soldier, do you think you would believe the arguments on the leaflet? Why or why not?

4. Think and Apply

Draw a poster that could have been used to call for support in the United States for the Allied Powers in World War I. Your poster should focus on the idea of "making the world safe for democracy."

1860   1870   1880

1867
• United States buys Alaska from Russia

CONNECT MAIN IDEAS

Use this graphic organizer to show how the chapter's main ideas are connected. Write the main idea of each lesson. A copy of the organizer appears on page 114 of the Activity Book.

Building an Empire

The United States and the World

The Great War

Progressives and Reform

WRITE MORE ABOUT IT

Write a Letter Imagine that you are living in the Hawaiian Islands during the late nineteenth century. Write a letter to a friend explaining why some people want the United States to annex Hawaii and others do not. Be sure to tell your friend how you feel about the issue.

Write a Newspaper Article Imagine that you are a newspaper reporter covering the fighting in Europe during World War I. Write a short newspaper article describing what you have seen. Tell how tanks, machine guns, barbed wire, mines, and poison gas are affecting the fighting.

1890	1900	1910	1920	1930

1898
• Spanish-American War

1909
• NAACP founded

1917
• United States enters World War I

1920
• Women gain right to vote

USE VOCABULARY ·······················

Write the term that correctly matches each definition. Then use the term in a sentence.

alliance	**imperialism**
civil rights	**isolation**
conservation	**progressive**

1. empire building

2. a person who wants to improve government and make life better

3. keeping natural resources from being wasted or destroyed

4. the rights guaranteed to all citizens by the Constitution

5. a partnership

6. remaining separate from other countries

CHECK UNDERSTANDING ···············

7. What territories became part of the United States as a result of the Spanish-American War?

8. How was President Roosevelt able to get permission from Panama to build a canal in that country?

9. How did the merit system prevent officials from giving government jobs to people who did favors for them?

10. Why were the NAACP and the National Urban League important?

11. What alliance of countries won World War I? What alliance was defeated?

12. Why did Congress vote not to join the League of Nations?

THINK CRITICALLY ·······················

13. **Cause and Effect** How did alliances help lead to World War I?

14. **Past to Present** What effect did the passage of the Nineteenth Amendment have on American women?

APPLY SKILLS ·······················

Compare Map Projections One kind of map projection shows the sizes of regions in correct relationship to one another but distorts shapes. Another kind of projection correctly shows directions but distorts sizes of places. Which kind is a conformal projection, and which kind is an equal-area projection?

Recognize Propaganda Choose a cause that concerns you. Create a leaflet that uses propaganda to call for support from others for your cause. Share your leaflet with a classmate.

READ MORE ABOUT IT ···············

Theodore Roosevelt Takes Charge by Nancy Whitelaw. Albert Whitman & Company. This book describes the life and accomplishments of the twenty-sixth President of the United States.

Theodore Roosevelt Takes Charge
Nancy Whitelaw

HARCOURT BRACE

Visit the Internet at
http://www.hbschool.com
for additional resources.

GOOD TIMES AND BAD

"Time and place have had their say. So you will have to know something about the time and place where I came from, in order that you may interpret the . . . directions of my life."

Zora Neale Hurston, writer and anthropologist, in her 1942 book *Dust Tracks on a Road*

The Roaring Twenties

LESSON

1

FOCUS
What words might be used to describe the present decade?

Main Idea As you read, find out why the 1920s were described as the Roaring Twenties.

Vocabulary
consumer good
installment buying
assembly line
aviation
commercial industry
jazz

After the serious days of World War I, the 1920s brought good times to many Americans. People were eager for change and wanted to enjoy themselves. For this reason, the 1920s are often called the Roaring Twenties.

The Boom Economy

When the United States entered World War I in 1917, the economy changed greatly. Factories began producing weapons and other war supplies. When the war was over, factories started to make new products. They made vacuum cleaners, washing machines, radios, and other appliances for the home. In the 1920s Americans bought more of these **consumer goods**—the name given to products made for personal use. Never before had there been such a variety of goods to choose from.

Americans learned about consumer goods through advertisements in newspapers and magazines and on the radio. Business owners used advertisements in the hopes of making people want to buy their goods.

It was hard for many people to pay for goods all at once, so installment buying became common. **Installment buying** allows a buyer to take home a product after paying only a part of the selling price. The buyer then makes an installment, or payment, each month until the full price of the product has been paid.

While business boomed, agriculture slumped. Farmers had produced large amounts of food during World War I, when food was badly needed overseas. But the end of the war meant the end of high wartime demand. Farmers now had too many crops and no one to buy them.

REVIEW *What led to a boom in the economy in the 1920s?*

Nipper, the dog on RCA Victor's label, first appeared on phonographs and records in 1901.

The Automobile

One reason for the boom of the 1920s was the growth of new industries. One of the most important of these was the automobile industry.

The first successful gasoline-powered automobile, or car, was built in the 1890s. By the time the United States entered World War I, automobile companies were producing about 1 million cars a year. By 1923 they were making more than 3 million a year.

Leading the American automobile industry was a man from Michigan named Henry Ford. Ford had found a way to produce automobiles less expensively. The Ford Motor Company's system of mass production used a moving **assembly line**. Instead of being built one at a time, Ford's cars were assembled, or put together, as they were moved past a line of workers. Each worker did only one task, such as putting in headlights or seats. The assembly line cut the amount of time it took to make a car from about 12 hours to less than 2 hours. Workers on the assembly line could now produce 6 cars in the time it once took to produce a single car. Ford passed on the savings to his customers. By 1925 a person could buy a new Ford car for about $260.

As more people bought automobiles the need for other new industries grew. The need for automobile tires led to the growth of the rubber industry. The need for gasoline as fuel led to the growth of the oil industry. Gas stations were built in cities and along roadsides, and hundreds of thousands of miles of roads were paved. The United States was becoming a nation on wheels.

REVIEW *How did Henry Ford change the automobile industry?*

LEARNING FROM GRAPHS As a young man Henry Ford (below) worked as a machine operator. His idea of producing cars on an assembly line (above) helped increase sales of automobiles.

■ *About how many cars were sold in 1920? in 1929?*

Automobile Sales,
1920–1929

Year	
1920	🚗🚗🚗🚗
1921	🚗🚗🚗
1922	🚗🚗🚗🚗🚗
1923	🚗🚗🚗🚗🚗🚗🚗
1924	🚗🚗🚗🚗🚗🚗🚗
1925	🚗🚗🚗🚗🚗🚗🚗
1926	🚗🚗🚗🚗🚗🚗🚗
1927	🚗🚗🚗🚗🚗🚗
1928	🚗🚗🚗🚗🚗🚗🚗
1929	🚗🚗🚗🚗🚗🚗🚗🚗

🚗 = 500,000 automobiles

The Wright brothers' *Flyer* (above) takes off on the first piloted flight in 1903. Charles Lindbergh (right) stands next to the *Spirit of St. Louis,* the airplane that he flew across the Atlantic Ocean in 1927.

Aviation

Air transportation, or **aviation**, also became an important industry in the 1920s. Two brothers, Orville and Wilbur Wright, made the first flight in 1903 at Kitty Hawk, North Carolina. Over the years, the airplane was improved. It was used in World War I, but after the war not many people traveled by plane. By 1927 that began to change.

On May 20, 1927, Charles Lindbergh, an American airmail pilot, took off from New York in a small plane named the *Spirit of St. Louis.* His goal was to be the first person to fly alone across the Atlantic Ocean. If he did, he would win a $25,000 prize. Fighting off sleep, Lindbergh kept to his course over the open ocean. "My back is stiff; my shoulders ache; my eyes smart," he wrote in his journal.

It seemed impossible for Lindbergh to go on, but he did. He landed in Paris, France, about 34 hours after leaving New York. As news of his flight spread, Charles Lindbergh became a hero all over the world.

Lindbergh's flight helped make people more interested in air travel, and soon commercial airlines were making flights. A **commercial industry** is one that is run to make a profit. Between 1926 and 1930, the number of people traveling by plane grew from about 6,000 to about 400,000.

REVIEW *Who was Charles Lindbergh?*

Entertainment

Many Americans heard the news of Lindbergh's flight on the radio. The first commercial radio stations began broadcasting in the 1920s. Detroit's WWJ and Pittsburgh's KDKA were two of the earliest commercial radio stations. By 1929 more than 800 stations were reaching about 10 million families.

Radio made possible an audience of millions of people at one time. Listening to the radio, Americans could follow sports around the country. In 1926, millions listened as Gene Tunney beat Jack Dempsey in a ten-round boxing match. Yankee fans cheered when Babe Ruth hit his sixtieth home run during the 1927 baseball season.

Over their radios Americans could also hear a new kind of music called jazz. **Jazz** grew out of the African American musical heritage. This heritage was made up of music brought from West Africa and spirituals sung by enslaved people in the United States. Jazz was so popular among both black and white Americans that some have called the 1920s the Jazz Age.

Movies were another new form of entertainment enjoyed by many people in the 1920s. The movie business, which was based in Hollywood, California, started with silent films. By 1927 many movies were being made with sound. D. W. Griffith, a film director, saw a bright future for what were known as talking pictures. Griffith predicted,

66 Talkies, squeakies, moanies, songies, squawkies . . . But whatever you call them, I'm absolutely serious in what I have to say about them. Just give them ten years to develop and you're going to see the greatest artistic medium the world has known. 99

REVIEW *What new forms of entertainment were popular in the 1920s?*

The Harlem Renaissance

In the 1920s the New York City neighborhood of Harlem became a center of artistic development for African Americans. So many writers, musicians, and artists lived in Harlem during the 1920s that this period is now known as the Harlem Renaissance. The French word *renaissance* (REH•nuh•sahns) means

A popular dance (right) during the 1920s was the Charleston. In the 1920s Americans went to the movies about once a week. Charlie Chaplin (above) was the most popular comic actor of the time.

"rebirth." It is used to describe a time of new interest and activity in the arts.

Among the best-known of the Harlem writers was the poet Langston Hughes. He described Harlem during the 1920s as a magnet for African Americans from across the country. Young writers such as Claude McKay, Countee Cullen, and Zora Neale Hurston came to Harlem to share their work and encourage one another. Many of these artists and writers painted and wrote about what it was like to be African American in the United States.

Large audiences of both black and white Americans came to Harlem to hear trumpeter Louis Armstrong, singer Billie Holiday, and bandleader Duke Ellington. They also came to see actors such as Paul Robeson perform.

REVIEW *What was the Harlem Renaissance?*

During the Harlem Renaissance, Langston Hughes (left) wrote poems about African American life. The Savoy Ballroom (above) was a popular dance club in Harlem.

LESSON 1 REVIEW

Check Understanding

1 **Remember the Facts** What new industries helped the nation's economy grow in the 1920s?

2 **Recall the Main Idea** Why were the 1920s described as the Roaring Twenties?

Think Critically

3 **Personally Speaking** Charles Lindbergh set for himself the goal of being the first person to fly alone across the Atlantic Ocean. Why is it a good idea for people to set goals?

4 **Explore Viewpoints** How do you think the viewpoints of farmers in the 1920s differed from those of people living in cities in the 1920s?

Show What You Know

Poster Activity Review what you learned about consumer goods, advertisements, and installment buying. Choose a product that was popular during the 1920s. Make a poster to advertise the product that might make people want to buy it. Display your poster in the classroom.

The Great Depression and the New Deal

Many Americans thought that the good times of the 1920s would go on forever. President Herbert Hoover, elected in 1928, shared that hope. He had gained fame for his efforts to help poor and hungry people in Europe after World War I. He saw a much happier picture in the United States in 1928. "We in America today are nearer to the final triumph over poverty than ever before in the history of any land," he said. Little did he know how quickly that would change.

The Good Times End

In the 1920s thousands of Americans pinned their hopes on a rich future by investing money in the stock market. The **stock market** is a place where people can buy and sell stocks. If more people want to buy than sell a certain stock, the price of shares goes up. If more people want to sell than buy, the price goes down.

During the 1920s the prices on one stock market, the New York Stock Exchange, kept going higher. By 1929 some stocks were being sold at prices three times higher than they were sold for in 1920. People began to borrow money to buy stocks. "How can you lose?" they asked. Before long they learned the answer.

Beginning in the fall of 1929, some people decided to take their money out of the stock market. This caused stock prices to fall. As prices fell, many investors got nervous and decided to sell, too. Soon panicked stockholders were trying to sell all of their stocks. On October 24, 1929, thousands of investors wanted to sell stocks instead of buy them. They all wanted to turn their stocks into cash. With many sellers and few buyers, prices fell fast. On October 29, 1929, stock prices could go no lower. The stock market crashed. Nearly everyone who owned stocks lost money.

During the Great Depression, some people without jobs sold apples on the street to make money.

On the day of the stock market crash, people gathered on New York City's Wall Street, where stocks are traded. Stock certificates like this one (right) had lost much of their value.

The crash of the stock market ended the good times of the Roaring Twenties. It was the beginning of a long, difficult period known as the Great Depression. During a **depression** there is little money, little economic growth, and many people are out of work.

REVIEW *What caused the stock market to crash in 1929?*

The Great Depression

As people lost their jobs after the stock market crash, many needed to spend their savings in order to live. When large numbers of people tried to take money out of the banks, many banks had to close. People who had money in these banks lost all of their savings.

Because people had little money, they bought few goods. Manufacturers could not sell what they had made. Factory workers then lost their jobs because the factory owners could not pay their wages. When workers lost their jobs, they could not pay what they owed to banks or businesses. So more banks and businesses began to fail.

During the Great Depression, poverty and hardship affected almost every American.

President Hoover tried to give everyone hope. "Prosperity," he said, "is just around the corner." But it was not. In fact, times got worse.

By 1932 thousands of businesses had closed. One of every four American workers was without a job. People were starving. Hungry people stood in line for bread or for free meals at soup kitchens. Because they could not pay their rent or house payments, many people lost their homes. Those who were homeless spent the night in public shelters or out on the streets. Entire families often had to live in shacks made of scraps of wood.

One woman, a teenager during the Great Depression, remembers being sent by her mother to wait in line for free soup.

❝ If you happened to be one of the first ones in line, you didn't get anything but the water on top. So we'd ask the guy that was putting the soup into the buckets . . . to please dip down to get some meat and potatoes from the bottom of the kettle. But he wouldn't do it. ❞

REVIEW *What hardships did the Great Depression cause for many Americans?*

Business Failures, 1929–1945

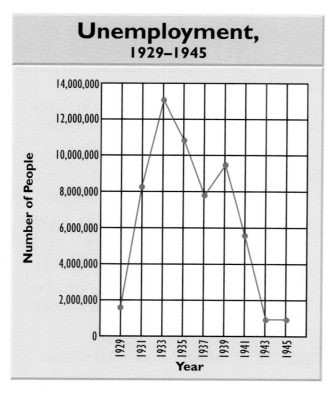

Number of Business Failures (y-axis): 0; 2,000; 4,000; 6,000; 8,000; 10,000; 12,000; 14,000; 16,000; 18,000; 20,000; 22,000; 24,000; 26,000; 28,000; 30,000

Year (x-axis): 1929 1931 1933 1935 1937 1939 1941 1943 1945

LEARNING FROM GRAPHS The bar graph shows the number of companies that went out of business from 1929 to 1945. The line graph shows the number of people who lost their jobs during the same period.

■ *Compare the trends shown on these graphs. Are the trends similar? Why or why not?*

Unemployment, 1929–1945

Number of People (y-axis): 0; 2,000,000; 4,000,000; 6,000,000; 8,000,000; 10,000,000; 12,000,000; 14,000,000

Year (x-axis): 1929 1931 1933 1935 1937 1939 1941 1943 1945

Franklin Roosevelt and the New Deal

In the summer of 1932, the Democratic party chose New York governor Franklin Delano Roosevelt as its presidential candidate. Roosevelt had served as the assistant secretary of the navy and had been his party's candidate for vice president in 1920. Roosevelt was a cheerful, likable person. Franklin Roosevelt told the Democrats, "I pledge you, I pledge myself to a new deal for the American people." The words became the name for his plan—the New Deal—to end the Great Depression. In November 1932 the American people elected Roosevelt to be President.

President Roosevelt believed that to end the Great Depression, the federal government needed to take bold, new action. On his inauguration day, Roosevelt told the American people,

66 The only thing we have to fear is fear itself. 99

He gave people hope that everything would be all right—that the government would do something to help. "This nation asks for action, and action now," he said.

In his speech Roosevelt called on Congress to act quickly. It did. Between March 9 and June 16, 1933, Congress passed many of Roosevelt's plans. During this time, later known as The 100 Days, more new laws were passed than at any other time since the founding of the nation.

The New Deal gave the federal government more authority. It also made it larger. The growing number of government workers formed a **bureaucracy**—the many workers and groups that are needed to run government programs.

REVIEW *What was the name of Franklin Roosevelt's plan to end the Great Depression?*

Government Programs

The New Deal's goal was to get people back to work. To provide jobs, it created a number of programs that were nicknamed Roosevelt's Alphabet Soup. The Civilian Conservation Corps, or CCC, hired young people to plant trees and take care of the many national parks. The Works Progress Administration, or WPA, hired workers to build roads, airports, and public buildings such as schools, libraries, and post offices. The WPA also hired writers and artists to record life during the Great Depression in words, paintings, and photographs.

Even with these government programs, **unemployment**, or the number of workers without jobs, stayed high. But at least unemployment did not get worse.

The government helped workers who had jobs by supporting labor unions. There had often been strikes and conflicts over the rights of workers to organize unions. New laws gave workers the right to form unions and the right to an hourly

This photograph from 1930 shows people waiting in line for free bread at a mission in New York City. Without money to pay for food, many people went hungry.

minimum wage, the lowest pay a worker can receive by law.

Workers were also helped by the Social Security Act. It was one of the most important programs of the New Deal. Social Security provides income for workers after

---

BIOGRAPHY

Franklin Delano Roosevelt
1882–1945

In 1921, eleven years before he won election as President, Franklin Roosevelt became ill with polio. The disease left him unable to walk. Polio forced him to leave politics for a time. But through hard work and the encouragement of his family, he recovered and learned to walk with the help of leg braces. In 1928 Roosevelt was elected governor of New York. In 1932 he was elected President of the United States. Roosevelt was reelected three more times, making him the only President to have been elected to four terms in office.

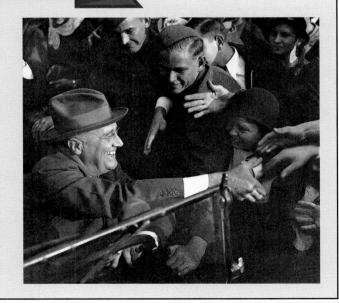

they have retired. In addition, it gives help to children of workers who have no means of support. Money for the program comes from taxes on workers' earnings.

The federal government also started huge building projects that put thousands of people back to work. Among these projects was the building of hydroelectric dams. These dams use the water they store to produce electricity. The government sold the electricity at low rates to users. The dams helped bring about growth in the regions where they were built.

In 1933 Congress created the Tennessee Valley Authority, or TVA. TVA workers built hydroelectric dams and locks on the Tennessee River. Also during the New Deal, workers built the Hoover Dam on the Colorado River. This dam supplied electricity to southern California and Arizona and helped these areas grow. The Grand Coulee and Bonneville dams on the Columbia River helped areas in eastern Washington and Oregon grow.

REVIEW *What was Roosevelt's Alphabet Soup?*

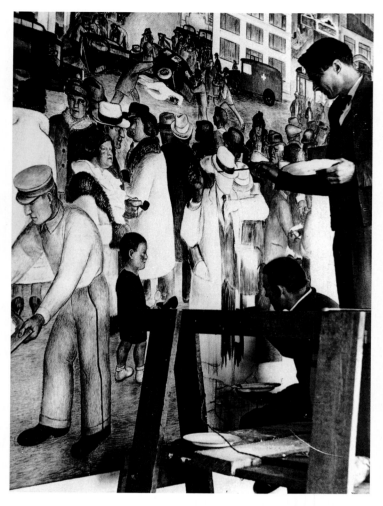

During the Great Depression, artists like the ones in this photograph were hired by the WPA to paint pictures of American life.

LESSON 2 REVIEW

Check Understanding
1 **Remember the Facts** What was the New Deal?

2 **Recall the Main Idea** How did the federal government help solve some of the problems of the Great Depression?

Think Critically
3 **Personally Speaking** Some people have said that the most valuable thing people lost during the Great Depression was hope. What do you think that means?

4 **Think More About It** How did the 1920s compare with the 1930s? Use the pictures in this chapter to help you.

Show What You Know
Newspaper Activity Have a family member help you look at the stock market report in the newspaper. Choose one stock and follow it for a week. Record the stock's closing price every day. With a classmate, figure out if you would have lost or made money by investing in the stock.

CHILDREN OF THE DUST BOWL

by Jerry Stanley

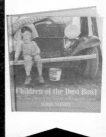

Farm families did not share in the good times of the 1920s. Crop and livestock prices dropped so low that farmers could not make a profit. When farmers could not pay off loans to the banks, they lost their farms. By the time of the New Deal, many farm families faced the same poverty and hardship as city families. The New Deal helped farmers by giving them loans so they would not lose their farms. But many farmers soon faced a new problem.

A drought came to the Great Plains early in the 1930s. Where healthy crops had grown, dry earth blew away in the strong winds. Dust storms turned day into night. The western Great Plains became known as the Dust Bowl. The Oklahoma Panhandle had the worst time. As you read the following account of life in the Dust Bowl, think about how the "Okies," the people of Oklahoma, learned to live in hard times.

A dust storm rises over the Texas Panhandle in March 1936 (background). The photograph of this family (left) who left the Texas Panhandle in 1939 and found work in California was taken by Dorothea Lange. Lange's famous photographs of the Dust Bowl showed Americans the misery of the people who lived there.

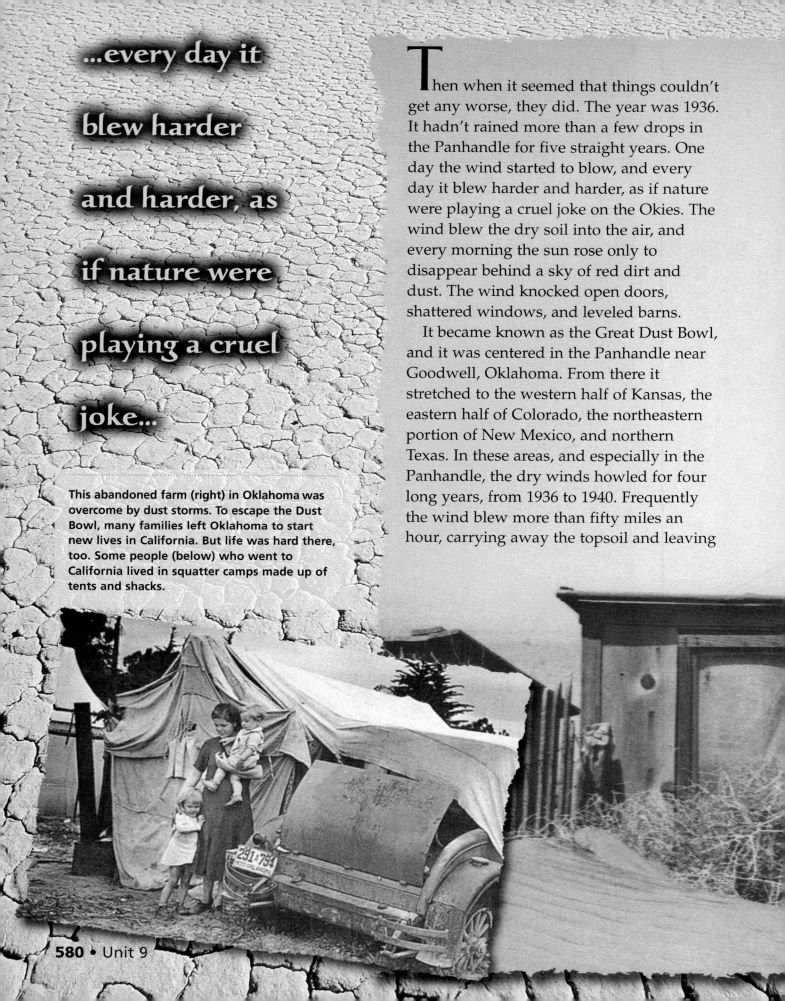

...every day it blew harder and harder, as if nature were playing a cruel joke...

This abandoned farm (right) in Oklahoma was overcome by dust storms. To escape the Dust Bowl, many families left Oklahoma to start new lives in California. But life was hard there, too. Some people (below) who went to California lived in squatter camps made up of tents and shacks.

Then when it seemed that things couldn't get any worse, they did. The year was 1936. It hadn't rained more than a few drops in the Panhandle for five straight years. One day the wind started to blow, and every day it blew harder and harder, as if nature were playing a cruel joke on the Okies. The wind blew the dry soil into the air, and every morning the sun rose only to disappear behind a sky of red dirt and dust. The wind knocked open doors, shattered windows, and leveled barns.

It became known as the Great Dust Bowl, and it was centered in the Panhandle near Goodwell, Oklahoma. From there it stretched to the western half of Kansas, the eastern half of Colorado, the northeastern portion of New Mexico, and northern Texas. In these areas, and especially in the Panhandle, the dry winds howled for four long years, from 1936 to 1940. Frequently the wind blew more than fifty miles an hour, carrying away the topsoil and leaving only hard red clay, which made farming impossible.

In the flatlands of the Panhandle people could see the dust storms coming from twenty to thirty miles away. The winds made the sky "boil red, blood red," said Horace Ray Conley of Foss, Oklahoma. "You could see the northers[1] coming," he recalled. "It carried that old red dirt, and the whole sky would be red. They were mean clouds, ugly clouds." As a child, Horace walked to school backward to keep the dirt from scraping him in the face. He remembered he was often let out of school to go to the family storm cellar where he would be safe.

As the clouds rose and roiled[2] each day, thousands of birds and rabbits raced in front of the approaching storms. That was the signal to the Okies to hurry before it was

too late. They had to herd their cows into the barn quickly, tie down farm equipment and whatever supplies they had outside, then run for cover. Cracks around windows and doors were taped or stuffed with wet towels, but it was impossible to escape the dust. At night families slept with wet washcloths or sponges over their faces to filter out the dust, but in the morning they would find their pillows and blankets caked with dirt, their tongues and teeth coated with grit.

Every morning the house had to be cleaned. Everett Buckland of Waynocka said, "If you didn't sweep the dust out right quick between storms, you'd end up scooping it out with a shovel." And every morning someone had to go check the animals. The fierce gales buried chickens, pigs, dogs, and occasionally cattle. Children were assigned the task of cleaning the nostrils of cows two or three times a day. . . .

---

[1] **norther:** windstorm blowing from the north
[2] **roiled:** stirred up

The Dust Bowl killed people who stayed out too long without shelter. Roland Hoeme of Hooker almost lost his grandmother to one storm. "I remember my grandmother hanging on to a fence post," he said. "The wind was blowin' so hard she looked like a pennant in a breeze." However, more people died from "dust pneumonia"—when the dust caused severe damage to the lungs. Bessie Zentz of Goodwell summed up the nightmare experienced by the "Dust Bowlers," as they came to be called: "The dust storms scared us to pieces," Bessie said. "It was dark as the middle of the night, and it stayed that way all day."

The storms ended any hope of farming in the Panhandle. The Okies planted mulberry trees for windbreaks and plowed furrows deep in the ground to help keep the soil in place. But the wind blasted the seeds from the furrows and whipped the crops from the earth. . . .

The Okies were broke, they were without land, and they were hungry. And still the wind blew day and night, scraping all life from the earth. It's little wonder that Okies named this period in their lives the Dirty Thirties.

An Oklahoma farmer and his son raise the height of a fence to keep it from being buried by drifts of blowing soil.

To help end conditions in the Dust Bowl, President Franklin Roosevelt started a conservation program as part of the New Deal. The goal was to stop the dust storms and save the land. An important part of the program was planting rows of large trees to stop the wind. These rows of trees are called windbreaks. In time, better plowing methods, more rainfall, and the new windbreaks ended the terrible dust.

LITERATURE REVIEW

1. What did people do to make it through the Dust Bowl days in Oklahoma?

2. How do you think you would have felt about living in the Dust Bowl?

3. Many people left Oklahoma to escape the Dust Bowl, but many stayed through all the hardships. With a partner, role-play a conversation between a person who is staying and a person who is leaving. Make sure the conversation gives the reasons for each person's decision. Present your conversation to the class.

World War II

FOCUS
What might cause conflict between countries today?

Main Idea As you read, look for the reasons that caused the United States and countries in Europe and Asia to go to war in the 1930s and 1940s.

Vocabulary
concentration camp
civilian
rationing
relocation camp

he United States was not the only country to suffer an economic depression in the 1930s. The depression was world-wide. Many Europeans, still rebuilding their countries after World War I, had a hard time finding jobs to support their families. In some places in Asia, countries were running out of the resources needed to make their economies grow. Strong leaders in both Europe and Asia promised to solve their coun-tries' problems by force. Another war was on its way. This second world war, or World War II, would be even worse than the first.

The Rise of Dictators

After World War I the Allied Powers expected Germany to pay for the costs of the war. But Germany did not have the money to do so. Its economy had been destroyed by the war and the depression that followed the war.

During the 1920s a German leader named Adolf Hitler tried to convince people that Germany had not been treated fairly after World War I. He believed that the Germans who had blond hair and blue eyes were the "true Germans" and were better than all other Germans and other peoples of the world. Hitler made life especially difficult for Germany's Jews, whom he blamed for many of Germany's problems.

Hitler became the leader of a political party in Germany called the National Socialists, or Nazis. The Nazi party grew in power and set up an army. Its soldiers, who called them-selves storm troopers, attacked Jewish people and others who were against Hitler. Soon the Nazis began to round up people who did not agree with them. They put some of these people in terrible prisons called **concentration camps**.

In 1933 the Nazi party, led by Adolf Hitler (inset, right), took control of Germany. Hitler addressed a crowd of 50,000 (below) at Nuremberg, Germany, in 1937.

The Nazis used force against Jews and other people whom they labeled as enemies.

In 1933 the Nazi party took control of the German government, and representative government in Germany came to an end. Hitler ruled as a dictator. He rebuilt Germany's economy by preparing for another war. Factories produced tanks, guns, and other war supplies. Hitler dreamed that Germany would one day rule the world.

Dictators came to power in other countries in Europe, too. Joseph Stalin ruled the Soviet Union, which had become a dictatorship—a country ruled by a dictator—after the Russian Revolution in 1917. Francisco Franco ruled Spain. In Italy Benito Mussolini (buh•NEE•toh moo•suh•LEE•nee) came to power in the 1920s. He wanted Italy to regain the power and glory it had in ancient times, when it was the center of the Roman Empire.

Dictators also ruled the Asian country of Japan. The emperor, Hirohito, had little authority after military officers took control of the government. Trade and industry were growing, but Japan did not have all the resources it needed. Japan's military leaders planned to get oil, rubber, and iron for their country by conquering other countries in Asia and the Pacific.

REVIEW *In what countries did dictators rule after World War I?*

The War Begins

In 1931 Japan invaded Manchuria, a part of China. In 1935 Italy took over the African country of Ethiopia. In 1937 Japan started a war against the rest of China. In 1938 Germany took over Austria and Czechoslovakia. Other countries, including the United States, did little to stop the fighting.

Then, on September 1, 1939, Germany invaded Poland. German forces attacked with tanks on land and planes in the air. They destroyed cities, roads, and communication lines. Leaders in Britain and France had finally had enough. They declared war on Germany on September 3, 1939. World War II had begun.

The British and French armies were not able to stop the Germans from taking over most of Europe. By 1940 German troops had conquered the Netherlands, Belgium, Luxembourg, Denmark, Norway, and most of France. German bombers attacked British cities, but Britain fought on.

Many people in the United States felt that their country should stay out of the war. President Franklin Roosevelt had promised to keep the United States out of the war, but he wanted the country to be prepared in case it was attacked. The United States started making tanks, bombers, and other war supplies. It also began to send equipment and supplies to help Britain.

In 1940 Japanese troops invaded French Indochina, which is now made up of the countries of Laos, Cambodia, and Vietnam.

American leaders feared that Japan would soon threaten the Philippines and other places in the Pacific. They were right.

REVIEW *When did World War II begin?*

The United States Enters the War

At 7:55 A.M. on Sunday, December 7, 1941, the roar of Japanese planes shattered the early morning calm over the Hawaiian Islands. The planes dropped bombs on American ships docked at Pearl Harbor. Pearl Harbor is an American naval base in the Hawaiian Islands. World War II had come to the United States.

In less than two hours, the attack was over. Much of the United States' Pacific fleet had sunk or lay burning in the harbor. At nearby Hickam Airfield, about 150 planes were destroyed. More than 2,000 sailors and soldiers and 68 civilians were killed. A **civilian** is a person who is not in the military.

German soldiers invaded Poland in 1939 and marched through Paris in 1940 (left). What do you suppose Americans of that time were thinking when they read headlines about the war?

Pearl Harbor

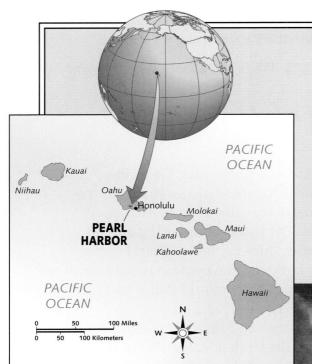

PACIFIC OCEAN

Kauai

Niihau

Oahu

Honolulu

PEARL HARBOR

Molokai

Lanai

Maui

Kahoolawe

PACIFIC OCEAN

Hawaii

0   50   100 Miles

0   50   100 Kilometers

N W E S

Pearl Harbor is one of the largest natural harbors in the world. It is located on the Hawaiian island of Oahu (oh•AH•hoo) and lies west of downtown Honolulu, the capital of Hawaii. The United States began using Pearl Harbor as a coal station for its steamships in 1887. The navy started using it as a base in 1902. The surprise attack on Pearl Harbor by Japanese forces led the United States to enter World War II. Today the USS *Arizona* Memorial stands above one of the ships sunk in the attack.

During the attack on Pearl Harbor, 19 American warships were sunk or disabled. Three others were damaged. The Japanese hoped that by the time the United States rebuilt its forces, Japan would have taken over more lands in Asia and the Pacific.

The day after the attack, President Roosevelt spoke to Congress:

❝ Yesterday, December 7, 1941—a date which will live in infamy—the United States of America was suddenly and deliberately attacked by naval and air forces of the Empire of Japan. . . . I ask that the Congress declare that since the . . . attack by Japan . . . a state of war has existed between the United States and the Japanese Empire. ❞

Congress declared war on Japan the same day. Three days later, when Japan's allies, Germany and Italy, declared war on the United States, Congress recognized a state of war with them, too. Germany, Italy, and Japan were known as the Axis Powers. The United States joined Britain and the Soviet Union. These three countries were known as the Allies.

REVIEW *When did the Japanese attack the American ships docked at Pearl Harbor?*

Americans at War

After the bombing at Pearl Harbor, the United States began to produce more airplanes, tanks, and other war supplies. This work gave many people jobs. Now instead of not enough jobs, there were not enough workers. World War II ended the Great Depression in the United States.

As they had in World War I, women took over jobs in factories, fields, and offices. Other women served in the armed forces. They made maps, drove ambulances, and worked as clerks or nurses. Some women trained as pilots and flew airplanes from factories to airfields in Europe and the Pacific.

The demands of fighting a war led to further growth in the federal government's authority. To produce war supplies and feed thousands of soldiers, the government took control of many businesses, setting prices and wages.

The new government rules also called for **rationing**, or limiting, what Americans could purchase, so that more supplies could be sent overseas. Government coupons were needed for such goods as butter, sugar, meat, home-heating oil, and gasoline. Each citizen had a coupon book for each kind of item. Without the coupons, people could not buy the rationed goods.

REVIEW *What did the government do to produce war supplies and feed its soldiers?*

Problems for Japanese Americans

War with Japan led to terrible problems for Japanese Americans. Some United States military officials believed that Japanese Americans would help Japan invade the United States.

In February 1942 President Roosevelt ordered the army to put about 110,000

LEARNING FROM GRAPHS The graph shows how the number of women who worked outside the home increased between the years 1900 and 1950. Many women, like the woman in the photograph (right), worked in airplane factories during World War II.

■ *By 1950, about how many American women were working outside the home?*

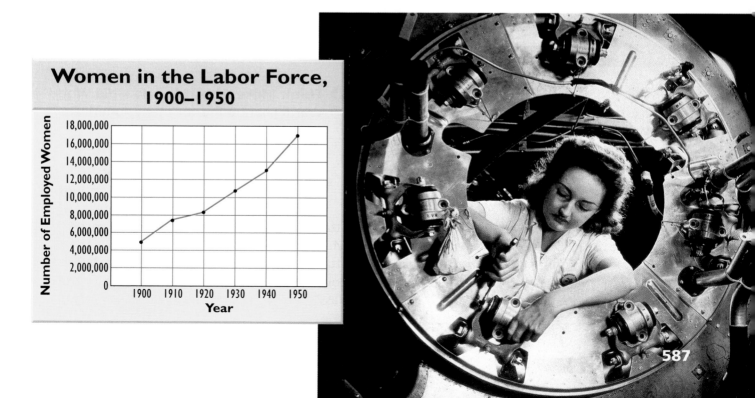

Women in the Labor Force, 1900–1950

These Japanese American soldiers arrived at Camp Shelby, Mississippi, in 1943. Like other United States citizens of Japanese origin, they fought bravely.

Japanese Americans in what were called **relocation camps**. These camps were like prisons. Barbed wire fenced people in. Soldiers with guns guarded the camps to keep people from leaving.

Even though most Japanese Americans were loyal United States citizens, they had to sell their homes, businesses, and belongings. They were moved to relocation camps in California, Arizona, Wyoming, Utah, Arkansas, and Idaho. Every Japanese American had to wear an identification tag.

"Our home was one room in a large army-style barracks, measuring 20 by 25 feet," remembers one woman. "The only furnishings were an iron pot-belly stove and cots." Another woman recalls, "Can you imagine the despair and utter desolation of all of us? Everybody was weeping, youngsters hanging onto parents, fear and terror all around."

While their families and friends were in the relocation camps, more than 17,000 Japanese Americans served in the army. Japanese Americans formed the 442nd Combat Team. This unit received more service awards than any other unit its size in World War II.

REVIEW *Why did President Roosevelt order the army to put Japanese Americans in relocation camps?*

LESSON 4 REVIEW

Check Understanding

1. **Remember the Facts**   What countries were ruled by dictators in the 1930s?

2. **Recall the Main Idea**   What caused different countries to take part in World War II?

Think Critically

3. **Personally Speaking**   How do you think you might feel as an American citizen if you were forced to live in a relocation camp?

4. **Think More About It**   How did World War II change life for many Americans?

Show What You Know

Interviewing Activity   Talk to people who are old enough to remember the Japanese attack on Pearl Harbor. Ask them to recall when they first heard the news about the attack and how they felt at the time. Write down your findings and report them to the class.

The Allies Win the War

FOCUS
How do events that happened in the past affect today's world?

Main Idea As you read, learn how World War II affected countries around the world.

Vocabulary
front
D day
Holocaust
island-hopping
communism
free world
cold war

World War II was a new kind of war. Soldiers did not fight from trenches, as they had in World War I. Instead, they moved quickly by tank, ship, and airplane. Bombs dropped in air raids destroyed factories, hospitals, and homes and killed hundreds of thousands of civilians. The war was fought over an area much larger than that of any other war—almost half the world. It was fought on two major **fronts**, or battle lines. The first was in Africa and Europe. The second was in the Pacific. Victory on both fronts would be needed to win the war.

War in Africa and Europe

The first step in the Allies' battle plan in Europe was to gain control of the Mediterranean Sea. To do this, the Allies had to fight the Germans and Italians in North Africa and then invade Italy. The Allies won North Africa in May 1943 and then started pushing north through Italy. In September the Italian government surrendered. However, heavy fighting went on until June 1944, when the Americans captured the city of Rome.

While the Allies were fighting in Italy, they were planning another invasion of Europe. On June 6, 1944, the date known as **D day**, the Allies worked together in the largest water-to-land invasion in history.

American General Dwight D. Eisenhower led the invasion. On the morning of June 6, he told his troops,

66 You are about to embark upon the great crusade. . . . The hopes and prayers of liberty-loving people everywhere march with you. 99

On D day American, British, and Canadian troops crossed the English Channel. They landed on the beaches of Normandy,

"Dog tags" were worn by soldiers for identification.

in France, where the German forces met them with heavy gunfire. One soldier remembered:

> 66 Everything was confusion. . . . Shells were coming in all the time; boats burning; vehicles with nowhere to go bogging down, getting hit; supplies getting wet; boats trying to come in all the time, some hitting mines, exploding. 99

Many soldiers died on D day, but the invasion was successful. The Allies broke through the German lines and began moving inland from the west, pushing back the enemy. At the same time, the Soviets were pushing back the German armies from the east. In April 1945, Allied troops met near Berlin, the German capital. There they learned that Hitler had killed himself.

Berlin fell to the Soviets on May 2, 1945, and the German military leaders asked to surrender. On May 8, the Allies accepted the surrender. This day was called V-E Day, or Victory in Europe Day. It marked the end of the war in Europe.

REVIEW *What happened on D day?*

The Holocaust

Only when the war in Europe was over did people discover everything that Hitler and the Nazis had done. Allied soldiers found the Nazis' concentration camps. The Allies learned that more than 12 million men, women, and children had been murdered in these camps. One of the largest of the death camps was at Auschwitz (OWSH•vits), in Poland.

BIOGRAPHY

Dwight D. Eisenhower
1890–1969

Dwight David Eisenhower grew up in Abilene, Kansas. He attended West Point Military Academy and spent more than 40 years as a soldier. In 1939 the Army put Eisenhower in charge of war planning. He headed the Allied invasion of North Africa in 1942. In 1944 Eisenhower became commander of all Allied forces in Europe. After the war he served as president of Columbia University. In 1952 Dwight Eisenhower was elected President of the United States.

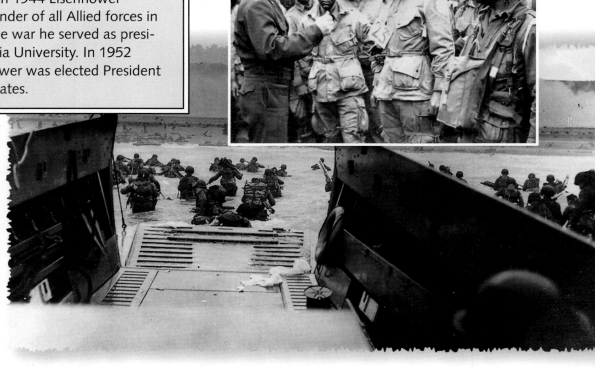

General Eisenhower talks with his troops (above right) before they leave for the D day invasion. On D day, 600 warships and 4,000 landing craft carried 176,000 soldiers across the English Channel (right).

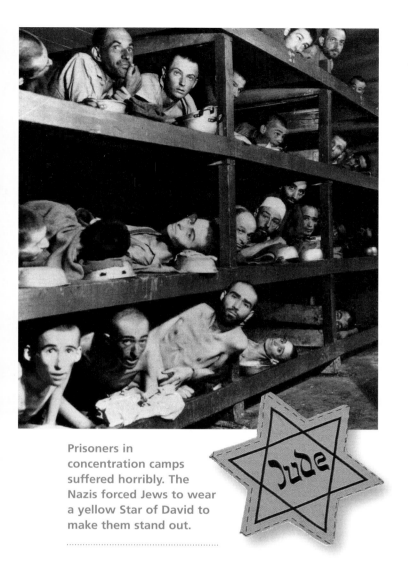

Prisoners in concentration camps suffered horribly. The Nazis forced Jews to wear a yellow Star of David to make them stand out.

The Nazis killed people for their religious and political beliefs. People who were ill or disabled and could not work were also killed. The largest group of victims were Jews, the people Hitler had blamed for Germany's problems.

During the war more than 6 million people were murdered on Hitler's orders because they were Jews. This terrible mass murder of European Jews came to be known as the **Holocaust** (HOH•luh•kawst). Hitler had called it the "final solution to the Jewish question." It was a deliberate attempt to destroy an entire people.

REVIEW *What was Hitler's "final solution"?*

War in the Pacific

In the Pacific, Allied leaders planned to defeat the Japanese by forcing them back from the lands and islands they had conquered. Allied leaders decided on a plan of **island-hopping**. This meant that Allied troops would take back the islands one at a time until they reached Tokyo. At the same time, the Allies would bomb Japan from the air.

Battles on the islands of Iwo Jima (EE•woh JEE•muh) and Okinawa (oh•kuh•NAH•wah) showed island-hopping to be a costly plan. At Iwo Jima, an island 750 miles (1,207 km) from Tokyo, Japan's capital, more than 4,000 American soldiers lost their lives. More than 20,000 Japanese soldiers died. At Okinawa, 350 miles (563 km) from Tokyo, 11,000 Americans died. The Japanese lost more than 100,000 people. As the Allies came closer to Tokyo, the losses grew.

By early April 1945 victory in the Pacific seemed near. But President Franklin Roosevelt did not live to see the end of the war. He died on April 12, 1945. Vice President Harry S. Truman became President.

After he became President, Truman learned that Roosevelt had agreed to the development of the most powerful bomb the world had ever known—the atom bomb. By the summer of 1945, this new weapon was ready. President Truman made the difficult decision to drop the atom bomb on Japan. He wanted to end the war quickly and save American lives.

On August 6, 1945, the American bomber *Enola Gay* flew over the industrial city of Hiroshima (hir•uh•SHEE•muh), Japan. A single bomb was dropped. There was a flash like an exploding sun. Then a mushroom-shaped cloud rose from the city. The bomb flattened a huge area of Hiroshima and killed more than 75,000 people, mostly civilians.

As terrible as the atom bomb was, Japan did not surrender. On August 9 the United States dropped a second bomb, this time on

World War II

UNION OF SOVIET SOCIALIST REPUBLICS

ASIA

ARCTIC OCEAN

ALASKA (U.S.)

CANADA

NORTH AMERICA

PACIFIC OCEAN

UNITED STATES

MONGOLIA

MANCHURIA

CHINA

KOREA

JAPAN

Hiroshima, 1945
Nagasaki, 1945
Okinawa 1945
Iwo Jima 1945

San Francisco

MEXICO

BURMA

THAILAND

FRENCH INDOCHINA

Bataan 1941–1942

Philippine Sea 1944

PHILIPPINES

Guam 1944

Peleliu 1944

Eniwetok 1944

Kwajalein 1944

Tarawa 1943

Pearl Harbor 1941

HAWAII (U.S.)

Midway 1942

Borneo

Java Sea 1942

DUTCH EAST INDIES

New Guinea

Coral Sea 1942

Guadalcanal 1942–1943

Aleutian Islands

Equator

AUSTRALIA

NEW ZEALAND

Legend:
- Allies and area controlled by Allies
- Axis Powers
- Neutral country
- Greatest area controlled by Axis Powers
- → Allied advance
- Major battle
- Atomic bombing

Location During the war, almost the whole world was divided between the Allies and the Axis Powers.

■ *How do you think the location of the United States was helpful to the country in the war?*

Nagasaki (nah•guh•SAH•kee). Only then did Japan agree to surrender. On August 15, Americans celebrated V-J Day, or Victory over Japan Day.

World War II was finally over. More than 300,000 American soldiers and close to 15 million soldiers from other countries had died in the fighting.

REVIEW *Why did Japan surrender to the United States?*

A Changed World

Just as they had after World War I, world leaders after World War II turned to the idea of an organization of nations. This time the United States supported the idea. In April 1945, delegates from 50 countries met in San Francisco to form the United Nations, or UN. The purpose of the UN is to keep world peace and promote cooperation among nations.

The United States came out of World War II as the strongest nation in the world. Americans used this strength to help other nations rebuild. Yet even as the war was ending and plans for peace were being made, new conflicts were beginning.

The United States and the Soviet Union were allies during World War II. After the war this quickly changed. The Soviet Union set up communist governments in the eastern European countries it had invaded during the war. **Communism** is a social and economic system in which all land and industries are owned by the government. Individuals have few rights and little freedom.

The United States saw the spread of communism as a threat to freedom. It began to help countries fight communism by giving them military and economic help. In the fight against communism, the United States and its allies were known as the **free world**.

Hostility, or unfriendliness, developed between the free world and the communist nations. This hostility became known as the Cold War. A **cold war** is fought with propaganda and money rather than with soldiers and weapons. For much of the second half of the 1900s, the Cold War shaped world events.

REVIEW *How did the United States help fight communism?*

Europe in 1945

* National capital

UNION OF SOVIET
SOCIALIST REPUBLICS

Place | World War II changed Europe in ways that would affect the
world for years to come.

■ *What does this map show about changes that took place in Germany after World War II?*

LESSON 5 REVIEW

Check Understanding

1 Remember the Facts   Who led the D day invasion? When did the invasion take place?

2 Recall the Main Idea   In what ways did World War II affect countries around the world?

Think Critically

3 Cause and Effect   How did differences between the United States and the Soviet Union cause problems after World War II?

4 Think More About It   How were the reasons for fighting in World War I different from the reasons for fighting in World War II?

Show What You Know

Writing Activity   Imagine that you are an Allied soldier who has helped free the people from a Nazi concentration camp. Use the picture in this lesson to write a letter home that describes what you saw there. Share your letter with a family member.

Read Parallel Time Lines

1. Why Learn This Skill?

When there are many events happening at about the same time, it can be difficult to put them in order. It even can be difficult to show them on one time line. Parallel time lines can help. Parallel time lines are two or more time lines that show the same period of time. Parallel time lines can also show events that happened in different places.

2. Understand the Process

The parallel time lines on this page show events that took place in 1945, the last year of World War II. Time Line A shows the important events that affected Europe. Time Line B shows the important events that affected the Pacific. You can use these parallel time lines to compare when different events happened.

❶ Which event took place first, V-E Day or V-J Day?

❷ Why do you think the label *Truman becomes President* is on both time lines?

❸ Did the United States drop the atom bomb on Hiroshima before or after Soviet troops surrounded Berlin?

❹ What was happening in Europe while the Battle of Iwo Jima was being fought?

3. Think and Apply

Create parallel time lines of events that have happened in your lifetime. Use one time line to show the important events in your life, beginning with the year you were born and ending with the present year. Use the other time line to show important events that have taken place in the United States during these same years.

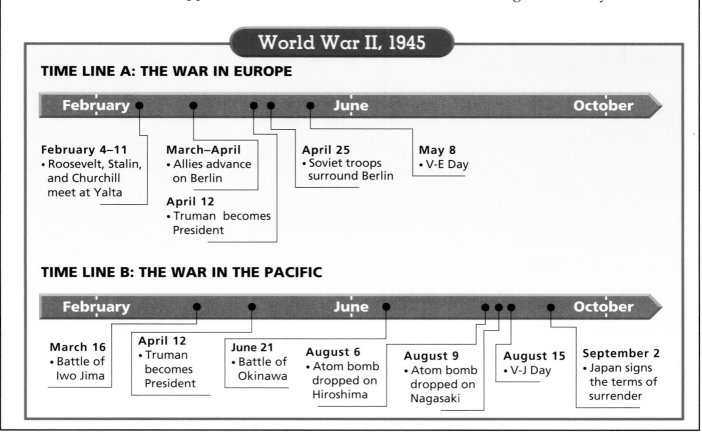

World War II, 1945

TIME LINE A: THE WAR IN EUROPE

February — June — October

February 4–11
• Roosevelt, Stalin, and Churchill meet at Yalta

March–April
• Allies advance on Berlin

April 12
• Truman becomes President

April 25
• Soviet troops surround Berlin

May 8
• V-E Day

TIME LINE B: THE WAR IN THE PACIFIC

February — June — October

March 16
• Battle of Iwo Jima

April 12
• Truman becomes President

June 21
• Battle of Okinawa

August 6
• Atom bomb dropped on Hiroshima

August 9
• Atom bomb dropped on Nagasaki

August 15
• V-J Day

September 2
• Japan signs the terms of surrender

CHAPTER 18
REVIEW

1900
1903
• First airplane flight
1910

CONNECT MAIN IDEAS

Use this graphic organizer to show how the chapter's main ideas are connected. Write three details to support each main idea. A copy of the organizer appears on page 121 of the Activity Book.

The Roaring Twenties brought good times to many Americans.

1. _____
2. _____
3. _____

World War II affected countries around the world.

1. _____
2. _____
3. _____

Good Times and Bad

The federal government helped Americans who were out of work during the Great Depression.

1. _____
2. _____
3. _____

The Dust Bowl made life very hard for people living on the Great Plains.

1. _____
2. _____
3. _____

The United States and countries in Europe and Asia entered into World War II.

1. _____
2. _____
3. _____

WRITE MORE ABOUT IT

Write a Short Story Imagine that you are living in the 1920s. Write a short story about your family getting its first automobile. In your story describe what it is like to ride in a car for the first time. Also tell how the car has changed your family's life.

Write a Diary Entry Imagine that you are living during World War II. Write a diary entry about going shopping with your family. Tell how the war has affected what you can buy. Also describe other ways the war has affected your family.

1929
• Stock market crashes

1939
• World War II begins

1941
• U.S. enters World War II

1945
• Germany and Japan surrender, ending World War II

USE VOCABULARY

For each group of terms, write a sentence or two explaining how the terms are related.

1. consumer good, installment buying
2. assembly line, commercial industry
3. stock market, depression, unemployment
4. civilian, rationing
5. front, D day, island-hopping
6. communism, free world, cold war

CHECK UNDERSTANDING

7. What advantage did installment buying offer the consumer?
8. How was Henry Ford able to produce cars less expensively?
9. What event helped make air travel a commercial industry?
10. How did jazz develop?
11. Why did Harlem attract so many people in the 1920s?
12. Why did many banks close during the Great Depression?
13. How did New Deal programs help workers?
14. What event caused the United States to enter the fighting in World War II?
15. Who were the largest group of victims in the Holocaust?
16. What did the United States see as a threat to freedom following World War II?

THINK CRITICALLY

17. **Personally Speaking** In the 1920s, movies and radio allowed Americans to learn about the world around them. How do you get information about the world?
18. **Cause and Effect** What effects did forced relocation have on the lives of Japanese Americans during World War II?

APPLY SKILLS

Read Parallel Time Lines Use the parallel time lines on page 595 to answer the questions.

19. What happened on April 12, 1945?
20. Did the Battle of Okinawa happen before or after Soviet troops surrounded Berlin?
21. Which happened first, the Battle of Iwo Jima or V-E Day?

READ MORE ABOUT IT

Rosie the Riveter by Penny Colman. Crown, 1995. This book uses primary sources to describe the American women who took over the jobs left behind by men during World War II.

Visit the Internet at **http://www.hbschool.com** for additional resources.

AMERICAN IDEAS AND PRODUCTS

During the 1900s the United States became a world power. As a result, American culture has spread. Today people everywhere are familiar with American ideas and products.

Millions of people around the world go to see American movies. They also watch the news on CNN, the Atlanta-based cable news network, and tune into American television shows.

American products are also popular internationally. Hundreds of millions of people outside the United States drink Coca-Cola. In fact, 95 percent of Coca-Cola's sales come from outside the country. People from Moscow to Singapore line up at McDonald's, often wearing American jeans and athletic shoes.

Think and Apply

With a partner, create a poster showing fifth graders in different countries using American products. Include American clothes, foods, and other products that you think children in other countries like. Share your poster with the class.

HARCOURT BRACE
Visit the Internet at **http://www.hbschool.com** for additional resources.

CNN Turner Le@rning
Check your media center or classroom video library for the Making Social Studies Relevant videotape of this feature.

UNIT 9
REVIEW

Summarize the Main Ideas
Study the pictures and captions to help you review the events you read about in Unit 9.

Write a Newspaper Article
Imagine that you are a newspaper reporter covering one of the events in this visual summary. Write an article describing the event.

1 By 1900 the United States had become a world power. It gained new territories after the Spanish-American War, in which Theodore Roosevelt's Rough Riders became famous.

3 The United States entered World War I in 1917. Most American soldiers fought from trenches.

6 During the Great Depression, millions of people lost their jobs. Many were forced to line up for free food. Drought on the Great Plains brought still more suffering.

2 The Panama Canal opened in 1914. It linked the Atlantic and Pacific oceans.

4 Women gained the right to vote in 1920, when the Nineteenth Amendment to the Constitution was ratified.

5 Automobiles became popular in the 1920s. During the Roaring Twenties, the United States economy boomed.

7 The United States entered World War II in 1941, when Pearl Harbor was attacked.

8 After World War II, the United Nations was formed to help keep world peace.

WOMEN'S RIGHT TO VOTE!

UNIT 9
REVIEW

USE VOCABULARY

Use each term in a sentence that will help explain its meaning.

1. merit system
2. military draft
3. aviation
4. jazz
5. bureaucracy
6. unemployment
7. minimum wage
8. concentration camp

CHECK UNDERSTANDING

9. What part did the battleship *Maine* play in the Spanish-American War?

10. How is the Panama Canal important to world trade?

11. How did transportation and communications change in the 1920s?

12. How did the Great Depression affect Americans?

13. What ended World War II in the Pacific?

THINK CRITICALLY

14. **Past to Present** How do alliances among countries affect the world today?

15. **Cause and Effect** What caused hostility to develop between the United States and the Soviet Union following World War II?

APPLY SKILLS

Compare Map Projections Map A is an azimuthal equal-area projection. Map B is an orthographic projection. Use these maps to answer the questions.

16. On which map does the United States look larger?

17. On which map can you more clearly see the North Pole?

18. What are the advantages and disadvantages of each type of projection?

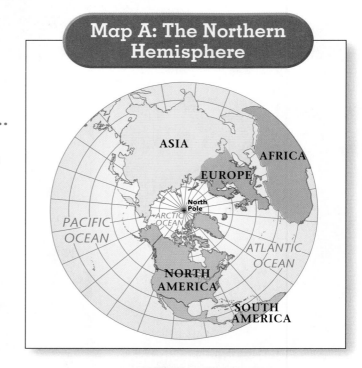

Map A: The Northern Hemisphere

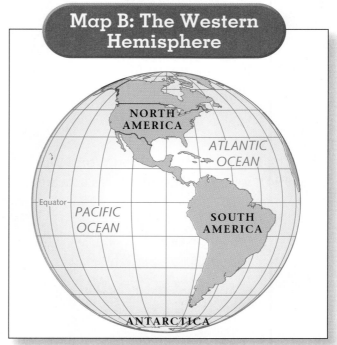

Map B: The Western Hemisphere

REMEMBER

- Share your ideas.
- Cooperate with others to plan your work.
- Take responsibility for your work.
- Help one another.
- Show your group's work to the class.
- Discuss what you learned by working together.

ACTIVITY

Give a Talk

Work in groups to research either the Roaring Twenties or the Great Depression. Find out how life in each decade was similar to and different from life today. When your research is complete, give a short talk to the class. If possible, play music from the 1920s or 1930s, and show pictures of people from the decade your group chose.

ACTIVITY

Invite Guest Speakers

Work in groups to invite several guest speakers to your class. With your teacher's help, choose a date and time for them to come. Then write a letter to a seniors' group in your community, inviting members to talk to your class about life during World War II.

Unit Project Wrap-Up

Make a Class Mural With your classmates, create a mural of American history from the 1890s through the 1940s. To complete this project, the class should divide into six groups, one for each decade. Members of each group should come up with scenes that illustrate important events that occurred during the decade. Be sure to think about the experiences of farmers, soldiers, industrial workers, women, and African Americans during your period. Group members should work together to paint or draw the scenes they have chosen.

THE AMERICAS TODAY

Throughout their history American citizens have been challenged in many ways—socially, politically, and economically. The years after World War II created even more challenges for Americans. As citizens of a world power, they had new responsibilities, and they needed to find new ways to respond to a changing world. In the last four decades, Americans have confronted the communist world, explored outer space, and worked to support democracy around the world. In facing these challenges, Americans have helped shape the future of their free and democratic society.

◄ The space shuttle *Discovery* takes off from Kennedy Space Center in Cape Canaveral, Florida.

UNIT THEMES

- Conflict and Cooperation
- Commonality and Diversity
- Continuity and Change
- Individualism and Interdependence

Unit Project

Create a Space Travel Exhibit
Complete this project with your classmates as you study Unit 10. As you read about space travel in the twentieth century, make a list of images to include in your exhibit. Find out what plans are being made for future space exploration. Make a classroom display of drawings, magazines, and other projects relating to space travel.

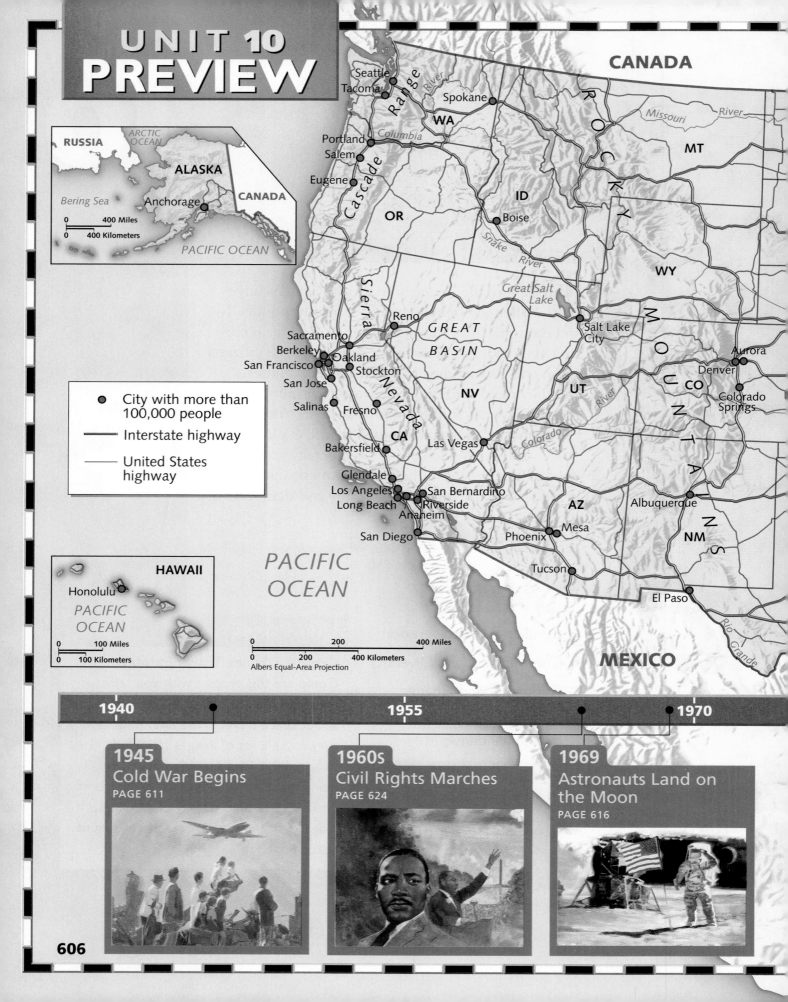

UNIT 10 PREVIEW

RUSSIA
ARCTIC OCEAN
ALASKA
Bering Sea
Anchorage
CANADA
PACIFIC OCEAN

0   400 Miles
0   400 Kilometers

CANADA

Seattle
Tacoma
Spokane
WA
Columbia
Portland
Salem
Eugene
Cascade Range
Range
River
Columbia
Missouri
River
MT
ID
Boise
Snake River
WY
Great Salt Lake
Salt Lake City
ROCKY
Reno
GREAT BASIN
Sacramento
Berkeley
Oakland
San Francisco
Stockton
San Jose
Salinas
Fresno
Sierra Nevada
NV
UT
Colorado River
Aurora
Denver
CO
Colorado Springs
MOUNTAINS
Bakersfield
CA
Las Vegas
Colorado
Glendale
Los Angeles
Long Beach
Anaheim
San Bernardino
Riverside
San Diego
AZ
Phoenix
Mesa
Tucson
Albuquerque
NM
El Paso
Rio Grande

- ● City with more than 100,000 people
- — Interstate highway
- — United States highway

HAWAII
Honolulu
PACIFIC OCEAN

0   100 Miles
0   100 Kilometers

PACIFIC OCEAN

0   200   400 Miles
0   200   400 Kilometers
Albers Equal-Area Projection

MEXICO

1940 — 1955 — 1970

1945
Cold War Begins
PAGE 611

1960s
Civil Rights Marches
PAGE 624

1969
Astronauts Land on the Moon
PAGE 616

The United States, 2000

CANADA

Lake Superior

Lake Michigan

Lake Huron

Lake Ontario

Lake Erie

ATLANTIC OCEAN

Gulf of Mexico

ND
MN
SD
WI
MI
ME
VT NH
MA
NY
CT RI

St. Paul
Minneapolis
Sioux Falls
Milwaukee
Madison
Grand Rapids
Flint
Lansing
Detroit
Buffalo
Albany
Worcester
Boston
Syracuse
Rochester
Hartford
Providence
New Haven
Bridgeport

NE
IA
Omaha
Lincoln
Cedar Rapids
Des Moines
Rockford
Aurora
Chicago
Ann Arbor
South Bend
Gary
Peoria
Fort Wayne
Toledo
Cleveland
Erie
Akron
Columbus
Dayton
Jersey City
Newark
New York City
Allentown
Pittsburgh
Philadelphia

Platte River
Mississippi River
Missouri River
Ohio R.

NE
KS
Kansas City
Topeka
Kansas City
Springfield
Wichita
IL
Springfield
Indianapolis
Cincinnati
IN
OH
WV
MD
Baltimore
Washington, D.C.
DE
PA

MO
St. Louis
Evansville
Louisville
Lexington
KY
Richmond
Newport News
Virginia Beach
VA
Norfolk

OK
Tulsa
Oklahoma City
Arkansas River
Little Rock
AR
Memphis
Nashville
TN
Knoxville
Chattanooga
Huntsville
Greensboro
Durham
Raleigh
Winston-Salem
NC
Charlotte
Columbia
SC

TX
Fort Worth
Dallas
Arlington
Abilene
Waco
Austin
San Antonio
Houston
Beaumont
Shreveport
LA
Baton Rouge
New Orleans
Jackson
MS
Birmingham
Montgomery
AL
Columbus
Macon
Atlanta
GA
Savannah
Jacksonville
Tallahassee
Mobile
FL
Orlando
Tampa
St. Petersburg

APPALACHIAN

N
W E
S

1985   **2000**

1975
Vietnam War Ends
PAGE 630

1989
The Berlin Wall is Torn Down
PAGE 636

1994
NAFTA Agreement Goes into Effect
PAGE 645

THE INAUGURAL POEM

ON
THE
PULSE
OF
MORNING

MAYA ANGELOU

On the pulse of morning

by
MAYA ANGELOU

Maya Angelou (AN•juh•loh) wrote her poem "On the Pulse of Morning" for the inauguration of Bill Clinton as President of the United States. Clinton took the oath of office on January 20, 1993. In her poem Angelou wanted to show that she loves her country despite its problems. She also wanted to celebrate the past while speaking hopefully about the future. As you read the poem, think about the problems and hopes Americans had in the years after World War II.

Lift up your eyes
Upon this day breaking for you.
Give birth again
To the dream.

Women, children, men,
Take it into the palms of your hands,
Mold it into the shape of your most
Private need. Sculpt it into
The image of your most public self.
Lift up your hearts.
Each new hour holds new chances
For a new beginning.
Do not be wedded forever
To fear, yoked eternally
To brutishness.

The horizon leans forward,
Offering you space
To place new steps of change.
Here, on the pulse of this fine day,
You may have the courage
To look up and out and upon me,
The Rock, the River, the Tree, your country.
No less to Midas than the mendicant [beggar].
No less to you now than the mastodon then.

Here, on the pulse of this new day,
You may have the grace to look up and out
And into your sister's eyes,
And into your brother's face,
        Your country,
        And say simply
        Very simply
        With hope—
        Good morning.

609

THE COLD WAR YEARS

"I have a dream that my four little children will one day live in a nation where they will not be judged by the color of their skin but by the content of their character."

Martin Luther King, Jr., Washington, D.C., August 28, 1963

The Cold War Begins

FOCUS
What can happen when powerful friends become enemies?

Main Idea   Read to find out what happened when two World War II Allies— the United States and the Soviet Union— became enemies after the war.

Vocabulary
superpower
airlift
cease-fire
missile
arms race

In the years after World War II, the United States and the Soviet Union became the world's most powerful nations. They were called **superpowers** because of the important roles they played in world events. The two superpowers were very different from one another, and there were many conflicts between them. These conflicts were fought mostly with words and economic weapons. Even so, the threat of a real war was always present. These years, from 1945 to 1991, have become known as the Cold War years. They were a frightening time for many people.

The Berlin Crisis

At the end of World War II, the Allies divided Germany into four parts. Each of the major Allies took charge of one part. The United States, Britain, and France worked together to build a strong West Germany out of their parts. The Soviet Union held East Germany and formed a communist country there. Under this system, the government took over land and businesses. The people had little freedom to make decisions about how their country should be run.

Berlin, the capital of Germany, was in East Germany. It was divided into four parts, too. But the Soviet Union would not let the Western Allies send supplies to the area the Allies controlled, which made up the city of West Berlin. The Soviets blocked highway, rail, and water routes so that no food or fuel could get into the city. They hoped to drive the Western Allies out of West Berlin.

To get around the blockade, the Allies started the Berlin Airlift in 1948. An **airlift** is a system of bringing in supplies by

These children in West Berlin are cheering as a plane carrying supplies flies over their city.

611

Europe and the Cold War

Communist country
Noncommunist country
— Iron Curtain

0   250   500 Miles
0   250   500 Kilometers
Azimuthal Equal-Area Projection

FINLAND
NORWAY
SWEDEN
North Sea
IRELAND
DENMARK
BRITAIN
Baltic Sea
NETHERLANDS
BRITISH ZONE
SOVIET ZONE
Berlin
POLAND
BELGIUM
EAST GERMANY
LUXEMBOURG
FRENCH ZONE
WEST GERMANY
CZECHOSLOVAKIA
AMERICAN ZONE
ATLANTIC OCEAN
FRANCE
SWITZERLAND
AUSTRIA
HUNGARY
ROMANIA
PORTUGAL
SPAIN
ITALY
YUGOSLAVIA
BULGARIA
Black Sea
ALBANIA
TURKEY
GREECE
Mediterranean Sea
AFRICA
ASIA

Division of Berlin

FRENCH SECTOR
BRITISH SECTOR
West Berlin
AMERICAN SECTOR
East Berlin
SOVIET SECTOR

UNION OF SOVIET SOCIALIST REPUBLICS

Regions Communist countries were said to be "behind the Iron Curtain." The Iron Curtain was a term used to express the idea that the people in communist countries were cut off from the rest of the world. This East German worker (right) is helping build the Berlin Wall.

■ *Which European countries were "behind the Iron Curtain?"*

airplane. For 11 months American and British pilots made more than 272,000 flights over East Germany to West Berlin. They carried more than 2 million tons of food and supplies to the people of West Berlin. Finally, the Soviets backed down and allowed supplies to be delivered over land.

After the blockade ended, many people tried to leave East Berlin to escape from communist rule. In 1961 the East German government, with Soviet help, built a fence to keep people from leaving. Then East Germany took down the fence and put up a concrete wall with barbed wire on the top.

The Berlin Wall, as it came to be known, was guarded by soldiers ready to shoot anyone who tried to cross it. The wall became one of the best-known symbols of the Cold War. It stood for the division between the free world and the communist countries.

REVIEW *How did the Western Allies solve the problem of getting supplies to West Berlin?*

The Korean War

Just as Germany was divided after World War II, Korea was divided into two parts. Soviet troops occupied North Korea, and American troops occupied South Korea. In 1948 North Korea formed a communist government, and South Korea formed a republic.

In 1950 the North Korean army, which had been trained and equipped by the Soviet Union, invaded South Korea. North Korea wanted to make all of Korea communist. North Korea was also helped by China, which had become communist in 1949.

United States President Harry S. Truman quickly sent more American soldiers to support South Korea. The United Nations also sent troops to stop the invasion. About 15 countries were now fighting a new war—the Korean War.

So many American soldiers died in the fighting that the Korean War became a major issue in the 1952 election for President of the United States. Dwight D. Eisenhower, the famous World War II general, promised that if he was elected, he would work to end the war. Soon after his election he kept his promise. By 1953 the North Korean troops had been pushed back into North Korea. A **cease-fire**, or an end to the shooting and bombing, was then declared, and an armistice was signed to stop the fighting. South Korea remained an independent country.

REVIEW *What were the results of the Korean War?*

The Cuban Missile Crisis

In 1961 John F. Kennedy took the oath of office as President of the United States. Only 43 years old, Kennedy was the youngest person ever elected President. At his inauguration, the new President tried to inspire

A Divided Korea

Movement At the end of World War II, Soviet troops in Korea were north of the 38th parallel, and American troops were south of it.

■ *How did the cease-fire line of 1953 change the northern boundary of South Korea?*

Americans to work for the good of their country. He said,

66 Ask not what your country can do for you; ask what you can do for your country. 99

His energy and his enthusiasm made him especially popular with young people. Soon

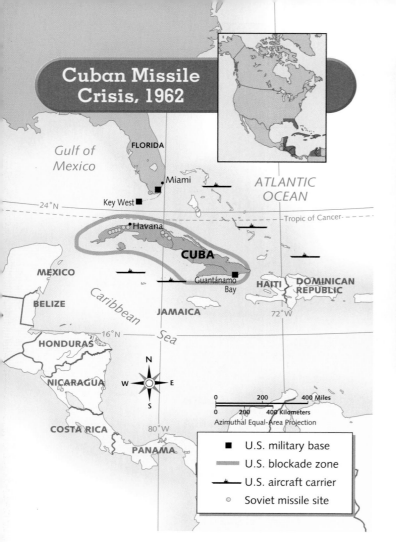

Cuban Missile Crisis, 1962

Gulf of Mexico

FLORIDA

Miami

Key West ■

24°N

ATLANTIC OCEAN

Tropic of Cancer

Havana

CUBA

Guantánamo Bay

HAITI

DOMINICAN REPUBLIC

MEXICO

72°W

BELIZE

Caribbean

JAMAICA

16°N

Sea

HONDURAS

N
W E
S

NICARAGUA

0   200   400 Miles
0   200   400 Kilometers
Azimuthal Equal-Area Projection

COSTA RICA   80°W

PANAMA

■ U.S. military base
▬ U.S. blockade zone
⊢ U.S. aircraft carrier
○ Soviet missile site

Human-Environment Interactions

President John F. Kennedy (above right) ordered a naval blockade of Cuba during the 1962 missile crisis. He often discussed problems with his brother Attorney General Robert F. Kennedy (above left).

■ *Why do you think U.S. aircraft carriers were placed where they were?*

after he took office, Cold War problems began to take up much of his time.

In October 1962 President Kennedy learned that the Soviet Union had built several launch sites for missiles in Cuba, just 90 miles (145 km) off the southern tip of Florida. A **missile** is a rocket that can carry a bomb over a long distance. Fidel Castro had taken control of Cuba in 1959. With the help of the Soviet Union, Castro had formed a communist government.

Worried that the Soviets would attack the United States from Cuba, Kennedy ordered a blockade of the island nation. The United States Navy would stop Soviet ships that were carrying missiles from reaching Cuba. Americans worried as they listened to the news on radio and television. What if the ships refused to stop? Would there be a war?

Finally, the Soviet Union agreed to stop sending missiles to Cuba and to remove all the missiles that were already there. The United States agreed to end the blockade.

Kennedy's success in handling the missile crisis increased his popularity. But he knew he would have to work hard to be elected President again. On November 22, 1963, the President and Jacqueline Kennedy, his wife, visited Dallas, Texas, to meet with supporters there. They were waving to the crowds as their car drove through the streets. Suddenly shots rang out. President Kennedy was killed. A few hours after the assassination, Vice President Lyndon Baines Johnson took the oath of office as the new President.

REVIEW *Why did the United States take action when the Soviet Union set up missile bases in Cuba?*

In the early 1960s, Americans worried about being attacked by Soviet missiles. During drills like the one shown here, students were trained to prepare for a missile attack.

The Arms Race

The Cold War helped start an arms race between the two superpowers. In an **arms race** one country builds weapons to protect itself against another country. The other country then builds even more weapons to protect itself. Both the United States and the Soviet Union believed that having the most and the strongest weapons would keep their people safe.

The arms race started with the atom bomb. The Soviet Union knew what atom bombs had done to the Japanese cities of Hiroshima and Nagasaki. It feared the power of the United States to destroy a whole city with one bomb. Soon the Soviet Union was building its own atom bombs.

After the Soviet Union had the atom bomb, however, the United States made an even more powerful bomb. Scientists said that the hydrogen bomb, or the H-bomb, was 1,000 times more powerful than the atom bombs dropped on Japan during World War II. Other atomic weapons were made, too. By the 1960s the superpowers had missiles that could carry bombs to targets halfway around the world.

Both the Americans and the Soviets lived in fear during the Cold War. Some Americans built special shelters below ground as protection in case of an attack. They stocked their shelters with flashlights, radios, first-aid kits, canned food, water, and other supplies. At schools across the country, "duck-and-cover" drills were held to teach children to get under their desks if a missile attack came.

REVIEW *What was each side's goal in the arms race?*

LESSON I REVIEW

Check Understanding

1. **Remember the Facts**   What events contributed to Cold War conflicts?

2. **Recall the Main Idea**   How did relations between the United States and the Soviet Union change after World War II?

Think Critically

3. **Think More About It**   Why do you think the Soviet Union wanted to drive the Western Allies out of West Berlin?

4. **Personally Speaking**   How do you think people in the United States and people in the Soviet Union felt about one another during the Cold War?

Show What You Know

Letter-Writing Activity
Imagine that you are living during the Cold War. Write a letter to President Kennedy telling him how you feel about the arms race. Read the letter to your classmates.

ONE GIANT LEAP

written by Mary Ann Fraser

The United States and the Soviet Union took the Cold War into space. In 1957 the Soviets surprised the United States by launching Sputnik (SPUT·nik). Sputnik was the world's first space satellite, an object sent by a rocket into an orbit around the Earth.

Because of Sputnik, the United States speeded up its own efforts to explore space. In 1958 Congress set up the National Aeronautics and Space Administration, or NASA, to develop the nation's space program. Then, in 1961, President John F. Kennedy set a goal for the United States. The goal was to put a person on the moon by the end of the 1960s.

In 1962 John Glenn became the first American astronaut to orbit the Earth. Then a series of explorations called the Apollo program prepared for a moon landing. In 1968 astronauts in Apollo 8 first circled the moon. By the next year NASA was ready to try a moon landing. On July 16, 1969, Apollo 11 blasted off from Cape Canaveral, Florida. On board were astronauts Neil Armstrong, Edwin "Buzz" Aldrin, Jr., and Michael Collins. NASA scientists at Mission Control in Houston, Texas, followed their flight closely. Now read the story of the first moon landing four days later.

The astronauts'
view of Earth
from the moon

July 20, 1969

As the sun rose in Houston, Mission Control gently woke the crew. "*Apollo 11, Apollo 11*—good morning from the Black Team."

Michael Collins replied, "Good morning, Houston . . . oh my, you guys wake up early."

The astronauts may not have been ready to wake up, but this was the day they had waited and trained for: landing day. After breakfast and a briefing from Mission Control, Aldrin and Armstrong put on their liquid-cooling undergarments. Grabbing hold of the handrails, they floated into *Eagle.* Collins remained behind so he could help his fellow astronauts if anything went wrong.

On *Apollo 11*'s thirteenth orbit, Collins pushed the switch to release the final latches. Gently the modules drifted apart to become two independent vehicles.

Houston broke through the static as *Eagle* soared from behind the moon. "Roger. How does it look?"

Armstrong was now controlling *Eagle.* He answered, "*Eagle* has wings."

One-and-a-half hours later tension mounted again as *Eagle* followed *Columbi* toward the back side of the moon to begin its descent. In less than 11 minutes Armstrong and Aldrin had to cross 300 miles of the moon's surface in *Eagle,* dropping in a long curve from 50,000 feet to touchdown.

Any equipment failure or miscalculatio would mean turning back or certain disaster. If a leg on the lunar module came to rest on a boulder or slope and the module toppled over, *Eagle* would not be able to take off. The men would be stranded. Some scientists thought that the moon's windless surface had a dangerously deep coating of dust. They worried that the module or men would sink into this loose lunar soil.

Apollo 11 blasts off.

Back on Earth, hundreds of journalists packed newsrooms while millions of TV viewers and radio listeners tuned in for word of the astronauts. The people of Mission Control waited for the static on their headsets to clear.

Eagle swung around from behind the moon, heading for the landing site on the Sea of Tranquility. Armstrong's voice finally came through. "The burn was on time."

"Current altitude about 46,000 feet, continuing to descend," reported the flight controller in Houston.

Just then ground control lost direct communication with *Eagle*. All commands had to be relayed through Mike Collins in *Columbia*. Armstrong adjusted *Eagle*'s position in flight, and Mission Control tried again to communicate directly. "*Eagle*, Houston. You are go. Take it all at four minutes. Roger, you are go—you are go to continue power descent."

"Roger." Aldrin had heard the message and commented, "And the earth right out our front window."

Suddenly an alarm went off in the cabin. "Twelve-o-two—twelve-o-two!" shouted Armstrong. "Give us the reading on the twelve-o-two program alarm."

The guidance computer was overloaded with data, but Mission Control decided *Eagle* should still proceed with landing. "Roger . . . we got—we're go on that alarm."

Armstrong peered through his small, triangular window. The computer was taking them to a stadium-size crater littered with ancient boulders, rock, and rubble. With the flip of a switch, Armstrong seized full manual control from the computer. Now he had to use all the flying skills he had learned as a pilot.

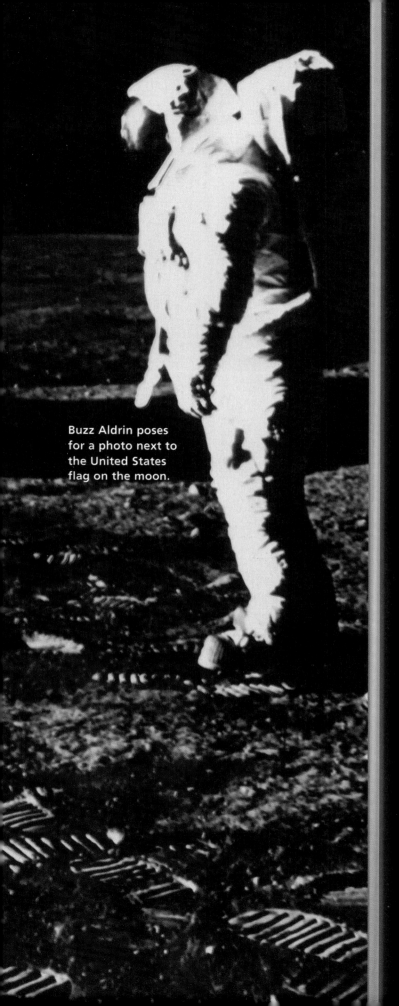

Buzz Aldrin poses for a photo next to the United States flag on the moon.

He adjusted the spacecraft's hovering position while Aldrin guided him. "Lights on. Forward. Good. Forty feet, down two and a half. Picking up some dust. Thirty feet, two and a half down. Faint shadow. Four forward. Four forward, drifting to the right a little." The rocket's firing was creating dust clouds, making it difficult to see.

Armstrong frantically searched for a site. Mission Control interrupted, "30 SECONDS!" Only 30 seconds of fuel for landing remained. Armstrong had to land immediately.

Slowly he lowered the craft. The blue light in the cockpit flashed. "Contact light," reported Aldrin. One of the three probes, like a feeler on a giant insect, had touched ground. "Okay, engine stop." They had landed four miles west of their original target, but still within the planned area.

"Houston, Tranquility Base here. The *Eagle* has landed," said Armstrong.

"Roger, Tranquility, we copy you on the ground," replied Mission Control. "You've got a bunch of guys about to turn blue. We're breathing again. Thanks a lot."

Back on Earth people of all nationalities celebrated the moon landing. But while Americans Armstrong and Aldrin had been skillfully piloting their spacecraft toward the Sea of Tranquility, the [Soviet Union's unmanned] *Luna 15* had crashed into the moon's Sea of Crises at nearly 300 miles per hour.

For several seconds Aldrin and Armstrong, the first humans on the moon, waited for the dust to settle about their spacecraft. Slowly they got their first glimpse of an alien world that had not changed for millions of years.

Armstrong (above left) and Aldrin (above right) are photographed on the moon's surface from a camera mounted in the lunar module. Neil Armstrong left his footprint (right) when he took the first step on the moon.

Meanwhile Collins in *Columbia* orbited to the back side of the moon, totally on his own for the first time.

A billion people from all over the world anxiously waited for the first steps onto the moon. Aldrin and Armstrong were no longer being viewed as Americans, but as representatives of all humanity.

With the last snap of their helmets in place, Armstrong and Aldrin could see but could no longer hear, taste, smell, or feel anything outside their space suits. The suits were their only protection against the moon's extreme temperatures, which ranged from –247 to 212 degrees Fahrenheit. Any tear in the suit could be fatal.

With Aldrin guiding him, Armstrong carefully stepped down the nine rungs of the ladder toward the moon's airless, waterless surface.

"I'm at the foot of the ladder. . . . The surface appears very, very fine grained as you get close to it." Armstrong could see that *Eagle*'s landing pads had barely sunk into the lunar dust. The moon's surface seemed safe. "I'm going to step off the LM [lunar module] now."

Exactly 109 hours, 24 minutes and 15 seconds into the mission, Armstrong stepped off the landing pad and placed the first human footprint on the moon.

"That's one small step for man, one giant leap for mankind," he said.

He had meant to say, "one small step for a man," but in his excitement and nervousness he left out the *a*. A few moments later Aldrin joined him.

With those first prints in the lunar dust the people of Earth proved they could reach beyond their planet and touch the moon. Neil Armstrong, Buzz Aldrin, and Michael Collins, through skill, courage, and teamwork, had helped realize centuries of dreams. Other men and women could now follow in their footsteps.

After a total of six moon landings, NASA began new space explorations. Unmanned spacecraft were launched far into the solar system to learn more about other planets. Today space shuttles and space stations orbit the Earth, and astronauts conduct scientific experiments in space.

The lunar module (right) allowed Armstrong and Aldrin to land safely on the moon's surface. A space suit (left) allows an astronaut to explore outside the spacecraft.

LITERATURE REVIEW

1. When did the first astronauts land on the moon?
2. What kinds of problems do you think the scientists at NASA had to solve in building a spacecraft to carry people to the moon?
3. Draw pictures about the space program. You may want to draw the *Apollo 11* astronauts landing on the moon or the space shuttle taking off or landing. Write captions for your pictures and share them with your classmates.

FOCUS

How do individuals today work to improve life in the United States?

Main Idea As you read, look for ways individuals worked to improve life in the United States in the twentieth century.

Vocabulary

nonviolence
integration

The Struggle for Equal Rights

In the years after World War II, Americans hoped for peace. Instead, they were in a cold war and an arms race with the Soviet Union. The struggle to bring peace to an uneasy world was not the only problem that Americans faced after World War II. People across the country continued to struggle for equal rights.

A Court Ruling

Seven-year-old Linda Brown of Topeka, Kansas, wanted to go to school with the other children in her neighborhood. She did not understand why state laws in Kansas said that African American children had to go to separate schools. Federal laws supported this segregation, or separation of the races, as long as the separate schools were equal. In most cases, however, they were not.

Thirteen African American families, among them Linda Brown's, decided to try to get these laws changed. The NAACP agreed to help them. One of its lawyers, Thurgood Marshall, presented the case before the United States Supreme Court. Marshall argued that separate schools did not provide equal education.

In 1954 the Supreme Court made a decision that supported what Thurgood Marshall had said. Chief Justice Earl Warren said, "In the field of education the doctrine [idea] of 'separate but equal' has no place." The Court ordered an end to segregation in public schools. However, many states were slow to obey that order. Their schools and other public places remained segregated.

REVIEW *What did the Supreme Court say about segregation in public schools?*

These lawyers—(left to right) George Hayes, Thurgood Marshall, and James Nabrit—argued against school segregation. They are standing outside the Supreme Court Building just after the Court's decision to end segregation in public schools.

The Montgomery Bus Boycott

On December 1, 1955, Rosa Parks of Montgomery, Alabama, got on a city bus and sat in the middle section. Under Alabama law, African Americans had to sit in the back. They could sit in the middle section only if the seats were not needed for white passengers.

As the bus filled up, the bus driver told Rosa Parks to give up her seat to a white man. She refused. The bus driver called the police, and Parks was arrested and taken to jail.

Many African Americans were angry when they heard what had happened. They held a meeting and decided to show the bus company's owners how they felt. They knew the company needed the money from African Americans' bus fares. So they passed the word—"Don't take the bus on Monday." A bus boycott began.

One of the leaders of the protest was Martin Luther King, Jr., a young minister in Montgomery. For more than a year, King and other African Americans boycotted the buses. King said that by working together they could bring about change peacefully. At last the Supreme Court ruled that all public transportation companies had to end segregation.

King believed in using **nonviolence**, or peaceful ways, to bring about change. He said that nonviolence would change people's minds and hearts, while violence would only make matters worse. So, many African Americans protested segregation in other public places—lunch counters, bus stations, schools, and other public buildings—in non-violent ways.

The protesters often used songs to tell their goals. They sang,

> 66 We shall overcome,
> We shall overcome,
> We shall overcome someday.
> Oh, deep in my heart, I do believe,
> We shall overcome someday. 99

REVIEW *What did the protesters hope the Montgomery bus boycott would do?*

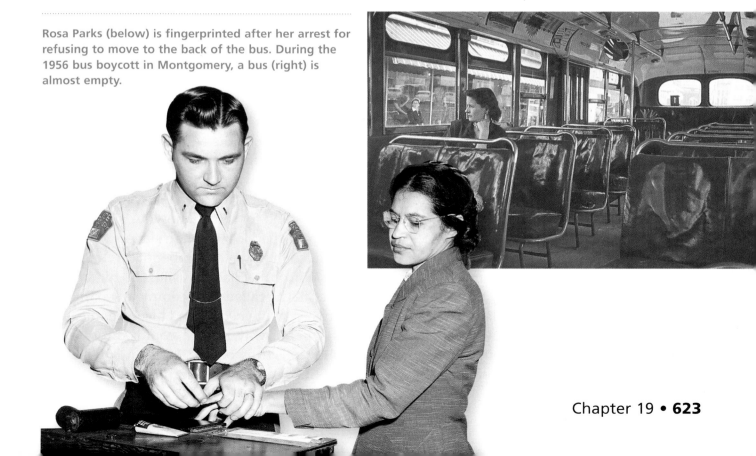

Rosa Parks (below) is fingerprinted after her arrest for refusing to move to the back of the bus. During the 1956 bus boycott in Montgomery, a bus (right) is almost empty.

Martin Luther King, Jr., Federal Holiday

Dr. Martin Luther King, Jr., was born on January 15, 1929, in Atlanta, Georgia. With the Montgomery bus boycott, he became a leader of the Civil Rights movement. He worked tirelessly for racial justice, despite many arrests and many threats on his life. On April 4, 1968, King was assassinated. Just four days later, people in Congress began working to make his birthday a federal holiday. But it was not until 1983 that a law was signed making the third Monday in January Martin Luther King, Jr., Day. The holiday was first observed on January 20, 1986. Today people celebrate the day with parades and other events. The special activities help them think about how they can keep alive King's dream of equality, justice, and peace.

Civil Rights Marches

Many African Americans looked to Martin Luther King, Jr., as their leader in the fight against segregation and for civil rights. In April 1963 King led marches in Birmingham, Alabama. The marchers wanted an end to all segregation. They called for **integration**, or the bringing together of people of all races in education, jobs, and housing.

For eight days there were marches. Many of the marchers were arrested, and King was one of those taken to jail. While King was held in jail, he wrote, "We know through painful experience that freedom is never voluntarily given. . . . It must be demanded."

Later that year 250,000 people from all different backgrounds gathered for a march in Washington, D.C. The marchers were showing their support for a new civil rights law that President Kennedy had asked the United States Congress to pass. As the marchers assembled in front of the Lincoln Memorial, Martin Luther King, Jr., spoke to them of his hopes. He said,

66 I have a dream that one day on the red hills of Georgia the sons of former slaves and the sons of former slaveowners will be able to sit down together at the table of brotherhood. . . . 99

In 1964 Congress passed the new civil rights law. The Civil Rights Act of 1964 made segregation in public places illegal. It also said that people of all races should have equal job opportunities.

REVIEW *What was the importance of the Civil Rights Act of 1964?*

Working for Change

In 1964 Martin Luther King, Jr., received the Nobel Peace Prize. He won the award for his use of nonviolent ways to bring about change. Not all African American leaders shared King's belief in nonviolent protest, however. One of them, Malcolm X, wanted change to happen faster.

Malcolm X was named Malcolm Little when he was born. He changed his last name to X to stand for the unknown African name his family had lost through slavery.

Malcolm X was a member of the Nation of Islam, or the Black Muslims. In his early speeches he called for a complete separation between white people and black people. Only in this way, he said, could African Americans truly be free. Malcolm X believed that freedom should be brought about "by

Proud of his African heritage, Malcolm X visited Egypt in 1964.

any means necessary." Later, after a trip to the Islamic holy city of Mecca in April 1964, he talked less about separation and more about cooperation among groups.

Malcolm X had little time to act on his ideas. In February 1965 he was assassinated. Then, in April 1968, Martin Luther King, Jr., also was assassinated.

Even though they had lost two important leaders, African Americans continued to work for change. Voting is one way that people bring about change. Knowing this, civil rights workers helped register African Americans to vote. By 1968 more than half of all African Americans who were old enough to vote were registered voters.

REVIEW *How did Malcolm X's views change later in his life?*

Other Groups Claim Their Rights

Following the lead of the African American Civil Rights movement, other groups of Americans began to organize for change. They, too, wanted equal rights under the law.

American Indians formed groups to work for the rights that they had been guaranteed in earlier treaties with the federal government. Although the government had promised these rights, in many cases the treaties had not been honored. Groups such as the National Congress of American Indians, the National Tribal Chairman's Association, and the American Indian Movement (AIM) began to work for American Indian rights. In 1975 the Indian Self-Determination and Educational Assistance Act was signed into law. For the first time Indian tribes were allowed to run their own businesses and health and education programs.

In the 1960s César Chávez organized a group that would become the United Farm Workers. Its members were mostly Mexican Americans. Like Martin Luther King, Jr., Chávez called for nonviolent action. In 1965 he called a strike of California grape pickers and started a boycott of grapes across the country. His goal was to get better wages and to improve working conditions. In 1970 Chávez reached agreement with the growers and helped the workers gain more rights.

REVIEW *What did groups such as the American Indian Movement and the United Farm Workers want to achieve?*

César Chávez (center) became a leader of labor organizations for farmworkers. Chávez was still working for the rights of farmworkers when he died in 1993.

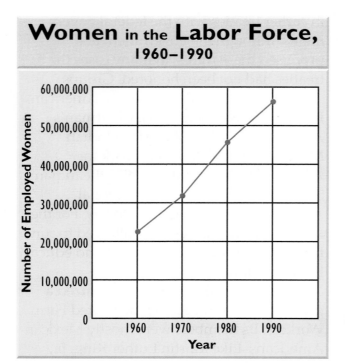

Women in the Labor Force, 1960–1990

Number of Employed Women (y-axis: 0 to 60,000,000)

Year (x-axis: 1960, 1970, 1980, 1990)

LEARNING FROM GRAPHS This graph shows how the number of women who worked outside the home increased from 1960 to 1990.

■ *About how many more women were employed in 1990 than in 1960? About how many times as many were employed in 1990 than in 1960?*

The Women's Rights Movement

Although the Civil Rights Act of 1964 said that all people should have equal job opportunities, many jobs still were not open to women. When men and women did have the same kind of job, women were often paid less than men. As a result, in 1966 writer Betty Friedan and others started the National Organization for Women, or NOW.

NOW and other women's rights groups helped elect many women to public office. They believed that these women would be able to get unfair laws changed.

By the 1970s new laws had been passed saying that employers must treat men and women equally. No job could be open to men only or women only. As a result, more women began careers in law, medicine, and business. Some became astronauts, construction workers, and firefighters. Others won elections and became members of Congress, governors of states, or mayors of cities. In 1981 Sandra Day O'Connor became the first woman appointed to the United States Supreme Court. In 1984 Geraldine Ferraro became the first woman nominated for Vice President by a major political party. Today women hold many important positions in government and in private companies.

REVIEW *What rights had women gained by the 1970s?*

LESSON 3 REVIEW

Check Understanding

❶ **Remember the Facts** Who were some of the main civil rights leaders in the United States in the twentieth century?

❷ **Recall the Main Idea** How did individuals work to improve life in the United States in the twentieth century?

Think Critically

❸ **Think More About It** Why is it important for everyone to be treated equally?

❹ **Past to Present** What rights do people have today as a result of the many struggles in the 1950s and 1960s?

Show What You Know

Simulation Activity
Imagine that it is 1963, and you are listening to Martin Luther King, Jr., speak at the march in Washington, D.C. With a partner, role-play a conversation between you and another marcher. Discuss how you feel about King's speech.

Act as a Responsible Citizen

1. Why Learn This Skill?

Democratic nations need responsible citizens. Citizens must know what is happening in their country, choose wise leaders, and take part in government. When a nation faces problems, its citizens may need to take action to solve those problems.

2. Remember What You Have Read

You have read about the struggle for civil rights in the United States during the 1950s and 1960s. Many citizens took part in the Civil Rights movement, which won important rights

Martin Luther King, Jr., used his skills as a public speaker to help the Civil Rights movement. Here he addresses a huge crowd during the March on Washington.

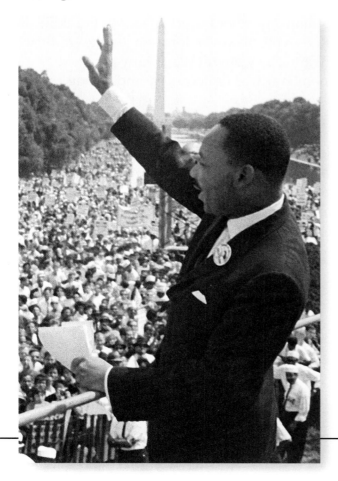

for African Americans. Martin Luther King, Jr., was a leader of this movement. The peaceful protests he led caught the attention of people around the world. King was not the only citizen to make a difference in the Civil Rights movement. Rosa Parks, who refused to give up her seat on a bus in Montgomery, Alabama, was one of hundreds of ordinary citizens to take part. Many risked their lives as they worked to gain civil rights for all.

3. Understand the Process

Acting as a responsible citizen is not always as difficult as it was during the struggle for civil rights. It can be as simple as listening to the news or voting. It does, however, require both thought and action.

Civil rights workers followed these five steps to act as responsible citizens:

1. They learned about the problems of prejudice and injustice in their country.
2. They thought about what could be done to bring about change.
3. They decided how to bring about change in a way that would be good for the whole country.
4. Each person decided what contribution he or she could best make.
5. People worked as individuals or with others to bring about change.

4. Think and Apply

Some acts of citizenship, such as voting, can be done only by adults. Others can be done by citizens of almost any age. The steps above can help anyone know how to act as a responsible citizen. Use the five steps as you decide on ways you and your classmates might act as responsible citizens of your community.

BUILDING CITIZENSHIP

FOCUS

How can people's opinions affect the actions of their government?

Main Idea As you read, think about how people's opinions brought about change during the 1960s and 1970s.

Vocabulary

hawk
dove
scandal

Vietnam War and Protests at Home

While many groups were trying to win better treatment and equal rights, President Lyndon Johnson was working on government programs to make life better for all Americans. These programs were part of Johnson's dream—what he called the Great Society. Johnson built on programs that President Franklin Roosevelt brought about during the New Deal. Johnson's Great Society programs included medical care for older people and help with education, housing, and jobs for those who needed it.

Between 1965 and 1968, President Johnson was able to get Congress to pass many new laws. In three years he got more programs started than any other President except Franklin Roosevelt. Like Roosevelt, however, Johnson led the country during a time of war—the Vietnam War. Many people thought the Vietnam War was unnecessary and wrong.

The Vietnam War

Like Korea, Vietnam was divided into two countries after World War II. North Vietnam became a communist country, and South Vietnam became a republic. In the late 1950s South Vietnamese communists, called the Vietcong, tried to take over the South Vietnamese government. They were helped by North

Many American soldiers reached Vietnam by ship. Soldiers' helmets (inset) were covered in different shades of green to help the soldiers blend in with the jungle.

Vietnam. Between 1956 and 1962, the United States sent money, war supplies, and soldiers to help South Vietnam fight the Vietcong.

By the time Johnson became President in 1963, the Vietcong were winning the war. Then, in August 1964, it was reported that a North Vietnamese gunboat attacked a United States Navy ship in the Gulf of Tonkin near Vietnam. Johnson sent more soldiers to South Vietnam to prevent another attack. The soldiers also fought the Vietcong.

When United States and South Vietnamese troops failed to defeat the Vietcong quickly, the United States sent planes to bomb North Vietnam. Johnson hoped the bombing would stop the flow of supplies from North Vietnam to the Vietcong. He also sent more troops to South Vietnam. By 1968 more than 500,000 United States soldiers were serving there.

The Vietnam War now was costing the United States billions of dollars each year. At the same time, President Johnson was starting many of his Great Society programs. Johnson said that the nation could afford both. As it turned out, he was wrong. To pay for both the Vietnam War and the programs of the Great Society, the government had to borrow a lot of money. This borrowing led to inflation. When there is inflation, people can buy less with the money they earn. A country's economy suffers.

REVIEW *How did the Vietnam War affect the economy of the United States?*

Americans Are Divided

The Vietnam War divided American public opinion. Some people said the war was needed to stop the spread of communism. Others said it was a civil war that should be settled by the Vietnamese without outside help.

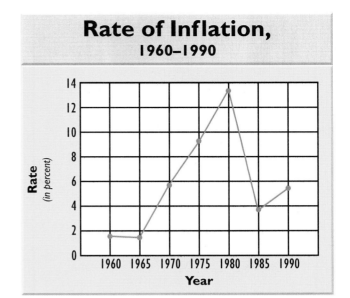

Rate of Inflation, 1960–1990

LEARNING FROM GRAPHS This graph shows how inflation increased during the 1960s and 1970s and then decreased during the 1980s.
■ *How was the rate of inflation related to the country's changing role in the war?*

This division was also seen in the government. Most government leaders were either hawks or doves. **Hawks** were people who supported the war. **Doves** were those who wanted the war to end.

As the number of Americans killed in Vietnam climbed into the thousands, more and more people began to oppose the war. All over the United States, protests and

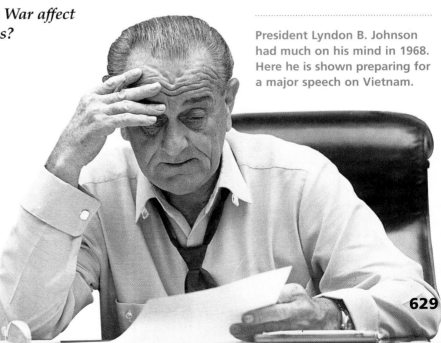

President Lyndon B. Johnson had much on his mind in 1968. Here he is shown preparing for a major speech on Vietnam.

629

A Divided Vietnam

CHINA

BURMA

Red River

Hanoi

NORTH VIETNAM

LAOS

Gulf of Tonkin

Hainan

Vientiane

Mekong River

HO CHI MINH TRAIL

Demilitarized Zone

South China Sea

THAILAND

Bangkok

CAMBODIA

SOUTH VIETNAM

Gulf of Thailand

Phnom Penh

Saigon

0 100 200 Miles
0 100 200 Kilometers
Mercator Projection

Mekong Delta

⊛ National capital

Movement The Ho Chi Minh Trail was a supply route from North Vietnam to South Vietnam. It was named for the communist leader of North Vietnam.

■ *Why do you think the trail went through other countries?*

marches against the war took place. Some young Americans resisted being drafted, or made to serve in the war. They burned their draft cards in protest. Some even moved out of the United States to avoid military service. Many of them went to Canada.

Because of the problems caused by the war, President Johnson decided not to run for reelection. In 1968 the American people elected a new President—Richard M. Nixon. Nixon tried to end the war by bombing North Vietnam even more than before. He also sent American soldiers into Cambodia, a country bordering Vietnam. Nixon's goal was to "bring an honorable end to the war." But the war did not end, and the protests against the war grew.

REVIEW *Why did some people protest the Vietnam War?*

Nixon Resigns

In 1972 President Nixon was reelected. In his second term, however, the Watergate scandal ended his presidency. A **scandal** is an action that brings disgrace. During the election campaign, some people working to help Nixon, who was a Republican, did some things that were against the law. One thing they did was to break into an office of the Democratic party in the Watergate Hotel. Many thought that President Nixon knew about this illegal act and tried to cover it up.

President Nixon and his family say farewell to White House staff members at the time of the President's resignation.

Veterans Day

To celebrate the signing of the armistice ending World War I, Armistice Day was first observed on November 11, 1919. In 1954 President Dwight D. Eisenhower changed the name of Armistice Day to Veterans Day. This day is dedicated to world peace and honors all veterans of the United States armed forces. Today Veterans Day is still observed on November 11. People celebrate with parades and speeches that honor the service that members of the military have given their country. Many European nations still celebrate Armistice Day.

A Vietnam veteran and his son search for people's names during a visit to the Vietnam Veterans Memorial.

Despite the scandal, President Nixon worked to end the Vietnam War. In 1969 he had begun to bring American troops home. But his plan to defeat the Vietcong by bombing North Vietnam harder failed. In January 1973 Nixon agreed to a cease-fire. He also agreed to bring the remaining American soldiers back from Vietnam.

The Watergate scandal, however, forced Nixon to step down. On August 9, 1974, he became the first President of the United States to resign. On that same day, Vice President Gerald Ford became President.

Without help from the United States, South Vietnamese soldiers could not win the war. On April 30, 1975, the government of South Vietnam surrendered. The government of North Vietnam gained control of the whole country. The unpopular war was finally over.

On Veterans Day in 1982, the Vietnam Veterans Memorial in Washington, D.C., was opened to visitors. Part of the memorial is a large wall of polished black stone. The wall lists the names of more than 58,000 American men and women who fought for their country and died or were reported missing during the Vietnam War.

REVIEW *How did the Vietnam War end?*

LESSON 4 REVIEW

Check Understanding

1 **Remember the Facts** Why did President Nixon resign?

2 **Recall the Main Idea** How did people's opinions bring about change during the 1960s and 1970s?

Think Critically

3 **Think More About It** What might have happened if people had not protested against the Vietnam War?

4 **Past to Present** Why do you think many Americans today have painful memories of the Vietnam War?

Show What You Know

Art Activity Write down your ideas about what different groups thought about the Vietnam War. Then make a mural that shows what these groups did to express how they felt about the conflict. Present your mural to the class.

Hawk or

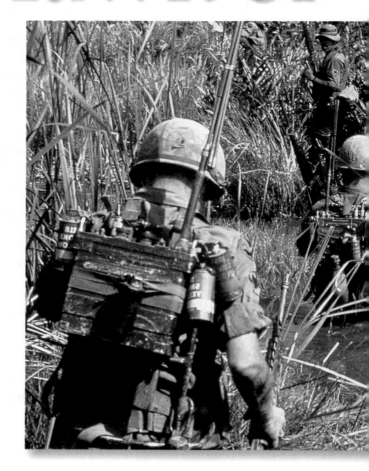

Like most wars in United States history, the Vietnam War had both supporters and nonsupporters. The hawks—named for the fierce bird of prey—wanted the war to continue until victory was achieved. They believed that communism would spread to other countries unless the United States helped South Vietnam win the conflict. The doves—named for the traditional symbol of peace—wanted the war to end immediately. They believed people were dying needlessly in a conflict that South Vietnam could not win. Each side strongly believed that it was right and the other side was wrong. There seemed to be no possible compromise.

Can you tell a hawk from a dove? Read the following quotations, and decide what each speaker believed about the Vietnam War.

President Lyndon B. Johnson

66 Why are we in South Vietnam? We are there because we have a promise to keep. Since 1954 every American President has offered support to the people of South Vietnam. We have helped to build, and we have helped to defend. Thus, over many years, we made a national pledge to help South Vietnam defend its independence. . . . To dishonor that pledge, to abandon this small and brave nation to its enemies, and to the terror that must follow, would be an unforgivable wrong. 99

Dove?

In this photo from 1970, United States soldiers patrol an area southwest of Saigon, South Vietnam, near the Cambodian border.

Senator J. William Fulbright

66 We are in a war to 'defend freedom' in South Vietnam. . . . When we talk about the freedom of South Vietnam, we may be thinking about how our pride would be injured if we settled for less than we set out to achieve; we may be thinking about our reputation as a great power, as though a compromise settlement would shame us before the world, marking us as a second-rate people with flagging [failing] courage and determination. Such fears are nonsensical. They are unworthy of the richest, most powerful, most productive, and best educated people in the world. 99

Compare Viewpoints

1. Was President Johnson a hawk or a dove? How do you know?
2. What viewpoint about the war did Senator Fulbright hold? How do you know?

Think and Apply

BUILDING CITIZENSHIP

Choose one of the wars you have studied in American history. Use encyclopedias and other references to identify some individuals or groups who were hawks and some who were doves during that war. Describe the point of view of each.

FOCUS

How do people help influence history?

Main Idea Read to learn how individuals helped bring the Cold War to an end.

Vocabulary

arms control
détente
terrorism
hostage
deficit

The Cold War Ends

Although he resigned in disgrace, President Nixon accomplished many important things while he was in office. His most important achievement may have been reducing tensions between the free world and the communist nations. Nixon became the first American President to visit both China and the Soviet Union. Later, Cold War tensions would rise and fall and then nearly disappear.

Nixon Visits China and the Soviet Union

The United States cut ties with China after the Asian nation became a communist country in 1949. Trade, travel, and communication between the two countries came to a complete end.

In 1972 President Nixon accepted an invitation from China's leader, Mao Zedong (MOW zeh•DOONG), to visit China. As a result of Nixon's visit, the two nations agreed to trade with each other and to allow visits from each other's scientific and cultural groups.

Three months after visiting China, Nixon flew to Moscow to meet with Soviet leader Leonid Brezhnev (BREZH•nef). Nixon told Brezhnev, "There must be room in the world for two great nations with different systems to live together and work together."

As a result of this meeting, the United States and the Soviet Union agreed to increase trade with each other and to work together on scientific and cultural projects. Most importantly, they agreed to **arms control**, or limiting the number of weapons that each

Standing on the Great Wall of China are (center) President Nixon and Patricia Nixon, his wife.

nation may have. The agreement signed by Nixon and Brezhnev limited the number of nuclear, or atomic, missiles on each side. This agreement marked the beginning of a period of **détente** (day•TAHNT), or an easing of tensions, between the United States and the Soviet Union. But this period of détente did not last long.

REVIEW *How did President Nixon ease tensions with China and the Soviet Union?*

Increased Tensions

Southwest Asia, or the Middle East, as Europeans and Americans have called the region, has long been a trouble spot. People there are divided by religious, cultural, and political differences. Some of the people have turned to **terrorism**, the use of violence to promote a cause. There have also been wars in the region. In 1948, 1956, 1967, and 1973, Israel fought wars with Egypt, Jordan, and Syria. In these wars the United States took the side of Israel. The Soviet Union took the side of the Arab nations. In taking sides, the United States and the Soviet Union increased Cold War tensions.

Then, in December 1979, Soviet troops invaded the country of Afghanistan (af•GAN•uh•stan) in Southwest Asia. The invasion moved Soviet troops much closer to the region's rich oil fields. President Jimmy Carter, who had been elected in 1976, called the invasion a threat to world peace.

President Carter insisted that the Soviets leave Afghanistan. When they did not, he cut back American trade with the Soviets and refused to agree to further arms control. He also said that American athletes would not take part in the 1980 Olympic games to be held in Moscow.

The fighting in Afghanistan continued for years. The Afghan rebels fought so fiercely that it was difficult for the Soviets to control the country. Finally, in 1988, the

President Carter (center) earned worldwide praise for bringing about a peace agreement between two old enemies, Egypt and Israel. Carter is shown with President Sadat (suh•DAHT) of Egypt (left) and Prime Minister Begin (BAY•gin) of Israel (right). The peace treaty they signed was known as the Camp David Accords.

Soviet Union began to withdraw its troops from Afghanistan.

Another problem in Southwest Asia proved to be even more troubling for President Carter. In 1979 a revolution took place in Iran. The shah, the country's leader, fled. Leaders of the revolution were angry at Americans because the United States had supported the shah. To show their anger, the revolutionaries attacked the United States embassy in Tehran, Iran's capital. They captured 53 Americans and made them hostages. **Hostages** are people held as prisoners until their captors' demands are met. President Carter was unable to win the release of the hostages. Many Americans lost confidence in him. In 1980 Carter ran again for President but lost. On the day the new President, Ronald Reagan, took the oath of office, the Iranians finally released the hostages.

REVIEW *What actions did Carter take when the Soviets invaded Afghanistan?*

Soviet leader Gorbachev (right) and President Reagan (far right) shake hands at their first meeting. They met each year from 1985 through 1988.

The Cold War Ends

In 1956, when the Soviet leader Nikita Khrushchev (krush•CHAWF) first learned about the destruction that hydrogen bombs could cause, he was so upset that he tossed and turned for nights, unable to sleep. "Then I became convinced," he said, "that we could never possibly use these weapons, and when I realized that I was able to sleep again."

Neither the Soviets nor the Americans used nuclear weapons during the Cold War. But throughout this period, both countries built more and more of them.

"Peace through strength" was Ronald Reagan's motto as he increased defense spending. He called the Soviet Union "an evil empire" and said that the Cold War was a "struggle between right and wrong, good and evil." Soviet leaders did not soften their stand, either. They continued building more weapons and helping communist rebels all over the world.

Then a new leader took over the Soviet Union, and nothing was the same again. Mikhail Gorbachev (mee•kah•EEL gawr•buh•CHAWF) became leader of the

Soviet Union in 1985. President Reagan said he would welcome the chance to meet the new Soviet leader in the "cause of world peace." In April 1985 Gorbachev agreed to a meeting. He said that better relations between the United States and the Soviet Union were "extremely necessary—and possible."

The first meeting between Reagan and Gorbachev in November 1985 marked the beginning of a real thaw in the Cold War. The President called it a "fresh start" in United States–Soviet relations. Soon the United States and the Soviet Union agreed to more treaties limiting nuclear missiles.

In the Soviet Union, Mikhail Gorbachev was already changing many of the old Soviet ways of doing things. He called for *perestroika* (pair•uh•STROY•kuh), or a "restructuring" of the Soviet government and economy. He also called for a new "openness," or *glasnost* (GLAZ•nohst). This would give the Soviet people more of the freedoms they wanted. Soviet citizens would be allowed to vote in free elections. They would be free to start and run their own businesses.

Reforms in the Soviet Union led to changes in many other communist nations. People in

Poland, Czechoslovakia, and Hungary gained new freedoms. In communist East Germany, government leaders removed the armed guards from the Berlin Wall and opened its gates. In 1989 the German people tore down the Berlin Wall. The next year they reunited their country.

In 1989 the new President of the United States, George Bush, met with Mikhail Gorbachev on a ship near Malta, a rocky island in the middle of the Mediterranean Sea. As a storm raged outside, the two men faced each other across a table. Years of mistrust between their countries made the outcome of the meeting uncertain. Neither one knew what to expect.

The two leaders talked about the many changes taking place in Europe and the Soviet Union. At the end Gorbachev looked Bush in the eye. "I have heard you say that you want *perestroika* to succeed," he said, "but frankly I didn't know this. Now I know." The Cold War was finally ending.

REVIEW *What changes did Gorbachev bring to the Soviet Union?*

A man standing on the newly opened Berlin Wall makes a peace sign as East Germans flood into West Berlin.

A New World Order

Talking about the idea of a world without the Cold War, President George Bush said,

66 Now we can see . . . the very real prospect of a new world order. A world in which freedom and respect for human rights find a home among all nations. 99

By "a new world order," President Bush meant a world without the alliances and conflicts of the past. However, conflicts in the world have continued.

In 1990 the nation of Iraq, led by its ruler, Saddam Hussein (hoo•SAYN), invaded neighboring Kuwait (koo•WAYT), a major oil producer. When Iraq refused to withdraw, the allied forces of the United States, Britain, France, Egypt, and Saudi Arabia attacked. During Operation Desert Storm the Iraqis were pushed back, and Kuwait's rulers were returned to power.

In the meantime the end of communism in eastern Europe set off fighting in what was once the nation of Yugoslavia. The civil war there has taken hundreds of thousands of lives. In 1991 the Soviet Union itself broke up into independent countries. Many of these countries are fighting one another for power and the right to self-government.

REVIEW *What did Bush mean by "a new world order"?*

New Challenges at Home

In 1993 Bill Clinton was elected President. In his 1995 State of the Union Address, Clinton said, "You know, tonight this is the first State of the Union Address ever delivered since the beginning of the Cold War when not a single Russian missile is pointed at the children of America."

After the Cold War ended, however, the United States faced many new challenges. Among the most important were to work for equality for all Americans, fight crime, and care for the environment.

Another important concern had to do with the economy. In the 1990s the United States remained a military superpower. But many Americans believed it was no longer the economic superpower it once was. It had the largest economy in the world, but it had economic problems. One reason was the government's budget **deficit**, or shortage. The government spent more money than it took in each year in taxes and other income. To help solve this problem, Congress passed a balanced-budget amendment to the Constitution in 1997. This amendment requires the government to spend no more money than it takes in each year.

By the end of the twentieth century, the economy of the United States had improved greatly. Under the leadership of President Clinton, the nation achieved a balanced budget. However, the United States is still challenged by an international trade deficit. It buys more goods from other countries than it sells. Inexpensive imports from countries

President Clinton held televised "town meetings" to listen to people's concerns and hear their views about the government.

such as Japan, South Korea, and Taiwan are snapped up by American consumers. As a result, American businesses producing similar goods have suffered.

According to many economists, what is needed to be a world leader today is different from what was needed during the Cold War. World leadership, they say, is based more and more on economic strength. Many Americans believe that one of the most important challenges for the United States today is to continue to be an economic superpower.

REVIEW *How can the United States remain a world leader?*

LESSON 5 REVIEW

Check Understanding

1 **Remember the Facts** President Nixon's visits to what two countries led to a time of détente?

2 **Recall the Main Idea** How did individuals help bring an end to the Cold War?

Think Critically

3 **Think More About It** What could have been some of the reasons Mao Zedong invited President Nixon to China?

4 **Cause and Effect** How did the reforms of the Soviet Union in the 1980s affect other communist nations in eastern Europe?

Show What You Know

Picture-Essay Activity Use information and pictures from current newspapers and magazines to make a picture essay titled *The World After the Cold War.* Share your picture essay with a partner, and discuss what it shows.

Understand Political Symbols

1. Why Learn This Skill?

People often recognize sports teams, clubs, and other organizations by their symbols. The same is true for political parties, the President, Congress, the Supreme Court, and even voters. Being able to identify political symbols and what they stand for can help you better understand news reports, political cartoons, and other sources of information.

2. Recognizing Symbols

Two of the country's most famous political symbols are animals. The donkey represents the Democratic party. The elephant represents the Republican party. The donkey was probably first used to represent President Andrew Jackson, a Democrat, in the 1830s. Later the donkey became a symbol for the entire party. Cartoonist Thomas Nast introduced the elephant as a symbol of the Republican party in 1874. Both symbols are still used today.

One of the symbols for the national government is Uncle Sam—a white-haired man wearing a red, white, and blue hat and suit. The bald eagle and the Statue of Liberty are other symbols for our government. Buildings are often used as political symbols. The White House is a symbol for the President, and the United States Capitol is a symbol for Congress.

3. Understand the Process

When you see a political symbol, answer these questions to help you understand its meaning:

1 Do you recognize the symbol? Does it stand for the national government as a whole or only part of the national government? Does it stand for a person or a group that is involved in government, such as a political party?

2 Where did you see the symbol? If it appeared in a newspaper, did the writer give you any clues about its meaning?

3 Are there any captions or other words that help explain what the symbol means? A symbol labeled "The Halls of Justice," for example, might tell you that it stands for a court.

4. Think and Apply

Look through current newsmagazines or the editorial pages of newspapers. Find an example of a political symbol. Cut out the example and paste it on a sheet of paper. Below the symbol, write a brief description of what it stands for.

The elephant is the symbol of the Republican party.

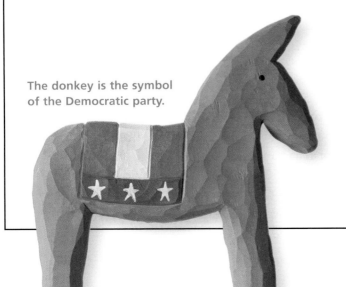

The donkey is the symbol of the Democratic party.

1940   1950   1960

1948
• Berlin Airlift

1962
• Cuban missile crisis

CONNECT MAIN IDEAS

Use this graphic organizer to show how the chapter's main ideas are connected. Write the main idea of each lesson. A copy of the organizer appears on page 130 of the Activity Book.

The Cold War Begins

_____

_____

_____

One Giant Leap

_____

_____

The Cold War Ends

_____

_____

_____

The Cold War Years

The Struggle for Equal Rights

_____

_____

_____

Vietnam War and Protests at Home

_____

_____

_____

WRITE MORE ABOUT IT

Write a Radio News Report Imagine that you are living in West Berlin during the Berlin Airlift. The radio station you work for has asked you to report on the conflict. Write what you will say about how the Allies are getting supplies to Berlin.

Write Your Opinion The three astronauts aboard *Apollo 11* faced many dangers during their trip to the moon, but they also made history. Write a paragraph or two telling why you would or would not have wanted to be an astronaut on board that historic flight.

1964
• Civil Rights Act is passed

1969
• Astronauts land on the moon

1975
• Vietnam War ends

1985
• The Cold War begins to come to an end

1991
• Soviet Union splits into independent countries

USE VOCABULARY

Write a term from this list to complete each of the sentences that follow.

détente   nonviolence

hawk   superpower

integration

1. The United States is a _____ because of the important role it plays in world events.

2. Working for change using _____ was important to Martin Luther King, Jr.

3. The bringing together of all races in education, jobs, and housing is called _____ .

4. President Johnson was a _____ because he wanted the United States to continue fighting the war in Vietnam.

5. In 1972 the United States and the Soviet Union began a period of _____ , the easing of military tensions between countries.

CHECK UNDERSTANDING

6. Why did President Kennedy order a blockade of Cuba?

7. How did a Supreme Court decision in 1954 change public schools?

8. How did the costs of the Great Society programs and the Vietnam War affect the economy of the United States?

9. Who was the first American President to visit both China and the Soviet Union? What was the important result of these visits?

10. What happened in eastern Europe after Mikhail Gorbachev became leader of the Soviet Union?

THINK CRITICALLY

11. **Explore Viewpoints** How were the views of Malcolm X different from the views of Martin Luther King, Jr.?

12. **Think More About It** In what ways has the women's rights movement changed the United States?

APPLY SKILLS

Act as a Responsible Citizen
Identify a person who you think is a responsible citizen. Write a paragraph telling why you think that person is acting responsibly.

Understand Political Symbols
A donkey, an elephant, the Capitol, the White House, and Uncle Sam are all political symbols. What does each represent?

READ MORE ABOUT IT

Rosa Parks: My Story by Rosa Parks. Dial. This autobiography describes the life of Rosa Parks, a woman whose struggle for racial equality helped start the Civil Rights movement.

ROSA PARKS: MY STORY
—by Rosa Parks—
with Jim Haskins

HARCOURT BRACE

Visit the Internet at
http://www.hbschool.com
for additional resources.

THE WESTERN HEMISPHERE TODAY

"With her friends in the United States she speaks English. . . . She dreams in both Spanish and English."

Kathleen Krull, author, describing a 12-year-old Mexican immigrant named Cinthya Guzman, shown here

Mexico Today

T he Republic of Mexico shares the North American continent with Canada and the United States. Mexico's lands are diverse—including coastal plains, rain forests, and mountains. These lands provide harvests of corn, wheat, and many other crops as well as natural resources such as silver, gold, and oil. All of these crops and resources have helped Mexico's economy in the past. In recent years, however, Mexico's economy has been troubled by many problems.

The Growth of Cities and the Middle Class

Seven out of every ten Mexicans live in urban areas. In the country's central and northern states, the urban population has boomed in recent years. Among the fastest-growing cities is Mexico City, in the central region.

Mexico City, ringed by volcanic mountains, stands on the site of the Aztec capital of Tenochtitlán. When the Aztecs built their capital in the 1300s, it was one of the world's largest cities. In the early 1500s, the Spanish conquered the Aztecs and destroyed Tenochtitlán. In its place they built Mexico City to be the capital of the Spanish colony of New Spain.

Today Mexico City remains the nation's capital, or Federal District. Its population is the largest of all the cities in the world. More than 8 million people live within Mexico City. Almost 21 million people live in the metropolitan area. A **metropolitan area** is a city and all the suburbs and other population areas around it. The largest metropolitan area in the United States is New York City. New York City's metropolitan area has about 20 million people.

Between 1940 and 1970 many factories were built in the northern region of Mexico. Cities there grew quickly. Hoping to find factory jobs, great numbers of people moved from rural areas to Monterrey, Ciudad Juárez (SEE•u•dahd HWAR•ays), Matamoros (mah•tah•MOH•rohs), and Tijuana (tee•WAH•nah).

LESSON
1

FOCUS
How might economic differences among people in a country cause problems?

Main Idea Read to learn how economic conditions have divided many of the people of Mexico.

Vocabulary
metropolitan area
middle class
interest rate
free-trade agreement

Mexico City, like all large cities, has crowded streets at rush hour.

Some members of Mexico's middle-class families have jobs making computers and other products in factories built along the United States–Mexico border.

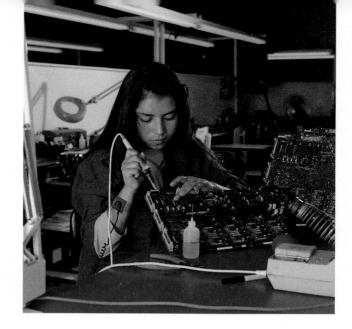

As in the United States, the growth of manufacturing in Mexico led to the growth of a large **middle class**, an economic level between the poor and the wealthy. Shopkeepers, factory managers, lawyers, and other workers and their families make up the middle class. By the 1990s Mexico's middle class was one of the largest in all the countries of the Americas.

For many years most middle-class families in Mexico had enough money to buy the many new products manufactured in their country. Then, in 1994, Mexico's money suddenly became devalued. That is, the value of Mexico's money suddenly dropped. This caused prices to rise sharply. Some prices doubled. Others tripled. **Interest rates**, or the amounts that banks charge customers to borrow money, rose as high as 80 percent.

Middle-class families found it very difficult to buy houses, cars, and most consumer products. The Mexicans called this economic disaster "the devaluation of 1994." The devaluation was caused by inflation and the Mexican government's need to pay its debts.

REVIEW *How did the devaluation of 1994 affect Mexico's middle class?*

HERITAGE

Colorfully dressed dancers celebrate Cinco de Mayo in Austin, Texas.

Cinco de Mayo

Cinco de Mayo, also known as Battle of Puebla Day, is a national holiday in Mexico. *Cinco de Mayo* means "fifth of May" in Spanish. On May 5, 1862, the Mexican army fought the French army in the Mexican city of Puebla. The French were trying to take control of the Mexican government. Although the French army was much larger, the Mexican army was able to hold off the French Army. Today the Mexican people and many Mexican Americans celebrate Cinco de Mayo with parades and fireworks. The holiday is important as a day to celebrate Mexican independence and national pride.

Regions Mexico is divided into 31 states.
■ *Which Mexican states border the United States?*

State	Capital City
1. AGUASCALIENTES	Aguascalientes
2. QUERÉTARO	Querétaro
3. TLAXCALA	Tlaxcala
4. MORELOS	Cuernavaca
5. MÉXICO	Toluca
6. DISTRITO FEDERAL	Mexico City

Reaction to NAFTA

Mexico's economy had caused problems for its people for many years. With the devaluation of 1994, the problems were made worse. People at all economic levels lost their jobs. Mexico's poor people, who make up 45 percent of the country's almost 98 million people, suffered the most. For them, even basic foods such as beans and eggs became luxuries.

Before the devaluation, the Mexican government had decided that one way the nation could make its economy stronger was to join the United States and Canada in signing the North American Free Trade Agreement, known as NAFTA. A **free-trade agreement** is a treaty in which countries agree to charge no tariffs on goods they buy from each other and

sell to each other. Such an agreement gives businesses in these countries the chance to compete more fairly.

But the NAFTA agreement did not make everyone in Mexico happy. Among those who were angry that the Mexican government had signed the NAFTA agreement were many of the country's farmers. On January 1, 1994, the date NAFTA went into effect, about 2,000 poor farmers in the southern Mexican state of Chiapas (chee•AH•pahs) took control of several towns. Fighting between the farmers and Mexican soldiers soon broke out, and more than 100 people were killed.

Most of the farmers in Chiapas are of American Indian heritage. They make up half the population of the state. They were afraid that free trade would bring large

This woman baking tortillas is from Oaxaca (wuh•HAH•kuh), a state in southern Mexico. Many people in southern Mexico depend on farming to make a living.

amounts of corn, soybeans, wheat, and other farm products to Mexico from the United States and Canada. These products could be sold more cheaply than the farmers of Chiapas could sell their crops. One leader of the farmers said, "The free-trade agreement is a death certificate for the Indian peoples of Mexico."

While many Mexicans living in the rural southern states are against NAFTA, those living in the more industrialized central and northern states support the free-trade agreement. Factory owners and other business people hope the agreement will help them sell more of their goods in the growing markets of the United States and Canada. They believe that this trade will create more jobs in Mexico and will strengthen the country's economy as a whole.

REVIEW *What is NAFTA?*

LESSON 1 REVIEW

Check Understanding

1 **Remember the Facts** Which city in Mexico has the largest population of all cities in the world?

2 **Recall the Main Idea** How have economic conditions divided many of the people of Mexico?

Think Critically

3 **Cause and Effect** What effects did the devaluation of 1994 have on Mexico's middle class? What effects did it have on Mexico's poor people?

4 **Explore Viewpoints** How did farmers in southern Mexico view the NAFTA agreement? How did Mexico's business people view the agreement?

Show What You Know

Map Activity Make a map that shows the states and major cities of Mexico. Add illustrations that show landforms and products. Discuss what you have learned about Mexico as you compare your map with those of your classmates.

Save My Rainforest

by Monica Zak
illustrations by Bengt-Arne Runnerström
English version by Nancy Schimmel

Omar Castillo lives in Mexico City, which is over an 800-mile (1,287 km) walk from the Selva Lacandona (SEL•*vuh* lah•kahn•DOH•*nah*), Mexico's last remaining rain forest. On the television news, Omar hears that the rain forest is in danger of being destroyed. He decides that he must try to do something to save the rain forest. With the help of his father, Omar sets out on foot to make a long, difficult journey that he will never forget.

Early one morning Omar and his father start walking. At first Omar is smiling and singing. On the road at last! And tonight, for the first time in his life, he will sleep in a tent.

For hours and hours they walk on the hot pavement. Finally, they leave the dirty yellow air of the city for the clear, clean air of the countryside. But Omar is too tired to notice. Then his feet begin to hurt. He goes a good ways before he says anything. When he does, his father stops and takes Omar's shoes off.

"You have blisters. I'll put a bandage on . . . there. Now we can get started again."

"But Papa, I'm too tired. I can't go on."

"I'm tired too," says his father, "but try to go a little farther. I'll buy us a cool drink at the next store." They find a fruit stand where a woman with long braids sells them tall glasses of pineapple drink.

She looks at them curiously and finally asks, "What does your banner say? I can't read."

Omar revives at once. "This side says 'Let's protect the rainforest' and the other side says 'Walk—Mexico City—Tuxtla Gutiérrez.'[1] Tuxtla's a long way south of here, but that's where we decided to go, to see the governor of the state of Chiapas, where the rainforest is. He is responsible for taking care of it. We need to tell him to save the rainforest so there will still be a rainforest in Mexico for us children when we grow up."

"You must be sent from heaven!" she says.

Omar's father smiles. "No, he's just a regular kid. All kids have good ideas, but usually people don't listen to them. It

---

[1] **Tuxtla Gutiérrez:** (TOOST•lah goo•TYAIR•ehs)

never made any difference to me that they were destroying the rainforest and the animals, but when I thought about what my son said, I realized that he knew what he was talking about. That's why I decided to come with him."

Another day, the sun beats down through the thin mountain air. This time it is Omar's father who has blisters. He calls, "Must you walk so fast, Omar?"

After walking more than a week, they come down out of the mountains. They can see banana plantations now, and *mango* trees. They camp by the side of the road.

Omar lies in the tent and listens. The night before, he heard coyotes howling near the tent: ah-ooo, ah-ooo, ah-ooo. He was afraid. Now he listens to the murmuring leaves. *What if a snake should get into the tent? What if robbers attack us?* he thinks. An enormous truck rumbles past and shakes the tent. *What if the driver fell asleep and . . .*

"Omar, are you awake?" his father asks.

"Mm-hm," answers Omar. "I can't sleep."

"Well," says Omar's father, "we really had a tough day. Heat, no shade, and traffic. Now it's pleasant. We won't be cold tonight."

"No," says Omar, smiling. "Remember the first night in the tent? I thought it would be wonderful, camping, but then the rain started . . ."

"Yes," says his father, "and the water came in. At three in the morning! Remember how good that hot *pozole* tasted after we walked in the dark and cold?"

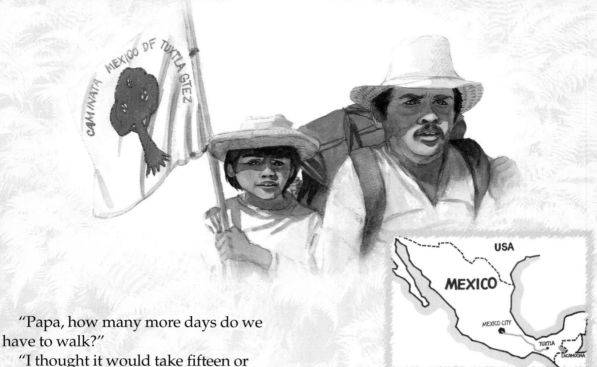

"Papa, how many more days do we have to walk?"

"I thought it would take fifteen or twenty days, but it will take much longer. I don't want to disappoint you, but I don't believe we can go on."

"But why?" asks Omar, astounded.

"We are running out of money."

They decide to keep going.

"We will have to beg for food," says Omar.

They go into a restaurant and Omar's father explains to the owner why they are walking. "We have no more money," Omar's father says, "and my son is awfully hungry." The owner turns them out without giving them even a glass of water. But then a woman sitting outside a little hut motions them in, makes a fresh pot of coffee, and serves them coffee and bread. It goes like that. Some days people give them food, but often they have to walk the whole day without eating anything. Those days are hard.

When Omar sees boys playing soccer, he stops and watches with envy, but they never ask him to play. Sometimes there are things to look at in the road: a huge scorpion or snakes run over by cars. But more often, walking is boring. Omar throws rocks at fenceposts, thinking *Why didn't I bring anything to play with?* Then somebody who hears he is going to the rainforest gives him a toy Tarzan. He passes the time pretending Tarzan is in the rainforest, swinging from vines.

People warn them not to take the shortest way to Tuxtla, the road that goes through poor villages. "They'll attack you and rob you. It's too dangerous!" But Omar and his father take that road anyway, because it is 125 miles shorter. At first they are a little afraid, but no one attacks them. In fact, women and children come out and give them oranges and *tortilla* chips. . . .

A few days later they stop in a little town to eat in a restaurant. An announcer comes on television to say there has been a terrible earthquake in Mexico City. They see a picture of a big pile of rubble and hear that it is the hospital where Omar's grandmother works! Omar starts to cry. His father has tears in his eyes. No one can reach Mexico City by telephone because the lines are out. Then a ham radio operator in the town promises he will help them get news.

After four days of waiting, the radio operator says, "Your *abuela* is alive, Omar. She wasn't in the hospital when the earthquake came. Your mother is well. She sends you kisses and says your house wasn't hurt at all. She wishes you a safe journey."

And now they can continue.

After thirty-nine days of walking, Omar and his father come to Tuxtla Gutiérrez. They have travelled 870 miles and they are tired. They have to wait the whole day outside the governor's office, but finally the moment comes that Omar has been hoping for.

His heart beats loudly as he faces the governor and says, "Save my rainforest and stop the hunting of the rainforest animals for the next twenty years." The governor pats Omar on the head and says there is nothing to worry about.

Omar still worries. *He is treating me like a kid*, he thinks. *He won't do anything.*

But Omar does get to see a rainforest. When Tuxtla was built, a piece of the rainforest was left as a park. At first, Omar is disappointed in the rainforest, too. There aren't lots of strange animals running around in plain sight. Just gigantic trees and a clean wet smell.

Omar stands quietly for a long time in the deep green light amid the huge trunks, listening to all the birds singing high above in the canopy of leaves. Then he knows that being in a real rainforest at last is worth the trouble of walking 870 miles.

LITERATURE REVIEW

1. Why did Omar and his father walk from Mexico City to Tuxtla Gutiérrez?
2. For what reasons might you take an action like Omar's?
3. In the years after his long journey, Omar Castillo continued to work with other children to save the rain forest. With a partner, brainstorm other environmental problems in the world today. Make a list of the actions you might take to help solve one of these problems.

Use Population Maps

1. Why Learn This Skill?

Like most other geographic information, population is shown on maps in many different ways. One way is with color. Another is with dots. A third way to show population is on a special kind of map called a cartogram. A **cartogram** is a map that shows information by changing the size of places. Knowing how to read different kinds of population maps can make it easier for you to find out the number of people who live in different areas.

2. Understand the Process

Look at the key on the population map of Mexico below. The key tells you that the colors on the map stand for different population densities. **Population density** is the number of people who live in 1 square mile or 1 square kilometer of land. On the map the color yellow stands for the least crowded areas. Red stands for the most crowded areas. Read the map key to find the areas in Mexico that have more than 250 people per square mile or more than 100 people per square kilometer. Is Mexico more populated in the central part of the country or in the northern part?

The population of cities is also given on the population map of Mexico. Different-sized dots stand for cities with different population sizes. The largest dot on the map stands for a city

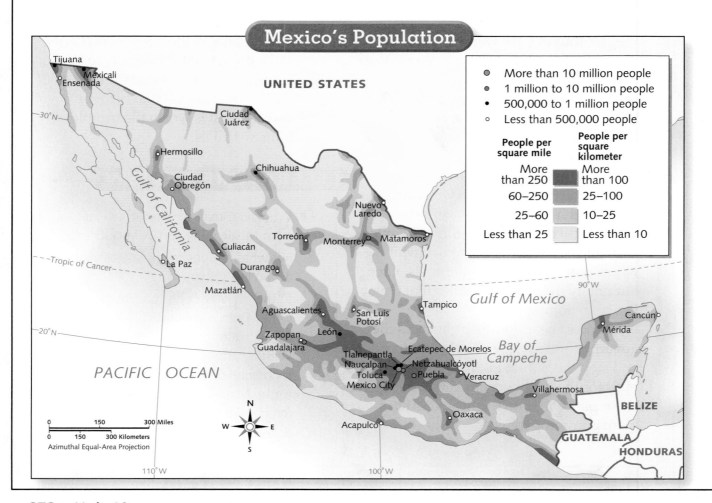

Mexico's Population

with a population of more than 10 million people. The next-smaller dot stands for cities of 1 to 10 million people. These symbols do not give the exact populations of cities. But they do help you compare the population sizes of cities. Find the dots for the cities of Guadalajara and Mérida. Which city has more people? Which city has fewer people, Monterrey or Oaxaca?

Now look at the cartogram of the Western Hemisphere. This cartogram also shows information about population, but in a very different way. On most maps, the size of a country is based on its land area. On a population cartogram, however, the size of a country is based on its population instead of its land area.

A cartogram does not show the number of people who live in each country. But it does show how each country's population compares with that of another country. Countries with larger populations are larger on a cartogram. Countries with smaller populations are smaller on a cartogram.

Find Canada and Mexico on a globe or a map. You will notice that Canada has a larger land area than Mexico, so it is larger in size. Which of these two countries is larger on the cartogram below? What does the cartogram show about these countries?

3. Think and Apply

Study the population information given on the map on page 652 and on the cartogram below. Then show some of the same information by using a chart, graph, or table. You might make a bar graph comparing the numbers of cities with different populations in Mexico or a table showing the five countries with the largest populations.

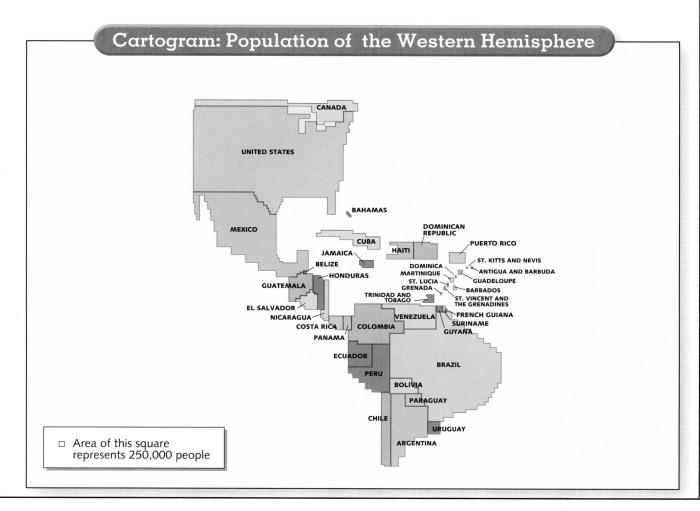

Cartogram: Population of the Western Hemisphere

☐ Area of this square represents 250,000 people

FOCUS

How might political
changes affect the way
people live in a
country?

Main Idea Read to
find out how political
changes have affected
the way people live in
the Caribbean and in
Central America.

Vocabulary

commonwealth
embargo
free election

Democracy in the Caribbean and in Central America

ike the United States, many nations in the Caribbean and in Central America have a history of democracy. Costa Rica has a long democratic tradition. So does Puerto Rico, with its ties to the United States. In other places in the region, however, people continue to struggle for democracy.

Puerto Rico

In 1898, after the Spanish-American War, the United States took control of Puerto Rico from Spain. In 1952 Puerto Rico became a kind of territory of the United States called a **commonwealth**. As citizens of a commonwealth, Puerto Ricans hold United States citizenship.

In 1993 the Puerto Rican people had to decide whether they wanted to change their political relationship with the United States. They had three choices. They could remain a commonwealth, declare independence, or become a state of the United States. Some Puerto Ricans who had lived in the United States said that statehood would be the best thing that could happen to Puerto Rico. Puerto Ricans who wanted their island to stay a commonwealth said they not only wanted to keep United States citizenship but also wanted Puerto Rico to keep its own identity. Puerto Ricans who wanted independence said they wanted Puerto Rico to be on its own as an independent country.

In this important vote, more than 48 percent of the voters decided that Puerto Rico should remain a commonwealth. A close second in the voting was the choice of statehood, with 46 percent of the vote. The vote showed that Puerto Ricans want to keep their strong ties with the United States.

REVIEW *What is Puerto Rico's relationship with the United States?*

Crowds of people wave Puerto Rican flags during a Puerto Rico Day parade in New York City.

The Caribbean and Central America

UNITED STATES

0   250   500 Miles
0   250   500 Kilometers
Azimuthal Equal-Area Projection

Gulf of Mexico

ATLANTIC OCEAN

— Tropic of Cancer

Nassau ★

BAHAMAS

★ Havana

CUBA

TURKS AND CAICOS ISLANDS (U.K.)

MEXICO

PUERTO RICO (U.S.)

BRITISH VIRGIN ISLANDS (U.K.)
ANGUILLA (U.K.)
ST. KITTS AND NEVIS

DOMINICAN REPUBLIC

HAITI

★ Bélmopan

BELIZE

Port-au-Prince ★

Santo Domingo

San Juan ★

ANTIGUA AND BARBUDA

GUATEMALA

JAMAICA ★

U.S. VIRGIN ISLANDS

GUADELOUPE (FRANCE)

Guatemala City ★

Kingston

MARTINIQUE (FRANCE)

PACIFIC OCEAN

HONDURAS

DOMINICA

San Salvador ★

★ Tegucigalpa

Caribbean Sea

ST. LUCIA

EL SALVADOR

NICARAGUA

BARBADOS

ST. VINCENT AND THE GRENADINES

Managua

GRENADA

Port-of-Spain ★

San José ★

Panama City

TRINIDAD AND TOBAGO

COSTA RICA

PANAMA

SOUTH AMERICA

★ National capital

Location Caribbean countries are on islands, and Central American countries are on the mainland.
■ *Which island is made up of more than one country?*

Cuba

Like Puerto Rico, Cuba came under the control of the United States after the Spanish-American War. However, Cuba became independent soon after the war. Leaders of the newly independent Cuba wanted to build a strong economy. Political control soon fell into the hands of landowners and other wealthy Cubans.

Over the years, differences in the rights of the rich and the poor angered many of Cuba's farmers and workers. In 1959 a group of rebels led by Fidel Castro took over Cuba's government. They said their goal was to bring equal rights to all citizens and to solve many of Cuba's social and economic problems. To reach this goal, however, Castro made Cuba a communist nation. He has ruled Cuba as a dictator ever since.

Under communism, Cuba's government took

Cuba's leader, Fidel Castro

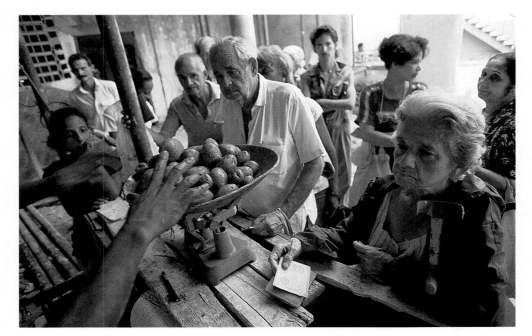

Economic conditions in Cuba have gotten worse since the end of the Cold War, and supplies have been scarce. These Cubans are waiting in line to receive potatoes according to a rationing system. The amount they receive is based on family size.

over people's property and businesses. In 1962 the United States, which feared having a communist nation so close to its borders, set up an embargo against Cuba. During an **embargo** one country refuses to trade its goods with another country.

Cut off from the United States, Cuba came to depend on the Soviet Union for money and supplies. When the Cold War ended, however, the former Soviet Union was no longer able to support Cuba. Life in Cuba became very difficult. Many factories closed, and people lost their jobs. "If you don't have work," said one unemployed worker, "you can't even eat an orange any more."

Today many Cubans believe that the best hope for their nation is for the United States to lift its embargo. Many Cubans now living in the United States want their homeland to return to the free-enterprise system. Free enterprise, they say, will encourage people to start businesses that will create jobs. For this to happen, Cuba will need a democratic government that will allow free enterprise.

REVIEW *What changes do some Cubans living in the United States want for Cuba?*

Haiti

Haiti shares the island of Hispaniola with the Dominican Republic. Haiti is the second-oldest republic in the Western Hemisphere, after the United States. During the Haitian Revolution, which began in 1791, the people of the island rebelled against their French rulers. Haiti became an independent country in 1804.

For much of its history, however, Haiti has been ruled by dictators.

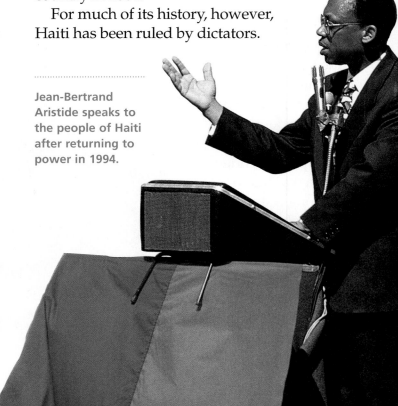

Jean-Bertrand Aristide speaks to the people of Haiti after returning to power in 1994.

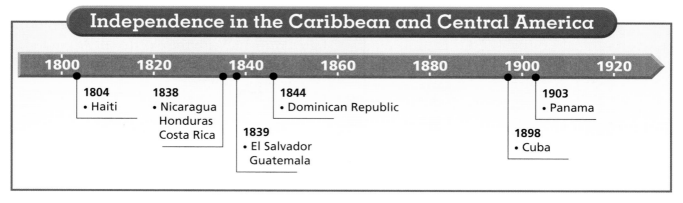

Independence in the Caribbean and Central America

1800	1820	1840	1860	1880	1900	1920

1804
• Haiti

1838
• Nicaragua
  Honduras
  Costa Rica

1839
• El Salvador
  Guatemala

1844
• Dominican Republic

1903
• Panama

1898
• Cuba

LEARNING FROM TIME LINES This time line shows when countries in the Caribbean and Central America became independent, after being controlled by other countries.

■ *In what year did Cuba become independent?*

In January 1988, Haitians chose new leaders by holding a **free election**—one in which there is a choice of candidates. It was the first free election held in Haiti in many years. But by June military leaders had overthrown the newly elected government and seized control of the country.

In 1990 a free election was held once again in Haiti. The people chose Jean-Bertrand Aristide (air•uh•STEED) as their president. But in 1991 his government, too, was overthrown by military leaders. He escaped to the United States.

The years of military rule in Haiti were harsh. Soldiers killed almost 4,000 of the country's 6 million people. Many Haitians wanted to go to the United States to escape the violence. Some risked death by traveling across the ocean in boats and on small rafts. When the Haitians arrived, however, the United States did not allow them to stay.

In 1994 the United States helped end military rule in Haiti by sending soldiers to Haiti. Soon President Aristide returned to office. He told his people,

66 Let us live in peace. All the guns must be silent. 99

In January 1996 the Haitian people held another free election. The people elected René Préval to be president. Although Préval replaced Aristide as President, the government continued as a democracy.

Haiti still faces hard times, however. Its people are among the poorest in the Western Hemisphere, and its economic problems have yet to be solved.

REVIEW *What important events happened in Haiti in 1988?*

An American soldier talks with students at the Saint Anne Elementary School, in Port-au-Prince, Haiti, in 1994. During Operation Restore Democracy, American troops helped end years of violent rule by the Haitian military in the island nation.

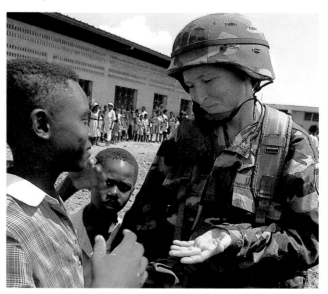

Nicaragua and Costa Rica

A dramatic change in government also took place in the Central American country of Nicaragua (nih•kah•RAH•gwah). In 1990, after years of civil war, voters elected Violeta Chamorro (vee•oh•LAY•tah chah•MAWR•oh) as Nicaragua's democratic president. Leaders in the United States were happy about Chamorro's victory. For many years the United States had helped democratic groups who wanted to end rule by Nicaraguan rebels known as Sandinistas. The United States had even placed an embargo against Nicaragua, as it had done against Cuba.

Years of fighting and natural disasters had hurt Nicaragua's economy. "War, hurricane, earthquake, tidal wave—Nicaragua has suffered all of that," explains one Nicaraguan citizen. "Now there is real hunger." After the election of Chamorro, the United States lifted the embargo and sent aid to help Nicaragua's economy and to strengthen the democratic government. With the election of Arnoldo Alemán in 1996, Nicaragua continued under democratic rule.

Unlike Nicaragua, neighboring Costa Rica has had a democratic government for many years. Its constitution was adopted in 1949.

One of Costa Rica's best-known leaders is former president Oscar Arias Sánchez. President Arias won the 1987 Nobel Peace Prize for his leadership in creating a peace plan for Central America.

REVIEW *In what year did rule by the Sandinistas in Nicaragua end?*

BIOGRAPHY

Violeta Barrios de Chamorro 1929–

Violeta Chamorro was born in the Nicaraguan town of Rivas. She spent her early adult years raising her family. Chamorro's husband was a respected politician and the editor of a major newspaper. In 1978 the Nicaraguan dictator, Anastasio Somoza, ordered her husband killed. After his death, Chamorro ran the newspaper. She also served for a short time in the Sandinista government. Until her election as president in 1990, Chamorro spoke openly against the Sandinistas. Many people think that her bravery helped her win the presidential election.

LESSON 3 REVIEW

Check Understanding

1. **Remember the Facts** Why have some people left countries in the Caribbean and in Central America to come to the United States?

2. **Recall the Main Idea** How have political changes affected the way people live in the Caribbean and in Central America?

Think Critically

3. **Explore Viewpoints** What different viewpoints did Puerto Ricans hold on the question of statehood?

4. **Cause and Effect** How did the end of the Cold War affect Cuba?

Show What You Know

Time Line Activity Gather news articles on how democratic reforms have affected a country in the Caribbean or in Central America. Use these articles and other resources to create a time line of political events in the country you chose. Share your time line with your classmates.

Challenges in South America

Native peoples lived in South America for thousands of years. Then, in the 1500s, Spain, Portugal, and other European countries began to build colonies there. European countries soon ruled most of the continent. By the mid-1800s most parts of South America had been **liberated**, or set free, from European rulers. Leaders of the independence movements included Simón Bolívar (see•MOHN boh•LEE•var) in Venezuela and José de San Martín (san mar•TEEN) in Argentina. Independence, however, did not solve all of the problems that many South American countries had faced as colonies.

New Countries with Old Problems

Disagreements based on social class and economic level have long caused conflicts in South America. In many places, small groups of wealthy European landowners wanted to run South American countries after they became independent. But much larger groups wanted an equal say in the new governments. These groups were native peoples, enslaved Africans, and **mestizos** (meh•STEE•zohz), people of mixed native and European backgrounds.

New leaders promised to solve their countries' problems. But almost all of these leaders were military rulers supported by the European landowners. In the late 1800s and early 1900s, dictators ruled many South American countries. They did not solve the problems of social and economic inequality that continue in many nations today.

Simón Bolívar began leading revolutions for independence in Caracas, Venezuela, his place of birth. He helped Venezuela, Bolivia, Colombia, Ecuador, and Peru gain independence from Spain.

REVIEW *What problems have many countries in South America faced since becoming independent?*

New Problems for All Countries

Perhaps the greatest problem South Americans face today is how best to use the continent's vast resources. Thousands of square miles of rain forest have been destroyed to clear the land for planting crops, raising cattle, and digging mines.

Clearing the forest land provides jobs for many people. But the burning has caused problems for the environment. Some scientists believe that it has led to a warming of the Earth. If average temperatures rise too high, the Earth's weather patterns could change.

That might harm the plants and animals on which people everywhere depend.

In Brazil the widespread cutting down of the forests, or **deforestation**, has left many native peoples homeless. Most of Brazil's native peoples live in the thick rain forests of the country's Amazon River region. Because of deforestation many native peoples are struggling to keep their way of life. "We must hold on to our land and culture," says Pedro Inácio Pinheiro, a leader of the Tikuna people. "We can never give these up." Today the Brazilian government is working on ways to use the resources of the rain forest while also preserving it.

Resources of South America

Regions

South America is a huge continent with many resources. People in most South American countries speak Spanish. In Brazil they speak Portuguese.

■ *Which country is the largest in South America?*

Legend:
- ⊛ National capital
- Iron ore
- Copper
- Gold
- Silver
- Forests
- Oil
- Sugarcane
- Bananas
- Coffee
- Grains
- Cattle

Modified Chambers Trimetric Projection

The powerful Iguazú (ee•gwah•zoo) Falls form part of the Argentina-Brazil border. Both Argentina and Brazil have established national parks near the falls to protect the surrounding lands. Although deforestation remains a problem in South America, some efforts have been made to prevent the destruction of natural resources.

Another problem in South America that affects other parts of the world is the production and sale of illegal drugs. In some areas of South America, especially in Bolivia and Colombia, farmers can earn more money by growing crops used to make harmful drugs than by producing other crops. People can make huge profits selling these illegal drugs in Europe and the United States. Conflicts have broken out between countries over stopping the trade in illegal drugs.

To build greater cooperation among the countries of the Western Hemisphere, the Organization of American States, or OAS, was formed in 1948. Almost all the countries of South America, Central America, and the Caribbean, along with Mexico, Canada, and the United States, have joined. The OAS helps settle disagreements and works to improve trade and understanding among its member nations.

REVIEW *What is the OAS?*

LESSON 4 REVIEW

Check Understanding

1 **Remember the Facts** What kinds of disagreements have caused conflicts all over South America?

2 **Recall the Main Idea** How have the problems of South America affected the United States and other parts of the world?

Think Critically

3 **Personally Speaking** How do you think the history of South America is like the history of the United States? How do the histories seem different?

4 **Think More About It** In what ways is the Organization of American States similar to the United Nations?

Show What You Know

News-Writing Activity With a partner, choose one country in South America. Work with your partner to prepare an article for a newsmagazine. The article should describe life in that country today. Focus on the important issues facing the people there. Compare your article with those written by your classmates.

FOCUS

How might a nation protect the rights of all its citizens?

Main Idea As you read, find out how Canada has worked to protect the rights of its diverse groups of citizens.

Vocabulary

province
separatist

The Peoples of Canada

C anada is the second-largest country in the world in area and covers almost half of North America. More than 29 million people live in this vast land. As in the United States, the first people in Canada were American Indians, who have lived there for thousands of years. In the 1500s the French arrived. In 1763, after Britain won the French and Indian War, Canada became a British colony. It remained a colony until 1867, when it was given limited independence. Not until 1982, when a new constitution was written, was Canada's independence complete.

The Constitution of 1982

The Constitution of 1982 is in many ways like the British constitution, which Canada had been using since 1867. But there is an important difference. Canada added a section called the Charter of Rights and Freedoms. This statement of rights is similar to the Bill of Rights in the United States Constitution.

The Canadian charter recognizes the rights of Canada's diverse peoples and promises to protect the country's multicultural heritage. The charter allows both French and English to be used in public schools and in the courts. It also states that treaties with American Indians in Canada will be upheld.

But not all Canadians in the nation's ten provinces and two territories were happy with the Constitution of 1982. The **provinces** are political regions much like states in the United States, but they have more authority. Each province has its own government and its own prime minister, or leader of the government. A province can take many actions without the approval of the national government. Many leaders in the provinces worried that they would lose some of their authority under the new constitution.

There were also regional divisions in the country. People in the western provinces —Manitoba, Saskatchewan, Alberta,

The flag of Canada shows a maple leaf, a symbol of the country.

Languages in Canada

Majority speak English
Majority speak French
American Indian languages
CREE Name of Indian language

Places While most Canadians speak English, many other languages can be heard in different places. Notice that Quebec has many French speakers.

■ *What language do most people living in Winnipeg, Manitoba speak?*

and British Columbia—felt they should have a greater say in the national government because the western provinces contain most of the country's natural resources. People in the eastern provinces—Ontario, Quebec, New Brunswick, Newfoundland, Nova Scotia, and Prince Edward Island—felt they should have more control because they have more people than the western provinces do.

REVIEW *Why were Canadian people divided over the country's Constitution of 1982?*

Quebec Opposes the Constitution

Of all the provinces, Quebec has objected most to the Constitution of 1982. The reason for this can be found in the province's history.

Quebec was the oldest and most important part of the colony of New France, which was founded in the early 1600s. Even after the British took control of New France in 1763, French culture remained strong in Quebec. French families there have kept alive their

A visit to Quebec City (above) allows people to experience French-Canadian culture firsthand. Signs in Quebec, like this stop sign (above right), are printed in both French and English.

language, laws, Catholic religion, and cultural traditions for hundreds of years. Today its French culture sets Quebec apart from Canada's other provinces. More than 82 percent of Quebec's people speak French. These French Canadians like to be called Québecois (kay•beh•KWAH).

While the other provinces have objected to the Constitution of 1982, only Quebec has refused to accept it. Many Québecois feel that the constitution does not recognize their special role in the founding of Canada. It does not give them the authority they have always had to veto national decisions. And it does not give them the right to use only French in schools, on public signs, and in the courts. Some Québecois even want to secede from Canada. Known as **separatists**, they want Quebec to become a separate, independent nation.

REVIEW *Why have French Canadians in Quebec refused to accept the constitution?*

LEARNING FROM TIME LINES An important event in Canada's history took place when the British Parliament passed the British North America Act, making Canada a self-governing nation partly under British control.
■ *When was this act passed? What type of nation was Canada called?*

Key Events in Canada's History

1750 — 1800 — 1850 — 1900 — 1950 — 2000

1763
• Britain takes control of New France

1867
• British North America Act creates Dominion of Canada

1982
• Constitution of 1982 completes Canada's independence

1994
• North American Free Trade Agreement takes effect

Standing Up for Native Rights

Like the Québecois, the native peoples of Canada want greater protection for their cultures and their rights. Even with the Charter of Rights and Freedoms, which clearly states the rights of American Indians to keep their own land and to form their own governments, some Indian groups feel these rights have been ignored.

In the summer of 1990, a violent conflict broke out in the town of Oka, in Quebec. Some people in Oka wanted to make a golf course larger, using part of a Mohawk burial ground. Mohawk men, women, and children put up a barrier to keep the builders away. Through their protests the Mohawks succeeded in stopping the construction on their land, but the deeper problem was not solved. "There is still great anger here," explains Mohawk artist Deborah Etienne. "The land is our identity, our life, and they wanted to take it away from us. . . . Our land claims are not settled. Nothing is resolved."

In other cases, native groups have persuaded the Canadian government to take

This Inuit family lives on Holman Island in the Northwest Territories. Native peoples make up a large part of the population in Canada's Arctic region.

action. In 1984 the Canadian government gave the Cree and Naskapi (NAS•kuh•pee) peoples greater self-government. In 1992 the Inuits of Canada's Northern Territories won the right to form their own self-governing region. The territory, which the Inuits call Nunavut, meaning "our land," split from the Northern Territories. By these and similar actions, the Canadian government supports cultures in the Americas that are thousands of years old.

REVIEW *What document lists the rights of the native peoples of Canada?*

LESSON 5 REVIEW

Check Understanding

1 Remember the Facts What are some of the diverse groups that live in Canada?

2 Recall the Main Idea How has Canada worked to protect the rights of its diverse groups of citizens?

Think Critically

3 Personally Speaking What might happen if Quebec decides to secede from Canada? What do you think might happen if a large state like California broke away from the United States?

4 Cause and Effect What caused the Indian groups to take action to protect their rights? What have been the effects of their actions?

Show What You Know

Writing Activity Study maps and other resource materials that give information about the geography of Canada. Find the province in Canada that is most like the state in which you live. Then write a paragraph comparing and contrasting the two places. Share your paragraph with a classmate.

1940   1950   1960

1948
• The OAS is formed

1952
• Puerto Rico becomes a United States territory

1959
• Fidel Castro becomes the leader of Cuba

CONNECT MAIN IDEAS

Use this organizer to show how the chapter's main ideas are connected. Complete the organizer by writing two or three sentences that summarize the main idea of each lesson. A copy of the organizer appears on page 142 of the Activity Book.

The Western Hemisphere Today

Mexico Today
_____
_____
_____

Democracy in the Caribbean and in Central America
_____
_____
_____

The Peoples of Canada
_____
_____
_____

Challenges in South America
_____
_____
_____

WRITE MORE ABOUT IT

Write a Poem Omar and his father carried a banner that said, "Let's protect the rainforest." Write a poem about saving forests or conserving the environment.

Write a Postcard Suppose that you are traveling through Canada on vacation. Write a postcard to a friend. Explain how Quebec is different from Canada's other provinces.

1970	1980	1990	2000

1982
• Canada's new constitution is written

1990
• Violeta Chamorro becomes president of Nicaragua

1994
• The NAFTA agreement goes into effect

USE VOCABULARY

Write the term that correctly matches each definition. Then use each term in a complete sentence.

deforestation   liberate

embargo   metropolitan area

interest rate   province

1 a city and all the suburbs and other population areas around it

2 the amount that a bank charges customers to borrow money

3 the refusal of one country to trade its goods with another country

4 to set free

5 the widespread cutting down of forests

6 a political region that is much like a state

CHECK UNDERSTANDING

7 How did the devaluation of 1994 affect Mexico's middle class?

8 What is a free-trade agreement? What three nations signed NAFTA?

9 What did the Puerto Rican people decide about their political relationship with the United States in the 1993 election?

10 Why has life in Cuba become very difficult since the end of the Cold War?

11 What is the chief purpose of the OAS?

12 What is the Charter of Rights and Freedoms?

13 What do the separatists in Canada want?

THINK CRITICALLY

14 Personally Speaking Omar walked 870 miles to be in a real rain forest. Describe a time when you had to work hard to do something. How did working hard to accomplish something make you feel?

15 Cause and Effect What effect did the election of Violeta Chamorro as president have on Nicaragua?

APPLY SKILLS

Use Population Maps Use the population map on page 652 and the cartogram on page 653 to answer these questions.

16 Which city has more people, Monterrey or Tijuana?

17 In what part of Mexico is the population density the greatest?

18 Which country has more people, Costa Rica or Haiti?

READ MORE ABOUT IT

Chico Mendes: Defender of the Rain Forest by Joann J. Burch. Millbrook. This book describes one man's efforts to protect the Amazon rain forest.

Visit the Internet at
http://www.hbschool.com
for additional resources.

DEMOCRACY
in the Americas

Since colonial times, the ideas of freedom and democracy have been important to the people of the United States. These ideas are also important to people of other countries in the Americas. The United States has set an example of democracy for its neighboring countries in the Western Hemisphere.

Today every country in the Americas except Cuba has a democratic form of government. The United States and Canada have had democratic governments for a long time. Canada's constitution guarantees its people many of the same freedoms as those found in the United States Constitution.

During much of the twentieth century, many Latin American countries were ruled by military dictators. These dictatorships began to fall in the 1980s and 1990s. Many of those countries now have written constitutions like that of the United States. By following the example of the United States and other democratic nations, people in the Americas have achieved greater freedom than they ever had before.

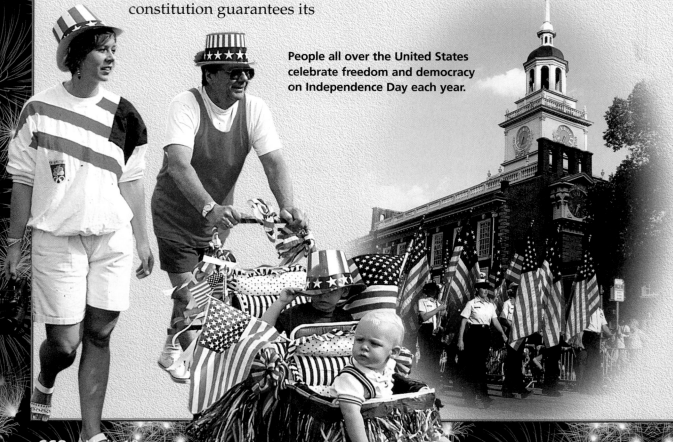

People all over the United States celebrate freedom and democracy on Independence Day each year.

Think and Apply

Choose a country in the Americas, other than the United States, that has a democratic government. Use the Internet, encyclopedias, and other resources to find out how the country's government is organized. Make a chart that shows the government's different parts and how they work together. Then write a paragraph that tells how the government of the country you researched is similar to and different from the government of the United States. Share your findings with the class.

Canadians (above) and many Latin Americans (below) also have special days to celebrate their independence and the freedoms they enjoy because of democracy. Today almost all countries in Latin America hold free elections (bottom right) in which people can vote for the candidates of their choice.

HARCOURT BRACE

Visit the Internet at **http://www.hbschool.com** for additional resources.

CNN Turner Le@rning

Check your media center or classroom video library for the Making Social Studies Relevant videotape of this feature.

DIPUTADOS   SENADORES   PRESIDENTE

UNIT 10 REVIEW

VISUAL SUMMARY

Summarize the Main Ideas
Study the pictures and captions to help you review the events you read about in Unit 10.

Choose an Event
From this visual summary, choose the event that you think will have the most important effect on the future. Write a paragraph to explain your choice.

1 The Cold War began after World War II. The Soviet Union cut off land routes to West Berlin in 1948, but an airlift brought in supplies.

3 In 1963 Martin Luther King, Jr., spoke for civil rights at a huge gathering in Washington, D.C.

4 The United States put the first person on the moon in 1969.

6 Changes in the Soviet Union brought an end to the Cold War. In 1989 the Berlin Wall was torn down.

2 War seemed near in 1962 when the Soviet Union sent missiles to Cuba. President Kennedy ordered a blockade of the island. Finally, Soviet leader Nikita Khrushchev agreed to remove the missiles.

5 Americans were divided over the Vietnam War. After many deaths, the war ended in 1975.

7 Today many of the countries in the Western Hemisphere face problems with their economies and governments. A major problem in South America is the clearing of rain forests.

8 Mexico, the United States, and Canada have signed the NAFTA agreement to remove tariffs on trade between these countries.

USE VOCABULARY

Use each term in a complete sentence that will help explain its meaning.

1. airlift
2. cease-fire
3. arms control
4. middle class
5. free election
6. mestizo

CHECK UNDERSTANDING

7. Which President ordered a naval blockade during the Cuban missile crisis?

8. Who was the first person to set foot on the moon?

9. How did Martin Luther King, Jr., work to bring about change?

10. How did Mikhail Gorbachev help change the Soviet Union?

11. How did the growth of manufacturing affect Mexico?

12. What are some important rights guaranteed by Canada's Charter of Rights and Freedoms?

THINK CRITICALLY

13. **Explore Viewpoints** Why do you think that Soviet leader Mikhail Gorbachev wanted to work toward better relations between the Soviet Union and the United States?

14. **Personally Speaking** Which United States President do you think made the greatest contributions to world peace? Explain your choice.

APPLY SKILLS

Use Population Maps Use the population map of South America below to answer the following questions.

15. Are there more areas of high population density in the coastal areas or in the central areas of South America?

16. Which country has the most areas of high population density?

17. Which countries have the least areas of high population density?

18. Which capital cities are surrounded by areas where there are only 2–25 people per square mile?

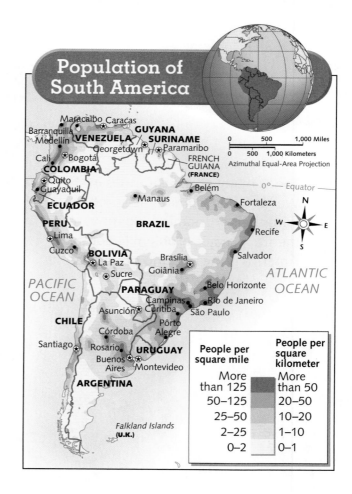

Population of South America

REMEMBER
- Share your ideas.
- Cooperate with others to plan your work.
- Take responsibility for your work.
- Help one another.
- Show your group's work to the class.
- Discuss what you learned by working together.

ACTIVITY

Create a Hall of Fame

People from different ethnic groups and cultures have worked to bring about change in the United States and in other countries in the Americas. Your class should list 25 of these people to include in a Hall of Fame. They may be people that you read about in this unit or earlier units. The 25 names on the list should then be divided among small groups. Each group should make a poster for each person assigned to the group. The poster should include a drawing and a short biography of the person. Display all the posters together on a classroom wall or in a hallway.

ACTIVITY

Prepare a Newscast

Work in a group to prepare a newscast that covers one of the following events: the Cuban missile crisis, the Montgomery bus boycott, the civil rights march in Washington, D.C., the Watergate scandal, Nixon's visit to China, or the 1985 Reagan and Gorbachev meeting. Each member of your group should have a job, such as researcher, writer, reporter, or set designer. When planning your newscast, include information that describes the changes that the event brought about. Present your newscast to your class.

Unit Project Wrap-Up

Create a Space Travel Exhibit

Continue working with your classmates on your exhibit about space travel. Make sure you find out what the United States and other countries are planning to do to explore space in the years to come. Among the items you may want to include are posters, drawings, books, magazines, photographs, and any other objects related to space exploration. When you are finished, invite another class to visit the exhibit.

For Your Reference

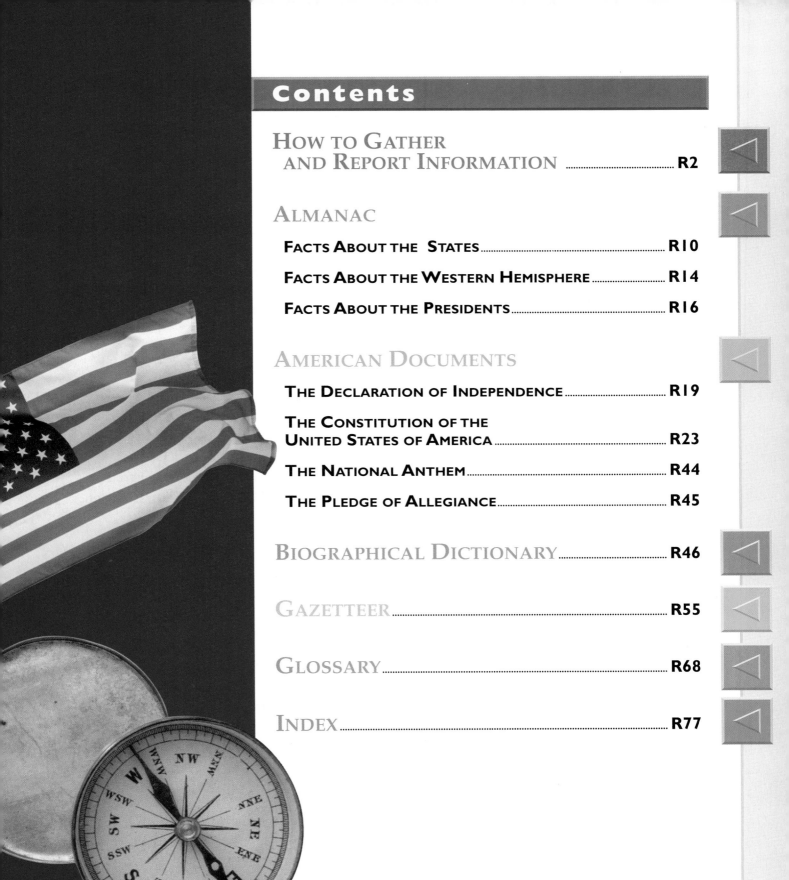

Contents

How to Gather and Report Information

To write a report, make a poster, or do many other social studies projects, you may need information that is not in your textbook. You would need to gather this information from reference books, electronic references, or community resources. The following guide can help you in gathering information from many sources and in reporting what you find.

HOW TO USE REFERENCE TOOLS

Reference works are collections of facts. They include books and electronic resources, such as almanacs, atlases, dictionaries, and encyclopedias. In a library a reference book has *R* or *REF*—for *reference*—on its spine with the call number. Most reference books are for use only in the library. Many libraries also have electronic references on CD-ROM and on the Internet.

▶ WHEN TO USE AN ENCYCLOPEDIA

An encyclopedia is a good place to begin to look for information. An encyclopedia has articles on nearly every subject. The articles are in alphabetical order. Each gives basic facts about people, places, and events. Some electronic encyclopedias allow you to hear music and speeches and see short movies.

▶ WHEN TO USE A DICTIONARY

A dictionary can give you information about words. Dictionaries explain word meanings and show the pronunciations of words. A dictionary is a good place to check the spelling of a word. Some dictionaries also include the origins of words and lists of foreign words, abbreviations, well-known people, and place names.

▶ WHEN TO USE AN ATLAS

You can find information about places in an atlas. An atlas is a book of maps. Some atlases have road maps. Others have maps of countries around the world. There are atlases with maps that show crops, population, products, and many other things. Ask a librarian to help you find the kind of atlas you need.

▶ WHEN TO USE AN ALMANAC

An almanac is a book or electronic resource of facts and figures. It shows information in tables and charts. However, the subjects are not in alphabetical order. You will need to use the index, which does list the subjects in alphabetical order. Most almanacs are brought up to date every year. So an almanac can give you the latest information.

These students are researching information that they need to prepare a report on the American Revolution.

A card file can help you find the nonfiction book you want.

▶ HOW TO FIND NONFICTION BOOKS

Nonfiction books give facts about real people and things. In a library, all nonfiction books are numbered and placed in order on the shelves. To find the nonfiction book you want, you need to know its call number. You can find this number by using a card file or a computer catalog, but you will need to know the book's title, author, or subject. Here are some sample entries for a book on American Indians.

Subject Card

```
              INDIANS OF NORTH AMERICA.
970.004   America's fascinating Indian heritage /
REA           [editor, James A. Maxwell]. -- Pleasantville,
          N.Y. : Reader's Digest Association, c1978.

              416 p. : ill. ; 29 cm.

              ISBN 0-89577-019-9
```

Author Card

```
              Maxwell, James A., 1912-
970.004   America's fascinating Indian heritage /
REA           [editor, James A. Maxwell]. -- Pleasantville,
          N.Y. : Reader's Digest Association, c1978.

              416 p. : ill. ; 29 cm.

E77.A56       ISBN 0-89577-019-9
```

```
970.004   America's fascinating Indian heritage /
REA           [editor, James A. Maxwell]. -- Pleasantville,
          N.Y. : Reader's Digest Association, c1978.

              416 p. : ill. ; 29 cm.

              At head of title: Reader's Digest.
E77.A56       Includes index.
              ISBN 0-89577-019-9



              1. Indians of North America.    I. Maxwell,
          James A., 1912-  II. Title: Reader's Digest.

          E77.A56                              970'.004
                                               78-55614
```

Title Card

Computer Catalog

▶ HOW TO FIND PERIODICALS

Libraries have special sections for periodicals—newspapers and magazines. Periodicals are good sources for the latest information and for topics not covered in books. New issues of periodicals are usually displayed on a rack. Older issues are stored away, sometimes on film. Most libraries have an index or guide that lists magazine articles by subject. The most widely used guides are the *Children's Magazine Guide* and the *Readers' Guide to Periodical Literature*.

The entries in these guides are usually in alphabetical order by subject, author, or title. Abbreviations may be used for many parts of an entry, such as the name of the magazine and the date of the issue. Here is a sample entry for an article on the Civil War.

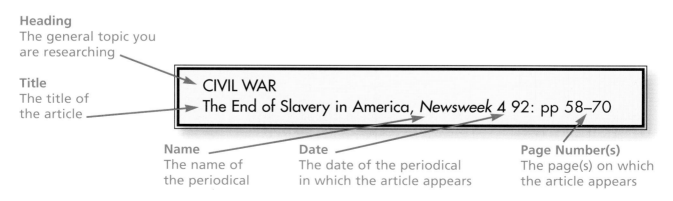

Heading
The general topic you are researching

Title
The title of the article

CIVIL WAR
The End of Slavery in America, *Newsweek* 4 92: pp 58–70

Name
The name of the periodical

Date
The date of the periodical in which the article appears

Page Number(s)
The page(s) on which the article appears

HOW TO FIND INTERNET RESOURCES

The World Wide Web, part of the Internet, is a rich resource for information. You can use the World Wide Web to read documents, see photographs and artworks, and examine other primary sources. You can also use it to listen to music, read electronic books, take a "tour" of a museum, or get the latest news.

Information on the World Wide Web changes all the time. What you find today may not be there tomorrow, and new information is always being added. Much of the information you find may be useful, but remember that some of it may not be accurate.

▶ PLAN YOUR SEARCH

1. Make a list of your research questions.
2. Think about possible sources for finding your answers.
3. Identify key words to describe your research topic.
4. Consider synonyms and variations of those terms.
5. Decide exactly how you will go about finding what you need.

▶ SEARCH BY SUBJECT

To search for topics, or subjects, choose a search engine. You can get a list of available search engines by clicking the SEARCH or NET SEARCH button at the top of your screen.

If you want to find Web sites for baseball, for example, enter "baseball" in the search engine field. Then click SEARCH or GO on the screen. You will see a list of sites all over the World Wide Web having to do with baseball. Because not all search engines list the same sites, you may need to use more than one search engine.

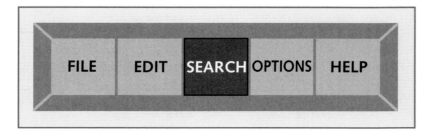

FILE   EDIT   SEARCH   OPTIONS   HELP

▶ SEARCH BY USING ADDRESSES

Each site on the World Wide Web has an address called a Uniform Resource Locator, or URL for short. A typical URL is shown in the box below.

To find URL listings, look in manuals, books, newspapers, magazines, and television and radio credits. To use a URL to go to a Web site, type the URL in the LOCATION/GO TO or NETSITE box in the upper left corner of the screen.

Go To http://www.hbschool.com

▶ BOOKMARK YOUR RESOURCES

Once you have found a site that you think will be helpful, you can bookmark it. Bookmarking makes a copy of a URL and keeps a record of it so you can easily go back to the site later.

While you are at the site you want to bookmark, click BOOKMARKS at the top of your screen and choose ADD BOOKMARK. Your list of bookmarks might look like this:

Knowing how to use the Internet can help you find a wide range of information on a topic quickly and easily.

BOOKMARKS

- Harcourt Brace School Publishers: The Learning Site

- Library of Congress Home Page

- The Smithsonian Institution Home Page

- National Archives Online Exhibit Hall

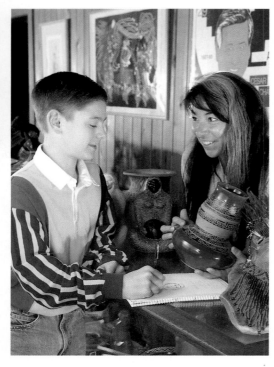

Conducting an interview can be a good way to gather firsthand information about a topic.

HOW TO CONDUCT AN INTERVIEW

Conducting interviews, or asking people questions, is a good way to get facts and points of view.

▶ PLANNING AN INTERVIEW

1. Make a list of people to interview.
2. Call or write to each person to request an interview. When you contact the person, identify yourself and let the person know what you want to talk about.
3. Ask the person you will interview to set a time and place to meet.

▶ BEFORE THE INTERVIEW

1. Read more about your topic, and, if possible, about the person. That way, you will be better able to talk with the person about your topic.
2. Make a list of questions to ask.

▶ DURING THE INTERVIEW

1. Listen carefully. Do not interrupt or argue with the person.
2. Take notes, and write down the person's exact words.
3. If you want to use a tape recorder, first ask the person if you may do so.

▶ AFTER THE INTERVIEW

1. Before you leave, thank the person you interviewed.
2. Follow up by writing a thank-you note.

HOW TO CONDUCT A SURVEY

A good way to get information about the views of people in your community is to conduct a survey.

1. Identify your topic, and make a list of questions. Write them so that they can be answered with "yes" or "no" or with "for" or "against." You may also want to give a "no opinion" or "not sure" choice.
2. Make a tally sheet for recording the responses.
3. Decide how many people you will ask and where you will conduct your survey.
4. During the survey, record the responses carefully on the tally sheet.
5. When you have finished your survey, count the responses and write a summary statement or conclusion that your survey supports.

HOW TO WRITE FOR INFORMATION

People in places far away can also give you information. You can write a letter to ask for information about a certain topic. When you write, be sure to do these things:

- Write neatly or use a computer.
- Say who you are and why you are writing.
- Make your request specific and reasonable.
- Provide a self-addressed, stamped envelope for the answer.

HOW TO WRITE A REPORT

You may be asked to write a report on the information you have gathered. Most reports are 300 to 500 words long.

▶ GATHER AND ORGANIZE YOUR INFORMATION

Gather information about your topic from reference books, electronic references, or community resources. Then organize the information you have gathered.

- Take notes as you find information for your report.
- Review your notes to make sure that you have all the information you need.
- Outline your information.
- Make sure the information is in the right order.

▶ DRAFT YOUR REPORT

- Review your information. Decide whether you need more.
- Remember that the purpose of your report is to share information about your topic.
- Write a draft of your report. Put all your ideas on paper.

▶ REVISE

- Check that you have followed the order of your outline. Move sentences that seem out of place.
- Add any information that seems needed.
- Add quotations that show people's exact words.
- Reword sentences if too many follow the same pattern.

▶ PROOFREAD AND PUBLISH

- Check for errors.
- Make sure nothing has been left out.
- Write a clean copy of your report, or use a computer.

A good report is well-organized and full of important information about a topic.

Almanac

FACTS ABOUT THE STATES

State Flag	State	Year of Statehood	Population*	Area (sq. mi.)	Capital	Origin of State Name
	Alabama	1819	4,319,000	51,609	Montgomery	Choctaw, *alba ayamule*, "one who clears land and gathers food from it"
	Alaska	1959	609,000	586,412	Juneau	Aleut, *alayeska*, "great land"
	Arizona	1912	4,555,000	113,909	Phoenix	Papago, *arizonac*, "place of the small spring"
	Arkansas	1836	2,523,000	53,104	Little Rock	Quapaw, "the downstream people"
	California	1850	32,268,000	158,693	Sacramento	Spanish, a fictional island
	Colorado	1876	3,893,000	104,247	Denver	Spanish, "red land" or "red earth"
	Connecticut	1788	3,270,000	5,009	Hartford	Mohican, *quinnitukqut*, "at the long tidal river"
	Delaware	1787	732,000	2,057	Dover	Named for Lord de la Warr
	Florida	1845	14,654,000	58,560	Tallahassee	Spanish, "filled with flowers"
	Georgia	1788	7,486,000	58,876	Atlanta	Named for King George II of England
	Hawaii	1959	1,187,000	6,450	Honolulu	Polynesian, *hawaiki* or *owykee*, "homeland"
	Idaho	1890	1,210,000	83,557	Boise	Shoshone, "light on the mountains"

State Flag	State	Year of Statehood	Population*	Area (sq. mi.)	Capital	Origin of State Name
	Illinois	1818	11,896,000	56,400	Springfield	Algonquian, *iliniwek*, "men" or "warriors"
	Indiana	1816	5,864,000	36,291	Indianapolis	*Indian + a*, "land of the Indians"
	Iowa	1846	2,852,000	56,290	Des Moines	Dakota, *ayuba*, "beautiful land"
	Kansas	1861	2,595,000	82,264	Topeka	Sioux, "land of the south wind people"
	Kentucky	1792	3,908,000	40,395	Frankfort	Cherokee, *kentake*, "meadowland"
	Louisiana	1812	4,352,000	48,523	Baton Rouge	Named for King Louis XIV of France
	Maine	1820	1,242,000	33,215	Augusta	Named after a French province
	Maryland	1788	5,094,000	10,577	Annapolis	Named for Henrietta Maria, Queen Consort of Charles I of England
	Massachusetts	1788	6,118,000	8,257	Boston	Algonquian, "at the big hill" or "place of the big hill"
	Michigan	1837	9,774,000	58,216	Lansing	Chippewa, *mica gama*, "big water"
	Minnesota	1858	4,686,000	84,068	St. Paul	Dakota Sioux, "sky-blue water"
	Mississippi	1817	2,731,000	47,716	Jackson	Chippewa, *mici sibi*, "big river"
	Missouri	1821	5,402,000	69,686	Jefferson City	Algonquian, "muddy water"or "people of the big canoes"

*These population figures are from the most recent available statistics.

Almanac

FACTS ABOUT THE STATES

State Flag	State	Year of Statehood	Population*	Area (sq. mi.)	Capital	Origin of State Name
	Montana	1889	879,000	147,138	Helena	Spanish, "mountainous"
	Nebraska	1867	1,657,000	77,227	Lincoln	Omaha, *ni-bthaska,* "river in the flatness"
	Nevada	1864	1,677,000	110,540	Carson City	Spanish, "snowy" or "snowed upon"
	New Hampshire	1788	1,173,000	9,304	Concord	Named for Hampshire County, England
	New Jersey	1787	8,053,000	7,836	Trenton	Named for the Isle of Jersey
	New Mexico	1912	1,730,000	121,666	Santa Fe	Named by Spanish explorers from Mexico
	New York	1788	18,137,000	49,576	Albany	Named after the Duke of York
	North Carolina	1789	7,425,000	52,586	Raleigh	Named after King Charles II of England
	North Dakota	1889	641,000	70,665	Bismarck	Sioux, *dakota,* "friend" or "ally"
	Ohio	1803	11,186,000	41,222	Columbus	Iroquois, *oheo,* "beautiful, beautiful water"
	Oklahoma	1907	3,317,000	69,919	Oklahoma City	Choctaw, "red people"
	Oregon	1859	3,243,000	96,981	Salem	Algonquian, *wauregan,* "beautiful water"
	Pennsylvania	1787	12,020,000	45,333	Harrisburg	*Penn + sylvania,* meaning "Penn's woods"

Almanac

State Flag	State	Year of Statehood	Population*	Area (sq. mi.)	Capital	Origin of State Name
	Rhode Island	1790	987,000	1,214	Providence	Dutch, "red-clay island"
	South Carolina	1788	3,760,000	31,055	Columbia	Named after King Charles II of England
	South Dakota	1889	738,000	77,047	Pierre	Sioux, *dakota*, "friend" or "ally"
	Tennessee	1796	5,368,000	42,244	Nashville	Name of a Cherokee village
	Texas	1845	19,439,000	267,338	Austin	Native American, *tejas*, "friend" or "ally"
	Utah	1896	2,059,000	84,916	Salt Lake City	Ute, "land of the Ute"
	Vermont	1791	589,000	9,609	Montpelier	French, *vert*, "green," and *mont*, "mountain"
	Virginia	1788	6,734,000	40,817	Richmond	Named after Queen Elizabeth I of England
	Washington	1889	5,610,000	68,192	Olympia	Named for George Washington
	West Virginia	1863	1,816,000	24,181	Charleston	From the English-named state of Virginia
	Wisconsin	1848	5,170,000	56,154	Madison	Possibly Algonquian, "grassy place" or "place of the beaver"
	Wyoming	1890	480,000	97,914	Cheyenne	Algonquian, *mache-weaming*, "at the big flats"
	District of Columbia		529,000	67		Named after Christopher Columbus

*These population figures are from the most recent available statistics.

FACTS ABOUT THE WESTERN HEMISPHERE

Country	Population*	Area (sq. mi.)	Capital	Origin of Country Name
North America				
Antigua and Barbuda	66,000	171	St. Johns	Named for the Church of Santa María la Antigua in Seville, Spain
Bahamas	262,000	5,382	Nassau	Spanish, *bajamar,* "shallow water"
Barbados	258,000	166	Bridgetown	Means "bearded"—probably referring to the beardlike vines early explorers found on its trees
Belize	225,000	8,867	Belmopan	Mayan, "muddy water"
Canada	29,123,000	3,849,674	Ottawa	Huron-Iroquois, *kanata,* "village" or "community"
Costa Rica	3,534,000	19,730	San José	Spanish, "rich coast"
Cuba	10,999,000	42,804	Havana	Origin unknown
Dominica	83,000	290	Roseau	Latin, *dies dominica,* "Day of the Lord"
Dominican Republic	8,228,000	18,704	Santo Domingo	Named after the capital city
El Salvador	5,662,000	8,124	San Salvador	Spanish, "the Savior"
Grenada	96,000	133	St. George's	Origin unknown
Guatemala	11,558,000	42,042	Guatemala City	Indian, "land of trees"
Haiti	6,611,000	10,695	Port-au-Prince	Indian, "land of mountains"
Honduras	5,751,000	43,277	Tegucigalpa	Spanish, "profundities"—probably referring to the depth of offshore waters
Jamaica	2,616,000	4,244	Kingston	Arawak, *xamayca,* "land of wood and water"
Mexico	97,563,000	756,066	Mexico City	Aztec, *mexliapan,* "lake of the moon"
Nicaragua	4,386,000	50,880	Managua	From *Nicarao,* the name of an Indian Chief
Panama	2,693,000	29,157	Panama City	From an Indian village's name

Almanac

Country	Population*	Area (sq. mi.)	Capital	Origin of Country Name
St. Kitts-Nevis	42,000	104	Basseterre	Named by Christopher Columbus—Kitts for St. Christopher, a Catholic saint; Nevis, for a cloud-topped peak that looked like las nieves, "the snows"
St. Lucia	160,000	238	Castries	Named by Christopher Columbus for a Catholic saint
St. Vincent and the Grenadines	119,000	150	Kingstown	May have been named by Christopher Columbus for a Catholic saint
Trinidad and Tobago	1,273,000	1,980	Port-of-Spain	Trinidad, from the Spanish word for "trinity"; Tobago, named for tobacco because the island has the shape of an Indian smoking pipe
United States of America	267,636,000	3,787,318	Washington, D.C.	Named after the explorer Amerigo Vespucci

South America

Country	Population*	Area (sq. mi.)	Capital	Origin of Country Name
Argentina	35,798,000	1,073,518	Buenos Aires	Latin, argentum, "silver"
Bolivia	7,670,000	424,164	La Paz/Sucre	Named after Simón Bolívar, the famed liberator
Brazil	164,511,000	3,286,470	Brasília	Named after a native tree that the Portuguese called "bresel wood"
Chile	14,508,000	292,135	Santiago	Indian, chilli, "where the land ends"
Colombia	37,418,000	440,831	Bogotá	Named after Christopher Columbus
Ecuador	11,691,000	105,037	Quito	From the Spanish word for equator, referring to the country's location
Guyana	706,000	83,044	Georgetown	Indian, "land of waters"
Paraguay	5,652,000	157,048	Asunción	Named after the Paraguay River, which flows through it
Peru	24,950,000	496,255	Lima	Quechua, "land of abundance"
Suriname	443,000	63,251	Paramaribo	From an Indian word, surinen
Uruguay	3,262,000	68,037	Montevideo	Named after the Uruguay River, which flows through it
Venezuela	22,396,000	352,144	Caracas	Spanish, "Little Venice"

*These population figures are from the most recent available statistics.

FACTS ABOUT THE

Presidents

1 George Washington

Birthplace:
  Westmoreland County, VA
Home State: *VA*
Political Party: *None*
Age at Inauguration: *57*
Served: *1789–1797*
Vice President:
  John Adams
1732–1799

2 John Adams

Birthplace: *Braintree, MA*
Home State: *MA*
Political Party: *Federalist*
Age at Inauguration: *61*
Served: *1797–1801*
Vice President:
  Thomas Jefferson
1735–1826

3 Thomas Jefferson

Birthplace: *Albemarle County, VA*
Home State: *VA*
Political Party:
  Democratic-Republican
Age at Inauguration: *57*
Served: *1801–1809*
Vice Presidents: *Aaron Burr, George Clinton*
1743–1826

4 James Madison

Birthplace: *Port Conway, VA*
Home State: *VA*
Political Party:
  Democratic-Republican
Age at Inauguration: *57*
Served: *1809–1817*
Vice Presidents:
  George Clinton, Elbridge Gerry
1751–1836

5 James Monroe

Birthplace:
  Westmoreland County, VA
Home State: *VA*
Political Party:
  Democratic-Republican
Age at Inauguration: *58*
Served: *1817–1825*
Vice President:
  Daniel D. Tompkins
1758–1831

6 John Quincy Adams

Birthplace: *Braintree, MA*
Home State: *MA*
Political Party:
  Democratic-Republican
Age at Inauguration: *57*
Served: *1825–1829*
Vice President:
  John C. Calhoun
1767–1848

7 Andrew Jackson

Birthplace: *Waxhaw settlement, SC*
Home State: *TN*
Political Party:
  Democratic
Age at Inauguration: *61*
Served: *1829–1837*
Vice Presidents:
  John C. Calhoun, Martin Van Buren
1767–1845

8 Martin Van Buren

Birthplace: *Kinderhook, NY*
Home State: *NY*
Political Party:
  Democratic
Age at Inauguration: *54*
Served: *1837–1841*
Vice President:
  Richard M. Johnson
1782–1862

9 William H. Harrison

Birthplace: *Berkeley, VA*
Home State: *OH*
Political Party: *Whig*
Age at Inauguration: *68*
Served: *1841*
Vice President:
  John Tyler
1773–1841

10 John Tyler

Birthplace: *Greenway, VA*
Home State: *VA*
Political Party: *Whig*
Age at Inauguration: *51*
Served: *1841–1845*
Vice President: *none*
1790–1862

11 James K. Polk

Birthplace: *near Pineville, NC*
Home State: *TN*
Political Party:
  Democratic
Age at Inauguration: *49*
Served: *1845–1849*
Vice President:
  George M. Dallas
1795–1849

12 Zachary Taylor

Birthplace: *Orange County, VA*
Home State: *LA*
Political Party: *Whig*
Age at Inauguration: *64*
Served: *1849–1850*
Vice President:
  Millard Fillmore
1784–1850

13 Millard Fillmore

Birthplace: *Locke, NY*
Home State: *NY*
Political Party: *Whig*
Age at Inauguration: *50*
Served: *1850–1853*
Vice President: *none*
1800–1874

Home state refers to the state of residence when elected.

Almanac

14 Franklin Pierce

Birthplace: *Hillsboro, NH*
Home State: *NH*
Political Party: *Democratic*
Age at Inauguration: *48*
Served: *1853–1857*
Vice President: *William R. King*

1804–1869

15 James Buchanan

Birthplace: *near Mercersburg, PA*
Home State: *PA*
Political Party: *Democratic*
Age at Inauguration: *65*
Served: *1857–1861*
Vice President: *John C. Breckinridge*

1791–1868

16 Abraham Lincoln

Birthplace: *near Hodgenville, KY*
Home State: *IL*
Political Party: *Republican*
Age at Inauguration: *52*
Served: *1861–1865*
Vice Presidents: *Hannibal Hamlin, Andrew Johnson*

1809–1865

17 Andrew Johnson

Birthplace: *Raleigh, NC*
Home State: *TN*
Political Party: *National Union*
Age at Inauguration: *56*
Served: *1865–1869*
Vice President: *none*

1808–1875

18 Ulysses S. Grant

Birthplace: *Point Pleasant, OH*
Home State: *IL*
Political Party: *Republican*
Age at Inauguration: *46*
Served: *1869–1877*
Vice Presidents: *Schuyler Colfax, Henry Wilson*

1822–1885

19 Rutherford B. Hayes

Birthplace: *near Delaware, OH*
Home State: *OH*
Political Party: *Republican*
Age at Inauguration: *54*
Served: *1877–1881*
Vice President: *William A. Wheeler*

1822–1893

20 James A. Garfield

Birthplace: *Orange, OH*
Home State: *OH*
Political Party: *Republican*
Age at Inauguration: *49*
Served: *1881*
Vice President: *Chester A. Arthur*

1831–1881

21 Chester A. Arthur

Birthplace: *Fairfield, VT*
Home State: *NY*
Political Party: *Republican*
Age at Inauguration: *51*
Served: *1881–1885*
Vice President: *none*

1829–1886

22 Grover Cleveland

Birthplace: *Caldwell, NJ*
Home State: *NY*
Political Party: *Democratic*
Age at Inauguration: *47*
Served: *1885–1889*
Vice President: *Thomas A. Hendricks*

1837–1908

23 Benjamin Harrison

Birthplace: *North Bend, OH*
Home State: *IN*
Political Party: *Republican*
Age at Inauguration: *55*
Served: *1889–1893*
Vice President: *Levi P. Morton*

1833–1901

24 Grover Cleveland

Birthplace: *Caldwell, NJ*
Home State: *NY*
Political Party: *Democratic*
Age at Inauguration: *55*
Served: *1893–1897*
Vice President: *Adlai E. Stevenson*

1837–1908

25 William McKinley

Birthplace: *Niles, OH*
Home State: *OH*
Political Party: *Republican*
Age at Inauguration: *54*
Served: *1897–1901*
Vice Presidents: *Garret A. Hobart, Theodore Roosevelt*

1843–1901

26 Theodore Roosevelt

Birthplace: *New York, NY*
Home State: *NY*
Political Party: *Republican*
Age at Inauguration: *42*
Served: *1901–1909*
Vice President: *Charles W. Fairbanks*

1858–1919

27 William H. Taft

Birthplace: *Cincinnati, OH*
Home State: *OH*
Political Party: *Republican*
Age at Inauguration: *51*
Served: *1909–1913*
Vice President: *James S. Sherman*

1857–1930

28 Woodrow Wilson

Birthplace: *Staunton, VA*
Home State: *NJ*
Political Party: *Democratic*
Age at Inauguration: *56*
Served: *1913–1921*
Vice President: *Thomas R. Marshall*

1856–1924

29 Warren G. Harding

Birthplace: *near Blooming Grove, OH*
Home State: *OH*
Political Party: *Republican*
Age at Inauguration: *55*
Served: *1921–1923*
Vice President: *Calvin Coolidge*
1865–1923

30 Calvin Coolidge

Birthplace: *Plymouth Notch, VT*
Home State: *MA*
Political Party: *Republican*
Age at Inauguration: *51*
Served: *1923–1929*
Vice President: *Charles G. Dawes*
1872–1933

31 Herbert Hoover

Birthplace: *West Branch, IA*
Home State: *CA*
Political Party: *Republican*
Age at Inauguration: *54*
Served: *1929–1933*
Vice President: *Charles Curtis*
1874–1964

32 Franklin D. Roosevelt

Birthplace: *Hyde Park, NY*
Home State: *NY*
Political Party: *Democratic*
Age at Inauguration: *51*
Served: *1933–1945*
Vice Presidents: *John N. Garner, Henry A. Wallace, Harry S. Truman*
1882–1945

33 Harry S. Truman

Birthplace: *Lamar, MO*
Home State: *MO*
Political Party: *Democratic*
Age at Inauguration: *60*
Served: *1945–1953*
Vice President: *Alben W. Barkley*
1884–1972

34 Dwight D. Eisenhower

Birthplace: *Denison, TX*
Home State: *NY*
Political Party: *Republican*
Age at Inauguration: *62*
Served: *1953–1961*
Vice President: *Richard M. Nixon*
1890–1969

35 John F. Kennedy

Birthplace: *Brookline, MA*
Home State: *MA*
Political Party: *Democratic*
Age at Inauguration: *43*
Served: *1961–1963*
Vice President: *Lyndon B. Johnson*
1917–1963

36 Lyndon B. Johnson

Birthplace: *near Stonewall, TX*
Home State: *TX*
Political Party: *Democratic*
Age at Inauguration: *55*
Served: *1963–1969*
Vice President: *Hubert H. Humphrey*
1908–1973

37 Richard M. Nixon

Birthplace: *Yorba Linda, CA*
Home State: *NY*
Political Party: *Republican*
Age at Inauguration: *56*
Served: *1969–1974*
Vice Presidents: *Spiro T. Agnew, Gerald R. Ford*
1913–1994

38 Gerald R. Ford

Birthplace: *Omaha, NE*
Home State: *MI*
Political Party: *Republican*
Age at Inauguration: *61*
Served: *1974–1977*
Vice President: *Nelson A. Rockefeller*
1913–

39 Jimmy Carter

Birthplace: *Plains, GA*
Home State: *GA*
Political Party: *Democratic*
Age at Inauguration: *52*
Served: *1977–1981*
Vice President: *Walter F. Mondale*
1924–

40 Ronald W. Reagan

Birthplace: *Tampico, IL*
Home State: *CA*
Political Party: *Republican*
Age at Inauguration: *69*
Served: *1981–1989*
Vice President: *George H. W. Bush*
1911–

41 George H. W. Bush

Birthplace: *Milton, MA*
Home State: *TX*
Political Party: *Republican*
Age at Inauguration: *64*
Served: *1989–1993*
Vice President: *Dan Quayle*
1924–

42 William Clinton

Birthplace: *Hope, AR*
Home State: *AR*
Political Party: *Democratic*
Age at Inauguration: *46*
Served: *1993–2001*
Vice President: *Albert Gore*
1946–

43 George W. Bush

Birthplace: *New Haven, CT*
Political Party: *Republican*
Age at Inauguration: *54*
Served: *2001–*
Vice President: *Richard Cheney*
1946–

Home state refers to the state of residence when elected.

Almanac

American Documents

The Declaration of Independence

In Congress, July 4, 1776.
The unanimous Declaration of the
thirteen United States of America,

When in the Course of human events it becomes necessary for one people to dissolve the political bands which have connected them with another, and to assume among the powers of the earth, the separate and equal station to which the Laws of Nature and of Nature's God entitle them, a decent respect to the opinions of mankind requires that they should declare the causes which impel them to the separation.

We hold these truths to be self-evident, that all men are created equal, that they are endowed by their Creator with certain unalienable Rights, that among these are Life, Liberty and the pursuit of Happiness.
That to secure these rights, Governments are instituted among Men, deriving their just powers from the consent of the governed,
That whenever any Form of Government becomes destructive of these ends, it is the Right of the People to alter or to abolish it, and to institute new Government, laying its foundation on such principles and organizing its powers in such form, as to them shall seem most likely to effect their Safety and Happiness. Prudence, indeed, will dictate that Governments long established should not be changed for light and transient causes; and accordingly all experience hath shown, that mankind are more disposed to suffer, while evils are sufferable, than to right themselves by abolishing the forms to which they are accustomed. But when a long train of abuses and usurpations, pursuing invariably the same Object evinces a design to reduce them under absolute Despotism, it is their right, it is their duty, to throw off such Government, and to provide new Guards for their future security.

Such has been the patient sufferance of these Colonies; and such is now the necessity which constrains them to alter their former Systems of Government. The history of the present King of Great Britain is a history of repeated injuries and usurpations, all having in direct object the establishment of an absolute Tyranny over these States. To prove this, let Facts be submitted to a candid world.

He has refused his Assent to Laws, the most wholesome and necessary for the public good.
He has forbidden his Governors to pass Laws of immediate and pressing importance, unless suspended in their operation till his Assent should be obtained; and when so suspended, he has utterly neglected to attend to them.

PREAMBLE
The Preamble tells why the Declaration was written. It states that the members of the Continental Congress believed the colonies had the right to break away from Britain and become a free nation.

STATEMENT OF RIGHTS
The opening part of the Declaration tells what rights the members of the Continental Congress believed that all people have. All people are equal and have the rights to life, liberty, and the pursuit of happiness. These rights cannot be taken away. When a government tries to take these rights away from the people, the people have the right to change the government or do away with it. The people can then form a new government that gives them these rights.

CHARGES AGAINST THE KING
The Declaration lists more than 25 charges against the king. He was mistreating the colonists, the Declaration says, in order to gain total control over the colonies.

The king rejected many laws passed by colonial legislatures.

American Documents

The king made the colonial legislatures meet at unusual times and places.

The king and the king's governors often dissolved colonial legislatures for disobeying their orders.

The king stopped people from moving to the colonies and into the western lands.

The king prevented the colonists from choosing their own judges. The king chose the judges, and they served only as long as the king was satisfied with them.

The king hired people to help collect taxes in the colonies.

The king appointed General Thomas Gage, commander of Britain's military forces in the Americas, as governor of Massachusetts.

The king expected the colonists to provide housing and supplies for the British soldiers in the colonies.

The king and Parliament demanded that colonists pay many taxes, even though the colonists did not agree to pay them.

Colonists were tried by British naval courts, which had no juries.

Colonists accused of treason were sent to Britain to be tried.

He has refused to pass other Laws for the accommodation of large districts of people, unless those people would relinquish the right of Representation in the Legislature, a right inestimable to them and formidable to tyrants only.

He has called together legislative bodies at places unusual, uncomfortable, and distant from the depository of their public Records, for the sole purpose of fatiguing them into compliance with his measures.

He has dissolved Representative Houses repeatedly, for opposing with manly firmness his invasions on the rights of the people.

He has refused for a long time, after such dissolutions, to cause others to be elected; whereby the Legislative powers, incapable of Annihilation, have returned to the People at large for their exercise; the State remaining in the mean time exposed to all the dangers of invasion from without, and convulsions within.

He has endeavored to prevent the population of these States; for that purpose obstructing the Laws for Naturalization of Foreigners; refusing to pass others to encourage their migrations hither, and raising the conditions of new Appropriations of Lands.

He has obstructed the Administration of Justice, by refusing his Assent to Laws for establishing Judiciary powers.

He has made Judges dependent on his Will alone, for the tenure of their offices, and the amount and payment of their salaries.

He has erected a multitude of New Offices, and sent hither swarms of Officers to harrass our people, and eat out their substance.

He has kept among us, in times of peace, Standing Armies without the Consent of our legislatures.

He has affected to render the Military independent of and superior to the Civil power.

He has combined with others to subject us to a jurisdiction foreign to our constitution, and unacknowledged by our laws; giving his Assent to their Acts of pretended Legislation:

For quartering large bodies of armed troops among us:

For protecting them, by a mock Trial, from punishment for any Murders which they should commit on the Inhabitants of these States:

For cutting off our Trade with all parts of the world:

For imposing Taxes on us without our Consent:

For depriving us in many cases, of the benefits of Trial by Jury:

For transporting us beyond Seas to be tried for pretended offences:

For abolishing the free System of English Laws in a neighboring Province, establishing therein an Arbitrary government, and enlarging its Boundaries so as to render it at once an example and fit instrument for introducing the same absolute rule into these Colonies:

For taking away our Charters, abolishing our most valuable Laws, and altering fundamentally the Forms of our Governments:

For suspending our own Legislatures, and declaring themselves invested with power to legislate for us in all cases whatsoever.

He has abdicated Government here, by declaring us out of his Protection and waging War against us.

He has plundered our seas, ravaged our Coasts, burnt our towns, and destroyed the lives of our people.

He is at this time transporting large Armies of foreign Mercenaries to complete the works of death, desolation and tyranny, already begun with circumstances of Cruelty & perfidy scarcely paralleled in the most barbarous ages, and totally unworthy the Head of a civilized nation.

He has constrained our fellow Citizens taken Captive on the high Seas to bear Arms against their Country, to become the executioners of their friends and Brethren, or to fall themselves by their Hands.

He has excited domestic insurrections amongst us, and has endeavored to bring on the inhabitants of our frontiers, the merciless Indian Savages, whose known rule of warfare, is an undistinguished destruction of all ages, sexes and conditions.

In every stage of these Oppressions We have Petitioned for Redress in the most humble terms: Our repeated Petitions have been answered only by repeated injury. A Prince, whose character is thus marked by every act which may define a Tyrant, is unfit to be the ruler of a free people.

Nor have We been wanting in attentions to our British brethren. We have warned them from time to time of attempts by their legislature to extend an unwarrantable jurisdiction over us. We have reminded them of the circumstances of our emigration and settlement here. We have appealed to their native justice and magnanimity, and we have conjured them by the ties of our common kindred to disavow these usurpations, which, would inevitably interrupt our connections and correspondence. They too have been deaf to the voice of justice and of consanguinity. We must, therefore, acquiesce in the necessity, which denounces our Separation, and hold them, as we hold the rest of mankind, Enemies in War, in Peace Friends.

We, therefore, the Representatives of the united States of America, in General Congress, Assembled, appealing to the Supreme Judge of the world for the rectitude of our intentions, do, in the Name, and by Authority of the good People of these Colonies, solemnly publish and declare, That these United Colonies are, and of Right ought to be Free and Independent States; that they are Absolved from all Allegiance to the British Crown, and that all political connection between them and the State of Great Britain, is and ought to be totally dissolved; and that as Free and Independent States, they have full Power to levy War, conclude Peace, contract Alliances, establish Commerce, and to do all other Acts and Things which Independent States may of right do.

The king allowed General Gage to take military action to enforce British laws in the colonies.

The king hired Hessian mercenaries and sent them to fight the colonists.

The king's governor in Virginia promised freedom to all enslaved people who joined the British forces. The British also planned to use Indians to fight the colonists.

The Declaration explained the efforts of the colonists to avoid separation from Britain. But the colonists said that the king had ignored their protests. Because of the many charges against the king, the writers of the Declaration concluded that he was not fit to rule free people.

A STATEMENT OF INDEPENDENCE
The writers declared that the colonies were now free and independent states. All ties with Britain were broken. As free and independent states, they had the right to make war and peace, to trade, and to do all the things free countries could do.

To support the Declaration, the signers promised one another their lives, their fortunes, and their honor.

And for the support of this Declaration, with a firm reliance on the protection of divine Providence, we mutually pledge to each other our Lives, our Fortunes and our sacred Honor.

John Hancock

NEW HAMPSHIRE
Josiah Bartlett
William Whipple
Matthew Thornton

MASSACHUSETTS
John Adams
Samuel Adams
Robert Treat Paine
Elbridge Gerry

NEW YORK
William Floyd
Philip Livingston
Francis Lewis
Lewis Morris

RHODE ISLAND
Stephen Hopkins
William Ellery

NEW JERSEY
Richard Stockton
John Witherspoon
Francis Hopkinson
John Hart
Abraham Clark

PENNSYLVANIA
Robert Morris
Benjamin Rush
Benjamin Franklin
John Morton
George Clymer
James Smith
George Taylor
James Wilson
George Ross

DELAWARE
Caesar Rodney
George Read
Thomas McKean

MARYLAND
Samuel Chase
William Paca
Thomas Stone
Charles Carroll of Carrollton

NORTH CAROLINA
William Hopper
Joseph Hewes
John Penn

VIRGINIA
George Wythe
Richard Henry Lee
Thomas Jefferson
Benjamin Harrison
Thomas Nelson, Jr.
Francis Lightfoot Lee
Carter Braxton

SOUTH CAROLINA
Edward Rutledge
Thomas Heyward, Jr.
Thomas Lynch, Jr.
Arthur Middleton

CONNECTICUT
Roger Sherman
Samuel Huntington
William Williams
Oliver Wolcott

GEORGIA
Button Gwinnett
Lyman Hall
George Walton

Members of the Continental Congress stated that copies of the Declaration should be sent to all Committees of Correspondence and to commanders of the troops and that it should be read in every state.

Resolved, That copies of the Declaration be sent to the several assemblies, conventions, and committees, or councils of safety, and to the several commanding officers of the continental troops; that it be proclaimed in each of the United States, at the head of the army.

THE CONSTITUTION OF THE UNITED STATES OF AMERICA

Preamble*

We the people of the United States, in order to form a more perfect Union, establish justice, insure domestic tranquillity, provide for the common defense, promote the general welfare, and secure the blessings of liberty to ourselves and our posterity, do ordain and establish this Constitution for the United States of America.

ARTICLE I
THE LEGISLATIVE BRANCH

SECTION 1. CONGRESS

All legislative powers herein granted shall be vested in a Congress of the United States, which shall consist of a Senate and House of Representatives.

SECTION 2. THE HOUSE OF REPRESENTATIVES

(1) The House of Representatives shall be composed of members chosen every second year by the people of the several states, and the electors in each state shall have the qualifications requisite for electors of the most numerous branch of the state legislature.

(2) No person shall be a Representative who shall not have attained to the age of twenty-five years, and been seven years a citizen of the United States, and who shall not, when elected, be an inhabitant of that state in which he shall be chosen.

(3) Representatives [and direct taxes]** shall be apportioned among the several states which may be included within this Union, according to their respective numbers [which shall be determined by adding to the whole number of free persons, including those bound to service for a term of years, and excluding Indians not taxed, three-fifths of all other persons]. The actual enumeration shall be made within three years after the first meeting of the Congress of the United States, and within every subsequent term of ten years, in such manner as they shall by law direct. The number of Representatives shall not exceed one for every 30,000, but each state shall have at least one Representative [; and until such enumeration shall be made, the State of New Hampshire shall be entitled to choose three; Massachusetts eight; Rhode Island and Providence Plantations one; Connecticut five; New York six; New Jersey four; Pennsylvania eight; Delaware one; Maryland six; Virginia ten; North Carolina five; South Carolina five; and Georgia three].

*Titles have been added to make the Constitution easier to read. They did not appear in the original document.
**The parts of the Constitution that no longer apply are printed in italics within brackets [ ]. These portions have been changed or set aside by later amendments.

PREAMBLE
The introduction to the Constitution states the purposes and principles for writing it. The writers wanted to set up a fairer form of government and to secure peace and freedom for themselves and for future generations.

CONGRESS
Congress has the authority to make laws. Congress is made up of two groups of lawmakers: the Senate and the House of Representatives.

(1) ELECTION AND TERM OF MEMBERS
Qualified voters are to elect members of the House of Representatives every two years. Each member of the House of Representatives must meet certain requirements.

(2) QUALIFICATIONS
Members of the House of Representatives must be at least 25 years old. They must have been citizens of the United States for at least seven years. They must live in the state that they will represent.

(3) DETERMINING APPORTIONMENT
The number of representatives a state may have depends on the number of people living in each state. Every ten years the federal government must take a census, or count, of the population in every state. Every state will have at least one representative.

(4) FILLING VACANCIES

If there is a vacancy in representation in Congress, the governor of the state involved must call a special election to fill it.

(5) SPECIAL AUTHORITY

The House of Representatives chooses a Speaker as its presiding officer. It also chooses other officers as appropriate. The House is the only government branch that may impeach, or charge, an official in the executive branch or a judge of the federal courts for failing to carry out his or her duties. These cases are tried in the Senate.

(1) NUMBER, TERM, AND SELECTION OF MEMBERS

Each state is represented by two senators. Until Amendment 17 was passed, state legislatures chose the senators for their states. Each senator serves a six-year term and has one vote in Congress.

(2) OVERLAPPING TERMS AND FILLING VACANCIES

One-third of the senators are elected every two years for a six-year term. This grouping allows at least two-thirds of the experienced senators to remain in the Senate after each election. Amendment 17 permits state governors to appoint a replacement to fill a vacancy until the next election is held.

(3) QUALIFICATIONS

Senators must be at least 30 years old. They must have been citizens of the United States for at least nine years. They must live in the state that they will represent.

(4) PRESIDENT OF THE SENATE

The Vice President acts as chief officer of the Senate but does not vote unless there is a tie.

(5) OTHER OFFICERS

The Senate chooses its other officers and a president pro tempore, who serves if the Vice President is not present or if the Vice President becomes President. *Pro tempore* is a Latin term meaning "for the time being."

(4) When vacancies happen in the representation from any state, the executive authority thereof shall issue writs of election to fill such vacancies.

(5) The House of Representatives shall choose their Speaker and other officers; and shall have the sole power of impeachment.

SECTION 3. THE SENATE

(1) The Senate of the United States shall be composed of two Senators from each state [*chosen by the legislature thereof*], for six years, and each Senator shall have one vote.

(2) [*Immediately after they shall be assembled in consequence of the first election, they shall be divided as equally as may be into three classes. The seats of the Senators of the first class shall be vacated at the expiration of the second year, of the second class at the expiration of the fourth year, and of the third class at the expiration of the sixth year, so that one-third may be chosen every second year; and if vacancies happen by resignation, or otherwise, during the recess of the legislature of any state, the executive thereof may make temporary appointments until the next meeting of the legislature, which shall then fill such vacancies.*]

(3) No person shall be a Senator who shall not have attained to the age of thirty years, and been nine years a citizen of the United States, and who shall not, when elected, be an inhabitant of that state for which he shall be chosen.

(4) The Vice President of the United States shall be President of the Senate, but shall have no vote, unless they be equally divided.

(5) The Senate shall choose their other officers, and also a President *pro tempore*, in the absence of the Vice President, or when he shall exercise the office of the President of the United States.

(6) The Senate shall have the sole power to try all impeachments. When sitting for that purpose, they shall be on oath or affirmation. When the President of the United States is tried, the Chief Justice shall preside; and no person shall be convicted without the concurrence of two-thirds of the members present.

(7) Judgment in cases of impeachment shall not extend further than to removal from office, and disqualification to hold and enjoy any office of honor, trust, or profit under the United States; but the party convicted shall nevertheless be liable and subject to indictment, trial, judgment and punishment, according to law.

SECTION 4. ELECTIONS AND MEETINGS

(1) The times, places, and manner of holding elections for Senators and Representatives shall be prescribed in each state by the legislature thereof; but the Congress may at any time by law make or alter such regulations, [*except as to the places of choosing Senators*].

(2) The Congress shall assemble at least once in every year, [*and such meeting shall be on the first Monday in December, unless they shall by law appoint a different day*].

SECTION 5. RULES OF PROCEDURE

(1) Each house shall be the judge of the elections, returns and qualifications of its own members, and a majority of each shall constitute a quorum to do business; but a smaller number may adjourn from day to day, and may be authorized to compel the attendance of absent members, in such manner and under such penalties as each house may provide.

(2) Each house may determine the rules of its proceedings, punish its members for disorderly behavior, and, with the concurrence of two-thirds, expel a member.

(3) Each house shall keep a journal of its proceedings, and from time to time publish the same, excepting such parts as may in their judgment require secrecy; and the yeas and nays of the members of either house on any question shall, at the desire of one-fifth of those present, be entered on the journal.

---

(6) IMPEACHMENT TRIALS
If the House of Representatives votes articles of impeachment, the Senate holds a trial. A two-thirds vote is required to convict a person who has been impeached.

(7) PENALTY FOR CONVICTION
If convicted in an impeachment case, an official is removed from office and may never hold office in the United States government again. The convicted person may also be tried in a regular court of law for any crimes.

(1) HOLDING ELECTIONS
Each state makes its own rules about electing senators and representatives. However, Congress may change these rules at any time. Today congressional elections are held on the Tuesday after the first Monday in November, in even-numbered years.

(2) MEETINGS
The Constitution requires Congress to meet at least once a year. That day is the first Monday in December, unless Congress sets a different day. Amendment 20 changed this date to January 3.

(1) ORGANIZATION
Each house of Congress may decide if its members have been elected fairly and are able to hold office. Each house may do business only when a quorum—a majority of its members—is present. By less than a majority vote, each house may compel absent members to attend.

(2) RULES
Each house may decide its own rules for doing business, punish its members, and expel a member from office if two-thirds of the members agree.

(3) JOURNAL
The Constitution requires each house to keep records of its activities and to publish these records from time to time. The House Journal and the Senate Journal are published at the end of each session. How each member voted must be recorded if one-fifth of the members ask for this to be done.

(4) ADJOURNMENT

When Congress is in session, neither house may take a recess for more than three days without the consent of the other.

(1) PAY AND PRIVILEGES

Members of Congress set their own salaries, which are to be paid by the federal government. Members cannot be arrested or sued for anything they say while Congress is in session. This privilege is called congressional immunity. Members of Congress may be arrested while Congress is in session only if they commit a crime.

(2) RESTRICTIONS

Members of Congress may not hold any other federal office while serving in Congress. A member may not resign from office and then take a government position created during that member's term of office or for which the pay has been increased during that member's term of office.

(1) MONEY-RAISING BILLS

All money-raising bills must be introduced first in the House of Representatives, but the Senate may suggest changes.

(2) HOW A BILL BECOMES A LAW

After a bill has been passed by both the House of Representatives and the Senate, it must be sent to the President. If the President approves and signs the bill, it becomes law. The President can also veto, or refuse to sign, the bill. Congress can override a veto by passing the bill again by a two-thirds majority. If the President does not act within ten days, two things may happen. If Congress is still in session, the bill becomes a law. If Congress ends its session within that same ten-day period, the bill does not become a law.

(3) ORDERS AND RESOLUTIONS

Congress can pass orders and resolutions, some of which have the same effect as a law. Congress may decide on its own when to end the session. Other such acts must be signed or vetoed by the President.

(4) Neither house, during the session of Congress, shall, without the consent of the other, adjourn for more than three days, nor to any other place than that in which the two houses shall be sitting.

SECTION 6. PRIVILEGES AND RESTRICTIONS

(1) The Senators and Representatives shall receive a compensation for their services, to be ascertained by law and paid out of the Treasury of the United States. They shall in all cases, except treason, felony, and breach of the peace, be privileged from arrest during their attendance at the session of their respective houses, and in going to and returning from the same; and for any speech or debate in either house, they shall not be questioned in any other place.

(2) No Senator or Representative shall, during the time for which he was elected, be appointed to any civil office under the authority of the United States, which shall have been created, or the emoluments whereof shall have been increased, during such time; and no person holding any office under the United States shall be a member of either house during his continuance in office.

SECTION 7. MAKING LAWS

(1) All bills for raising revenue shall originate in the House of Representatives; but the Senate may propose or concur with amendments as on other bills.

(2) Every bill which shall have passed the House of Representatives and the Senate shall, before it become a law, be presented to the President of the United States; if he approve, he shall sign it, but if not, he shall return it, with his objections, to that house in which it shall have originated, who shall enter the objections at large on their journal, and proceed to reconsider it. If after such reconsideration two-thirds of that house shall agree to pass the bill, it shall be sent, together with the objections, to the other house, by which it shall likewise be reconsidered, and, if approved by two-thirds of that house, it shall become a law. But in all such cases the votes of both houses shall be determined by yeas and nays, and the names of the persons voting for and against the bill shall be entered on the journal of each house respectively. If any bill shall not be returned by the President within ten days (Sundays excepted) after it shall have been presented to him, the same bill shall be a law, in like manner as if he had signed it, unless the Congress by their adjournment prevent its return, in which case it shall not be a law.

(3) Every order, resolution, or vote to which the concurrence of the Senate and House of Representatives may be necessary (except on a question of adjournment) shall be presented to the President of the United States; and before the same shall take effect, shall be approved by him, or being disapproved by him, shall be repassed by two-thirds of the Senate and House of Representatives, according to the rules and limitations prescribed in the case of a bill.

SECTION 8. POWERS DELEGATED TO CONGRESS
The Congress shall have power
    (1) To lay and collect taxes, duties, imposts and excises, to pay the debts and provide for the common defense and general welfare of the United States; but all duties, imposts and excises shall be uniform throughout the United States;

    (2) To borrow money on the credit of the United States;

    (3) To regulate commerce with foreign nations, and among the several states [*and with the Indian tribes*];

    (4) To establish a uniform rule of naturalization, and uniform laws on the subject of bankruptcies throughout the United States;

    (5) To coin money, regulate the value thereof, and of foreign coin, and fix the standard of weights and measures;

    (6) To provide for the punishment of counterfeiting the securities and current coin of the United States;

    (7) To establish post offices and post roads;

    (8) To promote the progress of science and useful arts by securing for limited times to authors and inventors the exclusive right to their respective writings and discoveries;

    (9) To constitute tribunals inferior to the Supreme Court;

    (10) To define and punish piracies and felonies committed on the high seas and offenses against the law of nations;

(1) TAXATION
Only Congress has the authority to raise money to pay debts, defend the United States, and provide services for its people by collecting taxes or tariffs on foreign goods. All taxes must be applied equally in all states.

(2) BORROWING MONEY
Congress may borrow money for national use. This is usually done by selling government bonds.

(3) COMMERCE
Congress can control trade with other countries and between states.

(4) NATURALIZATION AND BANKRUPTCY
Congress decides what requirements people from other countries must meet to become United States citizens. Congress can also pass laws to protect people who are bankrupt, or cannot pay their debts.

(5) COINS, WEIGHTS, AND MEASURES
Congress can print and coin money and decide its value. Congress also decides on the system of weights and measures to be used throughout the nation.

(6) COUNTERFEITING
Congress may pass laws to punish people who make fake money, bonds, or stamps.

(7) POSTAL SERVICE
Congress can build post offices and make rules about the postal system and the roads used for mail delivery.

(8) COPYRIGHTS AND PATENTS
Congress can issue patents and copyrights to inventors and authors to protect the ownership of their works.

(9) FEDERAL COURTS
Congress can establish a system of federal courts under the Supreme Court.

(10) CRIMES AT SEA
Congress can pass laws to punish people for crimes committed at sea. Congress may also punish United States citizens for breaking international law.

(11) DECLARING WAR
Only Congress can declare war.

(12) THE ARMY
Congress can establish an army, but it cannot vote enough money to support it for more than two years. This part of the Constitution was written to keep the army under civilian control.

(13) THE NAVY
Congress can establish a navy and vote enough money to support it for as long as necessary. No time limit was set because people thought the navy was less of a threat to people's liberty than the army was.

(14) MILITARY REGULATIONS
Congress makes the rules that guide and govern all the armed forces.

(15) THE MILITIA
Each state has its own militia, now known as the National Guard. The National Guard can be called into federal service by the President, as authorized by Congress, to enforce laws, to stop uprisings against the government, or to protect the people in case of floods, earthquakes, and other disasters.

(16) CONTROL OF THE MILITIA
Congress helps each state support the National Guard. Each state may appoint its own officers and train its own guard according to rules set by Congress.

(17) NATIONAL CAPITAL AND OTHER PROPERTY
Congress may pass laws to govern the nation's capital (Washington, D.C.) and any land owned by the government.

(18) OTHER NECESSARY LAWS
The Constitution allows Congress to make laws that are necessary to enforce the powers listed in Article I. This clause allows Congress to stretch its authority when new situations arise.

(11) To declare war, [*grant letters of marque and reprisal,*] and make rules concerning captures on land and water;

(12) To raise and support armies, but no appropriation of money to that use shall be for a longer term than two years;

(13) To provide and maintain a navy;

(14) To make rules for the government and regulation of the land and naval forces;

(15) To provide for calling forth the militia to execute the laws of the Union, suppress insurrections and repel invasions;

(16) To provide for organizing, arming, and disciplining the militia, and for governing such part of them as may be employed in the service of the United States, reserving to the states, respectively, the appointment of the officers, and the authority of training the militia according to the discipline prescribed by Congress;

(17) To exercise exclusive legislation in all cases whatsoever, over such district (not exceeding ten miles square) as may, by cession of particular states, and the acceptance of Congress, become the seat of government of the United States, and to exercise like authority over all places purchased by the consent of the legislature of the state in which the same shall be, for the erection of forts, magazines, arsenals, dock-yards, and other needful buildings; —and

(18) To make all laws which shall be necessary and proper for carrying into execution the foregoing powers, and all other powers vested by this Constitution in the government of the United States, or in any department or officer thereof.

SECTION 9. POWERS DENIED TO CONGRESS

(1) [*The migration or importation of such persons as any of the states now existing shall think proper to admit shall not be prohibited by the Congress prior to the year 1808; but a tax or duty may be imposed on such importation, not exceeding 10 dollars for each person.*]

(2) The privilege of the writ of habeas corpus shall not be suspended, unless when in cases of rebellion or invasion the public safety may require it.

(3) No bill of attainder or ex post facto law shall be passed.

(4) [*No capitation or other direct tax shall be laid, unless in proportion to the census or enumeration herein before directed to be taken.*]

(5) No tax or duty shall be laid on articles exported from any state.

(6) No preference shall be given by any regulation of commerce or revenue to the ports of one state over those of another; nor shall vessels bound to, or from, one state, be obliged to enter, clear, or pay duties in another.

(7) No money shall be drawn from the Treasury, but in consequence of appropriations made by law; and a regular statement and account of the receipts and expenditures of all public money shall be published from time to time.

---

(1) SLAVE TRADE
Some authority is not given to Congress. Congress could not prevent the slave trade until 1808, but it could put a tax of ten dollars on each slave brought into the United States. After 1808, when a law was passed to stop slaves from being brought into the United States, this section no longer applied.

(2) HABEAS CORPUS
A writ of habeas corpus is a privilege that entitles a person to a hearing before a judge. The judge must then decide if there is good reason for that person to have been arrested. If not, that person must be released. The government is not allowed to take this privilege away except during a national emergency, such as an invasion or a rebellion.

(3) SPECIAL LAWS
Congress cannot pass laws that impose punishment on a named individual or group, except in cases of treason. Article III sets limits to punishments for treason. Congress also cannot pass laws that punish a person for an action that was legal when it was done.

(4) DIRECT TAXES
Congress cannot set a direct tax on people, unless it is in proportion to the total population. Amendment 16, which provides for the income tax, is an exception.

(5) EXPORT TAXES
Congress cannot tax goods sent from one state to another or from a state to another country.

(6) PORTS
When making trade laws, Congress cannot favor one state over another. Congress cannot require ships from one state to pay a duty to enter another state.

(7) PUBLIC MONEY
The government cannot spend money from the treasury unless Congress passes a law allowing it to do so. A written record must be kept of all money spent by the government.

(8) TITLES OF NOBILITY AND GIFTS

The United States government cannot grant titles of nobility. Government officials cannot accept gifts from other countries without the permission of Congress. This clause was intended to prevent government officials from being bribed by other nations.

(1) COMPLETE RESTRICTIONS

The Constitution does not allow states to act as if they were individual countries. No state government may make a treaty with other countries. No state can print its own money.

(2) PARTIAL RESTRICTIONS

No state government can tax imported goods or exported goods without the consent of Congress. States may charge a fee to inspect these goods, but profits must be given to the United States Treasury.

(3) OTHER RESTRICTIONS

No state government may tax ships entering its ports unless Congress approves. No state may keep an army or navy during times of peace other than the National Guard. No state can enter into agreements called compacts with other states without the consent of Congress.

(1) TERM OF OFFICE

The President has the authority to carry out our nation's laws. The term of office for both the President and the Vice President is four years.

(2) THE ELECTORAL COLLEGE

This group of people is to be chosen by the voters of each state to elect the President and Vice President. The number of electors in each state is equal to the number of senators and representatives that state has in Congress.

(3) ELECTION PROCESS

This clause describes in detail how the electors were to choose the President and Vice President. In 1804 Amendment 12 changed the process for electing the President and the Vice President.

---

(8) No title of nobility shall be granted by the United States; and no person holding any office of profit or trust under them, shall, without the consent of the Congress, accept of any present, emolument, office, or title, of any kind whatever, from any king, prince, or foreign state.

SECTION 10. POWERS DENIED TO THE STATES

(1) No state shall enter into any treaty, alliance, or confederation; grant letters of marque and reprisal; coin money; emit bills of credit; make anything but gold and silver coin a tender in payment of debts; pass any bill of attainder, ex post facto law, or law impairing the obligation of contracts, or grant any title of nobility.

(2) No state shall, without the consent of the Congress, lay any imposts or duties on imports or exports, except what may be absolutely necessary for executing its inspection laws; and the net produce of all duties and imposts, laid by any state on imports or exports, shall be for the use of the Treasury of the United States; and all such laws shall be subject to the revision and control of the Congress.

(3) No state shall, without the consent of Congress, lay any duty of tonnage, keep troops, or ships of war in time of peace, enter into any agreement or compact with another state, or with a foreign power, or engage in war, unless actually invaded, or in such imminent danger as will not admit of delay.

ARTICLE II
THE EXECUTIVE BRANCH

SECTION 1. PRESIDENT AND VICE PRESIDENT

(1) The executive power shall be vested in a President of the United States of America. He shall hold his office during the term of four years, and together with the Vice President, chosen for the same term, be elected as follows:

(2) Each state shall appoint, in such manner as the legislature thereof may direct, a number of electors, equal to the whole number of Senators and Representatives to which the state may be entitled in the Congress; but no Senator or Representative, or person holding an office of trust or profit under the United States, shall be appointed an elector.

(3) [The electors shall meet in their respective states, and vote by ballot for two persons, of whom one at least shall not be an inhabitant of the same state with themselves. And they shall make a list of all the persons voted for, and of the number of votes for each; which list they shall sign and certify, and transmit sealed to the seat of the government of the United States, directed to the president of the Senate. The president of the Senate shall, in the presence of the Senate and House of Representatives, open all the certificates, and the votes shall then be counted. The person having the greatest number of votes shall be the President, if such number be a majority of the whole number of electors appointed; and if

there be more than one who have such majority, and have an equal number of votes, then the House of Representatives shall immediately choose by ballot one of them for President; and if no person have a majority, then from the five highest on the list the said House shall in like manner choose the President. But in choosing the President the votes shall be taken by states, the representation from each state having one vote: A quorum for this purpose shall consist of a member or members from two-thirds of the states, and a majority of all the states shall be necessary to a choice. In every case, after the choice of the President, the person having the greatest number of votes of the electors shall be the Vice President. But if there should remain two or more who have equal votes, the Senate shall choose from them by ballot the Vice President.]

(4) The Congress may determine the time of choosing the electors, and the day on which they shall give their votes; which day shall be the same throughout the United States.

(4) TIME OF ELECTIONS
Congress decides the day the electors are to be elected and the day they are to vote.

(5) No person except a natural-born citizen *[or a citizen of the United States, at the time of the adoption of this Constitution,]* shall be eligible to the office of the President; neither shall any person be eligible to that office who shall not have attained to the age of thirty-five years, and been fourteen years a resident within the United States.

(5) QUALIFICATIONS
The President must be at least 35 years old, be a citizen of the United States by birth, and have been living in the United States for 14 years or more.

(6) *[In case of the removal of the President from office, or of his death, resignation, or inability to discharge the powers and duties of the said office, the same shall devolve on the Vice President, and the Congress may by law provide for the case of removal, death, resignation or inability, both of the President and Vice President, declaring what officer shall then act as President, and such officer shall act accordingly, until the disability be removed, or a President shall be elected.]*

(6) VACANCIES
If the President dies, resigns, or is removed from office, the Vice President becomes President.

(7) The President shall, at stated times, receive for his services, a compensation, which shall neither be increased nor diminished during the period for which he shall have been elected, and he shall not receive within that period any other emolument from the United States, or any of them.

(7) SALARY
The President receives a salary that cannot be raised or lowered during a term of office. The President may not be paid any additional salary by the federal government or any state or local government. Today the President's salary is $200,000 a year, plus expenses for things such as housing, travel, and entertainment.

(8) Before he enter on the execution of his office, he shall take the following oath or affirmation:—"I do solemnly swear (or affirm) that I will faithfully execute the office of President of the United States, and will to the best of my ability, preserve, protect, and defend the Constitution of the United States."

(8) OATH OF OFFICE
Before taking office, the President must promise to perform the duties faithfully and to protect the country's form of government. Usually the Chief Justice of the Supreme Court administers the oath of office.

SECTION 2. POWERS OF THE PRESIDENT

(1) The President shall be Commander in Chief of the Army and Navy of the United States, and of the militia of the several states, when called into the actual service of the United States; he may require the opinion, in writing, of the principal officer in each of the executive departments, upon any subject relating to the duties of their respective offices, and he shall have power to grant reprieves and pardons for offenses against the United States, except in cases of impeachment.

(1) THE PRESIDENT'S LEADERSHIP
The President is the commander of the nation's armed forces and of the National Guard when it is in service of the nation. All government officials of the executive branch must report their actions to the President when asked. The President can excuse people from punishment for crimes committed.

(2) TREATIES AND APPOINTMENTS
The President has the authority to make treaties, but they must be approved by a two-thirds vote of the Senate. The President appoints justices to the Supreme Court, ambassadors to other countries, and other federal officials with the Senate's approval.

(3) FILLING VACANCIES
If a government official's position becomes vacant when Congress is not in session, the President can make a temporary appointment.

DUTIES
The President must report to Congress on the condition of the country. This report is now presented in the annual State of the Union message.

IMPEACHMENT
The President, the Vice President, or any government official will be removed from office if impeached, or accused, and then found guilty of treason, bribery, or other serious crimes. The Constitution protects government officials from being impeached for unimportant reasons.

FEDERAL COURTS
The authority to decide legal cases is granted to a Supreme Court and to a system of lower courts established by Congress. The Supreme Court is the highest court in the land. Justices and judges are in their offices for life, subject to good behavior.

(1) GENERAL AUTHORITY
Federal courts have the authority to decide cases that arise under the Constitution, laws, and treaties of the United States. They also have the authority to settle disagreements among states and among citizens of different states.

(2) SUPREME COURT
The Supreme Court can decide certain cases being tried for the first time. It can review cases that have already been tried in a lower court if the decision has been appealed, or questioned, by one side.

(2) He shall have power, by and with the advice and consent of the Senate, to make treaties, provided two-thirds of the senators present concur; and he shall nominate, and by and with the advice and consent of the Senate, shall appoint ambassadors, other public ministers and consuls, judges of the Supreme Court, and all other officers of the United States, whose appointments are not herein otherwise provided for, and which shall be established by law; but the Congress may by law vest the appointment of such inferior officers, as they think proper, in the President alone, in the courts of law, or in the heads of departments.

(3) The President shall have power to fill up all vacancies that may happen during the recess of the Senate, by granting commissions which shall expire at the end of their next session.

SECTION 3. DUTIES OF THE PRESIDENT
He shall from time to time give to the Congress information of the state of the Union, and recommend to their consideration such measures as he shall judge necessary and expedient; he may, on extraordinary occasions, convene both houses, or either of them, and in case of disagreement between them, with respect to the time of adjournment, he may adjourn them to such time as he shall think proper; he shall receive ambassadors and other public ministers; he shall take care that the laws be faithfully executed, and shall commission all the officers of the United States.

SECTION 4. IMPEACHMENT
The President, Vice President and all civil officers of the United States, shall be removed from office on impeachment for, and conviction of, treason, bribery, or other high crimes and misdemeanors.

ARTICLE III
THE JUDICIAL BRANCH

SECTION 1. FEDERAL COURTS
The judicial power of the United States shall be vested in one Supreme Court, and in such inferior courts as the Congress may from time to time ordain and establish. The judges, both of the supreme and inferior courts, shall hold their offices during good behavior, and shall, at stated times, receive for their services a compensation, which shall not be diminished during their continuance in office.

SECTION 2. AUTHORITY OF THE FEDERAL COURTS
(1) The judicial power shall extend to all cases, in law and equity, arising under this Constitution, the laws of the United States, and treaties made or which shall be made, under their authority; to all cases affecting ambassadors, other public ministers and consuls; to all cases of admiralty and maritime jurisdiction; to controversies to which the United States shall be a party; to controversies between two or more states; [*between a state and citizens of another state;*] between citizens of different states; —between citizens of the same state claiming lands under grants of different states, [*and between a state or the citizens thereof, and foreign states, citizens, or subjects.*]

(2) In all cases affecting ambassadors, other public ministers and consuls, and those in which a state shall be party, the Supreme Court shall have original jurisdiction. In all the other cases before mentioned, the Supreme Court shall have appellate jurisdiction, both as to law and fact, with such exceptions, and under such regulations as the Congress shall make.

(3) The trial of all crimes, except in cases of impeachment, shall be by jury; and such trial shall be held in the state where the said crimes shall have been committed; but when not committed within any state, the trial shall be at such place or places as the Congress may by law have directed.

SECTION 3. TREASON

(1) Treason against the United States shall consist only in levying war against them, or in adhering to their enemies, giving them aid and comfort. No person shall be convicted of treason unless on the testimony of two witnesses to the same overt act, or on confession in open court.

(2) The Congress shall have power to declare the punishment of treason, but no attainder of treason shall work corruption of blood, or forfeiture except during the life of the person attainted.

ARTICLE IV
RELATIONS AMONG STATES

SECTION 1. OFFICIAL RECORDS

Full faith and credit shall be given in each state to the public acts, records, and judicial proceedings of every other state. And the Congress may by general laws prescribe the manner in which such acts, records, and proceedings shall be proved, and the effect thereof.

SECTION 2. PRIVILEGES OF THE CITIZENS

(1) The citizens of each state shall be entitled to all privileges and immunities of citizens in the several states.

(2) A person charged in any state with treason, felony, or other crime, who shall flee from justice, and be found in another state, shall on demand of the executive authority of the state from which he fled, be delivered up, to be removed to the state having jurisdiction of the crime.

(3) [*No person held to service or labor in one state, under the laws thereof, escaping into another, shall in consequence of any law or regulation therein, be discharged from such service or labor, but shall be delivered up on claim of the party to whom such service or labor may be due.*]

---

(3) TRIAL BY JURY
The Constitution guarantees a trial by jury for every person charged with a federal crime. Amendments 5, 6, and 7 extend and clarify a person's right to a trial by jury.

(1) DEFINITION OF TREASON
Acts that may be considered treason are making war against the United States or helping its enemies. A person cannot be convicted of attempting to overthrow the government unless there are two witnesses to the act or the person confesses in court to treason.

(2) PUNISHMENT FOR TREASON
Congress can decide the punishment for treason, within certain limits.

OFFICIAL RECORDS
Each state must honor the official records and judicial decisions of other states.

(1) PRIVILEGES
A citizen moving from one state to another has the same rights as other citizens living in that person's new state of residence. In some cases, such as voting, people may be required to live in their new state for a certain length of time before obtaining the same privileges as citizens there.

(2) EXTRADITION
At the governor's request, a person who is charged with a crime and who tries to escape justice by crossing into another state may be returned to the state in which the crime was committed.

(3) FUGITIVE SLAVES
The original Constitution required that runaway slaves be returned to their owners. Amendment 13 abolished slavery, eliminating the need for this clause.

(1) ADMISSION OF NEW STATES
Congress has the authority to admit new states to the Union. All new states have the same rights as existing states.

(2) FEDERAL PROPERTY
The Constitution allows Congress to make or change laws governing federal property. This applies to territories and federally owned land within states, such as national parks.

GUARANTEES TO THE STATES
The federal government guarantees that every state have a republican form of government. The United States must also protect the states against invasion and help the states deal with rebellion or local violence.

AMENDING THE CONSTITUTION
Changes to the Constitution may be proposed by a two-thirds vote of both the House of Representatives and the Senate or by a national convention called by Congress when asked by two-thirds of the states. For an amendment to become law, the legislatures or conventions in three-fourths of the states must approve it.

(1) PUBLIC DEBT
Any debt owed by the United States before the Constitution went into effect was to be honored.

(2) FEDERAL SUPREMACY
This clause declares that the Constitution and federal laws are the highest in the nation. Whenever a state law and a federal law are found to disagree, the federal law must be obeyed so long as it is Constitutional.

(3) OATHS OF OFFICE
All federal and state officials must promise to follow and enforce the Constitution. These officials, however, cannot be required to follow a particular religion or satisfy any religious test.

SECTION 3. NEW STATES AND TERRITORIES

(1) New states may be admitted by the Congress into this Union; but no new state shall be formed or erected within the jurisdiction of any other state; nor any state be formed by the junction of two or more states, or parts of states, without the consent of the legislatures of the states concerned as well as of the Congress.

(2) The Congress shall have power to dispose of and make all needful rules and regulations respecting the territory or other property belonging to the United States; and nothing in this Constitution shall be so construed as to prejudice any claims of the United States, or of any particular state.

SECTION 4. GUARANTEES TO THE STATES

The United States shall guarantee to every state in this Union a republican form of government, and shall protect each of them against invasion; and on application of the legislature, or of the executive (when the legislature cannot be convened) against domestic violence.

ARTICLE V
AMENDING THE CONSTITUTION

The Congress, whenever two-thirds of both houses shall deem it necessary, shall propose amendments to this Constitution, or, on the application of the legislatures of two-thirds of the several states, shall call a convention for proposing amendments, which, in either case, shall be valid to all intents and purposes, as part of this Constitution, when ratified by the legislatures of three-fourths of the several states, or by conventions in three-fourths thereof, as the one or the other mode of ratification may be proposed by the Congress; provided that [*no amendment which may be made prior to the year 1808 shall in any manner affect the first and fourth clauses in the Ninth Section of the First Article; and that*] no state, without its consent, shall be deprived of its equal suffrage in the Senate.

ARTICLE VI
GENERAL PROVISIONS

(1) All debts contracted and engagements entered into, before the adoption of this Constitution, shall be as valid against the United States under this Constitution, as under the Confederation.

(2) This Constitution, and the laws of the United States which shall be made in pursuance thereof, and all treaties made, or which shall be made, under the authority of the United States, shall be the supreme law of the land; and the judges in every state shall be bound thereby, anything in the Constitution or laws of any state to the contrary notwithstanding.

(3) The Senators and Representatives before mentioned, and the members of the several state legislatures, and all executive and judicial officers, both of the United States and of the several states, shall be bound by oath or affirmation, to support this Constitution; but no religious test shall ever be required as a qualification to any office or public trust under the United States.

ARTICLE VII
RATIFICATION

The ratification of the conventions of nine states, shall be sufficient for the establishment of this Constitution between the states so ratifying the same.

Done in convention by the unanimous consent of the states present the seventeenth day of September in the year of our Lord one thousand seven hundred and eighty seven and of the independence of the United States of America the Twelfth. In witness whereof we have hereunto subscribed our names.
George Washington—President and deputy from Virginia

DELAWARE
George Read
Gunning Bedford, Jr.
John Dickinson
Richard Bassett
Jacob Broom

MARYLAND
James McHenry
Daniel of St. Thomas Jenifer
Daniel Carroll

VIRGINIA
John Blair
James Madison, Jr.

NORTH CAROLINA
William Blount
Richard Dobbs Spaight
Hugh Williamson

SOUTH CAROLINA
John Rutledge
Charles Cotesworth Pinckney
Charles Pinckney
Pierce Butler

GEORGIA
William Few
Abraham Baldwin

NEW HAMPSHIRE
John Langdon
Nicholas Gilman

MASSACHUSETTS
Nathaniel Gorham
Rufus King

CONNECTICUT
William Samuel Johnson
Roger Sherman

NEW YORK
Alexander Hamilton

NEW JERSEY
William Livingston
David Brearley
William Paterson
Jonathan Dayton

PENNSYLVANIA
Benjamin Franklin
Thomas Mifflin
Robert Morris
George Clymer
Thomas FitzSimons
Jared Ingersoll
James Wilson
Gouverneur Morris

ATTEST: William Jackson, secretary

RATIFICATION
In order for the Constitution to become law, 9 of the 13 states had to approve it. Special conventions were held for this purpose. The process took 9 months to complete.

BASIC FREEDOMS

The Constitution guarantees our five basic freedoms of expression. It provides for the freedoms of religion, speech, the press, peaceable assembly, and petition for redress of grievances.

WEAPONS AND THE MILITIA

This amendment was included to prevent the federal government from taking away guns used by state militias.

HOUSING SOLDIERS

The federal government cannot force people to house soldiers in their homes during peacetime. However, Congress may pass laws allowing this during wartime.

SEARCHES AND SEIZURES

This amendment protects people's privacy and safety. Subject to certain exceptions, a law officer cannot search a person or a person's home and belongings unless a judge has issued a valid search warrant. There must be good reason for the search. The warrant must describe the place to be searched and the people or things to be seized, or taken.

RIGHTS OF ACCUSED PERSONS

If a person is accused of a crime that is punishable by death or of any other crime that is very serious, a grand jury must decide if there is enough evidence to hold a trial. People cannot be tried twice for the same crime, nor can they be forced to testify against themselves. No person shall be fined, jailed, or executed by the government unless the person has been given a fair trial. The government cannot take a person's property for public use unless fair payment is made.

AMENDMENT 1 (1791)***
BASIC FREEDOMS

Congress shall make no law respecting an establishment of religion, or prohibiting the free exercise thereof; or abridging the freedom of speech, or of the press; or the right of the people peaceably to assemble, and to petition the government for a redress of grievances.

AMENDMENT 2 (1791)
WEAPONS AND THE MILITIA

A well-regulated militia, being necessary to the security of a free state, the right of the people to keep and bear arms shall not be infringed.

AMENDMENT 3 (1791)
HOUSING SOLDIERS

No soldier shall, in time of peace, be quartered in any house, without the consent of the owner; nor in time of war, but in a manner to be prescribed by law.

AMENDMENT 4 (1791)
SEARCHES AND SEIZURES

The right of the people to be secure in their persons, houses, papers, and effects, against unreasonable searches and seizures, shall not be violated; and no warrants shall issue but upon probable cause, supported by oath or affirmation, and particularly describing the place to be searched, and the persons or things to be seized.

AMENDMENT 5 (1791)
RIGHTS OF ACCUSED PERSONS

No person shall be held to answer for a capital, or otherwise infamous crime, unless on a presentment or indictment of a grand jury, except in cases arising in the land or naval forces, or in the militia, when in actual service in time of war or public danger; nor shall any person be subject for the same offense to be twice put in jeopardy of life or limb; nor shall be compelled in any criminal case to be a witness against himself; nor be deprived of life, liberty, or property, without due process of law; nor shall private property be taken for public use without just compensation.

*** The date beside each amendment is the year that the amendment was ratified and became part of the Constitution.

AMENDMENT 6 (1791)
RIGHT TO A FAIR TRIAL

In all criminal prosecutions, the accused shall enjoy the right to a speedy and public trial, by an impartial jury of the state and district wherein the crime shall have been committed, which district shall have been previously ascertained by law, and to be informed of the nature and cause of the accusation; to be confronted with the witnesses against him; to have compulsory process for obtaining witnesses in his favor, and to have the assistance of counsel for his defense.

AMENDMENT 7 (1791)
JURY TRIAL IN CIVIL CASES

In suits at common law, where the value in controversy shall exceed 20 dollars, the right of trial by jury shall be preserved, and no fact tried by a jury shall be otherwise re-examined in any court of the United States, than according to the rules of the common law.

AMENDMENT 8 (1791)
BAIL AND PUNISHMENT

Excessive bail shall not be required, nor excessive fines imposed, nor cruel and unusual punishments inflicted.

AMENDMENT 9 (1791)
RIGHTS OF THE PEOPLE

The enumeration in the Constitution, of certain rights, shall not be construed to deny or disparage others retained by the people.

AMENDMENT 10 (1791)
POWERS OF THE STATES AND THE PEOPLE

The powers not delegated to the United States by the Constitution, nor prohibited by it to the states, are reserved to the states respectively, or to the people.

AMENDMENT 11 (1798)
SUITS AGAINST STATES

The judicial power of the United States shall not be construed to extend to any suit in law or equity, commenced or prosecuted against one of the United States or citizens of another state, or by citizens or subjects of any foreign state.

RIGHT TO A FAIR TRIAL
A person accused of a crime has the right to a public trial by an impartial jury, locally chosen. The trial must be held within a reasonable amount of time. The accused person must be told of all charges and has the right to see, hear, and question any witnesses. The federal government must provide a lawyer free of charge to a person who is accused of a serious crime and who is unable to pay for legal services.

JURY TRIAL IN CIVIL CASES
In most federal civil cases involving more than 20 dollars, a jury trial is guaranteed. Civil cases are those disputes between two or more people over money, property, personal injury, or legal rights. Usually civil cases are not tried in federal courts unless much larger sums of money are involved or unless federal courts are given the authority to decide a certain type of case.

BAIL AND PUNISHMENT
Courts cannot treat harshly people accused of crimes or punish them in unusual or cruel ways. Bail is money put up as a guarantee that an accused person will appear for trial. In certain cases bail can be denied altogether.

RIGHTS OF THE PEOPLE
The federal government must respect all natural rights, whether or not they are listed in the Constitution.

POWERS OF THE STATES AND THE PEOPLE
Any rights not clearly given to the federal government or denied to the states belong to the states or to the people.

SUITS AGAINST STATES
A citizen of one state cannot sue another state in federal court.

AMENDMENT 12 (1804)
ELECTION OF PRESIDENT AND VICE PRESIDENT

The electors shall meet in their respective states, and vote by ballot for President and Vice President, one of whom, at least, shall not be an inhabitant of the same state with themselves; they shall name in their ballots the person voted for as President, and in distinct ballots the person voted for as Vice President, and they shall make distinct lists of all persons voted for as President, and of all persons voted for as Vice President, and of the number of votes for each, which lists they shall sign and certify, and transmit, sealed, to the seat of government of the United States, directed to the President of the Senate; the President of the Senate shall, in the presence of the Senate and House of Representatives, open all the certificates, and the votes shall then be counted; the person having the greatest number of votes for President shall be the President, if such a number be a majority of the whole number of electors appointed; and if no person have such majority; then from the persons having the highest numbers not exceeding three on the list of those voted for as President, the House of Representatives shall choose immediately, by ballot, the President. But in choosing the President, the votes shall be taken by states, the representation from each state having one vote; a quorum for this purpose shall consist of a member or members from two thirds of the states, and a majority of all the states shall be necessary to a choice. [*And if the House of Representatives shall not choose a President whenever the right of choice shall devolve upon them, before the fourth day of March next following, then the Vice President shall act as President, as in the case of the death or other constitutional disability of the President.*] The person having the greatest number of votes as Vice President, shall be the Vice President, if such number be a majority of the whole number of electors appointed, and if no person have a majority, then, from the two highest numbers on the list the Senate shall choose the Vice President; a quorum for the purpose shall consist of two thirds of the whole number of Senators, and a majority of the whole number shall be necessary to a choice. But no person constitutionally ineligible to the office of President shall be eligible to that of Vice President of the United States.

AMENDMENT 13 (1865)
END OF SLAVERY

SECTION 1. ABOLITION
Neither slavery nor involuntary servitude, except as a punishment for crime whereof the party shall have been duly convicted, shall exist within the United States, or any place subject to their jurisdiction.

SECTION 2. ENFORCEMENT
Congress shall have power to enforce this article by appropriate legislation.

AMENDMENT 14 (1868)
RIGHTS OF CITIZENS

SECTION 1. CITIZENSHIP
All persons born or naturalized in the United States and subject to the jurisdiction thereof, are citizens of the United States and of the state wherein they reside. No state shall make or enforce any law which shall abridge the privileges or immunities of citizens of the United States, nor shall any state deprive any person of life, liberty, or property, without due process of law; nor deny to any person within its jurisdiction the equal protection of the laws.

SECTION 2. NUMBER OF REPRESENTATIVES

Representatives shall be apportioned among the several states according to their respective numbers, counting the whole number of persons in each state, [*excluding Indians not taxed*]. But when the right to vote at any election for the choice of electors for President and Vice President of the United States, representatives in Congress, the executive and judicial officers of a state, or the members of the legislature thereof, is denied to any of the [*male*] inhabitants of such state, being [*twenty-one years of age and*] citizens of the United States, or in any way abridged, except for participation in rebellion or other crime, the basis of representation therein shall be reduced in the proportion which the number of such [*male*] citizens shall bear to the whole number of [*male*] citizens [*twenty-one years of age*] in such state.

SECTION 3. PENALTY FOR REBELLION

No person shall be a Senator or Representative in Congress, or elector of President and Vice President, or hold any office, civil or military, under the United States, or under any state, who, having previously taken an oath, as a member of Congress, or as an officer of the United States, or as a member of any state legislature, or as an executive or judicial officer of any state, to support the Constitution of the United States, shall have engaged in insurrection or rebellion against the same, or given aid or comfort to the enemies thereof. But Congress may, by a vote of two thirds of each house, remove such disability.

SECTION 4. GOVERNMENT DEBT

The validity of the public debt of the United States, authorized by law, including debts incurred for payment of pensions and bounties for services in suppressing insurrection or rebellion, shall not be questioned. But neither the United States nor any state shall assume or pay any debt or obligation incurred in aid of insurrection or rebellion against the United States, [*or any claim for the loss or emancipation of any slave;*] but all such debts, obligations, and claims shall be held illegal and void.

SECTION 5. ENFORCEMENT

The Congress shall have power to enforce, by appropriate legislation, the provisions of this article.

AMENDMENT 15 (1870)
VOTING RIGHTS

SECTION 1. RIGHT TO VOTE

The right of citizens of the United States to vote shall not be denied or abridged by the United States or by any state on account of race, color, or previous condition of servitude.

SECTION 2. ENFORCEMENT

The Congress shall have power to enforce this article by appropriate legislation.

AMENDMENT 16 (1913)
INCOME TAX

The Congress shall have power to lay and collect taxes on incomes, from whatever source derived, without apportionment among the several states, and without regard to any census or enumeration.

NUMBER OF REPRESENTATIVES
Each state's representation in Congress is based on its total population. Any state denying eligible citizens the right to vote will have its representation in Congress decreased. This clause abolished the Three-fifths Compromise in Article 1, Section 2. Later amendments granted women the right to vote and lowered the voting age to 18.

PENALTY FOR REBELLION
No person who has rebelled against the United States may hold federal office. This clause was originally added to punish the leaders of the Confederacy for failing to support the Constitution of the United States.

GOVERNMENT DEBT
The federal government is responsible for all public debts. It is not responsible, however, for Confederate debts or for debts that result from any rebellion against the United States.

ENFORCEMENT
Congress may enforce these provisions by law.

RIGHT TO VOTE
No state may prevent a citizen from voting simply because of race or color or condition of previous servitude. This amendment was designed to extend voting rights to enforce this by law.

INCOME TAX
Congress has the power to collect taxes on its citizens, based on their personal incomes rather than on the number of people living in a state.

DIRECT ELECTION OF SENATORS
Originally, state legislatures elected senators. This amendment allows the people of each state to elect their own senators directly. The idea is to make senators more responsible to the people they represent.

PROHIBITION
This amendment made it illegal to make, sell, or transport liquor within the United States or to transport it out of the United States or its territories. Amendment 18 was the first to include a time limit for approval. If not ratified within seven years, it would be repealed, or canceled. Many later amendments have included similar time limits.

WOMEN'S VOTING RIGHTS
This amendment granted women the right to vote.

TERMS OF OFFICE
The terms of the President and the Vice President begin on January 20, in the year following their election. Members of Congress take office on January 3. Before this amendment newly elected members of Congress did not begin their terms until March 4. This meant that those who had run for reelection and been defeated remained in office for four months.

AMENDMENT 17 (1913)
DIRECT ELECTION OF SENATORS

SECTION 1. METHOD OF ELECTION
The Senate of the United States shall be composed of two Senators from each state, elected by the people thereof, for six years; and each Senator shall have one vote. The electors in each state shall have the qualifications requisite for electors of the most numerous branch of the state legislatures.

SECTION 2. VACANCIES
When vacancies happen in the representation of any state in the Senate, the executive authority of such state shall issue writs of election to fill such vacancies: *Provided,* that the legislature of any state may empower the executive thereof to make temporary appointments until the people fill the vacancies by election as the legislature may direct.

SECTION 3. EXCEPTION
[*This amendment shall not be so construed as to affect the election or term of any Senator chosen before it becomes valid as part of the Constitution.*]

AMENDMENT 18 (1919)
BAN ON ALCOHOLIC DRINKS

SECTION 1. PROHIBITION
[*After one year from the ratification of this article the manufacture, sale, or transportation of intoxicating liquors within, the importation thereof into, or the exportation thereof from the United States and all territory subject to the jurisdiction thereof for beverage purposes is hereby prohibited.*]

SECTION 2. ENFORCEMENT
[*The Congress and the several states shall have concurrent power to enforce this article by appropriate legislation.*]

SECTION 3. RATIFICATION
[*This article shall be inoperative unless it shall have been ratified as an amendment to the Constitution by the legislatures of the several states as provided in the Constitution, within seven years from the date of the submission hereof to the states by the Congress.*]

AMENDMENT 19 (1920)
WOMEN'S VOTING RIGHTS

SECTION 1. RIGHT TO VOTE
The right of citizens of the United States to vote shall not be denied or abridged by the United States or by any state on account of sex.

SECTION 2. ENFORCEMENT
Congress shall have power to enforce this article by appropriate legislation.

AMENDMENT 20 (1933)
TERMS OF OFFICE

SECTION 1. BEGINNING OF TERMS
The terms of the President and Vice President shall end at noon on the 20th day of January, and the terms of Senators and Representatives at noon on the 3rd day of January, of the years in which such terms would have ended if this article had not been ratified; and the terms of their successors shall then begin.

SECTION 2. SESSIONS OF CONGRESS

The Congress shall assemble at least once in every year, and such meeting shall begin at noon on the 3rd day of January, unless they shall by law appoint a different day.

SECTION 3. PRESIDENTIAL SUCCESSION

If, at the time fixed for the beginning of the term of the President, the President-elect shall have died, the Vice President-elect shall become President. If a President shall not have been chosen before the time fixed for the beginning of his term, or if the President-elect shall have failed to qualify, then the Vice President-elect shall act as President until a President shall have qualified; and the Congress may by law provide for the case wherein neither a President-elect nor a Vice President-elect shall have qualified, declaring who shall then act as President, or the manner in which one who is to act shall be selected and such person shall act accordingly until a President or Vice President shall be qualified.

SECTION 4. ELECTIONS DECIDED BY CONGRESS

The Congress may by law provide for the case of the death of any of the persons from whom the House of Representatives may choose a President whenever the right of choice shall have devolved upon them, and for the case of the death of any of the persons from whom the Senate may choose a Vice President whenever the right of choice shall have devolved upon them.

SECTION 5. EFFECTIVE DATE

[*Sections 1 and 2 shall take effect on the 15th day of October following the ratification of this article.*]

SECTION 6. RATIFICATION

[*This article shall be inoperative unless it shall have been ratified as an amendment to the Constitution by the legislatures of three fourths of the several states within seven years from the date of its submission.*]

AMENDMENT 21 (1933)
END OF PROHIBITION

SECTION 1. REPEAL OF AMENDMENT 18

The eighteenth article of amendment to the Constitution of the United States is hereby repealed.

SECTION 2. STATE LAWS

The transportation or importation into any state, territory, or possession of the United States for delivery or use therein of intoxicating liquors, in violation of the laws thereof, is hereby prohibited.

SECTION 3. RATIFICATION

[*This article shall be inoperative unless it shall have been ratified as an amendment to the Constitution by conventions in the several states, as provided in the Constitution within seven years from the date of the submission hereof to the states by Congress.*]

SESSIONS OF CONGRESS
Congress meets at least once a year, beginning at noon on January 3. Congress had previously met at least once a year beginning on the first Monday of December.

PRESIDENTIAL SUCCESSION
If the newly elected President dies before January 20, the newly elected Vice President becomes President on that date. If a President has not been chosen by January 20 or does not meet the requirements for being President, the newly elected Vice President becomes President. If neither the newly elected President nor the newly elected Vice President meets the requirements for office, Congress decides who will serve as President until a qualified President or Vice President is chosen.

END OF PROHIBITION
This amendment repealed Amendment 18. This is the only amendment to be ratified by state conventions instead of by state legislatures. Congress felt that this would give people's opinions about prohibition a better chance to be heard.

A President may not serve more than two full terms in office. Any President who serves less than two years of a previous President's term may be elected for two more terms.

PRESIDENTIAL ELECTORS FOR DISTRICT OF COLUMBIA
This amendment grants three electoral votes to the national capital.

BAN ON POLL TAXES
No United States citizen may be prevented from voting in a federal election because of failing to pay a tax to vote. Poll taxes had been used in some states to prevent African Americans from voting.

PRESIDENTIAL VACANCY
If the President is removed from office or resigns from or dies while in office, the Vice President becomes President.

AMENDMENT 22 (1951)
TWO-TERM LIMIT FOR PRESIDENTS

SECTION 1. TWO-TERM LIMIT

No person shall be elected to the office of the President more than twice, and no person who has held the office of President, or acted as President, for more than two years of a term to which some other person was elected President shall be elected to the office of the President more than once. [*But this article shall not apply to any person holding the office of President when this article was proposed by the Congress, and shall not prevent any person who may be holding the office of President, or acting as President, during the term within which this article becomes operative from holding the office of President, or acting as President, during the remainder of such term.*]

SECTION 2. RATIFICATION

[*This article shall be inoperative unless it shall have been ratified as an amendment to the Constitution by the legislatures of three-fourths of the several states within seven years from the date of its submission to the states by the Congress.*]

AMENDMENT 23 (1961)
PRESIDENTIAL ELECTORS FOR DISTRICT OF COLUMBIA

SECTION 1. NUMBER OF ELECTORS

The District constituting the seat of Government of the United States shall appoint in such manner as Congress may direct:

A number of electors of President and Vice President equal to the whole number of Senators and Representatives in Congress to which the District would be entitled if it were a state, but in no event more than the least populous state; they shall be in addition to those appointed by the states, but they shall be considered, for the purposes of the election of President and Vice President, to be electors appointed by a state, and they shall meet in the District and perform such duties as provided by the twelfth article of amendment.

SECTION 2. ENFORCEMENT

The Congress shall have power to enforce this article by appropriate legislation.

AMENDMENT 24 (1964)
BAN ON POLL TAXES

SECTION 1. POLL TAX ILLEGAL

The right of citizens of the United States to vote in any primary or other election for President or Vice President, for electors for President or Vice President, or for Senator or Representative in Congress, shall not be denied or abridged by the United States or any state by reason of failure to pay any poll tax or other tax.

SECTION 2. ENFORCEMENT

The Congress shall have power to enforce this article by appropriate legislation.

AMENDMENT 25 (1967)
PRESIDENTIAL SUCCESSION

SECTION 1. PRESIDENTIAL VACANCY

In case of the removal of the President from office or of his death or resignation, the Vice President shall become President.

SECTION 2. VICE PRESIDENTIAL VACANCY

Whenever there is a vacancy in the office of the Vice President, the President shall nominate a Vice President who shall take the office upon confirmation by a majority vote of both houses of Congress.

SECTION 3. PRESIDENTIAL DISABILITY

Whenever the President transmits to the President pro tempore of the Senate and the Speaker of the House of Representatives his written declaration that he is unable to discharge the powers and duties of his office, and until he transmits to them a written declaration to the contrary, such powers and duties shall be discharged by the Vice President as Acting President.

SECTION 4. DETERMINING PRESIDENTIAL DISABILITY

Whenever the Vice President and a majority of either the principal officers of the executive departments or of such other body as Congress may by law provide, transmit to the President pro tempore of the Senate and the Speaker of the House of Representatives their written declaration that the President is unable to discharge the powers and duties of his office, the Vice President shall immediately assume the powers and duties of the office as Acting President.

Thereafter, when the President transmits to the President pro tempore of the Senate and the Speaker of the House of Representatives his written declaration that no inability exists, he shall resume the powers and duties of his office unless the Vice President and a majority of either the principal officers of the executive department or of such other body as Congress may by law provide, transmit within four days to the President pro tempore of the Senate and the Speaker of the House of Representatives their written declaration that the President is unable to discharge the powers and duties of his office. Thereupon Congress shall decide the issue, assembling within 48 hours for that purpose if not in session. If the Congress, within 21 days after receipt of the latter written declaration, or, if Congress is not in session, within 21 days after Congress is required to assemble, determines by two-thirds vote of both houses that the President is unable to discharge the powers and duties of his office, the Vice President shall continue to discharge the same as Acting President; otherwise the President shall resume the powers and duties of his office.

AMENDMENT 26 (1971)
VOTING AGE

SECTION 1. RIGHT TO VOTE

The right of citizens of the United States, who are 18 years of age or older, to vote shall not be denied or abridged by the United States or any state on account of age.

SECTION 2. ENFORCEMENT

The Congress shall have the power to enforce this article by appropriate legislation.

AMENDMENT 27 (1992)
CONGRESSIONAL PAY

No law, varying the compensation for the services of the Senators and Representatives, shall take effect, until an election of Representatives shall have intervened.

VICE PRESIDENTIAL VACANCY
If the office of the Vice President becomes open, the President names someone to assume that office and that person becomes Vice President if both houses of Congress approve by a majority vote.

PRESIDENTIAL DISABILITY
This section explains in detail what happens if the President cannot continue in office because of sickness or any other reason. The Vice President takes over as acting President until the President is able to resume office.

DETERMINING PRESIDENTIAL DISABILITY
If the Vice President and a majority of the Cabinet inform the Speaker of the House and the president pro tempore of the Senate that the President cannot carry out his or her duties, the Vice President then serves as acting President. To regain the office, the President has to inform the Speaker and the president pro tempore in writing that he or she is again able to serve. But, if the Vice President and a majority of the Cabinet disagree with the President and inform the Speaker and the president pro tempore that the President is still unable to serve, then Congress decides who will hold the office of President.

VOTING AGE
All citizens 18 years or older have the right to vote. Formerly, the voting age was 21.

CONGRESSIONAL PAY
A law raising or lowering the salaries for members of Congress cannot be passed for that session of Congress.

THE NATIONAL ANTHEM

The Star-Spangled Banner

"The Star-Spangled Banner" was written by Francis Scott Key in September 1814 and adopted as the national anthem in March 1931. The army and navy had recognized it as such long before Congress approved it.

During the War of 1812, Francis Scott Key spent a night aboard a British warship in the Chesapeake Bay while trying to arrange for the release of an American prisoner. The battle raged throughout the night, while the Americans were held on the ship. The next morning, when the smoke from the cannons finally cleared, Francis Scott Key was thrilled to see the American flag still waving proudly above Fort McHenry. It symbolized the victory of the Americans.

There are four verses to the national anthem. In these four verses, Key wrote about how he felt when he saw the flag still waving over Fort McHenry. He wrote that the flag was a symbol of the freedom for which the people had fought so hard. Key also told about the pride he had in his country and the great hopes he had for the future of the United States.

(1)

Oh, say can you see by the dawn's early light
What so proudly we hail'd at the twilight's last gleaming,
Whose broad stripes and bright stars through the perilous fight
O'er the ramparts we watch'd were so gallantly streaming?
And the rockets' red glare, the bombs bursting in air,
Gave proof through the night that our flag was still there.
Oh, say does that star-spangled banner yet wave
O'er the land of the free and the home of the brave?

(2)

On the shore dimly seen through the mists of the deep,
Where the foe's haughty host in dread silence reposes,
What is that which the breeze, o'er the towering steep,
As it fitfully blows, half conceals, half discloses?
Now it catches the gleam of the morning's first beam,
In full glory reflected now shines in the stream.
'Tis the star-spangled banner, oh, long may it wave
O'er the land of the free and the home of the brave!

(3)

And where is that band who so vauntingly swore
That the havoc of war and the battle's confusion
A home and a country should leave us no more?
Their blood has wash'd out their foul footstep's pollution.
No refuge could save the hireling and slave
From the terror of flight or the gloom of the grave,
And the star-spangled banner in triumph doth wave
O'er the land of the free and the home of the brave.

(4)

Oh, thus be it ever when freemen shall stand
Between their lov'd home and the war's desolation!
Blest with vict'ry and peace may the heav'n-rescued land
Praise the power that hath made and preserv'd us a nation!
Then conquer we must, when our cause it is just,
And this be our motto, "In God is our Trust,"
And the star-spangled banner in triumph shall wave
O'er the land of the free and the home of the brave.

THE PLEDGE OF ALLEGIANCE

I pledge allegiance to the Flag

of the United States of America,

and to the Republic

for which it stands,

one Nation under God, indivisible,

with liberty and justice for all.

The flag is a symbol of the United States of America. The Pledge of Allegiance says that the people of the United States promise to stand up for the flag, their country, and the basic beliefs of freedom and fairness upon which the country was established.

American Documents

Biographical Dictionary

The Biographical Dictionary lists many of the important people introduced in this book. The page number tells where the main discussion of each person starts. See the Index for other page references.

A

Adams, Abigail *1744–1818* Patriot who wrote about women's rights in letters to John Adams, her husband. p. 257, 284

Adams, John *1735–1826* 2nd U.S. President and one writer of the Declaration of Independence. p. 253

Adams, Samuel *1722–1803* American Revolutionary leader who set up a Committee of Correspondence in Boston and helped form the Sons of Liberty. p. 238

Addams, Jane *1860–1935* American reformer who brought the idea of settlement houses from Britain to the United States. With Ellen Gates Starr, she founded Hull House in Chicago. p. 506

Aldrin, Edwin, Jr. *1930–* American astronaut who was one of the first people to set foot on the moon. p. 616

Anderson, Robert *1805–1871* Union commander of Fort Sumter who was forced to surrender to the Confederacy. p. 432

Anthony, Susan B. *1820–1906* Women's suffrage leader who worked to enable women to have the same rights as men. pp. 395, 396

Aristide, Jean-Bertrand (air•uh•STEED, ZHAHN bair•TRAHN) *1953–* Freely elected president of Haiti who was over-thrown in 1991 but was returned to office in 1994. p. 656

Armstrong, Louis *1901–1971* Noted jazz trumpeter who helped make jazz popular in the 1920s. p. 573

Armstrong, Neil *1930–* American astronaut who was the first person to set foot on the moon. p. 616

Arnold, Benedict *1741–1801* Continental army officer who became a traitor and worked for the British army. p. 267

Atahuallpa (ah•tah•WAHL•pah) *1502?–1533* Inca ruler who was killed in the Spanish conquest of the Incas. p. 137

Attucks, Crispus *1723?–1770* Patriot and former slave who was killed during the Boston Massacre. p. 237

Austin, Moses *1761–1821* American pioneer who wanted to start an American colony in Texas. p. 383

Austin, Stephen F. *1793–1836* Moses Austin's son. He carried out his father's dream of starting an American colony in Texas. p. 383

B

Balboa, Vasco Núñez de (bahl•BOH•ah, NOON•yes day) *1475–1519* Explorer who in 1513 became the first European to reach the western coast of the Americas—proving to Europeans that the Americas were separate from Asia. p. 128

Banneker, Benjamin *1731–1806* African who helped survey the land for the new capital of the United States. p. 329

Barker, Penelope *1700s* One of the first politically active women in the American colonies, she led the women of Edenton, North Carolina, in a "tea party" of their own to boycott British tea. p. 240

Barrett, Janie Porter *1865–1948* African American teacher who founded a settlement house in Hampton, Virginia. p. 506

Barton, Clara *1821–1912* Civil War nurse and founder of the American Red Cross. p. 445

Beauregard, Pierre Gustave (BOH•ruh•gard) *1818–1893* Confederate army officer. p. 411

Bee, Barnard Elliott *1824–1861* Confederate army officer. p. 412

Behaim, Martin (BAY•hym) *1436?–1507* German geographer who in 1492 made the first world globe in Europe. p. 113

Bessemer, Henry *1813–1898* British inventor of a way to produce steel more easily and cheaply than before. p. 484

Bienville, Jean Baptiste Le Moyne, Sieur de (byan•VEEL, ZHAHN ba•TEEST luh MWAHN) *1680–1747* French explorer who—with his brother, Pierre Le Moyne, Sieur d'Iberville—started an early settlement at the mouth of the Mississippi River. p. 181

Bolívar, Simón (boh•LEE•var, see•MOHN) *1783–1830* Leader of independence movements in Bolivia, Colombia, Ecuador, Peru, and Venezuela. p. 659

Bonaparte, Napoleon (BOH•nuh•part, nuh•POH•lee•uhn) *1769–1821* French leader who sold all of the Louisiana region to the United States. p. 353

Boone, Daniel *1734–1820* American who was one of the first pioneers to cross the Appalachians. p. 205, 349

Booth, John Wilkes *1838–1865* Actor who assassinated President Abraham Lincoln. p. 458

Bowie, James *1796–1836* American soldier killed at the Alamo. p. 384

Bradford, William *1590–1657* Governor of Plymouth Colony. p. 155

Breckinridge, John *1821–1875* Democrat from Kentucky who ran against Abraham Lincoln in the 1860 presidential election. p. 431

Brendan *485?–578* Irish monk who is said to have sailed to an unknown land between Europe and Asia. p. 111

Brezhnev, Leonid (BREZH•nef) *1906–1982* Leader of the Soviet Union from 1964 until his death in 1982. President Nixon's 1972 visit with him in the Soviet Union led to arms control and began a period of détente. p. 634

Brown, John *1800–1859* American abolitionist who seized a weapons storehouse to help slaves rebel. He was caught and hanged. p. 422

Brown, Linda *1943–* African American student whose family was among a group that challenged public-school segregation. p. 622

Brown, Moses *1738–1836* Textile pioneer who built the first textile mill in the United States, using Samuel Slater's plans. p. 373

Burgoyne, John (ber•GOYN) *1722–1792* British general who lost a battle to the Continental army on October 17, 1777, at Saratoga, New York. p. 266

Burnet, David G. *1788–1870* 1st president of the Republic of Texas, when it was formed in 1836. p. 385

Bush, George *1924–* 41st U.S. President. He was President at the end of the Cold War and during Operation Desert Storm. p. 637

Byrd, William, II *1674–1744* Early Virginia planter who kept a diary of his daily life. p. 202

Cabeza de Vaca, Álvar Núñez (kah•BAY•sah day VAH•kuh) *1490?–1560?* Spanish explorer who went to Mexico City and told stories of the Seven Cities of Gold. p. 140

Caboto, Giovanni *1450?–1499?* Italian explorer who in 1497 sailed from England and landed in what is now Newfoundland, though he thought he had landed in Asia. The English gave him the name John Cabot. p. 126

Calhoun, John C. *1782–1850* Vice President under John Quincy Adams and Andrew Jackson. He was a strong believer in states' rights. p. 380

Calvert, Cecilius *1605–1675* First proprietor of the Maryland colony. p. 184

Cameahwait (kah•MEE•ah•wayt) *1800s* Chief of the Shoshones during the Lewis and Clark expedition. He was Sacagawea's brother. p. 356

Carnegie, Andrew *1835–1919* Entrepreneur who helped the steel industry grow in the United States. p. 484

Carter, Jimmy *1924–* 39th U.S. President. He brought about a peace agreement between Israel and Egypt. p. 635

Cartier, Jacques (kar•TYAY, ZHAHK) *1491–1557* French explorer who sailed up the St. Lawrence River and began a fur-trading business with the Hurons. p. 147

Castro, Fidel *1926–* Leader who took over Cuba in 1959 and made it a communist nation. p. 614

Cavelier, René-Robert (ka•vuhl•YAY) *See* La Salle.

Chamorro, Violeta (chuh•MAWR•oh, vee•oh•LET•uh) *1929–* Nicaragua's democratic president, elected in 1990, after years of communist rule. p. 658

Champlain, Samuel de (sham•PLAYN) *1567?–1635* French explorer who founded the first settlement at Quebec. p. 148

Charles I *1500–1558* King of Spain. p. 144

Charles I *1600–1649* British king who chartered the colonies of Massachusetts and Maryland. p. 184

Charles II *1630–1685* British king who granted a charter for the Carolina colony. Son of Charles I and Henrietta Maria. p. 189

Chávez, César *1927–1993* Labor leader and organizer of the United Farm Workers. p. 625

Clark, William *1770–1838* American explorer who aided Meriwether Lewis in an expedition through the Louisiana Purchase. p. 355

Clay, Henry *1777–1852* Representative from Kentucky who worked for compromises on the slavery issue. p. 426

Clinton, George *1739–1812* American politician who helped form the Democratic-Republican party. p. 316

Clinton, William *1946–* 42nd U.S. President. p. 637

Cody, William (Buffalo Bill) *1846–1917* Cowhand known for shooting many buffalo. p. 528

Collins, Michael *1930–* American astronaut who remained in the lunar orbiter during the *Apollo 11* moon landing. p. 616

Columbus, Christopher *1451–1506* Italian-born Spanish explorer who in 1492 sailed west from Spain and thought he had reached Asia but had actually reached islands near the Americas, lands that were unknown to Europeans. p. 111

Cooper, Peter *1791–1883* American manufacturer who built *Tom Thumb,* one of the first locomotives made in the United States. p. 378

Cornish, Samuel *1795–1858* African who in 1827 helped John Russwurm found an abolitionist newspaper called *Freedom's Journal.* p. 393

Cornwallis, Charles *1738–1805* British general who surrendered at the Battle of Yorktown, resulting in victory for the Americans in the Revolutionary War. p. 267

Coronado, Francisco Vásquez de (kawr•oh•NAH•doh) *1510?–1554* Spanish explorer who led an expedition from Mexico City into what is now the southwestern United States in search of the Seven Cities of Gold. p. 140

Cortés, Hernando (kawr•TEZ) *1485–1547* Spanish conquistador who conquered the Aztec Empire. p. 135

Crazy Horse *1842?–1877* Sioux leader who fought against General George Custer. p. 529

Crockett, Davy *1786–1836* American pioneer who was killed at the Alamo. p. 384

Custer, George *1839–1876* U.S. army general who led an attack against Sioux and Cheyenne Indians. Custer and all of his men were killed in the battle. p. 529

da Gama, Vasco (dah GAH•muh) *1460?–1524* Portuguese navigator who sailed from Europe, around the southern tip of Africa, and on to Asia between 1497 and 1499. p. 119

Dare, Virginia *1587–?* First child born of English parents in America. She vanished with the other settlers of the Lost Colony. p. 152

Davis, Jefferson *1808–1889* United States senator from Mississippi who became president of the Confederacy. p. 432

Dawes, William *1745–1799* American who, along with Paul Revere, warned the Patriots that the British were marching toward Concord. p. 241

de Soto, Hernando (day SOH•toh) *1496?–1542* Spanish explorer who led an expedition into what is today the southeastern United States. p. 141

de Triana, Rodrigo Sailor on the *Pinta* during Columbus's first voyage; he was the first to sight land. p. 122

Dekanawida (deh•kahn•uh•WIH•duh) *1500s* Legendary Iroquois holy man who called for an end to the fighting among the Iroquois, a view that led to the formation of the Iroquois League. p. 86

Dewey, George *1837–1917* American naval commander who destroyed the Spanish fleet and captured Manila Bay in the Spanish-American War. p. 550

Dias, Bartholomeu (DEE•ahsh) *1450?–1500* Portuguese navigator who in 1488 became the first European to sail around the southern tip of Africa. p. 119

Dickinson, John *1732–1808* Member of the Continental Congress who wrote most of the Articles of Confederation, adopted in 1781. p. 285

Douglas, Stephen A. *1813–1861* American legislator who wrote the Kansas-Nebraska Act and debated Abraham Lincoln in a race for a Senate seat from Illinois. p. 429

Douglass, Frederick *1817–1895* Abolitionist speaker and writer who had escaped from slavery. p. 394

Drake, Francis *1543–1596* English explorer who sailed around the world. p. 151

Du Bois, W. E. B. (doo•BOYS) *1868–1963* African American teacher, writer, and leader who helped form the National Association for the Advancement of Colored People (NAACP). p. 558

E

Edison, Thomas *1847–1931* American who invented the phonograph and the electric lightbulb; he also built the first power station to supply electricity to New York City. p. 480

Eisenhower, Dwight D. *1890–1969* 34th U.S. President and, earlier, American general who led the D day invasion. pp. 589, 590

Elizabeth I *1533–1603* Queen of England during the middle to late 1500s. p. 151

Ellicott, Andrew *1754–1820* American surveyor who helped survey land for the new United States capital. p. 329

Ellington, Edward Kennedy (Duke) *1899–1974* Band leader who became well-known playing jazz during the 1920s. p. 573

Emerson, Ralph Waldo *1803–1882* American poet who wrote the "Concord Hymn." p. 242

Equiano, Olaudah (ek•wee•AHN•oh, OHL•uh•dah) *1750–1797* African who was kidnapped from his village and sold into slavery. He later wrote a book describing his experiences. p. 202

Eriksson, Leif (AIR•ik•suhn, LAYV) *?–1020?* Viking explorer who sailed from Greenland to North America in the A.D. 1000s. p. 112

Eriksson, Thorvald (AIR•ik•suhn, TUR•val) *1000s* Brother of Leif Eriksson. Thorvald Eriksson led one trip to Vinland. p. 112

Estéban (ehs•TAY•bahn) *1500–1539* African explorer who went with Cabeza de Vaca to Mexico City and told stories of the Seven Cities of Gold. Estéban was killed on a later expedition, the purpose of which was to find out whether the stories were true. p. 140

F

Farragut, Jorge (FAIR•uh•guht, HAWR•hay) *1755–1817* Spanish-born man who fought in the Continental army and the navy. p. 266

Ferdinand II *1452–1516* King of Spain who—with Queen Isabella, his wife—sent Christopher Columbus on his voyage to find a western route to Asia. p. 120

Ferraro, Geraldine *1935–* First woman to be nominated as a major party's candidate for Vice President of the United States. p. 626

Finley, John Fur trader who helped Daniel Boone find the way across the Appalachian Mountains to Kentucky. p. 349

Ford, Gerald *1913–* 38th U.S. President. The Vietnam War ended during his term. p. 631

Ford, Henry *1863–1947* American automobile manu-facturer who mass-produced cars at low cost by using assembly lines. p. 570

Forten, James *1766–1842* Free African in Philadelphia who ran a busy sail factory and became wealthy. p. 425

Franklin, Benjamin *1706–1790* American leader who was sent to Britain to ask Parliament for representation. He was a writer of the Declaration of Independence, a delegate to the Constitutional Convention, and a respected scientist and business leader. p. 235

Frémont, John C. *1813–1890* Surveyor who led an early expedition to make maps of the West. His careful descriptions helped thousands of settlers. p. 386

Frick, Henry Clay *1849–1919* Manager of a steel mill in Homestead, Pennsylvania. His announcement of a pay cut led to a violent strike. p. 492

Friedan, Betty *1921–* Writer who helped set up the National Organization for Women to work for women's rights. p. 626

Frontenac, Louis de Buade, Count de (FRAHN•tuh•nak) *1622–1698* French leader who was appointed governor-general of New France. p. 178

G

Gage, Thomas *1721–1787* Head of the British army in North America and colonial governor. p. 239

Gálvez, Bernardo de (GAHL•ves) *1746–1786* Spanish governor of Louisiana who sent supplies to the Patriots in the Revolutionary War and led his own soldiers in taking a British fort in Florida. p. 266

Garrison, William Lloyd *1805–1879* American abolitionist who started a newspaper called *The Liberator*. p. 393

Gates, Horatio *1728–1806* American general who defeated the British in 1777, at Saratoga, New York. p. 266

George II *1683–1760* British king who chartered the Georgia colony. p. 189

George III *1738–1820* King of England during the Revolutionary War. p. 227

Geronimo *1829–1909* Apache chief who fought one of the longest wars between Native Americans and the United States government. p. 531

Gerry, Elbridge *1744–1814* Massachusetts delegate to the Constitutional Convention. p. 309

Glenn, John H., Jr. *1921–* American astronaut who was the first person to orbit the Earth. p. 616

Glidden, Joseph *1813–1906* Inventor of barbed wire. p. 523

Gompers, Samuel *1850–1924* Early labor union leader who formed the American Federation of Labor. p. 491

Gorbachev, Mikhail (gawr•buh•CHAWF, myik•uh•EEL) *1931–* Leader of the Soviet Union from 1985 to 1991. He improved relations with the United States and expanded freedom in the Soviet Union. p. 636

Gorham, Nathaniel *1738–1796* Massachusetts delegate to the Constitutional Convention. p. 310

Granger, Gordon Union general who read the order declaring all slaves in Texas to be free. p. 463

Grant, Ulysses S. *1822–1885* 18th U.S. President and, earlier, commander of the Union army in the Civil War. p. 453

Grenville, George *1712–1770* British prime minister who passed the Stamp Act in 1765. p. 231

Hallidie, Andrew S. *1836–1900* American inventor of the cable car. p. 508

Hamilton, Alexander *1755–1804* American leader in calling for the Constitutional Convention and winning support for it. He favored a strong national government. p. 291

Hammond, James Henry *1807–1864* Senator from South Carolina. p. 418

Hancock, John *1737–1793* Leader of the Sons of Liberty in the Massachusetts colony. p. 241

Harrison, William Henry *1773–1841* 9th U.S. President. Earlier he directed U.S. forces against the Indians at the Battle of Tippecanoe and was a commander in the War of 1812. p. 359

Hays, Mary Ludwig *1754?–1832* Known as Molly Pitcher, she carried water to American soldiers during the Battle of Monmouth; when her husband fell during the battle, she began firing his cannon. p. 257

Henrietta Maria *1609–1669* Queen of Charles I of England. The Maryland colony was named in her honor. p. 184

Henry *1394–1460* Henry the Navigator, prince of Portugal, who set up the first European school for training sailors in navigation. p. 118

Henry, Patrick *1736–1799* American colonist who spoke out in the Virginia legislature against paying British taxes. His views became widely known, and Loyalists accused him of treason. p. 233

Henry IV *1553–1610* King of France. p. 148

Hiawatha (hy•uh•WAH•thuh) *1500s* Onondaga chief who persuaded other Iroquois tribes to form the Iroquois League. p. 86

Hirohito *1901–1989* Emperor of Japan from 1926 until his death. p. 584

Hitler, Adolf *1889–1945* Nazi dictator of Germany. His actions led to World War II and the killing of millions of people. p. 583

Holiday, Billie *1915–1945* Jazz singer who sang in Harlem during the Harlem Renaissance. p. 573

Hooker, Thomas *1586?–1647* Minister who helped form the Connecticut colony. His democratic ideas were adopted in the Fundamental Orders. p. 185

Hoover, Herbert *1874–1964* 31st U.S. President. When the Depression began, he thought that the economy was healthy and conditions would improve. p. 574

Houston, Sam *1793–1863* President of the Republic of Texas and, later, governor of the state of Texas. p. 385

Huascar (WAHS•kar) Brother of Atahuallpa, who killed him to become the last Inca king of Peru. p. 137

Hudson, Henry *?–1611* Explorer who sailed up the Hudson River, giving the Dutch a claim to the area. p. 149

Hughes, Langston *1902–1967* Poet and one of the best-known Harlem writers. p. 573

Huishen *500s* Chinese Buddhist monk said to have sailed to an unknown land between Europe and Asia. p. 111

Hurston, Zora Neale *1903–1960* Novelist and one of the best-known Harlem writers. p. 573

Hutchinson, Anne Marbury *1591–1643* English-born woman who left Massachusetts because of her religious beliefs. She settled near Providence, which joined with other settlements to form the Rhode Island colony. p. 186

Iberville, Pierre Le Moyne, Sieur d' (ee•ber•VEEL) *1661–1706* French explorer who—with his brother, Jean Baptiste Le Moyne, Sieur de Bienville—started an early settlement at the mouth of the Mississippi River. p. 181

Idrisi, al- (uhl•ih•DREE•see) *1100–1165* Arab geographer and cartographer. p. 113

Isabella I *1451–1504* Queen of Spain who—with King Ferdinand, her husband—sent Columbus on his voyage to find a western route to Asia. p. 120

Jackson, Andrew *1767–1845* 7th U.S. President and, earlier, commander who won the final battle in the War of 1812. As President he favored a strong Union and ordered the removal of Native Americans from their lands. p. 361, 379

Jackson, Thomas (Stonewall) *1824–1863* Confederate general. p. 410

James I *1566–1625* King of England in the early 1600s. The James River and Jamestown were named after him. p. 153

Jay, John *1745–1829* American leader who wrote letters to newspapers, defending the Constitution. He became the first chief justice of the Supreme Court. p. 318

Jefferson, Thomas *1743–1826* 3rd U.S. President and the main writer of the Declaration of Independence. p. 253

Jenney, William *1832–1907* American engineer who developed the use of steel frames to build tall buildings. p. 507

John I *1357–1433* King of Portugal during a time of great exploration. Father of Prince Henry, who set up a school of navigation. p. 118

Johnson, Andrew *1808–1875* 17th U.S. President. Differences with Congress about Reconstruction led to his being impeached, though he was found not guilty. p. 465

Johnson, Lyndon B. *1908–1973* 36th U.S. President. He started Great Society programs and expanded the Vietnam War. p. 614

Joliet, Louis (zhohl•YAY, loo•EE) *1645–1700* French fur trader who explored lakes and rivers for France, with Marquette and five others. p. 179

Jones, Jehu Free African who owned one of South Carolina's best hotels before the Civil War. p. 425

Joseph *1840–1904* Nez Perce chief who tried to lead his people to Canada after they were told to move onto a reservation. p. 530

Kalakaua (kah•lah•KAH•ooh•ah) *1836–1891* Hawaiian king who tried but failed to keep Americans from taking over the Hawaiian Islands. p. 548

Kalb, Johann, Baron de *1721–1780* German soldier who helped the Patriots in the Revolutionary War. p. 264

Kennedy, John F. *1917–1963* 35th U.S. President. He helped pass the Civil Rights Act of 1964. p. 613

Key, Francis Scott *1779–1843* American lawyer and poet who wrote the words to "The Star-Spangled Banner." p. 365

King, Martin Luther, Jr. *1929–1968* African American civil rights leader who worked for integration in nonviolent ways. King won the Nobel Peace Prize in 1964. pp. 470, 624

King, Richard *1825–1885* Rancher in South Texas who founded the country's largest ranch. p. 522

King, Rufus *1755–1827* Massachusetts delegate to the Constitutional Convention. p. 310

Knox, Henry *1750–1806* Secretary of war in the first government under the Constitution. p. 326

Kosciuszko, Thaddeus (kawsh•CHUSH•koh) *1746–1817* Polish officer who helped the Patriots in the Revolutionary War. He later returned to Poland and led a revolution there. p. 264

Kublai Khan (KOO•bluh KAHN) *1215–1294* Ruler of China who was visited by Marco Polo. p. 115

La Follette, Robert *1855–1925* Wisconsin governor who began many reforms in his state, including a merit system for government jobs. p. 557

La Salle, René-Robert Cavelier, Sieur de (luh•SAL) *1643–1687* French explorer who found the mouth of the Mississippi River and claimed the whole Mississippi Valley for France. p. 180

Lafayette, Marquis de (lah•fee•ET) *1757–1834* French noble who fought alongside the Americans in the Revolutionary War. p. 264

Lafon, Thomy *1810–1893* Free African who made a fortune from businesses in New Orleans. p. 425

Las Casas, Bartolomé de (lahs KAH•sahs, bar•toh•luh•MAY day) *1474–1566* Spanish missionary who spent much of his life trying to help Native Americans. p. 144

Law, John *1671–1729* Scottish banker who was appointed proprietor of the Louisiana region in 1717. p. 181

Lazarus, Emma *1849–1887* Poet who wrote, in 1883, the poem now on the base of the Statue of Liberty. p. 534

Le Moyne, Jean-Baptiste (luh•MWAHN, ZHAHN ba•TEEST) *See* Bienville.

Le Moyne, Pierre *See* Iberville.

Lee, Charles *1731–1782* American officer during the Revolutionary War. p. 247

Lee, Richard Henry *1732–1794* American Revolutionary leader who said to the Continental Congress that the colonies should become independent from Britain. p. 252

Lee, Robert E. *1807–1870* United States army colonel who gave up his post and became commander of the Confederate army in the Civil War. p. 443

L'Enfant, Pierre Charles *1754–1825* French-born American engineer who planned the buildings and streets of the new capital of the United States. p. 329

Lewis, Meriwether *1774–1809* American explorer chosen by Thomas Jefferson to be a pathfinder in the territory of the Louisiana Purchase. p. 355

Liliuokalani, Lydia (li•lee•uh•woh•kuh•LAH•nee) *1838–1917* Hawaiian queen who tried but failed to bring back the Hawaiian monarchy's authority. p. 548

Lincoln, Abraham *1809–1865* 16th U.S. President, leader of the Union in the Civil War, and signer of the Emancipation Proclamation. pp. 429, 431, 435, 445, 446

Lincoln, Benjamin *1733–1810* Continental army general. p. 267

Lincoln, Mary Todd *1818–1882* Wife of Abraham Lincoln. p. 443

Lindbergh, Charles *1902–1974* Airplane pilot who was the first to fly solo between the United States and Europe. p. 571

Livingston, Robert R. *1746–1813* One of the writers of the Declaration of Independence. p. 253

Louis XIV *1638–1715* King of France. p. 178

Lowell, Francis Cabot *1775–1817* Textile pioneer who set up an American mill in which several processes were completed under one roof. p. 374

Lucas, Eliza *1722?–1793* South Carolina settler who experimented with indigo plants. She gave away seeds, and indigo then became an important cash crop in the colonies. p. 189

Madison, Dolley *1768–1849* James Madison's wife and First Lady during the War of 1812. p. 361

Madison, James *1751–1836* 4th U.S. President. He was a leader in calling for the Constitutional Convention, writing the Constitution, and winning support for it. p. 290

Magellan, Ferdinand (muh•JEH•luhn) *1480?–1521* Portuguese explorer who in 1519 led a fleet of ships from Spain westward to Asia. He died on the voyage, but one of the ships made it back to Spain, completing the first trip around the world. p. 129

Malcolm X *1925–1965* African American leader who disagreed with the views of Martin Luther King, Jr., on nonviolence and integration. p. 624

Malintzin (mah•LINT•suhn) *1501?–1550* Aztec princess who interpreted for Hernando Cortés and helped him in other ways to conquer Mexico. p. 136

Mann, Horace *1796–1859* American school reformer in the first half of the 1800s. p. 392

Mao Zedong (MOW zeh•DOONG) *1893–1976* Leader of China from 1949 until his death. President Nixon's 1972 visit with him in China led to trade and cultural exchange with the United States. p. 634

Marion, Francis *1732?–1795* Known as the Swamp Fox, he led Continental soldiers through the swamps of South Carolina on daring raids against the British. p. 259

Marquette, Jacques (mar•KET, ZHAHK) *1637–1675* Catholic missionary who knew several American Indian languages. With Joliet, he explored lakes and rivers for France. p. 179

Marshall, James *1810–1885* Carpenter who found gold at John Sutter's sawmill near Sacramento, California, leading to the California gold rush of 1849. p. 389

Marshall, John *1755–1835* Chief Justice of the Supreme Court in 1832; Marshall ruled that the United States should protect the Cherokees and their lands in Georgia. p. 382

Marshall, Thurgood *1908–1993* NAACP lawyer who argued the school segregation case that the Supreme Court ruled on in 1954 and, later, was the first African American to serve on the Supreme Court. p. 622

Martí, José (mar•TEE) *1853–1895* Cuban leader who did much to win Cuban independence from Spain. p. 550

Mason, George *1725–1792* Virginia delegate to the Constitutional Convention who argued for an end to the slave trade. p. 300

Massasoit (ma•suh•SOYT) *?–1661* Chief of the Wampanoags, who lived in peace with the Pilgrims. p. 156

McCormick, Cyrus *1809–1884* Inventor of a reaping machine for harvesting wheat. p. 517

McCoy, Joseph *1837–1915* Cattle trader who arranged to move large herds by using stockyards near railroad tracks. p. 520

McKinley, William *1843–1901* 25th U.S. President. The Spanish-American War was fought during his term. p. 549

Menéndez de Avilés, Pedro (meh•NEN•des day ah•vee•LAYS) *1519–1574* Spanish leader of settlers in St. Augustine, Florida, the first permanent European settlement in what is now the United States. p. 173

Mongoulacha (mahn•goo•LAY•chah) *1700s* Indian leader who helped Bienville and Iberville. p. 181

Monroe, James *1758–1831* 5th U.S. President. He established the Monroe Doctrine, which said that the United States would stop any European nation from expanding its American empire. p. 362

Morris, Gouverneur (guh•vuh•NIR) *1752–1816* American leader who was in charge of the final wording of the United States Constitution. p. 293

Morse, Samuel F. B. *1791–1872* American who developed the telegraph and invented Morse code. p. 484

Motecuhzoma (maw•tay•kwah•SOH•mah) *1466–1520* Emperor of the Aztecs when they were conquered by the Spanish. He is also known as Montezuma. p. 135

Mott, Lucretia *1793–1880* American reformer who, with Elizabeth Cady Stanton, organized the first convention for women's rights. p. 395

Muhlenberg, Peter *1746–1807* Young minister, son of the colonies' Lutheran leader, who became a Patriot militia officer. p. 256

Murray, John *1732–1809* Royal governor of Virginia during the Revolutionary War. He promised enslaved Africans their freedom if they would fight for the British government. p. 259

Mussolini, Benito (moo•suh•LEE•nee, buh•NEE•toh) *1883–1945* Dictator of Italy from 1925 until 1943. p. 584

Nixon, Richard M. *1913–1994* 37th President. He tried to end the Vietnam War, he reduced tensions with communist nations, and he resigned the presidency because of the Watergate scandal. pp. 630, 634

Niza, Marcos de (day NEE•sah) *1495–1558* Spanish priest who was sent with Estéban to confirm stories of the Seven Cities of Gold. When he returned to Mexico City, he said he had seen a golden city. p. 140

O'Connor, Sandra Day *1930–* First woman to be appointed to the United States Supreme Court. p. 626

Oglethorpe, James *1696–1785* English settler who was given a charter to settle Georgia. He wanted to bring in debtors from England to help settle it. p. 189

Osceola *1804–1838* Leader of the Seminoles in Florida. p. 381

Oswald, Richard *1705–1784* British merchant who met with Benjamin Franklin to negotiate terms between America and Britain at the end of the Revolutionary War. p. 268

Otis, James *1725–1783* Massachusetts colonist who spoke out against British taxes and called for "no taxation without representation." p. 232

Paine, Thomas *1737–1809* Author of a widely read pamphlet called *Common Sense*, in which he attacked King George III and called for a revolution to make the colonies independent. p. 252

Parks, Rosa *1913–* African American woman whose refusal to give up her seat on a Montgomery, Alabama, bus started a year-long bus boycott. p. 623

Paterson, William *1745–1806* Constitutional delegate from New Jersey who submitted the New Jersey Plan, under which each state would have one vote, regardless of population. p. 297

Penn, William *1644–1718* Proprietor of Pennsylvania under a charter from King Charles II of Britain. Penn was a Quaker who made Pennsylvania a refuge for settlers who wanted religious freedom. p. 187

Perry, Oliver Hazard *1785–1819* American naval commander who won an important battle in the War of 1812. p. 361

Pickett, Bill *1870–1932* Cowhand who was the first African American elected to the National Cowboy Hall of Fame and Western Heritage Center. p. 522

Pike, Zebulon *1779–1813* American who led an expedition down the Arkansas River to explore the southwestern part of the Louisiana Purchase. p. 357

Pinzón, Martín Captain of the *Pinta*. Brother of Vincente Pinzón. p. 122

Pinzón, Vincente Captain of the *Niña*. Brother of Martín Pinzón. p. 122

Pizarro, Francisco (pee•ZAR•oh) *1475?–1541* Spanish conquistador who conquered the Inca Empire. p. 137

Pocahontas (poh•kuh•HAHN•tuhs) *1595–1617* Indian chief Powhatan's daughter. p. 153

Polk, James K. *1795–1849* 11th U.S. President. He gained land for the United States by setting a northern boundary in 1846 and winning a war with Mexico in 1848. p. 386

Polo, Maffeo Trader from Venice; uncle of Marco Polo. p. 115

Polo, Marco *1254–1324* Explorer from Venice who spent many years in Asia in the late 1200s. He wrote a book about his travels that gave Europeans information about Asia. p. 115

Polo, Niccolò Trader from Venice; father of Marco Polo. p. 115

Ponce de León, Juan (PAHN•say day lay•OHN) *1460–1521* Spanish explorer who landed on the North American mainland in 1513, near what is now St. Augustine, Florida. p. 139

Powhatan (pow•uh•TAN) *1550?–1618* Chief of a federation of Indian tribes that lived in the Virginia territory. Pocahontas was his daughter. p. 153

Ptolemy, Claudius (TAH•luh•mee) *100s* Astronomer in ancient Egypt. p. 127

Pulaski, Casimir (puh•LAS•kee) *1747–1779* Polish noble who came to the British colonies to help the Patriots in the Revolutionary War. p. 264

R

Raleigh, Sir Walter (RAH•lee) *1554–1618* English explorer who used his own money to set up England's first colony in North America, on Roanoke Island near North Carolina. p. 151

Randolph, Edmund *1753–1813* Virginia delegate to the Constitutional Convention who wrote the Virginia Plan, which stated that the number of representatives a state would have in Congress should be based on the population of the state. p. 297

Read, George *1733–1798* Delaware delegate to the Constitutional Convention who thought the states should be done away with in favor of a strong national government. p. 296

Reagan, Ronald *1911–* 40th U.S. President. His meetings with Soviet leader Mikhail Gorbachev led to a thaw in the Cold War, including advances in arms control. p. 635

Red Cloud *1822–1909* Sioux chief who led his people on a three-year fight to keep miners and army troops off a road that ran through Sioux land. p. 529

Revere, Paul *1735–1818* American who warned the Patriots that the British were marching toward Concord, where Patriot weapons were stored. pp. 241, 242

Riis, Jacob (REES) *1849–1914* Reformer and writer who described the living conditions of the poor in New York City. p. 505

Robeson, Paul *1898–1976* African American actor and singer who performed in Harlem and outside the United States. p. 573

Rockefeller, John D. *1839–1937* American oil entrepreneur who joined many refineries into one business, called the Standard Oil Company. p. 485

Roosevelt, Franklin Delano *1882–1945* 32nd U.S. President. He began New Deal programs to help the nation out of the Depression, and he was the nation's leader during World War II. pp. 576, 577

Roosevelt, Theodore *1858–1919* 26th U.S. President. He showed the world America's strength, made it possible to build the Panama Canal, and worked for progressive reforms and conservation. pp. 550, 556

Ross, John *1790–1866* Chief of the Cherokee nation. He fought in United States courts to prevent the loss of the Cherokees' lands in Georgia. Though he won the legal battle, he still had to lead his people along the Trail of Tears to what is now Oklahoma. p. 381

Ruffin, Edmund *1794–1865* Agriculturist from Virginia. He fired the first shot on Fort Sumter. p. 436

Russwurm, John *1799–1851* Helped Samuel Cornish found an abolitionist newspaper called *Freedom's Journal* in 1827. p. 393

Rutledge, John *1739–1800* Delegate to the Constitutional Convention, South Carolina governor, and Supreme Court Justice. p. 300

Sacagawea (sak•uh•juh•WEE•uh) *1786?–1812?* Shoshone woman who acted as an interpreter for the Lewis and Clark expedition. pp. 355, 356

Salem, Peter *1750?–1816* African who fought with the Minutemen at Concord and at the Battle of Bunker Hill. p. 258

Samoset *1590?–1653?* Native American chief who spoke English and who helped the settlers at Plymouth. p. 155

San Martín, José de (san mar•TEEN) *1778–1850* Leader of an independence movement in Argentina. p. 659

Santa Anna, Antonio López de *1794–1876* Dictator of Mexico; defeated Texans at the Alamo. p. 384

Scott, Dred *1795?–1858* Enslaved African who took his case for freedom to the Supreme Court and lost. p. 428

Scott, Winfield *1786–1866* American general in the war with Mexico. p. 388

Seguín, Juan (say•GEEN) Defender of the Alamo, where he was killed. p. 384

Sequoyah (sih•KWOY•uh) *1765?–1843* Cherokee leader who in 1921 created a writing system for the Cherokee language. p. 381

Serra, Junípero *1713–1784* Spanish missionary who helped build a string of missions in California. p. 175

Seward, William H. *1801–1872* Secretary of state in the cabinet of Abraham Lincoln. p. 450

Shays, Daniel *1747?–1825* Leader of Shays's Rebellion, which showed the weakness of the government under the Articles of Confederation. p. 287

Shen Tong Student from Beijing University in China who compared the Tiananmen Square massacre with the Boston Massacre. p. 272

Sherman, Roger *1721–1793* One of the writers of the Declaration of Independence. Connecticut delegate to the Constitutional Convention who worked out the compromise in which Congress would have two houses—one based on state population and one with two members from each state. pp. 253, 301

Sherman, William Tecumseh *1820–1891* Union general who, after defeating Confederate forces in Atlanta, led the March to the Sea, on which his troops caused great destruction. p. 456

Sitting Bull *1831–1890* Sioux leader who fought against General George Custer. p. 529

Slater, Samuel *1768–1835* Textile pioneer who helped bring the Industrial Revolution to the United States by providing plans for a new spinning machine. p. 373

Slocumb, Mary *1700s* North Carolina colonist who fought in the Revolutionary War. p. 257

Smith, John *1580–1631* English explorer who, as leader of the Jamestown settlement, saved its people from starvation. p. 153

Smith, Joseph *1805–1844* Mormon leader who settled his people in Illinois and was killed there. p. 387

Spalding, Eliza *1807–1851* American missionary and pioneer in the Oregon country. p. 386

Spalding, Henry *1801–1874* American missionary and pioneer in the Oregon country. p. 386

Sprague, Frank *1857–1934* American inventor who built the trolley car, an electric streetcar. p. 508

Squanto *See* Tisquantum.

Stalin, Joseph *1879–1953* Dictator of the Soviet Union from 1929 until his death. p. 584

Stanton, Elizabeth Cady *1815–1902* American reformer who, with Lucretia Mott, organized the first convention for women's rights. p. 395

Starr, Ellen Gates *1860–1940* Reformer who, with Jane Addams, founded Hull House in Chicago. p. 506

Steuben, Friedrich, Baron von (vahn SHTOY•buhn) *1730–1794* German soldier who helped train Patriot troops in the Revolutionary War. p. 264

Stinson, Katherine *1891–1977* American pilot who wanted to become a fighter pilot in World War I but was not allowed to fly in battle. p. 562

Stowe, Harriet Beecher *1811–1896* American abolitionist who in 1852 wrote the book *Uncle Tom's Cabin*. p. 393

Stuyvesant, Peter (STY•vuh•suhnt) *1610?–1672* Last governor of the Dutch colony of New Netherland. p. 187

Sutter, John *1803–1880* American pioneer who owned the sawmill where gold was discovered, leading to the California gold rush. p. 389

Taney, Roger B. (TAW•nee) *1777–1864* Supreme Court Chief Justice who wrote the ruling against Dred Scott. p. 428

Tascalusa (tuhs•kah•LOO•sah) *1500s* Leader of the Mobile people when they battled with Spanish troops led by Hernando de Soto. p. 141

Tecumseh (tuh•KUHM•suh) *1768–1813* Shawnee leader of Indians in the Northwest Territory. He wanted to form a strong Indian confederation. p. 358

Tenskwatawa (ten•SKWAHT•uh•wah) *1768–1834* Shawnee leader known as the Prophet. He worked with his brother Tecumseh and led the Indians at the Battle of Tippecanoe in 1811. p. 358

Tisquantum *1585?–1622* Native American who spoke English and who helped the Plymouth colony. p. 156

Tompkins, Sally *1833–1916* Civil War nurse who eventually ran her own private hospital in Richmond, Virginia. She was a captain in the Confederate army, the only woman to achieve such an honor. p. 444

Tonti, Henri de (TOHN•tee, ahn•REE duh) *1650–1704* French explorer with La Salle. p. 181

Toussaint-Louverture, Pierre (TOO•san LOO•ver•tur) *1743–1803* Haitian revolutionary and general who took over the government of St. Domingue from France and became the ruler of Haiti. p. 354

Travis, William B. *1809–1836* Commander of the Texas force at the Alamo, where he was killed. p. 384

Truman, Harry S. *1884–1972* 33rd U.S. President. He sent American soldiers to support South Korea in 1950. p. 591

Truth, Sojourner *1797?–1883* Abolitionist and former slave who became a leading preacher against slavery. p. 394

Tubman, Harriet *1820–1913* Abolitionist and former slave who became a conductor on the Underground Railroad. She led about 300 slaves to freedom. p. 424

Turner, Nat *1800–1831* Enslaved African who led a rebellion against slavery. More than 100 slaves were killed, and Turner was caught and hanged. p. 422

Tweed, William (Boss) *1823–1878* New York City political boss who robbed the city of millions of dollars. p. 557

Vanderbilt, Cornelius *1843–1899* American railroad owner during the railroad boom of the late 1800s. p. 484

Vespucci, Amerigo (veh•SPOO•chee, uh•MAIR•ih•goh) *1454–1512* Italian explorer who made several voyages from Europe to what many people thought was Asia. He determined that he had landed on another continent, which was later called America in his honor. p. 126

Wald, Lillian *1867–1940* Reformer who started the Henry Street Settlement in New York City. p. 506

Waldseemüller, Martin (VAHLT•zay•mool•er) *1470–1518?* German cartographer who published a map in 1507 that first showed a continent named America. p. 127

Ward, Artemas *1727–1800* American commander during the Revolutionary War. p. 247

Warren, Earl *1891–1974* Chief Justice of the Supreme Court who wrote the 1954 decision against school segregation. p. 622

Warren, Mercy Otis *1728–1814* Massachusetts colonist who spoke out against new British taxes on goods. p. 232

Washington, Booker T. *1856–1915* African American who founded Tuskegee Institute in Alabama. p. 558

Washington, George *1732–1799* 1st U.S. President, leader of the Continental army during the Revolutionary War, and president of the Constitutional Convention. pp. 247, 325

Westinghouse, George *1846–1914* American inventor who designed an air brake for stopping trains. p. 483

Wheatley, John *1700s* Boston slave owner who bought a young African girl to be maidservant to his wife; the family educated the girl and freed her. She became one of the earliest American poets, Phillis Wheatley. p. 258

Wheatley, Phillis *1753?–1784* American poet who wrote poems that praised the Revolution. pp. 257, 258

White, John *?–1593?* English painter and cartographer who led the second group that settled on Roanoke Island. p. 152

Whitman, Marcus *1802–1847* American missionary and pioneer in the Oregon Country. p. 386

Whitman, Narcissa *1808–1847* American missionary and pioneer in the Oregon Country. p. 386

Whitney, Eli *1765–1825* American inventor who was most famous for his invention of the cotton gin and his idea of interchangeable parts, which made mass production possible. pp. 374, 417

Williams, Roger *1603?–1683* Founder of Providence in what is now Rhode Island. He had been forced to leave Massachusetts because of his views. p. 186

Wilson, James *1742–1798* Pennsylvania delegate to the Constitutional Convention who argued for a single chief executive elected by an electoral college. p. 303

Wilson, Woodrow *1856–1924* 28th U.S. President. He brought the country into World War I after trying to stay neutral. He favored the League of Nations, but the Senate rejected U.S. membership in the league. p. 559

Woods, Granville T. *1856–1910* African American who improved the air brake and developed a telegraph system for trains. p. 483

Wright, Orville *1871–1948* Pioneer in American aviation who—with his brother, Wilbur—made and flew the first successful airplane, at Kitty Hawk, North Carolina. p. 571

Wright, Wilbur *1867–1912* Pioneer in American aviation who—with his brother, Orville—made and flew the first successful airplane, at Kitty Hawk, North Carolina. p. 571

York *1800s* Enslaved African whose hunting and fishing skills contributed to the Lewis and Clark expedition. p. 355

Young, Brigham *1801–1877* Mormon leader who came after Joseph Smith. He moved his people west to the Great Salt Lake valley. p. 387

Gazetteer

The Gazetteer is a geographical dictionary that will help you locate places discussed in this book. The page number tells where each place appears on a map.

Abilene A city in central Kansas on the Smoky Hill River; a major railroad town. (39°N, 97°W) p. 514

Acadia Original name of Nova Scotia, Canada; once a part of New France. p. 169

Adena (uh•DEE•nuh) An ancient settlement of the Mound Builders; located in southern Ohio. (40°N, 81°W) p. 64

Adirondack Mountains (a•duh•RAHN•dak) A mountain range in northeastern New York. p. 86

Alamo A mission in San Antonio, Texas; located in the southeastern part of the state; used as a fort during the Texas Revolution. (29°N, 98°W) p. 385

Alaska Range A mountain range in central Alaska. p. 40

Albany The capital of New York; located in the eastern part of the state, on the Hudson River. (43°N, 74°W) p. 188

Albemarle Sound (AL•buh•marl) An inlet of the Atlantic Ocean; located in northeastern North Carolina. p. 152

Alcatraz Island (AL•kuh•traz) A rocky island in San Francisco Bay, California; formerly a U.S. penitentiary, closed in 1963. (38°N, 123°W) p. 498

Aleutian Islands (uh•LOO•shuhn) A chain of volcanic islands; located between the North Pacific and the Bering Sea, extending west from the Alaska Peninsula. (52°N, 177°W) p. 40

Allegheny River (a•luh•GAY•nee) A river in the northeastern United States; flows southwest to join the Monongahela River in Pennsylvania, forming the Ohio River. p. 86

Altamaha River (AWL•tuh•muh•haw) A river that begins in southeastern Georgia and flows into the Atlantic Ocean. p. 189

Amazon River The longest river in South America, flowing from the Andes Mountains across Brazil and into the Atlantic Ocean. p. 137

American Samoa (suh•MOH•uh) A United States territory in the Pacific Ocean. p. 551

Anastasia Island (an•uh•STAY•zhuh) An island in northeastern Florida; located south of St. Augustine, off the coast of St. Johns County. (30°N, 81°W) p. 174

Andes Mountains (AN•deez) The longest chain of mountains in the world; located along the entire western coast of South America. p. 137

Angel Island An island in San Francisco Bay, California. (38°N, 123°W) p. 498

Annapolis (uh•NA•puh•luhs) The capital of Maryland; located on Chesapeake Bay; home of the United States Naval Academy. (39°N, 76°W) p. 189

Antietam (an•TEE•tuhm) A creek near Sharpsburg in north central Maryland; site of a Civil War battle in 1862. (39°N, 78°W) p. 457

Antigua An island in the eastern part of the Leeward Islands, in the eastern West Indies. p. 655

Appalachian Mountains (a•puh•LAY•chuhn) A mountain system of eastern North America; extends from southeastern Quebec, Canada, to central Alabama. p. 40

Appomattox (a•puh•MA•tuhks) A village in central Virginia; site of the battle that ended the Civil War in 1865; once known as Appomattox Courthouse. (37°N, 79°W) p. 409

Arkansas River A tributary of the Mississippi River, beginning in central Colorado and ending in southeastern Arkansas. p. 40

Asunción A city in South America, located on the eastern bank of the Paraguay river where the Paraguay and Pilcomayo rivers join. (25°S, 57°W) p. 660

Athabasca River A southern tributary of the Mackenzie River in Alberta, west central Canada; flows northeast and then north into Lake Athabasca. p. 168

Atlanta Georgia's capital and largest city; located in the northwest central part of the state; site of a Civil War battle in 1864. (33°N, 84°W) p. 34

Augusta A city in eastern Georgia; located on the Savannah River. (33°N, 82°W) p. 189

Baffin Bay A large inlet of the Atlantic Ocean between western Greenland and the Northwest Territories, Canada. p. 41

Baffin Island The largest and easternmost island in the Canadian Arctic Islands; once known as Helluland. p. 41

Bahamas An island group in the North Atlantic; located southeast of Florida and north of Cuba. p. 40

Baja California A peninsula in northwestern Mexico extending south-southeast between the Pacific Ocean and the Gulf of California. (32°N, 115°W) p. 40

Baltimore A major seaport in Maryland; located on the upper end of Chesapeake Bay. (39°N, 77°W) p. 169

Barbados An island in the Lesser Antilles, West Indies; located east of the central Windward Islands. p. 655

Barbuda A flat coral island in the eastern West Indies. p. 655

Baxter Springs A city in the southeastern corner of Kansas. (37°N, 94°W) p. 521

Beaufort Sea (BOH•fert) That part of the Arctic Ocean between northeastern Alaska and the Canadian Arctic Islands. p. 40

Beijing (BAY•JING) The capital of China; located on a large plain in northeastern China; once known as Khanbalik. (40°N, 116°E) p. 272

Gazetteer • **R55**

Belém A seaport city in northern Brazil, on the Pará River. (1°S, 48°W) p. 660

Belmopan A town in Central America; capital of Belize. (17°N, 88°W) p. 655

Belo Horizonte A city in eastern Brazil. (20°S, 44°W) p. 660

Benin (buh•NEEN) A former kingdom in West Africa; located along the Gulf of Guinea; present-day southern Nigeria. p. 145

Bennington A town in the southwestern corner of Vermont; site of a major Revolutionary War battle in 1777. (43°N, 73°W) p. 265

Bering Strait A narrow strip of water; separates Asia from North America. p. 48

Beringia (buh•RIN•gee•uh) An ancient land bridge that once connected Asia and North America. p. 48

Big Hole A national battlefield in southwestern Montana; site of the battle on August 9, 1877, between U.S. troops and Nez Perce Indians under Chief Joseph. p. 529

Birmingham A city in north central Alabama. (34°N, 87°W) p. 343

Black Hills A group of mountains in South Dakota; its highest peak, more than 7,000 feet (2,134 m), is the highest point in the Plains states p. 527

Black Sea A large inland sea between Europe and Asia. p. 116

Bogotá A city in South America located on the plateau of the Andes; capital of Colombia. (4°N, 74°W) p. 660

Boise (BOY•zee) Idaho's capital and largest city; located in the southwestern part of the state. (44°N, 116°W) p. 527

Bonampak An ancient settlement of the Mayan civilization; located in present-day southeastern Mexico. (16°N, 91°W) p. 92

Boone's Trail Daniel Boone's trail that began in North Carolina and ended in Tennessee. p. 350

Boonesborough (BOONZ•buhr•oh) A village in east central Kentucky; site of a fort founded by Daniel Boone; now called Boonesboro. (38°N, 84°W) p. 350

Boston The capital and largest city of Massachusetts; a port city located on Massachusetts Bay. (42°N, 71°W) p. 169

Boston Harbor The western section of Massachusetts Bay; located in eastern Massachusetts; the city of Boston is located at its western end. p. 241

Brainerd A town in southeastern Tennessee; once part of the Cherokee Nation. (35°N, 85°W) p. 381

Brandywine A battlefield on Brandywine Creek in southeastern Pennsylvania; site of a major Revolutionary War battle in 1777. (40°N, 76°W) p. 265

Brasília A city in South America on the Paraná River; capital of Brazil. (15°S, 48°W) p. 660

Brazos River (BRAH•zuhs) A river in central Texas; flows southeast into the Gulf of Mexico. p. 140

British Columbia One of Canada's ten provinces; located on the west coast of Canada and bordered by the Yukon Territory, the Northwest Territories, Alberta, the United States, and the Pacific Ocean. p. 663

Brookline A town in eastern Massachusetts; west-southwest of Boston. (42°N, 71°W) p. 241

Brooklyn A borough of New York City, New York; located on the western end of Long Island. (41°N, 74°W) p. 498

Brooks Island An island off the coast of California, in San Francisco Bay. (39°N, 122°W) p. 498

Brooks Range A mountain range crossing northern Alaska; forms the northwestern end of the Rocky Mountains. p. 40

Buenos Aires The capital of Argentina. (34°S, 58°W) p. 660

Buffalo A city in western New York; located on the northeastern point of Lake Erie. (43°N, 79°W) p. 343

Bull Run A stream in northeastern Virginia; flows toward the Potomac River; site of a Civil War battle in 1861 and in 1862. p. 457

Butte (BYOOT) A city in southwestern Montana; located on the plateau of the Rocky Mountains. (46°N, 112°W) p. 527

Cahokia (kuh•HOH•kee•uh) A village in southwestern Illinois; site of an ancient settlement of the Mound Builders. (39°N, 90°W) p. 64

Cajamarca (kah•hah•MAR•kah) A town in northern Peru; located on the Cajamarca River, northwest of Lima. (7°S, 79°W) p. 137

Calgary A city in southern Alberta, Canada; located on the Bow River. (51°N, 114°W) p. 663

Calicut (KA•lih•kuht) A city in southwestern India; located on the Malabar Coast. (11°N, 76°E) p. 107

Cambridge A city in northeastern Massachusetts; located near Boston. (42°N, 71°W) p. 241

Camden A city in north central South Carolina, near the Wateree River; site of a major Revolutionary War battle in 1780. (34°N, 81°W) p. 265

Canal Zone A strip of territory in Panama. p. 552

Canary Islands An island group in the Atlantic Ocean off the northwest coast of Africa. (28°N, 16°W) p. 125

Canton A port city in southeastern China; located on the Canton River; known in China as Guangzhou. (23°N, 113°E) p. 107

Cape Cod A peninsula of southeastern Massachusetts, extending into the Atlantic Ocean and enclosing Cape Cod Bay. (42°N, 70°W) p. 186

Cape Fear A cape at the southern end of Smith Island; located off the coast of North Carolina, at the mouth of the Cape Fear River. (34°N, 78°W) p. 189

Cape Fear River A river in central and southeastern North Carolina; formed by the Deep and Haw rivers; flows southeast into the Atlantic Ocean. p. 189

Cape Hatteras (HA•tuh•ruhs) A cape on southeastern Hatteras Island; located off the coast of North Carolina. (35°N, 75°W) p. 189

Cape Horn A cape on the southern tip of South America, on Horn Island; named by Dutch explorers. p. 660

Cape of Good Hope A cape located on the southernmost tip of Africa. (34°S, 18°E) p. 119

Cape Verde Islands (VERD) A group of volcanic islands off the western coast of Africa. (16°N, 24°W) p. 119

Caracas A city in northern Venezuela; capital of Venezuela. (10°N, 67°W) p. 660

Gazetteer

Caribbean Sea A part of the Atlantic Ocean between the West Indies and Central and South America. p. 41

Carson City The capital of Nevada; located in the western part of the state, near the Carson River. (39°N, 120°W) p. 538

Cartagena (kahr•tah•HAY•nah) A seaport on the northwestern coast of Colombia. (10°N, 75°W) p. 660

Cascade Range A mountain range in the western United States; a continuation of the Sierra Nevada; extends north from California to Washington. p. 40

Cayenne A city on the northwestern coast of Cayenne Island, in northern South America; capital of French Guiana. (5°N, 52°W) p. 660

Cemetery Hill A hill where much of the fighting of the first two days of the Battle of Gettysburg took place; located in Gettysburg, Pennsylvania, at the end of Cemetery Ridge. p. 460

Chachapoyas (chah•chah•POH•yahs) A town in northern Peru. (6°S, 78°W) p. 137

Chaco Canyon (CHAH•koh) An ancient settlement of the Anasazi; located in present-day northwestern New Mexico. (37°N, 108°W) p. 64

Chancellorsville (CHAN•suh•lerz•vil) A location in northeastern Virginia, just west of Fredericksburg; site of a Civil War battle in 1863. (38°N, 78°W) p. 457

Chapultepec (chah•POOL•teh•pek) An ancient settlement of the Aztec civilization; located in present-day south central Mexico. (32°N, 116°W) p. 92

Charles River A river in eastern Massachusetts; separates Boston from Cambridge; flows into Boston Bay. p. 241

Charleston A city in southeastern South Carolina; a major port on the Atlantic Ocean; once known as Charles Towne. (33°N, 80°W) p. 169

Charleston Harbor An inlet of the Atlantic Ocean in eastern South Carolina; located near Charleston. (33°N, 80°W) p. 433

Charlestown A city in Massachusetts; located on Boston Harbor between the mouths of the Charles and Mystic rivers. p. 241

Charlotte The largest city in North Carolina; located in the south central part of the state. (35°N, 81°W) p. 265

Charlottetown The capital of Prince Edward Island, Canada; located in the central part of the island, on Hillsborough Bay. (46°N, 63°W) p. 663

Chattanooga (cha•tuh•NOO•guh) A city in southeastern Tennessee; located on the Tennessee River; site of a Civil War battle in 1863. (35°N, 85°W) p. 457

Chattooga Village A town in northwestern Georgia; once part of the Cherokee Nation. (35°N, 85°W) p. 381

Cherokee Nation (CHAIR•uh•kee) A Native American nation located in present-day northern Georgia, eastern Alabama, southern Tennessee, and western North Carolina. p. 381

Chesapeake Bay An inlet of the Atlantic Ocean; surrounded by Virginia and Maryland. p. 156

Cheyenne (shy•AN) The capital of Wyoming; located in the southeastern part of the state. (41°N, 105°W) p. 521

Chicago A city in Illinois; located on Lake Michigan; the third-largest city in the United States. (42°N, 88°W) p. 343

Chickamauga (chik•uh•MAW•guh) A city in northwestern Georgia; site of a Civil War battle in 1863. (35°N, 85°W) p. 457

Chihuahua A city in northern Mexico. (28°N, 85°W) p. 645

Cholula (choh•LOO•lah) An ancient settlement of the Aztec civilization, located in present-day south central Mexico. (19°N, 98°W) p. 92

Cincinnati (sin•suh•NA•tee) A large city in southwestern Ohio; located on the Ohio River. (39°N, 84°W) p. 409

Cleveland The largest city in Ohio; located in the northern part of the state, at the mouth of the Cuyahoga River on Lake Erie. (41°N, 82°W) p. 343

Coast Mountains A mountain range in western British Columbia and southern Alaska; a continuation of the Cascade Range. p. 40

Coast Ranges Mountains along the Pacific coast of North America, extending from Alaska to Baja California. p. 40

Cold Harbor A location in east central Virginia, north of the Chickahominy River; site of a Civil War battle in 1862 and in 1864. (38°N, 77°W) p. 457

Colorado River A river in the southwestern United States; its basin extends from the Rocky Mountains to the Sierra Nevada; flows into the Gulf of California. p. 40

Columbia River A river that begins in the Rocky Mountains in southwestern Canada, forms the Washington–Oregon border, and empties into the Pacific Ocean below Portland; supplies much of that area's hydroelectricity. p. 40

Columbus The capital of Ohio; located in the central part of the state, on the Scioto River. (40°N, 83°W) p. 543

Compostela (kahm•poh•STEH•lah) A city in west central Mexico. (21°N, 105°W) p. 140

Comstock Lode A mining area near Virginia City, Nevada, that once supplied half the silver output of the United States. p. 527

Concord A town in northeastern Massachusetts, near Boston; site of a major Revolutionary War battle in 1775. (42°N, 71°W) p. 186

Concord River A river in northeastern Massachusetts; formed by the junction of the Sudbury and Assabet rivers; flows north into the Merrimack River at Lowell. p. 241

Connecticut River The longest river in New England; begins in New Hampshire, flows south, and empties into Long Island Sound in New York. p. 186

Constantinople (kahn•stant•uhn•OH•puhl) A port city in northwestern Turkey. (41°N, 29°E) p. 107

Copán (koh•PAHN) An ancient settlement of the Mayan civilization; located in present-day Honduras, in northern Central America. (15°N, 89°W) p. 92

Cowpens A town in northwestern South Carolina; located near the site of a major Revolutionary War battle in 1781. (35°N, 82°W) p. 265

Coxcatlán (kohs•kaht•LAHN) An ancient settlement of the Aztec civilization; located in present-day south central Mexico. p. 92

Cozumel (koh•soo•MEL) An island in the Caribbean Sea; located east of the Yucatán Peninsula; part of present-day Mexico. (21°N, 87°W) p. 92

Crab Orchard An ancient settlement of the Mound Builders; located in present-day southern Illinois. (38°N, 89°W) p. 64

Cuba An island country in the Caribbean; the largest island of the West Indies. (22°N, 79°W) p. 41

Gazetteer

Culp's Hill A hill in Pennsylvania where much of the fighting of the first two days of the Battle of Gettysburg took place; located at the end of Cemetery Ridge. p. 460

Cumberland Gap A pass through the Appalachian Mountains; located in northeastern Tennessee. p. 350

Cumberland River A river in southern Kentucky and northern Tennessee; flows west to the Ohio River. p. 265

Cuzco (KOOS•koh) The ancient capital of the Inca empire; a city located in present-day Peru, in western South America. (14°S, 72°W) p. 106

Dahlonega (duh•LAHN•uh•guh) A city in northern Georgia; once part of the Cherokee Nation. (35°N, 85°W) p. 381

Dallas A city in northeastern Texas; located on the Trinity River. (33°N, 97°W) p. 343

Dawson A city in the Yukon Territory, Canada; located on the right bank of the Yukon River, near the joining of the Yukon and Klondike rivers. (64°N, 139°W) p. 527

Deadwood A city in western South Dakota; located in Deadwood Gulch in the northern Black Hills. (44°N, 106°W) p. 527

Deerfield A town in northwestern Massachusetts. (43°N, 73°W) p. 186

Delaware Bay An inlet of the Atlantic Ocean; located between southern New Jersey and Delaware. p. 188

Delaware River A river in the northeastern United States; begins in southern New York and flows into the Atlantic Ocean at Delaware Bay. p. 86

Denver Colorado's capital and largest city. (40°N, 105°W) p. 514

Des Moines (dih•MOYN) Iowa's capital and largest city. (42°N, 94°W) p. 181

Detroit The largest city in Michigan; located in the southeastern part of the state, on the Detroit River. (42°N, 83°W) p. 169

Dickson An ancient settlement of the Mound Builders; located in present-day central Illinois. p. 64

Dodge City A city in southern Kansas; located on the Arkansas River; once a major railroad center on the Santa Fe Trail. (38°N, 100°W) p. 521

Dominica An island and a republic in the West Indies; located in the center of the Lesser Antilles between Guadeloupe and Martinique; used to be a self-governing state in association with Britain. p. 655

Dominican Republic A country in the West Indies, occupying the eastern part of Hispaniola. p. 549

Dover (DE) The capital of Delaware; located in the central part of the state. (39°N, 76°W) p. 188

Dover (NH) A city in southeastern New Hampshire. (43°N, 71°W) p. 186

Durango A city in northwestern central Mexico. (24°N, 104°W) p. 645

East River A strait located in New York; connects Long Island Sound and New York Bay. p. 498

Edenton (EE•duhn•tuhn) A town in northeastern North Carolina; located on Albemarle Sound, near the mouth of the Chowan River. (36°N, 77°W) p. 189

Edmonton The capital of Alberta, Canada; located in the south central part of the province on both banks of the north Saskatchewan River. (53°N, 113°W) p. 663

El Paso A city at the western tip of Texas; located on the Rio Grande. (32°N, 106°W) p. 342

Ellesmere Island (ELZ•mir) An island located in the northeastern part of the Northwest Territories; the northernmost point of Canada. p. 40

Ellis Island An island in Upper New York Bay; located southwest of Manhattan. (40°N, 74°W) p. 498

Ellsworth A city in central Kansas. p. 521

Emerald Mound An ancient settlement of the Mound Builders; located in present-day southwestern Mississippi. (32°N, 91°W) p. 64

Erie Canal The longest canal in the world; located in New York; connects Buffalo (on Lake Erie) with Troy (on the Hudson River). p. 377

Fairbanks A city in central Alaska. (65°N, 148°W) p. 527

Falkland Islands A British colony in the Atlantic Ocean; located east of the Strait of Magellan p. 660

Falmouth (FAL•muhth) A town in southwestern Maine. (44°N, 70°W) p. 186

Fort Atkinson A fort in southern Kansas; located on the Sante Fe Trail. (43°N, 89°W) p. 390

Fort Boise (BOY•zee) A fort in eastern Oregon; located on the Snake River and on the Oregon Trail. p. 390

Fort Bridger A present-day village in southwestern Wyoming; once an important station on the Oregon Trail. (41°N, 110°W) p. 390

Fort Crevecoeur (KREEV•KER) A fort in central Illinois; located on the Illinois River; built by La Salle in 1680. (41°N, 90°W) p. 180

Fort Crown Point A French fort; located in northeastern New York, on the shore of Lake Champlain. p. 227

Fort Cumberland A British fort located in northeastern West Virginia, on its border with Maryland. p. 227

Fort Dearborn A fort in northeastern Illinois; built in 1803; eventually became part of Chicago; site of a major battle in the War of 1812. (42°N, 88°W) p. 360

Fort Donelson A fort located in northwestern Tennessee; site of a major Civil War battle in 1862. p. 457

Fort Duquesne (doo•KAYN) A French fort in present-day Pittsburgh, southwestern Pennsylvania; captured and renamed Fort Pitt in 1758. (40°N, 80°W) p. 227

Fort Edward A British fort in eastern New York, on the Hudson River; a present-day village. (43°N, 74°W) p. 227

Fort Frontenac (FRAHNT•uhn•ak) A French fort once located on the site of present-day Kingston, Ontario, in southeastern Canada; destroyed by the British in 1758. (44°N, 76°W) p. 180

Fort Gibson A fort in eastern Oklahoma; end of the Trail of Tears. (36°N, 95°W) p. 404

Fort Hall A fort in southeastern Idaho; located on the Snake River, at a junction on the Oregon Trail. p. 390

Fort Laramie A fort in southeastern Wyoming; located on the Oregon Trail. (42°N, 105°W) p. 390

Fort Ligonier (lig•uh•NIR) A British fort; located in southern Pennsylvania near the Ohio River. p. 227

Fort Louisbourg (LOO•is•berg) A French fort; located in eastern Canada on the coast of the Atlantic Ocean. (46°N, 60°W) p. 227

Fort Mackinac (MA•kuh•naw) A fort located on the tip of present-day northern Michigan; site of a major battle in the War of 1812. (46°N, 85°W) p. 360

Fort Mandan A fort in present-day central North Dakota, on the Missouri River; site of a winter camp for the Lewis and Clark Expedition. (48°N, 104°W) p. 354

Fort McHenry A fort in central Maryland; located on the harbor in Baltimore; site of a major battle in the War of 1812. (39°N, 77°W) p. 360

Fort Miamis A French fort located on the southern shore of Lake Michigan, in present-day southwestern Michigan. p. 180

Fort Necessity A British fort located in southwestern Pennsylvania; located in present-day Great Meadows. (38°N, 80°W) p. 227

Fort Niagara A fort located in western New York, at the mouth of the Niagara River. (43°N, 79°W) p. 227

Fort Oswego A British fort; located in western New York, on the coast of Lake Ontario. (43°N, 77°W) p. 227

Fort Sumter A fort on a human-made island, off the coast of South Carolina, in Charleston Harbor; site of the first Civil War battle in 1861. (33°N, 80°W) p. 433

Fort Ticonderoga (ty•kahn•der•OH•gah) A historic British fort on Lake Champlain, in northeastern New York. (44°N, 73°W) p. 227

Fort Vancouver A fort in southwestern Washington, on the Columbia River; the western end of the Oregon Trail; present-day Vancouver. (45°N, 123°W) p. 390

Fort Walla Walla A fort in southeastern Washington; located on the Oregon Trail. (46°N, 118°W) p. 390

Fort William Henry A British fort located in eastern New York. (43°N, 74°W) p. 227

Fort Worth A city in northern Texas; located on the Trinity River. (33°N, 97°W) p. 521

Fortaleza A port in northern Brazil. (3°S, 38°W) p. 660

Fox River Located in southeast central Wisconsin; flows southwest toward the Wisconsin River, and then flows northeast and empties into Green Bay. p. 180

Franklin (MO) A city in central Missouri, on the Missouri River. (39°N, 93°W) p. 377

Franklin (TN) A city in central Tennessee; site of a major Civil War battle in 1864. (36°N, 87°W) p. 525

Fredericksburg A city in northeastern Virginia; located on the Rappahannock River; site of a Civil War battle in 1862. (38°N, 77°W) p. 189

Fredericton The capital of New Brunswick, Canada; located in the southwestern part of the province. (46°N, 66°W) p. 663

Frenchtown A town in present-day eastern Michigan; site of a major battle in the War of 1812. (42°N, 83°W) p. 360

Gatun Lake (gah•TOON) A lake in Panama; part of the Panama Canal system. p. 552

Georgetown A city in South America located at the mouth of the Demerara River; capital of Guyana. (6°N, 58°W) p. 660

Germantown A residential section of present-day Philadelphia, on Wissahickon Creek, in southeastern Pennsylvania; site of a major Revolutionary War battle in 1777. (40°N, 75°W) p. 265

Gettysburg A town in southern Pennsylvania; site of a Civil War battle in 1863. (40°N, 77°W) p. 409

Golconda (gahl•KAHN•duh) A city in the southeastern corner of Illinois; a point on the Trail of Tears. (37°N, 88°W) p. 404

Gonzales (gohn•ZAH•lays) A city in south central Texas; site of the first battle of the Texas Revolution. (30°N, 97°W) p. 385

Governors Island An island in New York Bay; located near the mouth of the East River. (41°N, 74°W) p. 498

Great Basin One of the driest parts of the United States; located in Nevada, Utah, California, Idaho, Wyoming, and Oregon; includes the Great Salt Lake Desert, the Mojave Desert, and Death Valley. p. 40

Great Bear Lake A lake located in northwest central Mackenzie district, Northwest Territories, Canada. p. 40

Great Lakes A chain of five lakes; located in central North America; the largest group of freshwater lakes in the world. p. 64

Great Plains A continental slope in western North America; borders the eastern base of the Rocky Mountains from Canada to New Mexico and Texas. p. 40

Great Salt Lake The largest lake in the Great Basin; located in northwestern Utah. p. 40

Great Slave Lake A lake in the south central mainland part of the Northwest Territories, Canada. p. 40

Greenland The largest island on Earth; located in the northern Atlantic Ocean, east of Canada. p. 41

Grenada (grah•NAY•duh) An island in the West Indies; the southernmost of the Windward Islands. p. 655

Groton (GRAH•tuhn) A town in southeastern Connecticut; located on Long Island Sound at the mouth of the Thames River. (41°N, 72°W) p. 186

Guadalajara A city in western central Mexico; capital of Jalisco state. (20°N, 103°W) p. 645

Guam (GWAHM) U.S. territory in the Pacific Ocean; largest of the Mariana Islands. p. 551

Guánica (GWAHN•ih•kah) A town in southwestern Puerto Rico; located on the Guánica Harbor. (18°N, 67°W) p. 549

Guantánamo Bay (gwahn•TAH•nah•moh) A bay in eastern Cuba; located on the southeastern coast of Oriente province. p. 614

Guatemala City A city in Central America; capital of Guatemala (the republic); largest city in Central America. (14°N, 90°W) p. 655

Guayaquil (gwy•ah•KEEL) A seaport in southwestern Ecuador; capital of Guayas province. (2°S, 80°W) p. 660

Guilford Courthouse (GIL•ferd) A location in north central North Carolina, near Greensboro; site of a major Revolutionary War battle in 1781. (36°N, 80°W) p. 265

Gulf of Alaska A northern inlet of the Pacific Ocean; located between the Alaska Peninsula and the southwestern coast of Canada. p. 40

Gulf of California An inlet of the Pacific Ocean located between Baja California and the northwestern coast of Mexico. p. 40

Gulf of Mexico An inlet of the Atlantic Ocean; located on the southeastern coast of North America; surrounded by the United States, Cuba, and Mexico. p. 40

Gulf of Panama A large inlet of the Pacific Ocean; located on the southern coast of Panama. p. 552

Gulf of St. Lawrence A deep gulf of the Atlantic Ocean, located on the eastern coast of Canada, between Newfoundland and the Canadian mainland. p. 148

Gunter's Landing A town in northeastern Alabama on the Tennessee River. (34°N, 86°W) p. 381

Haiti A country in the West Indies, occupying the western part of the island of Hispaniola. p. 549

Halifax The capital of the province of Nova Scotia, Canada; a major port on the Atlantic Ocean; remains free of ice all year. (44°N, 63°W) p. 663

Hampton Roads A channel in southeastern Virginia that flows into Chesapeake Bay; site of a Civil War naval battle in 1862 between two iron-clad ships, the *Monitor* and the *Merrimack*. p. 457

Harrodsburg A city in central Kentucky; located at an end of the Wilderness Road. (38°N, 85°W) p. 350

Hartford The capital of Connecticut. (42°N, 73°W) p. 186

Havana The capital of Cuba; located on the northwestern coast of the country. (23°N, 82°W) p. 140

Hawaiian Islands A chain of volcanic and coral islands; located in the north central Pacific Ocean. p. 551

Hawikuh (hah•wee•KOO) A former village in southwestern North America; located on the route of the Spanish explorer Coronado in present-day northwestern New Mexico. p. 140

Helena The capital of Montana (47°N, 112°W) p. 527

Hispaniola (ees•pah•NYOH•lah) An island in the West Indies made up of Haiti and the Dominican Republic; located in the Caribbean Sea between Cuba and Puerto Rico. p. 41

Honolulu (hahn•nuhl•OO•loo) Hawaii's capital and largest city. (21°N, 158°W) p. 586

Hopewell An ancient settlement of the Mound Builders; located in present-day southern Ohio. (39°N, 83°W) p. 64

Horseshoe Bend A location in eastern Alabama; site of a battle in the War of 1812; a present-day national military park. p. 360

Houston A city in southeastern Texas; third-largest port in the United States; leading industrial center in Texas. (30°N, 95°W) p. 343

Hudson Bay An inland sea in east central Canada surrounded by the Northwest Territories, Manitoba, Ontario, and Quebec. p. 41

Hudson River A river in the northeastern United States beginning in upper New York and flowing into the Atlantic Ocean; named for the explorer Henry Hudson. p. 86

Iceland An island country in the northern Atlantic Ocean, between Greenland and Norway. p. 593

Illinois River A river in western and central Illinois; flows southwest into the Mississippi River. p. 180

Independence A city in western Missouri; the starting point of the Oregon Trail. (39°N, 94°W) p. 390

Indianapolis Indiana's capital and largest city. (39°N, 86°W) p. 343

Isthmus of Panama (IHS•muhs) A narrow strip of land that connects North America and South America. p. 129

Jacksonville A city in northeastern Florida; located near the mouth of the St. Johns River. (30°N, 82°W) p. 343

Jamaica (juh•MAY•kuh) An island country in the West Indies, south of Cuba. p. 125

James River A river in central Virginia; begins where the Jackson and Cowpasture rivers join; flows east into Chesapeake Bay. p. 156

Jamestown The first permanent English settlement in the Americas; located in eastern Virginia, on the shore of the James River. (37°N, 76°W) p. 156

Jerusalem The capital of Israel; located in the central part of the country. (32°N, 35°E) p. 107

Juneau (JOO•noh) The capital of Alaska; located in the southeastern part of the state. (58°N, 134°W) p. 527

Kahoolawe (kah•hoh•uh•LAY•vay) One of the eight main islands of Hawaii; located west of Maui. p. 586

Kansas City The largest city in Missouri; located in the west central part of the state, on the Missouri River. (39°N, 95°W) p. 487

Kaskaskia (ka•SKAS•kee•uh) A village in southwestern Illinois; site of a major Revolutionary War battle in 1778. (38°N, 90°W) p. 265

Kauai (KOW•eye) The fourth-largest of the eight main islands of Hawaii. p. 586

Kennebec River (KEN•uh•bek) A river in west central and southern Maine; flows south from Moosehead Lake to the Atlantic Ocean. p. 186

Kennesaw Mountain (KEN•uh•saw) An isolated peak in northwestern Georgia, near Atlanta; site of a Civil War battle in 1864. p. 457

Kentucky River A river in north central Kentucky; flows northwest into the Ohio River. p. 350

Key West A city in southwestern Florida, on Key West Island. (25°N, 82°W) p. 549

Kings Mountain A ridge in northern South Carolina and southern North Carolina; site of a Revolutionary War battle in 1780. p. 265

Kingston A commercial seaport in the West Indies; capital of Jamaica. (18°N, 76°W) p. 655

Klondike An area in the Yukon Territory, Canada; gold was discovered there in 1896. p. 527

Gazetteer

La Paz A city in South America; capital of Bolivia. (16°S, 68°W) p. 660

La Venta An ancient settlement of the Olmecs; located in present-day southern Mexico, on an island near the Tonalá River. (18°N, 94°W) p. 64

Labrador A peninsula in northeastern North America; once known as Markland. p. 41

Labrador Sea Located south of Greenland and northeast of North America. p. 41

Lake Champlain (sham•PLAYN) A lake between New York and Vermont. p. 86

Lake Erie The fourth-largest of the Great Lakes; borders Canada and the United States. p. 41

Lake Huron The second-largest of the Great Lakes; borders Canada and the United States. p. 41

Lake Michigan The third-largest of the Great Lakes; borders Michigan, Illinois, Indiana, and Wisconsin. p. 41

Lake Ontario The smallest of the Great Lakes; borders Canada and the United States. p. 41

Lake Superior The largest of the Great Lakes; borders Canada and the United States. p. 41

Lake Texcoco (tes•KOH•koh) A dry lake in present-day Mexico City; site of the ancient Aztec capital city of Tenochtitlán. p. 95

Lake Titicaca (tih•tih•KAH•kah) The highest navigable lake in the world; located on the border between Peru and Bolivia. p. 137

Lake Winnipeg A lake located in south central Manitoba, Canada. p. 41

Lanai (luh•NY) An island in central Hawaii; a major pineapple-producing area. p. 586

Lancaster A city in southeastern Pennsylvania. (40°N, 76°W) p. 188

Las Vegas (lahs VAY•guhs) A city in the southeastern corner of Nevada. (36°N, 115°W) p. 538

Lava Beds A national monument located in northern California; made of lava and ice caves; battleground of the Modoc Wars in 1873. p. 529

Leadville (LED•vil) A town in Colorado. (39°N, 106°W) p. 527

Leticia A town in southeastern Colombia, on the Amazon River. (4°S, 70°W) p. 660

Lexington A town in northeastern Massachusetts; site of the first battle of the Revolutionary War in 1775. (42°N, 71°W) p. 241

Liberty Island A small island in Upper New York Bay; the Statue of Liberty is located there; once known as Bedloe's Island. p. 498

Lima (LEE•mah) The capital of Peru; located on the Rimac River (12°S, 77°W) p. 660

Lisbon The capital of Portugal; a port city located in the western part of the country. (39°N, 9°W) p. 107

Little Bighorn A location near the Little Bighorn River in southern Montana; site of a fierce battle between Sioux and Cheyenne Indians and U.S. Army soldiers led by General George Armstrong Custer. p. 529

London A city located in the southern part of England; capital of present-day Britain. (52°N, 0°) p. 107

Long Island An island located east of New York City and south of Connecticut; lies between Long Island Sound and the Atlantic Ocean. p. 188

Los Adaes Site of a mission of New Spain; located in present-day eastern Texas. p. 175

Los Angeles The largest city in California; second-largest city in the United States; located in the southern part of the state. (34°N, 118°W) p. 280

Louisiana Purchase A territory in the west central United States; it doubled the size of the nation when it was purchased from France in 1803; extended from the Mississippi River to the Rocky Mountains, and from the Gulf of Mexico to Canada. p. 354

Louisville (LOO•ih•vil) The largest city in Kentucky; located in the north central part of the state, on the Ohio River. (38°N, 86°W) p. 343

Machu Picchu (mah•choo PEEK•choo) The site of an ancient Inca city on a mountain in the Andes, northwest of Cuzco, Peru. (13°S, 73°W) p. 137

Mackenzie River A river located in western Mackenzie district, Northwest Territories, Canada; flows north-northwest into Mackenzie Bay; second-longest river in North America. p. 40

Macon (MAY•kuhn) A city in central Georgia; located on the Ocmulgee River. (33°N, 84°W) p. 377

Madeira (mah•DAIR•uh) An island group in the eastern Atlantic Ocean, off the coast of Morocco. p. 125

Managua A city in Central America; capital of Nicaragua; located on the south shore of Lake Managua. (12°N, 86°W) p. 655

Manaus (mah•NOWS) A city located in western Brazil on the left bank of Rio Negro. (3°S, 60°W) p. 660

Manhattan An island in southeastern New York; located at the mouth of the Hudson River. (41°N, 74°W) p. 498

Manitoba (ma•nuh•TOH•buh) A province in central Canada; bordered by Hudson Bay, Ontario, the United States, and Saskatchewan; located on the Interior Plains of Canada. p. 663

Massachusetts Bay An inlet of the Atlantic Ocean on the eastern coast of Massachusetts; extends from Cape Ann to Cape Cod. p. 186

Matamoros (mah•tah•MOH•rohs) A town in Coahuila state, northeastern Mexico. (26°N, 97°W) p. 652

Maui (MOW•ee) The second-largest island in Hawaii. p. 586

Maumee River (maw•MEE) A river located in Indiana and Ohio; flows east and then northeast into Lake Erie. p. 265

Meadowcroft The site of an archaeological dig in southwestern Pennsylvania. p. 53

Medford A city in northeastern Massachusetts, north of Boston. (42°N, 71°W) p. 241

Mediterranean Sea (meh•duh•tuh•RAY•nee•uhn) An inland sea, enclosed by Europe on the west and north, Asia on the east, and Africa on the south. p. 116

Memphis A city in the southwestern corner of Tennessee; located on the Mississippi River. (35°N, 90°W) p. 409

Mendoza A city located southeast of Aconcagua in Argentina. (33°S, 69°W) p. 660

Menotomy Located in northeastern Massachusetts. p. 241

Mérida A city in southeastern Mexico; capital of Yucatán state. (21°N, 89°W) p. 645

Merrimack River A river in southern New Hampshire and northeastern Massachusetts; formed by the junction of the Pemigewasset and Winnipesaukee rivers; empties into the Atlantic. p. 186

Mesa Verde (MAY•suh VAIR•day) An ancient settlement of the Anasazi; located in present-day southwestern Colorado. (37°N, 108°W) p. 64

Mexico City A city on the southern edge of the Central Plateau; the present-day capital of Mexico. (19°N, 99°W) p. 168

Miami A city in southeastern Florida; located on Biscayne Bay. (26°N, 80°W) p. 614

Midway Islands A United States territory in the Pacific Ocean. p. 551

Milwaukee (mil•WAW•kee) The largest city in Wisconsin; located in the southeast part of the state, on Lake Michigan. (43°N, 88°W) p. 343

Minneapolis The largest city in Minnesota; located in the southeast central part of the state, on the Mississippi River; twin city with St. Paul. (45°N, 93°W) p. 487

Mississippi River The longest river in the United States; located centrally, its source is Lake Itasca in Minnesota; flows south into the Gulf of Mexico. p. 40

Missouri River A tributary of the Mississippi River; located centrally, it begins in Montana and ends at St. Louis, Missouri. p. 40

Mobile (moh•BEEL) The only seaport city in southern Alabama; located at the mouth of the Mobile River. (31°N, 88°W) p. 409

Mobile Bay An inlet of the Gulf of Mexico; located off the coast of southern Alabama; the site of a Civil War naval battle in 1864. p. 457

Mohawk River A river in central New York that flows east to the Hudson River. p. 86

Molokai (mah•luh•KY) An island in Hawaii. p. 586

Monte Albán (MAHN•tay ahl•BAHN) An ancient settlement of the Aztec civilization; located in present-day south central Mexico. (17°N, 97°W) p. 92

Monterrey A city in northeastern Mexico; capital of Nuevo León state. (25°N, 100°W) p. 645

Montevideo A seaport city located in the southern part of the north shore of La Plata estuary; capital of Uruguay. (35°S, 56°W) p. 660

Montgomery The capital of Alabama; located in the southeast central part of the state. (32°N, 86°W) p. 409

Montreal The largest city in present-day Canada; located in southern Quebec, on Montreal Island at the north bank of the St. Lawrence River. (46°N, 73°W) p. 148

Morristown A town in northern New Jersey, located west-northwest of Newark. (41°N, 74°W) p. 188

Moscow The capital and largest city of Russia; located in the western part of the country. (56°N, 38°E) p. 107

Moundville An ancient settlement of the Mound Builders; located in present-day central Alabama. (33°N, 88°W) p. 64

Mount Vernon The home and burial place of George Washington; located in Fairfax County, Virginia, on the Potomac River, below Washington, D.C. (39°N, 77°W) p. 329

Murfreesboro A city in central Tennessee; located on the west fork of the Stones River; a site on the Trail of Tears. (36°N, 86°W) p. 404

Mystic River A short river rising in the Mystic Lakes; located in northeastern Massachusetts; flows southeast into Boston Harbor north of Charlestown. p. 241

Narragansett Bay An inlet of the Atlantic Ocean in southeastern Rhode Island. (41°N, 71°W) p. 186

Nashville The capital of Tennessee. (36°N, 87°W) p. 343

Nassau A city on the northeastern coast of New Providence Island; capital of the Bahamas. (25°N, 77°W) p. 655

Natal A seaport city in northeastern Brazil. (5°S, 35°W) p. 660

Natchez A city in southwestern Mississippi; located on the Mississippi River. (32°N, 91°W) p. 281

Natchitoches (NAH•kuh•tahsh) The first settlement in present-day Louisiana; located in the northwest central part of the state. (32°N, 93°W) p. 354

Nauvoo (naw•VOO) A city in western Illinois; located on the Mississippi River; beginning of the Mormon Trail. (41°N, 91°W) p. 390

Nazca (NAHS•kah) Site of an Indian civilization; located on the west central coast of Peru. (15°S, 75°W) p. 137

New Amsterdam A Dutch city on Manhattan Island that later became New York City. (41°N, 74°W) p. 156

New Bern A city and port in southeastern North Carolina. (35°N, 77°W) p. 189

New Brunswick One of Canada's ten provinces; bordered by Quebec, the Gulf of St. Lawrence, Northumberland Strait, the Bay of Fundy, the United States, and Nova Scotia. p. 663

New Echota (ih•KOHT•uh) A Native American town in northwestern Georgia; chosen as the capital of the Cherokee Nation in 1819. (34°N, 85°W) p. 381

New France The possessions of France in North America from 1534 to 1763; included Canada, the Great Lakes region, and Louisiana. p. 169

New Guinea (GIH•nee) An island of the eastern Malay Archipelago; located in the western Pacific Ocean, north of Australia. p. 592

New Haven A city in southern Connecticut; located on New Haven Harbor. (41°N, 73°W) p. 186

New London A city in southeastern Connecticut; located on Long Island Sound at the mouth of the Thames River. (41°N, 72°W) p. 208

New Orleans The largest city in Louisiana; a major port located between the Mississippi River and Lake Pontchartrain. (30°N, 90°W) p. 169

New River A river in southwestern Virginia and southern West Virginia; flows north across Virginia and into south central West Virginia. p. 350

New Spain The former Spanish possessions from 1535 to 1821; included the southwestern United States, Mexico, Central America north of Panama, the West Indies, and the Philippines. p. 168

New York City The largest city in the United States; located in southeastern New York at the mouth of the Hudson River. (41°N, 74°W) p. 169

Newark A port in northeastern New Jersey; located on the Passaic River and Newark Bay. (41°N, 74°W) p. 188

Newfoundland (NOO·fuhn·luhnd) One of Canada's ten provinces; among the earliest Viking settlements in North America; once known as Vinland. p. 41

Newport A city on the southern end of Rhode Island; located at the mouth of Narragansett Bay. (41°N, 71°W) p. 186

Newton A city in south-central Kansas. (38°N, 97°W) p. 521

Niihau (NEE·how) An island in northwestern Hawaii. p. 586

Nome A city on the southern side of the Seward Peninsula; located in western Alaska. (65°N, 165°W) p. 527

Norfolk (NAWR·fawk) A city in southeastern Virginia; located on the Elizabeth River. (37°N, 76°W) p. 189

North Pole The northernmost point on the Earth. p. 124

Northwest Territories One of Canada's two territories; located in northern Canada. p. 663

Norwich A city located in east central Vermont. p. 294

Nova Scotia (NOH·vuh·SKOH·shuh) A province of Canada; located in the eastern part of the country, on a peninsula. p. 148

Nueces River (noo·AY·says) A river in southern Texas; flows into Nueces Bay, which is at the head of Corpus Christi Bay. p. 385

Oahu (oh·AH·hoo) The third-largest of eight main islands of Hawaii; Honolulu is located there. p. 586

Oakland A city in western California; located on the eastern side of San Francisco Bay. (38°N, 122°W) p. 498

Oaxaca (wuh·HAH·kuh) A city and state in southern Mexico. (17°N, 96°W) p. 645

Ocmulgee (ohk·MUHL·gee) An ancient settlement of the Mound Builders; located in present-day central Georgia. p. 64

Ocmulgee River (ohk·MUHL·gee) A river in central Georgia; formed by the junction of the Yellow and South rivers; flows south to join the Altamaha River. p. 189

Ogallala (oh•guh•LAHL•uh) A city in western Nebraska on the South Platte River. (41°N, 102°W) p. 521

Ohio River A tributary of the Mississippi River, beginning in Pittsburgh, Pennsylvania, and ending at Cairo, Illinois. p. 41

Omaha (OH·muh·hah) The largest city in Nebraska; located in the eastern part of the state, on the Missouri River. (41°N, 96°W) p. 390

Ontario (ahn•TAIR•ee•oh) One of Canada's ten provinces; located between Quebec and Manitoba. p. 663

Oregon Country A former region in western North America; located between the Pacific coast and the Rocky Mountains, from the northern border of California to Alaska. p. 269

Oregon Trail A former route to the Oregon Country; extending from the Missouri River northwest to the Columbia River in Oregon. p. 391

Orinoco River A river in Venezuela; flows west then north forming a section of the Colombia–Venezuela boundary, then turns east in central Venezuela and empties through a wide delta into the Atlantic Ocean. p. 660

Ottawa (AH•tuh•wuh) The capital of Canada; located in Ontario on the St. Lawrence Lowlands. (45°N, 75°W) p. 663

Outer Banks A chain of narrow peninsulas and islands off the coast of North Carolina. p. 152

Palenque (pah·LENG·kay) An ancient settlement of the Mayan civilization; located in present-day Chiapas, in southern Mexico. (18°N, 92°W) p. 92

Palmyra Island (pal•MY•ruh) One of the northernmost of the Line Islands; located in the central Pacific Ocean. p. 551

Palo Duro Canyon A canyon on the Red River; located in northwestern Texas; contains a state park. p. 529

Panama Canal A canal across the Isthmus of Panama; extends from the Caribbean Sea to the Gulf of Panama. p. 552

Panama City The capital of Panama; located in Central America. (9°N, 80°W) p. 655

Paraguay River A river in south central South America; empties into the Paraná at the southwestern corner of Paraguay. p. 660

Paramaribo A seaport city located on the Suriname River; capital of Suriname. (5°N, 55°W) p. 660

Paraná River A river in southeast central South America; formed by the joining of the Rio Grande and the Paranaíba River in south central Brazil. p. 660

Pearl Harbor An inlet on the southern coast of Oahu, Hawaii; the Japanese attacked an American naval base there on December 7, 1941. p. 586

Pecos River (PAY•kohs) A river in eastern New Mexico and western Texas; empties into the Rio Grande. p. 521

Pee Dee River A river in North Carolina and South Carolina; forms where the Yadkin and Uharie rivers meet; empties into Winyah Bay. p. 189

Perryville A city in east central Kentucky; site of a major Civil War battle in 1862. (38°N, 90°W) p. 409

Perth Amboy A port city in central New Jersey; located on Raritan Bay. (40°N, 74°W) p. 188

Petersburg A port city in southeastern Virginia; located on the Appomattox River; site of a series of Civil War battles from 1864 to 1865. (37°N, 77°W) p. 457

Philadelphia A city in southeastern Pennsylvania, on the Delaware River; a major United States port. (40°N, 75°W) p. 169

Philippine Islands A group of more than 7,000 islands off the coast of southeastern Asia, making up the country of the Philippines. p. 129

Pikes Peak A mountain in east central Colorado; part of the Rocky Mountains. p. 354

Pittsburgh The second-largest city in Pennsylvania; located in the southwestern part of the state, on the Ohio River. (40°N, 80°W) p. 281

Platte River (PLAT) A river in central Nebraska; flows east into the Missouri River below Omaha. p. 168

Plattsburg A city in northeastern New York; located on the western shore of Lake Champlain; site of a major battle in the War of 1812. (45°N, 73°W) p. 360

Plymouth A town in southeastern Massachusetts, on Plymouth Bay; site of the first settlement built by the Pilgrims, who sailed on the *Mayflower*. (42°N, 71°W) p. 156

Port Royal A town in western Nova Scotia, Canada; name changed to Annapolis Royal in honor of Queen Anne; capital city until 1749. (45°N, 66°W) p. 148

Port-au-Prince A seaport located on Hispaniola Island, in the West Indies, on the southeastern shore of the Gulf of Gonave; capital of Haiti. (18°N, 72°W) p. 655

Portland (ME) A port city in southwestern Maine; located on the Casco Bay. (44°N, 70°W) p. 294

Portland (OR) Oregon's largest city and principal port; located in the northwestern part of the state on the Willamette River. (46°N, 123°W) p. 514

Pôrto Alegre A seaport city in southern Brazil; located on an inlet at the northern end of Lagoa dos Patos. p. 660

Port-of-Spain A seaport in the northwestern part of the island of Trinidad on the Gulf of Paria; capital of Trinidad and Tobago. (10°N, 61°W) p. 655

Portsmouth (NH) (PAWRT·smuhth) A port city in southeastern New Hampshire; located at the mouth of the Picataqua River. (43°N, 71°W) p. 186

Portsmouth (RI) A town in southeastern Rhode Island; located on the Sakonnet River. (42°N, 71°W) p. 186

Potomac River (puh·TOH·muhk) A river on the Coastal Plain of the United States; begins in West Virginia and flows into Chesapeake Bay; Washington, D.C., is located on this river. p. 189

Potosí (poh·toh·SEE) One of the highest cities in the world; located in present-day south central Bolivia. (20°S, 66°W) p. 137

Prince Edward Island One of Canada's ten provinces; located in the Gulf of St. Lawrence. p. 663

Princeton A borough in west central New Jersey; site of a major Revolutionary War battle. (40°N, 75°W) p. 265

Providence Rhode Island's capital and largest city; located in the northern part of the state, at the head of the Providence River. (42°N, 71°W) p. 169

Puebla A city in southeastern central Mexico. (19°N, 98°W) p. 645

Pueblo (PWEH·bloh) A city in Colorado. p. 521

Pueblo Bonito (pweh•bloh boh•nee•toh) Largest of the prehistoric pueblo ruins; located in Chaco Canyon National Monument, New Mexico. p. 102

Puerto Rico An island of the West Indies; located southeast of Florida; a commonwealth of the United States. p. 41

Put-in-Bay A bay on South Bass Island, north of Ohio in Lake Erie; site of a major battle in the War of 1812. (42°N, 83°W) p. 360

Q

Quebec (kwih·BEK) The capital of the province of Quebec, Canada; located on the northern side of the St. Lawrence River; the first successful French settlement in the Americas; established in 1608. (47°N, 71°W) p. 148

Queens A borough of New York City; located on the western end of Long Island. (41°N, 74°W) p. 498

Quito (KEE·toh) A city in northwestern South America; located near the equator; present-day capital of Ecuador. (0°, 79°W) p. 137

Raleigh (RAW·lee) The capital of North Carolina; located in the east central part of the state. (36°N, 79°W) p. 34

Recife (rih·SEE·fee) A seaport located in eastern Brazil at the mouth of the Capibaribe River, near Point Plata. (8°S, 35°W) p. 660

Red Clay A town located in southeastern Tennessee; once part of the Cherokee Nation. p. 381

Red River A tributary of the Mississippi River; rises in eastern New Mexico, flows across Louisiana and into the Mississippi River; forms much of the Texas–Oklahoma border. p. 354

Regina (rih·JY·nuh) The capital of Saskatchewan, Canada; located in the southern part of the province. (50°N, 104°W) p. 663

Richmond The capital of Virginia; a port city located in the east central part of the state, on the James River. (38°N, 77°W) p. 189

Rio Balsas (BAHL·sahs) A river in southern Mexico. p. 40

Rio de Janeiro A commercial seaport in southeastern Brazil on the southwestern shore of Guanabara Bay. (23°S, 43°W) p. 660

Rio de la Plata A river on the southeastern coast of South America. p. 660

Rio Grande A river in southwestern North America; it begins in Colorado and flows into the Gulf of Mexico; forms the border between Texas and Mexico. p. 40

Rio Usumacinta (oo·sooh·mah·SIN·tah) A river located in southern Mexico; forms part of the border between Mexico and Guatemala. p. 92

Roanoke Island (ROH·uh·nohk) An island near the coast of North Carolina; the site of the lost colony. (36°N, 76°W) p. 152

Roanoke River A river in southern Virginia and northeastern North Carolina; flows east and southeast across the North Carolina border and into Albemarle Sound. p. 189

Rochester (RAH·chuh·stər) A port city located in western New York. (43°N, 78°W) p. 395

Rocky Mountains A range of mountains in the western United States and Canada, extending from Alaska to New Mexico; these mountains divide rivers that flow east from those that flow west. p. 40

Roxbury A residential district in southern Boston, Massachusetts; formerly a city, but became part of Boston in 1868; founded in 1630. (42°N, 71°W) p. 241

S

Sabine River (suh·BEEN) A river in eastern Texas and western Louisiana; flows southeast to the Gulf of Mexico. p. 385

Sacramento The capital of California; located in the north central part of the state, on the Sacramento River. (39°N, 121°W) p. 342

Sacramento River A river in northwestern California; rises near Mt. Shasta and flows south into Suisun Bay. p. 390

Salem A city on the northeastern coast of Massachusetts. (43°N, 71°W) p. 186

Salisbury (SAWLZ•bair•ee) A city in central North Carolina; the beginning of Boone's Trail. (36°N, 80°W) p. 294

Salt Lake City Utah's capital and largest city; located in the northern part of the state, on the Jordan River. (41°N, 112°W) p. 390

Salvador A seaport city in eastern Brazil, located on All Saints Bay. (13°S, 38°W) p. 660

San Antonio A city in south central Texas; located on the San Antonio River; site of the Alamo. (29°N, 98°W) p. 280

San Antonio River A river in southern Texas; flows southeast and empties into San Antonio Bay. p. 385

San Diego A large port city in southern California; located on San Diego Bay. (33°N, 117°W) p. 175

San Francisco The second-largest city in California; located in the northern part of the state, on San Francisco Bay. (38°N, 123°W) p. 175

San Francisco Bay An inlet of the Pacific Ocean, located in west central California. p. 498

San Jacinto (jah•SIN•toh) A location in southeastern Texas; site of a battle in the Texas Revolution in 1836. (31°N, 95°W) p. 385

San José A city in Central America; capital of Costa Rica. (10°N, 84°W) p. 655

San Jose A city in western California; located southeast of San Francisco Bay. (37°N, 122°W) p. 606

San Juan (san•WAHN) Puerto Rico's capital and largest city. (18°N, 66°W) p. 549

San Juan Hill (san•WAHN) A hill in eastern Cuba; captured by Cuban and American troops during the Spanish-American War in 1898. p. 549

San Juan River (san•WAHN) A river in Colorado, New Mexico, and Utah; flows southwest across the Colorado–New Mexico border, bends west and then northwest across southwestern Colorado, flows into Utah, and then empties into the Colorado River. p. 102

San Lorenzo An ancient settlement of the Olmecs; located in present-day southern Mexico. (29°N, 113°W) p. 64

San Salvador One of the islands in the southern Bahamas; Christopher Columbus landed there in 1492. p. 125

Santa Fe (SAN•tah FAY) The capital of New Mexico; located in the north central part of the state. (36°N, 106°W) p. 168

Santa Fe Trail A former commercial route to the western United States; extended from western Missouri to Santa Fe, in central New Mexico. p. 390

Santee River A river in southeast central South Carolina; formed by the junction of the Congaree and Wateree rivers; flows southeast into the Atlantic Ocean. p. 189

Santiago (san•tee•AH•goh) A seaport on the southern coast of Cuba; second-largest city in Cuba. (20°N, 75°W) p. 549

Santo Domingo The capital city of the Dominican Republic. (18°N, 70°W) p. 655

São Francisco River A river in eastern Brazil; flows north, northeast, and east into the Atlantic Ocean south of Maceió. p. 660

São Paulo A city in southeastern Brazil; capital of São Paulo state. p. 660

Saratoga A village on the western bank of the Hudson River in eastern New York; site of a major Revolutionary War battle in 1777; present-day Schuylerville. (43°N, 74°W) p. 265

Saskatchewan (suh•SKA•chuh•wahn) One of Canada's ten provinces; located between Alberta and Manitoba. p. 663

Savannah The oldest city and a principal seaport in Georgia; located in the southeastern part of the state, at the mouth of the Savannah River. (32°N, 81°W) p. 169

Savannah River A river that forms the border between Georgia and South Carolina; flows into the Atlantic Ocean at Savannah, Georgia. p. 189

Schenectady (skuh•NEK•tuh•dee) A city in eastern New York; located on the Mohawk River. (43°N, 74°W) p. 188

Seattle The largest city in Washington; a port city located in the west central part of the state, on Puget Sound. (48°N, 122°W) p. 514

Sedalia (suh•DAYL•yuh) A city in west central Missouri. (39°N, 93°W) p. 521

Seneca Falls (SEN•uh•kuh) A town located in west central New York on the Seneca River. (43°N, 77°W) p. 395

Serpent Mound An ancient settlement of the Mound Builders; located in present-day southern Ohio. (39°N, 83°W) p. 64

Shiloh (SHY•loh) A location in southwestern Tennessee; site of a major Civil War battle in 1862; also known as Pittsburg Landing. (35°N, 88°W) p. 457

Siberia A region in north central Asia, mostly in Russia. p. 48

Sierra Madre Occidental (see•AIR•ah MAH•dray ahk•sih•den•TAHL) A mountain range in western Mexico, running parallel to the Pacific coast. p. 40

Sierra Madre Oriental (awr•ee•en•TAHL) A mountain range in eastern Mexico, running parallel to the coast along the Gulf of Mexico. p. 40

Sierra Nevada A mountain range in eastern California that runs parallel to the Coast Ranges. p. 40

Silver City A town in southwestern New Mexico. (33°N, 108°W) p. 527

Snake River A river that begins in the Rocky Mountains and flows west into the Pacific Ocean; part of the Oregon Trail ran along this river. p. 168

Sonoran Desert An arid region in western North America; includes southwestern Arizona and southeastern California; in Mexico includes western Sonora and northern Baja California. p. 40

South Pass A pass in southwestern Wyoming; crosses the Continental Divide; part of the Oregon Trail. p. 390

South Pole The southernmost point on the Earth. p. 124

Spiro An ancient settlement of the Mound Builders; located in eastern Oklahoma. (35°N, 95°W) p. 64

Spokane (spoh•KAN) A city in eastern Washington on the falls of the Spokane River. (48°N, 117°W) p. 527

Spring Place A town in northwestern Georgia; once part of the Cherokee Nation. (35°N, 85°W) p. 381

Springfield (MA) A city in southwestern Massachusetts; located on the Connecticut River. (42°N, 73°W) p. 186

Springfield (MO) A city in southwestern Missouri. (37°N, 93°W) p. 404

St. Augustine (AW•guh•steen) A city on the coast of northeastern Florida; the oldest city founded by Europeans in the United States. (30°N, 81°W) p. 140

St. Croix (KROY) A city in Maine; located west of Port Royal. (45°N, 67°W) p. 148

St. Ignace (IG•nuhs) A city in Michigan; located on the southeastern side of Michigan's upper peninsula. (46°N, 85°W) p. 180

St. John's A city on the southeastern coast of Canada, on the Atlantic Ocean; the capital of Newfoundland. (47°N, 52°W) p. 663

St. Joseph A city in northwestern Missouri on the Missouri River. (40°N, 95°W) p. 521

St. Lawrence River A river in northeastern North America; begins at Lake Ontario and flows into the Atlantic Ocean; forms part of the border between the United States and Canada. p. 41

St. Louis A major port city in east central Missouri; known as the Gateway to the West. (38°N, 90°W) p. 181

St. Lucia An island and an independent state of the Windward Islands; located in the eastern West Indies, south of Martinique and north of St. Vincent. p. 655

St. Marys A village in southern Maryland; the capital until 1694; present-day St. Marys City. (38°N, 76°W) p. 189

St. Paul The capital of Minnesota; located in the eastern part of the state, on the Mississippi River. (45°N, 93°W) p. 487

Strait of Magellan (muh•JEH•luhn) The narrow waterway between the southern tip of South America and Tierra del Fuego; links the Atlantic Ocean with the Pacific Ocean. p. 129

Sucre A city in Bolivia, South America. (19°S, 65°W) p. 660

Sudbury River A river in western Massachusetts; connects with the Concord River. p. 241

Suriname A country in north-central South America. p. 660

Susquehanna River (suhs•kwuh•HA•nuh) A river in Maryland, Pennsylvania, and central New York; rises in Otsego Lake, New York, and empties into northern Chesapeake Bay. p. 86

Tampa A city in western Florida; located on the northeastern end of Tampa Bay. (28°N, 82°W) p. 549

Tegucigalpa A city in Central America; capital of Honduras. (14°N, 87°W) p. 655

Tennessee River A tributary of the Mississippi River; begins in eastern Tennessee and flows into the Ohio River in Kentucky. p. 181

Tenochtitlán (tay•nohch•teet•LAHN) The ancient capital of the Aztec Empire, on the islands of Lake Texcoco; located in present-day Mexico City, in southern Mexico. (19°N, 99°W) p. 92

Tiahuanaco (tee•ah•wah•NAH•koh) A site of prehistoric ruins, located in western South America, in present-day Bolivia. (17°S, 69°W) p. 137

Tikal (tih•KAHL) An ancient settlement of the Mayan civilization; located in present-day southern Central America. (17°N, 89°W) p. 92

Timbuktu A town in Mali; located in western Africa, near the Niger River. (17°N, 3°W) p. 107

Toledo (tuh•LEE•doh) A port city located in northwestern Ohio, at the southwestern corner of Lake Erie. (42°N, 84°W) p. 487

Tombstone A city in the southeastern corner of Arizona; formerly a mining center widely known for its rich silver mines. (32°N, 110°W) p. 527

Toronto The capital of the province of Ontario, in Canada; located near the northwestern end of Lake Ontario; third-largest city in Canada. (43°N, 79°W) p. 663

Trail of Tears A trail that was the result of the Indian Removal Act of 1830; extended from the Cherokee Nation to Fort Gibson, in the Indian Territory. p. 404

Treasure Island An artificial island in San Francisco Bay, California; present-day naval base. (38°N, 122°W) p. 498

Trenton The capital of New Jersey; located in the west central part of the state; site of a major Revolutionary War battle in 1776. (40°N, 75°W) p. 265

Tres Zapotes (TRAYS sah•POH•tays) An ancient settlement of the Olmecs; located in southern Mexico. (18°N, 95°W) p. 64

Trinidad and Tobago An independent state made up of the islands of Trinidad and Tobago; located in the Atlantic Ocean off the northeastern coast of Venezuela. p. 655

Troy A city in eastern New York; located on the eastern bank of the Hudson River and on the Erie Canal. (43°N, 74°W) p. 343

Tucson (TOO•sahn) A city in southern Arizona; located on the Santa Cruz River. (32°N, 111°W) p. 168

Tula An ancient settlement of the Aztec civilization; located in present-day central Mexico, north of Tenochtitlán. (23°N, 100°W) p. 92

Tumbes (TOOM•bays) A town in northwestern Peru; located on the Tumbes River, near the Peru-Ecuador border. (4°S, 80°W) p. 137

Turkey Town A town in eastern Alabama; once part of the Cherokee Nation. (34°N, 86°W) p. 381

Turtle Mound An ancient settlement of the Mound Builders; located on the present-day east central coast of Florida. (29°N, 81°W) p. 64

Uxmal (oosh•MAHL) An ancient settlement of the Mayan civilization; located in the northern Yucatán Peninsula. (20°N, 90°W) p. 92

Valdivia A city located in the Los Lagos region in south central Chile, on the Valdivia River. (39°S, 73°W) p. 660

Gazetteer

Valley Forge A location in southeastern Pennsylvania, on the Schuylkill River; site of General George Washington's winter headquarters during the Revolutionary War. (40°N, 77°W) p. 265

Valparaíso A seaport located in Chile, west-northwest of Santiago on the Bay of Valparaíso; capital of Valparaíso. (33°S, 71°W) p. 660

Vancouver Canada's eighth-largest city; located where the northern arm of the Fraser River empties into the Pacific Ocean. (49°N, 123°W) p. 663

Vancouver Island An island off the southwestern coast of British Columbia, Canada. p. 40

Vandalia (van•DAYL•yuh) A city in south central Illinois. (39°N, 89°W) p. 377

Venice A port city in northeastern Italy; located on 118 islands in the Lagoon of Venice. (45°N, 12°E) p. 107

Veracruz (veh•rah•KROOZ) A seaport in Veracruz, Mexico; located in the eastern part of the country, on the Gulf of Mexico. (19°N, 96°W) p. 136

Vicksburg A city in western Mississippi; located on the Mississippi River; site of a major Civil War battle in 1863. (32°N, 91°W) p. 409

Victoria The capital of British Columbia, Canada; located on Vancouver Island. (48°N, 123°W) p. 663

Victoria Island The third-largest of Canada's Arctic Islands; located north of the central mainland part of the Northwest Territories. p. 40

Vincennes (vihn•SENZ) A town in southwestern Indiana; oldest town in Indiana. (39°N, 88°W) p. 169

Virginia City A village in western Nevada. (39°N, 119°W) p. 527

Wabash River (WAW•bash) A river in western Ohio and Indiana; flows west and south to the Ohio River, to form part of the Indiana–Illinois border. p. 265

Wake Island A United States territory in the Pacific Ocean. p. 551

Warrior's Path A Native American path that began in North Carolina and crossed the Appalachian Mountains to Kentucky and Ohio. p. 350

Washington, D.C. The capital of the United States; located between Maryland and Virginia, on the Potomac River in a special district that is not part of any state. (39°N, 77°W) p. 281

West Indies The islands stretching from Florida in North America to Venezuela in South America. p. 198

West Point A United States military post since the Revolutionary War; located in southeastern New York on the western bank of the Hudson River p. 265

Whitehorse The capital of the Yukon Territory, Canada; located on the southern bank of the Yukon River. (60°N, 135°W) p. 663

Whitman Mission Site of a Native American mission, established in 1836 by Marcus Whitman and his wife; located in present-day southeastern Washington. p. 390

Wilderness Road A pioneer road that began in Tennessee and crossed the Appalachian Mountains into Kentucky. p. 350

Williamsburg A city in southeastern Virginia; located on a peninsula between the James and York rivers. (37°N, 77°W) p. 169

Wilmington A city in northern Delaware; located where the Delaware and Christina rivers meet Brandywine Creek. (40°N, 76°W) p. 169

Winchester A city in northern Virginia; located in the Shenandoah Valley. (39°N, 78°W) p. 294

Winnipeg The capital of the province of Manitoba, in Canada; located on the Red River; fourth-largest city in Canada. (50°N, 97°W) p. 663

Wisconsin River A river located in central Wisconsin that flows south and southeast to the Mississippi River. p. 180

Yadkin River The upper course of the Pee Dee River; flows south across North Carolina. p. 350

Yagul An ancient settlement of the Aztec civilization; located in present-day southern Mexico. p. 92

Yellowknife A town in southern Mackenzie district, Canada; located on the northwestern shore of Great Slave Lake at the mouth of the Yellowknife River; capital of the Northwest Territories. (62°N, 114°W) p. 663

Yellowstone River A river in northwestern Wyoming, southeastern Montana, and northwestern North Dakota; flows northwest to the Missouri River. p. 354

Yorktown A small town in southeastern Virginia; located on Chesapeake Bay; site of the last major Revolutionary War battle in 1781. (37°N, 76°W) p. 265

Yucatán Peninsula (yoo•kah•TAN) A peninsula in south-eastern Mexico and northeastern Central America; separated from Cuba by the Yucatán Channel. p. 41

Yukon River A river that begins in the southwestern part of the Yukon Territory, Canada; flows through Alaska, and empties into the Bering Sea. p. 40

Yukon Territory One of Canada's two territories; bordered by the Arctic Ocean, the Northwest Territories, British Columbia, and Alaska. p. 663

Glossary

The Glossary contains important social studies words and their definitions. Each word is respelled as it would be in a dictionary. When you see this mark (') after a syllable, pronounce that syllable with more force than the other syllables. The page number at the end of the definition tells where to find the word in your book.

add, āce, câre, pälm; end, ēqual; it, īce; odd, ōpen, ôrder; tŏŏk, pōōl; up, bûrn; yōō as *u* in *fuse*; oil; pout; ə as *a* in *above*, *e* in *sicken*, *i* in *possible*, *o* in *melon*, *u* in *circus*; check; ring; thin; this; zh as in *vision*

abolish (ə•bä′lish) To end. p. 393

abolitionist (a•bə•li′shən•ist) A person who wants to abolish slavery. p. 393

absolute location (ab′sə•lōōt lō•kā′shən) Exact location on the Earth. p. 31

adobe (ä•dō′bā) A mixture of sand and straw that is dried into bricks. p. 66

agent (ā′jənt) A person who does business for other people. p. 149

agriculture (a′grə•kul•chər) Farming. p. 59

airlift (âr′lift) A system of delivering supplies by airplane. p. 611

allegiance (ə•lē′jənts) Loyalty. p. 252

alliance (ə•lī′əns) Partnership. p. 559

ally (al′ī) A friend, especially in time of war. p. 226

ambassador (am•ba′sə•dər) A representative from one country to another. p. 286

amendment (ə•mend′mənt) An addition or change to the Constitution. p. 322

analyze (a′nəl•īz) To break something into its parts and look closely at how those parts connect with one another. p. 29

annex (ə•neks′) To add on. p. 362

Anti-Federalist (an′tī•fe′də•rə•list) A citizen who was against ratification of the Constitution. p. 318

apprentice (ə•pren′təs) A person who learns a trade by living with the family of a skilled worker and working for several years. p. 198

archaeologist (är•kē•o′lə•jist) A scientist who studies the cultures from people from long ago. p. 49

arid (âr′əd) Very dry. p. 76

armada (är•mä′dä) A fleet of warships. p. 152

armistice (är′mə•stis) An agreement to stop fighting. p. 550

arms control (ärmz kən•trōl′) A limit to the number of weapons nations can have. p. 634

arms race (ärmz rās) Competition between countries for the most bombs and the most powerful weapons. p. 615

artifact (är′tə•fakt) An object that early people had made. p. 49

assassination (ə•sa•sən•ā′shən) The murder of a political leader such as a President. p. 458

assembly line (ə•sem′blē līn) A system of mass production in which parts of a product, such as a car, are put together as they move past a line of workers. p. 570

auction (ôk′shən) A public sale. p. 202

authority (ə•thär′ə•tē) Control over someone or something. p. 228

aviation (ā•vē•ā′shən) Air transportation. p. 571

backcountry (bak′kən•trē) An area beyond settled lands. p. 204

band (band) A small group of people who work together to do activities. p. 48

barbed wire (bärbd wīr) A wire with sharp points or barbs along it used to make fences. p. 523

barrio (bär′ē•ō) A neighborhood of Spanish-speaking people. p. 497

barter (bär′tər) To exchange goods with other people. p. 74

bill (bil) An idea for a new law. p. 298

Bill of Rights (bil uv rīts) A list of freedoms that was added to the Constitution as the first ten amendments. p. 322

blockade (blä•kād′) To use warships to prevent other ships from entering or leaving a harbor. p. 239

bonanza farm (bə•nan′zə färm) A large farm on the Great Plains in which people from the East invested money. p. 515

boom (bōōm) A time of quick economic growth. p. 526

border state (bôr′dər stāt) During the Civil War, a state between the North and the South that allowed slavery but did not secede from the Union. p. 441

borderlands (bôr′dər•landz) Areas of land on or near the borders of two adjoining countries, colonies, or regions. p. 173

boycott (boi′kät) A refusal to buy goods or services. p. 234

broker (brō′kər) A person who is paid to buy and sell for someone else. p. 201

buffer (bu′fər) An area of land that serves as a barrier. p. 173

bureaucracy (byŏŏ•rok′rə•sē) The many workers and groups needed to run government programs. p. 576

bust (bust) A time of quick economic decline. p. 526

Cabinet (kab′nit) The group of the President's most important advisers. p. 326

campaign (kam•pān′) A race for office. p. 329

canal (kə•nal′) A human-made waterway. p. 375

capital resource (kap′ə•təl rē′sôrs) Money to run a business. p. 484

cardinal direction (kär′də•nəl də•rek′shən) One of the main directions: north, south, east, or west. p. 35

carpetbagger (kär′pət•ba•gər) A Northerner who went to the South after the Civil War to try to help with Reconstruction or to make money buying land or opening a business. p. 467

cartogram (kär′tə•gram) A map that shows information by changing the sizes of places. p. 652

cartographer (kär•tä′grə•fər) A person who makes maps. p. 113

cash crop (kash krop) A crop that people raise to sell rather than to use themselves. p. 183

cause (coz) Any action that makes something happen. p. 29

cease-fire (sēs•fīr′) An end to shooting and bombing. p. 613

census (sen′səs) A population count. p. 302

century (sen′chə•rē) A period of 100 years. p. 61

ceremony (ser′ə•mō•nē) A service performed for a special purpose, such as for a religion. p. 77

charter (chär′tər) A document giving a person or group official approval to take a certain action. p. 183

checks and balances (cheks and ba′lən•səz) A system that gives each branch of government different powers so that each branch can check the authority of the others. p. 305

chronology (krə•nä′lə•jē) Time order. p. 29

citizen (si′tə•zən) A member of a town, state, or country. p. 19

city-state (si′tē•stāt) A city that has its own ruler and government. p. 90

civil rights (si′vəl rīts) The rights guaranteed to all citizens by the Constitution. p. 558

civil war (si′vəl wôr) A war between people of the same country. p. 137

civilian (sə•vil′yən) A person who is not in the military. p. 586

civilization (si•və•lə•zā′shən) A culture that has developed forms of government, religion, and learning. p. 62

claim (klām) To declare that you or your country owns something. p. 141

clan (klan) A group of families that are related to one another. p. 73

class (klas) A group of people treated with the amount of respect that is given to the group's place in society. p. 90

classify (kla′sə•fī) To sort. p. 191

climograph (klī′mə•graf) A graph that shows the average monthly temperature and the average monthly precipitation for a place. p. 518

cold war (kōld wôr) A war fought with propaganda and money rather than with soldiers and weapons. p. 593

colonist (kä′lə•nist) A person who lives in a colony. p. 143

colony (kä′lə•nē) A settlement ruled by another country. p. 143

commercial industry (kə•mûr′shəl in′dəs•trē) An industry run to make a profit. p. 571

commission (kə•mi′shən) A special committee. p. 556

Committee of Correspondence (kə•mi′tē uv kôr•ə•spän′dəns) A group set up in each of the colonies to quickly share information about taxes and other issues by writing letters to groups in the other colonies. p. 238

common (kä′mən) An open area where sheep and cattle grazed. p. 195

commonwealth (kom′ən•welth) An area whose people have the rights of citizens of the mother country but that functions mostly independently. p. 654

communism (kom′yə•niz•əm) A social and economic system in which all industries, land, and businesses are owned by a government. p. 593

compact (käm′pakt) An agreement. p. 155

compass (kəm′pəs) An instrument used to find direction. It has a needle that always points north. p. 117

compass rose (kəm′pəs rōz) A direction marker on a map. p. 35

compromise (käm′prə•mīz) To give up some of what you want in order to reach an agreement. p. 296

concentration camp (kon•sən•trā′shən kamp) A guarded camp where prisoners are held. p. 583

conclusion (kən•klōō′zhən) A decision or an idea reached by thoughtful study. p. 127

Conestoga (kä•nə•stō′gə) A large covered wagon used by farmers to carry their produce to market towns. p. 196

Confederacy (kən•fe′də•rə•sē) The Confederate States of America, a new country that was formed by Southern states that seceded from the Union after Abraham Lincoln was elected President in 1860. p. 432

confederation (kən•fe•də•rā′shən) A loosely united group of governments. p. 86

congress (kän′grəs) A meeting of representatives who have the authority to make decisions. p. 236

conquistador (kän•kēs′tə•dôr) Any of the Spanish conquerors in the Americas during the early 1500s. p. 136

consequence (kän′sə•kwens) The result of an action. p. 239

conservation (kon•sər•vā′shən) Keeping resources and the environment from being wasted or destroyed. p. 556

consolidate (kən•sä′lə•dāt) To join one business with another. p. 485

constitution (kän•stə•tōō′shən) A plan of government. p. 285

consumer good (kən•sōō′mər gŏŏd) A product made for personal use. p. 569

Continental (kän•tən•en′təl) A soldier in the first colonial army, which was headed by George Washington. p. 249

Continental Congress (kän•tən•en′təl kän′grəs) A meeting of representatives of the British colonies. p. 240

convention (kən•ven′shən) An important meeting. p. 291

corporation (kôr•pə•rā′shən) A business that sells shares of stock to investors. p. 484

cotton gin (kä′tən jin) A machine that removes the seeds from cotton fibers. p. 417

council (koun′səl) A group that makes laws. p. 86

county (koun′tē) A large part of a colony. Today, it is a part of a state. A county has its own local government. p. 197

county seat (koun′tē sēt) The main town for a large part of a colony. Today, it is the city where a county government is located. p. 197

coureur de bois (kŏŏ•rûr′də bwä) A French word meaning "runner of the woods." This was a person who traded with American Indians for furs. p. 207

cultural diffusion (kul′chə•rəl di•fyōō′zhən) The spread of a culture from one place to another. p. 63

cultural region (kul′chə•rəl rē′jən) An area where peoples share some ways of life. p. 71

culture (kul′chər) A people's way of life. pp. 21, 49

D day (dē dā) June 6, 1944, the day the World War II Allies worked together in the largest water-to-land invasion in history. p. 589

debate (di•bāt′) To argue opposite sides of an issue. p. 298

debtor (de′tər) A person who had been in prison for owing money. p. 189

decade (de′kād) A period of ten years. p. 61

declaration (de•klə•rā′shən) An official statement. p. 253

deficit (def′ə•sit) A budget shortage caused by spending more money than is earned. p. 638

deforestation (dē•fôr•ə•stā′shən) The widespread cutting down of forests. p. 660

delegate (de′li•gət) A representative. p. 291

democracy (di•mä′krə•sē) A government in which the people take part. p. 225

depression (di•presh′ən) A period during which there is little money and little economic growth, and many people are out of work. p. 575

desertion (di•zûr′shən) Running away from duties, such as military service. p. 142

détente (dā•tänt′) The easing of military tensions between countries. p. 635

dictator (dik′tā•tər) A leader who has total authority. p. 384

distortion (di•stôr′shən) An area that is not accurate on a map. p. 554

diversity (də•vûr′sə•tē) Differences, such as those among different peoples. p. 71

doctrine (däk′trən) A government plan of action. p. 362

dove (duv) A person who supports an end to the fighting of a war. p. 629

drought (drout) A long dry spell. p. 67

due process of law (dōō prä′ses uv lä) A process that guarantees the right to a fair public trial. p. 322

dugout (dug′out) A boat made from a large, hollowed-out log. p. 73

earthwork (ərth′wərk) A mound, or hill of earth, that people have built. p. 63

economy (i•kä′nə•mē) The way people use resources to meet their needs. p. 37

effect (i•fekt′) What happens because of an action. p. 29

electoral college (i•lek′tə•rəl kä′lij) A group of electors chosen by citizens to vote for the President. p. 303

elevation (e•lə•vā′shən) The height of land. p. 391

Emancipation Proclamation (i•man•sə•pā′shən prä•klə•mā′shən) The presidential order of 1863 that freed enslaved people in the Confederate states. p. 445

embargo (im bär′gō) A refusal by one country to trade its goods with another country. p. 656

emperor (em′pər•ər) The ruler of an empire. p. 93

empire (em′pīr) A conquered land of many peoples and places governed by one ruler. p. 93

encounter (in•koun′tər) A meeting, such as one between peoples who have never met before. p. 112

encroach (in•krōch′) To move onto without asking permission. p. 258

enlist (in•list′) To join. p. 250

entrepreneur (än•trə•prə•nûr′) A person who sets up a new business, taking a chance on making or losing money. p. 484

equality (i•kwä′lə•tē) The same rights for all people. p. 393

evidence (e′və•dəns) Proof. p. 50

executive branch (ig•ze′kyə•tiv branch) The branch of government that carries out the laws. p. 302

expedition (ek•spə•di′shən) A journey made for a special reason. p. 129

exploration (ek•splə•rā′shən) Searching the unknown. p. 113

export (ek′spôrt) A good sent from one country to another to be sold. p. 197

extinct (ik•stingkt′) No longer living, like a kind of animal that has died out. p. 58

fact (fakt) A statement that can be proved true. p. 131

fall line (fôl līn) A location where the land drops sharply, causing the rivers to form waterfalls. p. 204

farm produce (färm prō′dōōs) Grains, fruits, and vegetables that farmers can trade for goods and services or sell for money. p. 196

federal system (fe′də•rəl sis′təm) A governing system in which the states share authority with the national government. p. 296

Federalist (fe′də•rə•list) A citizen who was in favor of ratifying the Constitution. p. 318

federation (fe•də•rā′shən) An organization made up of many related groups. p. 492

forty-niner (fôr•tē•nī′nər) A gold seeker who arrived in California in the year 1849. p. 389

free election (frē i•lek′shən) An election in which there is a choice of candidates. p. 657

free enterprise (frē en′tər•prīz) An economic system in which people are able to start and run their own businesses with little control by the government. p. 483

free state (frē stāt) A state that did not allow slavery. p. 426

free world (frē wûrld) The United States and its allies who worked together to fight communism. p. 593

free-trade agreement (frē•trād ə•grē′mənt) A treaty in which countries agree to charge no tariffs, or taxes, on goods they buy from and sell to each other. p. 645

front (frunt) A battle line. p. 589

Fundamental Orders (fən•də•men′təl ôr′dərz) The first written system of government in North America. It was adopted in Connecticut. p. 186

generalization (jen•rə•lə•zā′shən) A statement that summarizes facts and shows how they are related. p. 208

geographer (jē•ä′grə•fər) A person whose work is to study geography. p. 31

Gettysburg Address (ge′tēz•bûrg ə•dres′) A short speech given by Abraham Lincoln in 1863 at the dedication of a cemetery at Gettysburg. p. 455

glacier (glā′shər) A huge sheet of ice. p. 48

grant (grant) A gift of money to be used for a special purpose. p. 139

grid (grid) On a map, the north-south and east-west lines that cross each other to form a pattern of squares. p. 36

grievance (grē′vəns) A complaint. p. 254

hacienda (ä•sē•en′dä) A large estate. p. 174

hatch lines (hach līnz) A pattern of lines often used on historical maps to indicate land that was claimed by two or more countries. p. 229

hawk (hôk) A person who supports the fighting of a war. p. 629

heritage (her′ə•tij) Culture that has come from the past and continues today. p. 37

historical empathy (hi•stôr′i•kəl em′pə•thē) Understanding the actions and feelings of people from other times and other places. p. 28

hogan (hō′gän) A cone-shaped house built by covering a log frame with mud or grass. p. 79

Holocaust (hol′ə•kôst) The murder of more than six million people in concentration camps during World War II. p. 591

homesteader (hōm′sted•ər) A person who settled government land between 1862 and 1900. p. 513

hostage (hos′tij) A person held as a prisoner by a captor until demands are met. p. 635

hub (hub) A city where many trains make stops on their way to different destinations. p. 487

human features (hyōō′mən fē′chərz) The buildings, bridges, farms, roads, and people themselves that are found in a place. p. 32

human resource (hyōō′mən rē′sôrs) A person who is a worker. p. 490

human rights (hyōō′mən rīts) Freedoms that all people should have. p. 323

hydroelectric dam (hī•drō•i•lek′trik dam) A dam that uses stored water to generate electricity. p. 578

immigrant (i′mi•grənt) A person who comes to live in a country from his or her home country. p. 188

impeach (im•pēch′) To accuse a government official, such as the President, of wrongdoing. p. 304

imperialism (im•pir′ē•ə•liz•əm) Empire building. p. 548

import (im′pôrt) A good brought into one country from another, to be sold. p. 196

impressment (im•pres′mənt) Forcing people into military service. p. 360

indentured servant (in•den'shərd sər'vənt) A person who agrees to work for another person without pay for a certain length of time in return for travel expenses. p. 201

independence (in•də•pen'dəns) Freedom to govern on one's own. p. 252

indigo (in'di•gō) A plant from which blue dye is made. p. 189

Industrial Revolution (in•dus'trē•əl re•və•lōō'shən) A time during the late 1700s and early 1800s when new inventions changed the way people lived, worked, and traveled. p. 373

inflation (in•flā'shən) An economic condition in which it takes more and more money to buy the same goods. p. 287

inset map (in'set map) A small map within a larger map. p. 36

installment buying (in•stôl'mənt bī'ing) Paying a small part of the purchase price for an item, taking it home, and paying the remaining cost on a schedule. p. 569

integration (in•tə•grā'shən) The bringing together of people of all races in education, jobs, and housing. p. 624

interchangeable parts (in•tər•chān'jə•bəl pärts) Identical copies of parts made by machines so that if one part breaks, an identical one can be installed. p. 374

interest rate (in'tə•rəst rāt) The amount that a bank charges customers to borrow money. p. 644

intermediate direction (in•tər•mē'dē•it də•rek'shən) One of the in-between directions: northeast, northwest, southeast, or southwest. p. 35

interpreter (in•tûr'prə•tər) A person who translates from one language to another. p. 156

invest (in•vest') To buy a share of a business in the hope of making a profit. p. 484

Iroquois League (ir'ə•kwoi lēg) A group of Iroquois tribes that worked together for peace. p. 86

island-hopping (ī'lənd•hä'ping) The process of the Allies capturing island after island as they advanced toward Japan. p. 591

isolation (ī•sə•lā'shən) Remaining separate from other countries. p. 563

isthmus (is'məs) A narrow strip of land that connects two larger land areas. p. 128

jazz (jaz) A kind of music that grew out of the African American musical heritage. p. 572

judicial branch (jōō•di'shəl branch) The branch of government that settles differences about the meaning of the laws. p. 302

jury (jûr'ē) A group of citizens who decide a case in court. p. 323

justice (jus'təs) A judge who serves on the Supreme Court. p. 304

kachina (kə•chē'nə) One of the spirits that are important in the religion of the Hopis and other Pueblo peoples. p. 77

kiva (kē'və) A special underground room where the Anasazi held religious services. p. 67

knoll (nōl) A small, round hill. p. 112

labor union (lā'bər yōōn'yən) A group of workers who take action to improve their working conditions. p. 491

legend (le'jənd) A story handed down over time, often to explain the past. p. 86

legislative branch (le'jəs•lā•tiv branch) The branch of government that makes the laws. p. 302

legislature (le'jəs•lā•chər) The lawmaking branch of a colony, a state government, or the national government. p. 226

liberate (li'bə•rāt) To set free. p. 659

liberty (lib'ər•tē) Freedom. p. 234

lines of latitude (līnz uv la'tə•tōōd) East-west lines on a map or globe that are always the same distance apart. Also called parallels. p. 36

lines of longitude (līnz uv lon'jə•tōōd) North-south lines on a map or globe that run from pole to pole. Also called meridians. p. 36

locator (lō'kā•tər) A small map or picture of a globe. It shows where the area shown on the main map is located in a state, in a country, on a continent, or in the world. p. 35

locomotive (lō•kə•mō'tiv) A railroad engine. p. 378

lodge (läj) A circular house built over a shallow pit and covered with sod. p. 81

loft (loft) The part of a house between the ceiling and the roof. p. 205

long drive (long drīv) A cattle drive in which Texas ranchers drove herds of cattle north to be sold in northern markets. p. 521

longhouse (long'hous) A long wooden building in which several Indian families lived together. p. 86

Loyalist (loi'ə•list) A colonist who supported the British monarch and laws. p. 232

mainland (mān'land) The main part of a continent, rather than an island near the continent. p. 139

maize (māz) Corn. p. 60

majority (mə•jôr'ə•tē) The greater part of a whole. p. 302

Glossary

Manifest Destiny (ma′nə•fest des′tə•nē) The belief shared by many Americans that it was the certain future of the United States to stretch from the Atlantic Ocean to the Pacific Ocean. p. 383

map key (map kē) A part of a map that explains what the symbols on the map stand for. Also called a legend. p. 35

map scale (map skāl) A part of a map that compares a distance on the map to a distance in the real world. p. 35

map title (map tī′təl) Words on a map that describe the subject of the map. p. 35

mass production (mas prə•duk′shən) A way of manufacturing that produces large amounts of goods at one time. p. 374

massacre (ma′si•kər) The killing of people who cannot defend themselves. p. 237

Mayflower Compact (mā′flou•ər käm′pakt) An agreement by those on the *Mayflower* to make and obey laws for their colony. This was the first example of self-rule by American colonists. p. 155

mercenary (mer′sən•âr•ē) A hired soldier. p. 249

meridians (mə•ri′dē•ənz) North-south lines on a map or globe that run from pole to pole. Also called lines of longitude. p. 124

merit system (mer′ət sis′təm) A way of making sure that the most qualified people get government jobs. p. 557

mesa (mā′sä) A high, flat-topped hill. p. 66

mestizo (me•stē′zō) A person of mixed Native American and European background. p. 659

metropolitan area (met•rə•pol′ə•tən âr′ē•ə) A city and all the suburbs and other population areas around it. p. 643

middle class (mid′əl klas) An economic level between the poor and the wealthy. p. 644

migration (mī•grā′shən) A movement of people from one place to another. p. 47

military draft (mil′ə•ter•ē draft) A way of bringing people into the military. p. 560

militia (mə•li′shə) A volunteer army. p. 195

millennium (mə•le′nē•əm) A period of 1,000 years. p. 61

minimum wage (min′ə•məm wāj) The lowest pay a worker can receive by law. p. 577

Minuteman (mi′nət•man) A member of the Massachusetts colony militia who could quickly be ready to fight the British. p. 241

missile (mi′səl) A rocket that can carry a bomb thousands of miles. p. 614

mission (mi′shən) A small religious community. p. 175

missionary (mi′shə•ner•ē) A person who teaches his or her religion to others. p. 143

monarch (mä′närk) A king or queen. p. 117

monopoly (mə•nop′ə•lē) To have almost complete control. p. 486

movement (mo̅o̅v′mənt) An effort by many people. p. 257

nationalism (na′shə•nəl•i•zəm) Pride in a country. p.362

naturalization (na•chə•rə•lə•zā′shən) The process of becoming an American citizen by living in the country for five years and then passing a test. p. 499

navigation (na•və•gā′shən) The study or act of planning and controlling the course of a ship. p. 118

negotiate (ni•gō′shē•āt) To talk with one another to work out an agreement. p. 269

neutral (no̅o̅′trəl) Not taking a side in a conflict. p. 256

noble (nō′bəl) A person from an important family. p. 91

nomad (nō′mad) A wanderer who has no settled home. p. 48

no-man's-land (nō′manz•land) In a war, land that is not held by either side but is filled with obstacles such as barbed wire and land mines. p. 561

nonviolence (nän•vī′ə•ləns) The use of peaceful ways to bring about change. p. 623

Northwest Passage (nôrth•west′ pa′sij) A water route that explorers wanted to find so that traders could cut through North America to Asia. p. 147

olive branch (ä′liv branch) A symbol of peace. p. 247

open range (ō′pən rānj) The huge unfenced grassland area of the Great Plains where cattle were allowed to roam and graze. p. 522

opinion (ə•pin′yən) A statement that tells what a person believes. p. 131

opportunity cost (ä•pər•to̅o̅′nə•tē kost) The cost of giving up one thing to get another. p. 243

oral history (ôr′əl his′tə•rē) Accounts that tell the experiences of people who did not have a written language or who did not write down what happened. p. 27

ordinance (ôr′də•nəns) A law or a set of laws. p. 289

origin story (ôr′ə•jən stōr′ē) A story that tells of a people's beliefs about the world and their place in it. p. 50

override (ō′və•rīd) A vote to cancel. p. 305

overseer (ō′vər•sē•ər) A person who was hired to watch slaves to see that they did their work. p. 421

pacifist (pa′sə•fist) A believer in a peaceful settlement of differences. p. 257

parallels (pâr′ə•lelz) East-west lines on a map or globe that are always the same distance apart. Also called lines of latitude. p. 124

Parliament (pär′lə•mənt) The part of the British government in which members make laws for the British people. p. 225

pathfinder (path′fīn•dər) Someone who finds a way through an unknown region. p. 355

Patriot (pā′trē•ət) A colonist who was against British rule. p. 241

patriotism (pā′trē•ə•ti•zəm) Love of one's country. p. 324

permanent (pər′mə•nənt) Long-lasting. p. 173

perspective (pər•spek′tiv) Point of view. p. 28

petition (pə•ti′shən) A request for action signed by many people. p. 234

physical features (fi′zi•kəl fē′chərz) The landforms, bodies of water, climate, soil, plant and animal life, and other natural resources that a place has. p. 32

pilgrim (pil′grəm) A person who makes a journey for a religious reason. p. 154

pioneer (pī•ə•nir′) A person who first settles a new place. p. 349

pit house (pit hous) A house built partly over a hole dug in the earth so that some of its rooms are under the ground. p. 73

plantation (plan•tā′shən) A huge farm. p. 143

political boss (pə•li′ti•kəl bôs) An elected official—especially a mayor—who has many dishonest employees and who is able to control the government. p. 557

political cartoon (pə•li′ti•kəl kär•toon′) A cartoon that expresses opinions about politics or about government. p. 251

political party (pə•li′ti•kəl pär′tē) A group of people involved in government who try to get others to agree with their ideas and who choose leaders who share the group's points of view. p. 327

population density (pop•yə•lā′shən den′sə•tē) The number of people who live in 1 square mile or 1 square kilometer of land. p. 652

portage (pôr′tij) The carrying of canoes and supplies around waterfalls and rapids or overland between rivers. p. 179

potlatch (pät′lach) A special Native American gathering at which the hosts give away valuable gifts. p. 74

Preamble (prē′am•bəl) The introduction to the Constitution. p. 293

prediction (pri•dik′shən) A telling beforehand of what will most likely happen next, based on what has happened before. p. 363

prejudice (pre′jə•dəs) A negative feeling some people have against others because of their race or culture. p. 495

presidio (prā•sē′dē•ō) A fort. p. 173

primary source (prī′mer•ē sôrs) A record made by people who saw or took part in an event. p. 26

prime meridian (prīm mə•ri′dē•ən) The meridian marked 0°. It runs north and south through Greenwich, England. p. 124

profit (prä′fət) In a business, money left over after everything has been paid for. p. 153

progressive (prə•gre′siv) A person who wants to improve government and make life better. p. 556

projection (prə•jek′•shən) One of many different views showing the round Earth on flat paper. p. 554

propaganda (prä•pə•gan′də) Information or ideas designed to help or harm a cause. p. 564

proprietary colony (prə•prī′ə•ter•ē kä′lə•nē) A colony that was owned and ruled by one person who was chosen by a king or queen. p. 181

proprietor (prə•prī′ə•tər) An owner. p. 181

prospector (prä′spek•tər) A person who searches for gold, silver, and other mineral resources. p. 525

province (prov′ins) A political region in Canada, much like an American state. p. 662

public opinion (pu′blik ə•pin′yən) What the people of a community think. p. 234

public school (pu′blik skool) A school paid for by taxes and open to all children. p. 392

pueblo (pwe′blō) A group of adobe houses that the Anasazi and other Pueblo peoples lived in. p. 66

purchase (pûr′chəs) To buy. p. 354

Puritan (pyûr′ə•tən) A member of the Church of England who settled in North America in order to follow Christian beliefs in a more "pure" way. p. 185

pyramid (pir′ə•mid) A building with three or more triangle-shaped sides that slant toward a point at the top. p. 62

quarter (kwôr′tər) To provide or pay for housing. p. 239

range war (rānj wôr) A fight between farmers and ranchers during the late 1800s. p. 524

ratify (ra′tə•fī) To agree to something and so make it a law. p. 315

rationing (rash′ə•ning) Limiting what people can buy. p. 587

Reconstruction (rē•kən•struk′shən) A time of rebuilding the country after the Civil War. p. 465

refinery (ri•fī′nə•rē) A factory where crude, or raw, oil is made into usable products. p. 485

reform (ri•fôrm′) A change for the better. p. 392

refuge (re′fyooj) A safe place. p. 184

regiment (re′jə•mənt) A troop of soldiers. p. 259

region (rē′jən) An area on the Earth with features that make it different from other areas. p. 33

Glossary

regulate (reg′yə•lāt) To control by the use of laws. p. 494

relative location (re′lə•tiv lō•kā′shən) The location of a place in relation to what it is near. p. 31

relief (ri•lēf′) Differences in height of an area of land. p. 390

religion (ri•li′jən) Beliefs about God or gods. p. 60

relocation camp (re•lō•kā′shən kamp) Prisonlike camps in which Japanese Americans were held after the bombing of Pearl Harbor. p. 588

repeal (ri•pēl′) To undo a law or tax. p. 236

representation (re•pri•zen•tā′shən) Acting or speaking on behalf of someone or something. p. 233

republic (ri•pu′blik) A form of government in which people elect representatives to run a country. p. 286

reservation (rez•ər•vā′shən) An area of land set aside by the government for American Indians. p. 529

resist (ri•zist′) To act against. p. 422

revolution (re•və•loo′shən) A sudden, complete change of government. p. 252

right (rīt) A freedom. p. 241

royal colony (roi′əl kä′lə•nē) A colony controlled by a king or queen. p. 178

ruling (roo′ling) A decision. p. 382

rumor (roo′mər) A story that has been told but has not been proved. p. 140

saga (sä′gə) An adventure story about brave deeds of people long ago. p. 111

scalawag (ska′li•wag) A person who supports something for his or her own gain. p. 467

scandal (skan′dəl) An action that brings disgrace. p. 630

scarce (skers) Not plentiful. p. 174

scurvy (skûr′vē) A sickness caused by not getting enough vitamin C, which is found in fruit and vegetables. p. 130

secede (si•sēd′) To leave the Union. p. 380

secondary source (se′kən•dâr•ē sôrs) A record of an event, written by someone who was not there at the time. p. 27

sectionalism (sek′shə•nəl•i•zəm) Regional loyalty. p. 380

segregation (se•gri•gā′shən) Separation. p. 467

self-government (self•gu′vərn•mənt) A system of government in which people make their own laws. p. 225

self-sufficient (self•sə•fish′ənt) Self-supporting. p. 175

separation of powers (se•pə•rā′shən əv pou′erz) The division of the national government into three branches instead of having one all-powerful branch. p. 302

separatist (se′pə•rə•tist) A person who wants to become or remain separate from a government or group. p. 664

settlement house (se′təl•mənt hous) A community center where people can learn new skills. p. 506

shaman (shä′mən) A religious leader and healer. p. 80

sharecropping (sher′krä•ping) A system of working the land, in which the worker was paid with a share of the crop. p. 464

siege (sēj) A long-lasting attack. p. 266

skyscraper (skī′skrā•pər) A tall steel-frame building. p. 507

slave code (slāv kōd) A group of laws that shaped the day-to-day lives of enslaved people. p. 421

slave state (slāv stāt) A state that allowed slavery. p. 426

slavery (slā′və•rē) The practice of holding people against their will and making them carry out orders. p. 91

society (sə•sī′ə•tē) A human group. p. 37

sod (sod) Earth cut into blocks or mats that are held together by grass and its roots. p. 81

specialize (spesh′əl•īz) To work mostly on one job that could be done well. p. 60

spiritual (spir′i•chə•wəl) A religious song based on Bible stories. p. 422

states' rights (stāts rīts) The idea that individual states have final authority over the national government. p. 380

stock (stok) A share in a company or business. p. 484

stock market (stok mär′kit) A place where people can buy and sell stocks, or shares in businesses. p. 574

strike (strīk) To stop work in protest of working conditions. p. 491

suffrage (su′frij) The right to vote. p. 395

superpower (soo′pər•pou•ər) A very powerful nation with an important role in world events. p. 611

surplus (sûr′pləs) More than is needed. p. 60

tariff (târ′əf) A tax on goods brought into a country. p. 232

tax (taks) Money that is paid by people to run the country. p. 227

technology (tek•nä′lə•jē) The use of scientific knowledge or tools to make or do something. p. 58

temple (tem′pəl) A place of worship. p. 62

tenement (te′nə•mənt) A poorly built apartment house. p. 498

tepee (tē′pē) A cone-shaped tent made of poles covered with animal skins. p. 83

territory (ter′ə•tôr•ē) Land that belongs to a national government but is not a state. p. 289

terrorism (ter′ə•riz•əm) The use of violence to promote a cause. p. 635

textile mill (tek′stīl mil) A factory where fibers such as cotton and wool are woven into cloth. p. 373

theory (thē′ə•rē) A possible explanation for something. p. 49

time line (tīm līn) A diagram that shows the events that took place during a certain period of time. p. 61

time zone (tīm zōn) A region in which a single time is used. p. 488

totem pole (tō'təm pōl) A wooden post that is carved with shapes of people and animals to show a family's history. p. 75

town meeting (toun mē'ting) An assembly in the New England colonies in which male landowners could take part in government. p. 195

township (toun'ship) A square of land in the Northwest Territory that measured 6 miles per side. p. 289

trade network (trād net'wərk) A system in which trade takes place between certain groups of people. p. 149

trade-off (trād'of) What you have to give up buying or doing in order to buy or do something else. p. 243

transcontinental railroad (trans•kän•tən•en'təl rāl'rōd) A railroad that crosses a continent, such as one that links the Atlantic and Pacific coasts of the United States. p. 483

transport (trans•pōrt') To carry. p. 375

travois (trə•voi') A kind of carrier that is made up of two poles fastened to the harness of an animal. p. 84

treason (trē'zən) Working against one's own government. p. 233

treaty (trē'tē) An agreement between countries. p. 268

trend (trend) A pattern of change over time. p. 420

triangular trade route (trī•ang'gyə•lər trād rōot) A shipping route that included Britain, the British colonies, and Africa. p. 197

tribe (trīb) A group made up of many bands of people with a shared culture and land. p. 60

tributary (tri'byə•ter•ē) A river or stream that feeds a larger river. p. 180

tribute (tri'byōot) Payments a ruler demands from his or her people. p. 93

unconstitutional (ən•kän•stə•tōō'shə•nəl) Going against the Constitution. p. 305

Underground Railroad (un'dər•ground rāl'rōd) A system of escape routes for enslaved people, leading to a free state or territory. p. 424

unemployment (un•im•ploi'mənt) The number of workers without jobs. p. 577

Union (yōōn'yən) The United States of America. p. 300

vaquero (bä•kā'rō) A Mexican cowhand. p. 522

veto (vē'tō) A power the President has to reject a bill passed by Congress. p. 304

vigilance (vi'jə•ləns) Watching over something or someone. p. 527

Glossary

Index

Page references for illustrations are set in italic type. An italic *m* indicates a map. Page references set in boldface type indicate the pages on which vocabulary terms are defined.

Index

Stowe, Harriet Beecher, 393 – 394, *394*, R53
Strait, A17, *A17*
Strait of Magellan, 129
Stranded at Plimoth Plantation (Bowen), 159
Strawberry Banke, 186
Streetcars, 507 – 508, *508*
Strikes, 491, 492 – 493, *493*, 625
Stuart, Gilbert, *314*
Stuyvesant, Peter, *187*, R53
Submarines, 559, 560, 564
Suffrage, 395 – 396
Sugar Act, 232
Sugar refineries, *m216*
Sugarcane, 143, 415, 548
Summary View of the Rights of British America, A (Jefferson), 253
Superior, Lake, 486
Superpower, 611, 638. *See also* Cold War; Soviet Union; United States
Supreme Court
  on civil rights, 622, *622*
  Constitution on, 302, 304
  on Indian rights, 382
  justices of, 304, 325
  on slavery, 428 – 429, *428*
  women on, 626
Suriname, R15
Surplus, food, 60, 77, *100*
Survey(s), R8
Surveyors, 289, *289*, 329, *329*, 386, *386*
Sutter, John, 389, R53
Sutter's Mill, 389
Swamp, A17, *A17*
Sweden, 111, 187
Symbols
  animals as, 251, *251*
  on maps, 35, *35*, 208 – 209, *m208*
  political, 639, *639*, 641
  in political cartoons, 251, *251*
  See also Flags; Patriotic symbols
Syria, 635

Tables, 142, 487
Taensas, 181
Taft, William H., R17
Tainos, 108 – 109, 111, 122 – 123
Taiwan, 638
Taney, Roger B., 428 – 429, *428*, R53
Tanks, 561, 585, 589
Tariffs, 232, 380
Tascalusa, 141, R53
Taxes, 227
  under Articles of Confederation, 286 – 287, 291

  as citizens' responsibility, 227, 230, 231, 232 – 235, *233*, 243, *243*, *274*, 286 – 287, 291, 297, *297*, 299, 323, 466
  colonies and, 227, 230, 231, 232 – 235, *233*, 243, *243*, *274*
  under federal system, 297, *297*, 299, 323
  during Reconstruction, 466
Taylor, Zachary, R16
Tea, 239 – 240, *239, 240*, 243, *243, 275*
Technology, 58
  agricultural, 515, 516, 517, *517*
  air brake, 483
  airplanes, 571, *571*, 596
  astrolabe, 117, *117, 126, 131*
  atlatl, 57, *57*
  Bessemer process (steel), 484, *537*
  canal lock, *376*, 552, *552 – 553*
  Clovis points, 57 – 58, *58*
  compass, 117, *117, 289*
  cotton gin, 417
  harvesting machines, 515, 516
  irrigation, 387
  lightbulb, 480 – 481, *481, 537*
  locomotives, *342*, 378, *378*, 398, *403*
  for ocean exploration, 400, *401*
  plow, 515
  printing press, *323*
  reaper, 517, *517*
  skyscrapers, 507, *507*
  for space exploration, 400, *400, 401*
  spinning machine, 373, *374*
  steamboats, 377, *403*
  telegraph, 483, 484, *484*
  telephone, 481, *537*
  windmills, 515, *515*
  See also Inventions
Tecumseh, 358 – 359, *359*, 361, R53
Tehuacán Valley, Mexico, 59 – 60
Telegraph, 483, 484, *484*
Telephone, 481, *537*
Television, 508, 598
Temples, 62, 87, 91
Tenements, 498, 505 – 506, *506*
Tennessee, 141, 205, *m350*, 351, 359, 379, 434, 442, *m442*, R13
Tennessee Valley Authority (TVA), 578
Tenochtitlán, 93 – 95, *93, 94, 95, m95, 100, 106,* 135 – 136, *136, m136,* 643
Tenskwatawa, 358, R53
Tenth Amendment, 323
Tepee, 83 – 84, *83*

Territory, 289
Terrorism, 635
Texas, 140, R13
  cattle industry in, 512, 520 – 521, 523
  in Civil War, 432, 434
  Dust Bowl in, *579*, 580
  early Indians in, 55
  flag of, 385
  freeing of slaves in, 463, *463*
  immigrants in, 496, *496*
  independence of, 372, *372,* 384 – 385, *m385*, 402
  settlement of, 175, 176, 177, 383 – 385, *383, 384, m385*
Texcoco, Lake, 93, *m95*
Textbooks, *392*
Textile industry, 373, 374 – 375, *374, 375,* 417 – 418, *419*, 444
Textile mill, 373
Thames, Battle of, 361
Thanksgiving Day, 155, *155*
Themes, of social studies, 19 – 21
Theodore Roosevelt Takes Charge (Whitelaw), 567
Theory, 49
Think and apply activities, 25, 30, 36, 53, 55, 61, 89, 99, 125, 131, 157, 161, 191, 199, 209, 213, 229, 231, 243, 251, 273, 295, 301, 321, 331, 335, 363, 391, 401, 435, 437, 461, 471, 489, 509, 519, 535, 555, 565, 595, 599, 627, 633, 639, 653, 669
Thinking skills. *See* Critical thinking skills
Third Amendment, 322
Thirteenth Amendment, 462, *462,* 465
This Man's War (Minder), 544 – 545
Thomas Alva Edison (Cousins), 480 – 481
Three-fifths Compromise, 298 – 299
Tiananmen Square, 272, *272 – 273*
Tijuana, Mexico, 643, *m652*
Tikal, 90
Timberline, *A16*, A17
Timbuktu, 114
Time, for travel, 294 – 295, *m294, 295,* 313, 338, *m338*
Time lines, 29
  activities, 531, 658
  of events during time of American Revolution, *268*
  identifying patterns on, 61, 69
  making, 277, 405, 407, 475
  parallel, 595, *595*
  vertical, 157, *157,* 159
Time zone, 488 – 489, *m489*
Time zone maps, 488 – 489, *m489,* 511, 538, *m538*
Tippecanoe, Battle of, 358, 359

Tisquantum (Squanto), 155–156, R53
Tobacco, 87, 143, 154, *168,* 183 – 184, *183,* 189, 200, 201, *m208,* 215, 415, *m478 – 479, m516*
Tobago, R15
Tokyo, Japan, 591
Tom Thumb (locomotive), 378, *378*
Tomb of the Unknowns, 459, *459*
Tompkins, Sally, 444, R53
Tonti, Henri de, 181, *182,* R53
Tools
  bone, 57
  stone, *50*
  See also Technology; Weapons
Tories (Loyalists), 232 – 233, 256, 257, 258, 267, 268 – 269
Tortillas, 91
Totem pole, 74, **75**
Toussaint-Louverture, Pierre Dominique, 354, *354,* R53
Town(s), *m288*
  colonial, 195 – 197, *195, 196*
  ghost towns, 526
  market, 196 – 197
  See also Cities
Town meetings, 195, *215,* 638
Townshend Acts, 236, 245
Township, 289
Trade
  with Africa, 119
  barter, 74, *100,* 352
  blockade and, 239, 444, 614, *671*
  boycotts and, 234 – 235, 623, *623,* 625
  between Britain and colonies, 230 – 231, 232 – 233, 235, 239 – 240
  in Civil War, 444
  in cotton, 417 – 418, 444, 445
  embargo on, 656
  between Europe and Asia, 116 – 117, *m116*
  exports and, 197, *235*
  by France, *107*
  free-trade agreements and, *607,* 645 – 646, 664, 667, *671*
  in furs, *107,* 147, 148, 149 – 150, *149, 150, 163,* 178, 207, *207, m208, 214,* 268
  in illegal drugs, 661
  imports and, 196, *235,* 638
  among Indians, 63, 64 – 65, 73, 74, 82, 92, 94, *100,* 108
  between Indians and Europeans, 147 – 150, *150, 163,* 175, 178, 207, *214*
  between Indians and pioneers, 352
  by Japan, 584, 638

For permission to reprint copyrighted material, grateful acknowledgment is made to the following sources:

Caroline House, Boyds Mills Press, Inc.: Cover photograph from *Erie Canal: Canoeing America's Great Waterway* by Peter Lourie. Copyright © 1997 by Peter Lourie.

Children's Book Press: From *The People Shall Continue* by Simon Ortiz. Text © 1977 by Children's Book Press; revised edition text © 1988 by Children's Book Press.

Childrens Press, Inc.: Cover illustration by Steven Gaston Dobson from *The World's Great Explorers: Jacques Marquette and Louis Jolliet* by Zachary Kent. Copyright © 1994 by Childrens Press®, Inc.

Clarion Books, a Houghton Mifflin Company imprint: Cover illustration by Jean Day Zallinger from *The Earliest Americans* by Helen Roney Sattler. Illustration copyright © 1993 by Jean Day Zallinger.

Crown Publishers, Inc.: Cover illustration from *Rosie the Riveter* by Penny Colman. Copyright © 1995 by Penny Colman. From *Children of the Dust Bowl: The True Story of the School at Weedpatch Camp* by Jerry Stanley, cover photograph by Russell Lee. Text copyright © 1992 by Jerry Stanley. Cover photograph courtesy of the Library of Congress.

Dial Books for Young Readers, a division of Penguin Putnam Inc.: Cover photograph from *Rosa Parks: My Story* by Rosa Parks, with Jim Haskins. Copyright © 1992 by Rosa Parks.

Farrar, Straus & Giroux, Inc.: "Prayer" and "House Blessing" from *In the Trail of the Wind*, edited by John Bierhorst. Published by Farrar, Straus & Giroux, Inc., 1971.

Jane Feder, on behalf of Julie Downing: Cover illustration by Julie Downing from *If You Were There In 1776* by Barbara Brenner. Illustration copyright © 1994 by Julie Downing. Cover illustration by Julie Downing from *If You Were There In 1492* by Barbara Brenner.

Harcourt Brace & Company: From *1787* by Joan Anderson. Text copyright © 1987 by Joan Anderson. Cover illustration by Stephen Alcorn from *Lincoln: In His Own Words*, edited by Milton Meltzer. Illustration copyright © 1993 by Stephen Alcorn. From *Guns for General Washington: A Story of the American Revolution* by Seymour Reit, cover illustration by Dan Andreasen. Text and cover illustration copyright © 1990 by Seymour Reit.

HarperCollins Publishers: Cover illustration from *Stranded at Plimoth Plantation 1626* by Gary Bowen. Illustration copyright © 1994 by Gary Bowen. *The Great Migration* by Jacob Lawrence. Text copyright © 1993 by The Museum of Modern Art, New York, and The Phillips Collection.

Holiday House, Inc.: From *Cassie's Journey: Going West in the 1860s* by Brett Harvey. Text copyright © 1988 by Brett Harvey. Cover photograph by Lawrence Migdale from *Potlatch: A Tsimshian Celebration* by Diane Hoyt-Goldsmith. Photograph copyright © 1997 by Lawrence Migdale.

Henry Holt and Company: From *One Giant Leap* by Mary Ann Fraser. Text copyright © 1993 by Mary Ann Fraser. "The Americas in 1492" from *The World in 1492* by Jean Fritz, Katherine Paterson, Patricia and Fredrick McKissack, Margaret Mahy and Jamake Highwater. Text copyright © 1992 by The Native Land Foundation.

Houghton Mifflin Company: Cover illustration by Heather Collins from *A Pioneer Sampler: The Daily Life of A Pioneer Family in 1840* by Barbara Greenwood. Illustration copyright © 1994 by Heather Collins/Glyphics. From *The Pueblo* by Charlotte and David Yue. Text copyright © 1986 by Charlotte and David Yue.

Lincoln Cathedral Library, Lincoln, England: From the 1630 handbill *Proportion of Provisions*.

Lothrop, Lee & Shepard Books, a division of William Morrow & Company, Inc.: Cover illustration by Giulio Maestro from *A More Perfect Union: The Story of Our Constitution* by Betsy and Giulio Maestro. Illustration copyright © 1987 by Giulio Maestro.

The McGraw-Hill Companies: From book #60660 *The Log of Christopher Columbus* by Robert Fuson. Text copyright © 1987 by Robert H. Fuson. Original English language edition published by International Marine Publishing Company, Camden, ME.

The Millbrook Press, Inc.: Cover photograph from *Chico Mendes* by Joann J. Burch. Photograph courtesy of Paulo Jares/Abril Imagens. Cover illustration from *Colonial Places* by Sarah Howarth. Copyright © 1994 by Sarah Howarth. Cover illustration from *The Boston Tea Party* by Laurie A. O'Neill. Copyright © 1996 by Laurie A. O'Neill.

Glenn Morris: From "Breaking the Bering Strait Barrier" by Glenn Morris. Originally published in *Indian Country Today*, October 27, 1993.

Morrow Junior Books, a division of William Morrow & Company, Inc.: Cover illustration from *Pioneer Girl: Growing Up On the Prairie* by Andrea Warren. Copyright © 1998 by Andrea Warren.

The Newborn Group: Cover illustrations by Teresa Fasolino from *1787* by Joan Anderson.

Pantheon Books, a division of Random House, Inc.: From *Hard Times: An Oral History of the Great Depression* by Studs Terkel. Text copyright © 1970 by Studs Terkel.

G. P. Putnam's Sons: From *Shh! We're Writing the Constitution* by Jean Fritz, illustrated by Tomie dePaola. Text copyright © 1987 by Jean Fritz; illustrations copyright © 1987 by Tomie dePaola. From *Stonewall* by Jean Fritz. Text copyright © 1979 by Jean Fritz. Cover illustration from *The Great Little Madison* by Jean Fritz. Copyright © 1989 by Jean Fritz.

Random House, Inc.: From "On the Pulse of Morning" in *On the Pulse of Morning* by Maya Angelou. Text and cover copyright © 1993 by Maya Angelou. From *The Story of Thomas Alva Edison* by Margaret Cousins, cover illustration by Dominick D'Andrea. Text copyright © 1965 by Margaret Cousins; text copyright renewed 1993 by Margaret Cousins and Random House, Inc.; cover illustration copyright © 1981 by Dominick D'Andrea.

Scholastic Inc.: Cover from *A House Divided: The Lives of Ulysses S. Grant and Robert E. Lee* by Jules Archer. Copyright © 1995 by Jules Archer. From *By the Dawn's Early Light* by Steven Kroll, illustrated by Dan Andreasen. Text copyright © 1994 by Steven Kroll; illustrations copyright © 1994 by Dan Andreasen.

Simon & Schuster Books for Young Readers, an imprint of Simon & Schuster: From "The Wilderness Is Tamed" in *Away Goes Sally* by Elizabeth Coatsworth. Text copyright 1934 by Macmillan Publishing Company; text copyright renewed © 1962 by Elizabeth Coatsworth Beston.

Volcano Press, Inc.: From *Save My Rainforest* by Monica Zak, illustrated by Bengt-Arne Runnerström, English version by Nancy Schimmel. Text © 1987 by Monica Zak; English language text © 1992 by Volcano Press, Inc. Originally published in Sweden under the title *Rädda Min Djungel* by Bokförlaget Opal, 1989.

Walker and Company, 435 Hudson St., New York, NY 10014: Cover illustration by Peter E. Hanson from *I, Columbus: My Journal 1492-1493*, edited by Peter and Connie Roop. Illustration copyright © 1990 by Peter E. Hanson.

Albert Whitman & Company: From *Samuel's Choice* by Richard Berleth. Text copyright © 1990 by Richard J. Berleth. Cover photograph from *Theodore Roosevelt Takes Charge* by Nancy Whitelaw. © 1992 by Nancy Whitelaw.

ILLUSTRATION CREDITS:

Dan Andreasen, pp. 364–369; Paul Bachem, pp. 222–223; Luigi Galante, pp. 73, 87, 351; Ben Garvie, p. 58; Jim Griffin, pp. 600–601; Dave Henderson, pp. 100–101, 274–275, 472–473, 668–671; Mark Hess, pp. 196, 201, 206; Uldis Klavins, pp. 162–163, 402–403; Mike Lamble, pp. 78–79, 176–177; Albert Lorenz, p. 330; Dennis Lyall, pp. 75, 266–267; Ed Martinez, pp. 344–347; Bill Maughan, pp. 208–209, 260–263, 336–337; Angus McBride, pp. 56–57; Ed Parker, pp. 298–299; Richard Schlecht, pp. 117, 128, 376–377, 507, 536–537; Steven Snider, pp. 418–419; John Suh, pp. 108–109.

COVER CREDITS:

Design Studio: Miriello Grafico Inc.; Photography: Ken West Photography.

All maps by GeoSystems

PHOTO CREDITS:

PAGE PLACEMENT KEY: (t)-top, (c)-center, (b)-bottom, (l)-left, (r)-right, (bg)-background.

COVER PHOTO CREDITS (by object):

Flag, Rafael Macia/Photo Researchers; Statue of Liberty, Kelly-mooney Photography/Corbis; all others, Ken West Photography/Miriello Grafico, Inc.

TABLE OF CONTENTS

HARCOURT BRACE & COMPANY iii (b) Harcourt Brace & Company/P & F Communications.
OTHER iv (tl) Werner Forman/Art Resouces; iv (bl) Michael Heron/Woodfin Camp and Associates; v (tl) Scala/Art Resource; v (bl) E. T. Archive; vi (tl) The Santa Barbara Mission; vi (bl) Founders Society Purchase, Gibbs-Williams Fund, The Detroit Institute of the Arts; vii (tl) Library of the Boston Athenaeum; vii (bl) Bequest of Winslow Warren/courtesy, Museum of Fine Arts, Boston; viii (tl) New York Historical Association, Cooperstown, Photo by Richard Walker; viii (bl) Corcoran Gallery of Art/Corbis Media; ix (tl) Colorado Historical Society; ix (bl) Archives Division-Texas State Library; x (tl) National Portrait Gallery, Smithsonian Institution/Art Resource, NY; x (bl) Library of Congress; xi (tl) Isiah West Tabor Photo; xi (bl) The Denver Public Library, Western History Department; xii (tl) Theodore Roosevelt Collection/Harvard College Library; xii (bl) Print Courtesy Stetson Kennedy; xiii (tl) Corbis-Bettmann; xiii (bl) David Hautzig; xiv (bl) Hartman-Dewit/Comstock.

INTRODUCTION

HARCOURT BRACE & COMPANY 18, 19 (br) Weronica Ankarorn/Harcourt Brace & Company; 21 (br) Victoria Bowen; 24 (b) Weronica Ankarorn; 26 (tr) (br) Victoria Bowen; 27 (br) Harcourt Brace & Company; 28 Weronica Ankarorn; 29 Terry Sinclair; 30 Terry Sinclair; 31 Victoria Bowen; 37 (tr) Victoria Bowen.
OTHER A-1 David Wagner/Phototake; 27 (tr) Archive Photos; 32 (tr) Superstock; 32 (c) Tony Stone Images; 32 (br) Joe Towers/The Stock Market; 37 (c) Chip Henderson/Tony Stone Images; 37 (br) Bob Daemmrich.

UNIT 1

HARCOURT BRACE & COMPANY: 42 (tl) Victoria Bowen; 97(b) Victoria Bowen; 103 Sheri O'Neal.
OTHER 38-39 Courtesy of Abell-Hanger Foundation and Permian Basin Petroleum Museum, Midland, Texas, where painting is on display. (c) 1973, Abell-Hanger Foundation; 42 (c) Courtesy: Richard Howard Collection/Jerry Jacka Photography; 42-43 (bg) Pete Saloutos/The Stock Market; 43 (bl) #3837(4) Courtesy of Library Services, American Museum of Natural History; 43 (tr) America Hurrah Archive; 44-45 (bg) David Muench/David Muench Photography; (b) Rota/American Museum of Natural History; 45 (tr) Lee Boltin; 46 Werner Forman/Art Resource, NY; 48 Mark Newman/Alaska Stock Images; 49 J.M. Adovasio/Mercyhurst Archaeological Institute; 50 (t) Dr. Thomas D. Dillehay, Department of Anthropology, The University of Kentucky; 50 (b) Mercyhurst Archaeological Institute; 51 (l) Amerind Foundation, Inc., Dragoon, Arizona; 51 (r) National Museum of American Art, Washington, DC; 54 John Maier, Jr./JB Pictures; 55 Tom Wolff/St. Remy Press; 57 Aiuppy Photographs; 59 Courtesy of the National Museum of the American Indian, Smithsonian Institution (slide #S3242); 50 (t) Vera Lentz; 62 Michael Zebe; 63 Felipe Davalos/National Geographic Image Collection; 65 (insert) Photograph (c) The Detroit Institute of Arts; 65 (tr) Tony Linck; 66-67 (bg) Jerry Jacka Photography; 67 (insert-l) Amerind Foundation, Dragoon, Arizona-Robin Starcliff Inc.; 67 (insert-r) Object from the Smithsonian National Museum of Natural History, photo by Mark Gulezian; 70 Michal Heron /Woodfin Camp & Associates; 71 Lynn Johnson Photographer; 73 Corbis Images; 74 #1 4075(2), Courtesy Department of Library Services, American Museum of Natural History; 76 John Doyle; 77 John Cancalosi/Stock Boston; 79 Colorado Historical Society; 80 Jerry Jacka; 81 Courtesy of The National Museum of the American Indian, Smithsonian Institution (#S3771); 82 (l) National Museum of American Art/Art Resource, NY; 82 (r) Courtesy of The National Museum of the American Indian, Smithsonian Institution (slide #S2600); 83 (tr) R. Webber/The Bata Shoe Museum; 83 (b) Detail of The Pecos Pueblo about 1500, By Tom Lovel, Artist. Courtesy of Abell-Hanger Foundation and Permian Basin Petroleum Museum, Midland, Texas, where painting is on display. (c) 1973, Abell-Hanger; 85 (bl) "Iroquois Bone Comb," Herbert Bigford, Sr. Collection, Longyear Museum of Anthropology/ Colgate University; 87 (tl) "Photo used courtesy of Pathways Productions, Inc. All rights reserved. Copyright 1994."; 88 (tl) Peabody Museum-Harvard University, photograph by Hillel Burger; 88 (tr) Rare Books & Manuscripts Division, The New York Public Library, Astor, Lenox, and Tilden Foundations; 90 Michael Zebe; 91 Peter Menzel/Stock, Boston; 92 (r) Justin Kerr; 93 (bl) Michael Zebe; 93 (br) Eric A. Weissman/Stock, Boston; 94-95 Detail of The Great City of Tenochtitlan, by Diego Rivera, 1945. Mural, 4.92 x 9.71 m. Patio Corridor, National Palace, Mexico City, D.F., Mexico. Schalkwijk/Art Resource; 98 (bc) First Light; 98 (br) Paul Grebliunas/Tony Stone Images; 98 (tc) Steve Dunwell/The Image Bank; 99 (cl) David Young Wolff/Tony Stone Images; 99 (bl) Harald Sund/The Image Bank; 99 (bc) Peter Hendrie Photo/The Image Bank; 99(c) Art Brewer/Tony Stone Images; 99 (tr) First Light.

UNIT 2

HARCOURT BRACE & COMPANY 108 (tl) Victoria Bowen; 120 Harcourt Brace & Company; 159 Victoria Bowen; 160-161 Harcourt Brace & Company; 165 Harcourt Brace & Company.
OTHER 104-105 Rijksmuseum Amsterdam; 110 Scala/Art Resource, NY; 111 Werner Forman/Art Resource, NY; 112 Werner Forman/Art Resource, NY; 113 The Granger Collection; 114 (tl) Giraudon/Art Resource, NY; 114 (tc) The New York Public Library Map Division, Astor, Lenox, & Tilden Foundations; 115 Giraudon/Art Resource, NY; 116 (tl) Collection of the National Palace Museum, Taipei, Taiwan, Republic of China; 117 (bc) Michael Holford; 117 (br) National Maritime Museum Picture Library; 118 (bl) Bibliotheque Nationale, Paris; 118 (br) Bibliotheque Nationale, Paris; 121 Rebecca E. Marvil/Light Sources Stock; 122 National Graphics, Inc.; 123 Scala/Art Resource, NY; 126 ZIN41924 Selection of Arab and European Astrolabes from the 14th to 16th century, copper, Museum of the History of Science, Oxford/Bridgeman Art Library, London; 127 The New York Public Library, Map Division; 130 AKG London; 131 The Bettman Archive; 134 E. T. Archive; 135 Scala/Art Resource; 136 American Museum of Natural History; 137 Werner Forman Archive, Museum fur Volkerkunde, Berlin/Art Resource; 138 Detail, Collection of the J. Paul Getty Museum, Malibu, California; 139 Courtesy of the Oakland Museum of California; 143 (c) Mel Fisher/Maritime Heritage Society, Key West, FL. Photo by Scott Nierling; 144 (tl) Courtesy of The Hispanic Society of America, New York; 144 (tr) Archivo Fotographico Sevillo; 145 Werner Forman, Art Resource, New York; 146 The Granger Collection, New York; 147 The Granger Collection, New York; 149 (l) "The Surveyor: Portrait of Captain John Henry Lefroy," Paul Kane, Glenbow Collection, Calgary, Alberta, Canada; 149 (r) From the Collection of the Minnesota Historical Society; 150 (l) The Minnesota Historical Society, #67.230.177; 150 (r) The Granger Collection, New York; 151 BAL1648 Elizabeth I, Armada portrait by Anonymous. Private Collection/Bridgeman Art Library, London; 152 (tl) the British Museum; 153 (l) The Library of Virginia; 153 (r) A.H. Robins, photo by Don Eiler; 155 Courtesy of The Pilgrim Society, Plymouth, Massachusetts.

UNIT 3

HARCOURT BRACE & COMPANY 193 (br) Victoria Bowen; 211 (br) Victoria Bowen; 217 Weronica Ankarorn.
OTHER 166-167 Print Collection, Miriam and Ira Wallach Division of Art, Prints, and Photographs, The New York Public Library, Astor, Lenox, and Tilden Foundations; 170 (tl) Rare Books & Manuscripts Division, The New York Public Library, Astor, Lenox, & Tilden Foundation; 170 (bl) Courtesy of The Pilgrim Society, Plymouth, Massachusetts; 171 (t) Courtesy of The Pilgrim Society, Plymouth, Massachusetts; 171 (r) Walter Meayers Edwards/National Geographic Image Collection; 171 (lr) The Pilgrim Society; 171 (bl) Courtesy of The Pilgrim Society, Plymouth, Massachusetts; 172 The Santa Barbara Mission; 173 Florida Museum of Natural History; 174 (tc) St. Augustine National Park Service; 177 George H.H. Huey; 178 Corbis-Bettmann; 179 (t) Courtesy of The Adirondack Museum, Photo by James Swedberg; 179 (b) Kevin Magee/Tom Stack & Associates; 182 The Historic New Orleans Collection, Accession No. 1991.60; 183 Science and Technology Section, Science, Industry & Business Library. The New York Public Library, Astor, Lenox, and Tilden Foundation; 184 Courtesy of the Jamestown-Yorktown Educational Trust; 185 (t) Worcester Art Museum, Worcester, Massachusetts. Gift of Mr. and Mrs. Albert Rice; 185 (b) Courtesy of The Pilgrim Society, Plymouth, Massachusetts; 186 (b) The Bettmann Archive; 187 (t) Culver Pictures, Inc.; 187 (b) Collection of the Albany Institute of History and Art, Bequest of Ledyard Cogswell, Jr.; 188 (bl) Giraudon/Art Resource, NY; 188 (c) The Historical Society of Pennsylvania; 194 Founders Society Purchase, Gibbs-Willams Fund, The Detroit Institute of the Arts; 195 New York Public Library Picture Collection; 197 Colonial Williamsburg Foundation; 200 Arthur C. Smith, III/Grant Heilman Photography; 202 (c) Courtesy, American Antiquarian Society; 202 (r) EX 17082 Negro Portrait: Olaudah Equiano by English School (18th Century). Royal Albert Memorial Museum, Exeter/Bridgeman Art Library, London; 203 The Metropolitan Museum, Gift of Edgar William and Bernice Chrysler Garbisch, 1963 (63.201.3). Photograph (c) 1984 The Metropolitan Museum of Art; 204 National Geographic Image Collection; 207 "American Beaver," by J.J. Audubon (detail). Taken from Plate XLVI Vivb., Quadrupeds of North America. Missouri Historical Society, St. Louis; 212-213 (bg) Chip Henderson/Tony Stone Images; 250 (bl) Mark E. Gibson; 251 (bl) Louis Grandadam/Tony Stone Images; 251 (br) Henley & Savage/The Stock Market.

UNIT 4

HARCOURT BRACE & COMPANY 222 (tl) Victoria Bowen; 225 Weronica Ankarorn; 238 Weronica Ankarorn; 245 Victoria Bowen; 260 (tl) Victoria Bowen; 271 Victoria Bowen; 277 Harcourt Brace & Company.
OTHER 218-219 Historical Society of Pennsylvania; 224 Library of Boston Athanaeum; 226 (bc) Library of Congress; 228 Dan McCoy/Rainbow; 230 The Granger Collection, New York; 231 By courtesy of the National Portrait Gallery, London; 232 Peabody Essex Museum, Salem, MA. Photo by Mark Sexton; 233 (c) Fraunces Tavern Museum, New York; 233 (bl) Massachusetts Historical Society; 233 (lc) Massachusetts Historical Society; 233 (cr) Corbis Media; 234 Virginia Historical Society; 235 Christie's Images; 236 (cr) Ed Eckstein for The Franklin Institute Science Museum; 236 (bl) Historical Society of Pennsylvania; 237 (tl) The Granger Collection, New York; 237 (tc) Stock Montage, Inc.; 237 (cr) Library Company of Philadelphia; 239 (tl) Deposited by the City of

Boston. Courtesy, Museum of Fine Arts, Boston; 239 (bc) Daughters of the American Revolution Museum, Washington, DC; 240 The Bridgeman Art Library International Ltd.; 241 (bc) Courtesy of the Concord Museum, Concord, Massachusetts, photograph by Chip Fanelli; 242 Gift of Joseph W. Revere, William B. Revere and Edward H.R. Revere. Courtesy, Museum of Fine Arts, Boston; 243 Archive Photos; 246 Bequest of Winslow Warren/Courtesy, Museum of Fine Arts, Boston; 247 The New York Public Library/Harcourt Brace and Company; 248 (tl) Historical Society of Pennsylvania; 249 (bl) Library of Congress; 249 (br) Yale University Art Gallery, Gift of the Associates; in Fine Arts and Mrs. Henry B. Loomis in Memory of Henry Bradford Loomis, B.A. 1875; 250 Delaware Art Museum, Howard Pyle Collection; 251 The Granger Collection, New York; 252 (portrait) Detail, Thomas Paine, John Wesley Jarvis, Gift of Marian B. Maurice (c) Board of Trustees, National Gallery of Art, Washington, DC; 253 (tl) Corbis-Bettmann; 253 (tr) Smithsonian Institution; 254 Yale University Art Gallery, Trumbull Collection; 255 Sisse Brimberg/Woodfin Camp & Associates; 256 Ted Spiegel; 257 (tr) Fraunces Tavern Museum, New York City; 258 (br) The Granger Collection, New York; 259 Amon Carter Museum, Fort Worth, Texas; 264 Ted Spiegel/National Geographic Society; 267 (inset) A detail, John Trumbull, "The Surrender of Lord Cornwallis At Yorktown, 19 October 1871," Yale University Art Gallery, Trumbull Collection; 272-273 Reuters/Bettmann.

UNIT 5

HARCOURT BRACE & COMPANY 282 Victoria Bowen; 292 (c) Harcourt Brace & Company; 301 Harcourt Brace & Company; 306 Victoria Bowen; 313 Victoria Bowen; 319 Weronica Ankarorn; 333 Victoria Bowen; 339 Weronica Ankarorn.
OTHER 278-279 Architect of the Capital/National Graphics Center; 284 New York Historical Association, Cooperstown, Photo by Richard Walker; 285 Historical Society of Pennsylvania; 286 Cranbrook Institute of Science; 287 (tl) Corbis-Bettmann; 287 (tr) Courtesy, American Antiquarian Society; 289 Smithsonian Institution, Division of Political History, Neg. #81-5397; 290 Courtesy Commonwealth of Massachusetts. Photo by Douglas Christian; 292 (b) Independence National Historical Park; 293 North Wind Picture Archives; 296 (tl) Courtesy of The National Archives; 296 (bl) The Granger Collection, New York; 297 (tc) The Library of Virginia; 297 (tr) Emmet Collection, Rare Books and Manuscripts Division, The New York Public Library, Astor, Lenox and Tilden Foundations; 298 (tl) New York Public Library; 298 (tc) Princeton University, Bequest of William Paterson, grandson of the subject, in 1899; 299 "Residences and Slave Quarters of Mulbery Plantation," by Thomas Coram, The Gibbes Museum of Art, Charleston, SC; 301 Ralph Earl Roger Sherman (1721-1793), M.A. (Hon.) 1786. Yale University Art Gallery, Gift of Roger Sherman White, B.A. 1899, L.L.B. 1902; 302 U.S. Senate Collection; 304 Wally McNamee/Woodfin Camp; 308 Michael Bryant/Woodfin Camp; 309 National Portrait Gallery, Smithsonian Institution/Art Resource, NY; 310 Metropolitan Museum of Art, New York City/Superstock; 311 Tom McHugh/Photo Researchers; 314 Corcoran Gallery of Art/Corbis; 315 Independence National Historical Park; 316 (tl) Michael

Bryant/Woodfin Camp; 316 (tr) Michael Bryant/Woodfin Camp; 316 (b) The Granger Collection, New York; 318 (bl) The Granger Collection, New York; 318 (br) Collection of The New York Historical Society; 320 (cl) Archive Photos; 320 (cr) Archive Photos; 320 (tl) Colonial Williamsburg Foundation; 320 (tr) The White House Historical Association; 322 The Smithsonian Institution, National Numismatic Collection; 323 The New York Historical Society; 324 Dover Publications; 325 Smithsonian Institution; 326 Mr. & Mrs. John Harney; 327 Sally Anderson-Bruce; 328 (tc) Independence National Historical Park Collection; 328 (tr) Independence National Historical Park Collection; 329 (bl) Maryland Historical Society; 331 American Numismatic Association; 334-335 Museum of Political Life, University of Hartford.

UNIT 6

HARCOURT BRACE & COMPANY 344 Victoria Bowen; 364 Victoria Bowen; 371 Victoria Bowen; 399 Victoria Bowen; 405 Harcourt Brace & Company.
OTHER 340-341 The National Cowboy Hall of Fame and Western Heritage Center, Oklahoma City, Oklahoma; 348 South Dakota State Archives; 349 Hulton Getty Picture Collection/Tony Stone Images; 350 (tl) George Caleb Bingham, Daniel Boone Escorting Settlers through the Cumberland Gap, 1851-52, detail. Oil on canvas, 36 1/2 x 50 1/4." Washington University Gallery of Art, St. Louis; 351 Reynolda House, Museum of American Art, Photography by Jackson Smith; 353 Collection of the New York Historical Society; 354 The Bettmann Archive; 355 (bl) Amon Carter Museum; 355 (br) North Wind Picture Archives; 356 Courtesy of The Montana Historical Society; 357 (l) Courtesy, Independence National Historical Park; 357 (r) Bob Thomason/Tony Stone Images; 358 National Portrait Gallery, Smithsonian Institution/Art Resource, NY; 359 (tl) The Field Museum Neg # A93851c; 359 (tr) Prophetstown used courtesy of Pathway Productions, Inc. All rights reserved. Copyright 1994; 361 (bl) The Granger Collection; 361 (br) Collection of the New York Historical Society; 362 The Bettmann Archive; 363 (bl) "Westward the Course of Empire Takes Its Way," ca. 1861, Oil on canvas, 0126.1615, from the Collection of Gilcrease Museum, Tulsa; 369 (bl) Library of Congress; 372 Archives Division-Texas State Library; 373 North Wind Picture Archives; 374 (l) Smithsonian Institution; 374 (r) Smithsonian Institution, Division of Engineering, Neg. #86-9625; 375 (bl) Progress for Cotton - No. 4 Carding, detail, Yale University Art Gallery, Mabel Brady Garvin Collection; 375 (br) Museum of American Textile History; 378 B&O Railroad Museum; 379 The Granger Collection; 381 (bc) National Portrait Gallery, Smithsonian Institution/Art Resource, NY; 382 Craig Smith/Philbrook Museum of Art, Tulsa, OK; 383 Archives Division-Texas State Library; 384 Friends of the Governor's Mansion, Austin, TX; 386 (t) National Portrait Gallery; 386 (bc) San Joaquin County Historical Society; 387 David W. Hawkinson/Brigham Young University Museum of Art; 389 California State Library; 391 (tl) The Kansas State Historical Society, Topeka, KS; 392 The Bettmann Archive; 393 State Archives of Michigan; 394 (r) State Archives of Michigan; 394 (l) Harriet Beecher Stowe Center, Hartford, CT; 395 (bl) The Bettmann Archives; 396 The Bettmann Archive; 400 (bl) Picture Perfect; (br) Charles Nicklin/Al Giddings' Images, Inc.; 401 (tl) Ron Church/Photo

Researchers, Inc.; 401 (bl) Photo Researchers, Inc.; 401 (br) World Perspectives/Tony Stone Images; 401 (tc) World Perspectives/Tony Stone Images.

UNIT 7

HARCOURT BRACE & COMPANY (bg) 406-407 High Impact Photography; 410 (tl) Victoria Bowen; 475 Weronica Ankarorn.
OTHER 410-411 (bg) Peter Gridley/FPG International; 410 (c) Brown Brothers; 411 Peter Gridley/FPG International; 412-413 (bg) Ellis-Sawyer/FPG International; 412 (bl) Valentine Museum, Richmond, VA; 412 (br) The Bettmann Archive; 413 (tc) Anne S.K. Brown Military Collection, Brown University Library; 413 (tr) Eleanor S. Brockenbrough Library/The Museum of the Confederacy, Richmond, Virginia, photograph by Katherine Wetzel; 414 National Portrait Gallery, Smithsonian Institution/Art Resource, NY; 415 James H. Karales/Peter Arnold, Inc.; 416 (t) Superstock; 416 (c) The Library of Congress; 417 (br) The Granger Collection, New York; 421 Courtesy of The Charleston Museum, Charleston, South Carolina; 422 "Last Sale of Slaves on the Courthouse Steps" by Thomas Satterwhite Noble, 1860. Oil on canvas. Missouri Historical Society, St. Louis, MO #1939.003.0001; 423 (bl) The Brooklyn Museum; 423 (br) The Bettmann Archive; 424 (br) The Bettmann Archive; 426 The Metropolitan Museum of Art, Gift of I.N. Phelps Stokes, Edward S. Hawes, Alice Mary Hawes, Marion Augusta Hawes, 1937; 428 (tl) Missouri Historical Society, St. Louis; 428 (tr) Library of Congress; 429 Courtesy of the Illinois State Historical Library; 430 Sophia Smith Collection, Smith College, Northampton, MA; 431 Museum of Political Life; 432 (bl) Stock Montage; 432 (bc) Museum of American Political Life, University of Hartford, West Hartford, CT; 433 (bc) Library of Congress; 435 (bl) The Granger Collection; 435 (br) National Portrait Gallery, Washington, DC/Art Resource, NY; 440 Library of Congress; 441 (t) NMAH, Smithsonian, TLB 2717. From Echoes of Glory: Arms and Equipment of the Union. (c) 1991 Time-Life Books, Inc.; 441 (b) The Museum of the Confederacy, Richmond, VA. Photo by Larry Sherer. TLB 2713. From Echoes of Glory: Arms and Equipment of the Confederacy. (c) 1991 Time-Life Books, Inc.; 443 (t) Library of Congress #LC-US2623794; 443 (c) High Impact Photography; 445 National Archives; 446-447 The Granger Collection, NY; 449 The Bettmann Archive; 450 (t) National Portrait Gallery, Smithsonian Institution, Washington, DC; 450-451 (c) The Library of Congress; 452, Peter Newark; 453 Chicago Historical Society; 454 (tl) Corbis-Bettmann; 454 (c) Salamander Books; 456 The National Archives/Corbis; 458 Tom Lovell (c) National Geographic Society; 459 Jeffrey Sylvester/FPG International; 462 In the Collection of The Corcoran Gallery of Art, Museum Purchase, Gallery Fund; 464 Cook Collection, Valentine Museum; 465 The Metropolitan Museum of Art, Morris K. Jesup Fund, 1940; 466 (bl) The Library of Congress; 466 (br) The Library of Congress; 467 The Granger Collection; 470-471 (bg) UPI/Bettmann.

UNIT 8

HARCOURT BRACE & COMPANY 480 (tl) Mark Switzer; 492 Victoria Bowen; 500 (tl) Victoria Bowen; 533 (br) Mark Switzer; 539 Weronica Ankarorn/Harcourt Brace and Company.
OTHER 476-477 Library of Congress; 481

Michael Freeman; 482 Isiah West Tabor Photo/California History Section, California State Library; 483 Stanford University Museum of Art/AAA Gift of David Hewes; 484 Smithsonian Institution, Division of Electricity, Neg. #27-979; 485 (l) The Bettmann Archive; 485 (r) Corbis-Bettmann; 486 The Granger Collection, New York; 488 (bl) Culver Pictures; 488 (br) The Granger Collection, New York; 490 Brown Brothers; 491 The Bettmann Archive; 492 The George Meany Memorial Archives; 493 Brown Brothers; 494 Library of Congress/Corbis; 495 National Archives, Washington, DC/Jonathan Wallen Photography; 496 The Institute of Texan Cultures, San Antonio, Texas; 497 Brown Brothers; 499 Calumet Regional Archives, Indiana University Northwest; 500 The Phillips Collection, Washington, DC; 501 (t) "The migrants arrived in great numbers." Panel No. 40 from The Great Migration Series by Jacob Lawrence (1940-41: text and title revised by the artist, 1993). Tempera on gesso on composition board, 12 x 18" (30.5 x 45.7 cm). The Museum of Modern Art, New York. Gift of Mrs. David M. Levy. Photograph (c) 1999 The Museum of Modern Art; 501 (b) "They also worked on the railroads." Panel No. 38 from The Great Migration Series by Jacob Lawrence (1940-41: text and title revised by the artist, 1993). Tempera on gesso on composition board, 12 x 18" (30.5 x 45.7 cm). The Museum of Modern Art, New York. Gift of Mrs. David M. Levy. Photograph (c) 1999 The Museum of Modern Art; 502 "The migration gained in momentum." Panel No. 18 from The Great Migration Series by Jacob Lawrence (1940-41: text and title revised by the artist, 1993). Tempera on gesso on composition board, 12 x 18" (30.5 x 45.7 cm). The Museum of Modern Art, New York. Gift of Mrs. David M. Levy. Photograph (c) 1999 The Museum of Modern Art; 503 (tl) "But living conditions were better in the North." Panel No. 44 from The Great Migration Series by Jacob Lawrence (1940-41: text and title revised by the artist, 1993). Tempera on gesso on composition board, 12 x 18" (30.5 x 45.7 cm). The Museum of Modern Art, New York. Gift of Mrs. David M. Levy. Photograph (c) 1999 The Museum of Modern Art; 503 (br) The Phillips Collection, Washington, DC; 504 "In the North the African American had more educational opportunities." Panel No. 58 from The Great Migration Series by Jacob Lawrence (1940-41: text and title revised by the artist, 1993). Tempera on gesso on composition board, 12 x 18" (30.5 x 45.7 cm). The Museum of Modern Art, New York. Gift of Mrs. David M. Levy. Photograph (c) 1999 The Museum of Modern Art; 505 The Library of Congress/Corbis; 506 The Jacob A. Riis Collection, Museum of the City of New York; 508 Detail, "Trolley Car, Brooklyn Trolley Car Strike, 1899," The Museum of the City of New York, The Byron Collection; 509 (bl) Stock Montage; 509 (br) University of Illinois at Chicago/The University Library/Jane Addams Memorial Collection; 511 Penguin Books; 512 The Denver Public Library, Western History Department; 513 (c) Corbis/Bettmann; 513 (b) H. Abernathy/H. Armstrong Roberts; 515 Nebraska State Historical Society; 517 The Bettmann Archive; 518 Grant Heilman Photography; 520-521 David Stoecklein/Adstock Photos; 522 (br) UPI/Bettmann; 523 Corbis/Bettmann; 524 (l) Scott Berner/Phototri; 524 (r) Smithsonian Institution, Division of Political History, Neg. #94-186; 525 FPG International; 526 (bl) California

State Library Neg. #912; 526 (r) Michael Friedman; 528 North Wind Picture Archive; 531 Culver Pictures; 534-535 (bg) Ken Biggs/Tony Stone Images; 535 (c) Joseph Pobereskin/Tony Stone Images; 535 (r) Jon Ortner/Tony Stone Images.

UNIT 9

HARCOURT BRACE & COMPANY 567 (br) Mark Switzer; 579 (tl) Mark Switzer; 597 (br) Mark Switzer; 351 (br) Harcourt Brace & Company.
OTHER 540-541 Fred Pansing/Image Bank; 544 FPG International; 545 Corbis/Bettmann; 546 Theodore Roosevelt Collection/Harvard College Library; 547 Gill C. Kenny, The Image Bank; 548 (t) Corbis-Bettmann; 548 (b) Jason Hailey/FPG International; 549 Ted Spiegel; 550 Brown Brothers; 553 The Bettmann Archive/Corbis-Bettmann; 556 Culver Pictures; 557 The Granger Collection; 558 (l) Corbis-Bettmann; 558 (r) Corbis-Bettmann; 559 Wood River Gallery, Mill Valley, CA; 560 (l) Culver Pictures; 560 (r) Culver Pictures; 562 Archive Photos; 563 National Portrait Gallery, Smithsonian Institute/Art Resource; 564 (l) James M. Flagg/The Granger Collection; 564 (r) Corbis; 565 Courtesy of The Library of Congress; 567 Mark Switzer; 568 Print Courtesy Stetson Kennedy; 569 Blank Archives/Archive Photos; 570 (t) From the Collections of the Henry Ford Museum & Greenfield Village; 570 (b) Culver Pictures; 571 (l) The Granger Collection; 571 (r) The Bettmann Archive/Corbis-Bettmann/; 572 (l) Archive Photos; 572 (r) Missouri State Historical Society; 573 (tr) Archive Photos; 573 (c) The Bettmann Archive/Corbis-Bettmann; 574 Archive Photos; 575 (l) New York Stock Exchange Archives; 575 (r) New York Stock Exchange Archives; 577 (bl) UPI/Bettmann; 577 (tr) The Bettmann Archive; 578 San Francisco History Room, San Francisco Public Library; 579-580 (bg) The Granger Collection; 579 (bl) The Library of Congress/Corbis; 580 (br) Dorothea Lange/Library of Congress; 581 (bg) Library of Congress/Corbis; 582 (bg) Library of Congress/Corbis; 582 (b) Arthur Rothstein/Library of Congress; 583 (b) UPI/Corbis-Bettmann; 583 (c) UPI/Corbis-Bettmann; 584 UPI/Bettmann Newsphotos; 585 (bl) UPI/Corbis-Bettmann; 585 (br) Culver Pictures; 586 (tl) UPI/Bettmann; 587 (br) Courtesy of The Library of Congress; 588 UPI/Corbis-Bettmann; 589 Private Collection; 590 (b) The Bettmann Archive; 590 (inset) UPI/Bettmann; 591 (l) Culver Pictures; 591 (r) Yellow Star, Germany, 1930s. Printed cotton. Gift of Moriah Artcraft Judaica. Photograph by Greg Staley, Courtesy of B'nai B'rith Klutznick National Jewish Museum; 598-599 Mark Richards/PhotoEdit; 599 (tl) Peter Morgan/Matrix International; 599 (tr) Tom Wagner/SABA; 599 (b) F. Hoffmann/The Image Works.

UNIT 10

HARCOURT BRACE & COMPANY 639 (l) Mark Switzer; 639 (r) Mark Switzer; 641 Harcourt Brace & Company; 673 Harcourt Brace & Company.
OTHER 604-605 Roger Ressmeyer/Corbis; 608 (t) Zane Williams/Tony Stone Images; 608 (l) Jim Stratford/Black Star; 609 (t) Jose L. Pelaez/Stock Market; 609 (bl) PhotoDisc; 609 (br) Ariel Skelley/Stock Market; 610 Corbis-Bettmann; 611

UPI/Corbis-Bettmann; 612 UPI/Bettmann; 614 Arthur Rickerby/Black Star; 615 (t) UPI/Bettmann/Corbis-Bettmann; 615 (tr) UPI/Corbis-Bettmann; 616-617 (bg) NASA Media Services; 617 NASA Media Services; 618-619 (bg) NASA Media Services; 620 (inset) Digital Vision; 620 (t) NASA Media Services; 621 (tr) NASA Media Services; 621 (bl) Digital Vision; 622 UPI/Bettmann; 623 (tl) AP/Wide World Photos; 623 (tr) Dan Weiner, Courtesy of Sandra Weiner; 624 (l) UPI/Corbis-Bettmann; 624 (br) John Lounois/Black Star; 625 Bob Fitch/Black Star; 627 UPI/Bettmann; 628 (bl) AP/Wide World Photos; 628 (br) UPI/Corbis-Bettmann; 629 UPI/Bettmann Newsphotos; 630 UPI/Corbis/Bettmann; 631 UPI/Bettmann Newsphotos; 632-633 (tc) UPI/Bettmann/Corbis-Bettmann; 632 (b) Dennis Brack/Black Star; 633 (b) UPI/Bettmann/Corbis-Bettmann; 634 UPI/Bettmann; 635 Dennis Brack/Black Star; 636 UPI/Bettmann; 637 AP/Wide World Photos; 638 AP/Wide World Photos; 642 David Hautzig; 643 Anthony Suau/Gamma Liaison; 644 (t) UPI/Bettmann; 644 (b) Bob Daemmerich; 646 Florence Parker/Archive Photos; 654 Comstock; 655 (bc) Tom Haley/Sipa Press; 656 (t) Cindy Karp/Black Star; 656 (b) Chantal Regnault/Gamma Liaison; 657 Alon Reininger/Contact Press; 658 Bill Gentile/Sipa Press; 659 Giraudon/Art Resource; 661 Will & Deni McIntyre/Photo Researchers; 662 John Brooks/Gamma Liaison; 664 (tl) Ron Watts/First Light; 664 (br) Paula Bronstein/TSW; 665 First Light; 668 (bl) B. Daemmrich/The Image Works; 668 (br) Joseph Nettis/Photo Researchers; 669 (t) Christopher Morris/SABA; 669 (c) Dante Busquets-Sordo/Gamma-Liaison; 669 (bl) S. Dooley/Liaison International; 669 (br) Paula Allen/Matrix International.

REFERENCE

Facing R1 Dennis Hallinan/FPG International; R1 (tl) Comstock; R1 (bl) Hartman-Dewit/Comstock; R2-R3 (b) Harcourt Brace & Company; R4 (t) Michael Heron/Woodfin Camp & Associates; R7 (br) Weronica Ankarorn; R9 (br) Harcourt Brace & Company; R16 Row 1 (tr) National Portrait Gallery; Row 2 (l) National Portrait Gallery; (c) Bettman; (r) National Portrait Gallery; Row 3 (l) National Portrait Gallery; (c) National Portrait Gallery; (r) The Granger Collection, New York; Row 4 (l) National Portrait Gallery; (c) National Portrait Gallery; (r) National Portrait Gallery; Row 5 (l) National Portrait Gallery; (c) The Granger Collection, New York; (r) The Granger Collection; R17 Row 1 (l) Bettmann; (c) National Portrait Gallery (r) The New York Historical Society; Row 2 (l) The Granger Collection; (c) The Granger Collection; (r) National Portrait Gallery; Row 3 (l) National Portrait Gallery; (c) National Portrait Gallery; (r) Harcourt Brace & Company; Row 4 (l) Harcourt Brace & Company; (c) Harcourt Brace & Company; (r) National Portrait Gallery; Row 5 (l) The Granger Collection; (c) Bettmann; (r) National Portrait Gallery; R18 Row 1 (l) National Portrait Gallery; (c) The Granger Collection; (r) The Granger Collection; Row 2 (l) The Granger Collection; (c) National Portrait Gallery; (r) Eisenhower Library; Row 3 (l) The Granger Collection, New York; (c) Wide World Photos; (r) The Granger Collection; Row 4 (l) National Portrait Gallery; (c) White House Historical Association; (r) Wide World Photos; Row 5 (l) David Valdez/The White House; (c) The White House.